Mail Order
Bride

Acknowledgements:

Special thanks to Jennifer Yuan, Michael Kalesniko, Nancy Ruff, and Glen Kalesniko

Dedicated to the artists, students, and teachers of David Thompson University Center. "Cloud hidden, whereabouts unknown."

Edited by Gary Groth
Designed by Carrie Whitney
Production Manager: Kim Thompson
Lettered by Paul Baresh, Carrie Whitney & Dan Dean
Promotion by Eric Reynolds
Published by Gary Groth & Kim Thompson

 Fantagraphics Books, 7563 Lake City Way, Seattle, WA 98115 USA.
For a free full-color catalogue of comics, including previous works by Mark Kalesniko, call 1-800-657-1100.
Our books may be viewed on our web site at www.fantagraphics.com.

First printing: February 2001
Second printing: March 2003

ISBN 1-56097-410-9
Printed in Canada

Mark Kalesniko

Mail Order
Bride

A Graphic Novel

FANTAGRAPHICS BOOKS

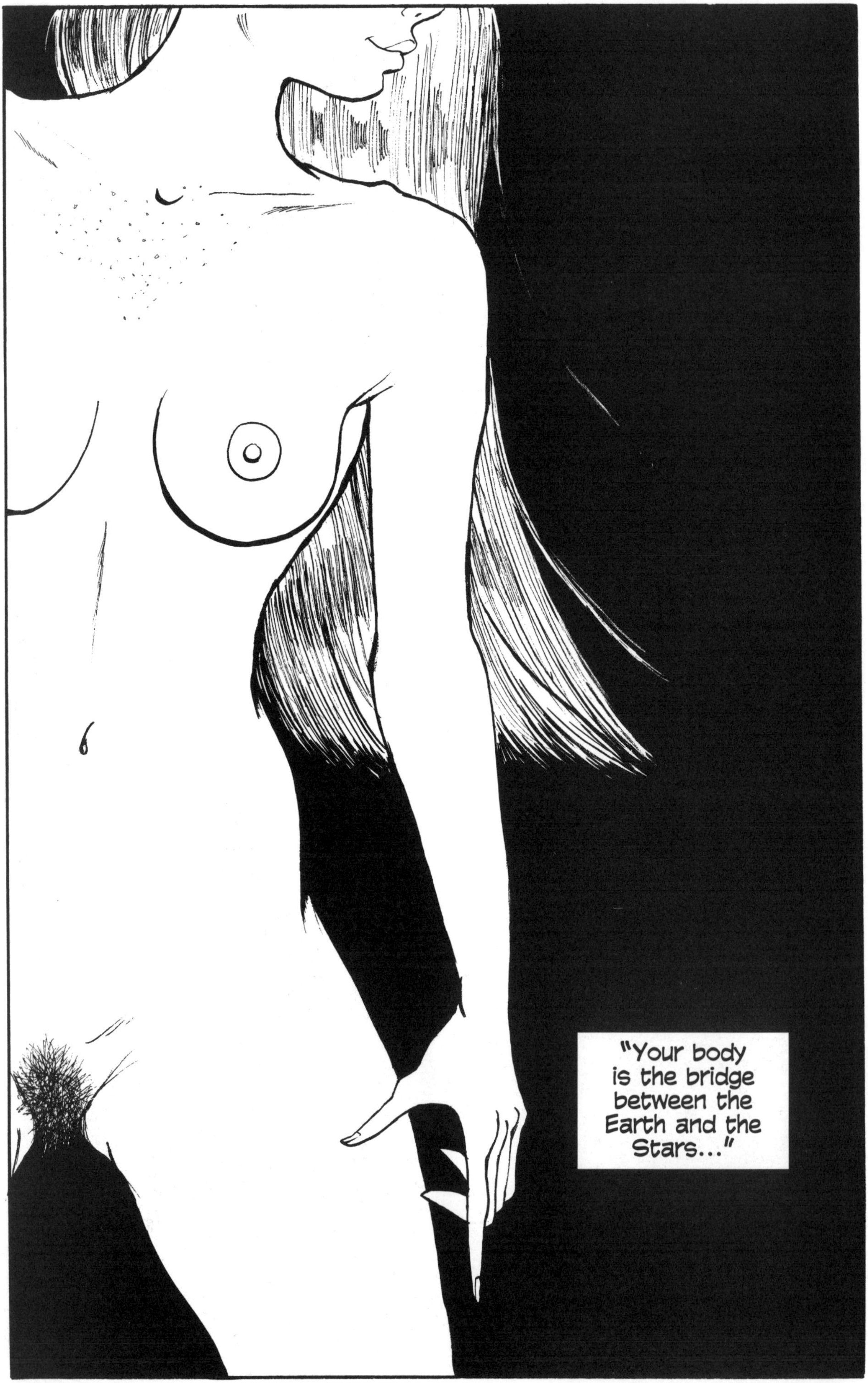
"Your body is the bridge between the Earth and the Stars..."

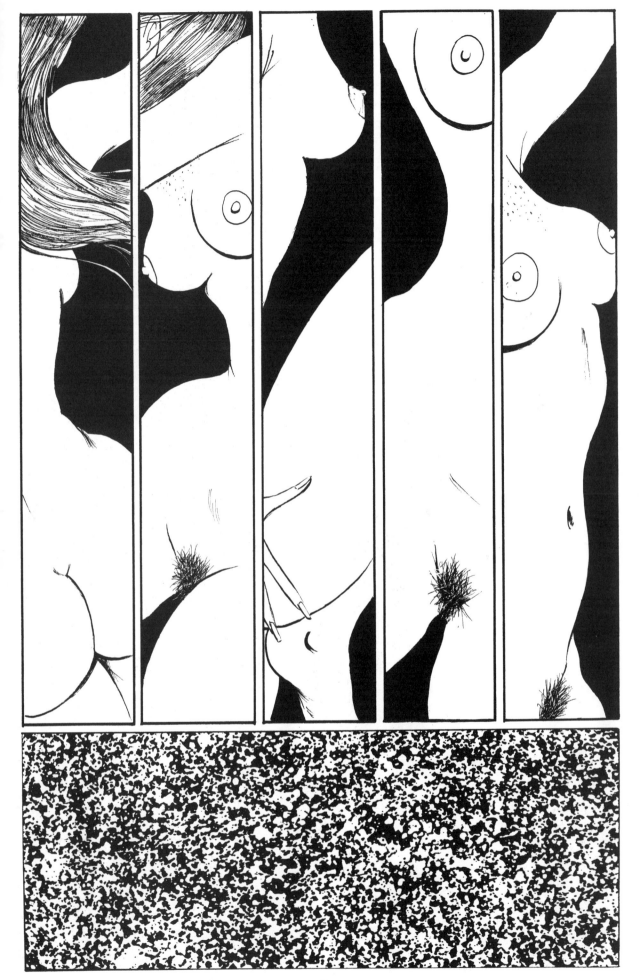

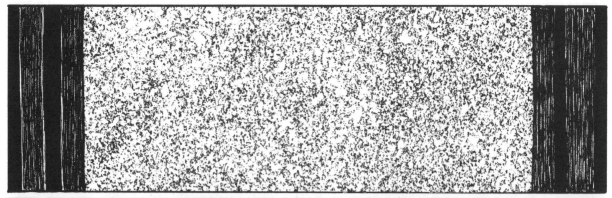

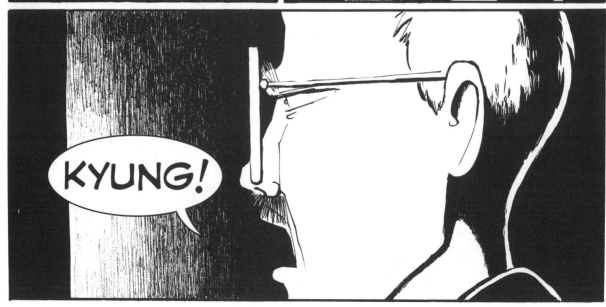

KYUNG!

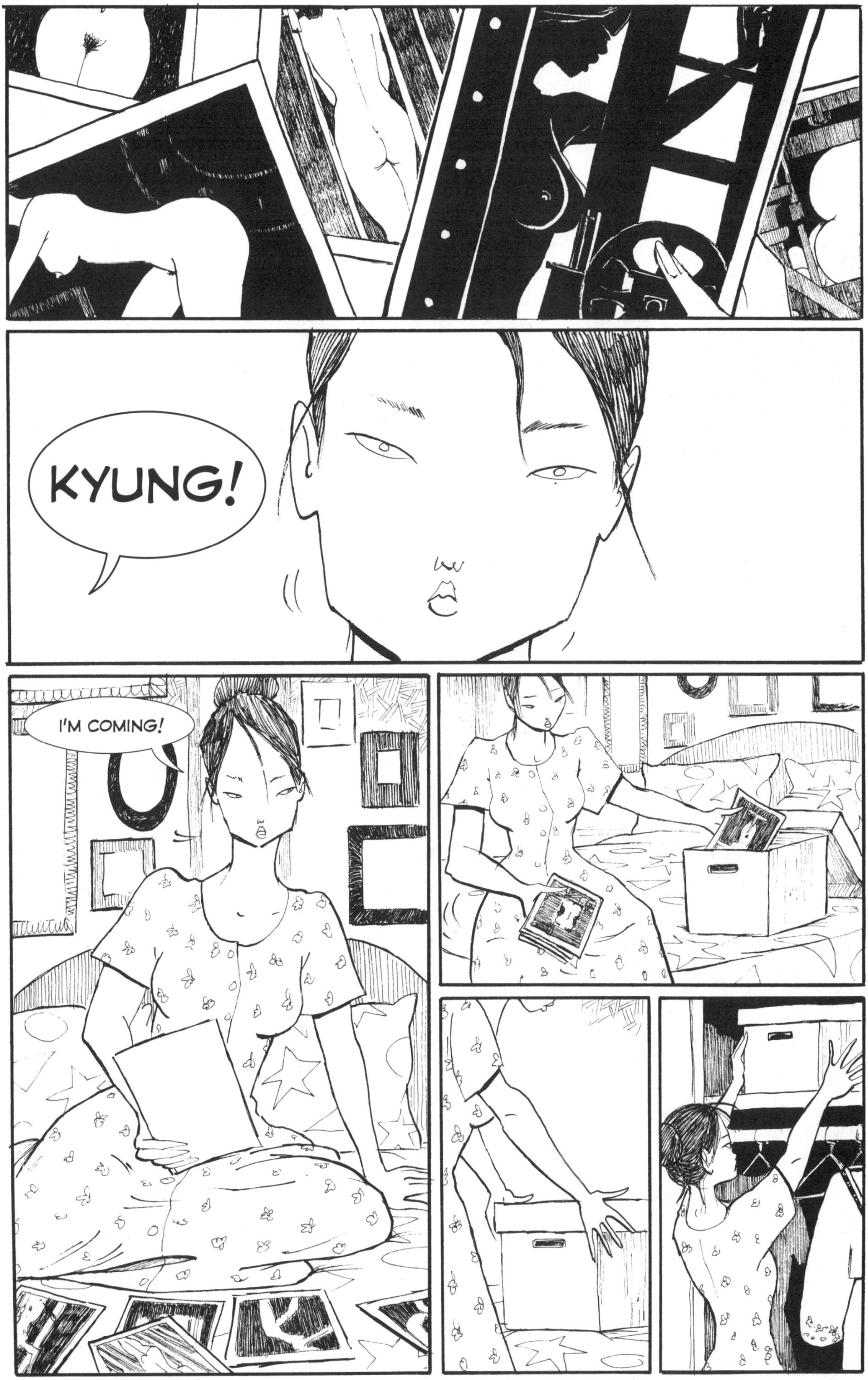

KYUNG!
I'M COMING!

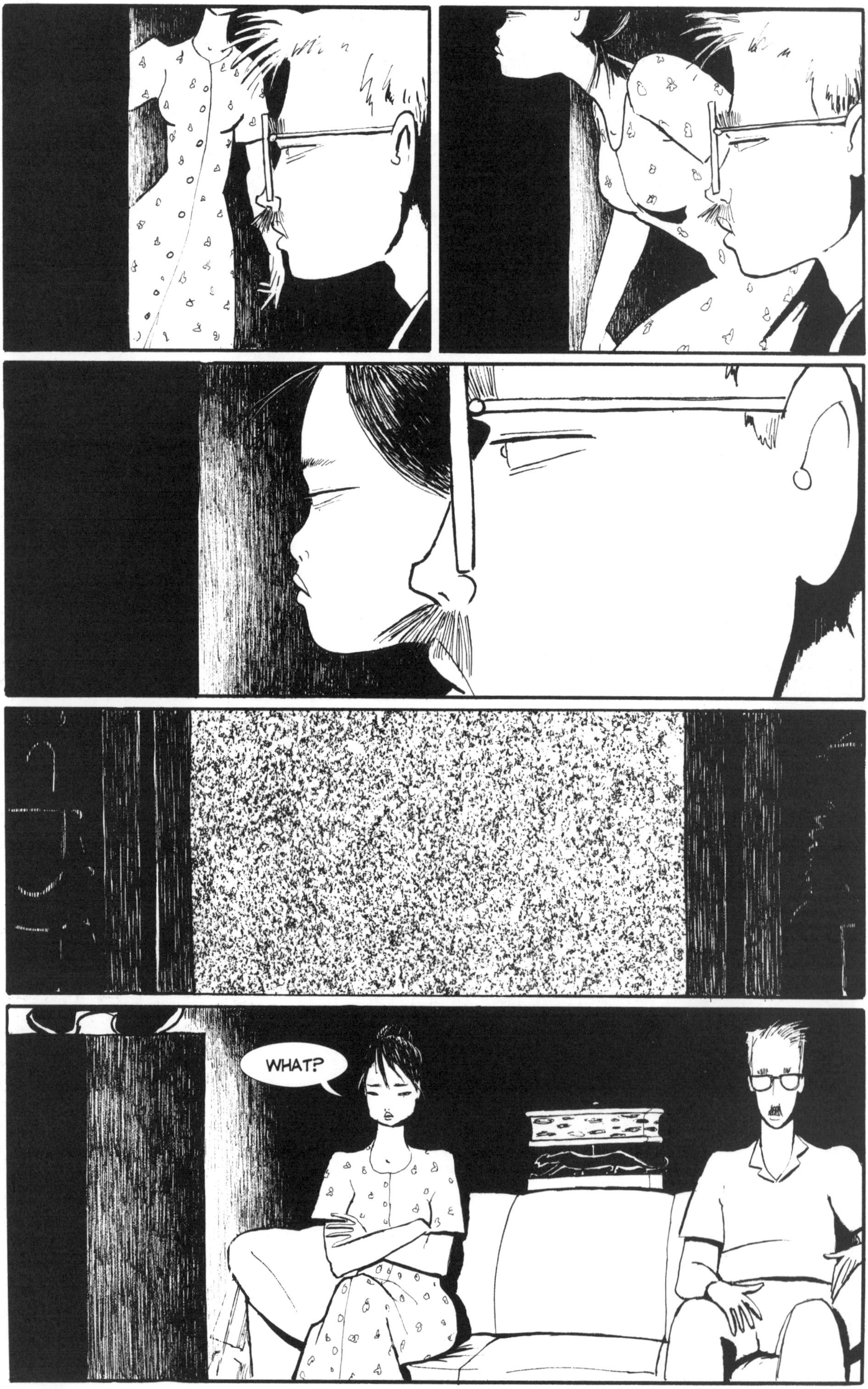
WHAT?

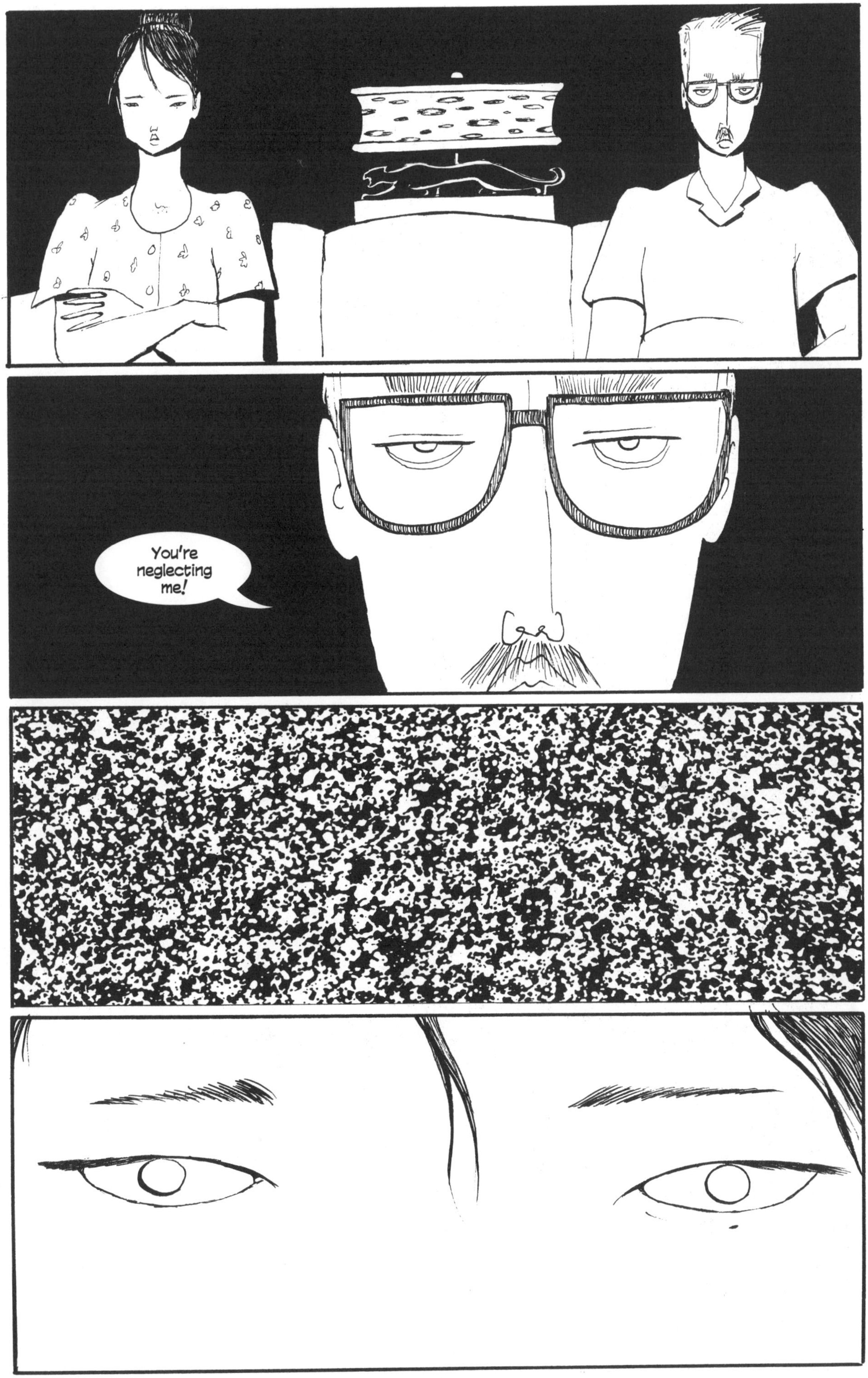
You're neglecting me!

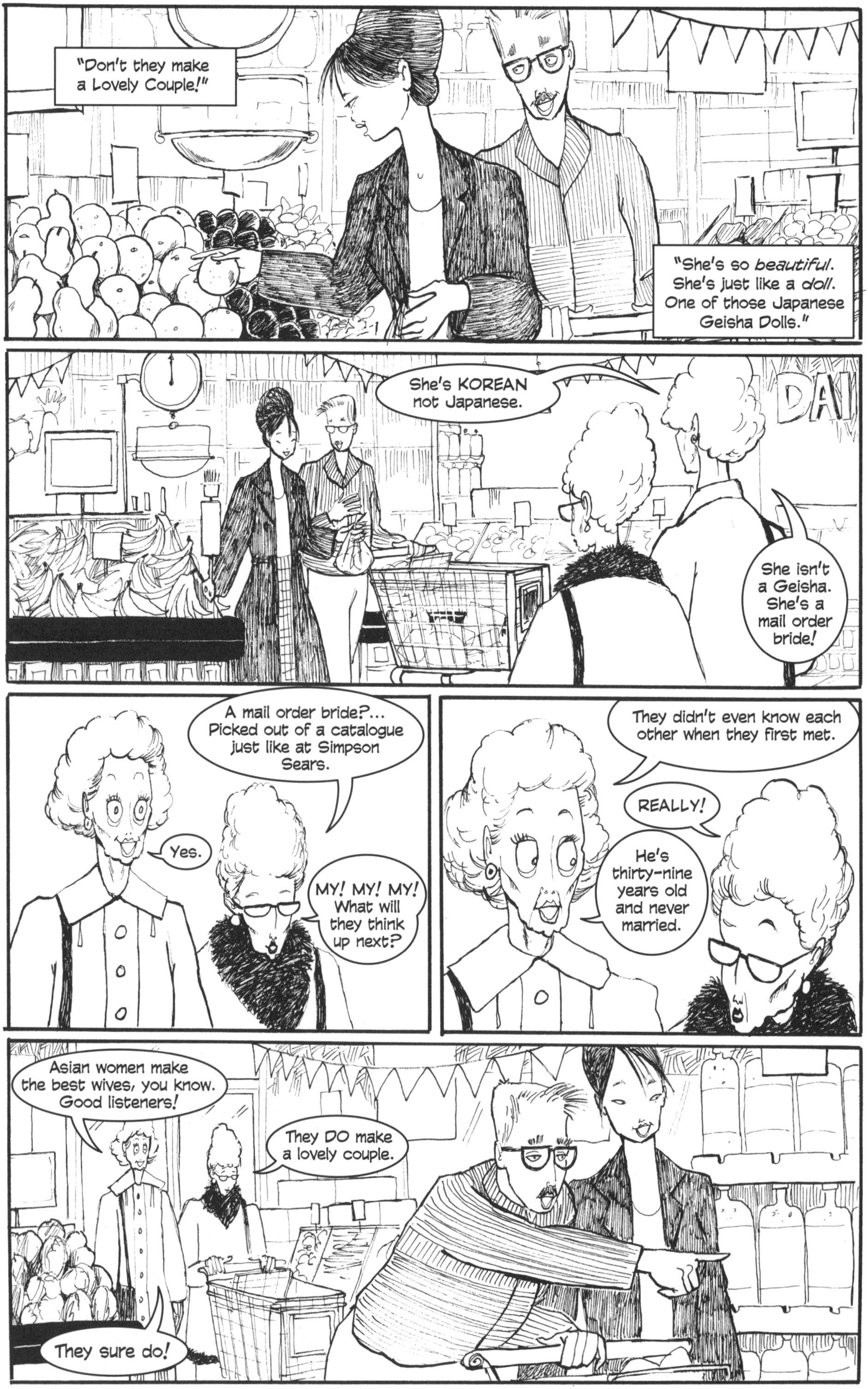
"Don't they make a Lovely Couple!"
"She's so *beautiful*. She's just like a *doll*. One of those Japanese Geisha Dolls."
She's KOREAN not Japanese.
She isn't a Geisha. She's a mail order bride!
A mail order bride?... Picked out of a catalogue just like at Simpson Sears.
Yes.
MY! MY! MY! What will they think up next?
They didn't even know each other when they first met.
REALLY!
He's thirty-nine years old and never married.
Asian women make the best wives, you know. Good listeners!
They DO make a lovely couple.
They sure do!

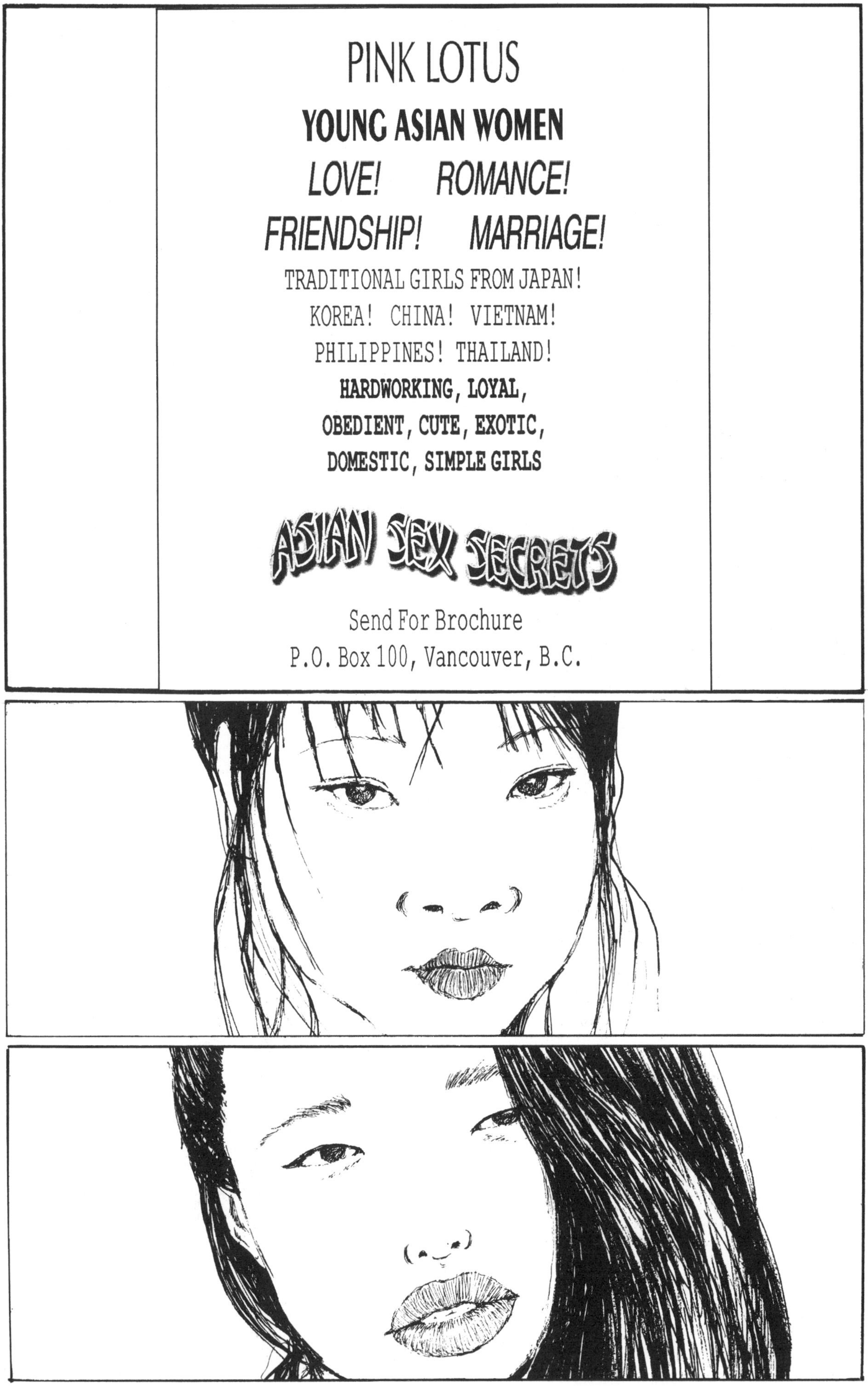
PINK LOTUS
YOUNG ASIAN WOMEN
LOVE! ROMANCE!
FRIENDSHIP! MARRIAGE!
TRADITIONAL GIRLS FROM JAPAN!
KOREA! CHINA! VIETNAM!
PHILIPPINES! THAILAND!
HARDWORKING, LOYAL,
OBEDIENT, CUTE, EXOTIC,
DOMESTIC, SIMPLE GIRLS
ASIAN SEX SECRETS
Send For Brochure
P.O. Box 100, Vancouver, B.C.

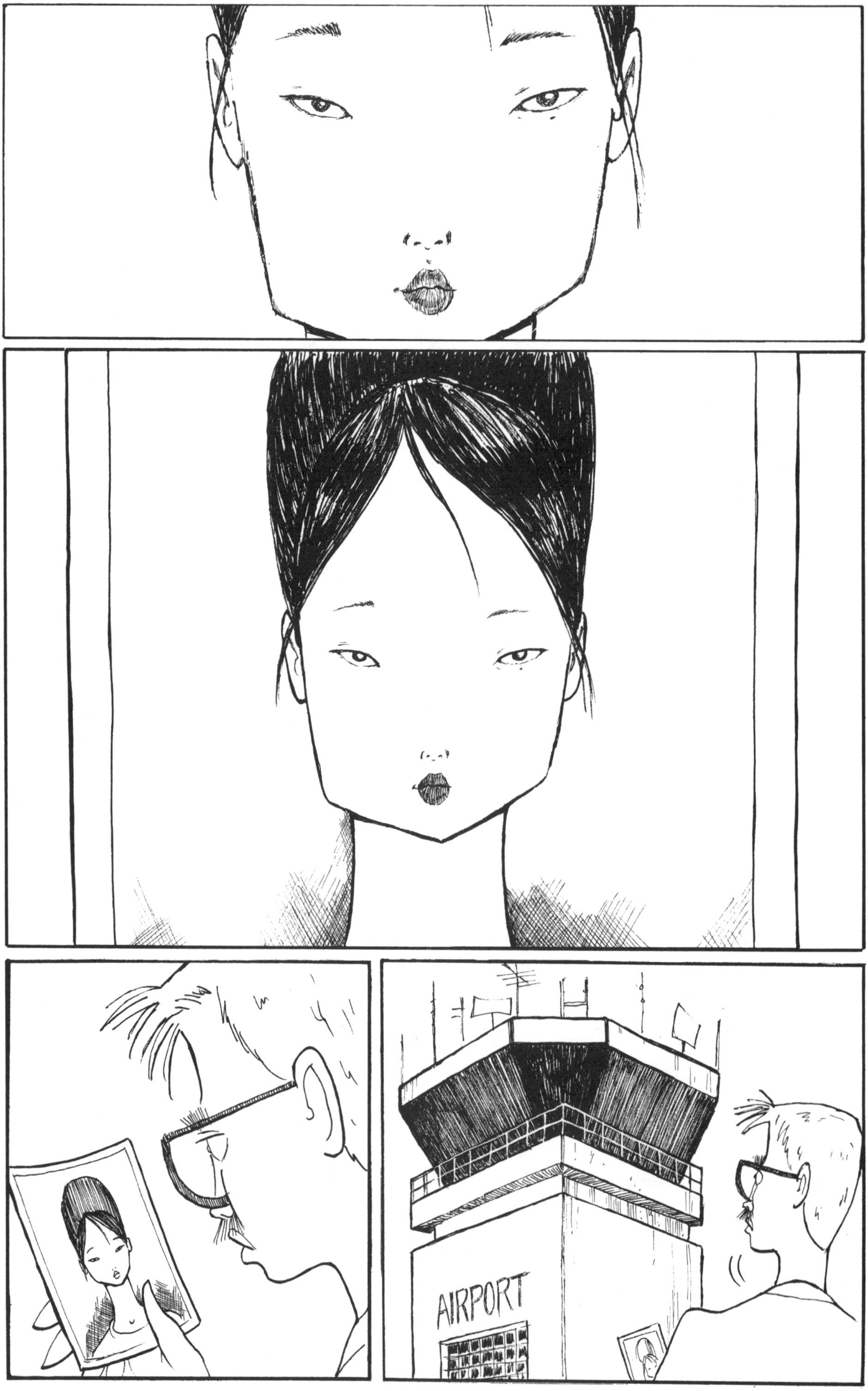
AIRPORT

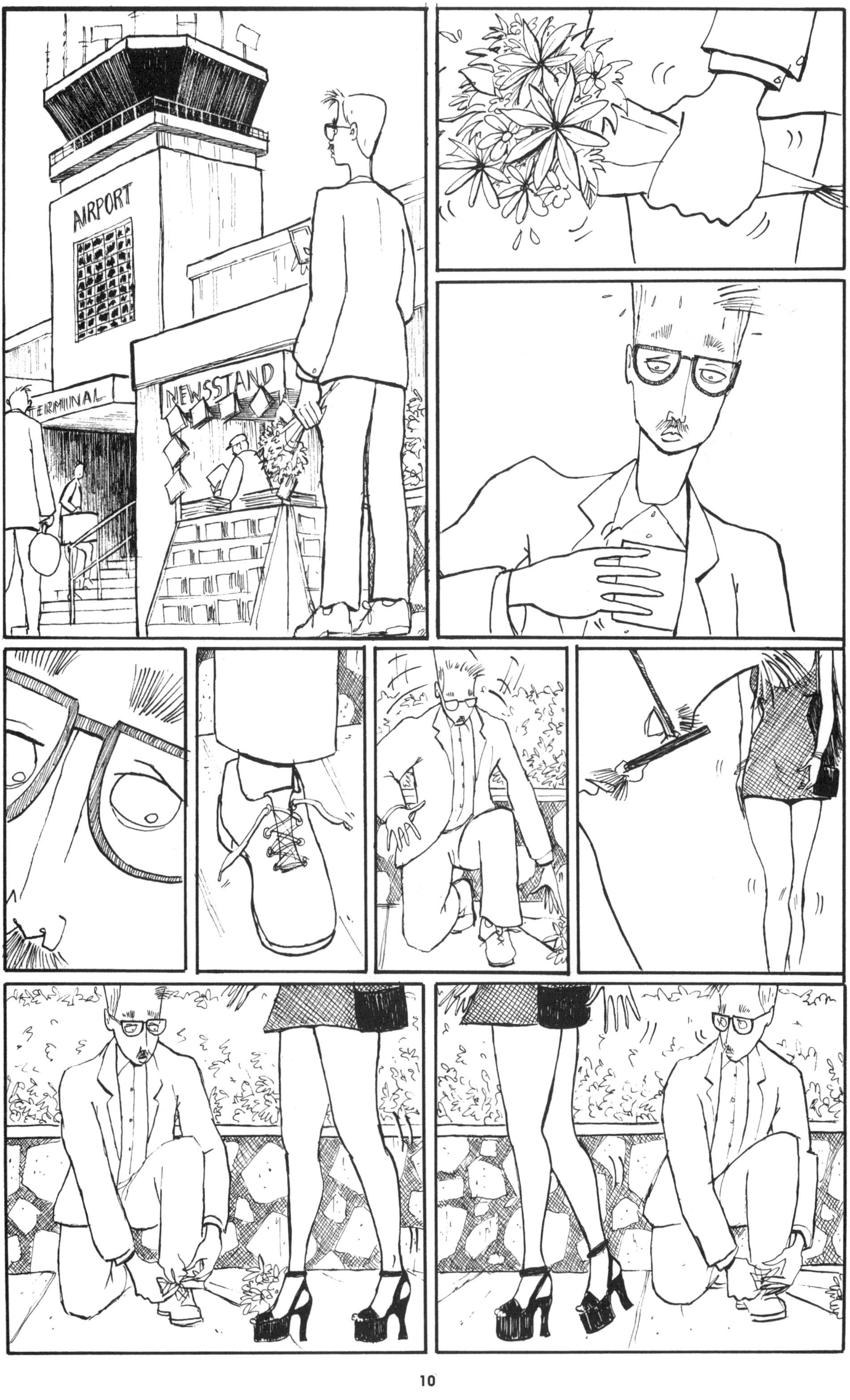
AIRPORT
TERMINAL
NEWSSTAND

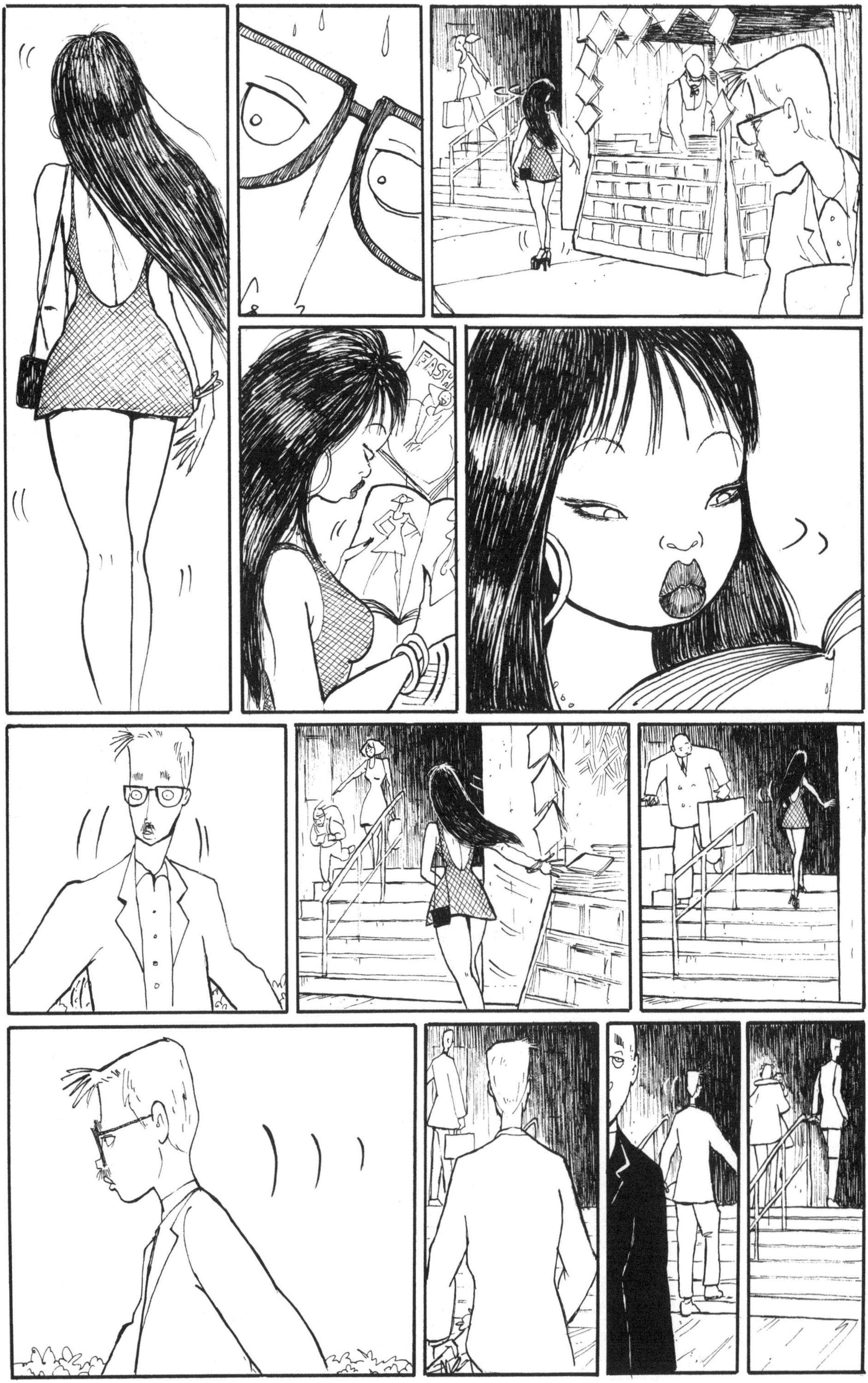

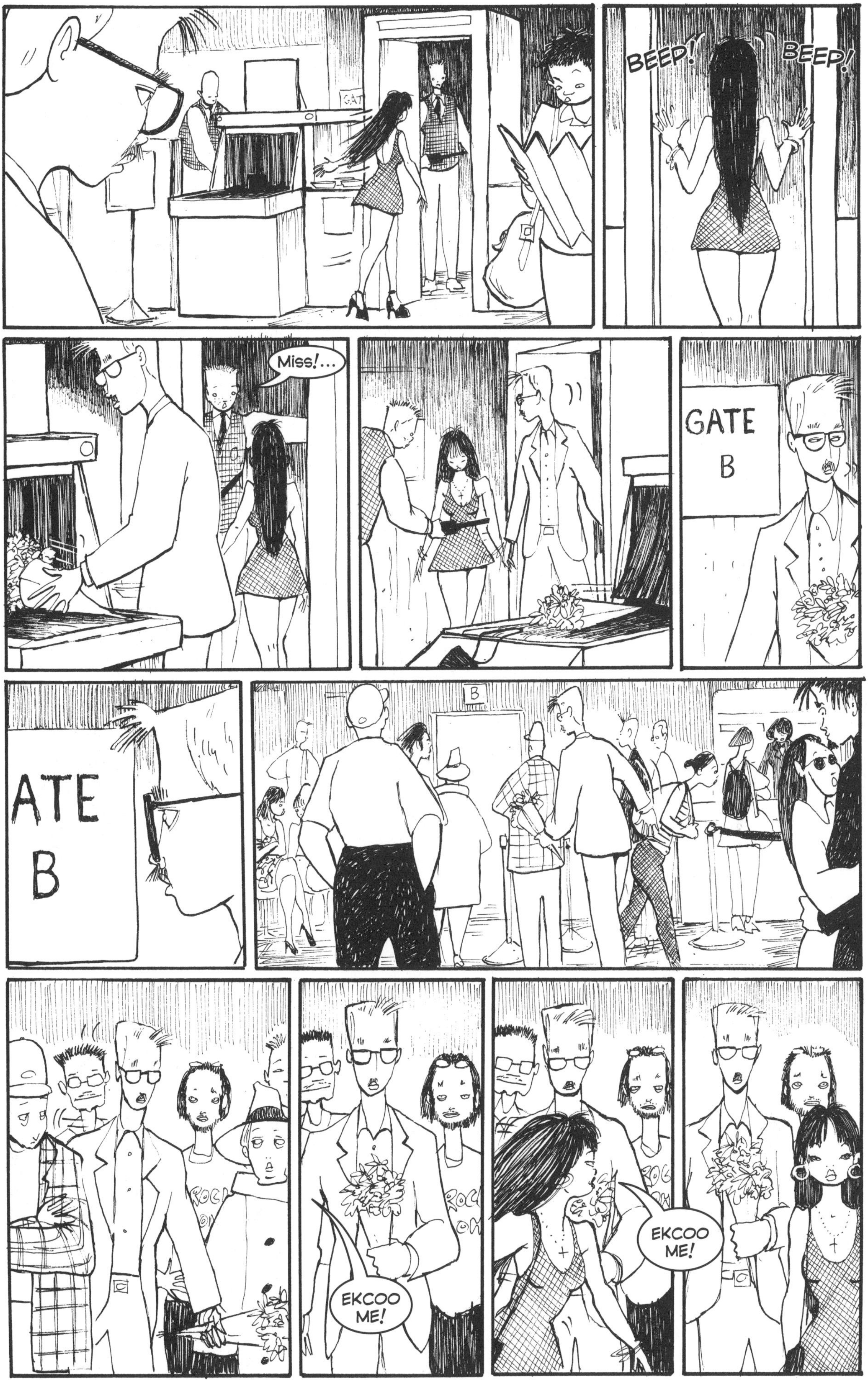
GAT
BEEP! BEEP!
Miss!...
GATE
B
ATE
B
B
EKCOO ME!
EKCOO ME!

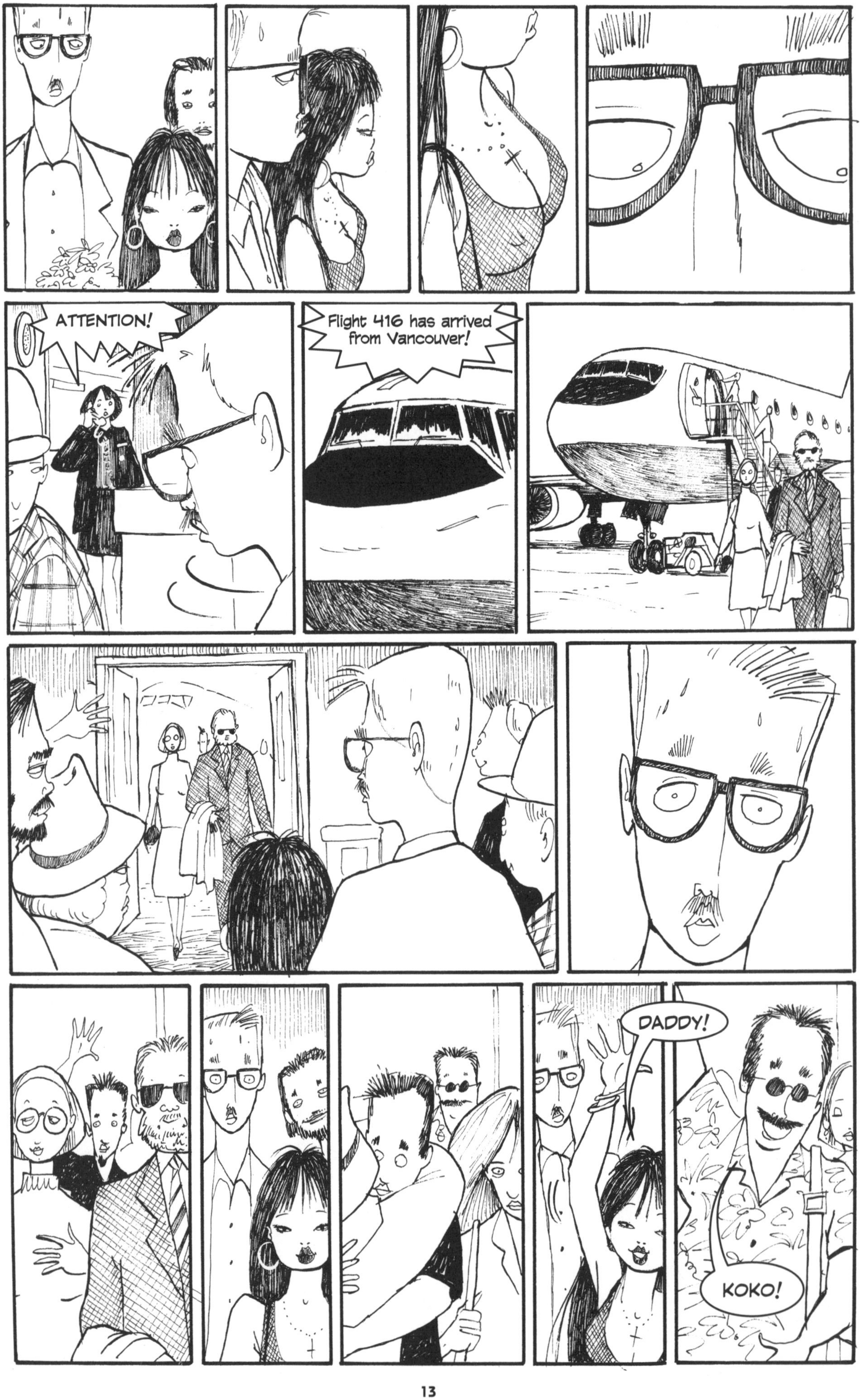
ATTENTION!
Flight 416 has arrived from Vancouver!
DADDY!
KOKO!

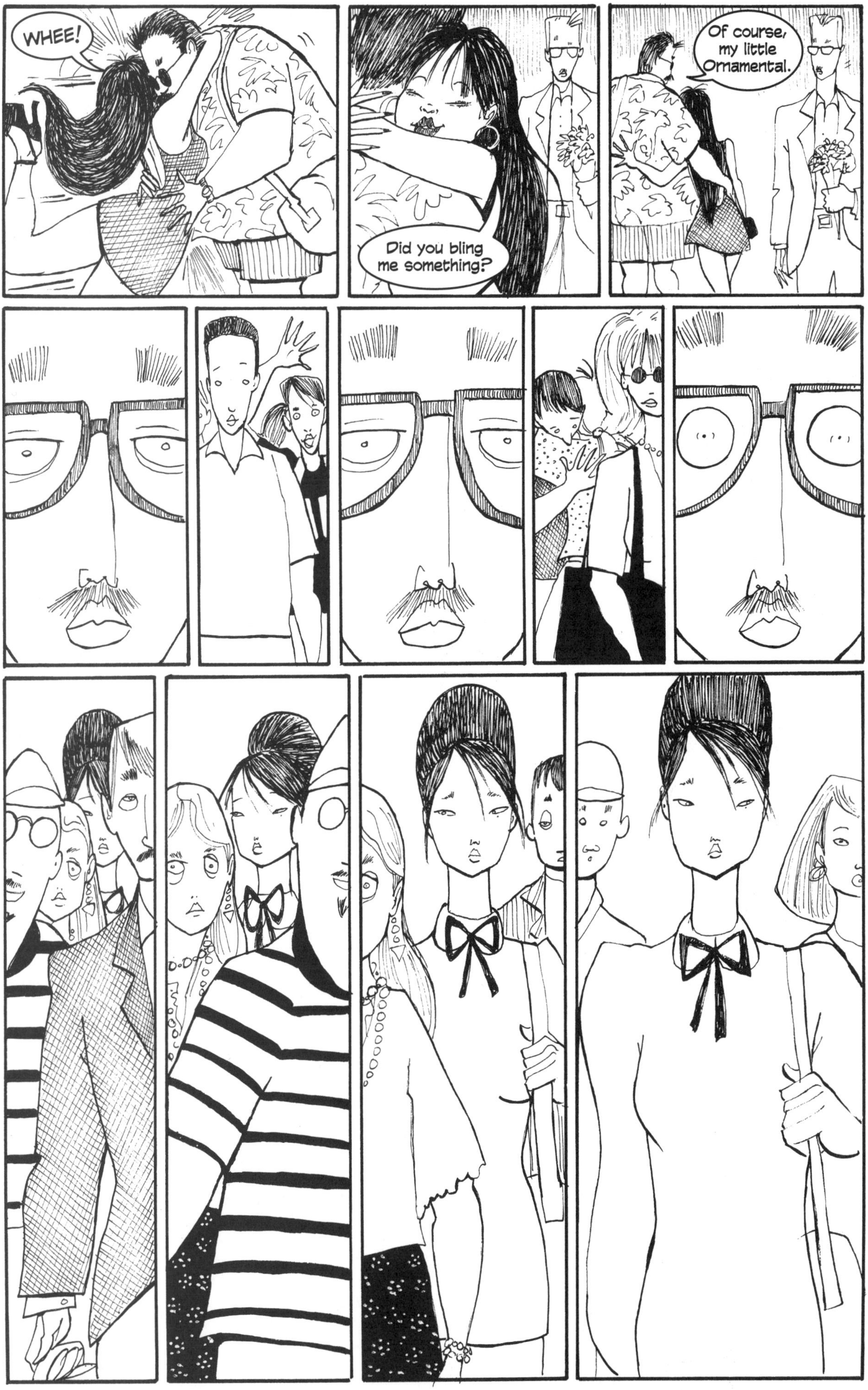
WHEE!
Did you bling me something?
Of course, my little Ornamental.

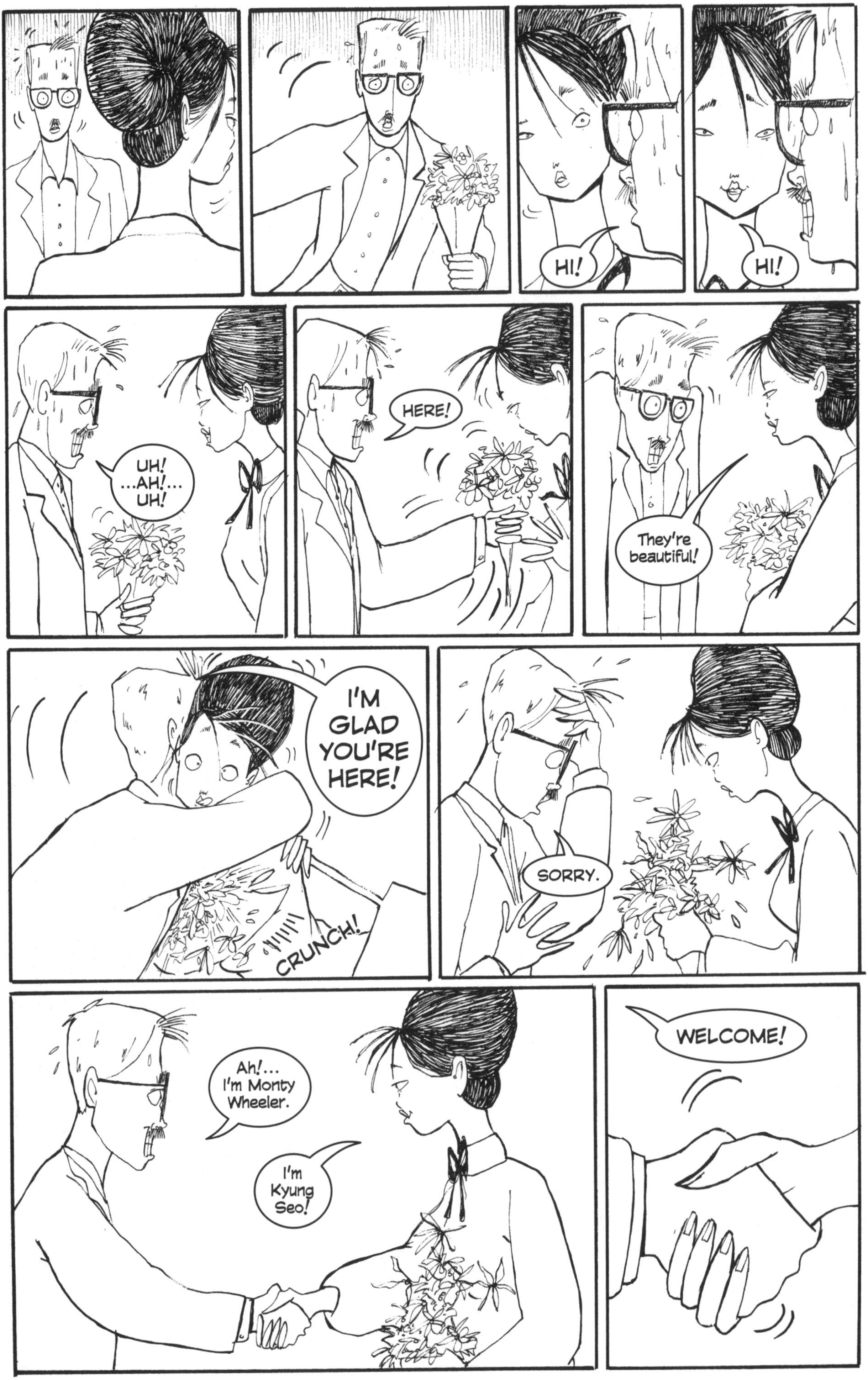
HI!
HI!
UH! ...AH!... UH!
HERE!
They're beautiful!
I'M GLAD YOU'RE HERE!
CRUNCH!
SORRY.
Ah!... I'm Monty Wheeler.
I'm Kyung Seo!
WELCOME!

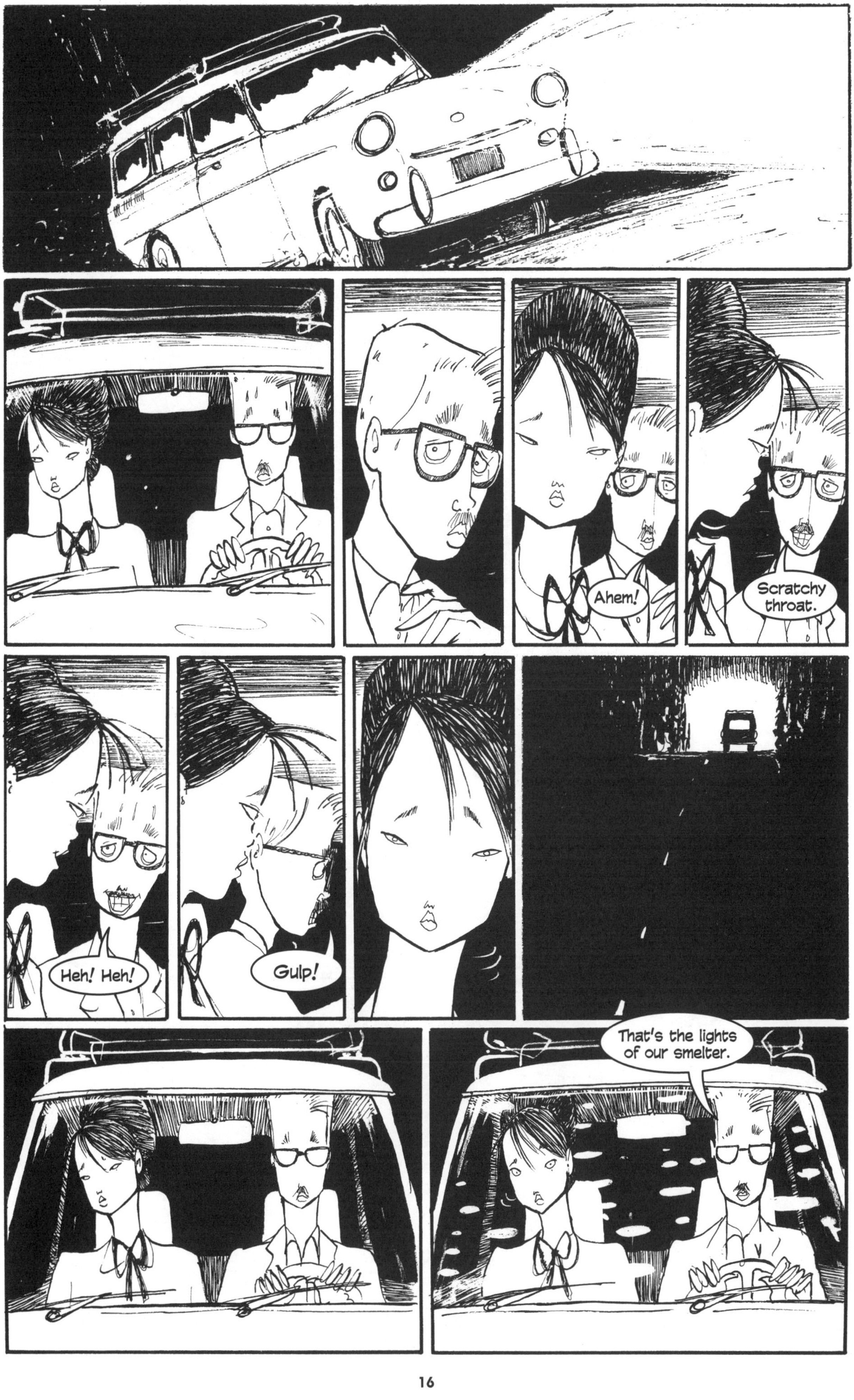
Ahem!
Scratchy throat.
Heh! Heh!
Gulp!
That's the lights of our smelter.

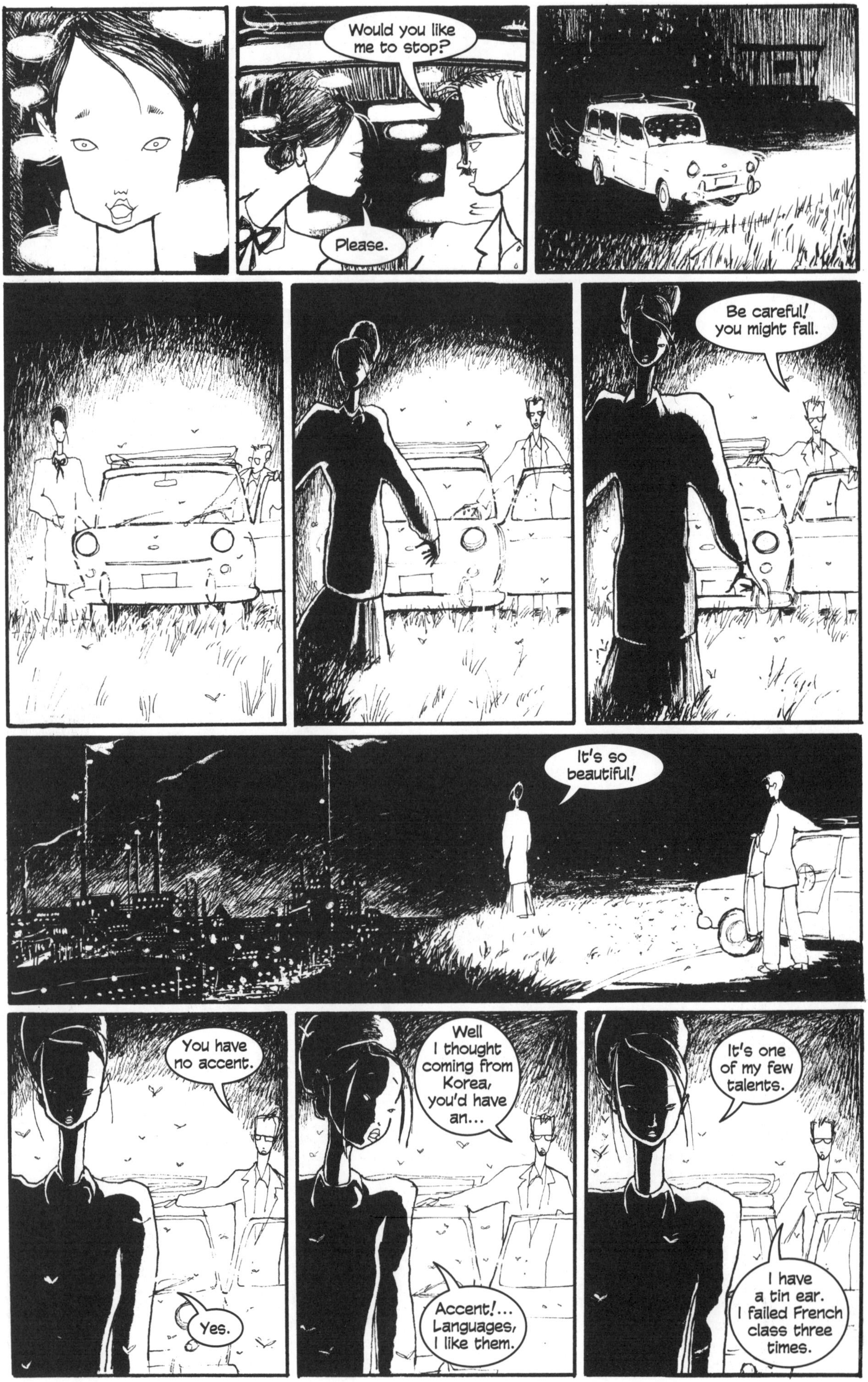
Would you like me to stop?
Please.
Be careful! you might fall.
It's so beautiful!
You have no accent.
Yes.
Well I thought coming from Korea, you'd have an...
Accent!... Languages, I like them.
It's one of my few talents.
I have a tin ear. I failed French class three times.

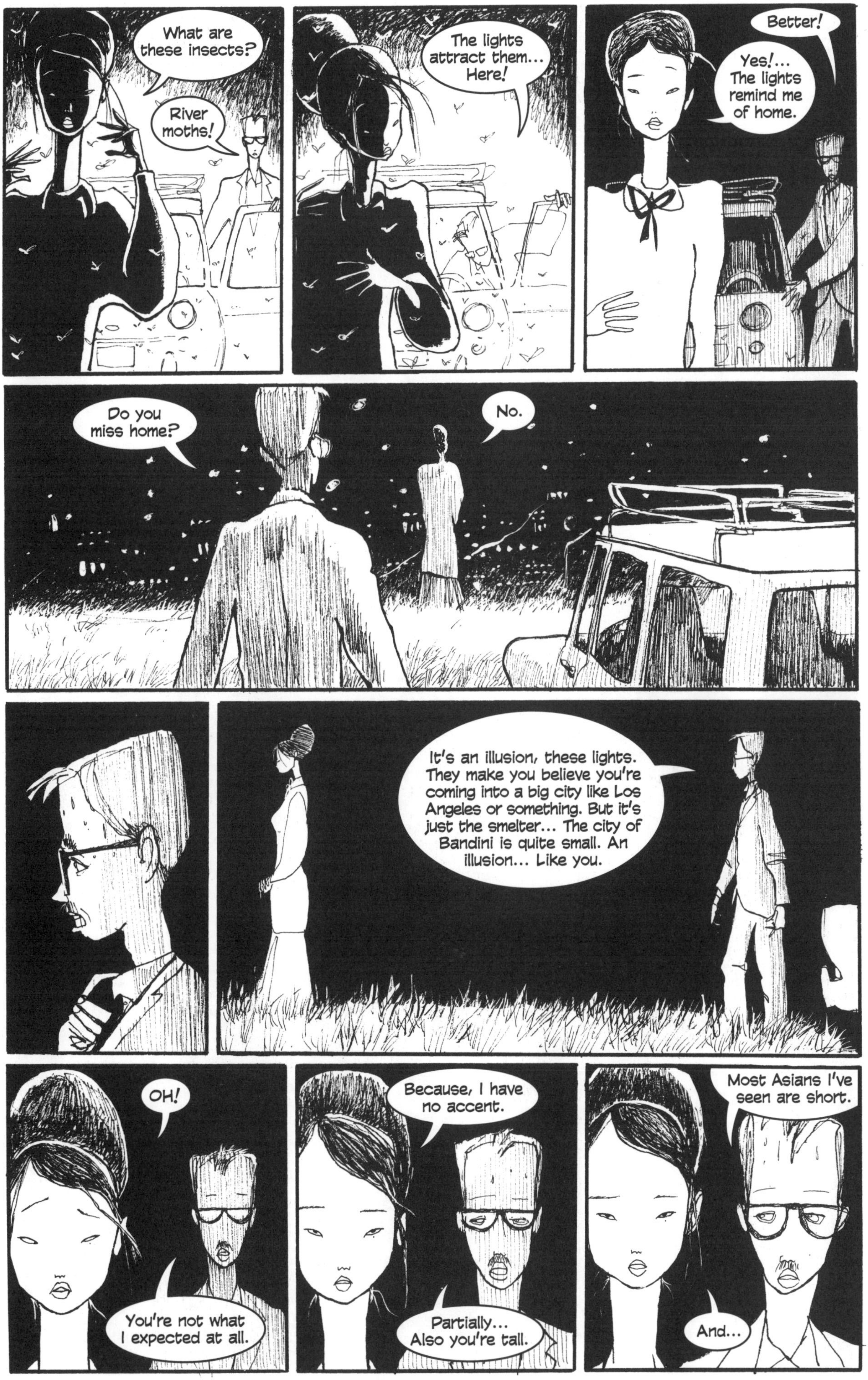
What are these insects?
River moths!
The lights attract them... Here!
Better!
Yes!... The lights remind me of home.
Do you miss home?
No.
It's an illusion, these lights. They make you believe you're coming into a big city like Los Angeles or something. But it's just the smelter... The city of Bandini is quite small. An illusion... Like you.
OH!
You're not what I expected at all.
Because, I have no accent.
Partially... Also you're tall.
Most Asians I've seen are short.
And...

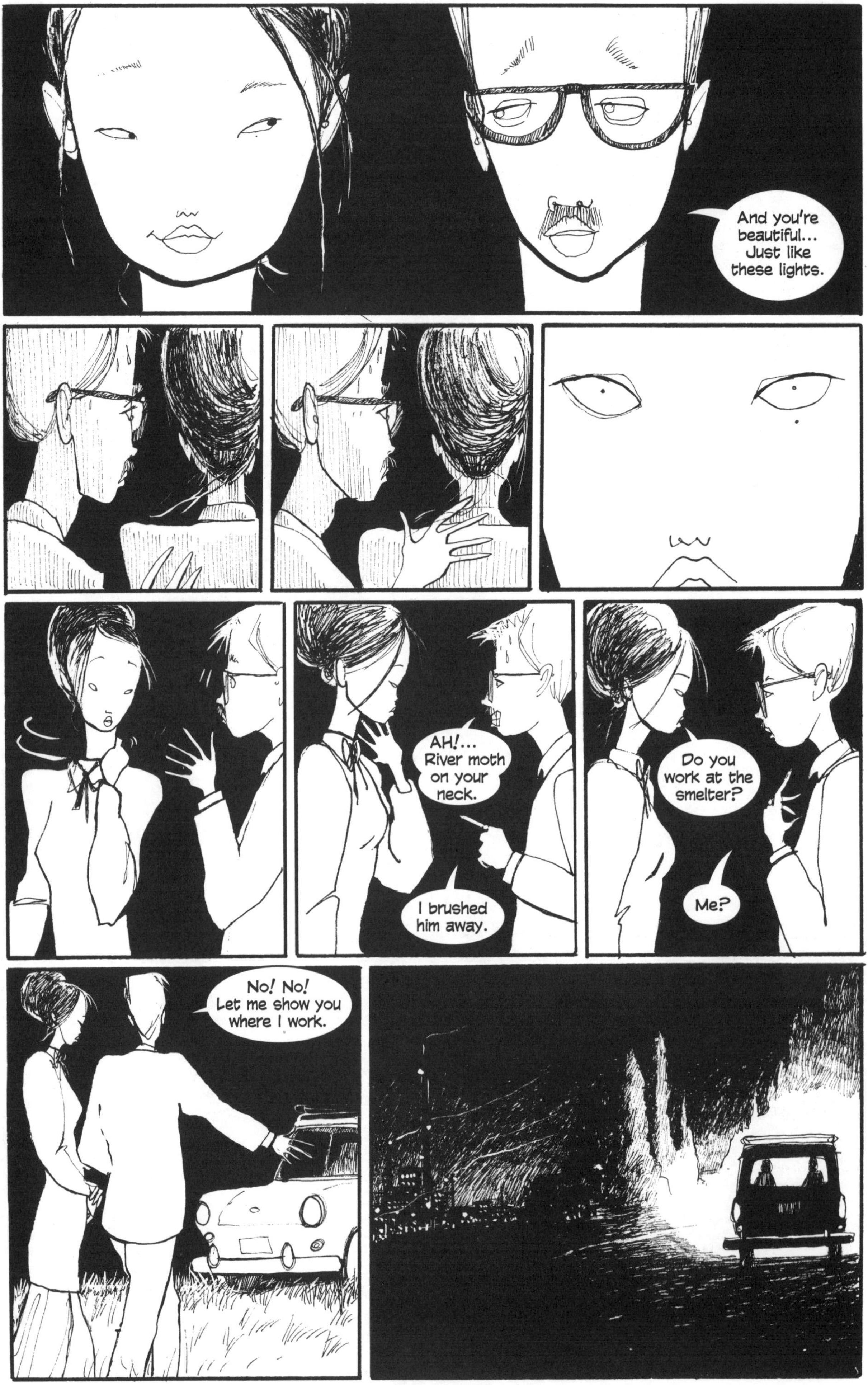
And you're beautiful... Just like these lights.
AH!... River moth on your neck.
I brushed him away.
Do you work at the smelter?
Me?
No! No! Let me show you where I work.

Come in.

I'll turn on the lights.

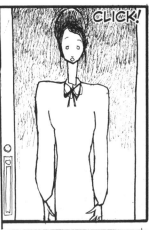

CLICK!

TA DAH! THIS IS WHERE I WORK!

ADULT

I sell comics, games, and toys!

I'm the biggest distributor in the area.

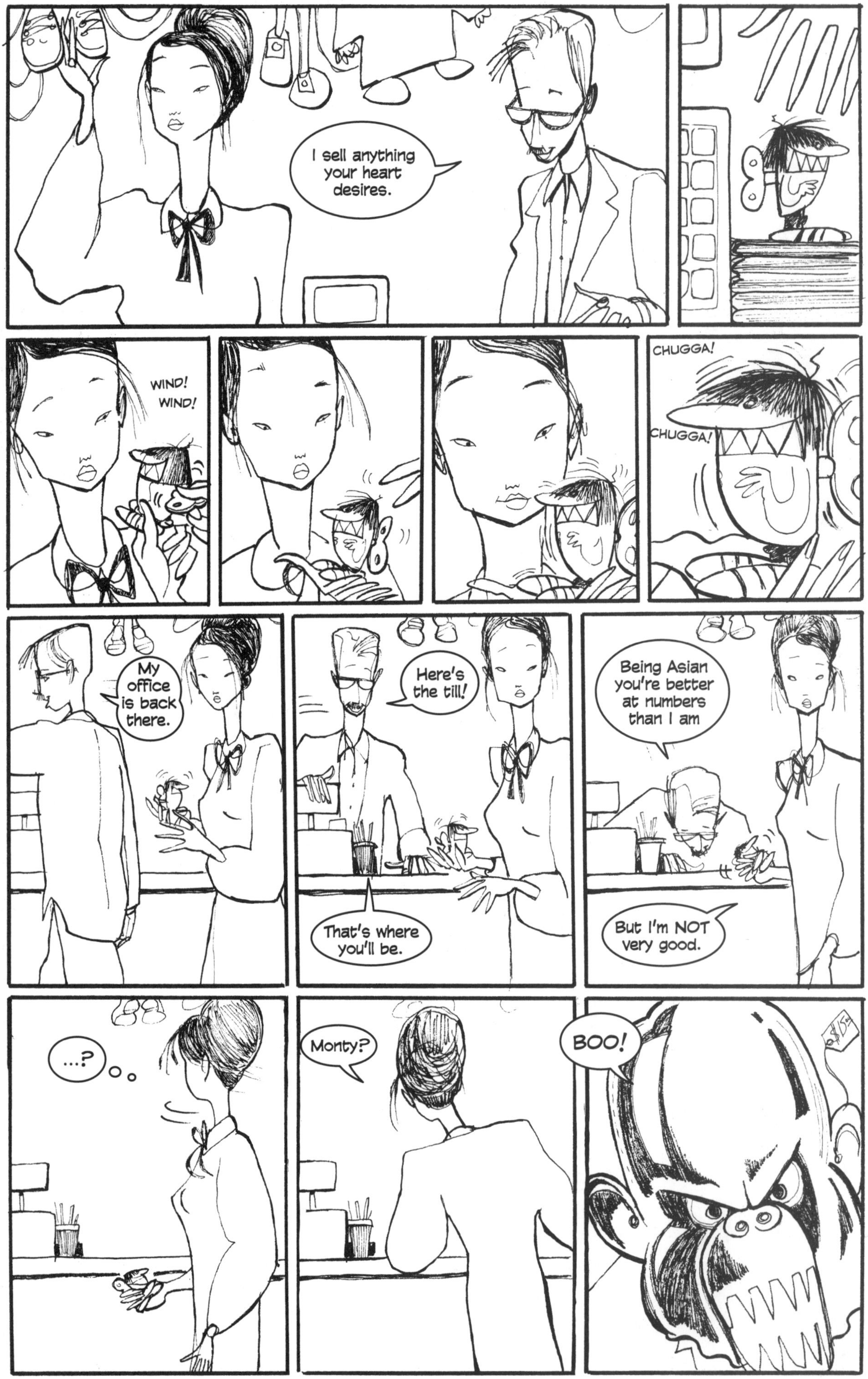

I sell anything your heart desires.
WIND! WIND!
CHUGGA! CHUGGA!
My office is back there.
Here's the till!
That's where you'll be.
Being Asian you're better at numbers than I am
But I'm NOT very good.
...?
Monty?
BOO!

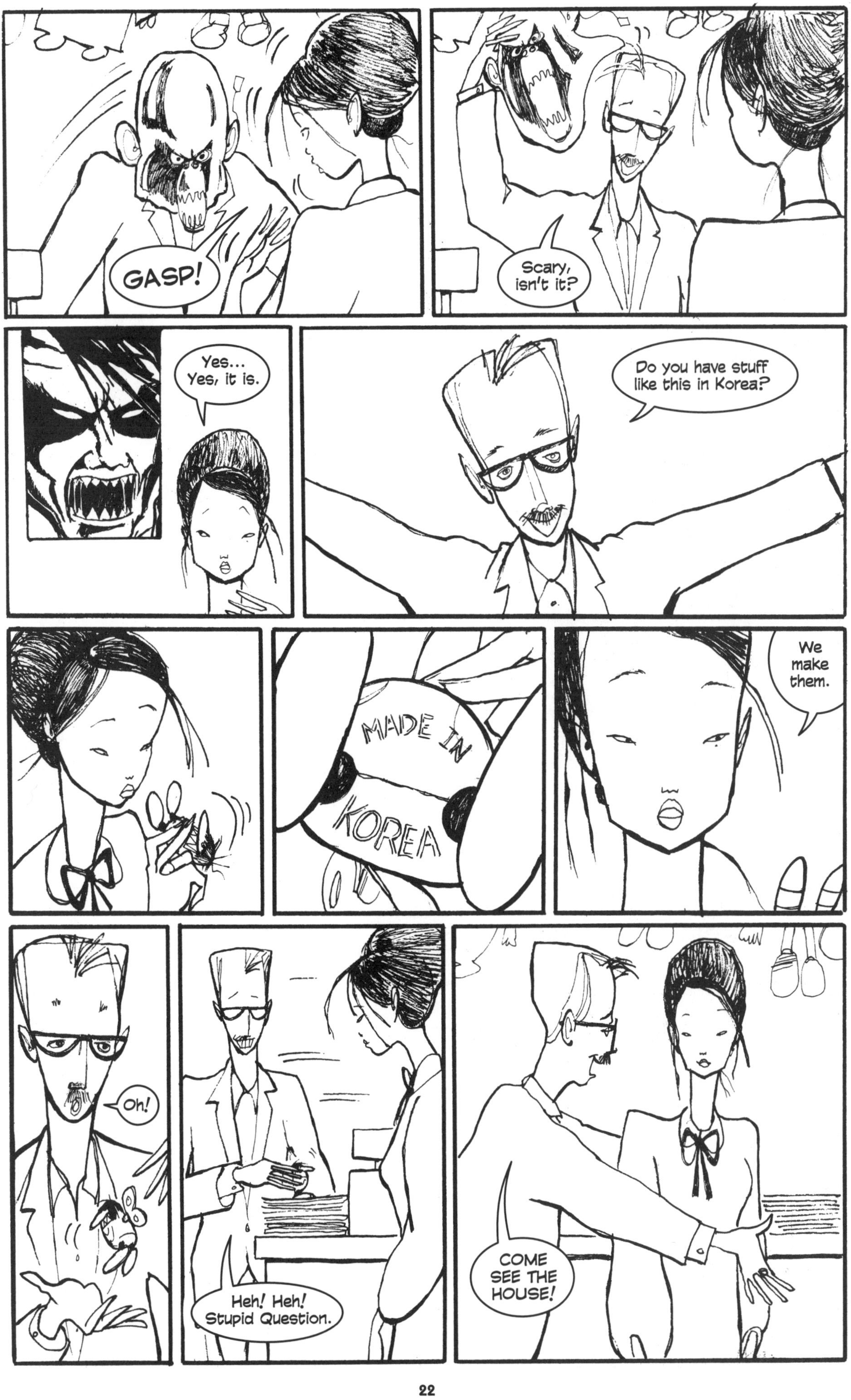
GASP!
Scary, isn't it?
Yes... Yes, it is.
Do you have stuff like this in Korea?
MADE IN KOREA
We make them.
Oh!
Heh! Heh! Stupid Question.
COME SEE THE HOUSE!

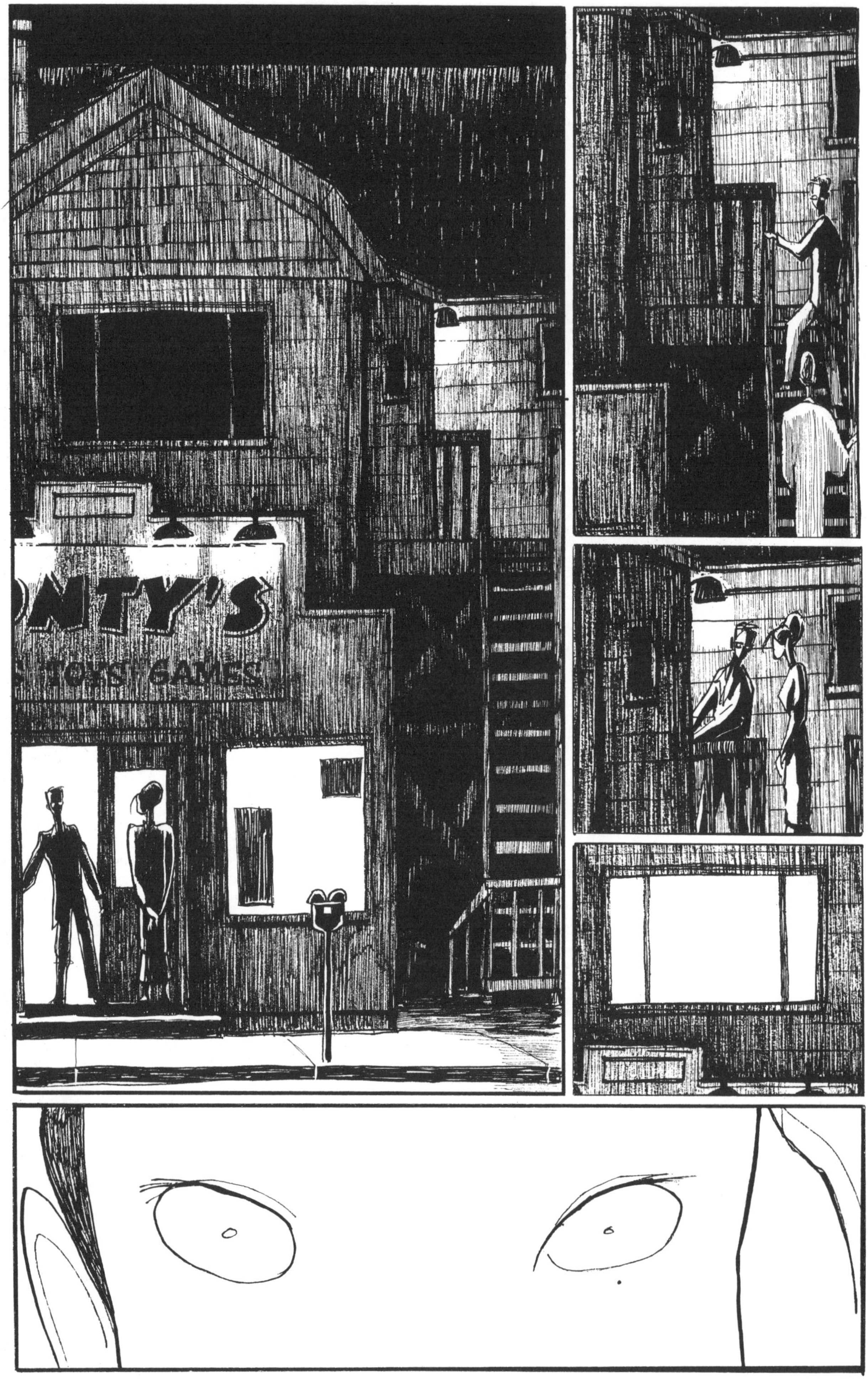
ONTY'S
TOYS GAMES

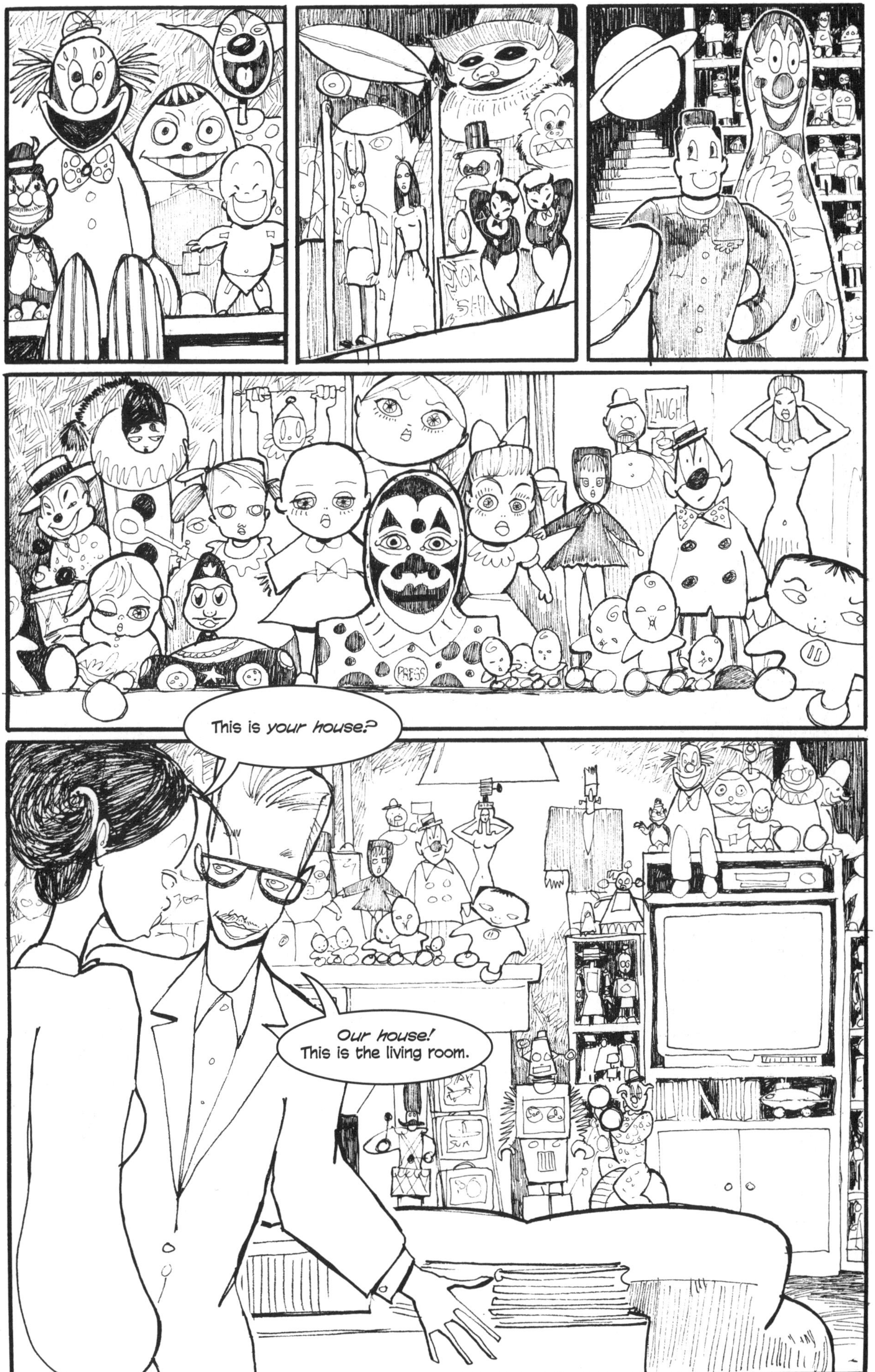
LAUGH!
PRESS
This is *your house?*
Our house!
This is the living room.

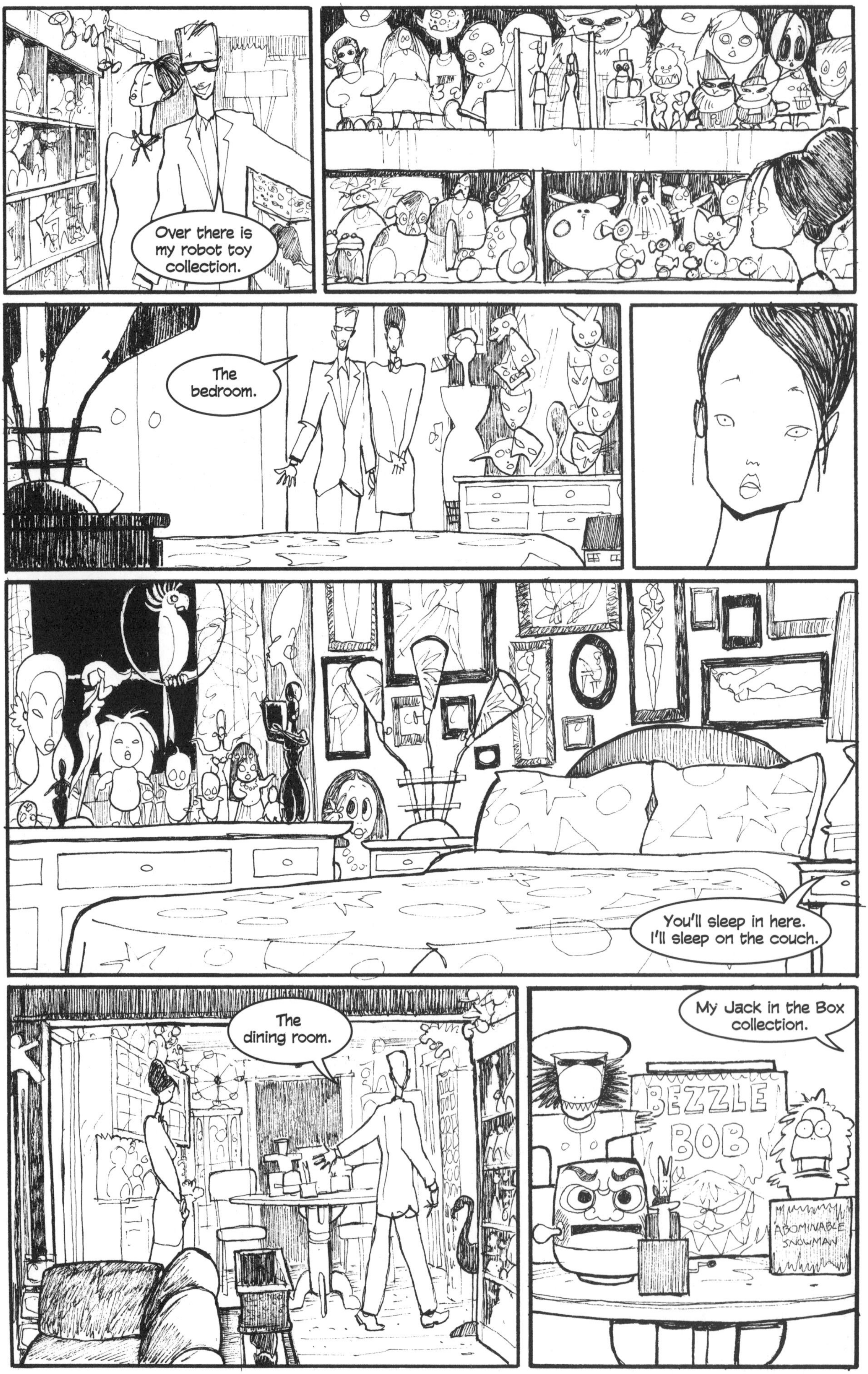
Over there is my robot toy collection.
The bedroom.
You'll sleep in here. I'll sleep on the couch.
The dining room.
My Jack in the Box collection.
BEZZLE BOB
ABOMINABLE SNOWMAN

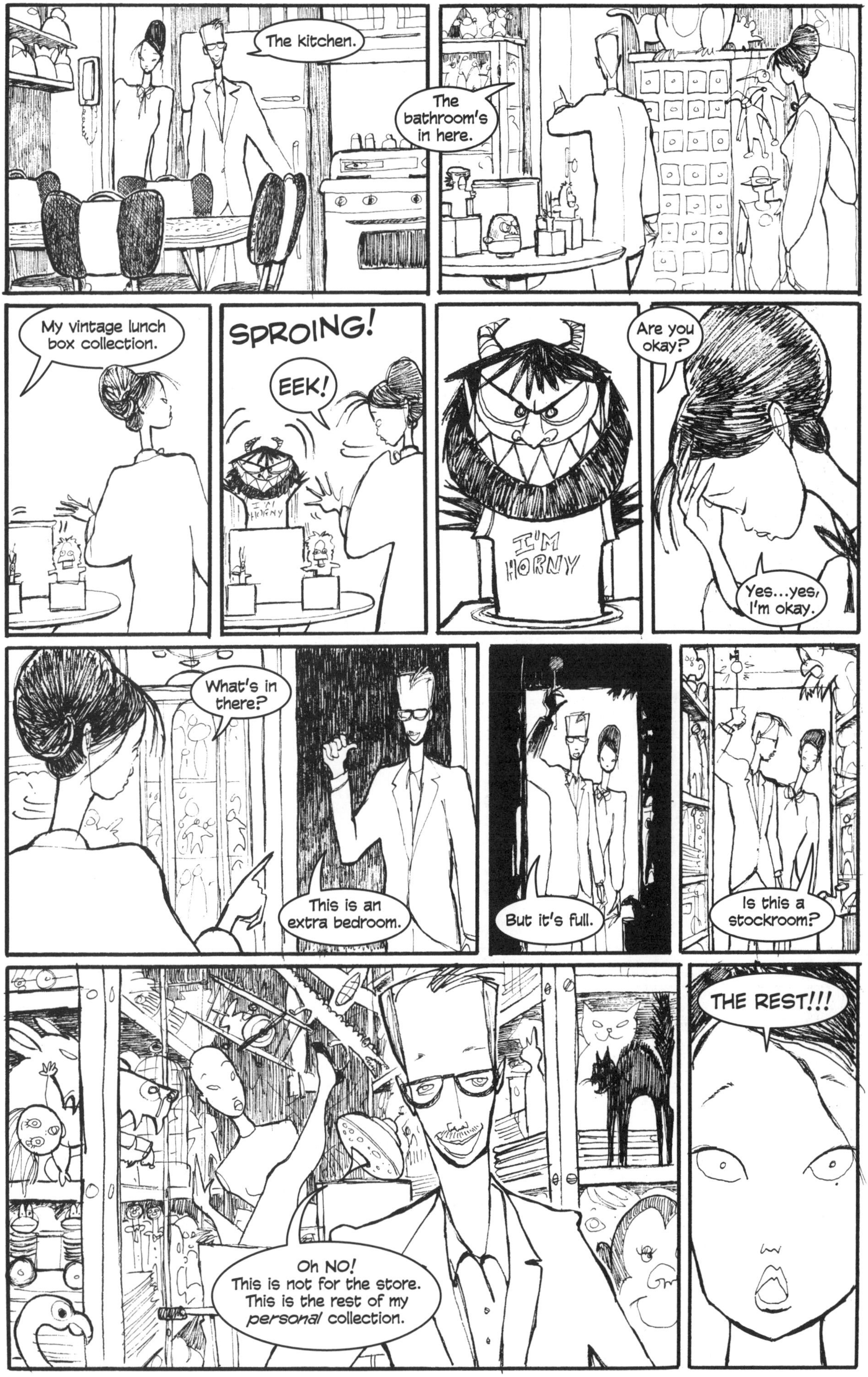
The kitchen.
The bathroom's in here.
My vintage lunch box collection.
SPROING!
EEK!
I'M HORNY
I'M HORNY
Are you okay?
Yes...yes, I'm okay.
What's in there?
This is an extra bedroom.
But it's full.
Is this a stockroom?
Oh NO! This is not for the store. This is the rest of my *personal* collection.
THE REST!!!

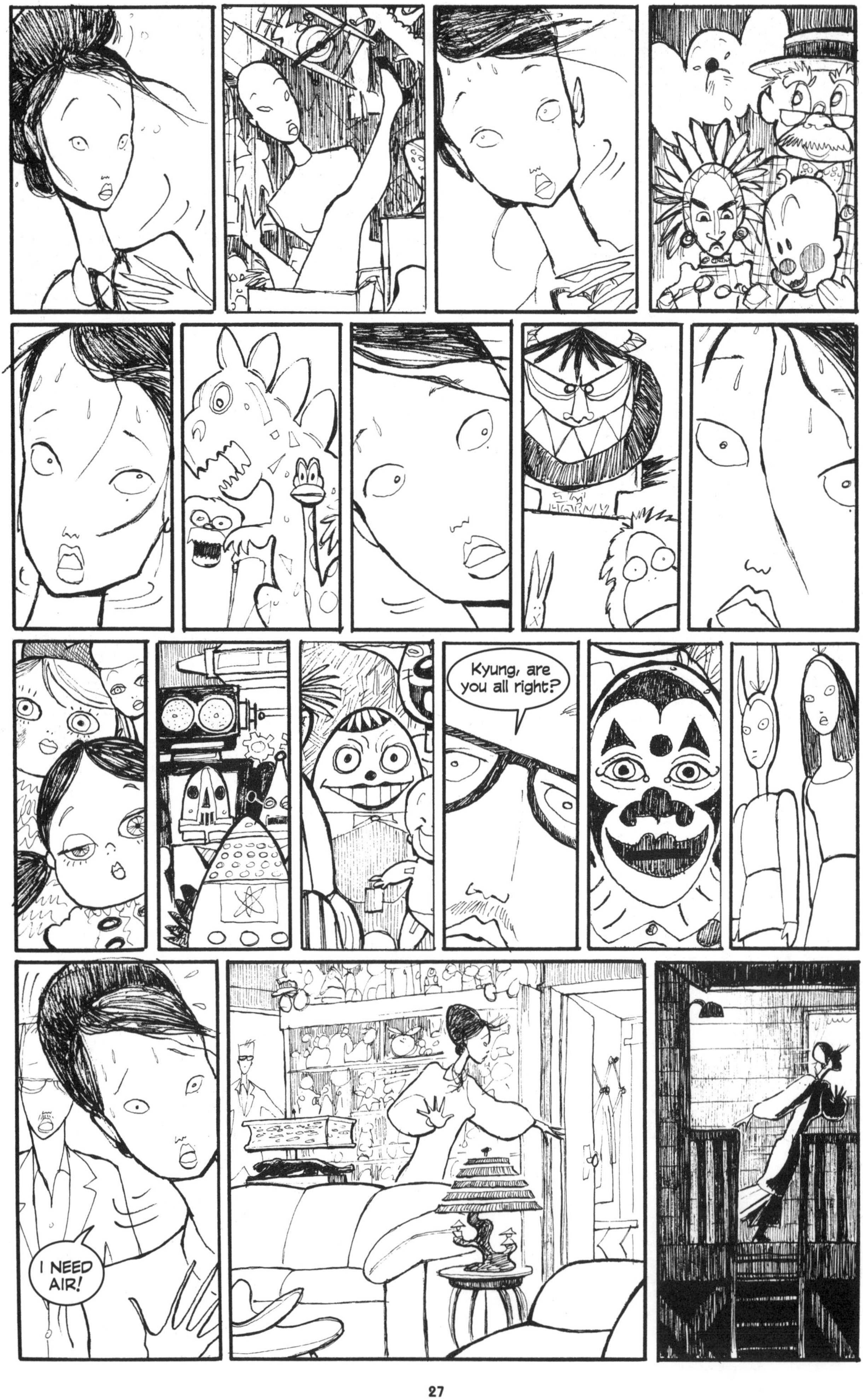
Kyung, are you all right?
I NEED AIR!

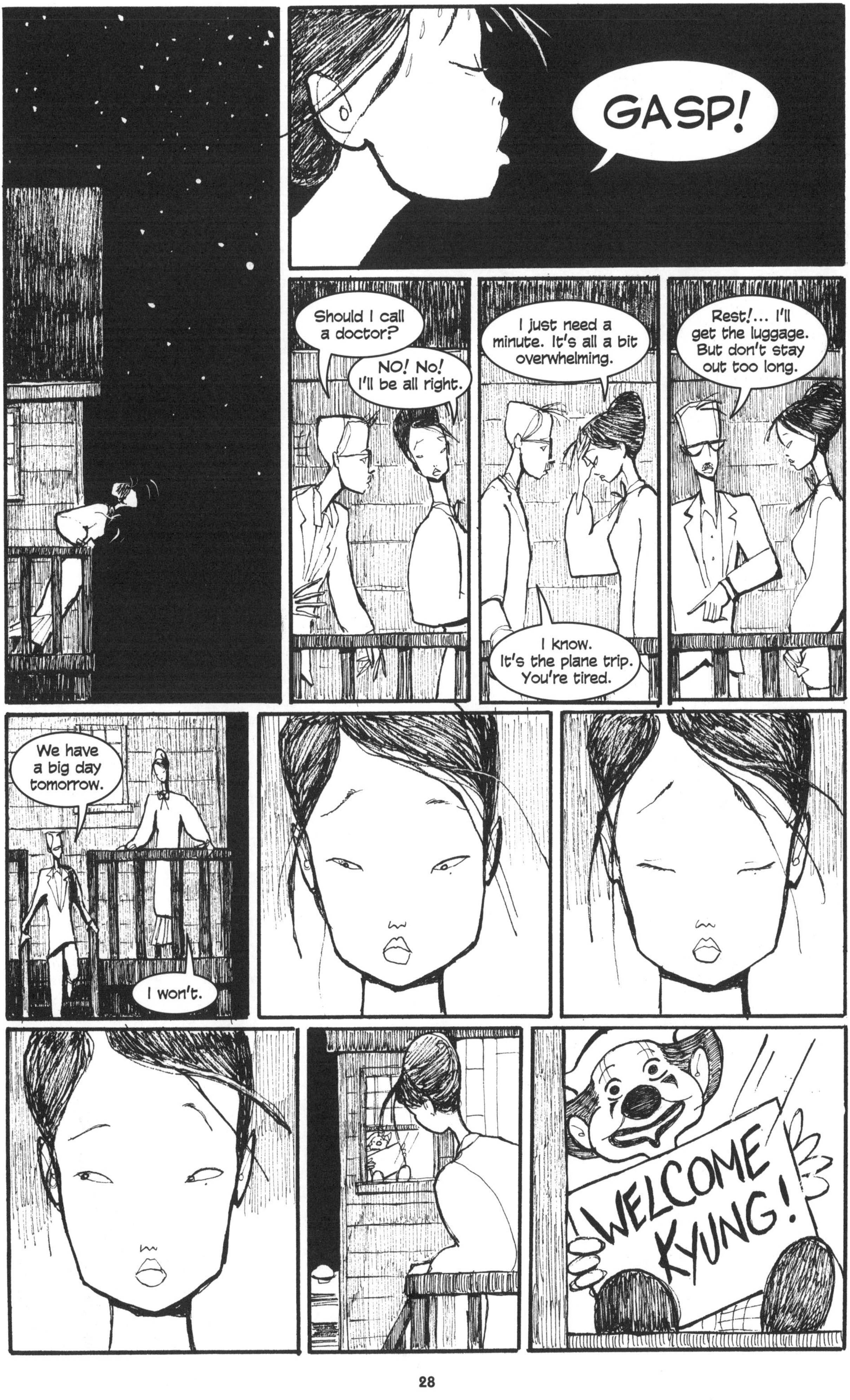
GASP!
Should I call a doctor?
NO! No! I'll be all right.
I just need a minute. It's all a bit overwhelming.
I know. It's the plane trip. You're tired.
Rest!... I'll get the luggage. But don't stay out too long.
We have a big day tomorrow.
I won't.
WELCOME KYUNG!

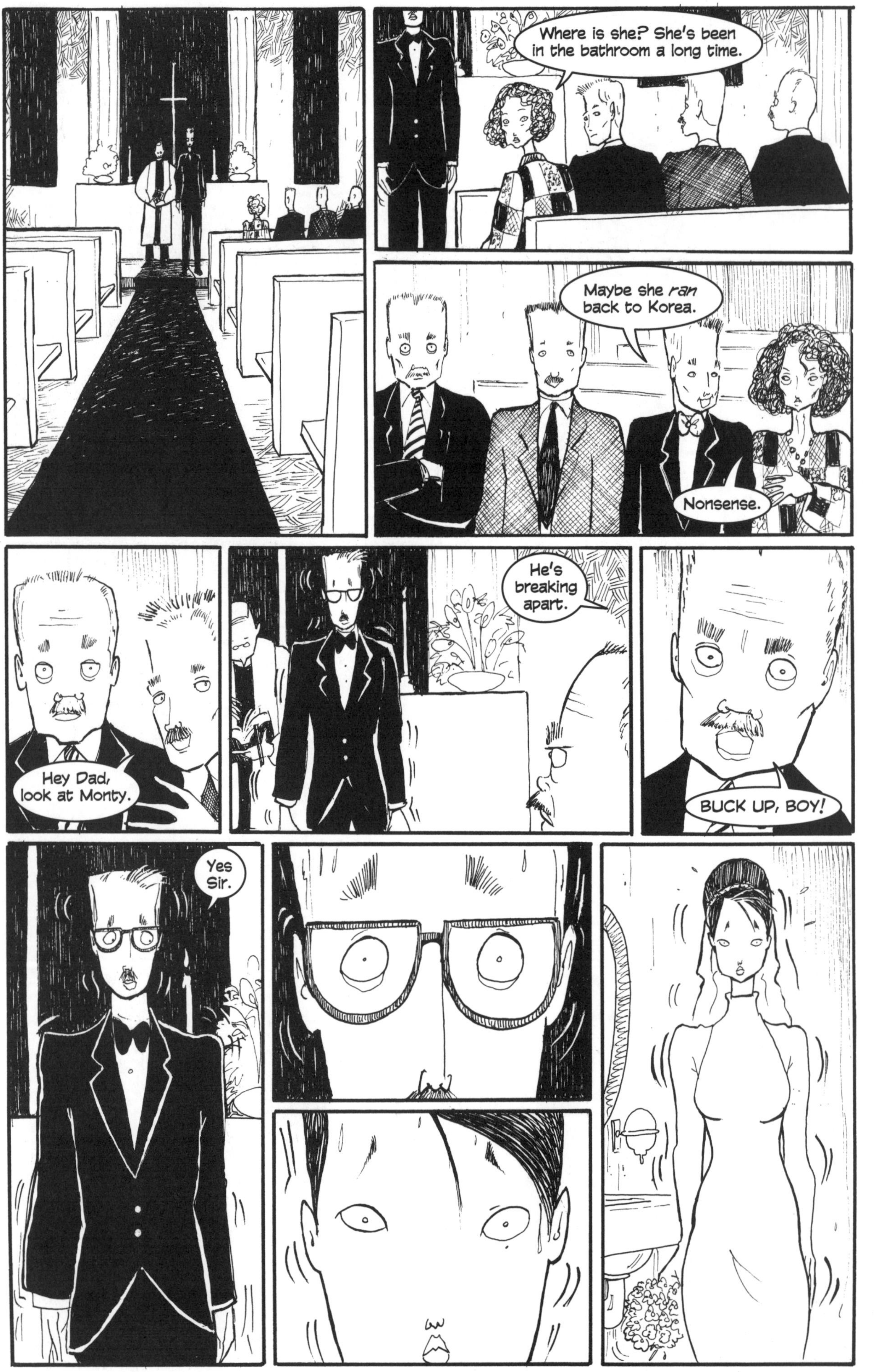
Where is she? She's been in the bathroom a long time.
Maybe she *ran* back to Korea.
Nonsense.
Hey Dad, look at Monty.
He's breaking apart.
BUCK UP, BOY!
Yes Sir.

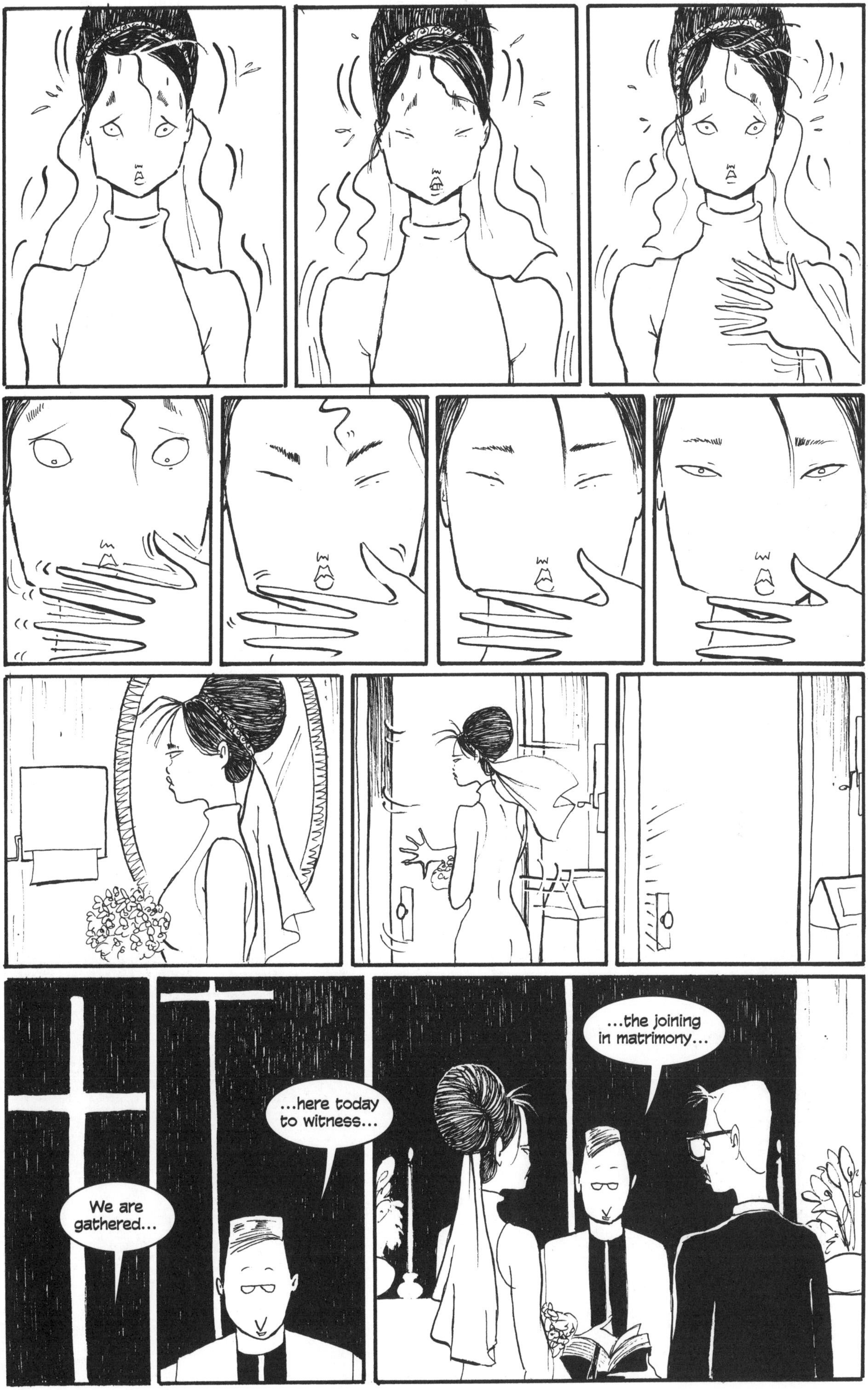
We are gathered...
...here today to witness...
...the joining in matrimony...

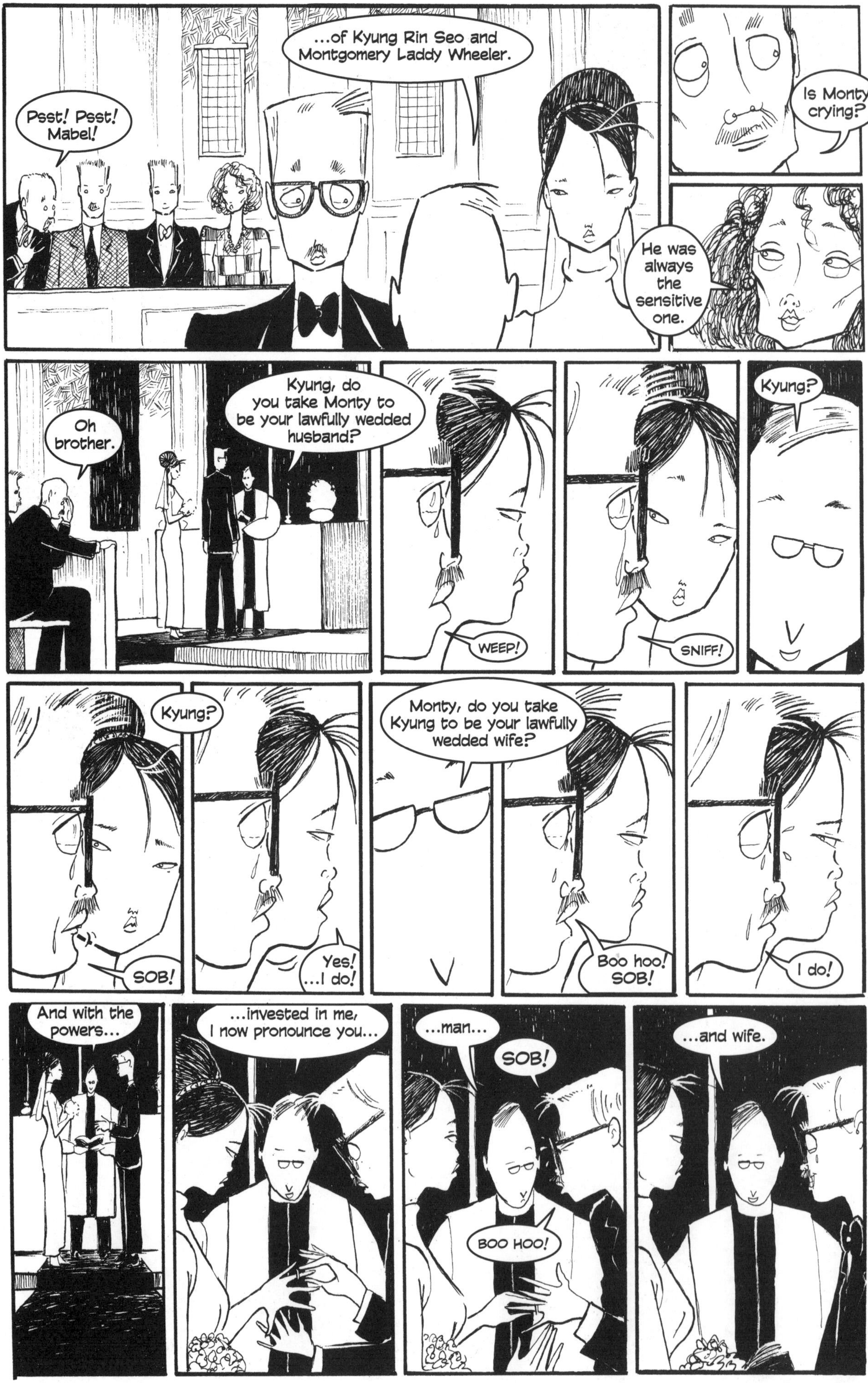
...of Kyung Rin Seo and Montgomery Laddy Wheeler.
Psst! Psst! Mabel!
Is Monty crying?
He was always the sensitive one.
Oh brother.
Kyung, do you take Monty to be your lawfully wedded husband?
WEEP!
SNIFF!
Kyung?
Kyung?
SOB!
Yes! ...I do!
Monty, do you take Kyung to be your lawfully wedded wife?
Boo hoo! SOB!
I do!
And with the powers...
...invested in me, I now pronounce you...
...man...
SOB!
BOO HOO!
...and wife.

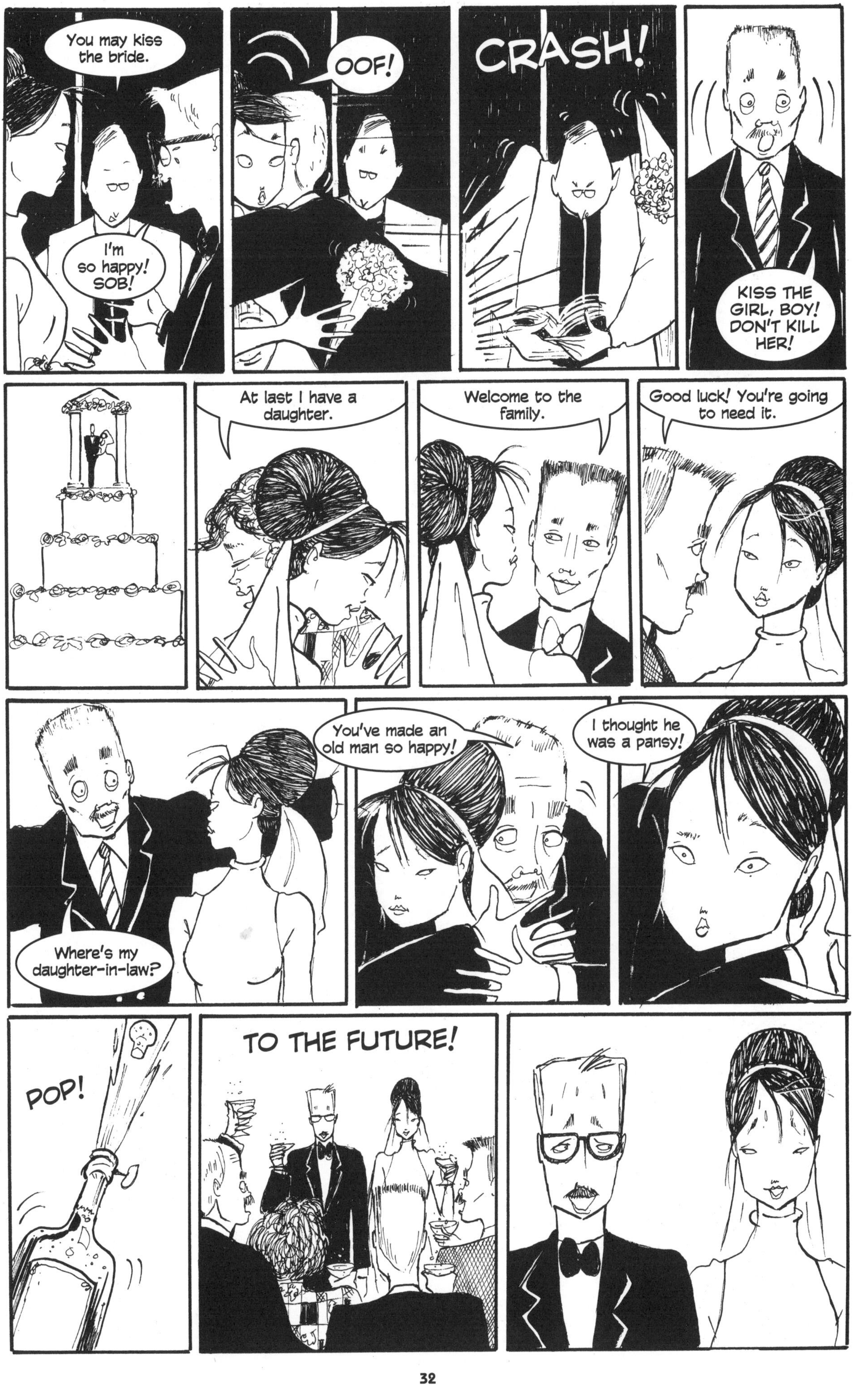
You may kiss the bride.
I'm so happy! SOB!
OOF!
CRASH!
KISS THE GIRL, BOY! DON'T KILL HER!
At last I have a daughter.
Welcome to the family.
Good luck! You're going to need it.
Where's my daughter-in-law?
You've made an old man so happy!
I thought he was a pansy!
POP!
TO THE FUTURE!

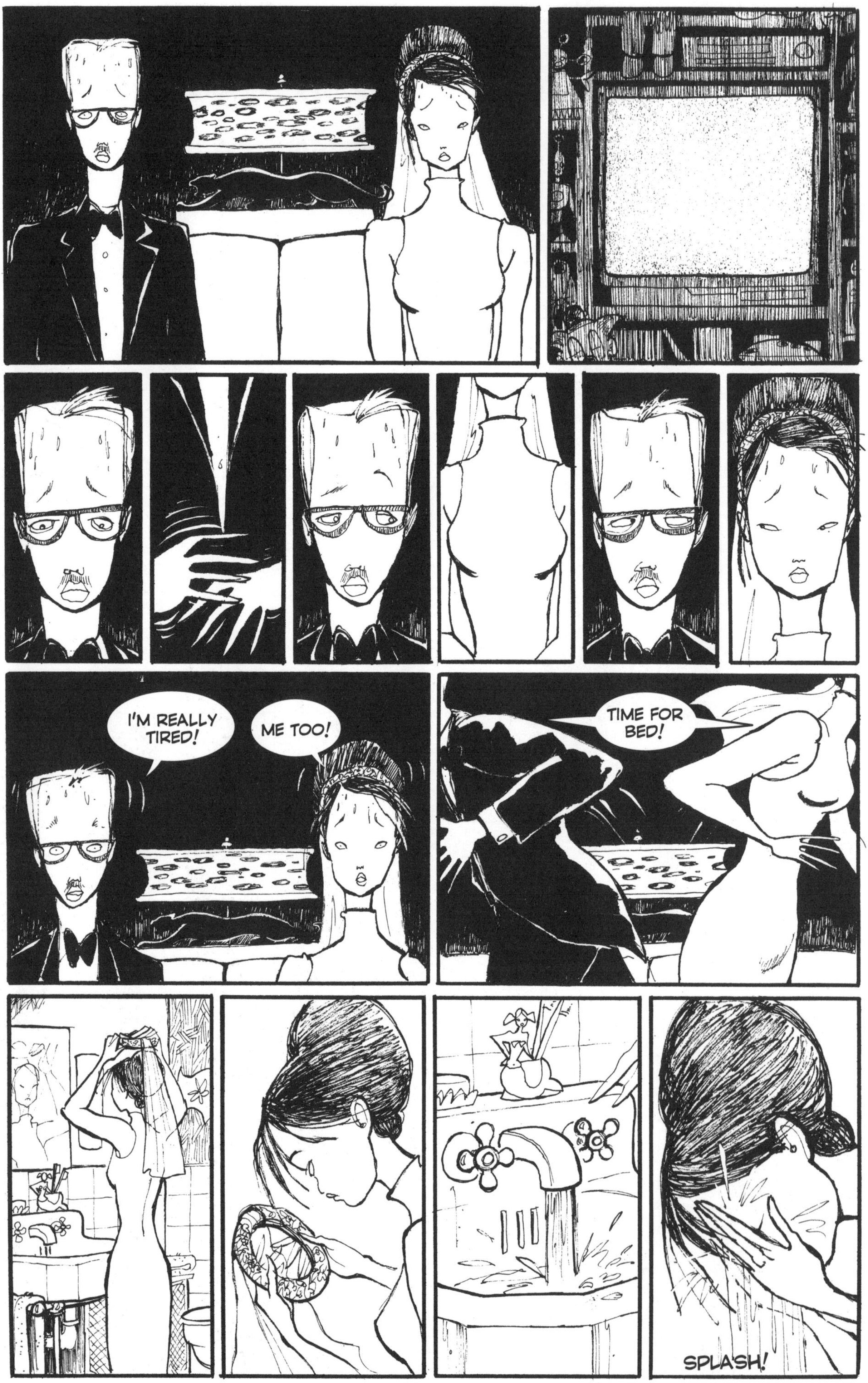
I'M REALLY TIRED!
ME TOO!
TIME FOR BED!
SPLASH!

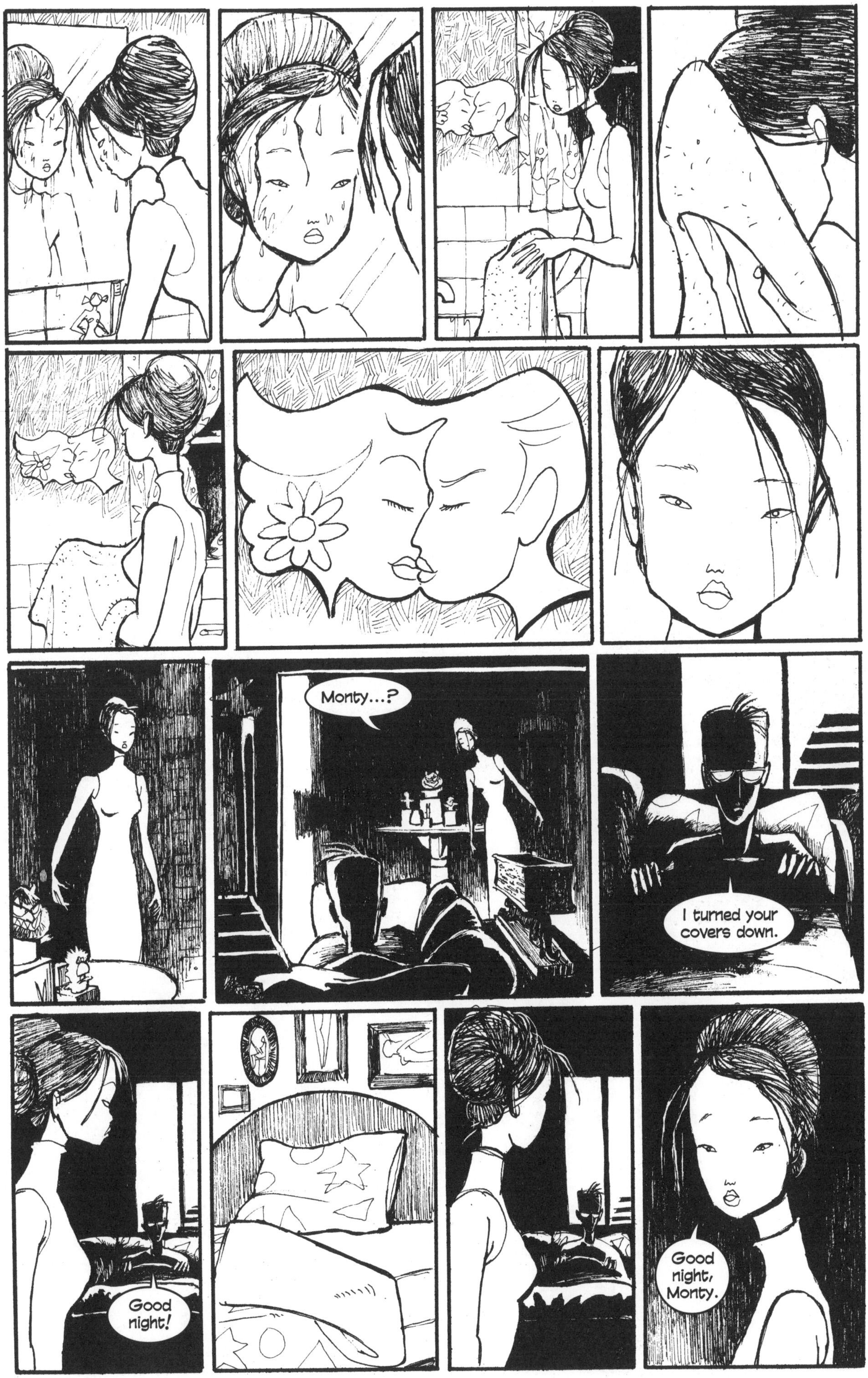
Monty...?
I turned your covers down.
Good night!
Good night, Monty.

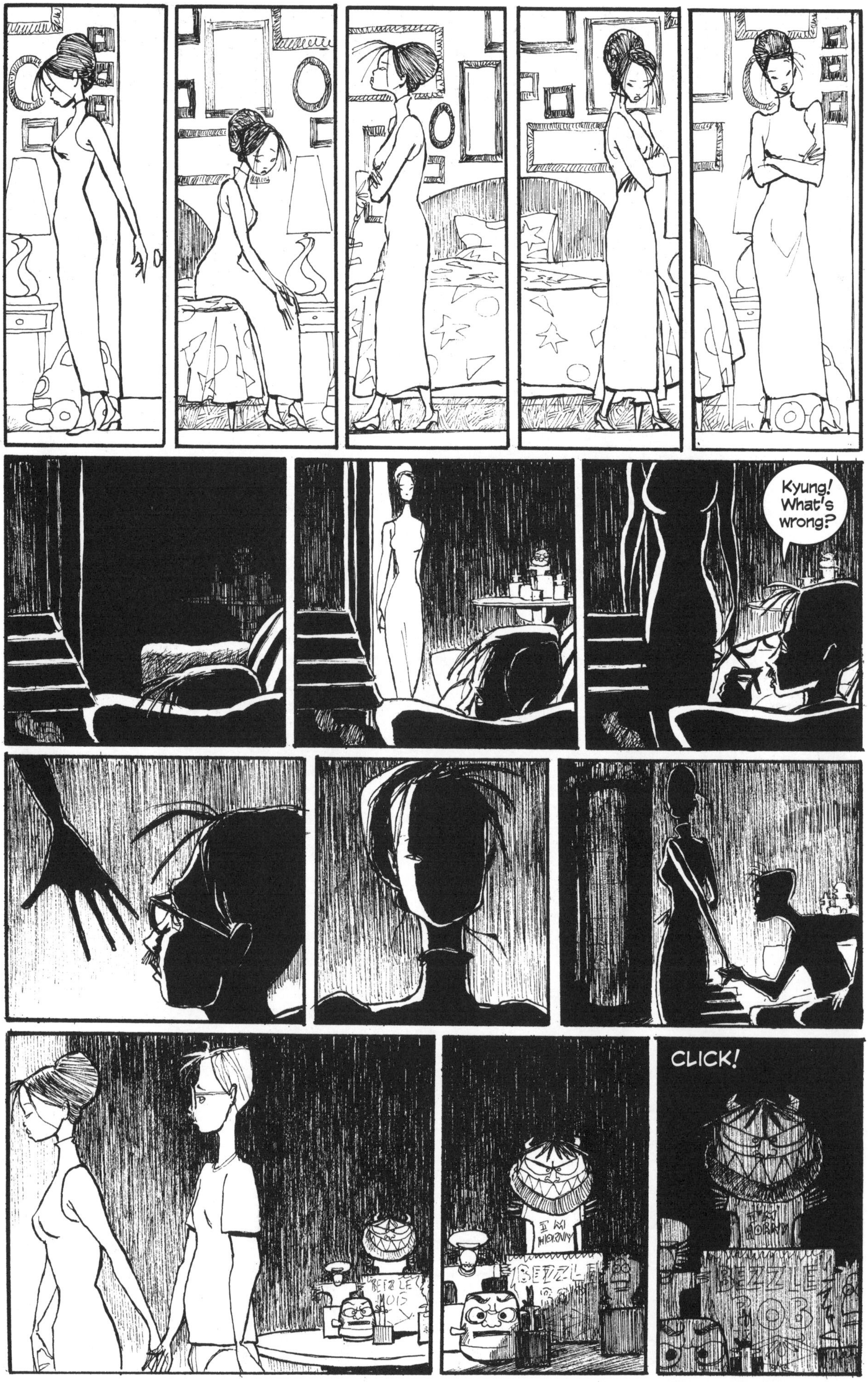
Kyung! What's wrong?
CLICK!

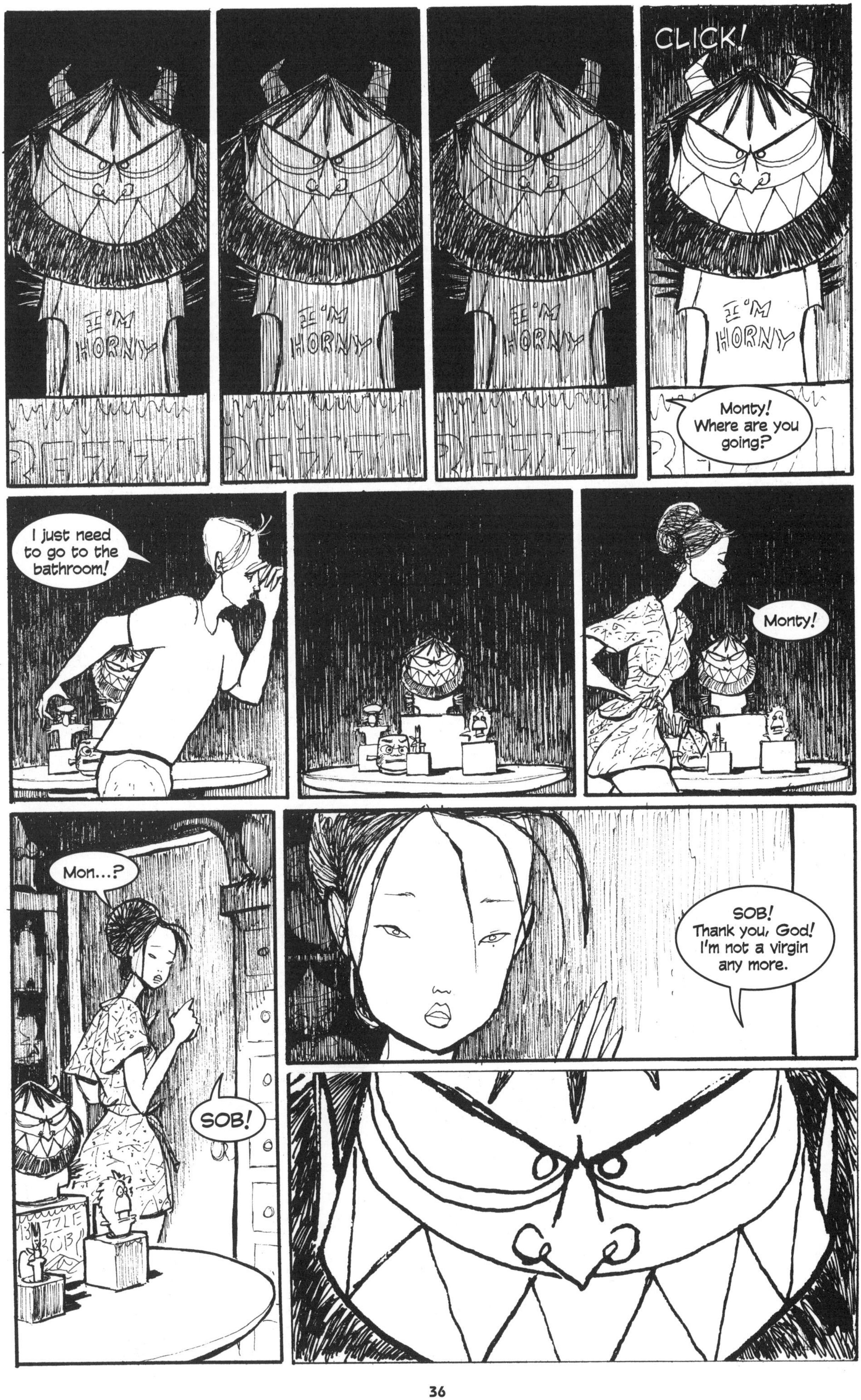
I'M HORNY
I'M HORNY
I'M HORNY
CLICK!
I'M HORNY
Monty! Where are you going?
I just need to go to the bathroom!
Monty!
Mon...?
SOB!
SOB! Thank you, God! I'm not a virgin any more.

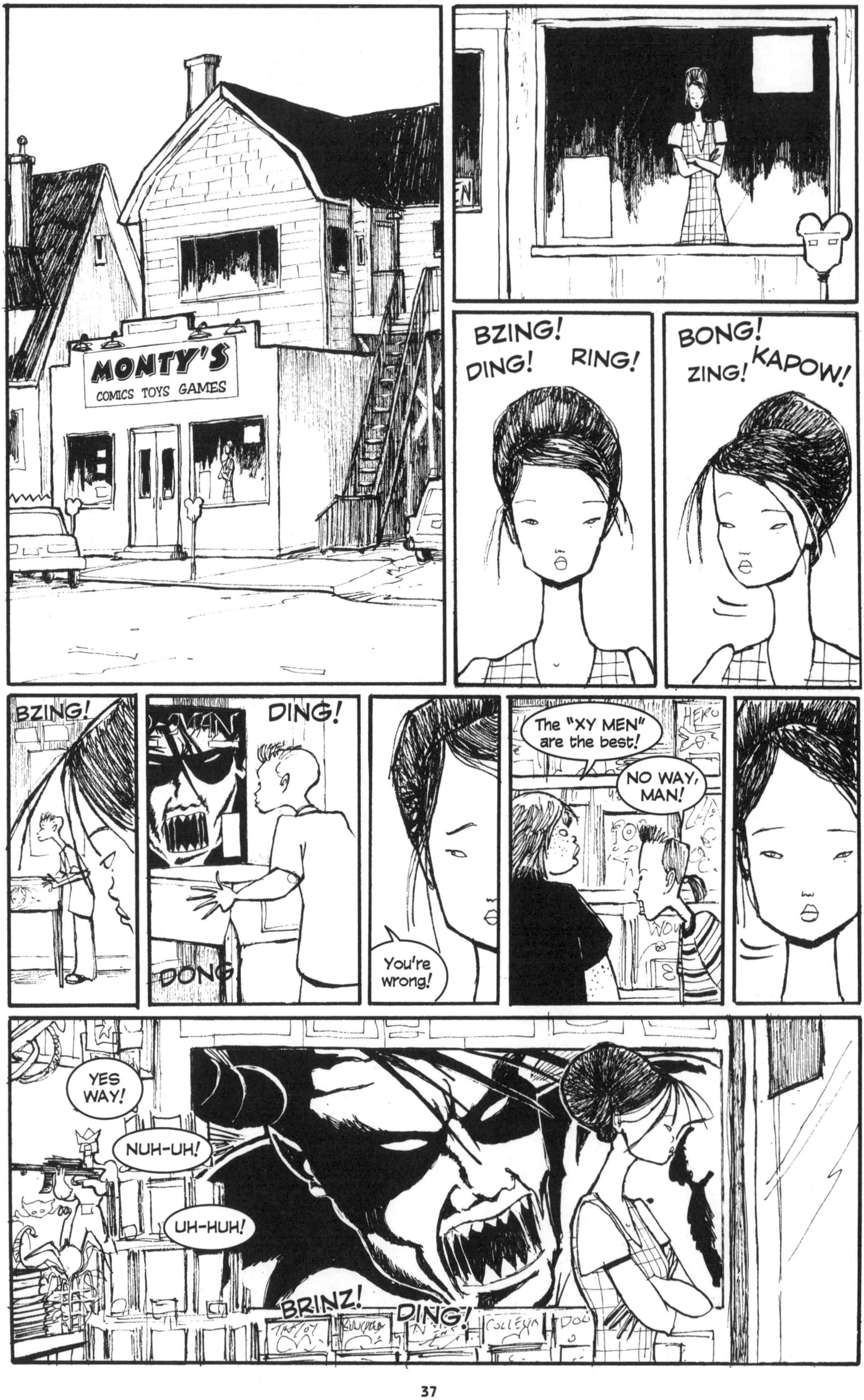
MONTY'S
COMICS TOYS GAMES
BZING!
DING!
RING!
BONG!
ZING!
KAPOW!
BZING!
DING!
DONG
You're wrong!
The "XY MEN" are the best!
NO WAY, MAN!
YES WAY!
NUH-UH!
UH-HUH!
BRINZ!
DING!

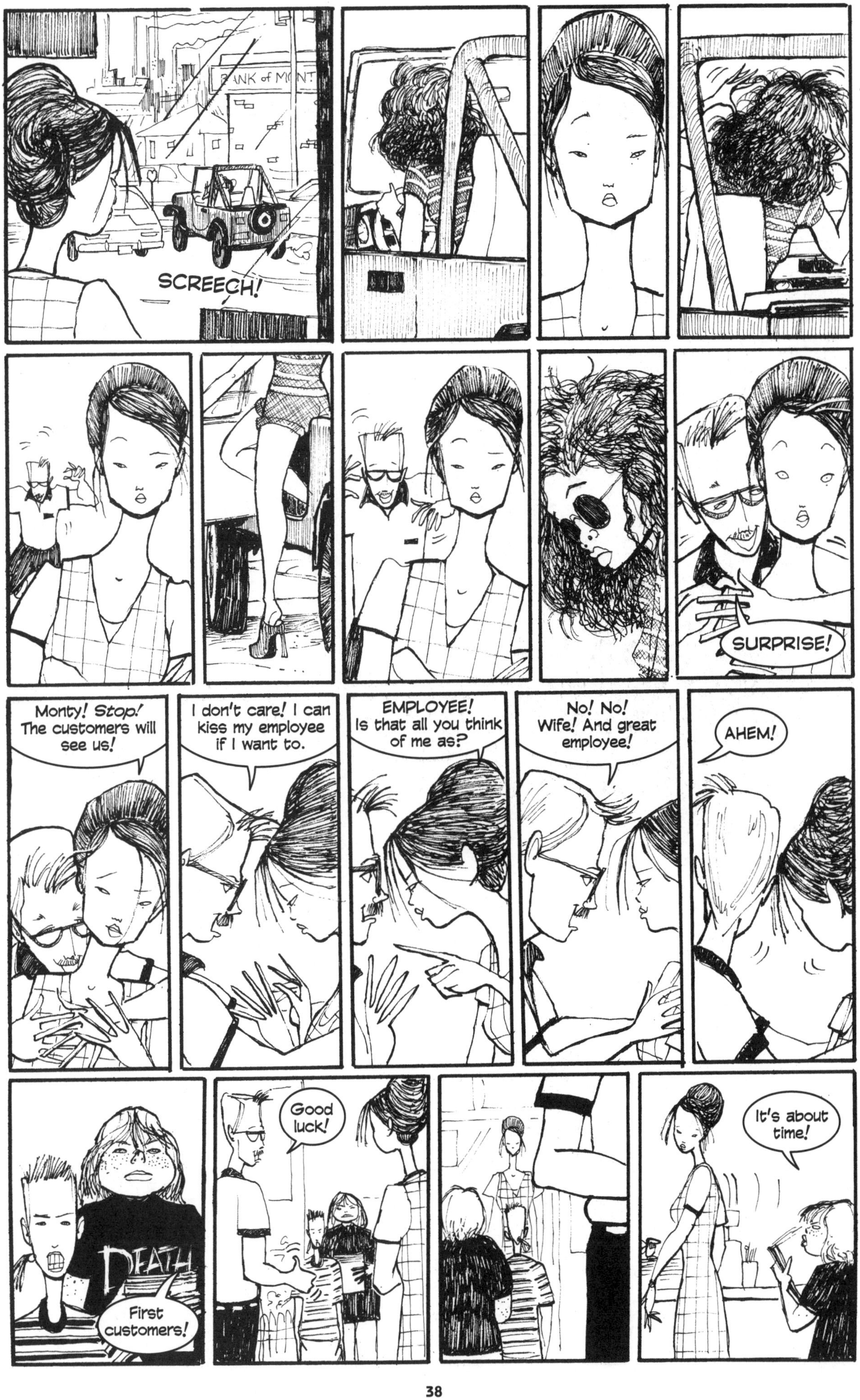
BANK of MONT
SCREECH!
SURPRISE!
Monty! Stop! The customers will see us!
I don't care! I can kiss my employee if I want to.
EMPLOYEE! Is that all you think of me as?
No! No! Wife! And great employee!
AHEM!
DEATH
First customers!
Good luck!
It's about time!

Clumsy!

Todd, do you have enough money for all of these?

No problem.

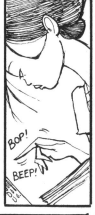

Mom gave me twenty dollars.

BOP!

BEEP!

Watch this. SHH!

$8.95 please.

Hey lady! This isn't right!

Pardon.

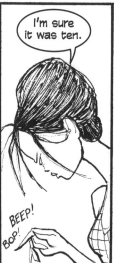

I gave you a twenty! You didn't give me enough change!

You saw me give her a twenty!

I SURE DID!

I'm sure it was ten.

BEEP!

BOP!

RIP-OFF JOINT!

RIP-OFF JOINT!

Let me think!

39

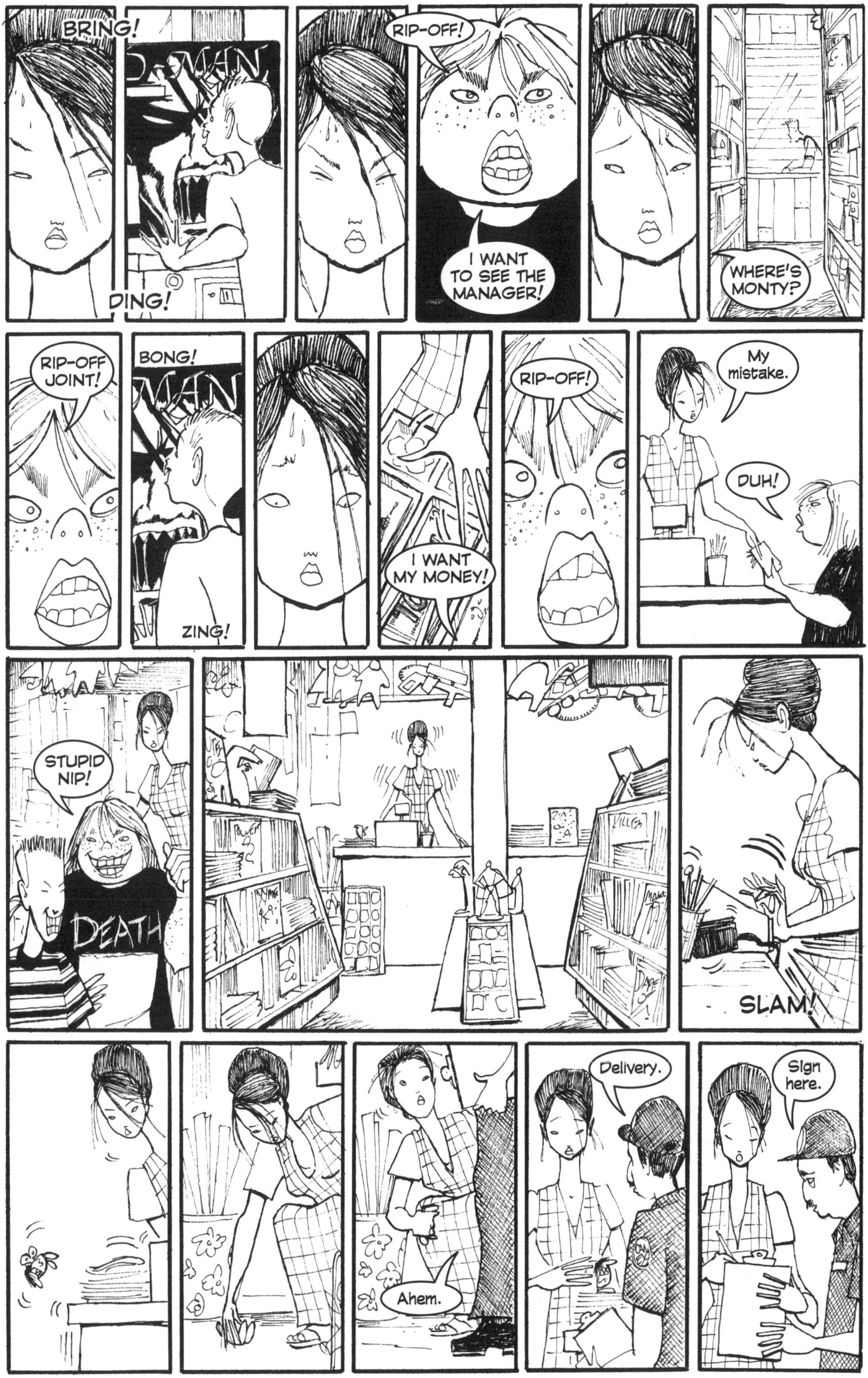
BRING!
DING!
RIP-OFF!
I WANT TO SEE THE MANAGER!
WHERE'S MONTY?
RIP-OFF JOINT!
BONG!
ZING!
RIP-OFF!
I WANT MY MONEY!
My mistake.
DUH!
STUPID NIP!
DEATH
SLAM!
Ahem.
Delivery.
Sign here.

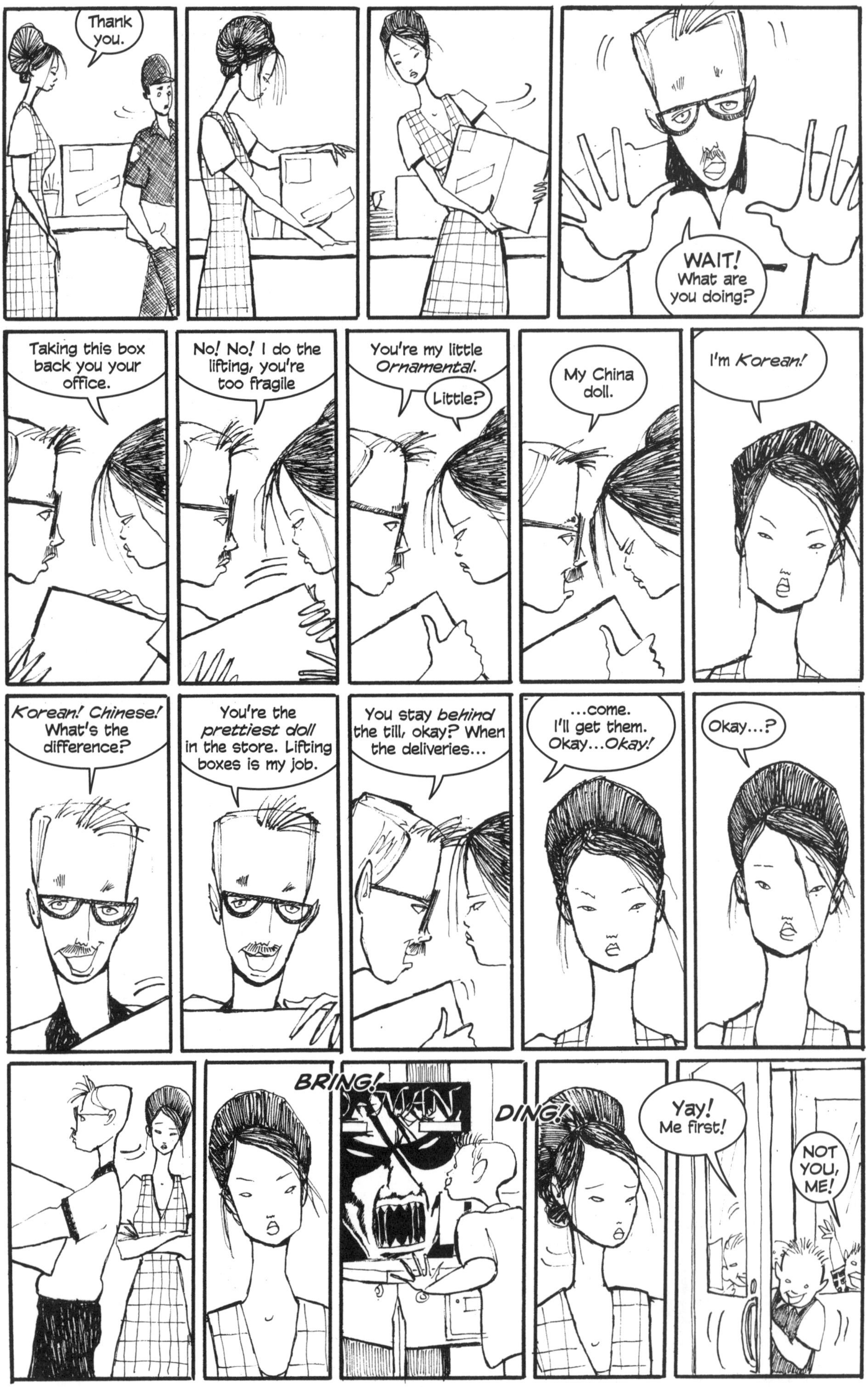
Thank you.
WAIT! What are you doing?
Taking this box back you your office.
No! No! I do the lifting, you're too fragile
You're my little *Ornamental*.
Little?
My China doll.
I'm *Korean!*
Korean! Chinese! What's the difference?
You're the *prettiest doll* in the store. Lifting boxes is my job.
You stay *behind* the till, okay? When the deliveries...
...come. I'll get them. Okay...*Okay!*
Okay...?
BRING!
DING!
Yay! Me first!
NOT YOU, ME!

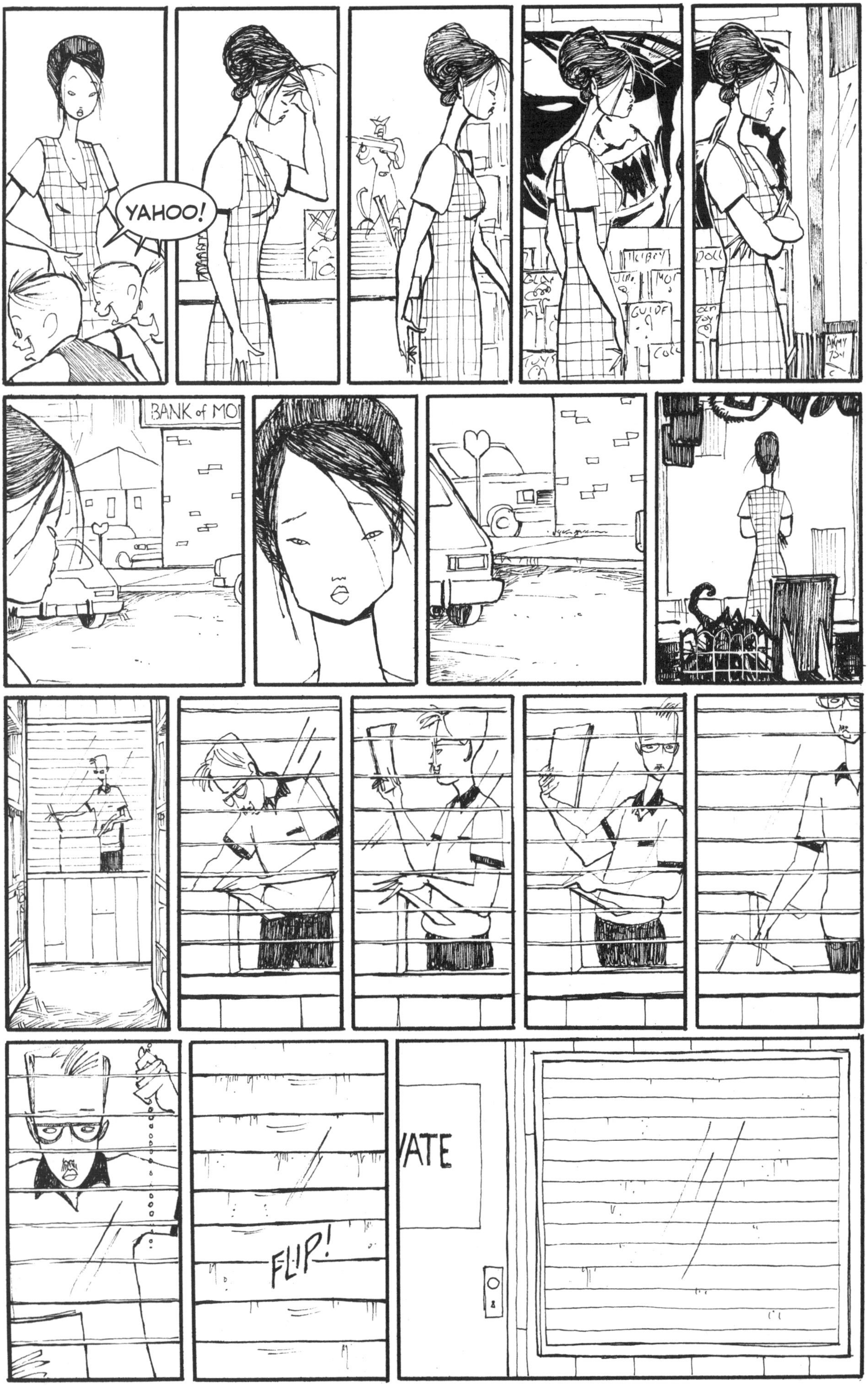
YAHOO!
BANK of MO
FLIP!
VATE

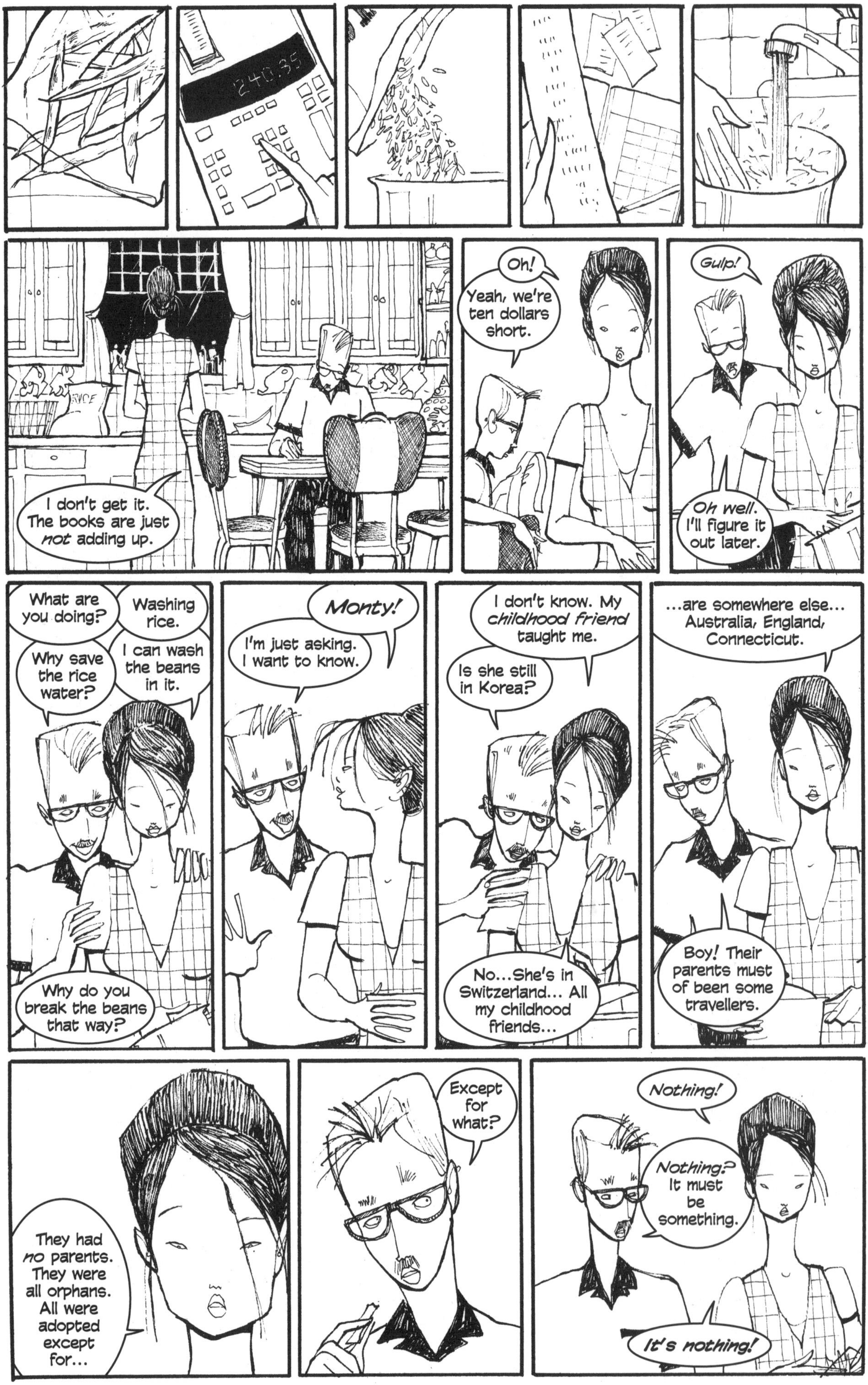
240.35
RICE
I don't get it. The books are just *not* adding up.
Oh!
Yeah, we're ten dollars short.
Gulp!
Oh well. I'll figure it out later.
What are you doing?
Washing rice.
Why save the rice water?
I can wash the beans in it.
Why do you break the beans that way?
Monty!
I'm just asking. I want to know.
I don't know. My *childhood friend* taught me.
Is she still in Korea?
No...She's in Switzerland... All my childhood friends...
...are somewhere else... Australia, England, Connecticut.
Boy! Their parents must of been some travellers.
They had *no* parents. They were all orphans. All were adopted except for...
Except for what?
Nothing!
Nothing? It must be something.
It's nothing!

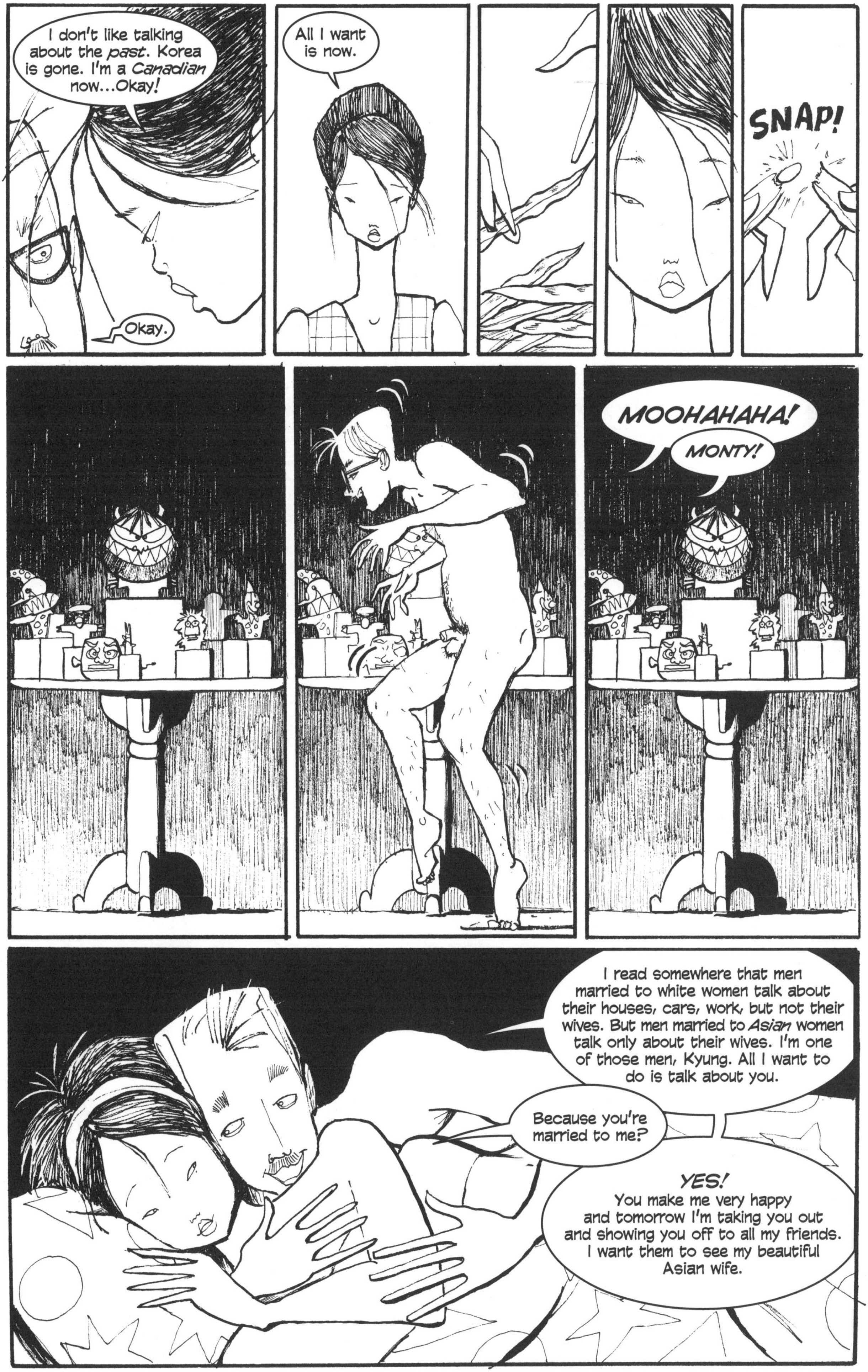
I don't like talking about the *past*. Korea is gone. I'm a *Canadian* now...Okay!
Okay.
All I want is now.
SNAP!
MOOHAHAHA!
MONTY!
I read somewhere that men married to white women talk about their houses, cars, work, but not their wives. But men married to *Asian* women talk only about their wives. I'm one of those men, Kyung. All I want to do is talk about you.
Because you're married to me?
YES!
You make me very happy and tomorrow I'm taking you out and showing you off to all my friends. I want them to see my beautiful Asian wife.

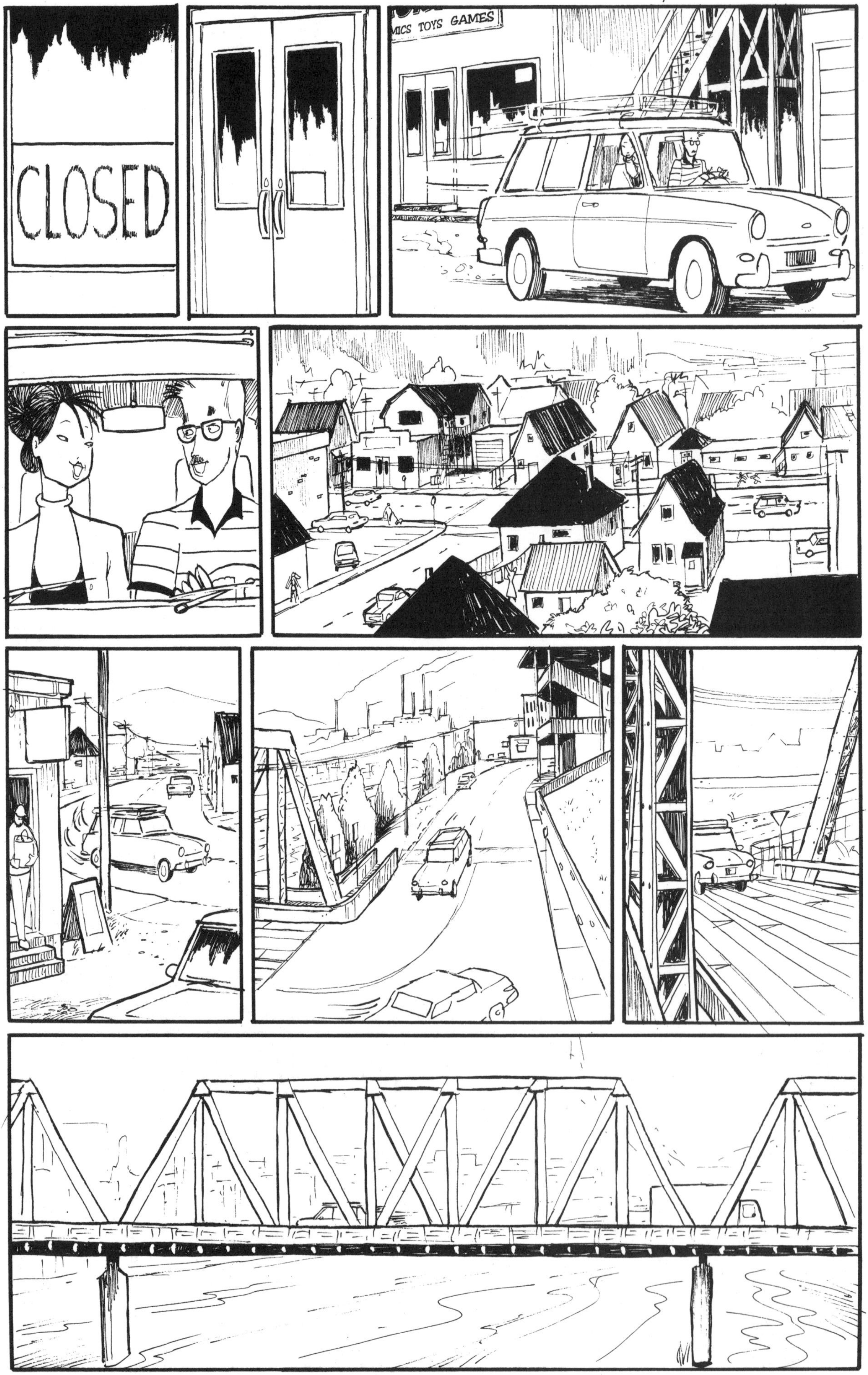
CLOSED
MICS TOYS GAMES

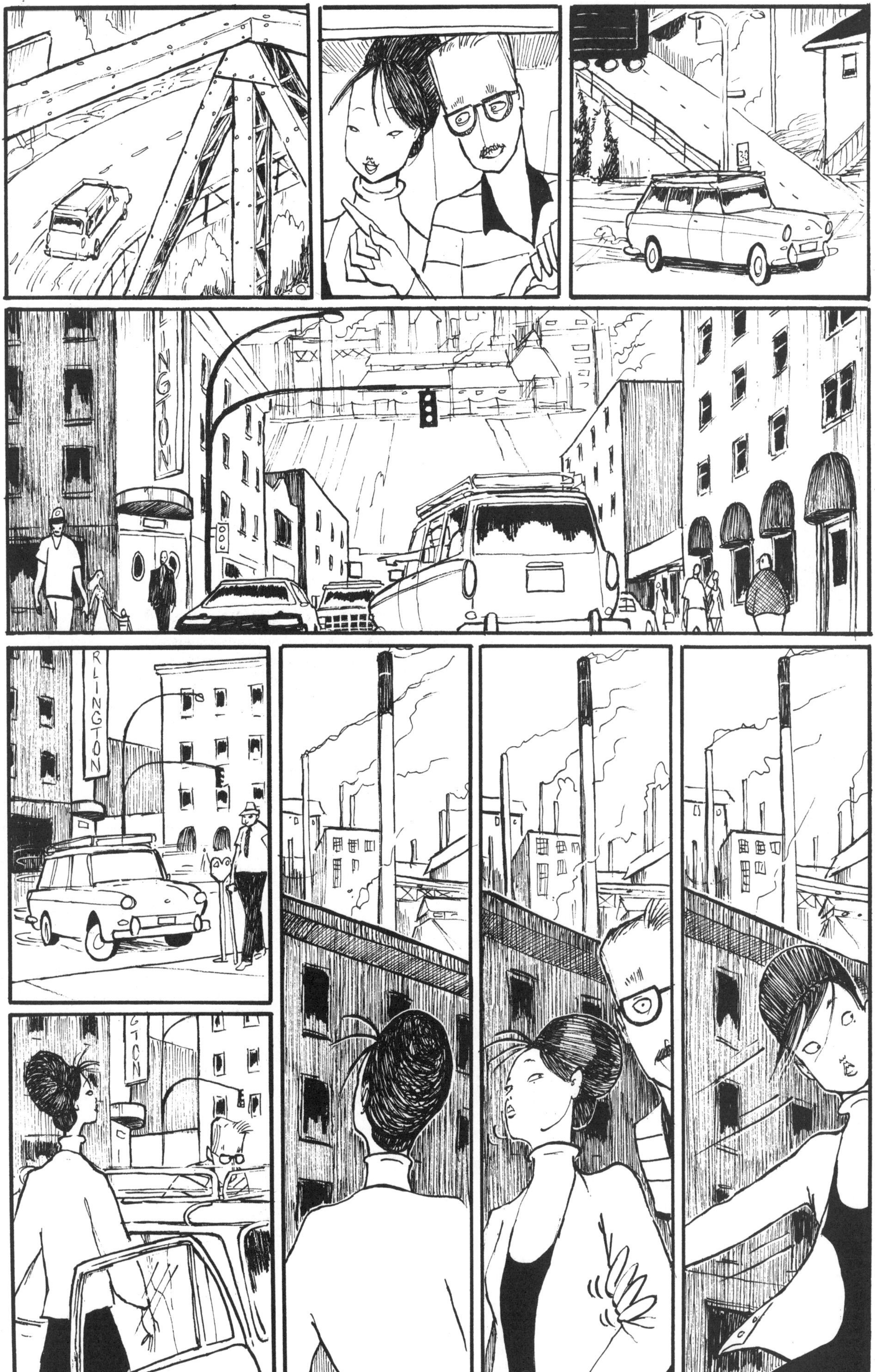
RLINGTON

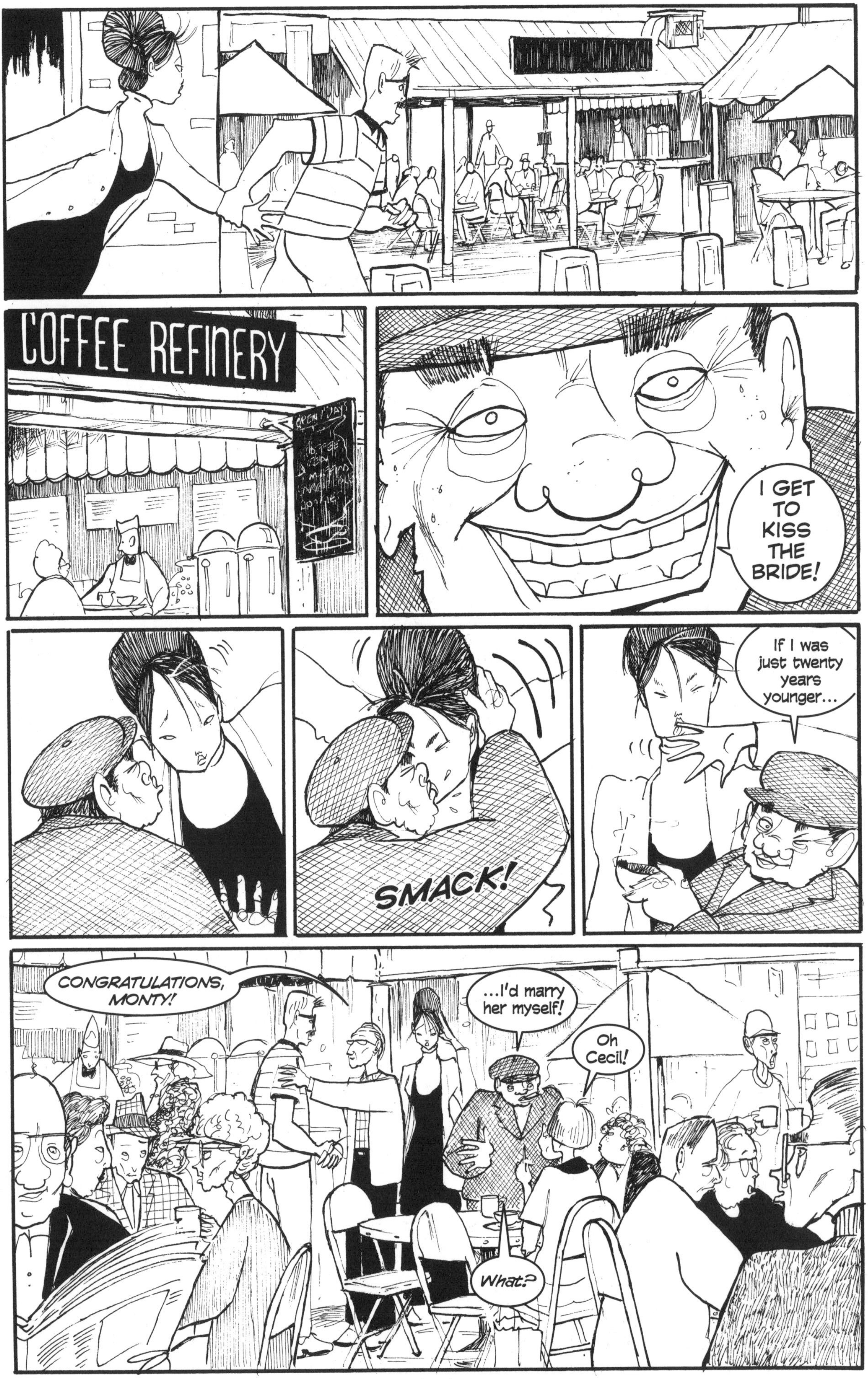
COFFEE REFINERY
I GET TO KISS THE BRIDE!
SMACK!
If I was just twenty years younger...
CONGRATULATIONS, MONTY!
...I'd marry her myself!
Oh Cecil!
What?

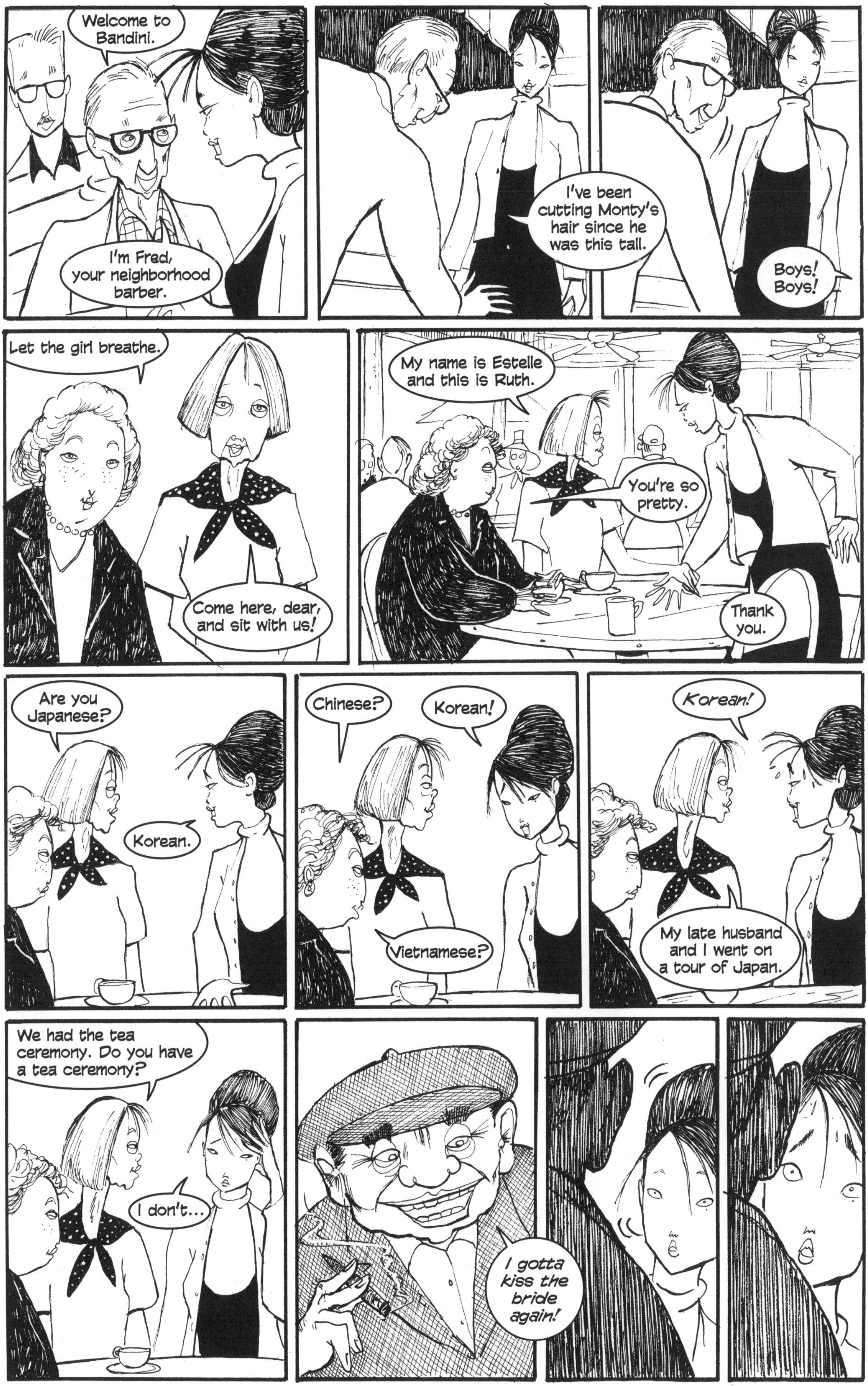
Welcome to Bandini.
I'm Fred, your neighborhood barber.
I've been cutting Monty's hair since he was this tall.
Boys! Boys!
Let the girl breathe.
Come here, dear, and sit with us!
My name is Estelle and this is Ruth.
You're so pretty.
Thank you.
Are you Japanese?
Korean.
Chinese?
Korean!
Vietnamese?
Korean!
My late husband and I went on a tour of Japan.
We had the tea ceremony. Do you have a tea ceremony?
I don't...
I gotta kiss the bride again!

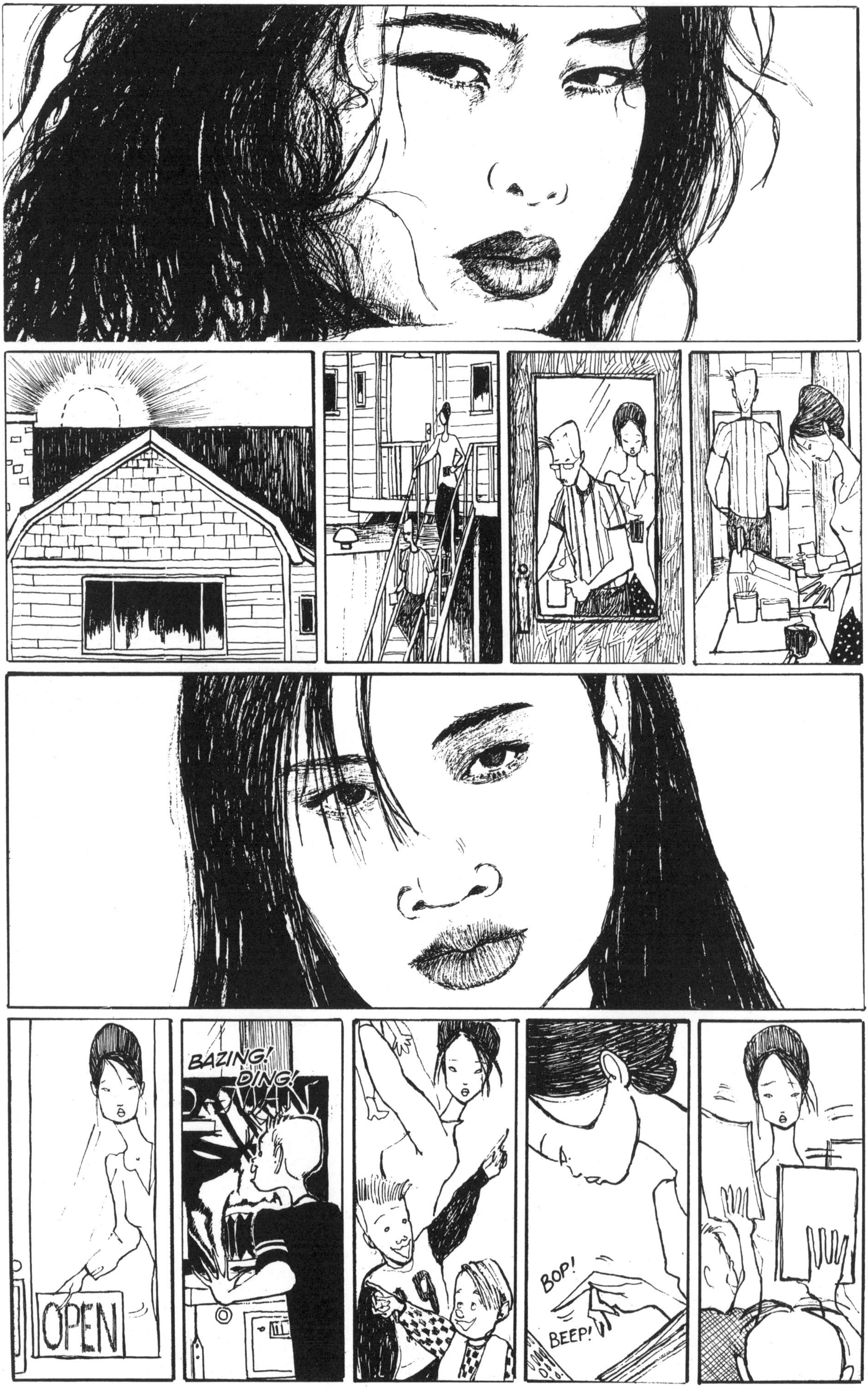
OPEN
BAZING!
DING!
BOP!
BEEP!

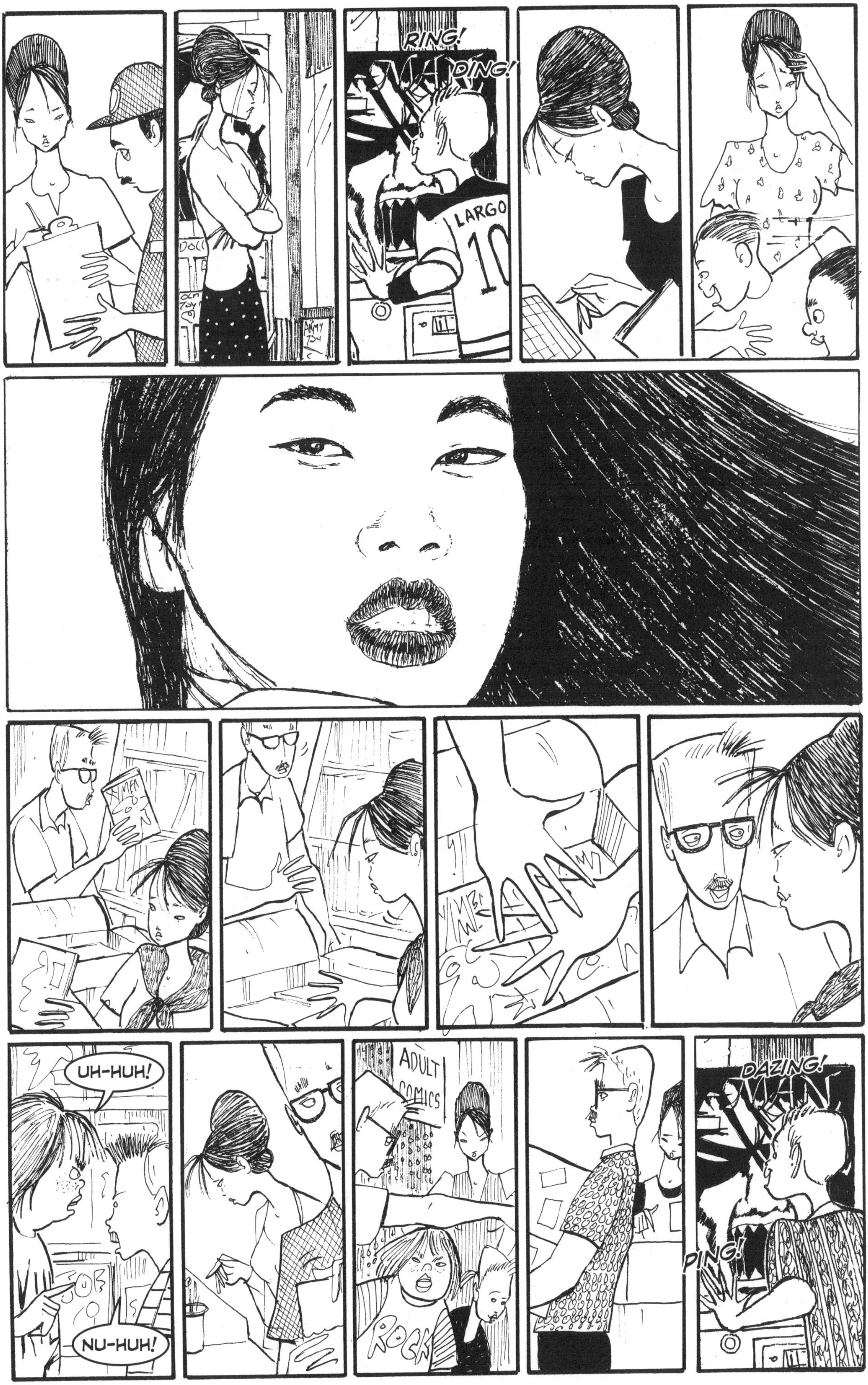
RING!
DING!
LARGO
10
UH-HUH!
NU-HUH!
ADULT COMICS
ROCK
DAZING!
PING!

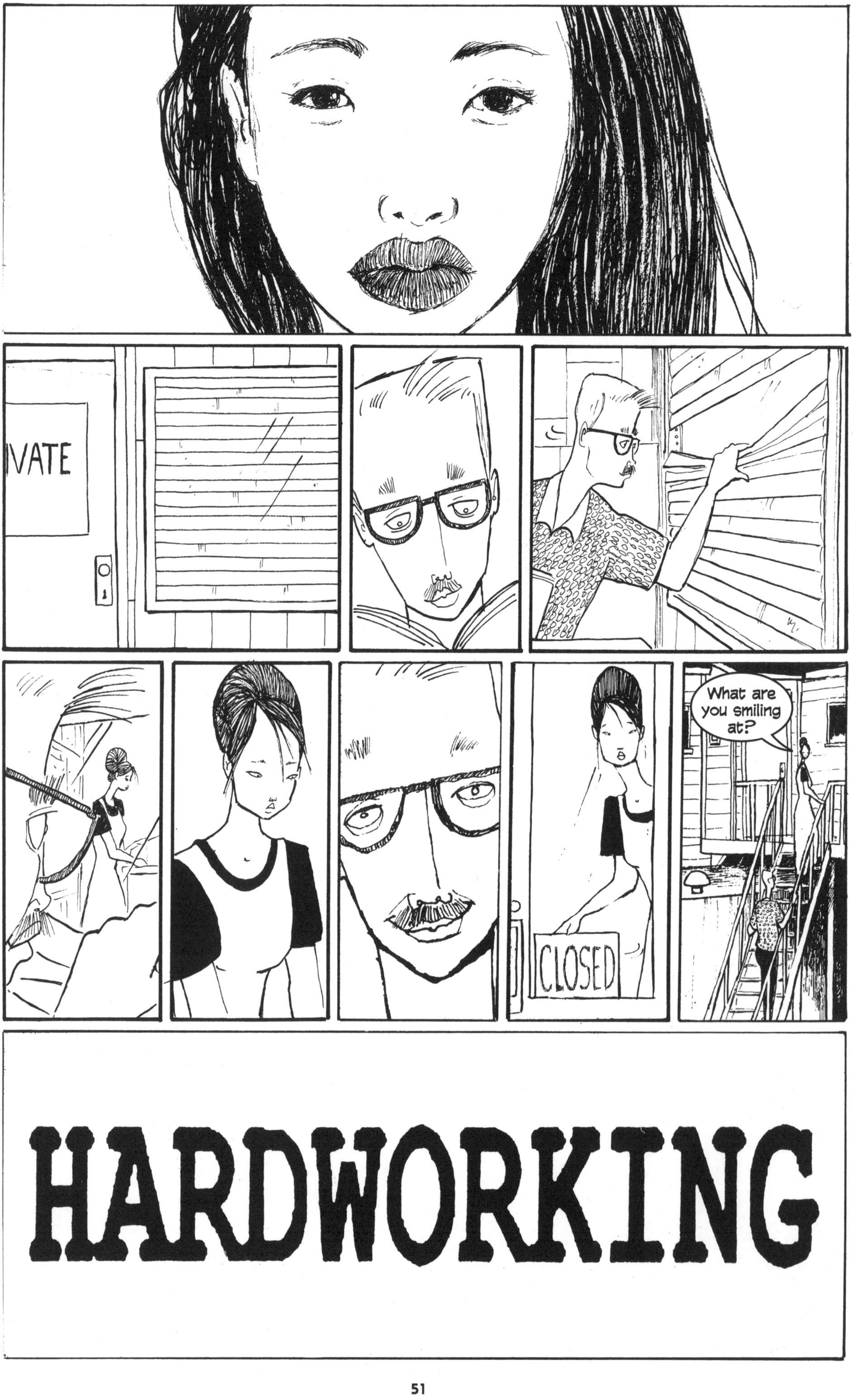
IVATE
What are you smiling at?
CLOSED

HARDWORKING

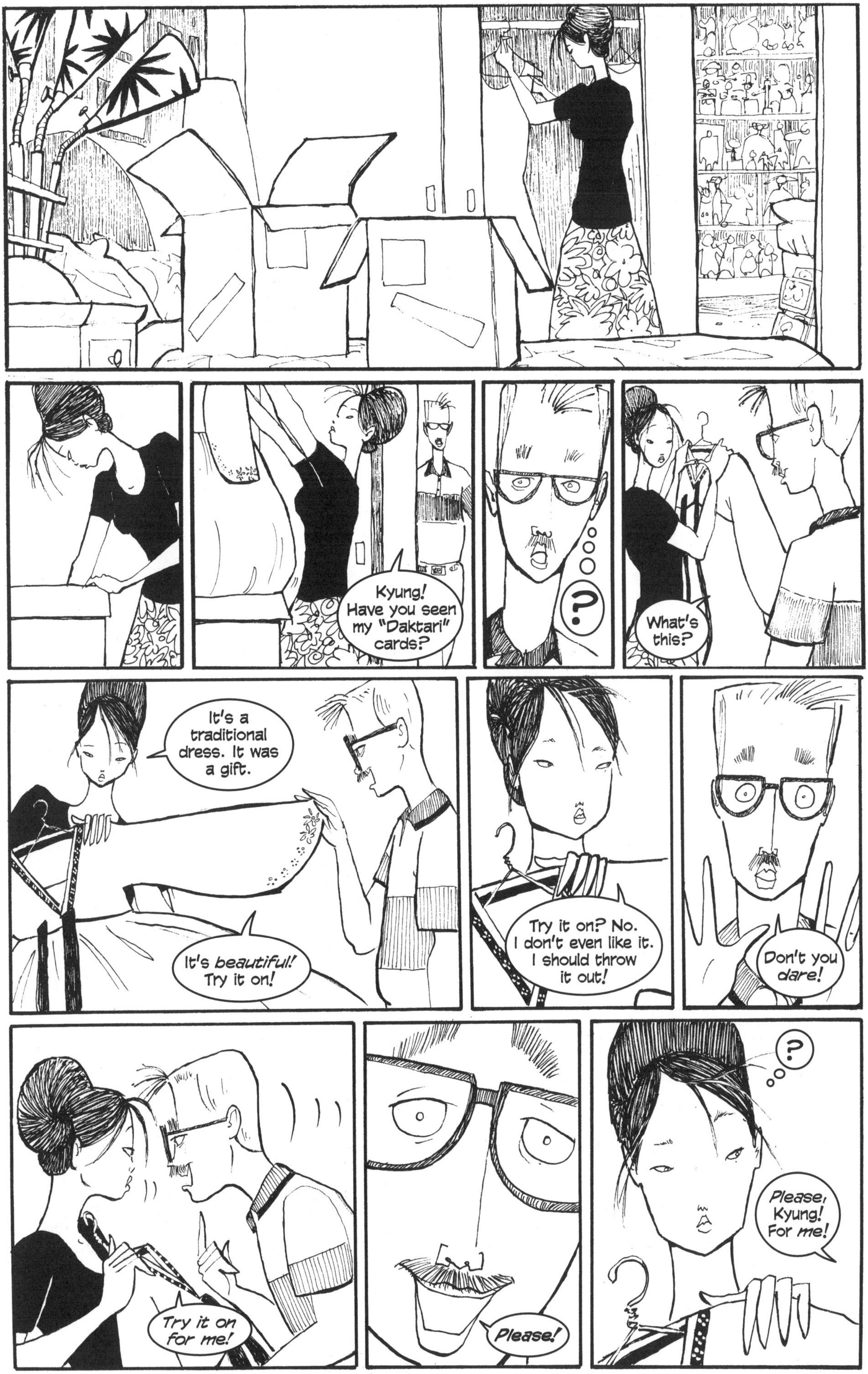
Kyung! Have you seen my "Daktari" cards?
?
What's this?
It's a traditional dress. It was a gift.
It's *beautiful!* Try it on!
Try it on? No. I don't even like it. I should throw it out!
Don't you *dare!*
Try it on for me!
Please!
?
Please, Kyung! For *me!*

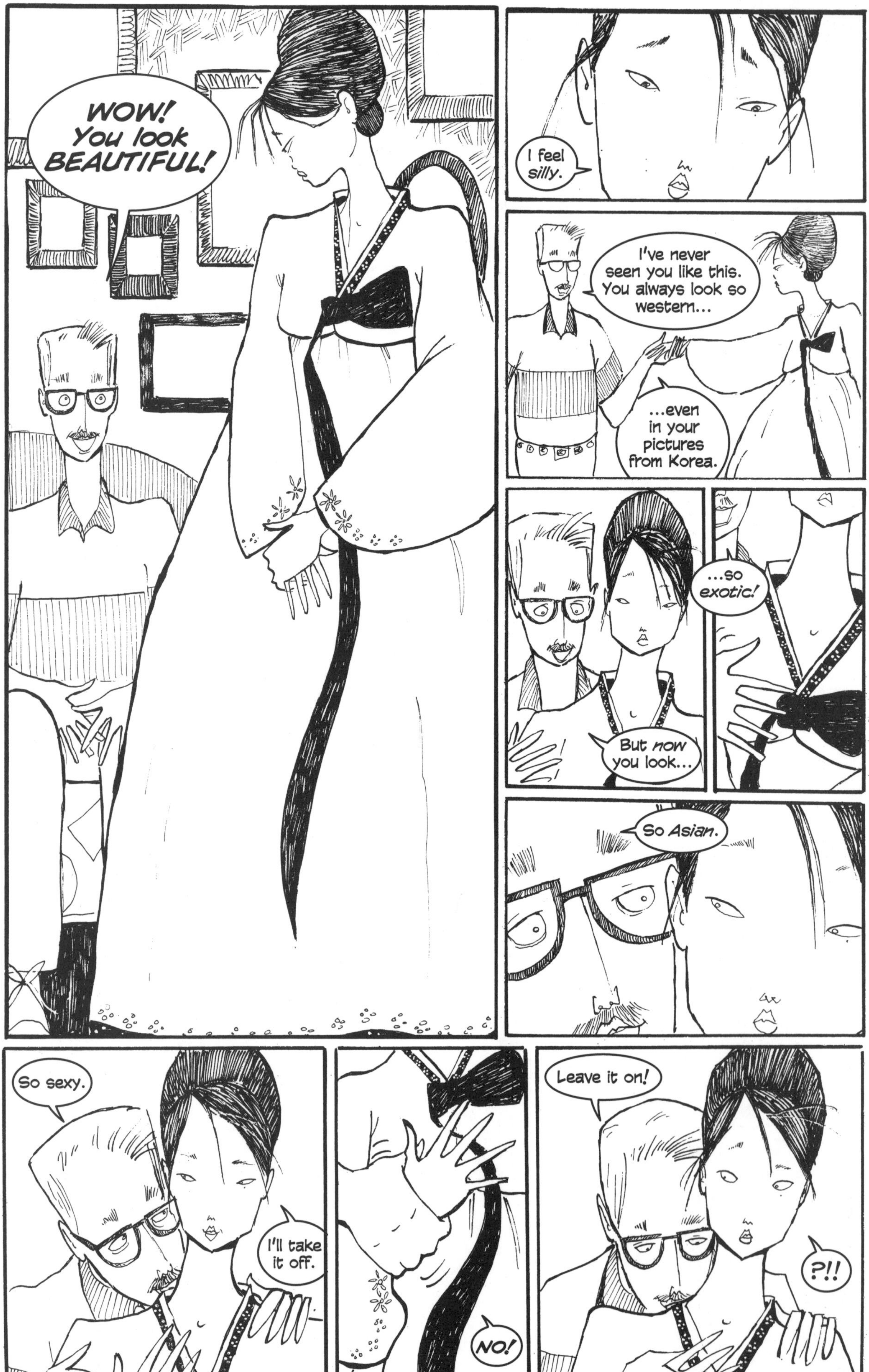
WOW! You look BEAUTIFUL!
I feel silly.
I've never seen you like this. You always look so western...
...even in your pictures from Korea.
But now you look...
...so exotic!
So Asian.
So sexy.
I'll take it off.
NO!
Leave it on!
?!!

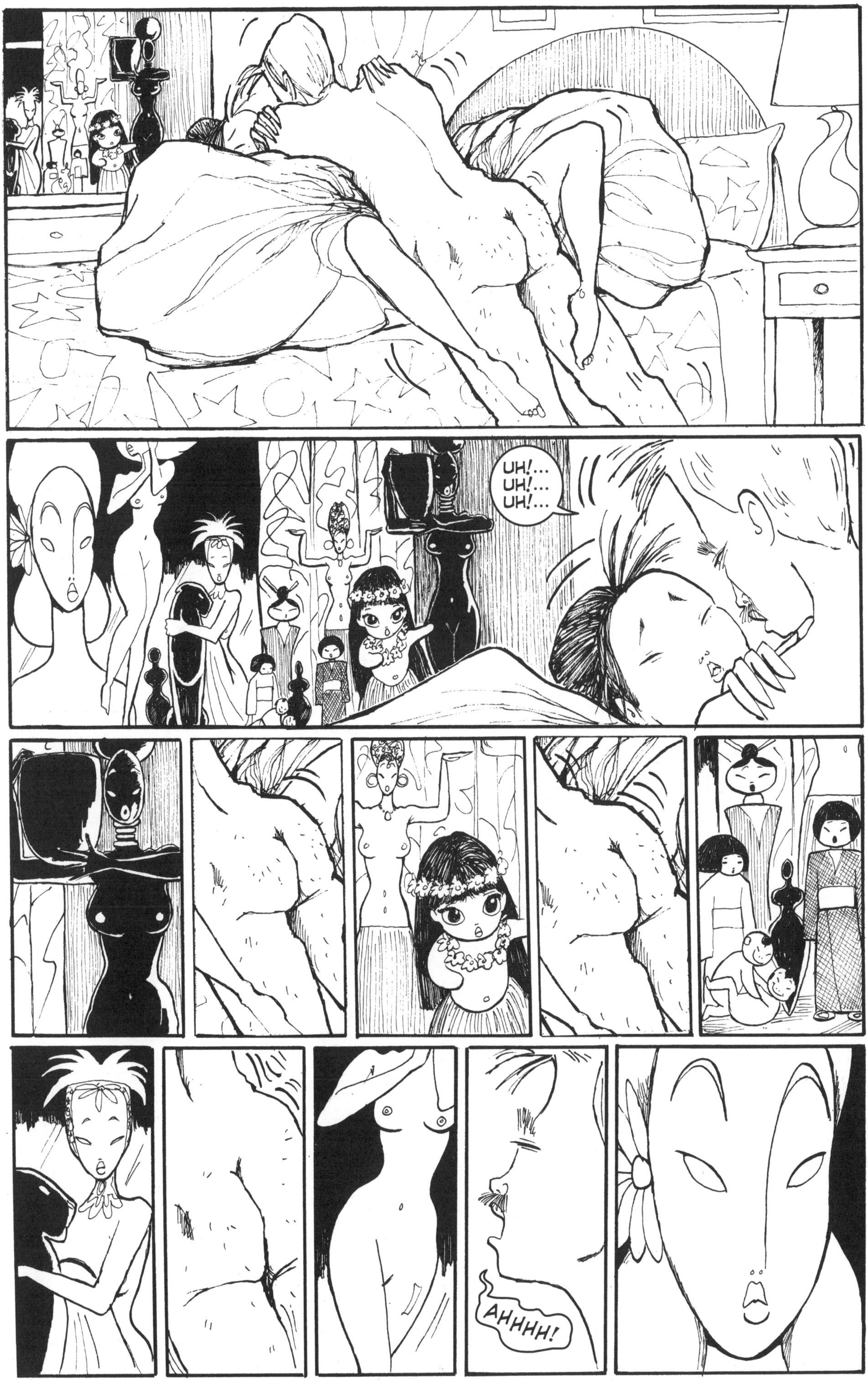
UH!... UH!... UH!...
AHHHH!

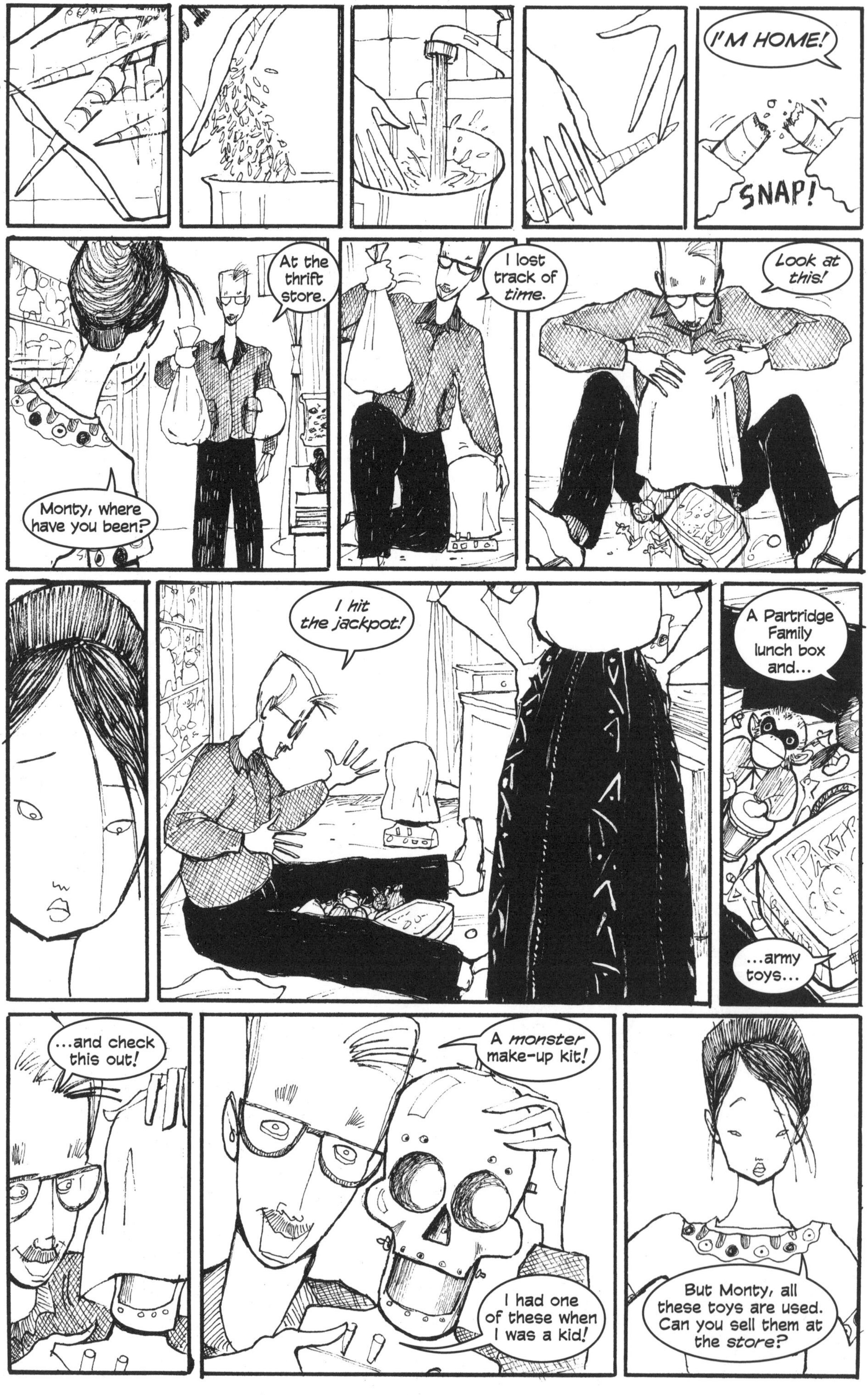
I'M HOME!
SNAP!
Monty, where have you been?
At the thrift store.
I lost track of *time*.
Look at this!
I hit the jackpot!
A Partridge Family lunch box and...
...army toys...
...and check this out!
A *monster* make-up kit!
I had one of these when I was a kid!
But Monty, all these toys are used. Can you sell them at the *store*?

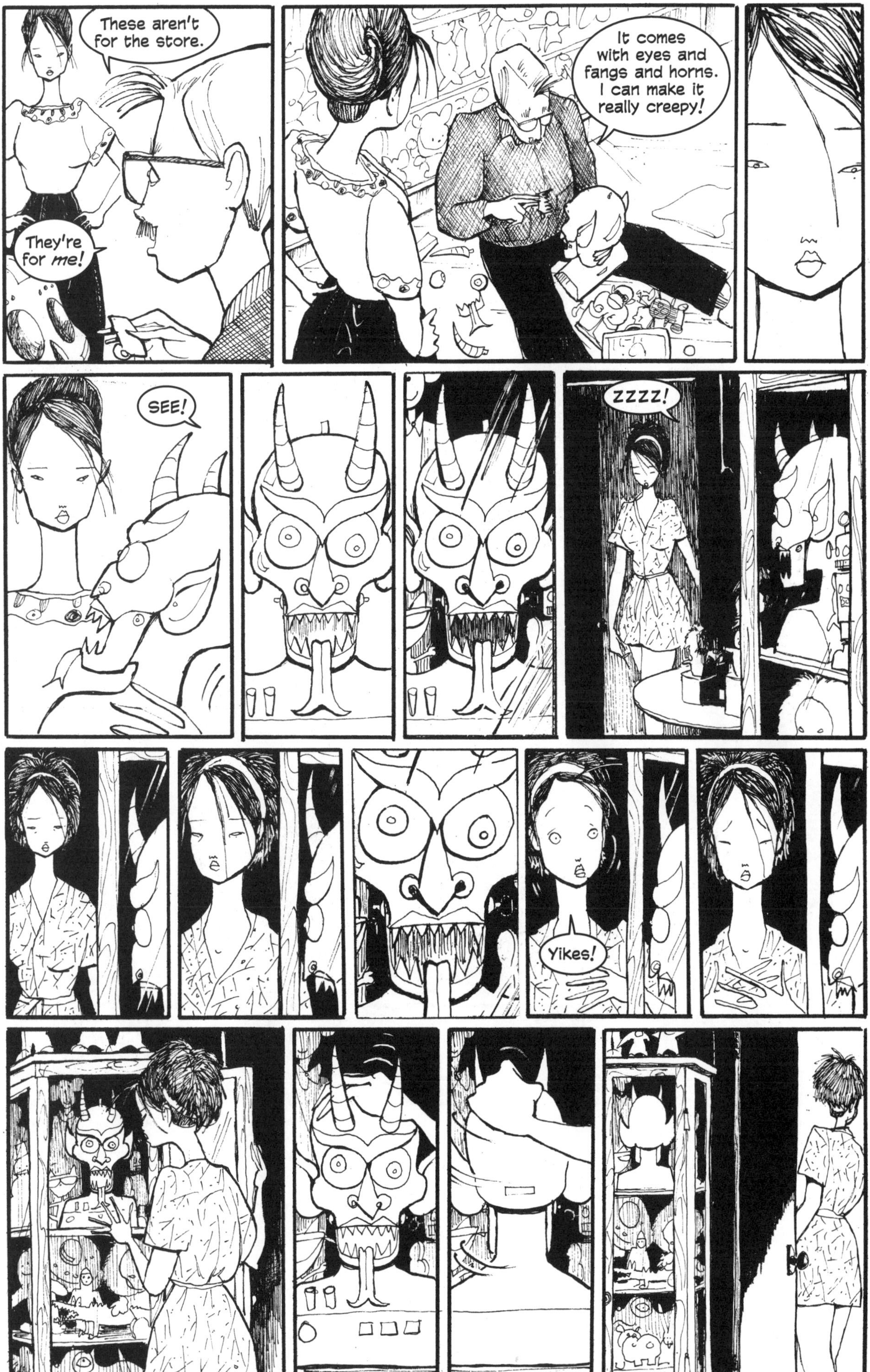
These aren't for the store.
They're for *me*!
It comes with eyes and fangs and horns. I can make it really creepy!
SEE!
ZZZZ!
Yikes!

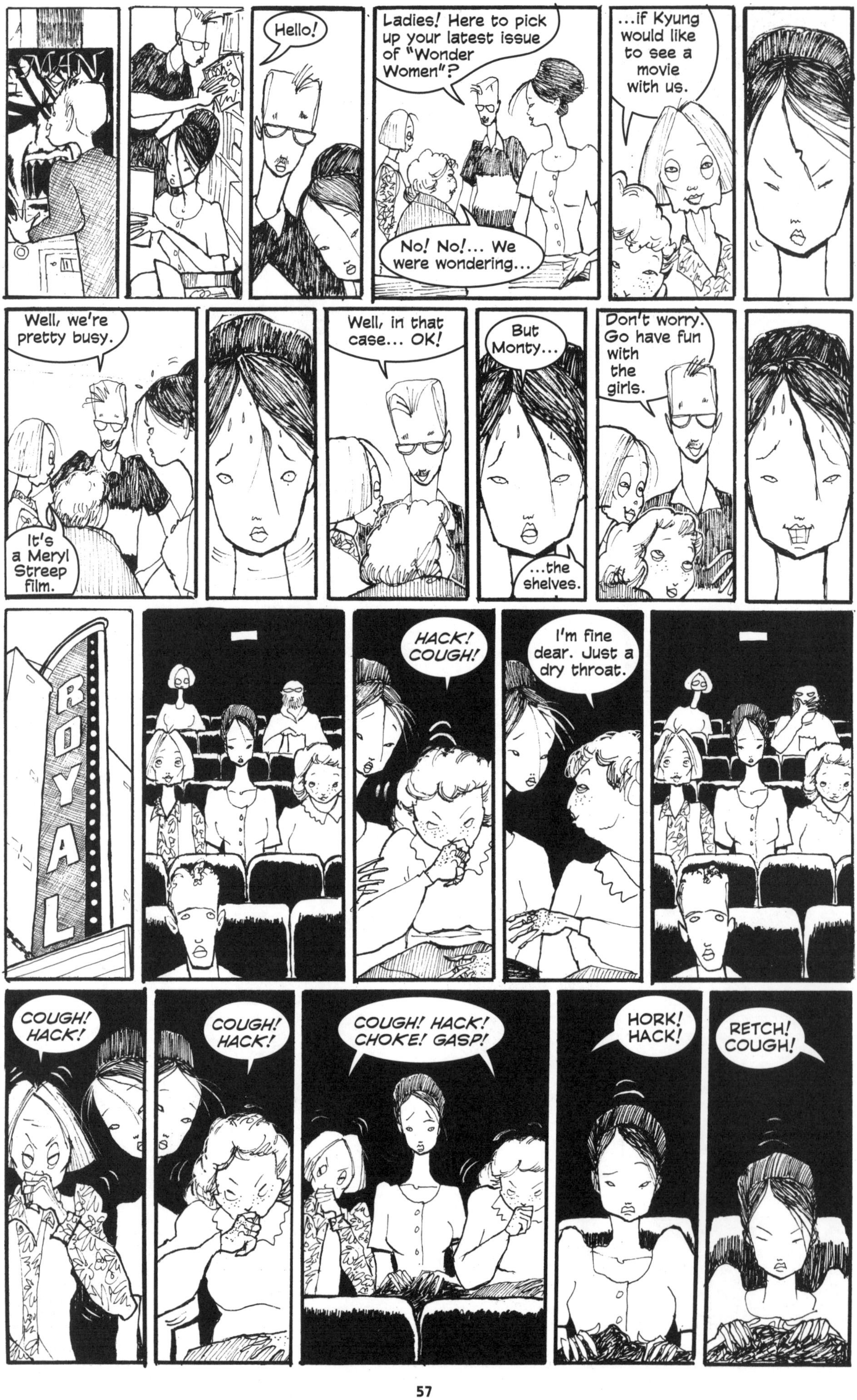

Hello!
Ladies! Here to pick up your latest issue of "Wonder Women"?
No! No!... We were wondering...
...if Kyung would like to see a movie with us.
Well, we're pretty busy.
It's a Meryl Streep film.
Well, in that case... OK!
But Monty...
...the shelves.
Don't worry. Go have fun with the girls.
ROYAL
HACK! COUGH!
I'm fine dear. Just a dry throat.
COUGH! HACK!
COUGH! HACK!
COUGH! HACK! CHOKE! GASP!
HORK! HACK!
RETCH! COUGH!

VAROOM!

VAROOM!

VAROOM!

Does he have to *rev* his car like that *every night?*

You'll get used to it.

But he's *filling* the house with *exhaust.*

He'll stop!

Why don't you tell him to stop?

GULP!

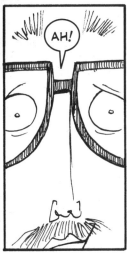

AH!

Your turn!

58

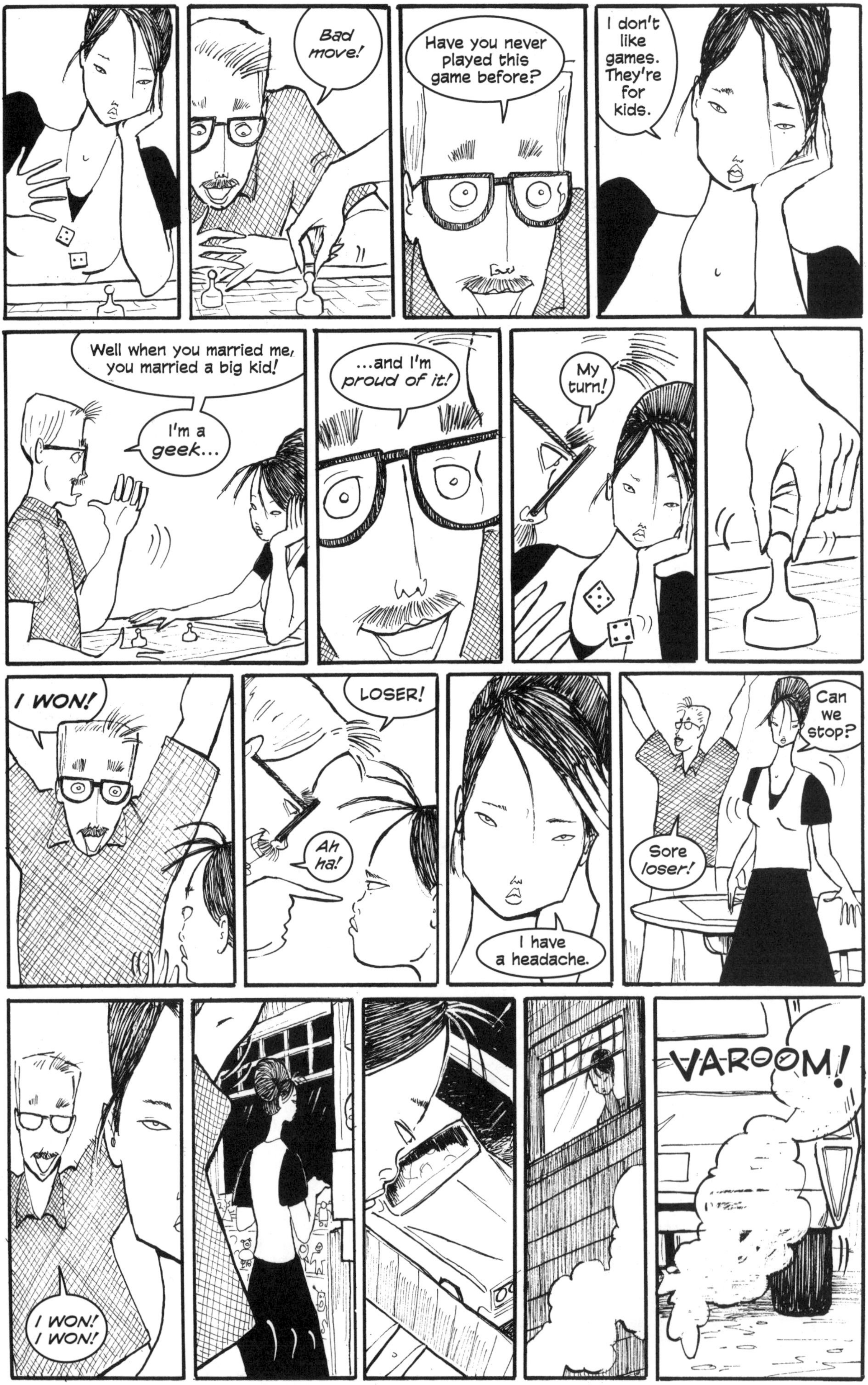
Bad move!
Have you never played this game before?
I don't like games. They're for kids.
Well when you married me, you married a big kid!
I'm a geek...
...and I'm proud of it!
My turn!
I WON!
LOSER!
Ah ha!
I have a headache.
Can we stop?
Sore loser!
I WON! I WON!
VAROOM!

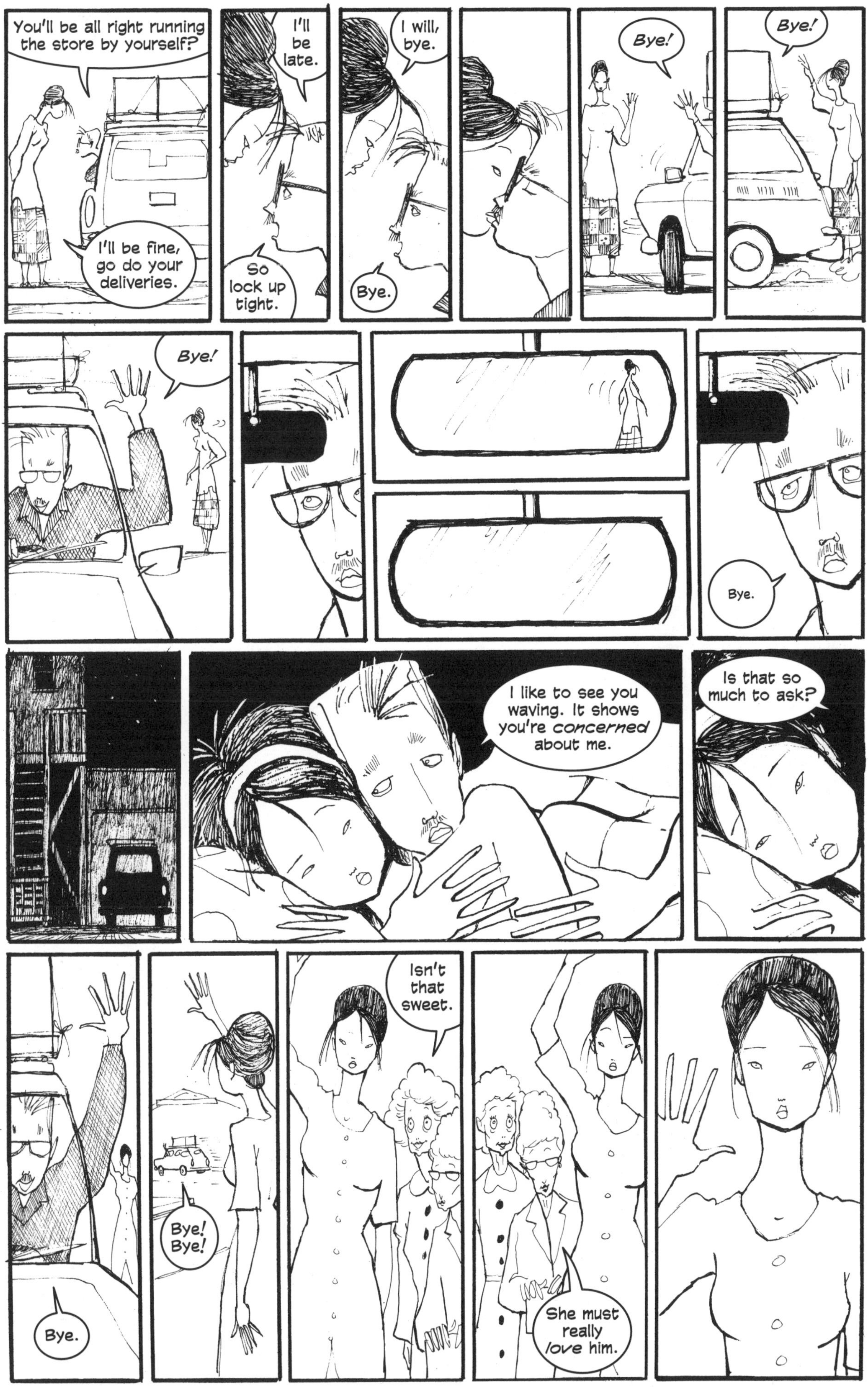
You'll be all right running the store by yourself?
I'll be fine, go do your deliveries.
I'll be late.
So lock up tight.
I will, bye.
Bye.
Bye!
Bye!
Bye!
Bye.
I like to see you waving. It shows you're *concerned* about me.
Is that so much to ask?
Bye!
Bye!
Bye.
Isn't that sweet.
She must really *love* him.

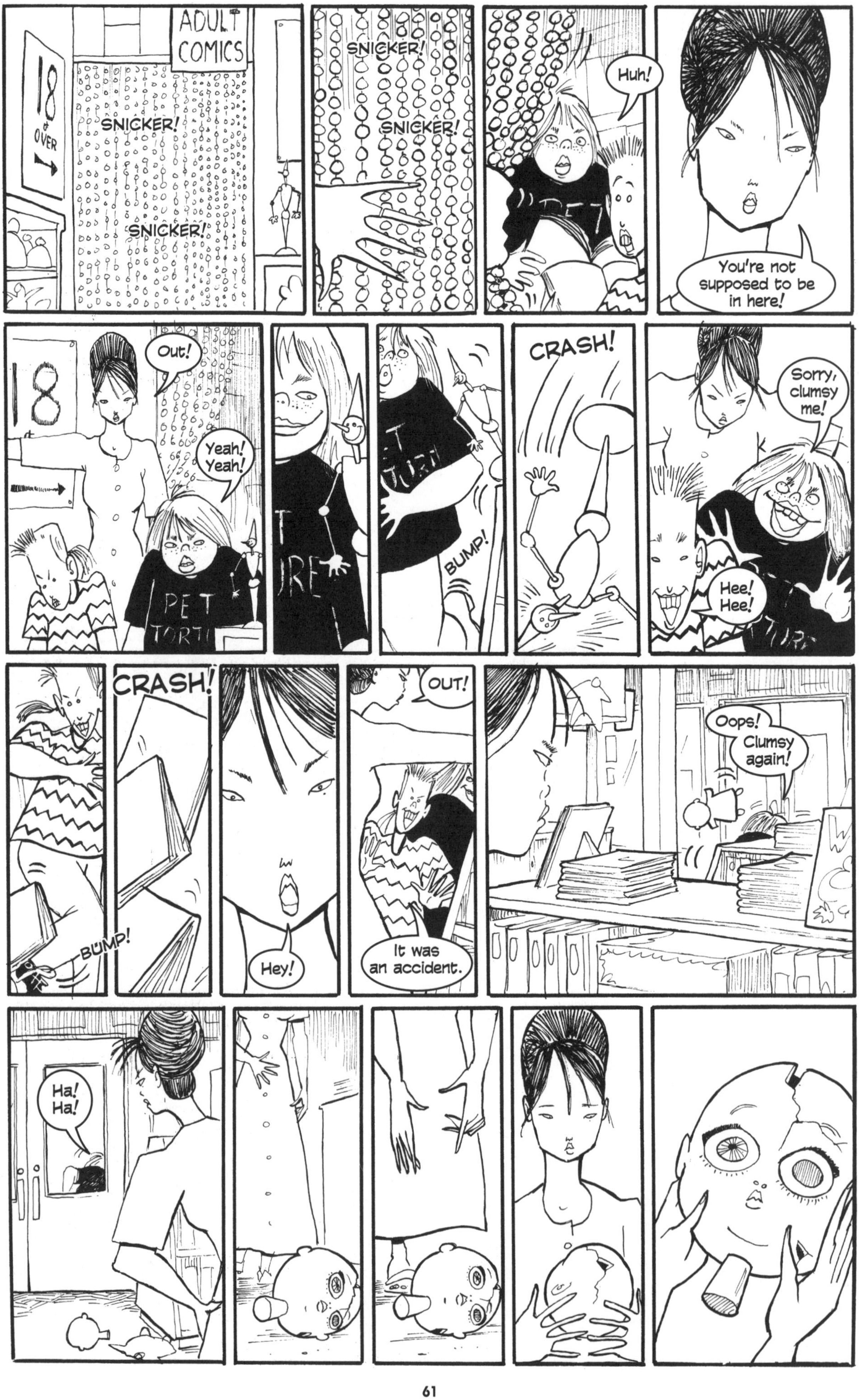
ADULT COMICS
18 & OVER
SNICKER!
SNICKER!
SNICKER!
SNICKER!
Huh!
PET
You're not supposed to be in here!
Out!
Yeah! Yeah!
PET TORTU
CRASH!
BUMP!
Sorry, clumsy me!
Hee! Hee!
CRASH!
BUMP!
Hey!
OUT!
It was an accident.
Oops! Clumsy again!
Ha! Ha!

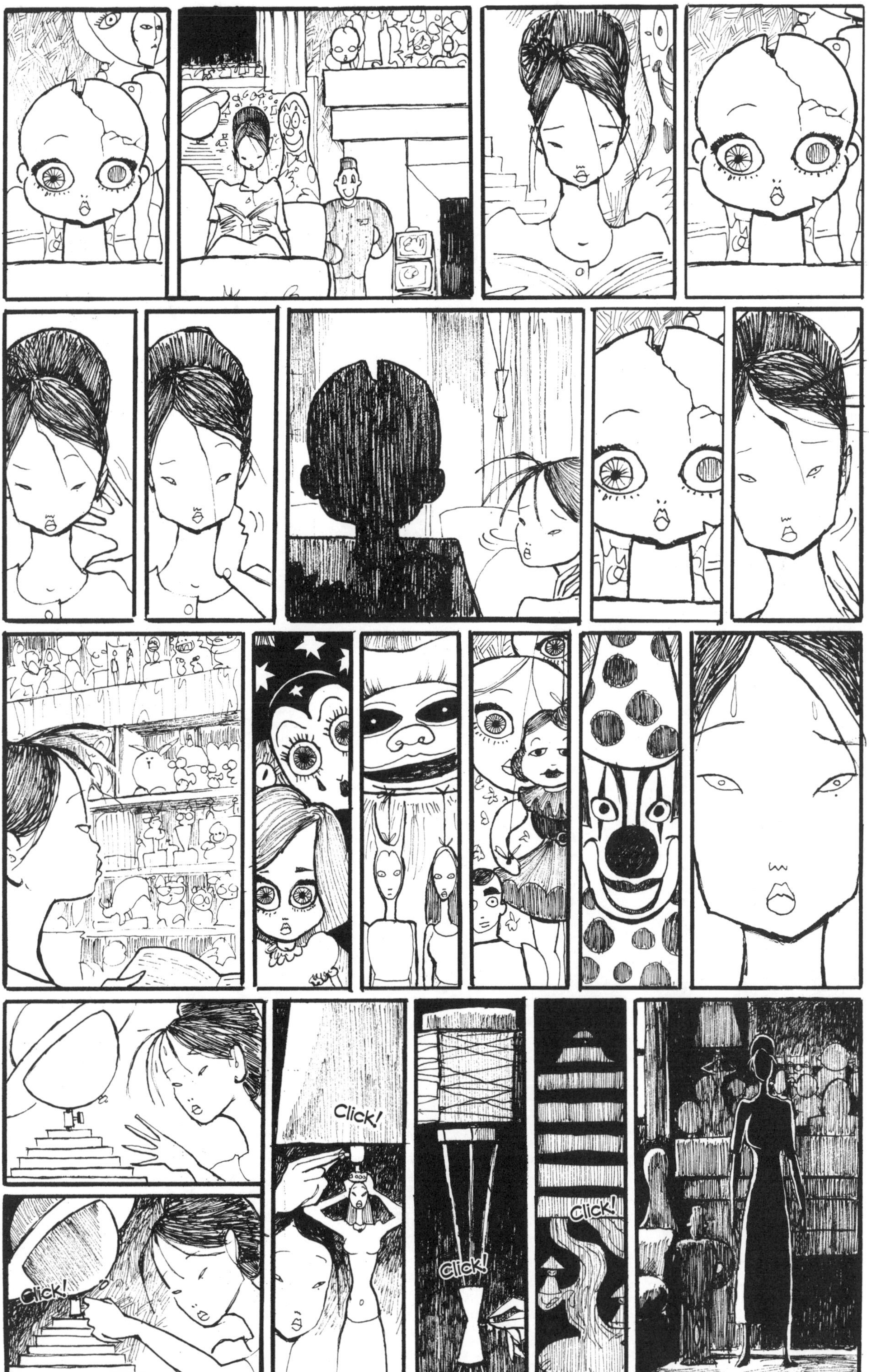
Click!
Click!
Click!
Click!

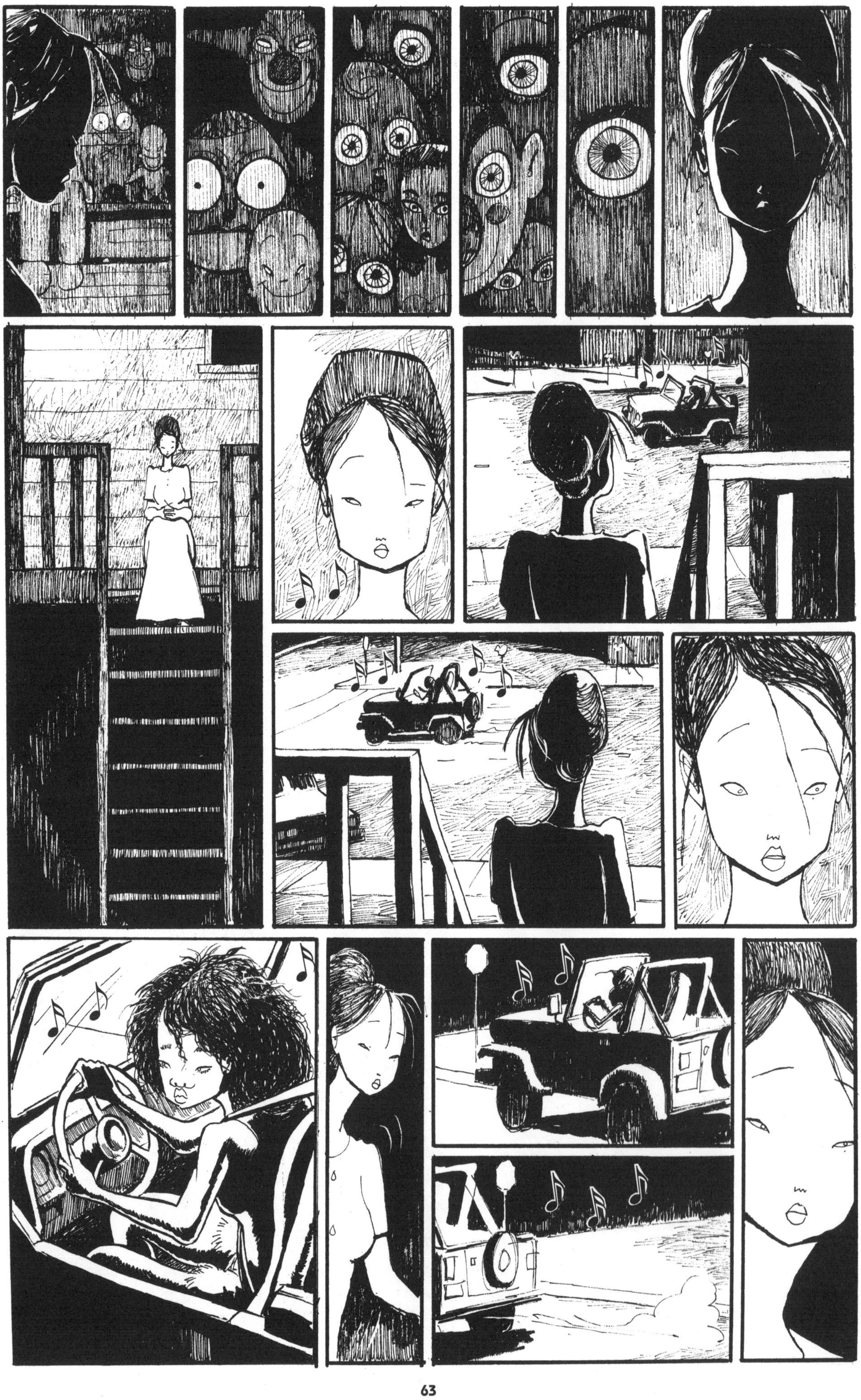

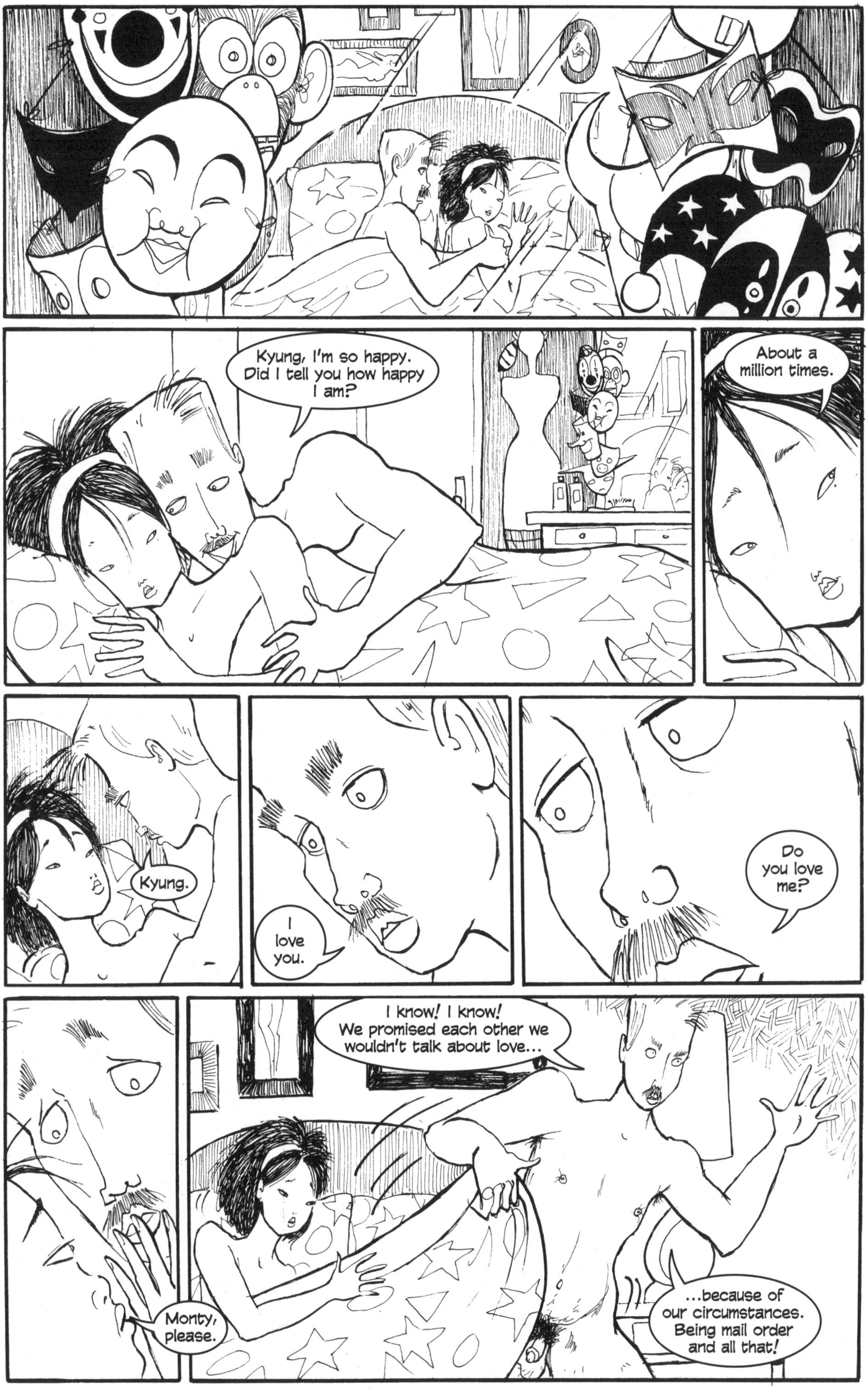
Kyung, I'm so happy. Did I tell you how happy I am?
About a million times.
Kyung.
I love you.
Do you love me?
I know! I know! We promised each other we wouldn't talk about love...
Monty, please.
...because of our circumstances. Being mail order and all that!

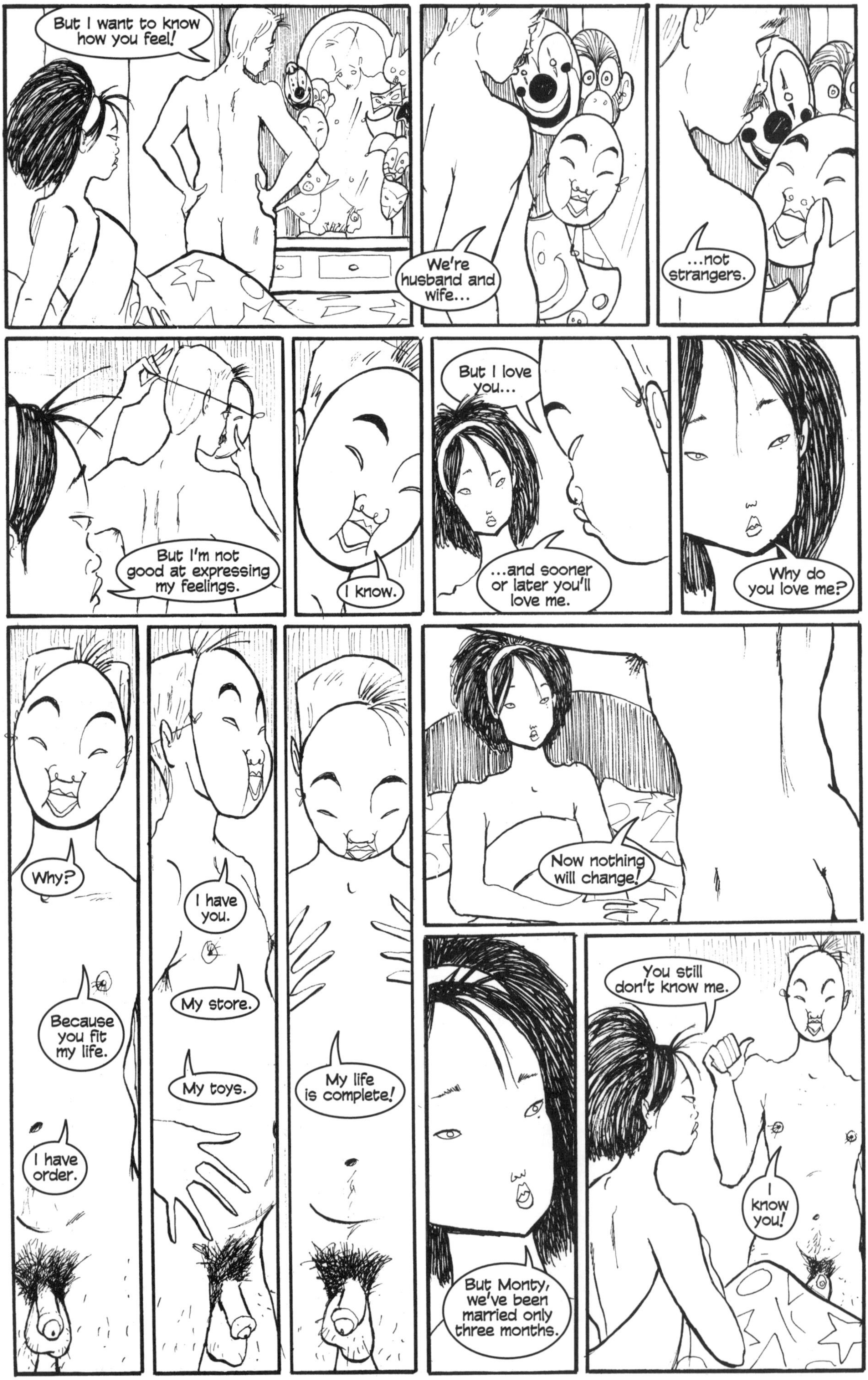
But I want to know how you feel!
We're husband and wife...
...not strangers.
But I'm not good at expressing my feelings.
I know.
But I love you...
...and sooner or later you'll love me.
Why do you love me?
Why?
Because you fit my life.
I have order.
I have you.
My store.
My toys.
My life is complete!
Now nothing will change!
But Monty, we've been married only three months.
You still don't know me.
I know you!

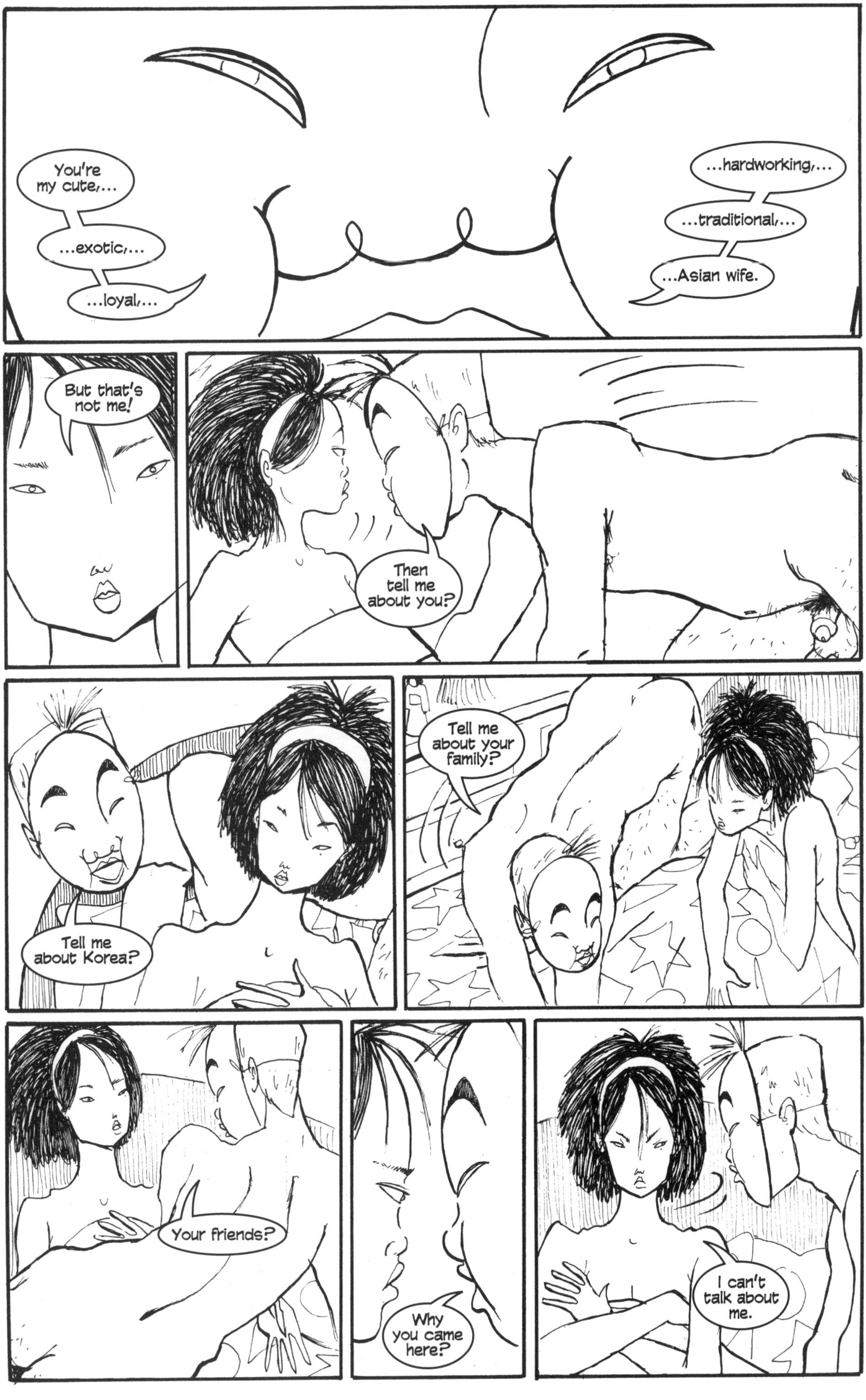
You're my cute,...
...exotic,...
...loyal,...
...hardworking,...
...traditional,...
...Asian wife.
But that's not me!
Then tell me about you?
Tell me about Korea?
Tell me about your family?
Your friends?
Why you came here?
I can't talk about me.

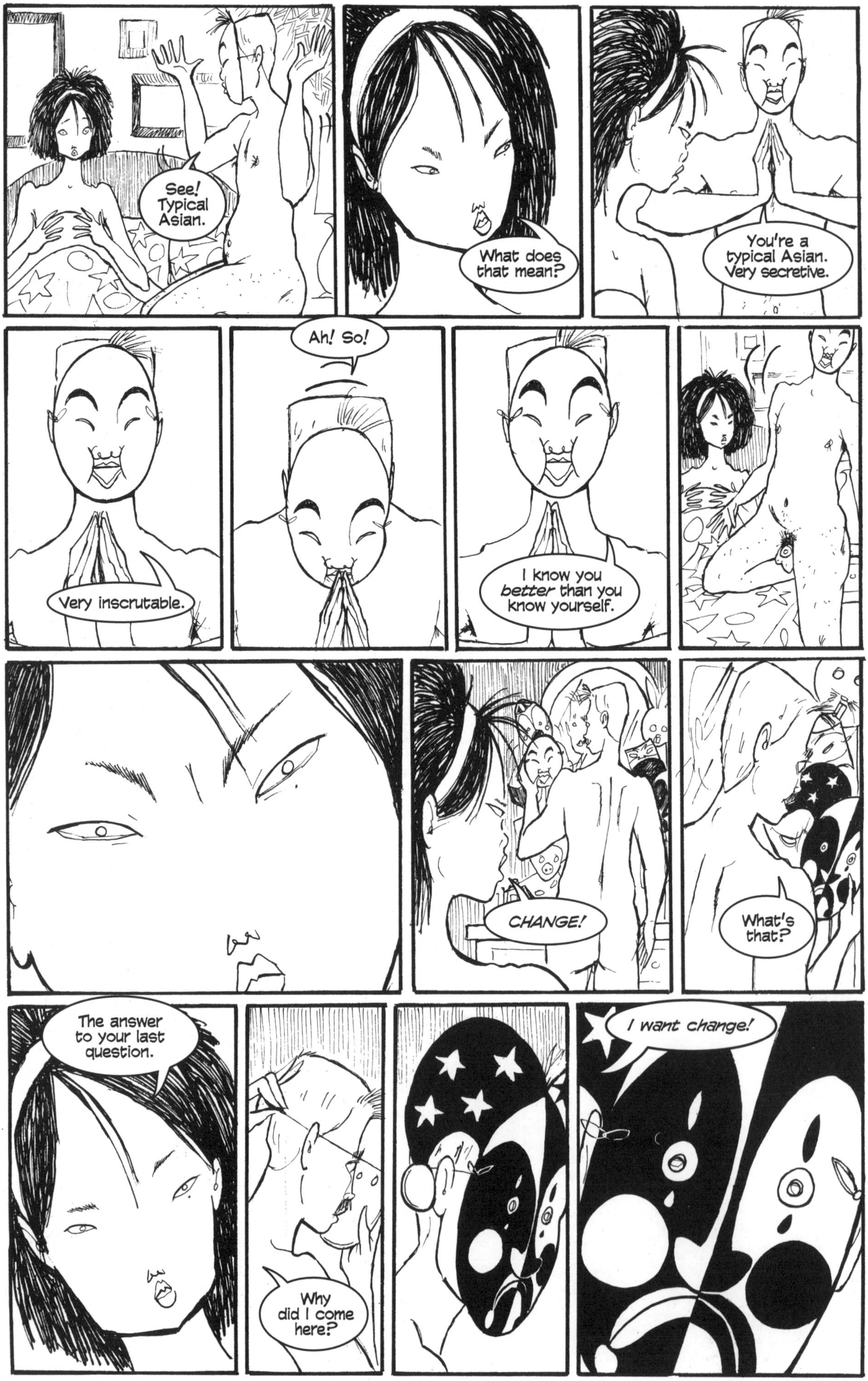
See! Typical Asian.
What does that mean?
You're a typical Asian. Very secretive.
Very inscrutable.
Ah! So!
I know you *better* than you know yourself.
CHANGE!
What's that?
The answer to your last question.
Why did I come here?
I want change!

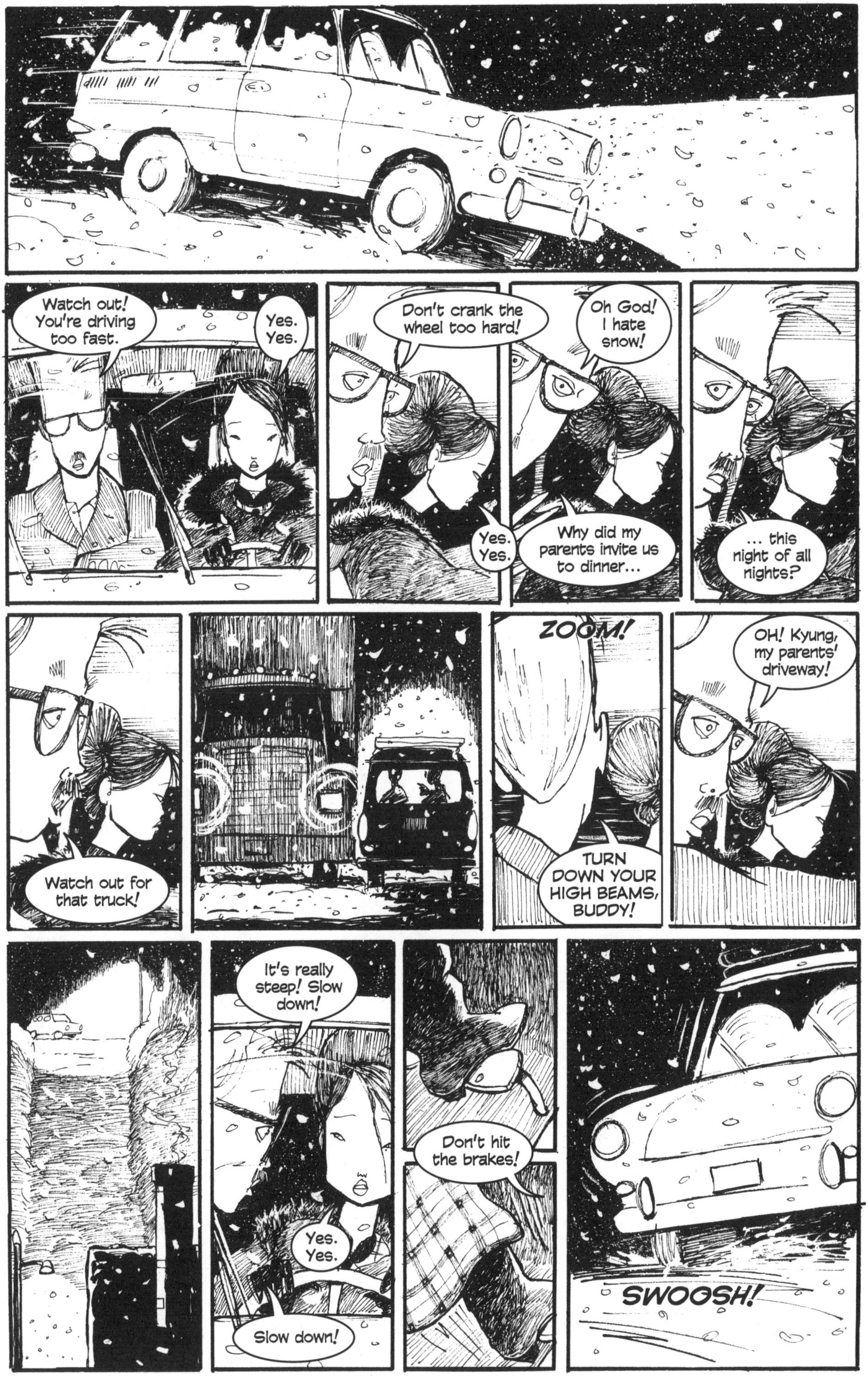
Watch out! You're driving too fast.
Yes. Yes.
Don't crank the wheel too hard!
Yes. Yes.
Oh God! I hate snow!
Why did my parents invite us to dinner...
... this night of all nights?
Watch out for that truck!
ZOOM!
TURN DOWN YOUR HIGH BEAMS, BUDDY!
OH! Kyung, my parents' driveway!
It's really steep! Slow down!
Yes. Yes.
Slow down!
Don't hit the brakes!
SWOOSH!

Turn into the skid!

SWISH!

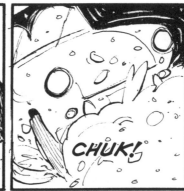

CHUK!

Oh shit! We're stuck!

I told you not to hit the brakes!

I should've driven.

Why didn't you?

Ah!... You needed the experience.

Well, now we have one.

Funny!

Let's see if we can get the car out before my dad and my brothers see this, or I'll never hear the end of it.

Shit.

Hi Kyung!

Hi Jack! Bob!

Hi Kyung!

HOW BAD IS IT?

69

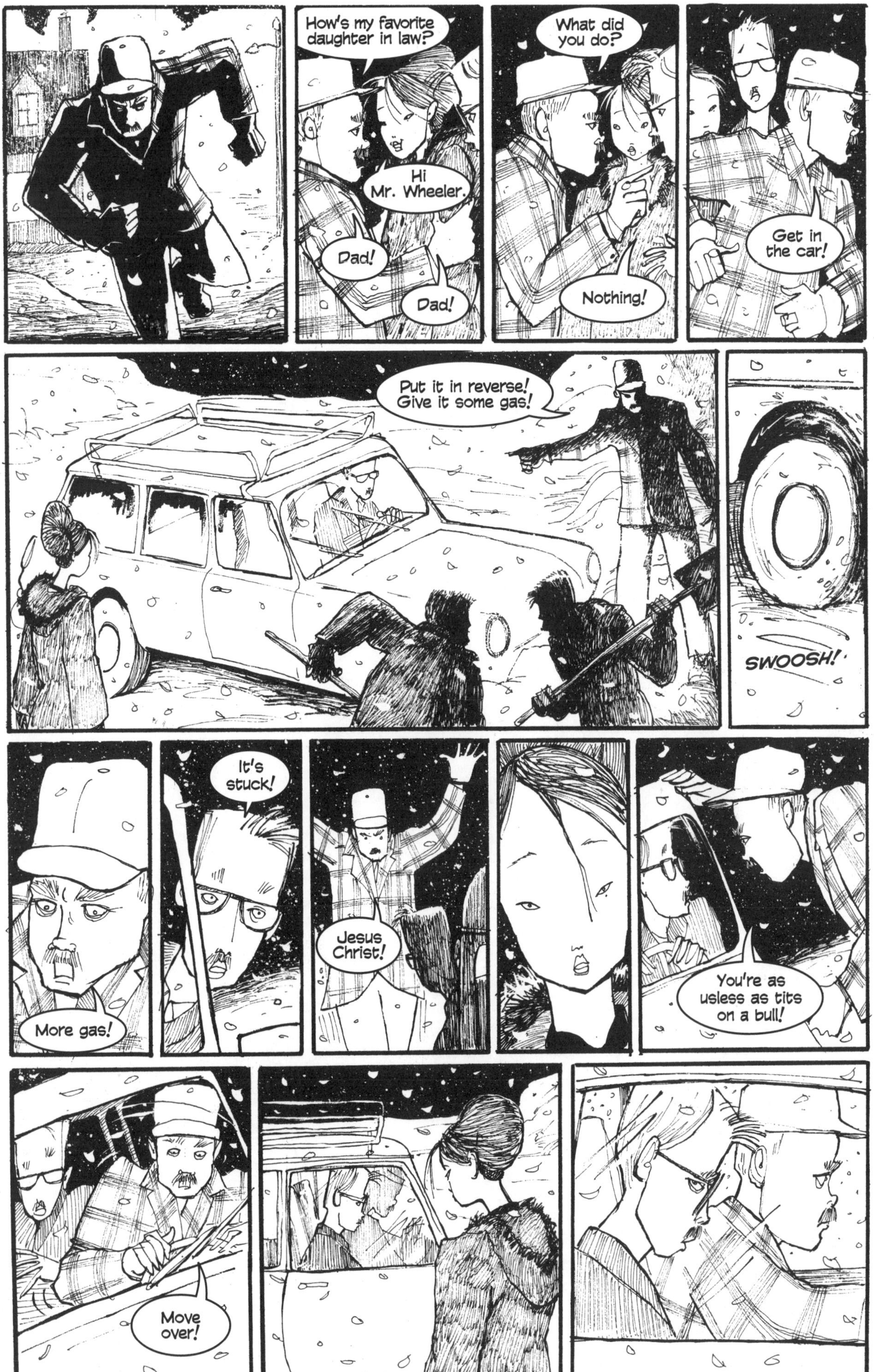
How's my favorite daughter in law?
Hi Mr. Wheeler.
Dad!
Dad!
What did you do?
Nothing!
Get in the car!
Put it in reverse! Give it some gas!
SWOOSH!
More gas!
It's stuck!
Jesus Christ!
You're as usless as tits on a bull!
Move over!

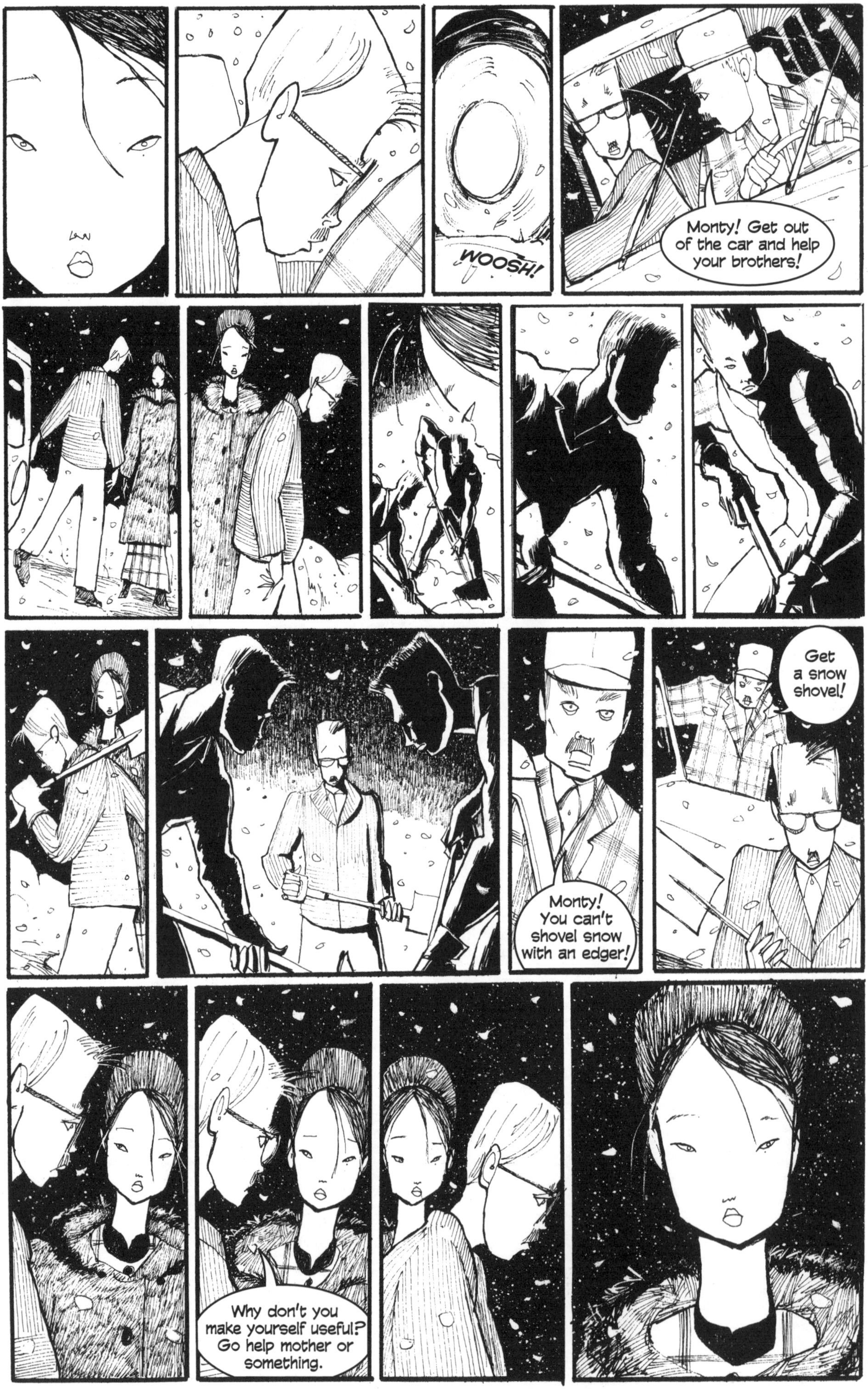
WOOSH!
Monty! Get out of the car and help your brothers!
Get a snow shovel!
Monty! You can't shovel snow with an edger!
Why don't you make yourself useful? Go help mother or something.

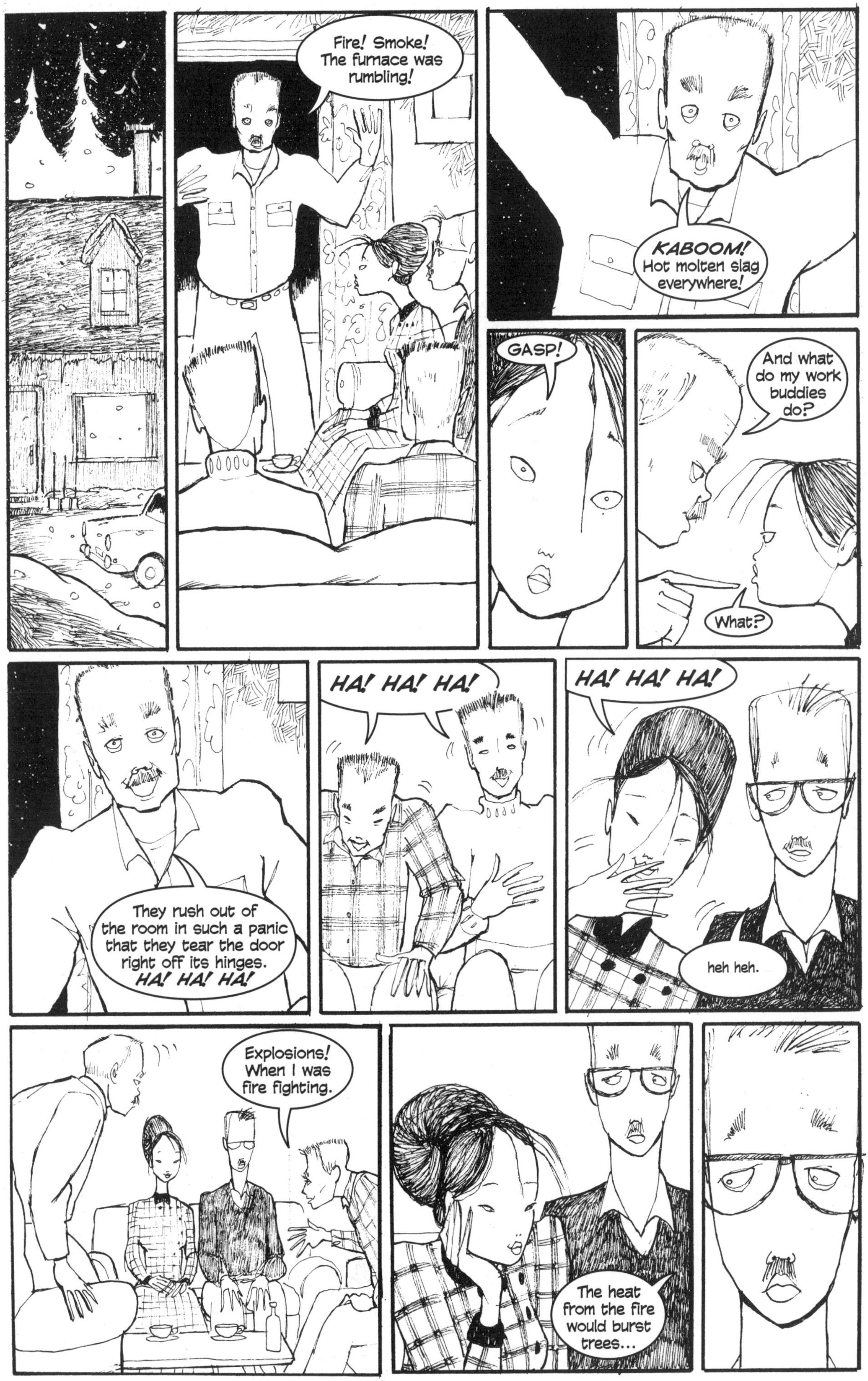
Fire! Smoke! The furnace was rumbling!
KABOOM! Hot molten slag everywhere!
GASP!
And what do my work buddies do?
What?
They rush out of the room in such a panic that they tear the door right off its hinges. HA! HA! HA!
HA! HA! HA!
HA! HA! HA!
heh heh.
Explosions! When I was fire fighting.
The heat from the fire would burst trees...

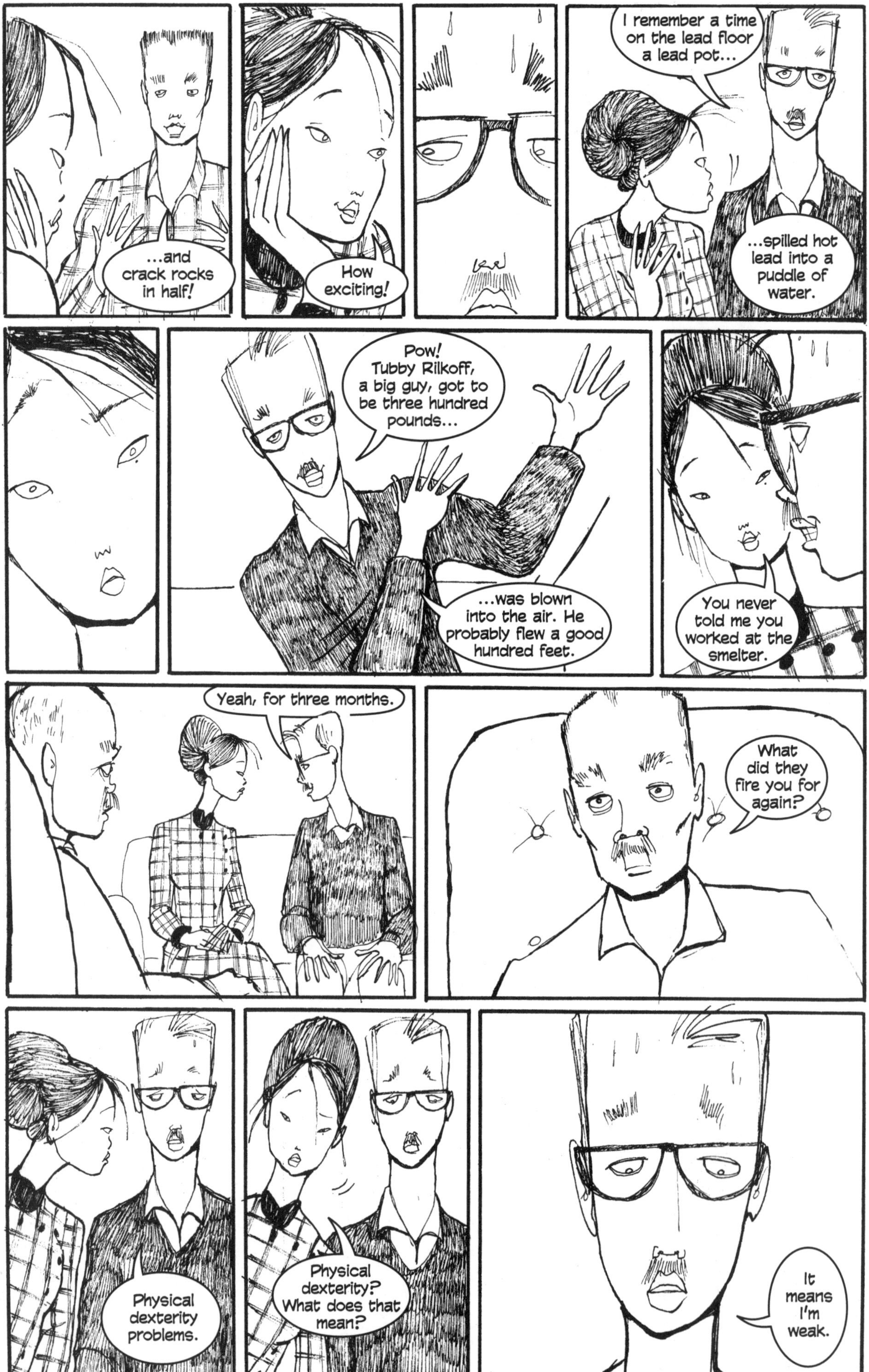
...and crack rocks in half!
How exciting!
I remember a time on the lead floor a lead pot...
...spilled hot lead into a puddle of water.
Pow! Tubby Rilkoff, a big guy, got to be three hundred pounds...
...was blown into the air. He probably flew a good hundred feet.
You never told me you worked at the smelter.
Yeah, for three months.
What did they fire you for again?
Physical dexterity problems.
Physical dexterity? What does that mean?
It means I'm weak.

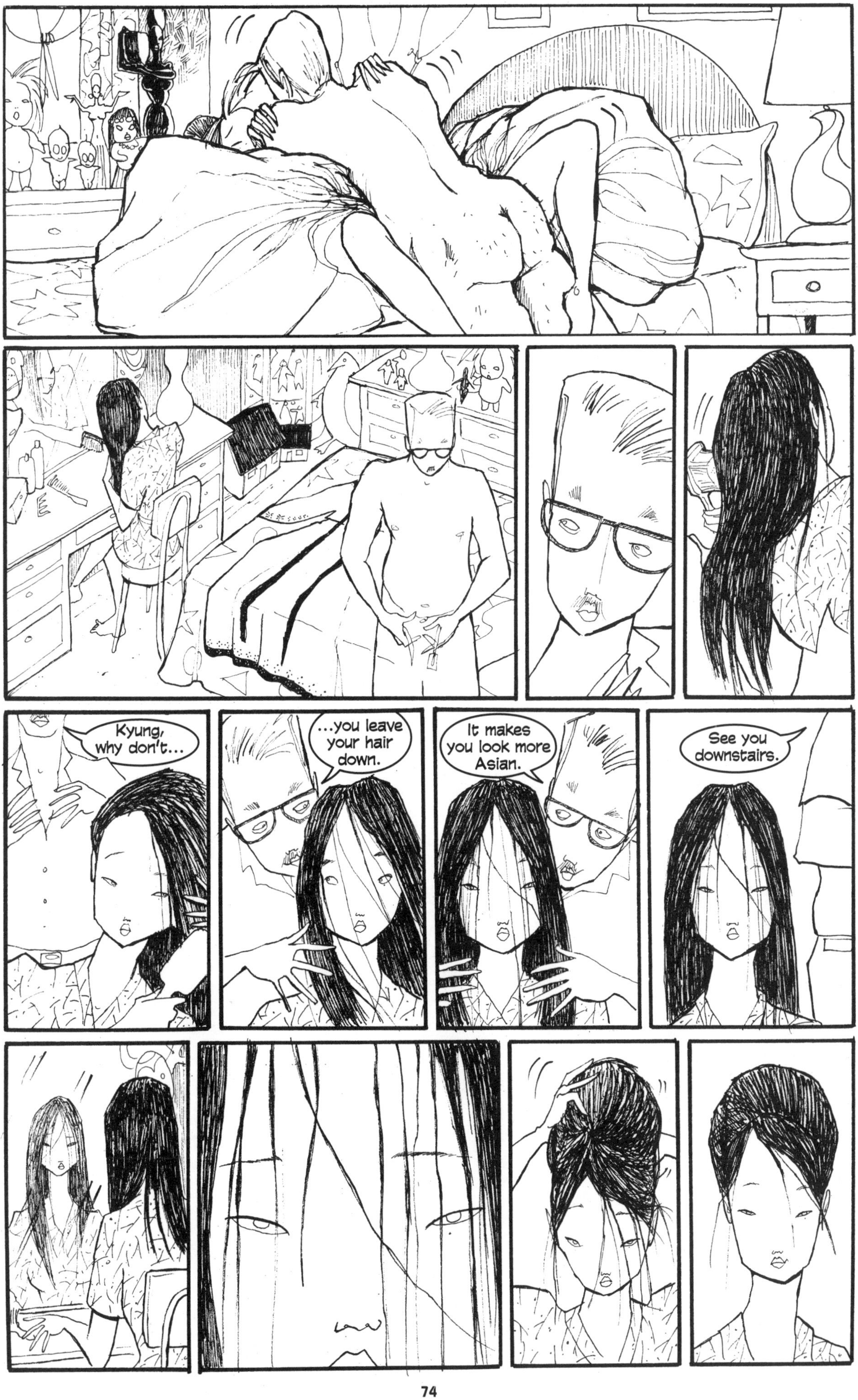

Kyung, why don't...
...you leave your hair down.
It makes you look more Asian.
See you downstairs.

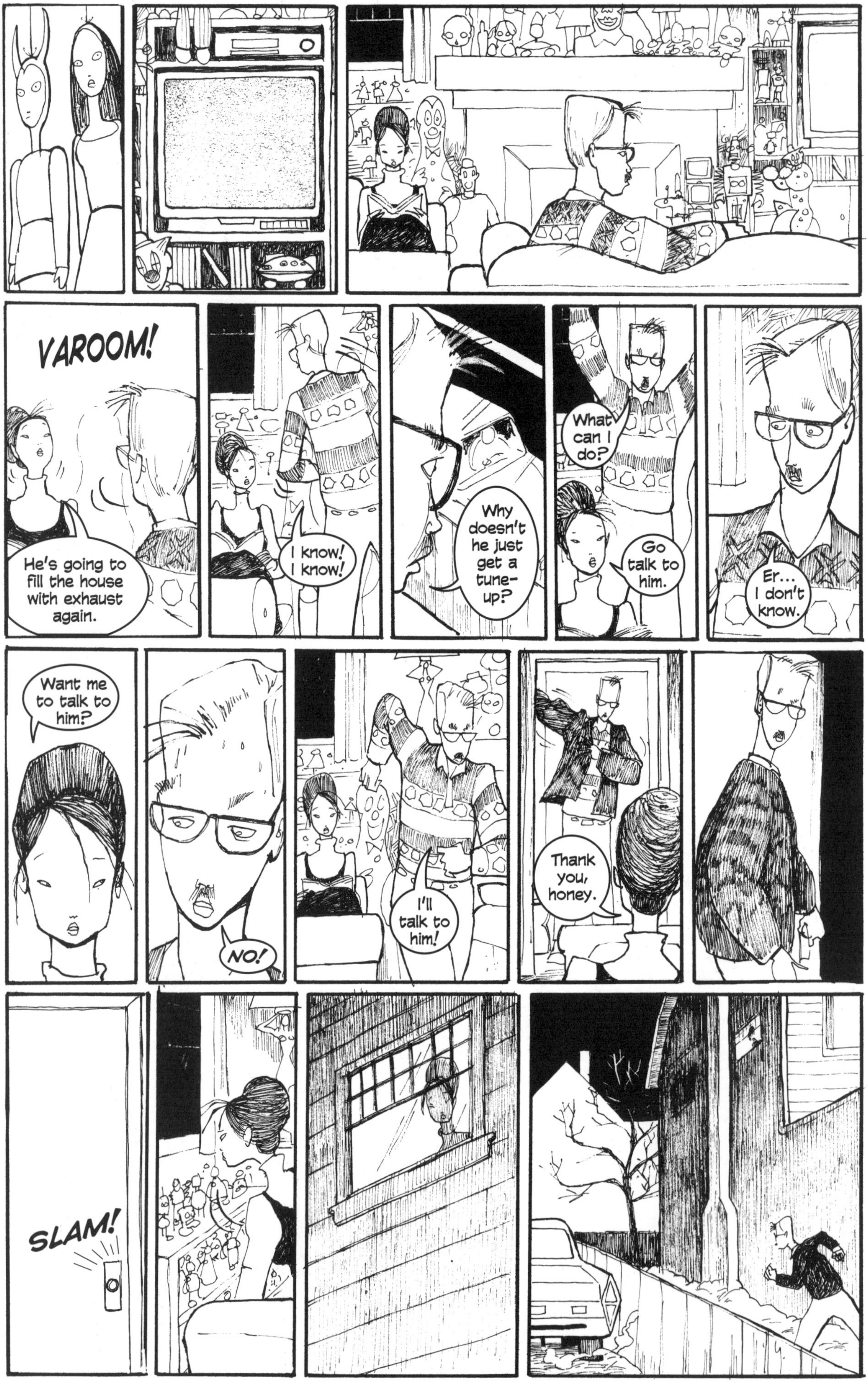
VAROOM!
He's going to fill the house with exhaust again.
I know! I know!
Why doesn't he just get a tune-up?
What can I do?
Go talk to him.
Er... I don't know.
Want me to talk to him?
NO!
I'll talk to him!
Thank you, honey.
SLAM!

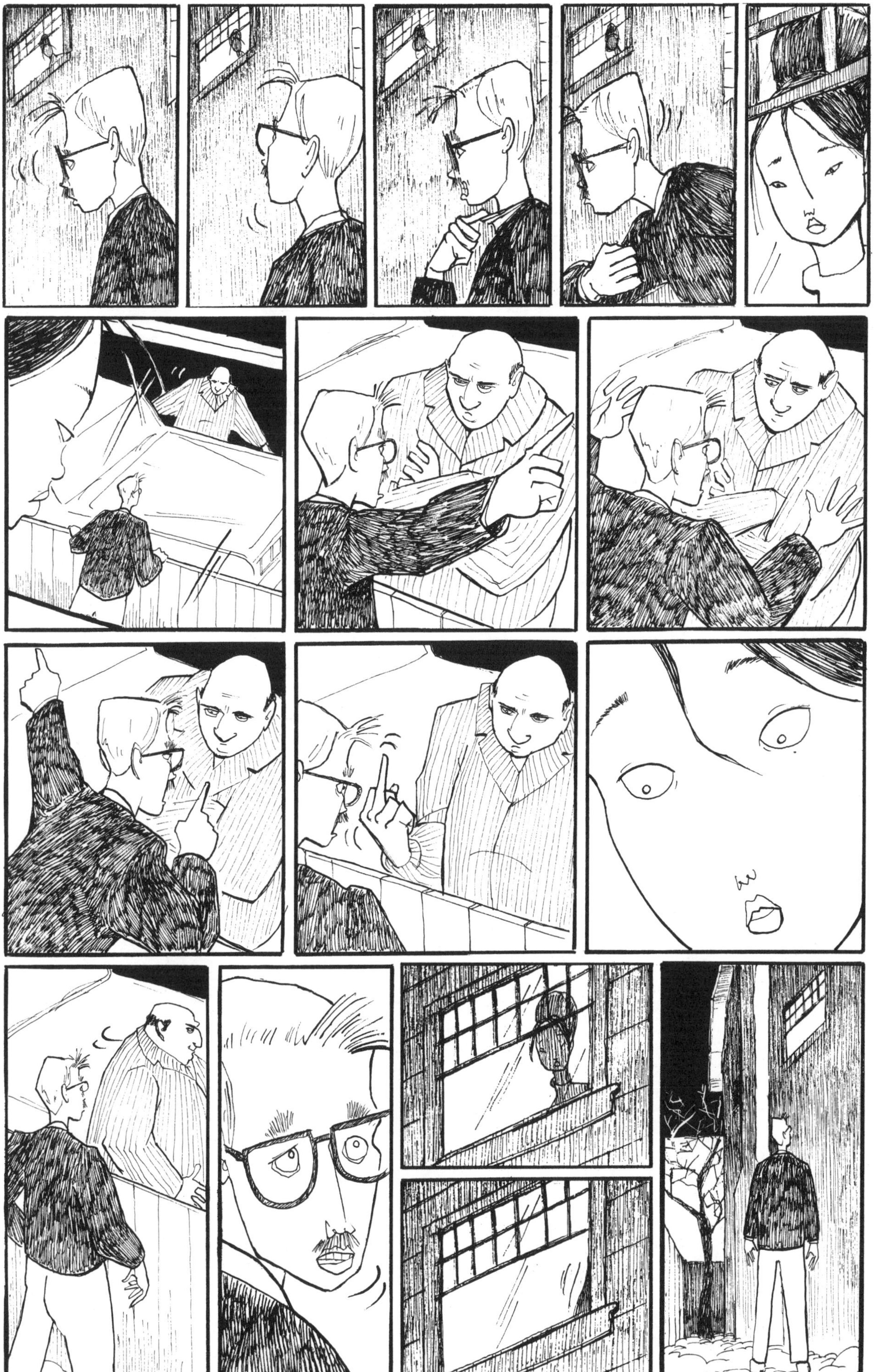

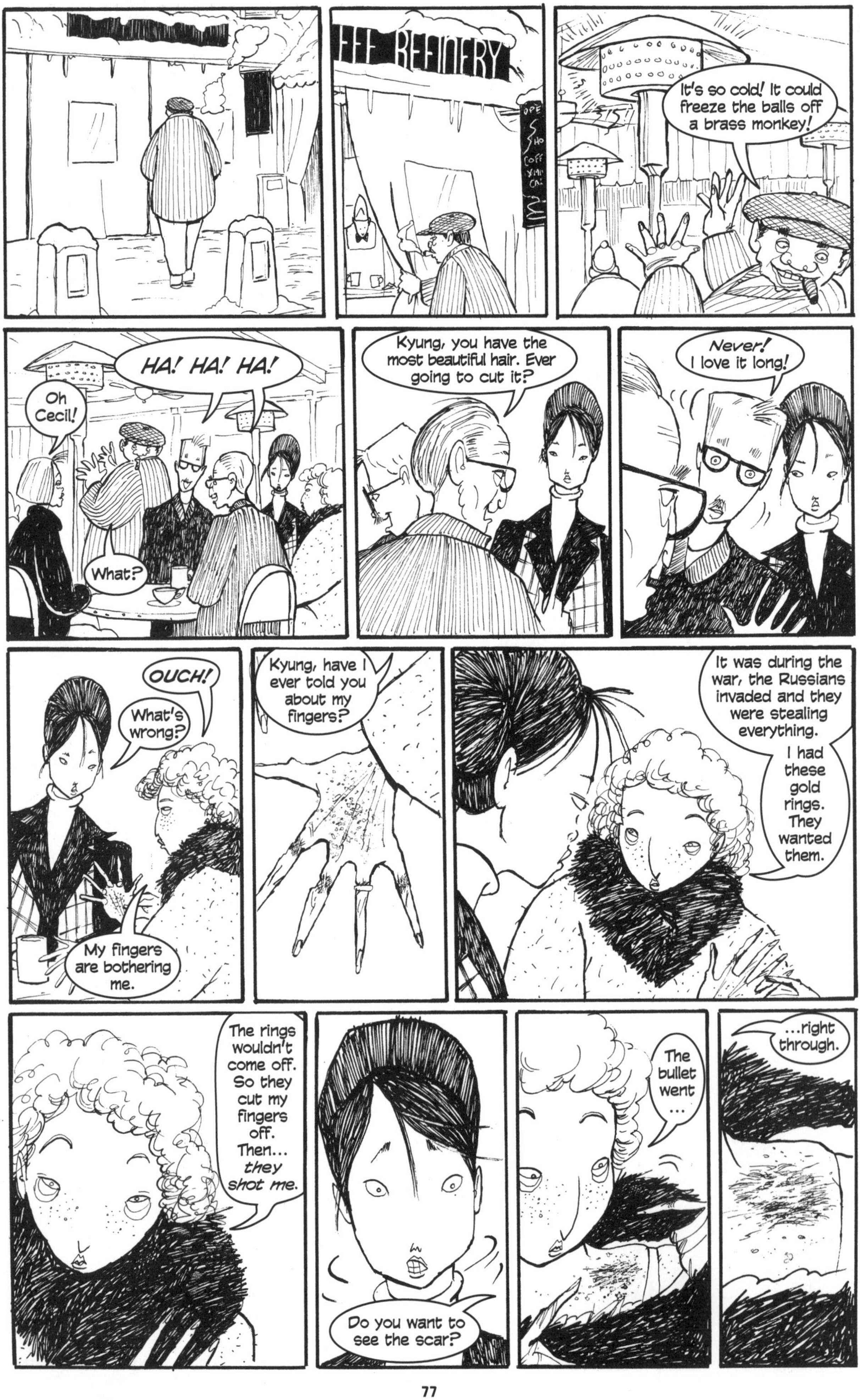
FFE REFINERY
It's so cold! It could freeze the balls off a brass monkey!
HA! HA! HA!
Oh Cecil!
What?
Kyung, you have the most beautiful hair. Ever going to cut it?
Never! I love it long!
OUCH!
What's wrong?
My fingers are bothering me.
Kyung, have I ever told you about my fingers?
It was during the war, the Russians invaded and they were stealing everything.
I had these gold rings. They wanted them.
The rings wouldn't come off. So they cut my fingers off. Then... they shot me.
Do you want to see the scar?
The bullet went ...
...right through.

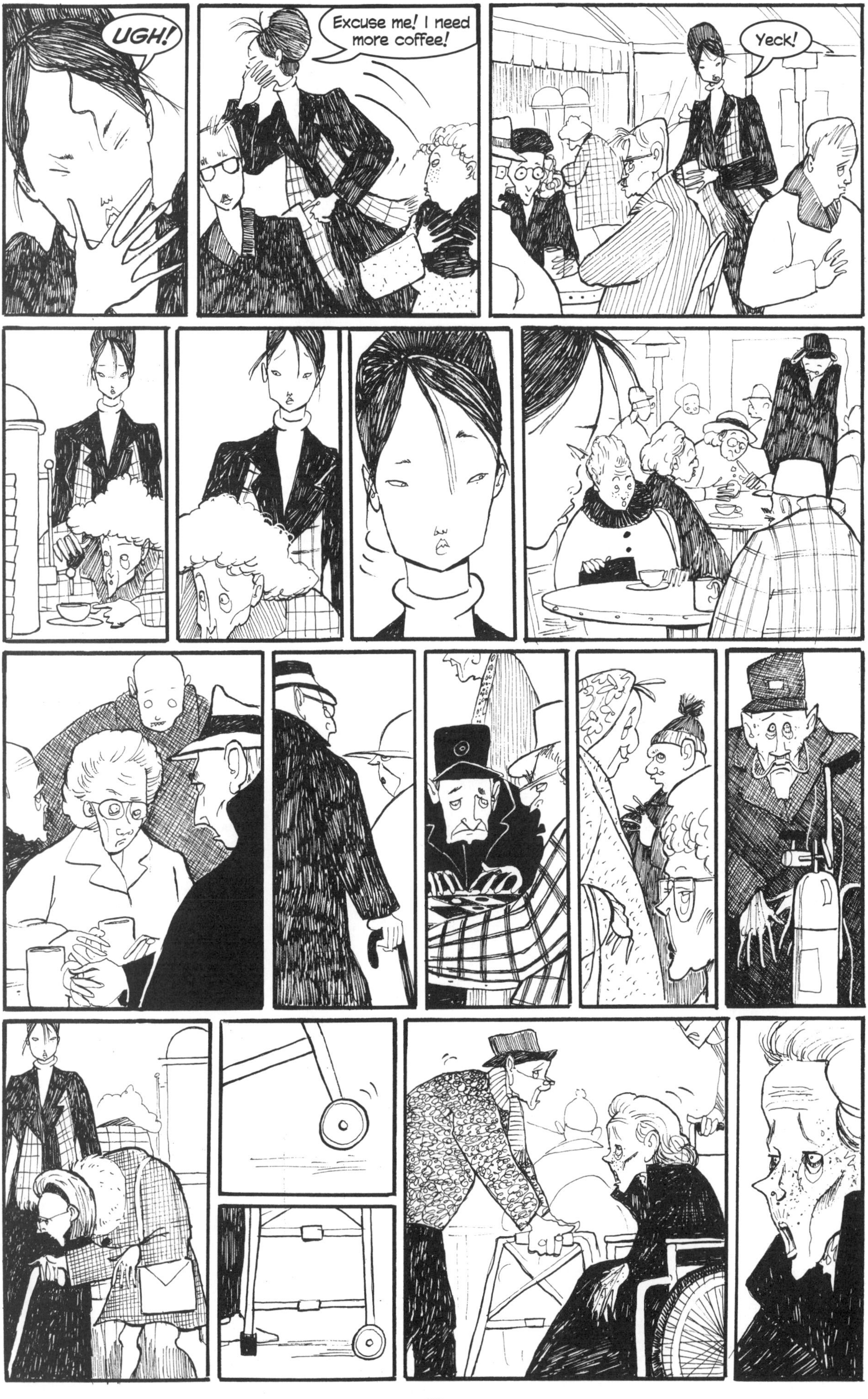
UGH!
Excuse me! I need more coffee!
Yeck!

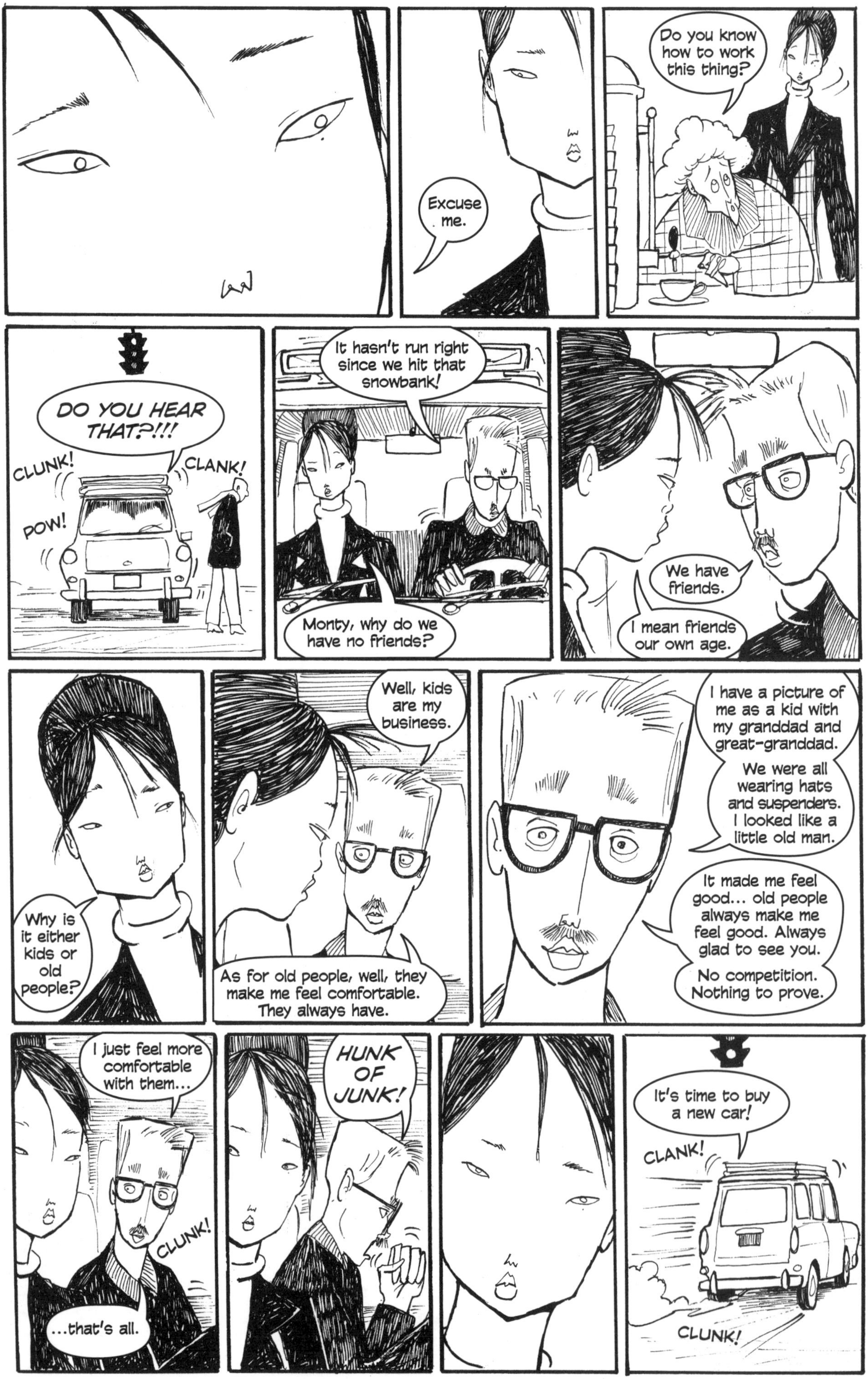
Excuse me.
Do you know how to work this thing?
DO YOU HEAR THAT?!!!
CLUNK!
CLANK!
POW!
It hasn't run right since we hit that snowbank!
Monty, why do we have no friends?
We have friends.
I mean friends our own age.
Why is it either kids or old people?
Well, kids are my business.
As for old people, well, they make me feel comfortable. They always have.
I have a picture of me as a kid with my granddad and great-granddad.
We were all wearing hats and suspenders. I looked like a little old man.
It made me feel good... old people always make me feel good. Always glad to see you.
No competition. Nothing to prove.
I just feel more comfortable with them...
CLUNK!
...that's all.
HUNK OF JUNK!
It's time to buy a new car!
CLANK!
CLUNK!

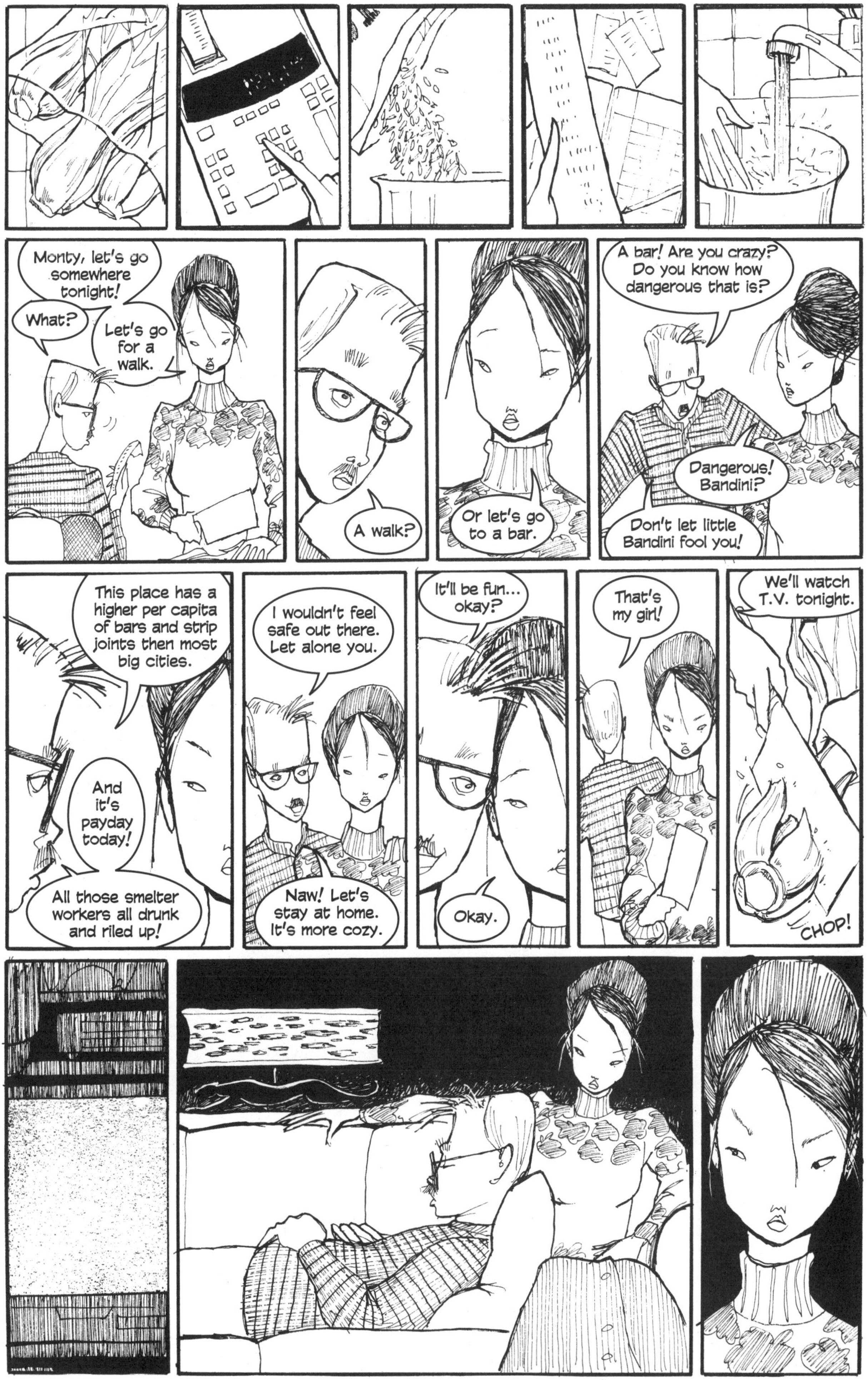

Monty, let's go somewhere tonight!
What?
Let's go for a walk.
A walk?
Or let's go to a bar.
A bar! Are you crazy? Do you know how dangerous that is?
Dangerous! Bandini?
Don't let little Bandini fool you!
This place has a higher per capita of bars and strip joints then most big cities.
And it's payday today!
All those smelter workers all drunk and riled up!
I wouldn't feel safe out there. Let alone you.
Naw! Let's stay at home. It's more cozy.
It'll be fun... okay?
Okay.
That's my girl!
We'll watch T.V. tonight.
CHOP!

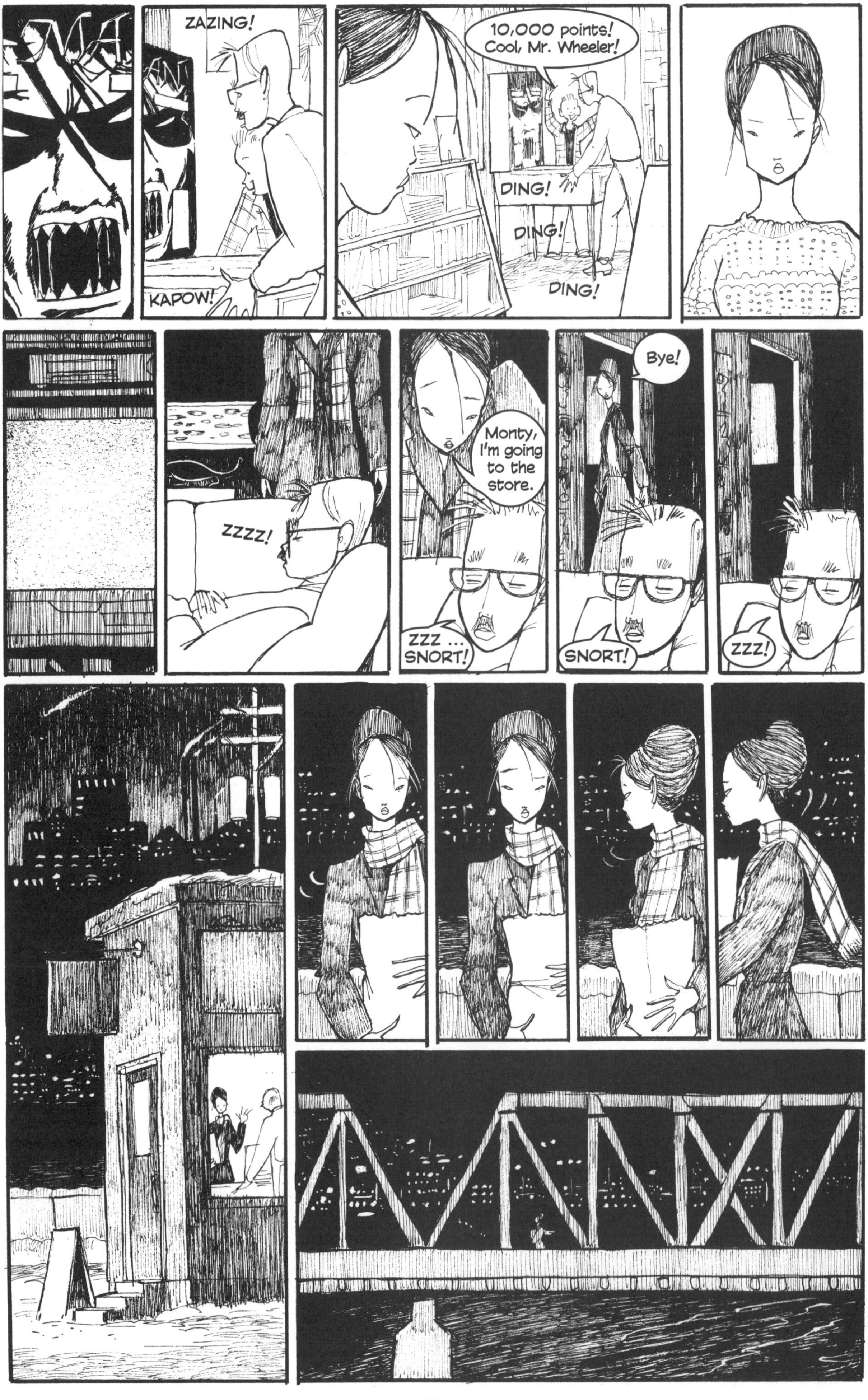
ZAZING!
KAPOW!
10,000 points! Cool, Mr. Wheeler!
DING!
DING!
DING!
ZZZZ!
Monty, I'm going to the store.
ZZZ ... SNORT!
Bye!
SNORT!
ZZZ!

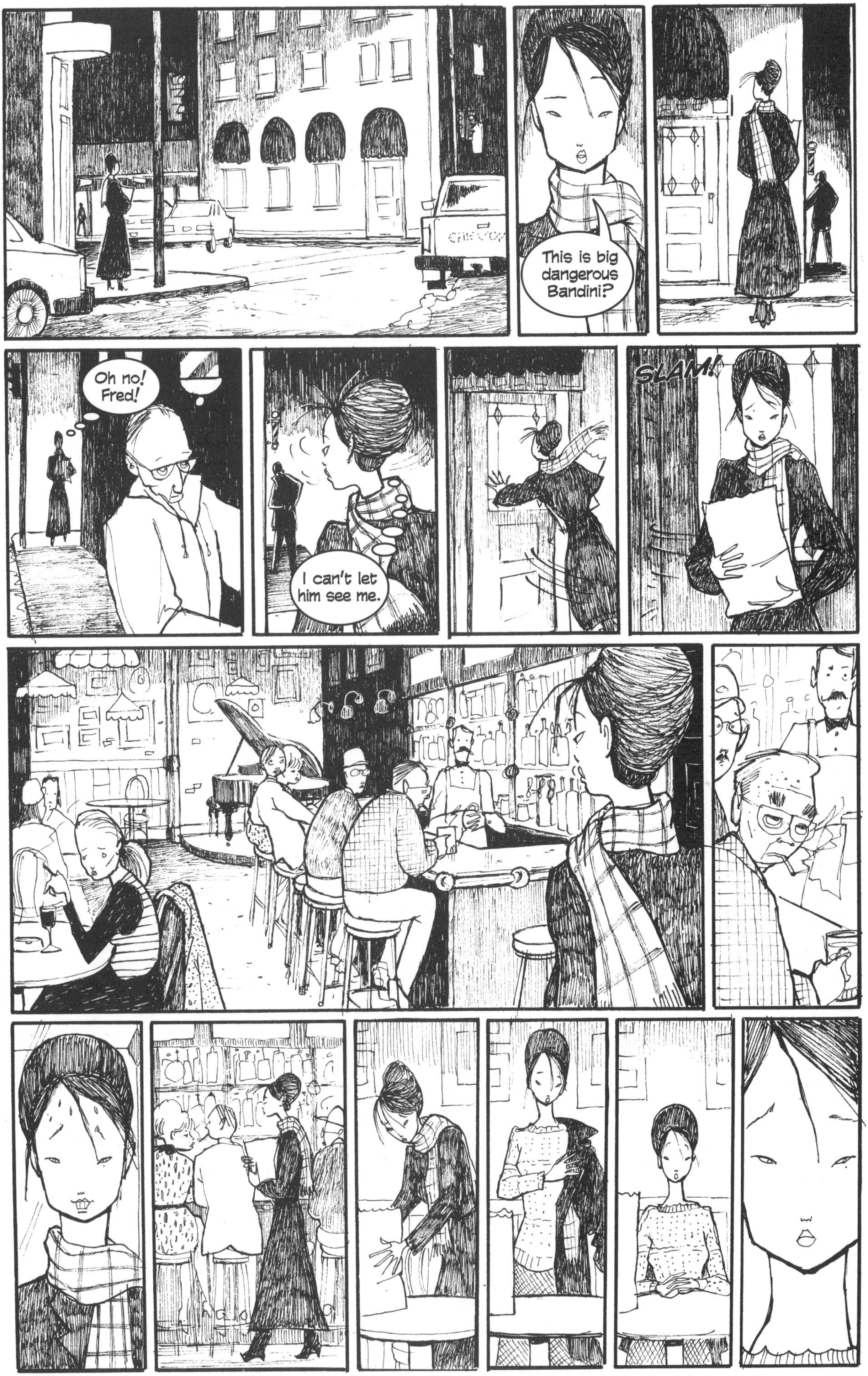
This is big dangerous Bandini?
Oh no! Fred!
I can't let him see me.
SLAM!

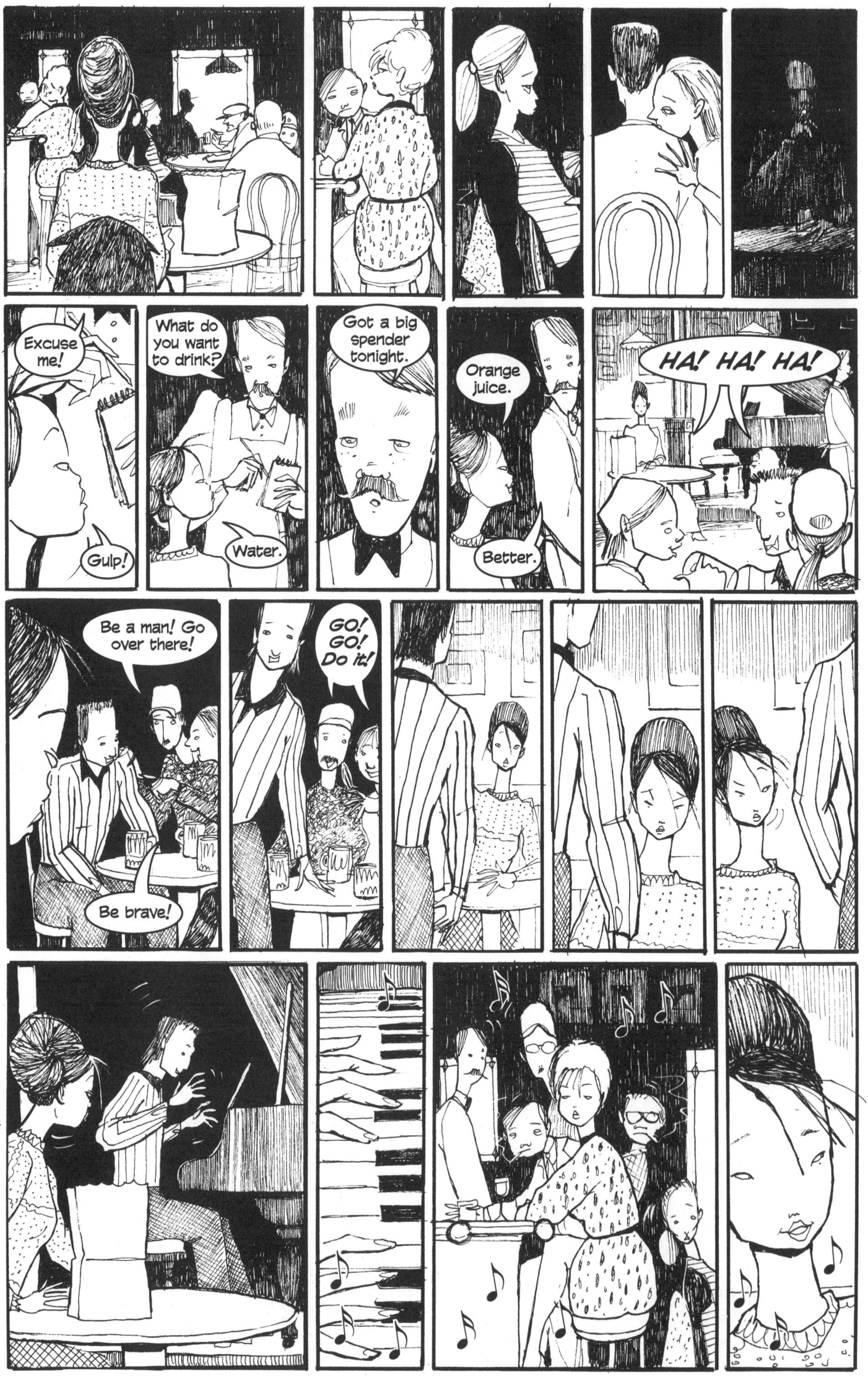
Excuse me!
Gulp!
What do you want to drink?
Water.
Got a big spender tonight.
Orange juice.
Better.
HA! HA! HA!
Be a man! Go over there!
Be brave!
GO! GO! Do it!

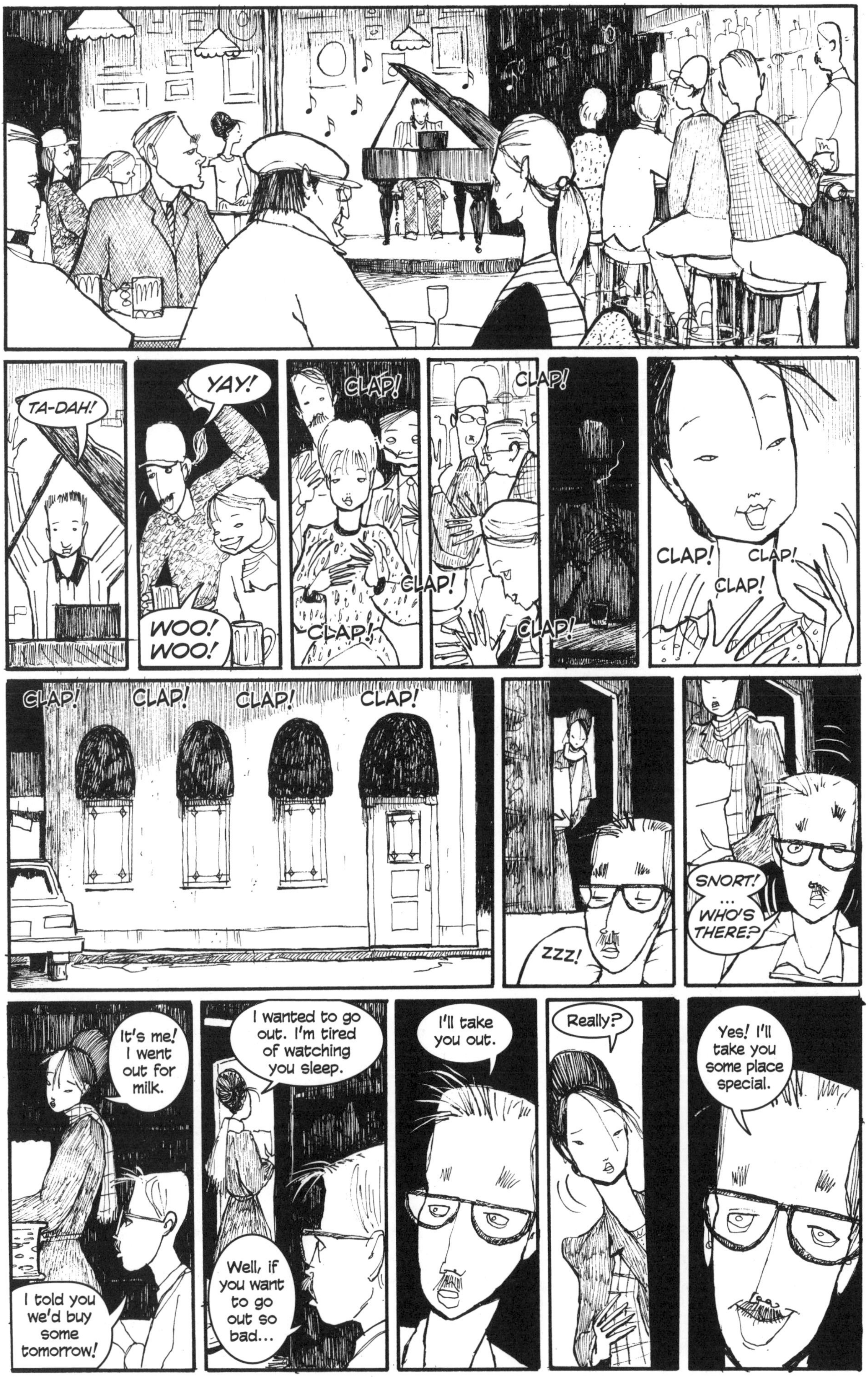
TA-DAH!
YAY!
WOO! WOO!
CLAP!
CLAP!
CLAP!
CLAP!
CLAP!
CLAP!
CLAP! CLAP!
CLAP!
CLAP! CLAP! CLAP! CLAP!
ZZZ!
SNORT! ... WHO'S THERE?
It's me! I went out for milk.
I told you we'd buy some tomorrow!
I wanted to go out. I'm tired of watching you sleep.
Well, if you want to go out so bad...
I'll take you out.
Really?
Yes! I'll take you some place special.

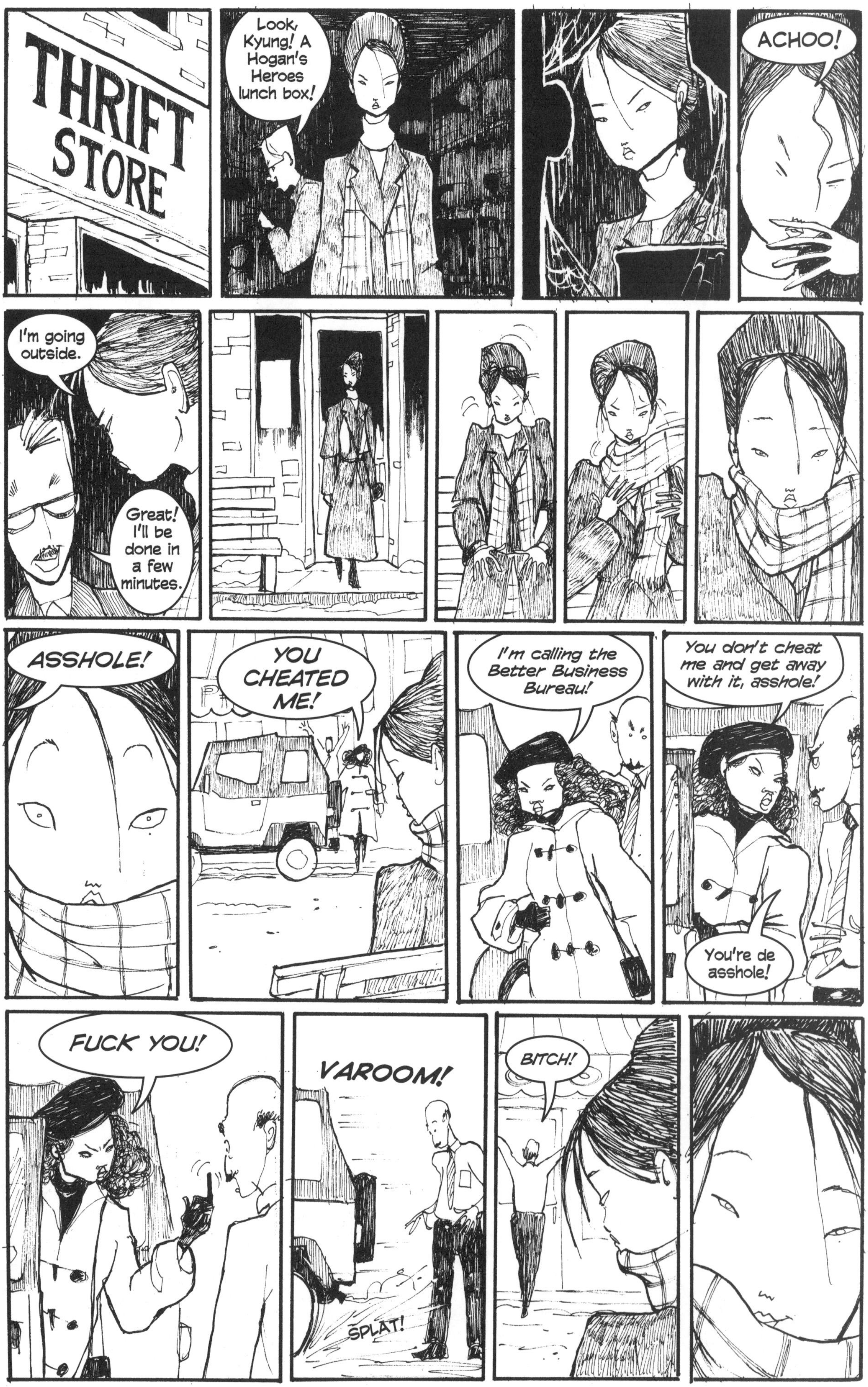
THRIFT STORE
Look, Kyung! A Hogan's Heroes lunch box!
ACHOO!
I'm going outside.
Great! I'll be done in a few minutes.
ASSHOLE!
YOU CHEATED ME!
I'm calling the Better Business Bureau!
You don't cheat me and get away with it, asshole!
You're de asshole!
FUCK YOU!
VAROOM!
SPLAT!
BITCH!

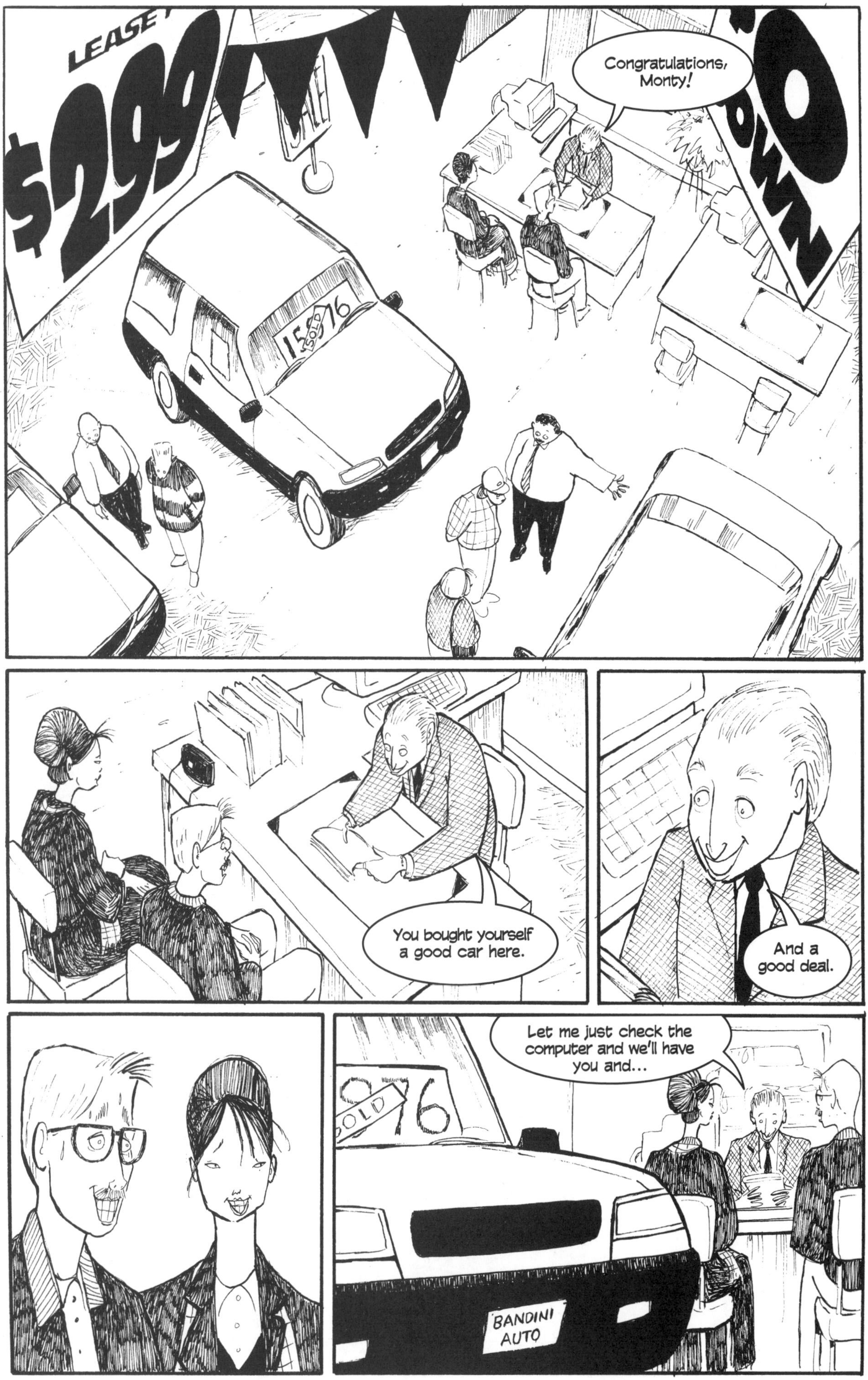
LEASE
$299
SALE
1559 SOLD 76
Congratulations, Monty!
DOWN
You bought yourself a good car here.
And a good deal.
9 SOLD 76
Let me just check the computer and we'll have you and...
BANDINI AUTO

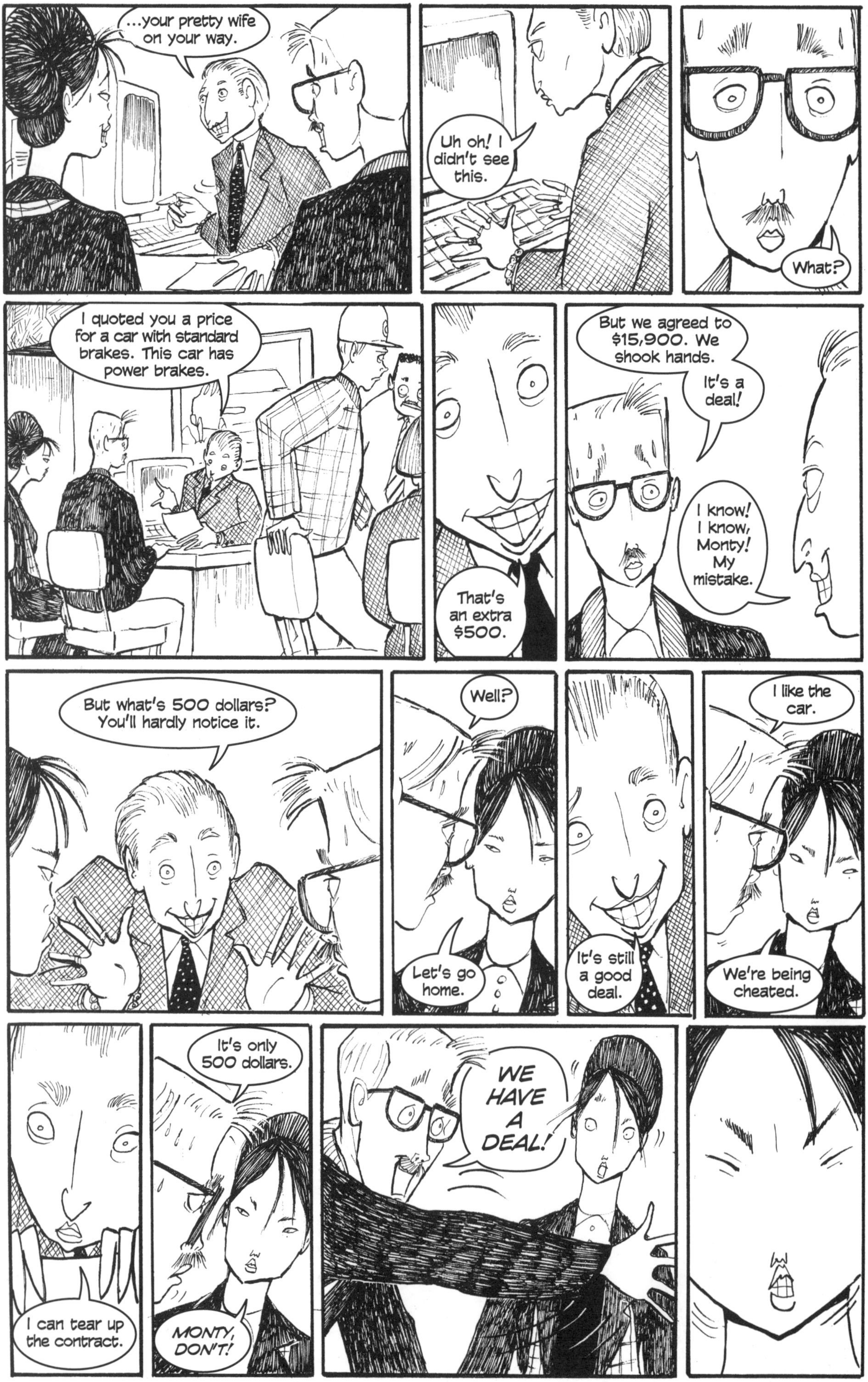
...your pretty wife on your way.
Uh oh! I didn't see this.
What?
I quoted you a price for a car with standard brakes. This car has power brakes.
That's an extra $500.
But we agreed to $15,900. We shook hands.
It's a deal!
I know! I know, Monty! My mistake.
But what's 500 dollars? You'll hardly notice it.
Well?
Let's go home.
It's still a good deal.
I like the car.
We're being cheated.
I can tear up the contract.
It's only 500 dollars.
MONTY, DON'T!
WE HAVE A DEAL!

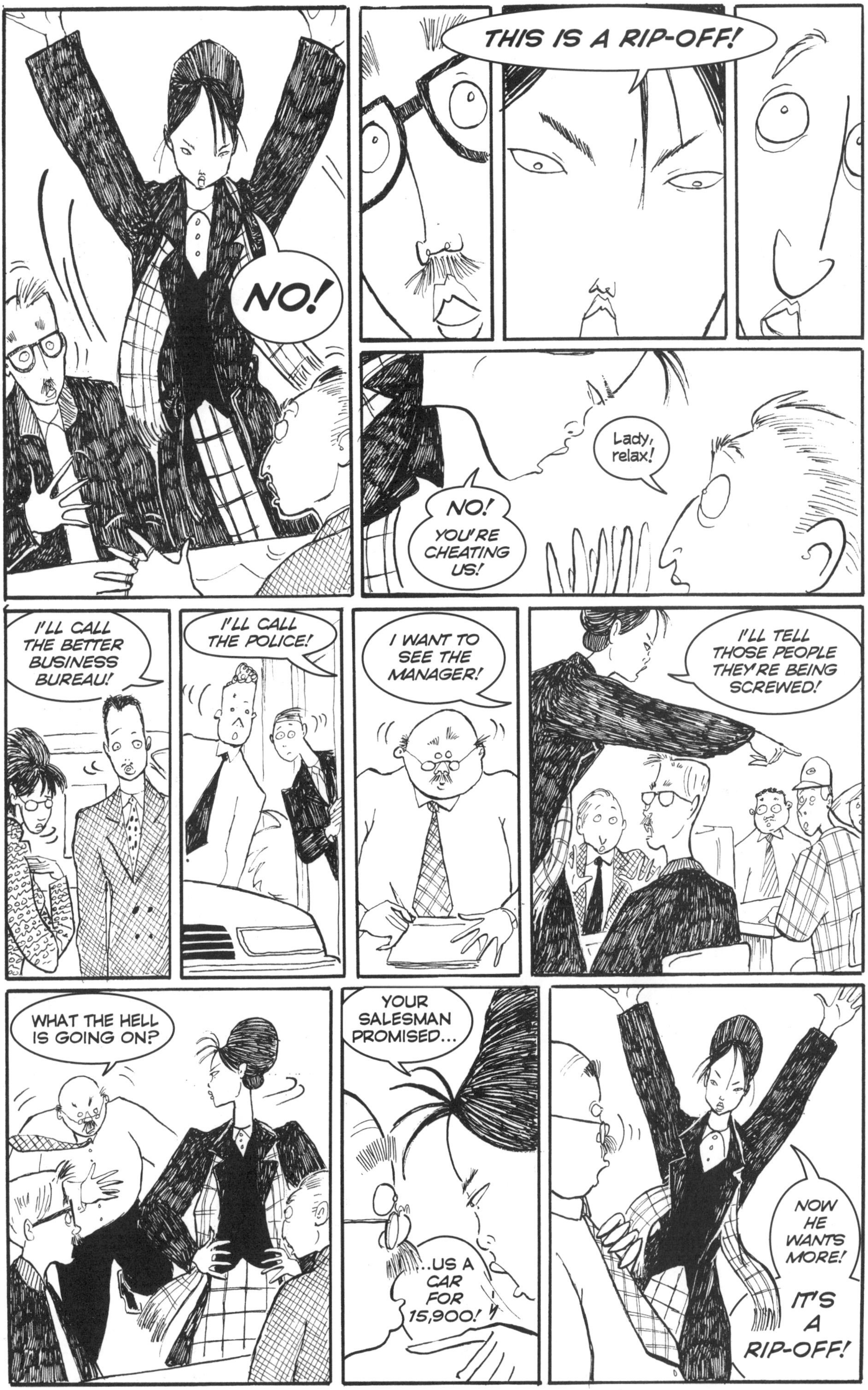
NO!
THIS IS A RIP-OFF!
Lady, relax!
NO! YOU'RE CHEATING US!
I'LL CALL THE BETTER BUSINESS BUREAU!
I'LL CALL THE POLICE!
I WANT TO SEE THE MANAGER!
I'LL TELL THOSE PEOPLE THEY'RE BEING SCREWED!
WHAT THE HELL IS GOING ON?
YOUR SALESMAN PROMISED...
...US A CAR FOR 15,900!
NOW HE WANTS MORE!
IT'S A RIP-OFF!

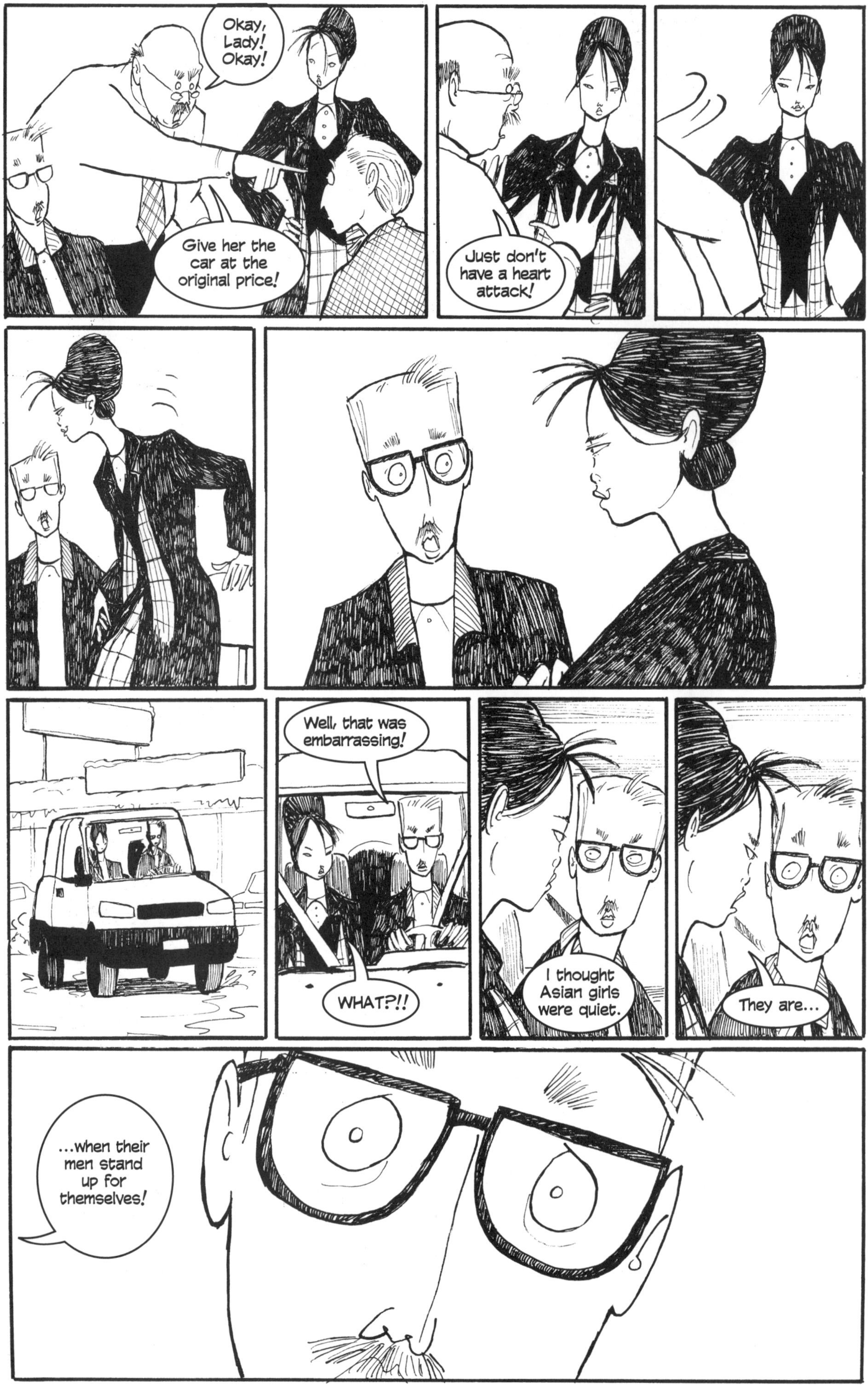
Okay, Lady! Okay!
Give her the car at the original price!
Just don't have a heart attack!
Well, that was embarrassing!
WHAT?!!
I thought Asian girls were quiet.
They are...
...when their men stand up for themselves!

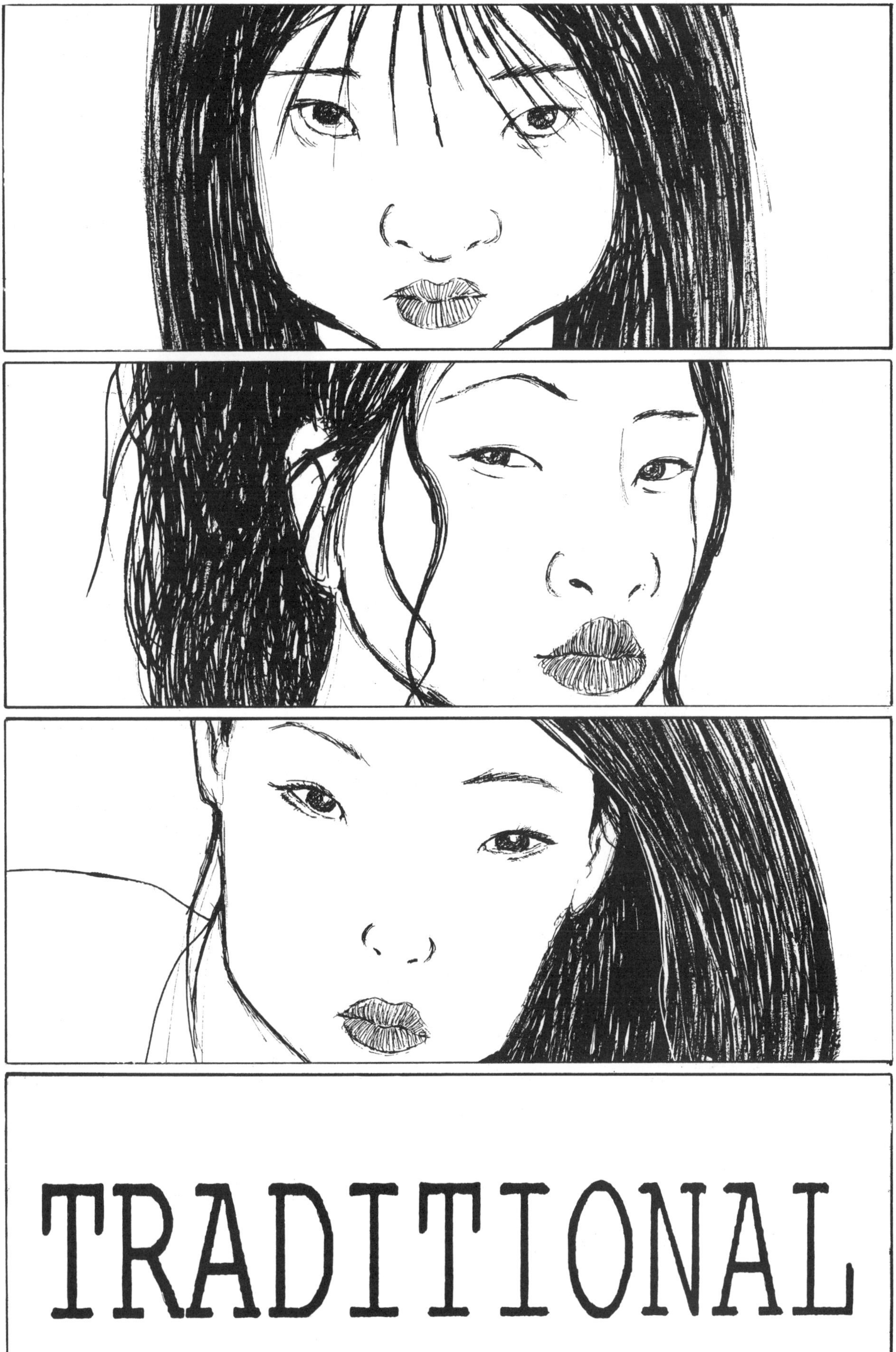
TRADITIONAL

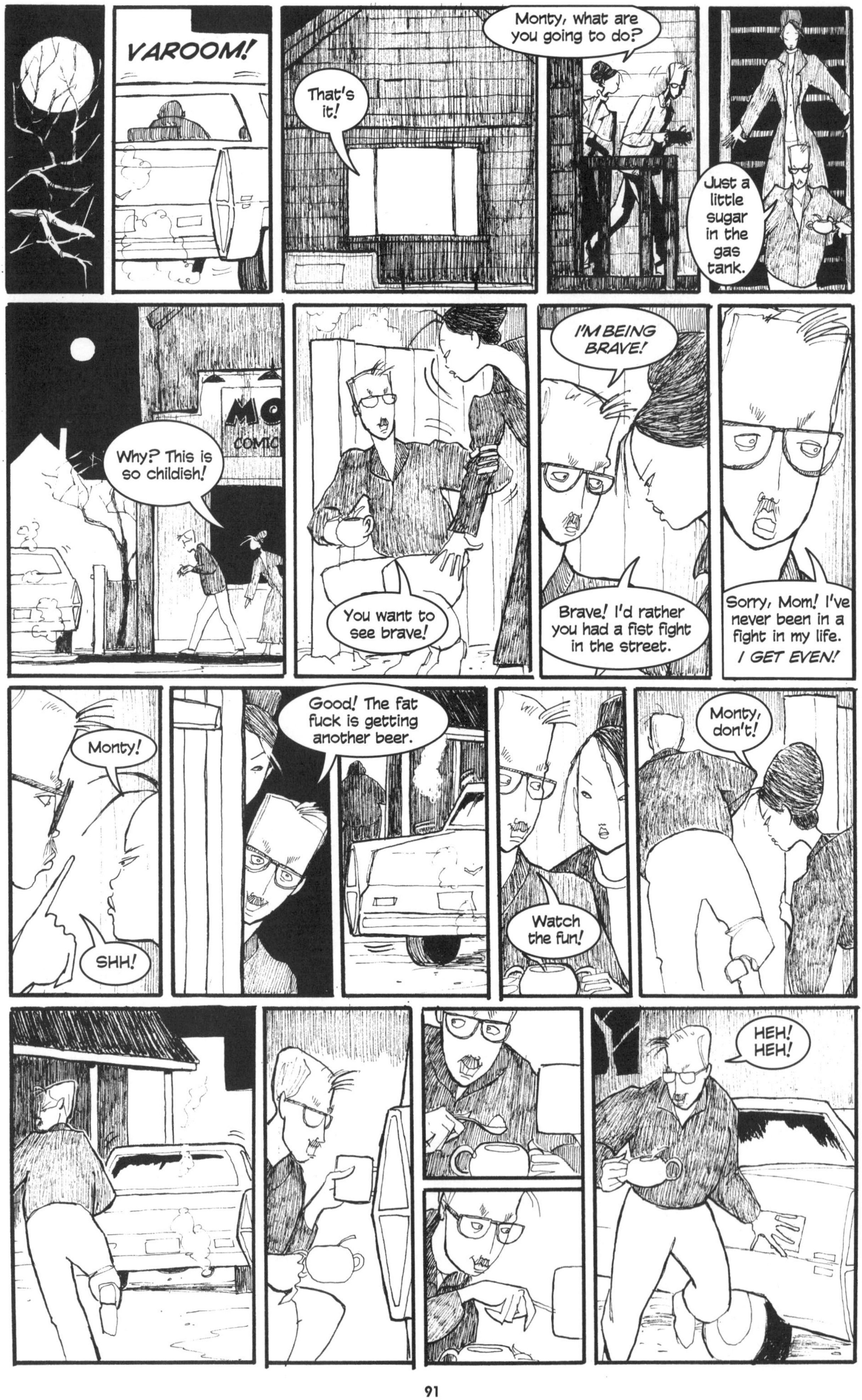

VAROOM!
That's it!
Monty, what are you going to do?
Just a little sugar in the gas tank.
Why? This is so childish!
MO
COMIC
You want to see brave!
I'M BEING BRAVE!
Brave! I'd rather you had a fist fight in the street.
Sorry, Mom! I've never been in a fight in my life.
I GET EVEN!
Monty!
SHH!
Good! The fat fuck is getting another beer.
Watch the fun!
Monty, don't!
HEH! HEH!

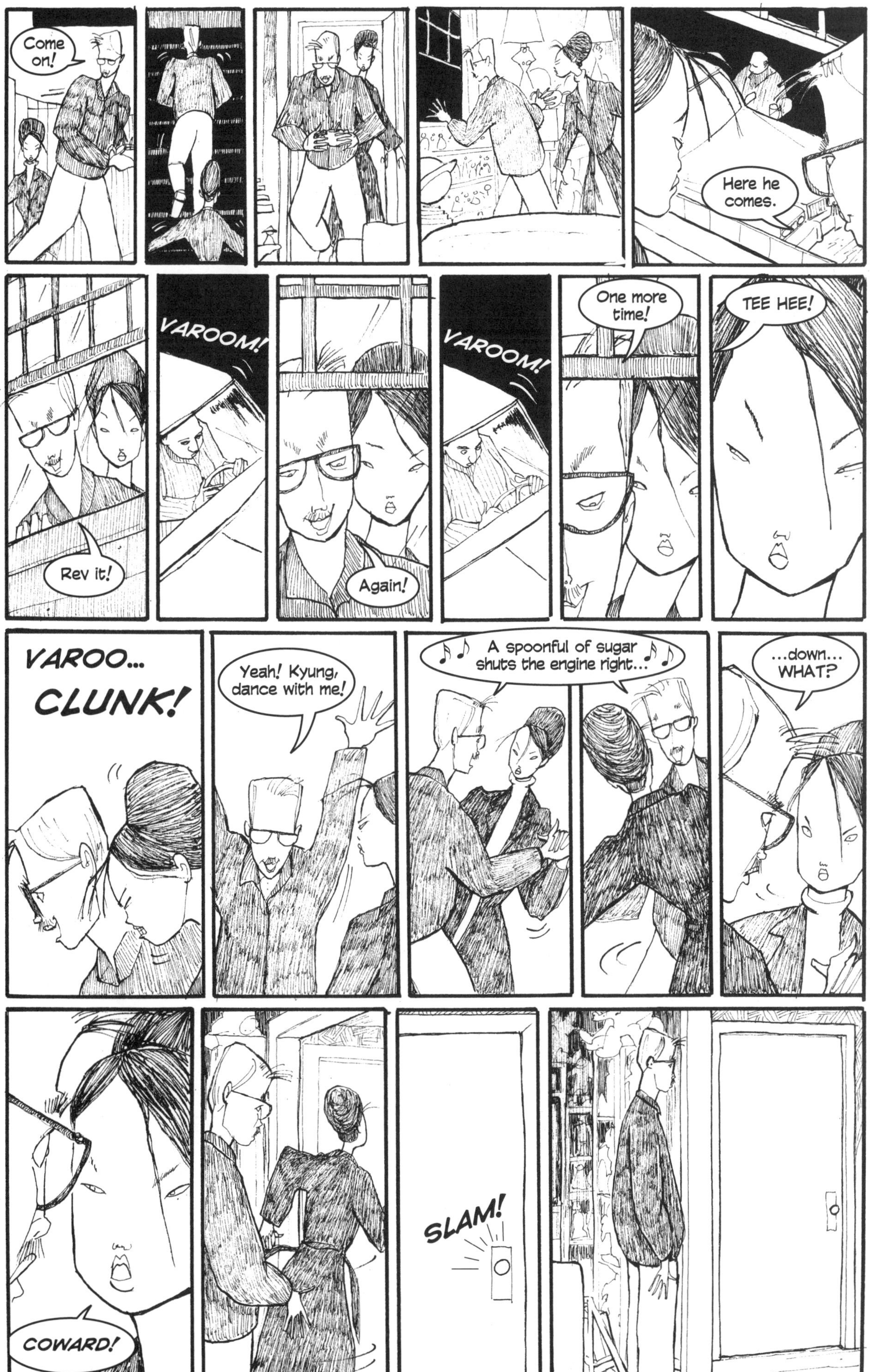
Come on!
Here he comes.
Rev it!
VAROOM!
Again!
VAROOM!
One more time!
TEE HEE!
VAROO... CLUNK!
Yeah! Kyung, dance with me!
A spoonful of sugar shuts the engine right...
...down... WHAT?
COWARD!
SLAM!

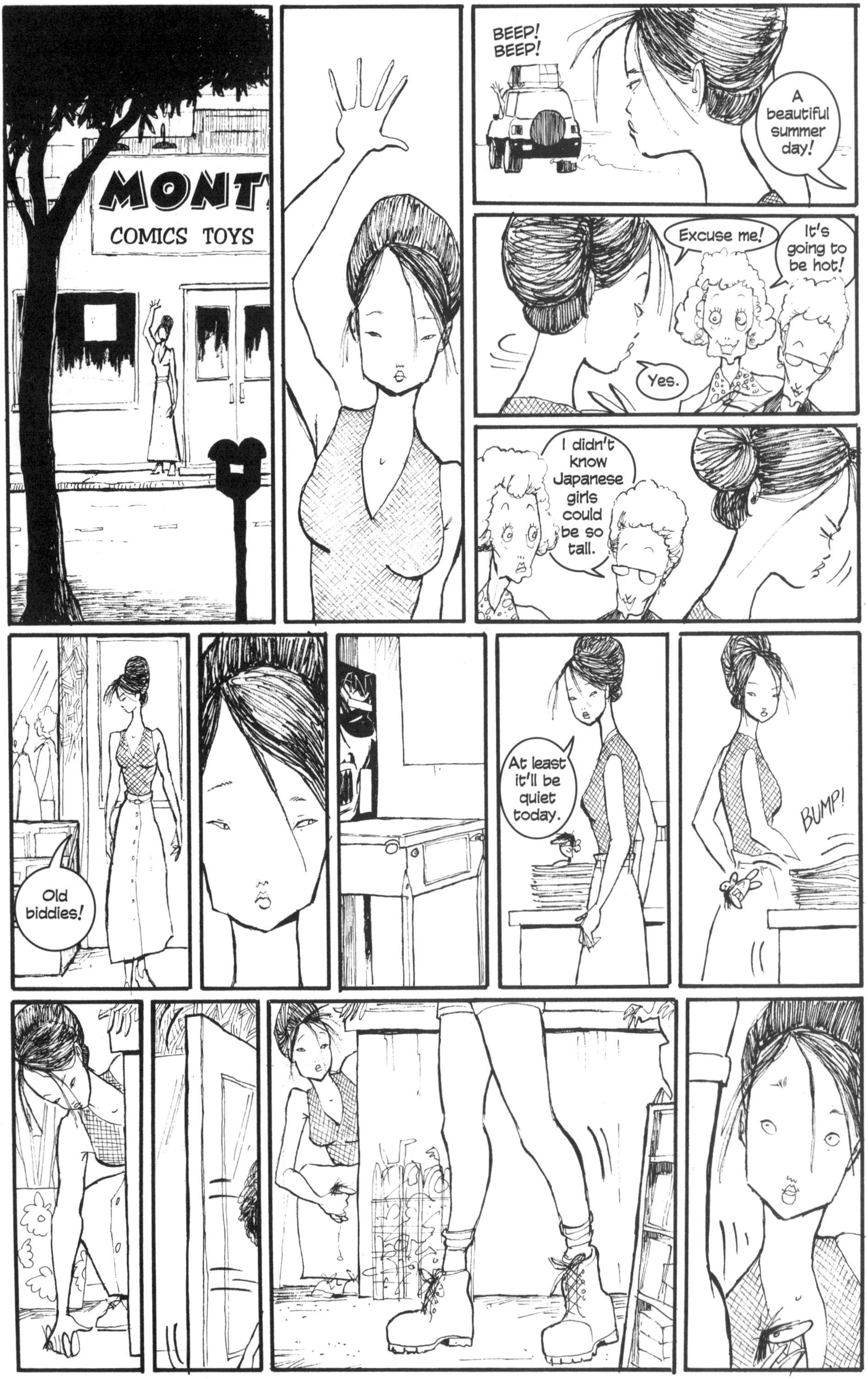
MONTY
COMICS TOYS
BEEP! BEEP!
A beautiful summer day!
Excuse me!
It's going to be hot!
Yes.
I didn't know Japanese girls could be so tall.
Old biddies!
At least it'll be quiet today.
BUMP!

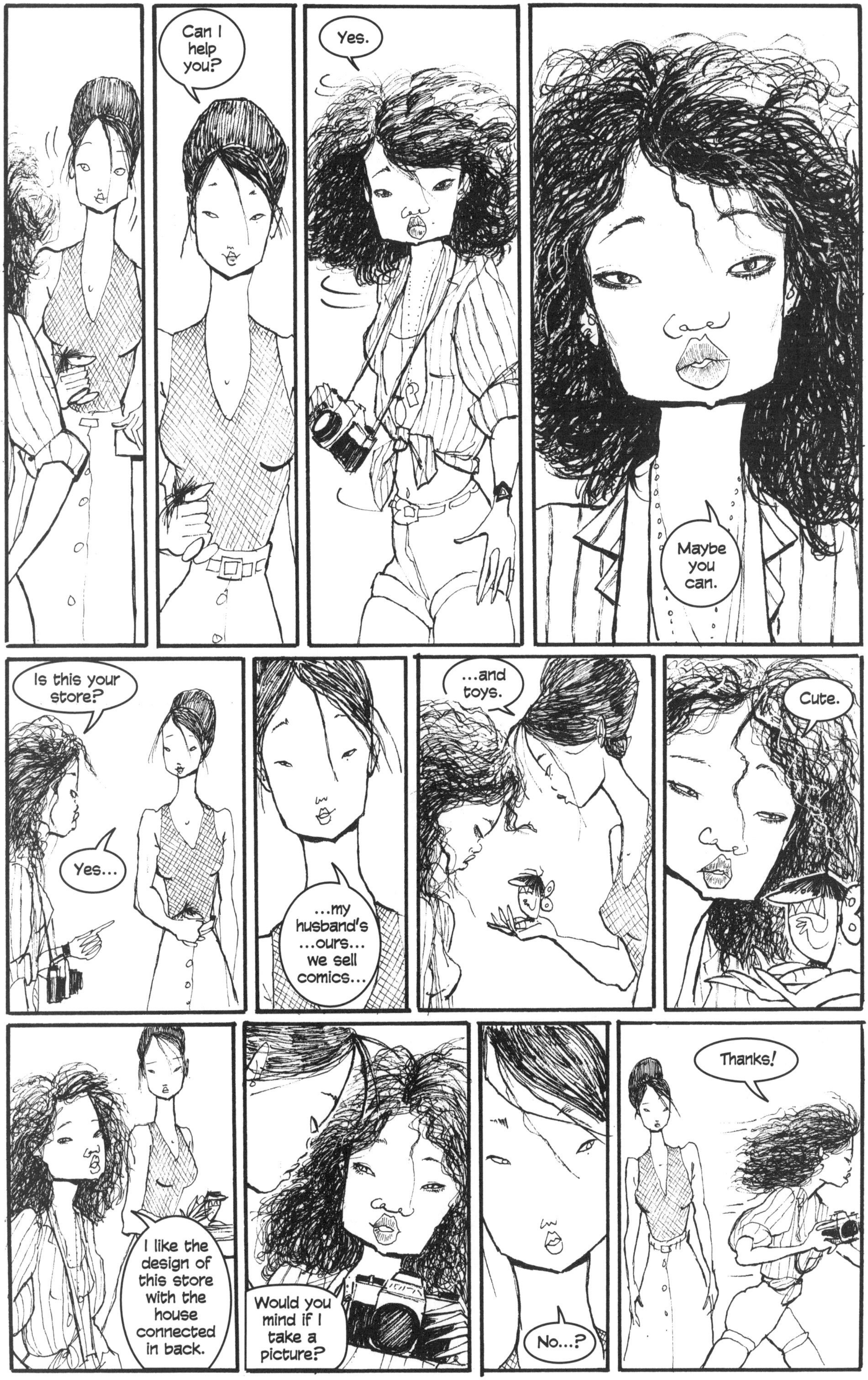
Can I help you?
Yes.
Maybe you can.
Is this your store?
Yes...
...my husband's ...ours... we sell comics...
...and toys.
Cute.
I like the design of this store with the house connected in back.
Would you mind if I take a picture?
No...?
Thanks!

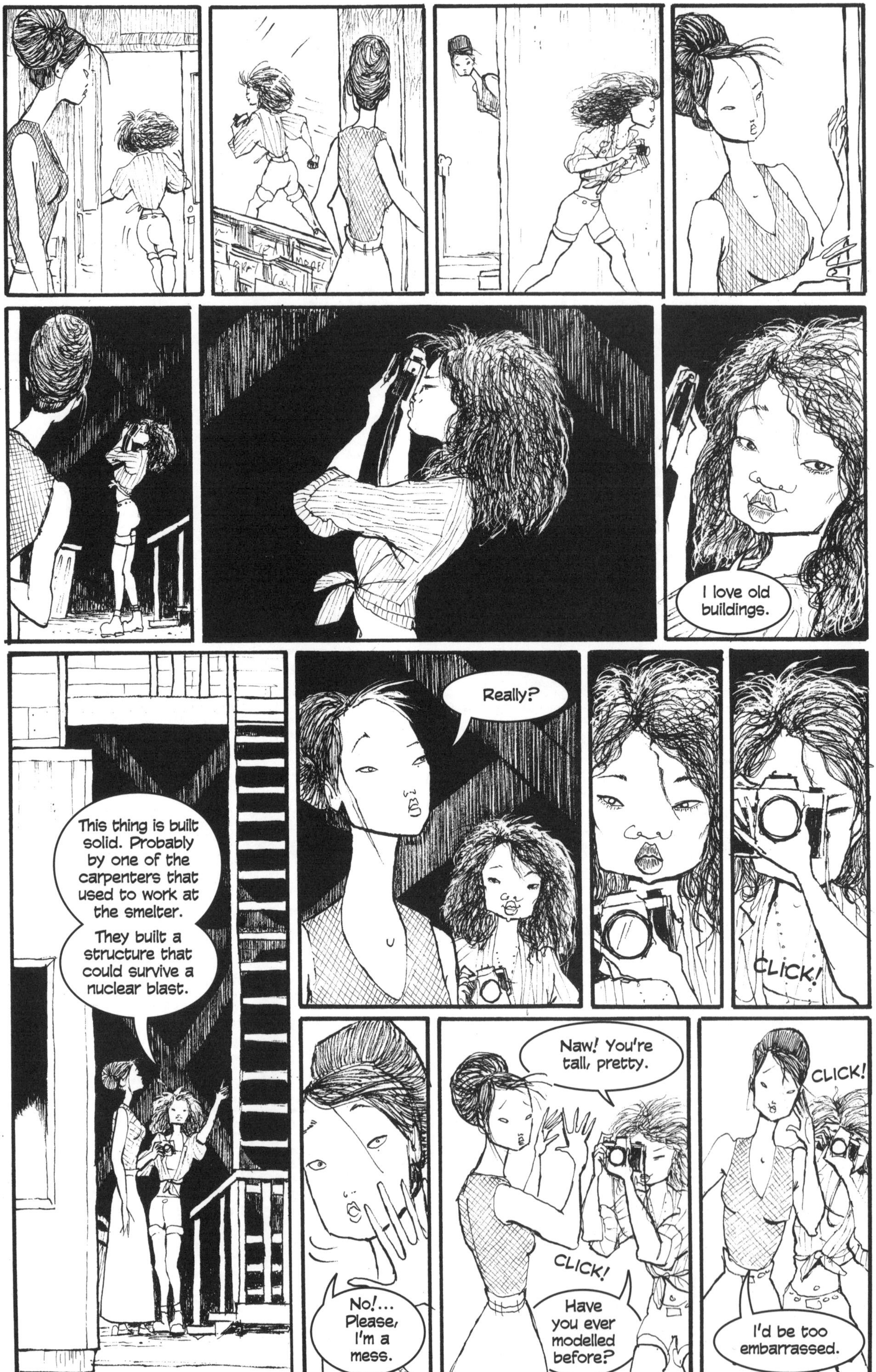
I love old buildings.
This thing is built solid. Probably by one of the carpenters that used to work at the smelter.
They built a structure that could survive a nuclear blast.
Really?
CLICK!
No!... Please, I'm a mess.
Naw! You're tall, pretty.
CLICK!
Have you ever modelled before?
CLICK!
I'd be too embarrassed.

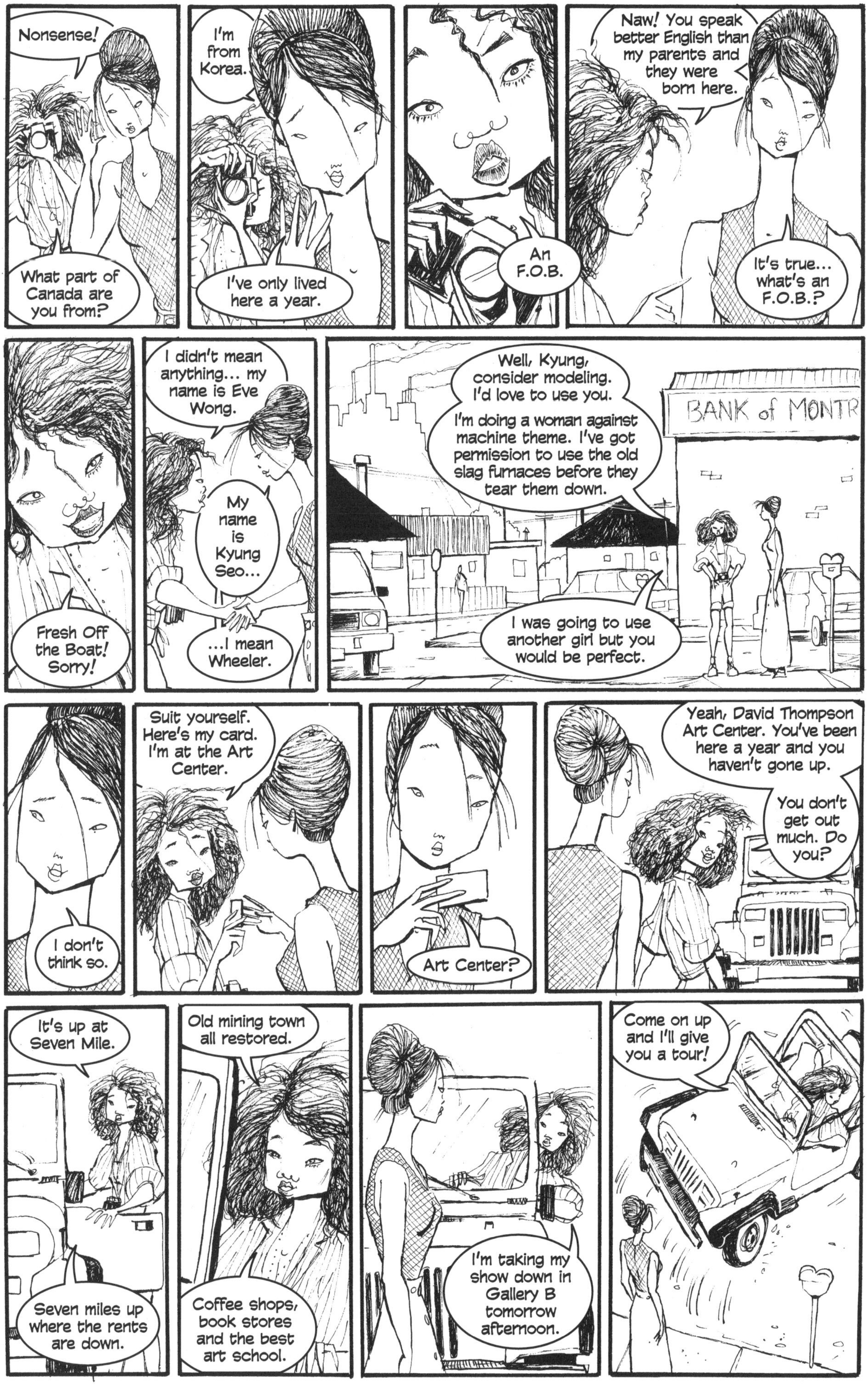
Nonsense!
What part of Canada are you from?
I'm from Korea.
I've only lived here a year.
An F.O.B.
Naw! You speak better English than my parents and they were born here.
It's true... what's an F.O.B.?
Fresh Off the Boat! Sorry!
I didn't mean anything... my name is Eve Wong.
My name is Kyung Seo...
...I mean Wheeler.
Well, Kyung, consider modeling. I'd love to use you.
I'm doing a woman against machine theme. I've got permission to use the old slag furnaces before they tear them down.
BANK of MONTR
I was going to use another girl but you would be perfect.
I don't think so.
Suit yourself. Here's my card. I'm at the Art Center.
Art Center?
Yeah, David Thompson Art Center. You've been here a year and you haven't gone up.
You don't get out much. Do you?
It's up at Seven Mile.
Seven miles up where the rents are down.
Old mining town all restored.
Coffee shops, book stores and the best art school.
I'm taking my show down in Gallery B tomorrow afternoon.
Come on up and I'll give you a tour!

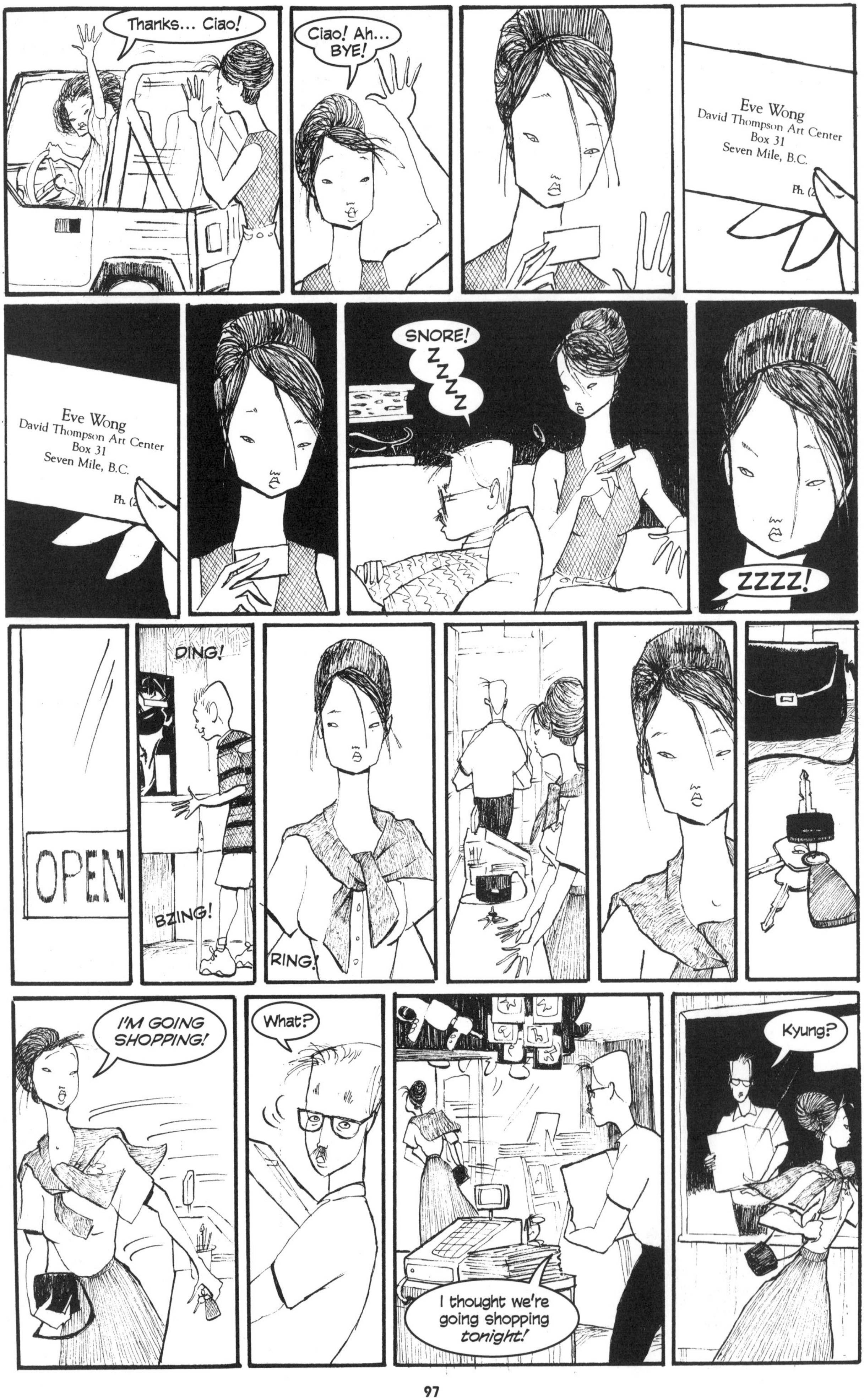
Thanks... Ciao!
Ciao! Ah... BYE!
Eve Wong
David Thompson Art Center
Box 31
Seven Mile, B.C.
Eve Wong
David Thompson Art Center
Box 31
Seven Mile, B.C.
SNORE! ZZZZ
ZZZZ!
OPEN
DING!
BZING!
RING!
I'M GOING SHOPPING!
What?
I thought we're going shopping *tonight!*
Kyung?

WOMEN!

Can't live with them. Can't live without them.

SCHREECH!

ZOOM!

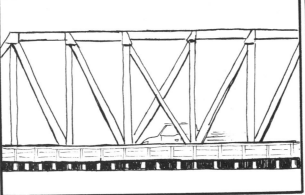

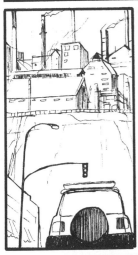

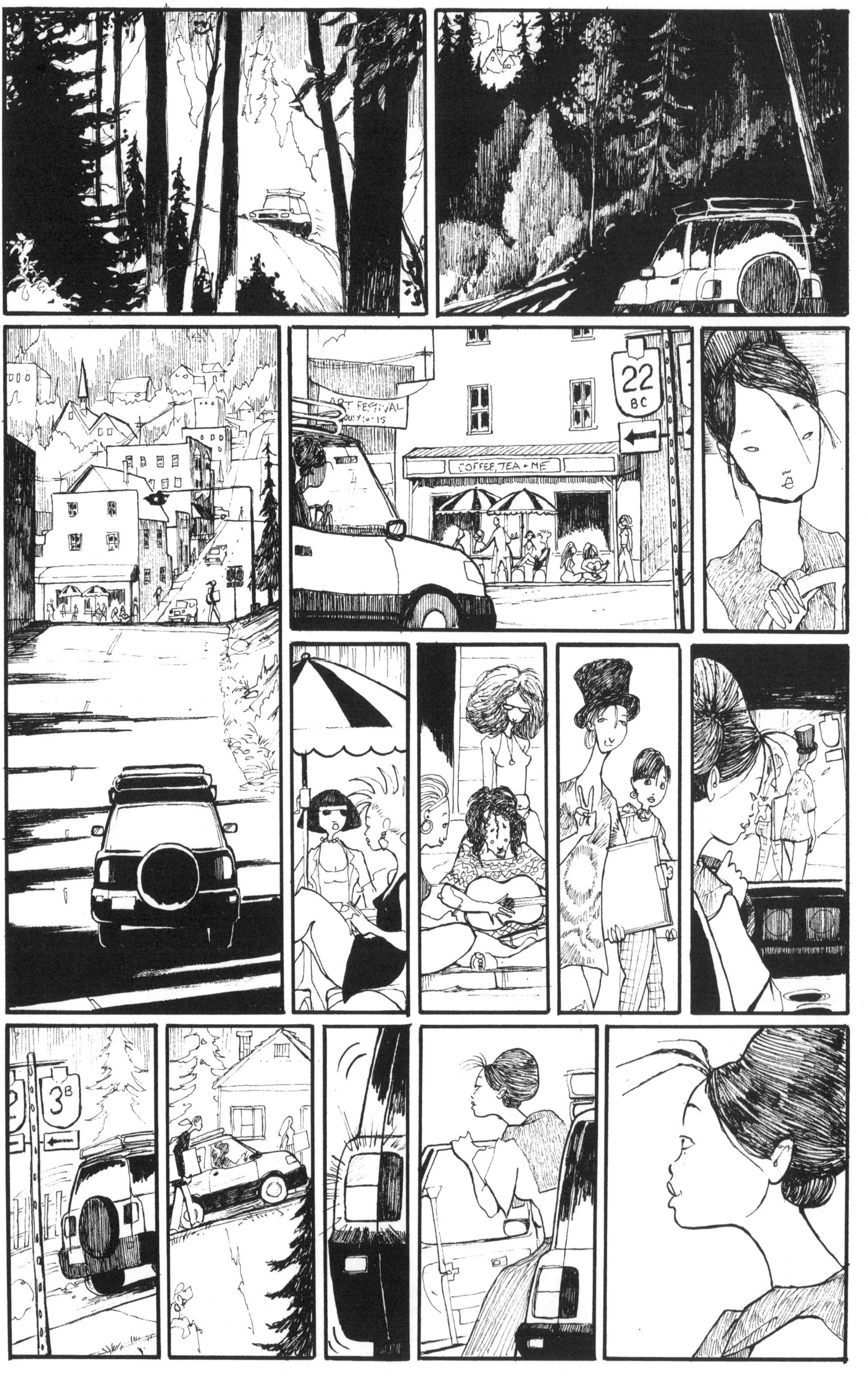
ART FESTIVAL
JULY 10-15
22
BC
COFFEE, TEA + ME
3B

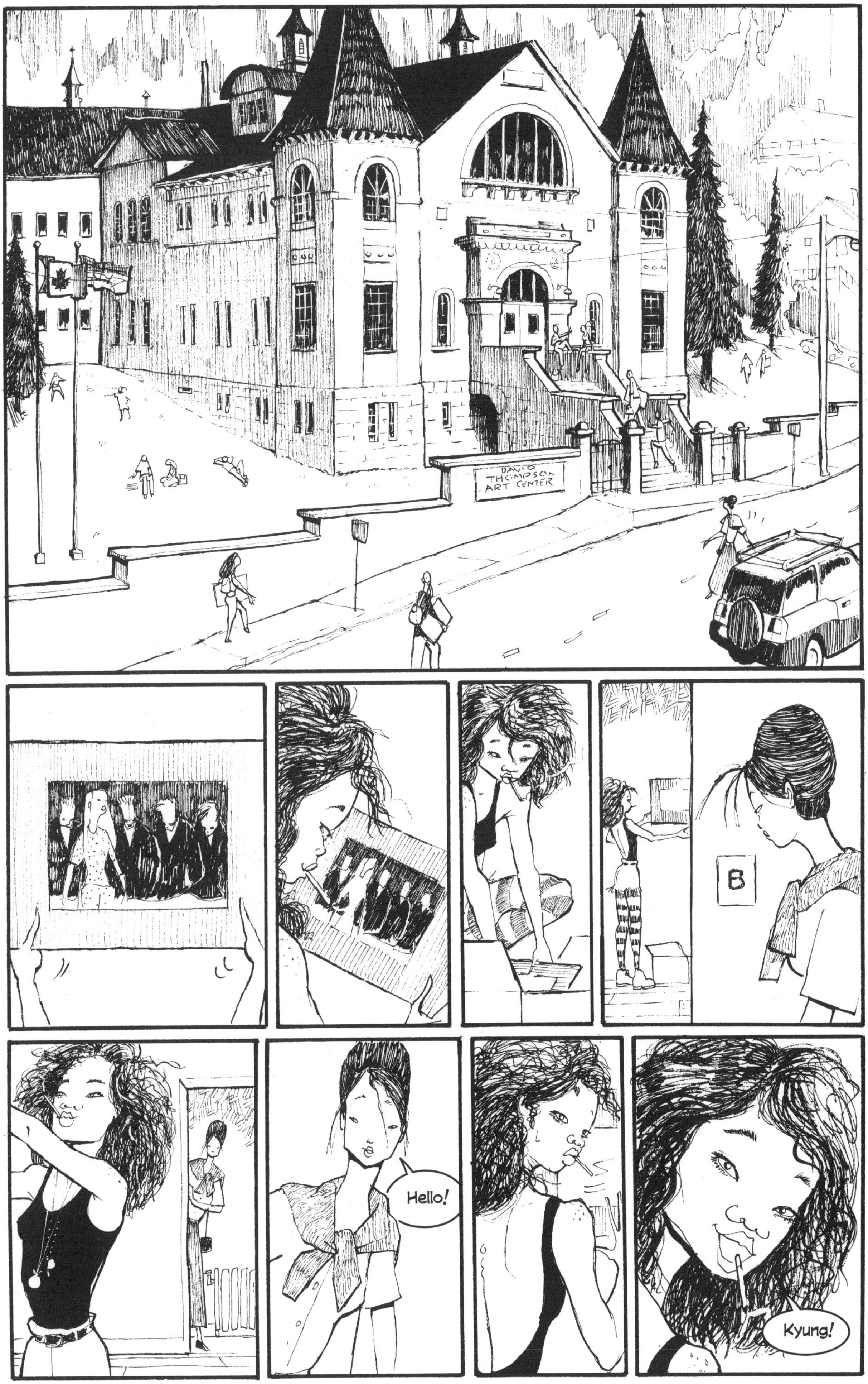
DAVID THOMPSON ART CENTER
B
Hello!
Kyung!

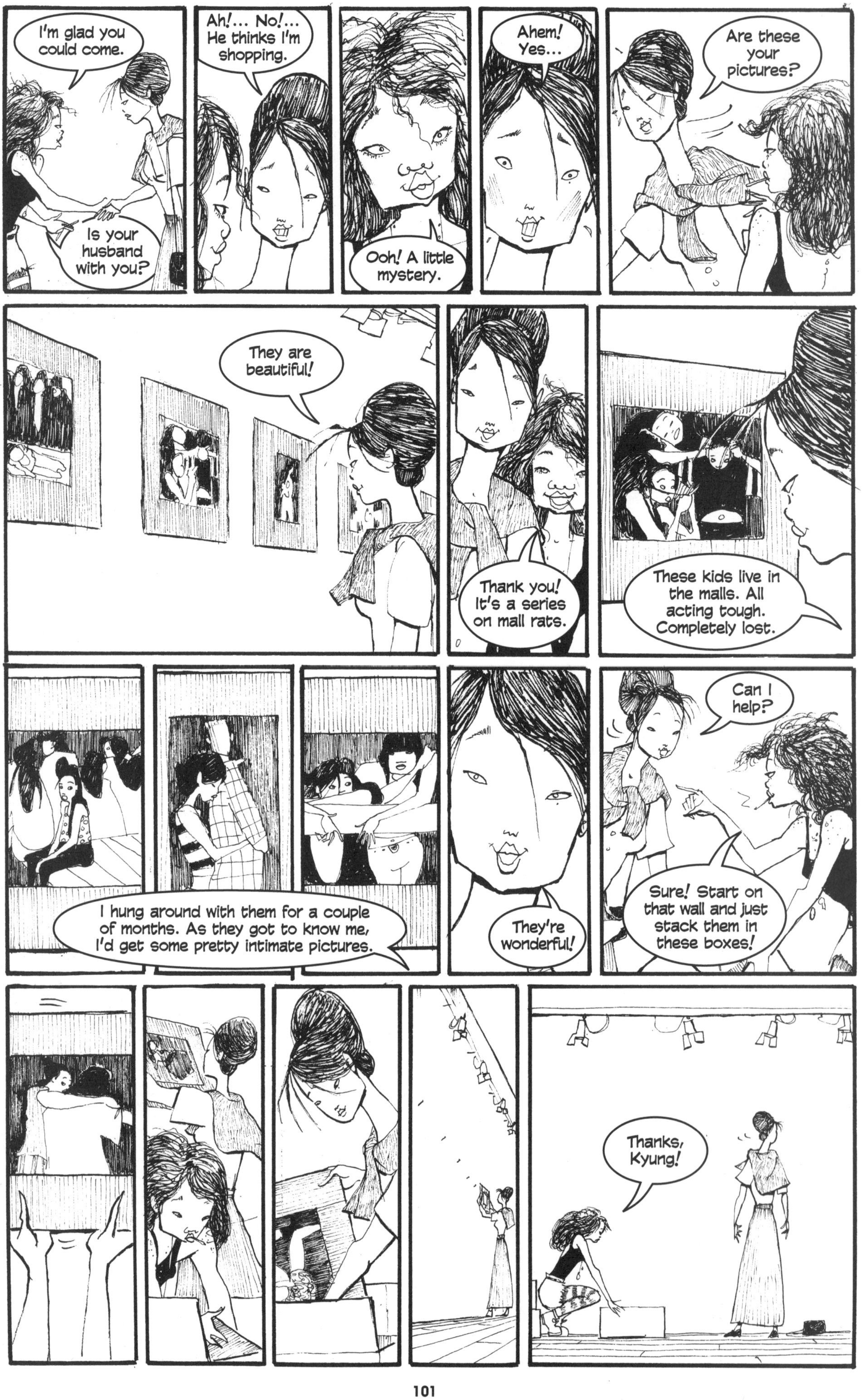
I'm glad you could come.
Is your husband with you?
Ah!... No!... He thinks I'm shopping.
Ooh! A little mystery.
Ahem! Yes...
Are these your pictures?
They are beautiful!
Thank you! It's a series on mall rats.
These kids live in the malls. All acting tough. Completely lost.
I hung around with them for a couple of months. As they got to know me, I'd get some pretty intimate pictures.
They're wonderful!
Can I help?
Sure! Start on that wall and just stack them in these boxes!
Thanks, Kyung!

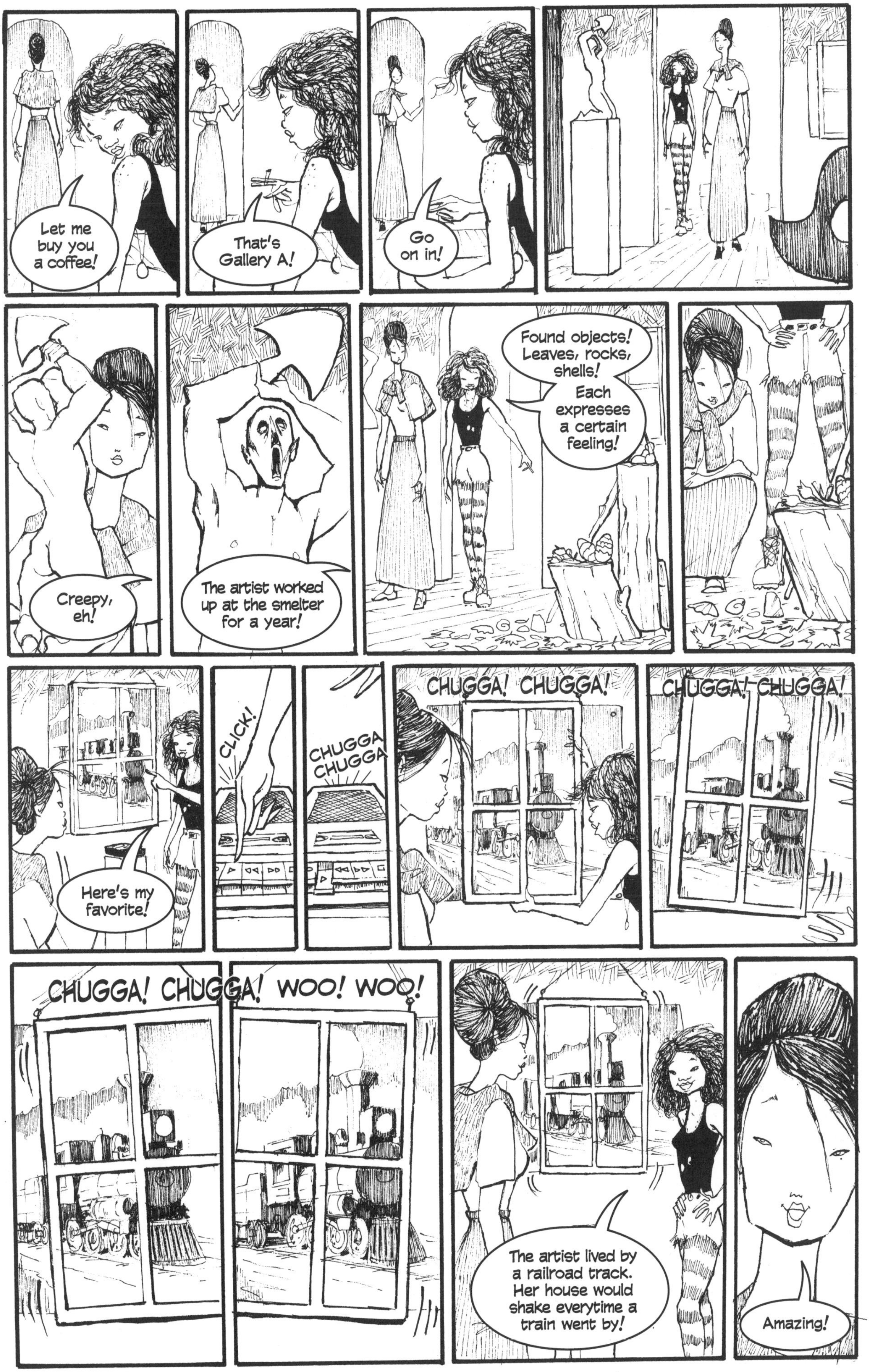
Let me buy you a coffee!
That's Gallery A!
Go on in!
Creepy, eh!
The artist worked up at the smelter for a year!
Found objects! Leaves, rocks, shells!
Each expresses a certain feeling!
Here's my favorite!
CLICK!
CHUGGA CHUGGA
CHUGGA! CHUGGA!
CHUGGA! CHUGGA!
CHUGGA! CHUGGA! WOO! WOO!
The artist lived by a railroad track. Her house would shake everytime a train went by!
Amazing!

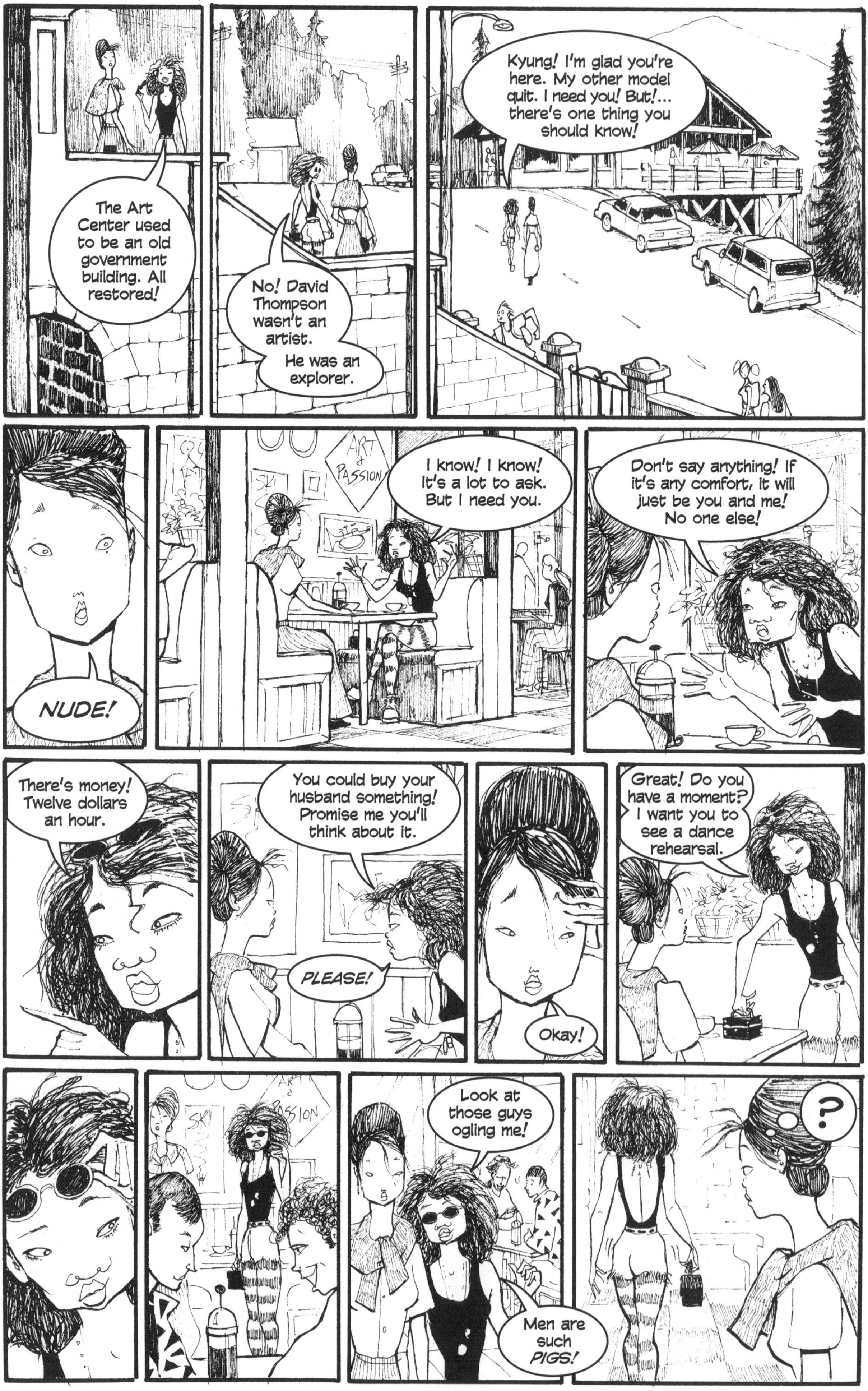
The Art Center used to be an old government building. All restored!
No! David Thompson wasn't an artist.
He was an explorer.
Kyung! I'm glad you're here. My other model quit. I need you! But!... there's one thing you should know!
NUDE!
ART & PASSION
SKI
I know! I know! It's a lot to ask. But I need you.
Don't say anything! If it's any comfort, it will just be you and me! No one else!
There's money! Twelve dollars an hour.
You could buy your husband something! Promise me you'll think about it.
PLEASE!
Okay!
Great! Do you have a moment? I want you to see a dance rehearsal.
SKI
PASSION
Look at those guys ogling me!
Men are such PIGS!
?

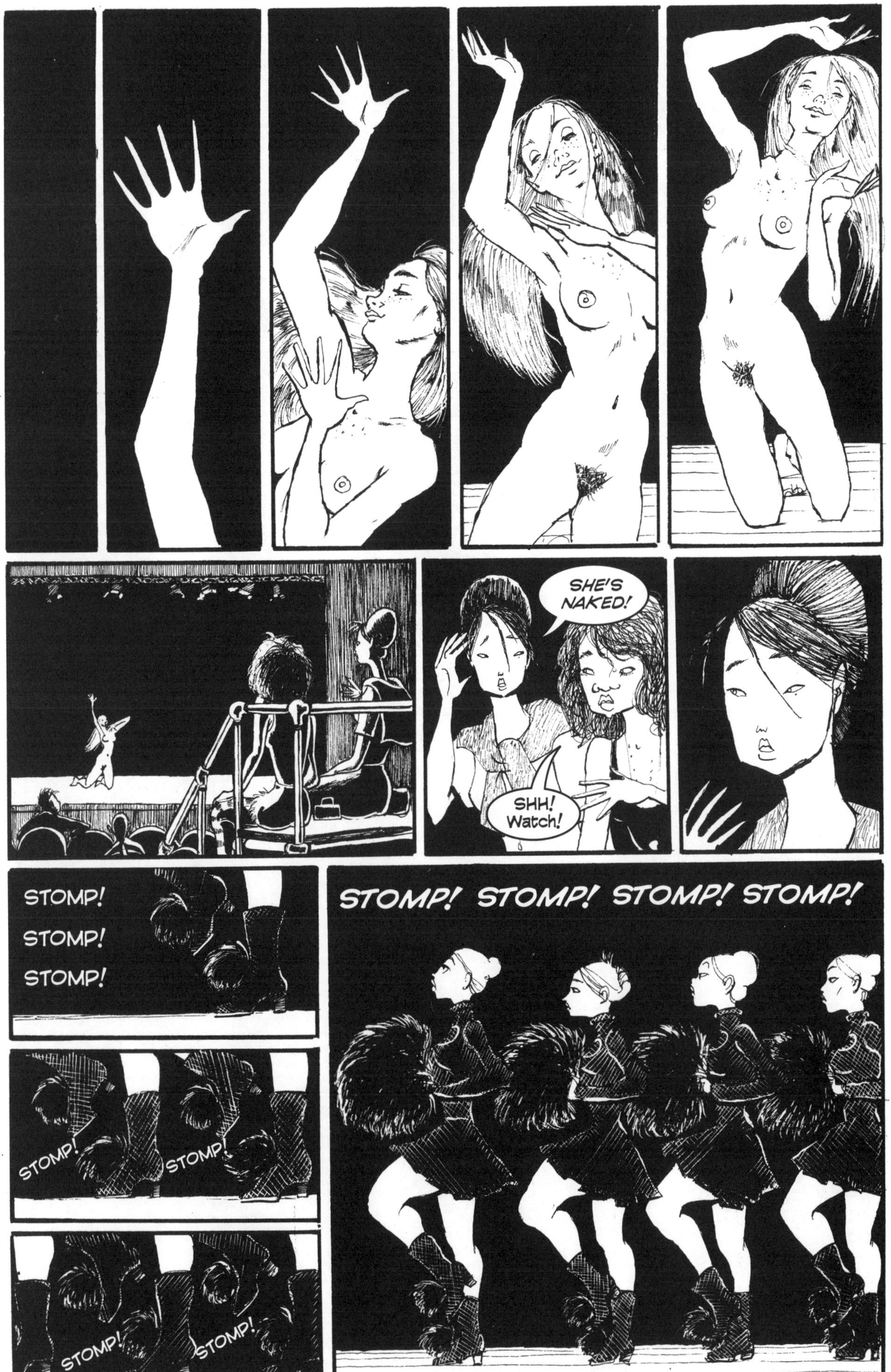
SHE'S NAKED!
SHH! Watch!
STOMP!
STOMP!
STOMP!
STOMP! STOMP! STOMP! STOMP!
STOMP!
STOMP!
STOMP!
STOMP!

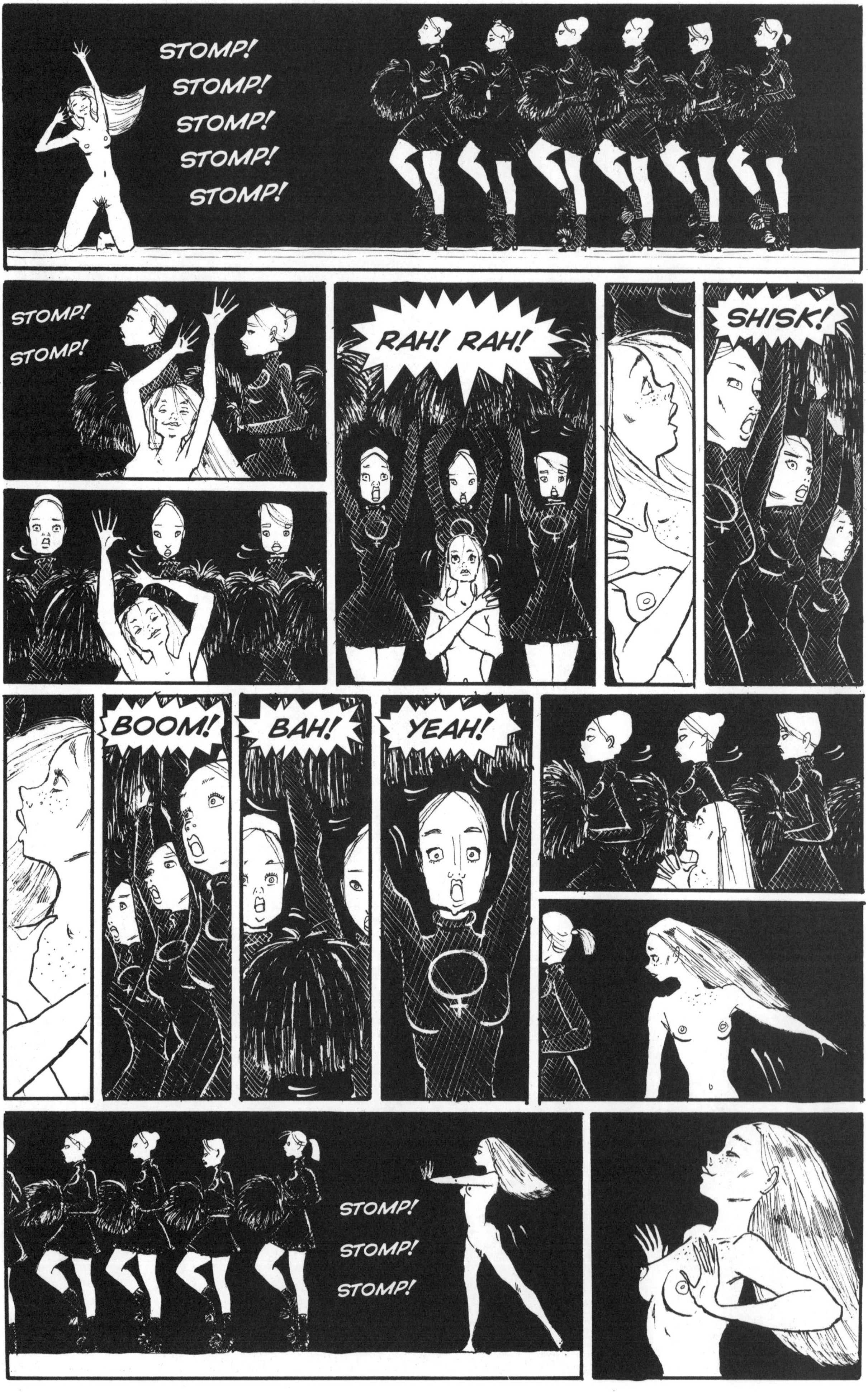
STOMP!
STOMP!
STOMP!
STOMP!
STOMP!
STOMP!
STOMP!
RAH! RAH!
SHISK!
BOOM!
BAH!
YEAH!
STOMP!
STOMP!
STOMP!

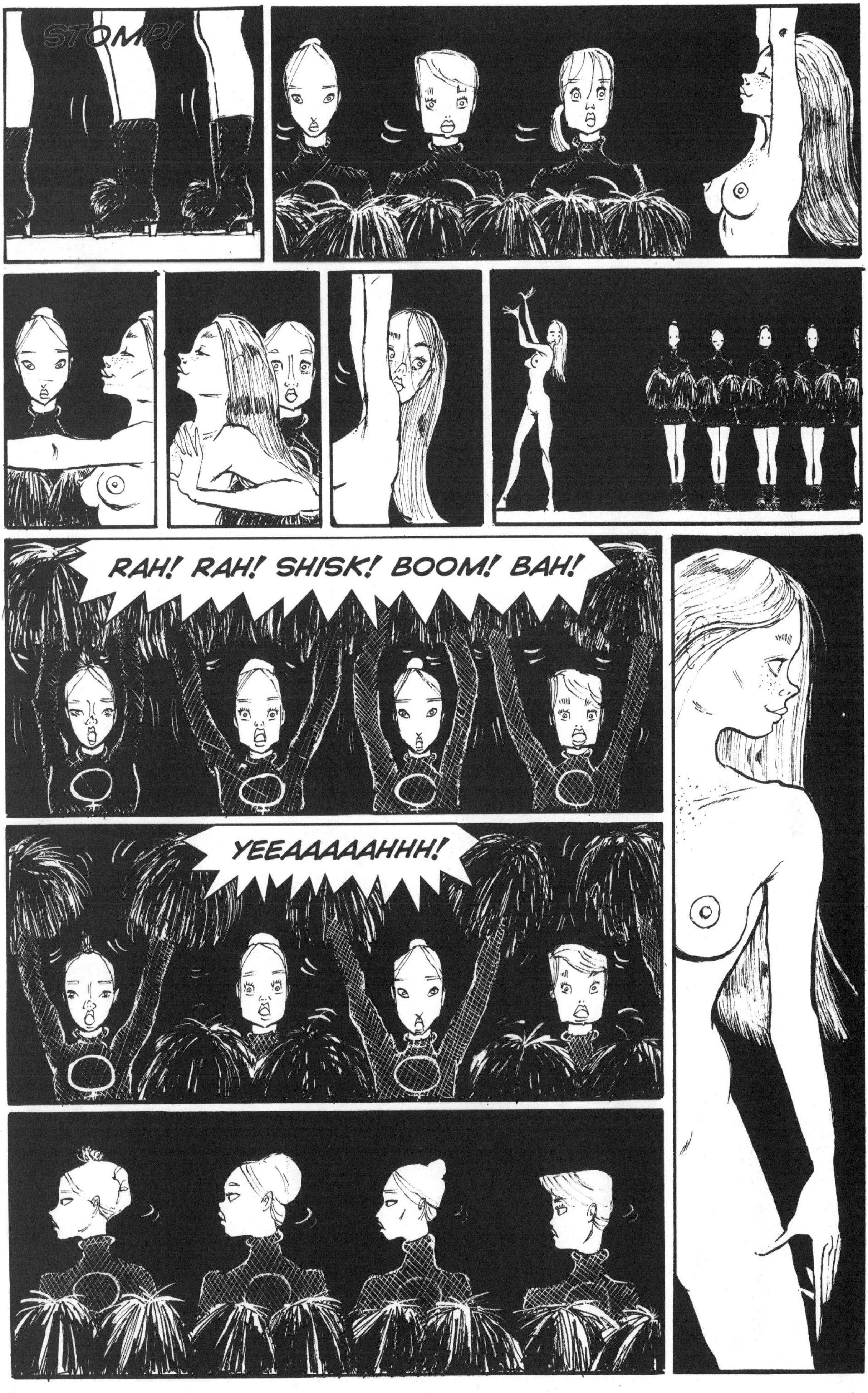
STOMP!
RAH! RAH! SHISK! BOOM! BAH!
YEEAAAAAHHH!

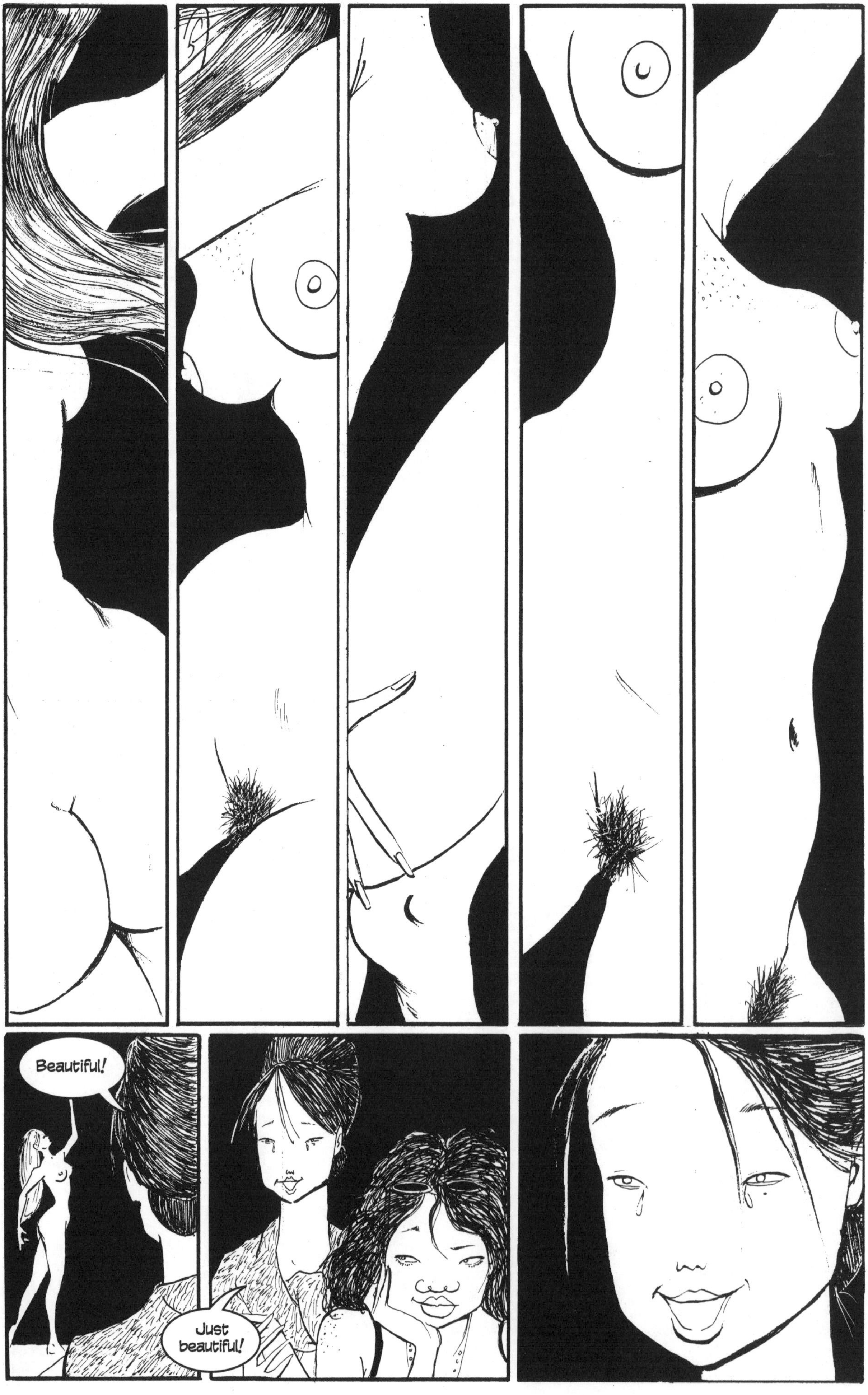
Beautiful!
Just beautiful!

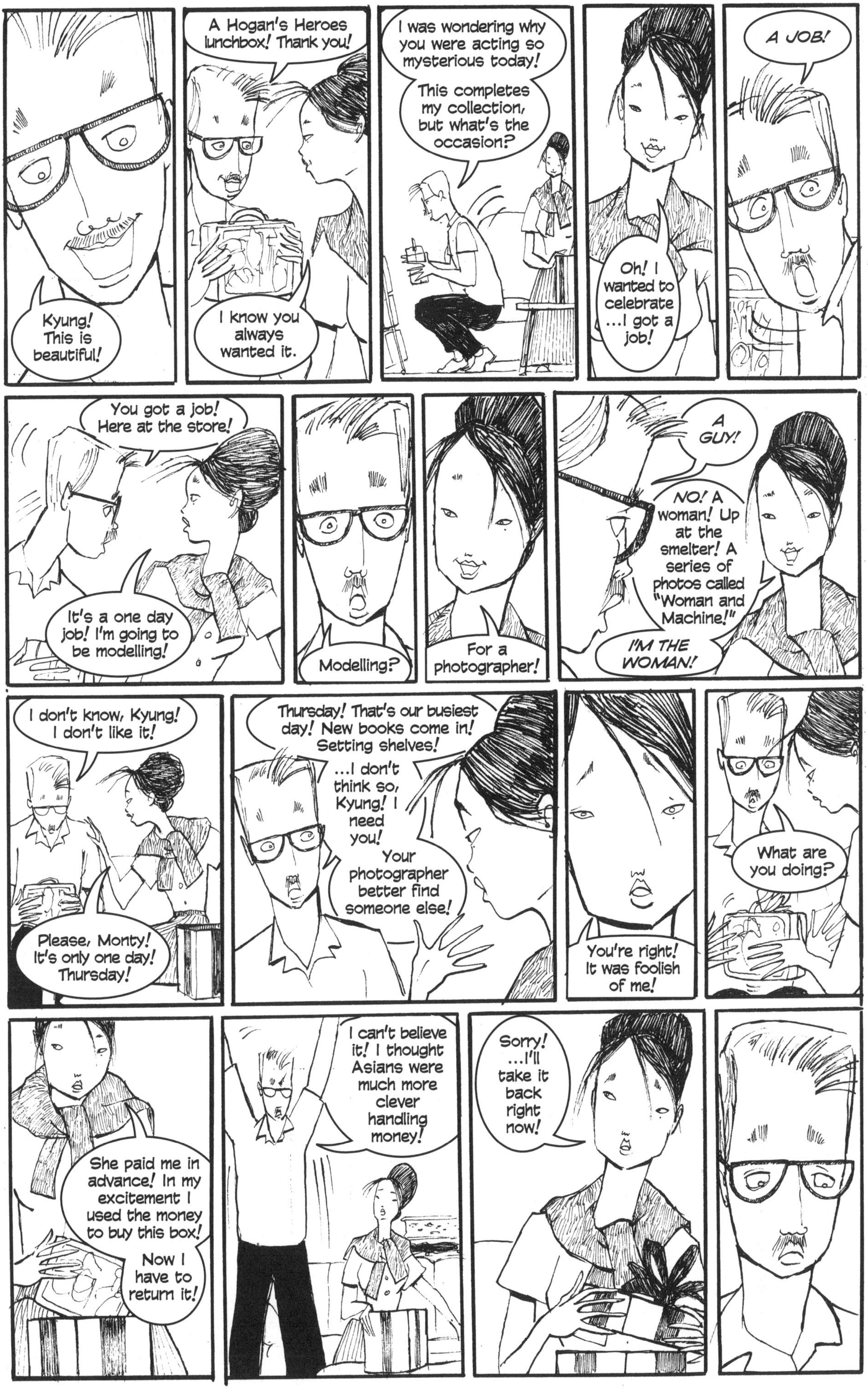
Kyung! This is beautiful!
A Hogan's Heroes lunchbox! Thank you!
I know you always wanted it.
I was wondering why you were acting so mysterious today!
This completes my collection, but what's the occasion?
Oh! I wanted to celebrate ...I got a job!
A JOB!
You got a job! Here at the store!
It's a one day job! I'm going to be modelling!
Modelling?
For a photographer!
A GUY!
NO! A woman! Up at the smelter! A series of photos called "Woman and Machine!"
I'M THE WOMAN!
I don't know, Kyung! I don't like it!
Please, Monty! It's only one day! Thursday!
Thursday! That's our busiest day! New books come in! Setting shelves!
...I don't think so, Kyung! I need you!
Your photographer better find someone else!
You're right! It was foolish of me!
What are you doing?
She paid me in advance! In my excitement I used the money to buy this box!
Now I have to return it!
I can't believe it! I thought Asians were much more clever handling money!
Sorry! ...I'll take it back right now!

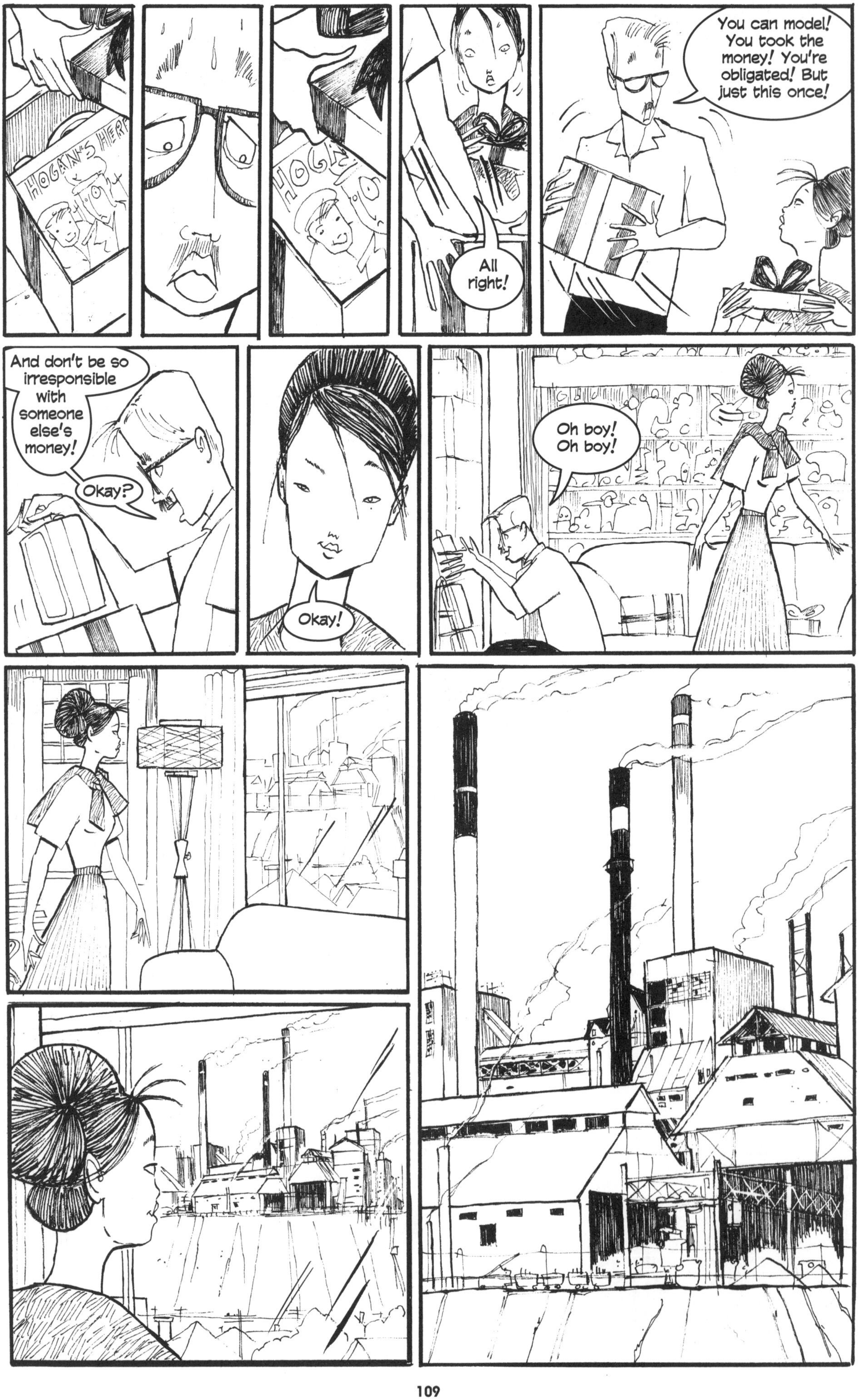
HOGAN'S HERO
HOG
All right!
You can model! You took the money! You're obligated! But just this once!
And don't be so irresponsible with someone else's money!
Okay?
Okay!
Oh boy! Oh boy!

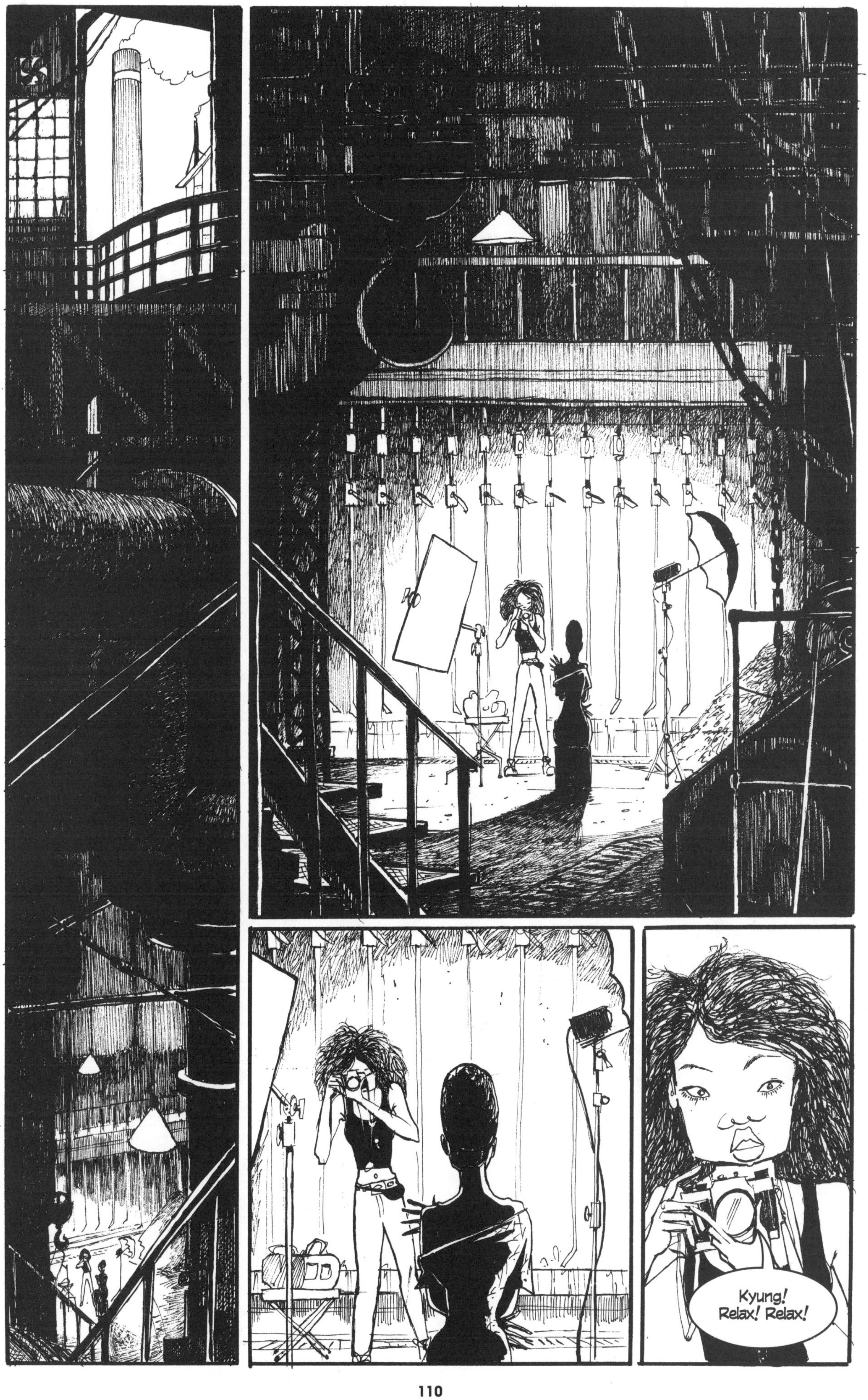
Kyung!
Relax! Relax!

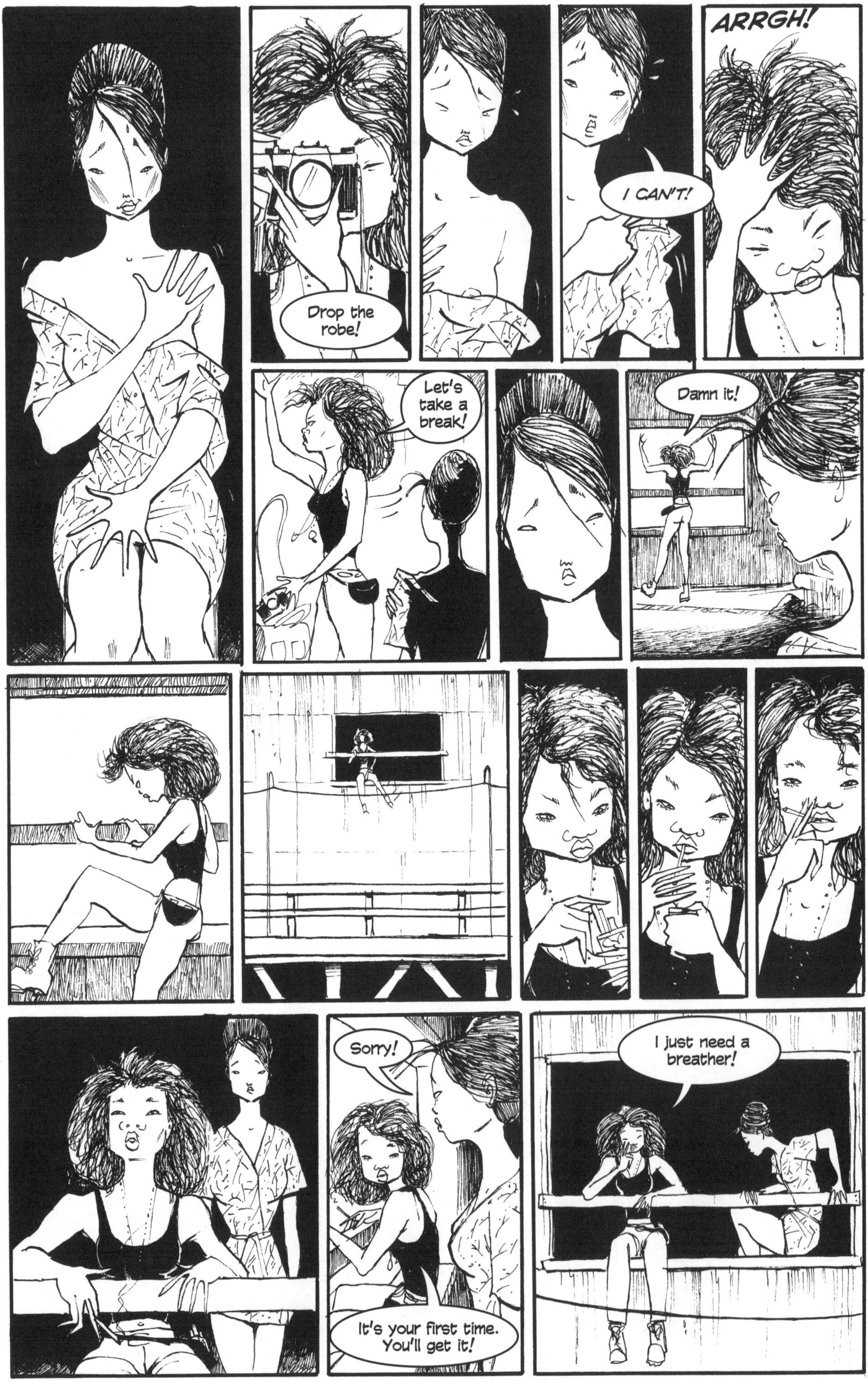

Drop the robe!
I CAN'T!
ARRGH!
Let's take a break!
Damn it!
Sorry!
It's your first time. You'll get it!
I just need a breather!

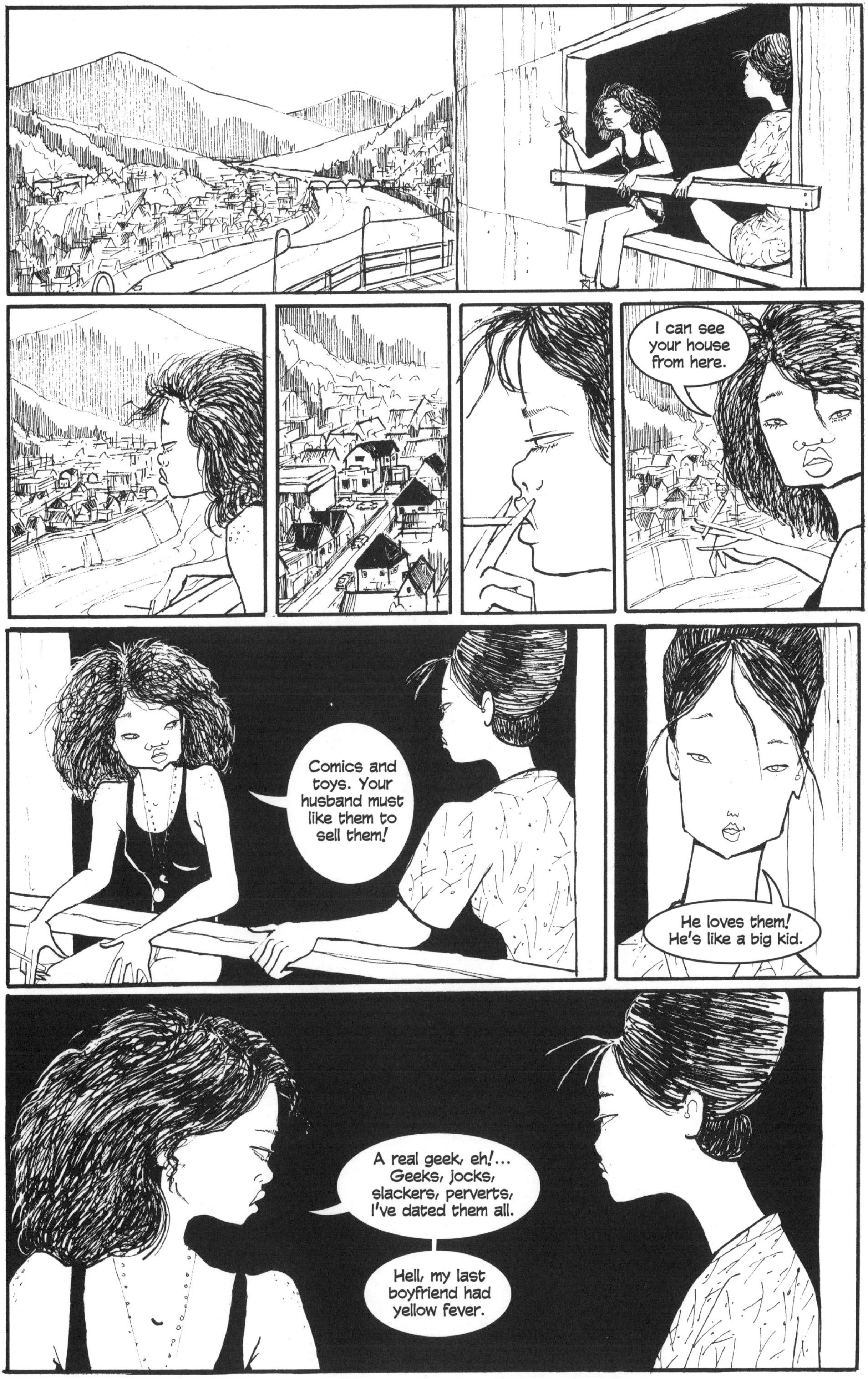
I can see your house from here.
Comics and toys. Your husband must like them to sell them!
He loves them! He's like a big kid.
A real geek, eh!... Geeks, jocks, slackers, perverts, I've dated them all.
Hell, my last boyfriend had yellow fever.

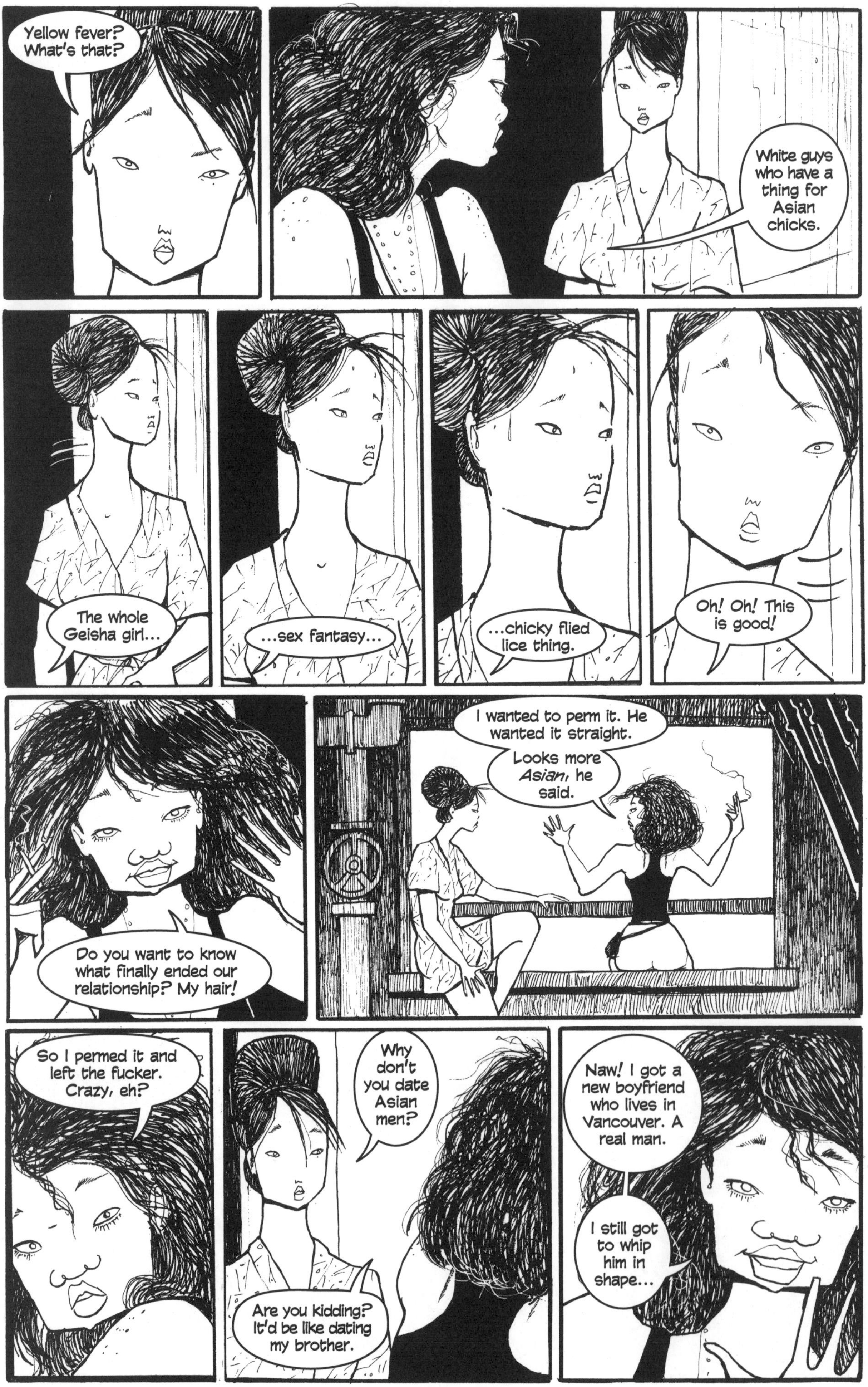
Yellow fever? What's that?
White guys who have a thing for Asian chicks.
The whole Geisha girl...
...sex fantasy...
...chicky flied lice thing.
Oh! Oh! This is good!
Do you want to know what finally ended our relationship? My hair!
I wanted to perm it. He wanted it straight.
Looks more *Asian*, he said.
So I permed it and left the fucker. Crazy, eh?
Why don't you date Asian men?
Are you kidding? It'd be like dating my brother.
Naw! I got a new boyfriend who lives in Vancouver. A real man.
I still got to whip him in shape...

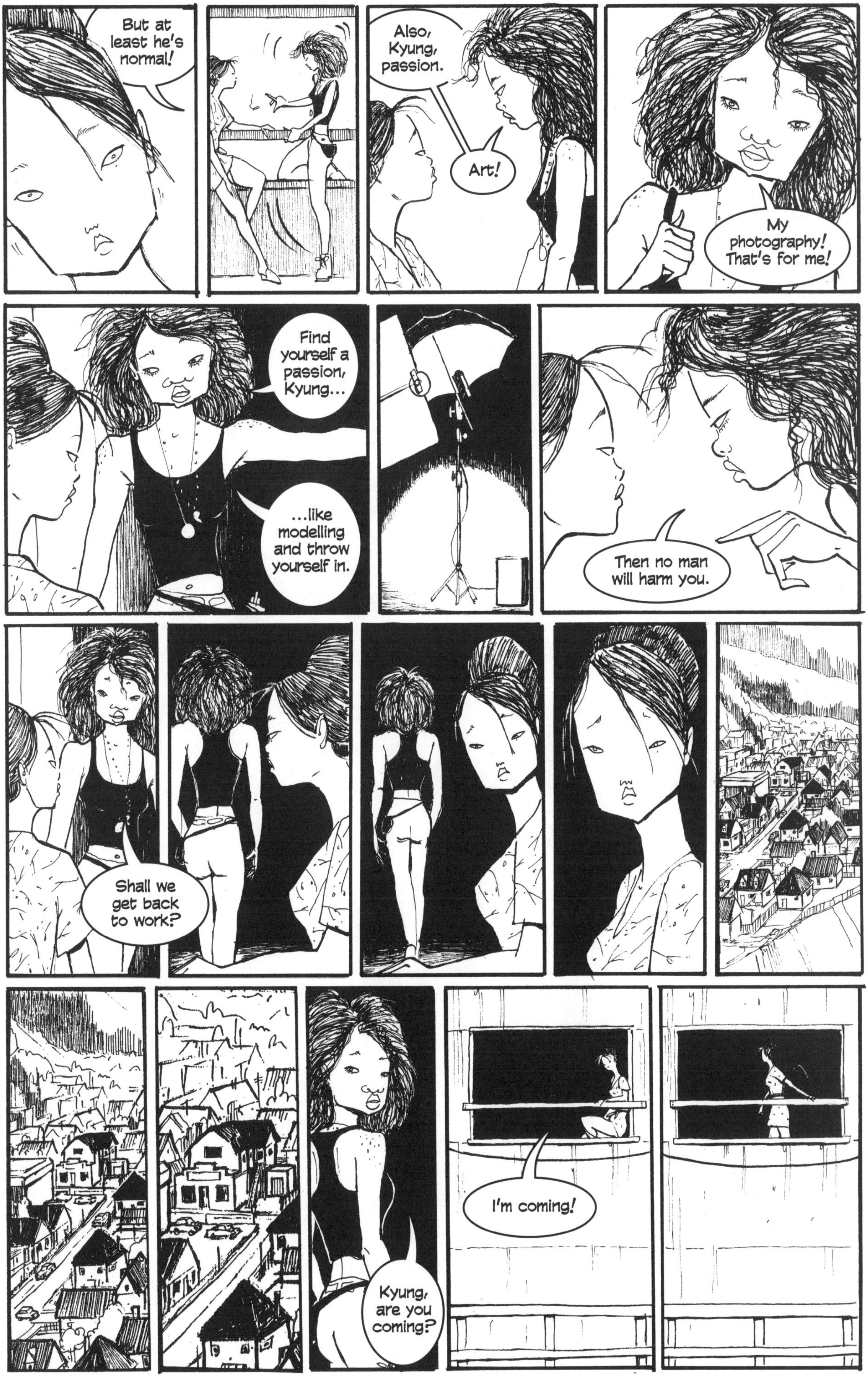
But at least he's normal!
Also, Kyung, passion.
Art!
My photography! That's for me!
Find yourself a passion, Kyung...
...like modelling and throw yourself in.
Then no man will harm you.
Shall we get back to work?
Kyung, are you coming?
I'm coming!

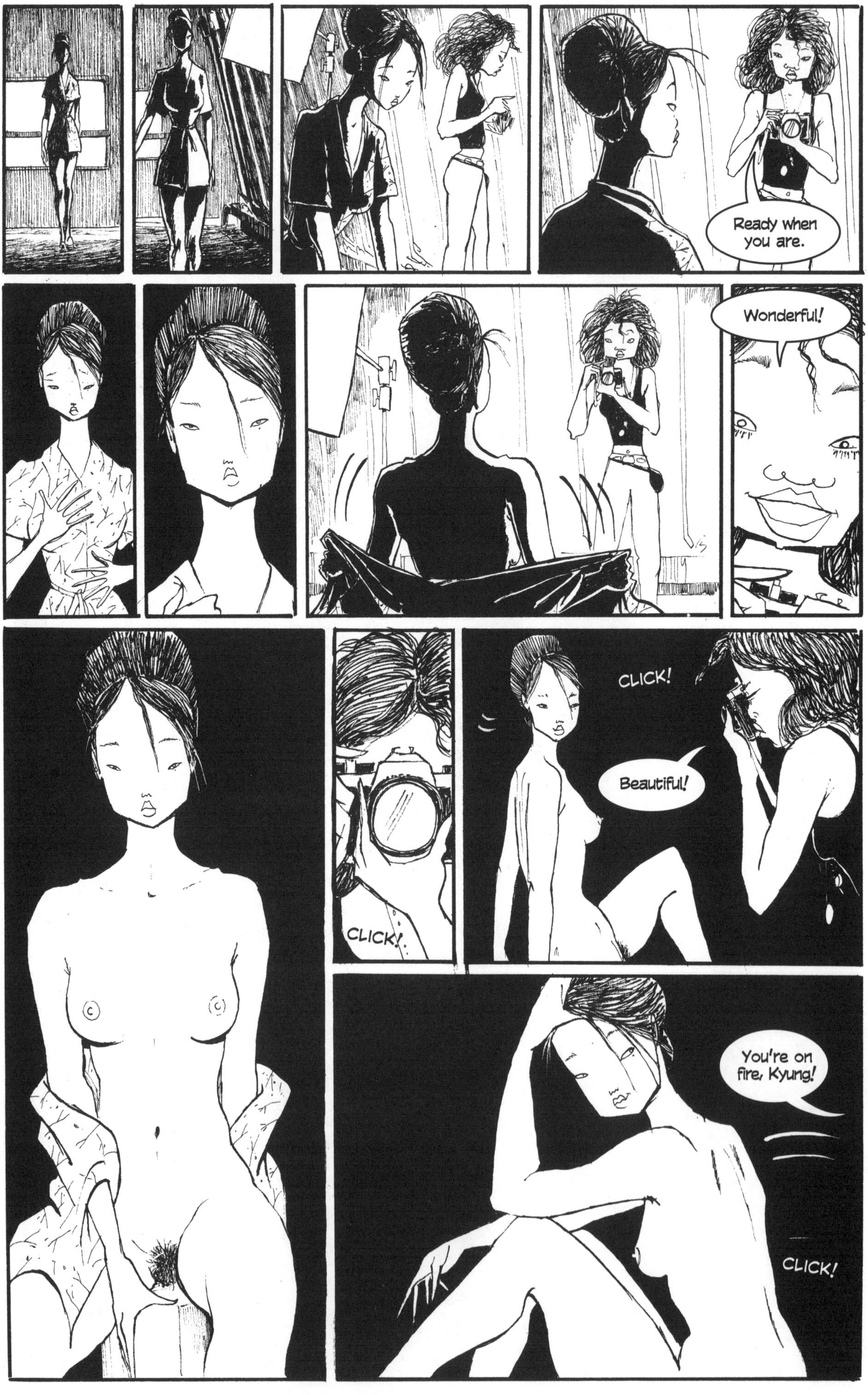
Ready when you are.
Wonderful!
CLICK!
CLICK!
Beautiful!
You're on fire, Kyung!
CLICK!

CLICK!

CLICK!

I have an idea!

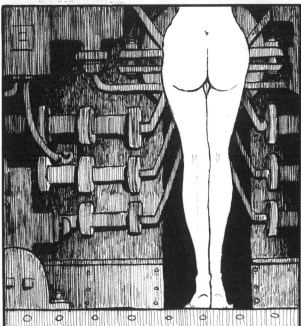

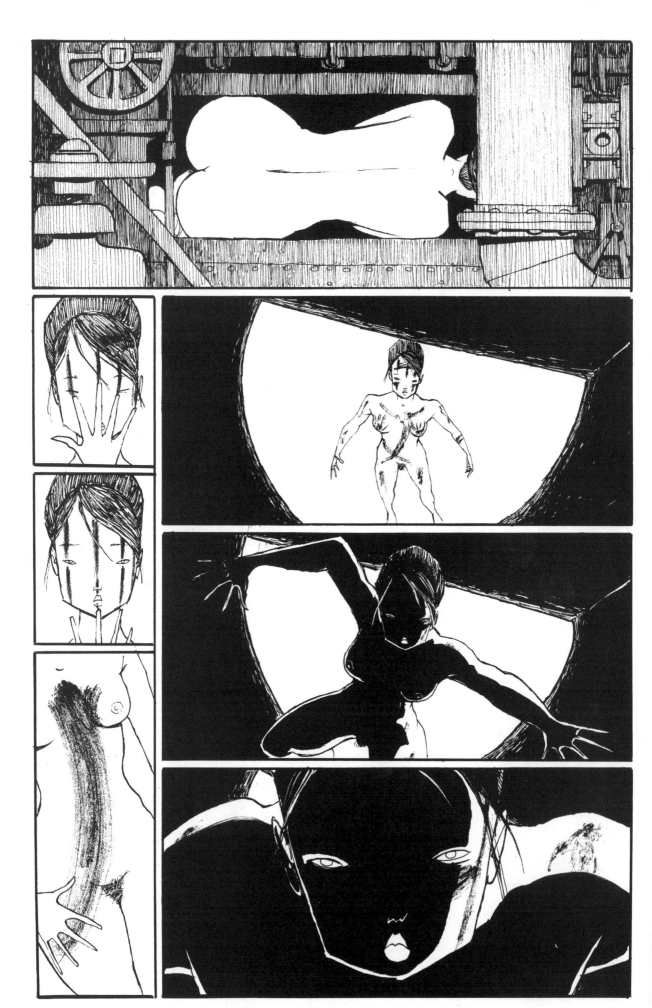

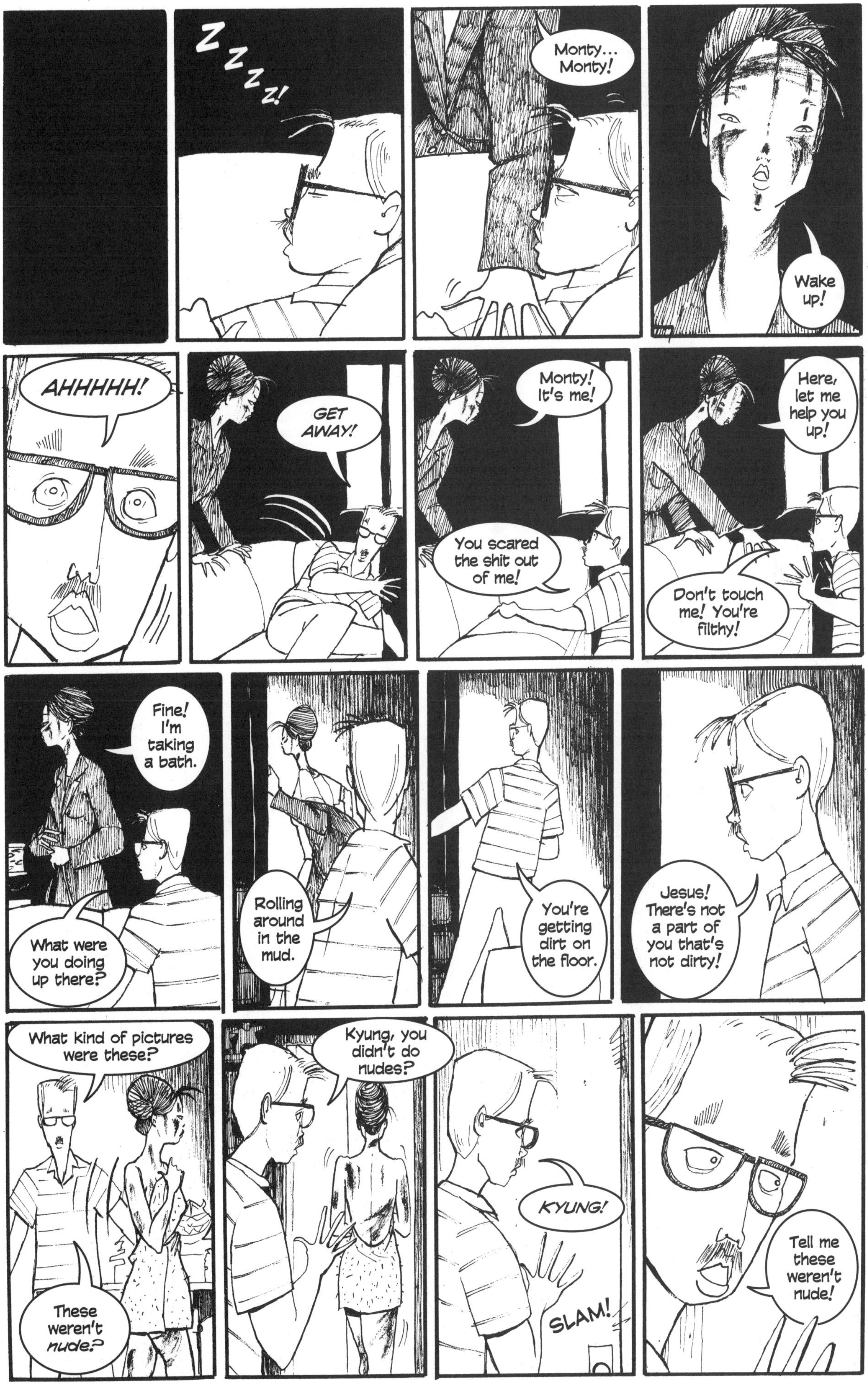
ZZZZ!
Monty... Monty!
Wake up!
AHHHHH!
GET AWAY!
Monty! It's me!
You scared the shit out of me!
Here, let me help you up!
Don't touch me! You're filthy!
Fine! I'm taking a bath.
What were you doing up there?
Rolling around in the mud.
You're getting dirt on the floor.
Jesus! There's not a part of you that's not dirty!
What kind of pictures were these?
These weren't *nude*?
Kyung, you didn't do nudes?
KYUNG!
SLAM!
Tell me these weren't nude!

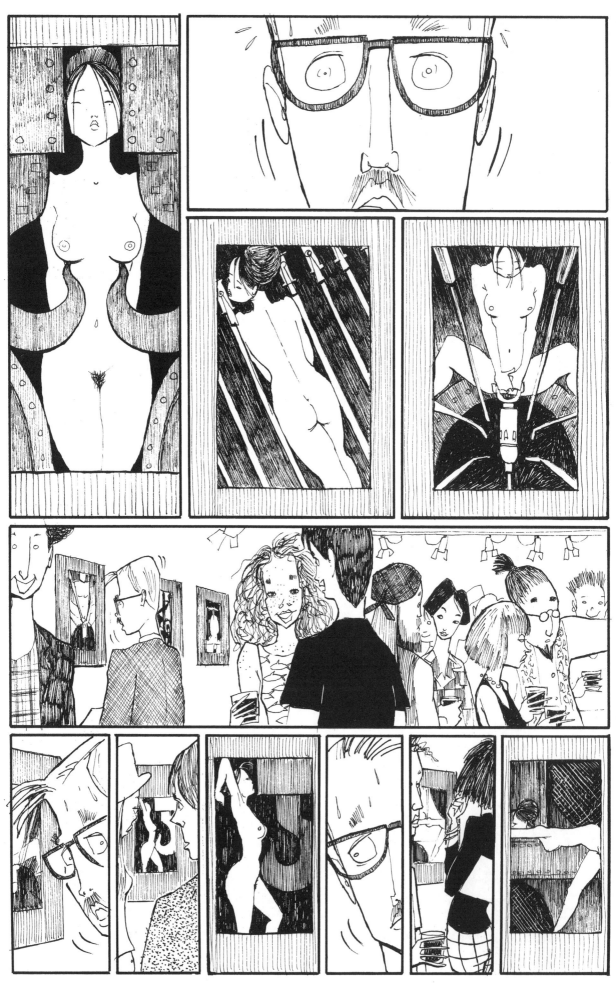

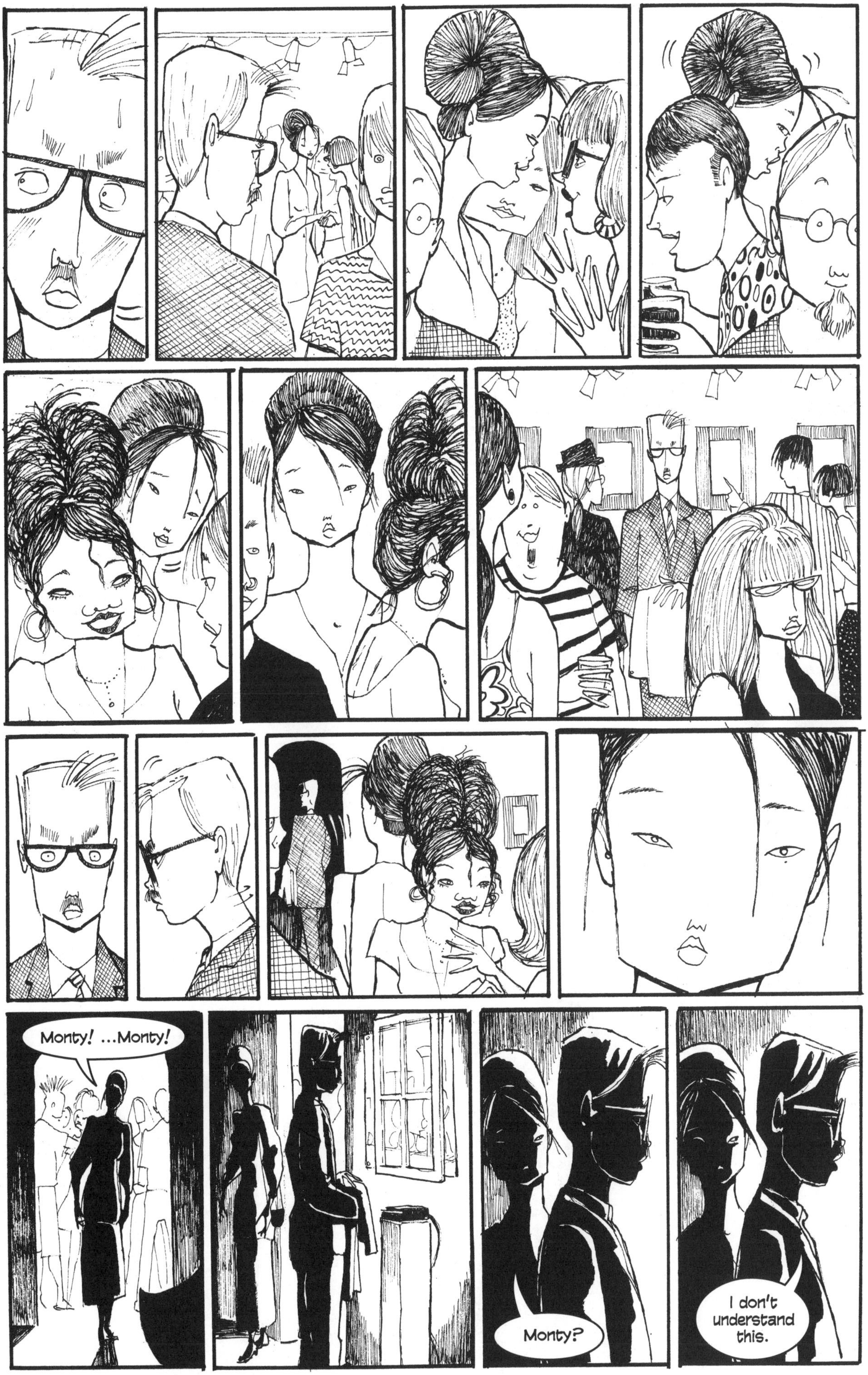
Monty! ...Monty!
Monty?
I don't understand this.

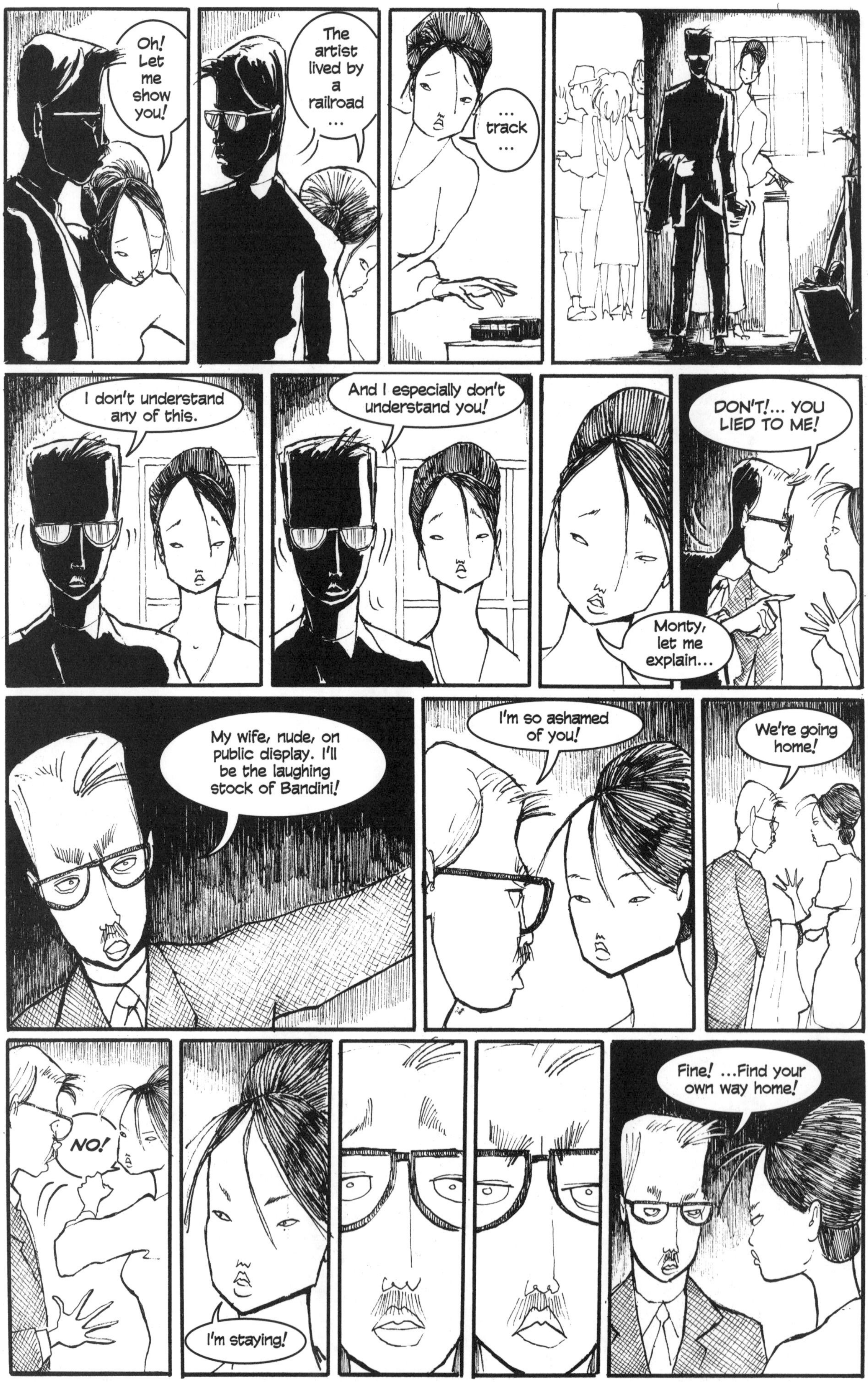
Oh! Let me show you!
The artist lived by a railroad ...
... track ...
I don't understand any of this.
And I especially don't understand you!
Monty, let me explain...
DON'T!... YOU LIED TO ME!
My wife, nude, on public display. I'll be the laughing stock of Bandini!
I'm so ashamed of you!
We're going home!
NO!
I'm staying!
Fine! ...Find your own way home!

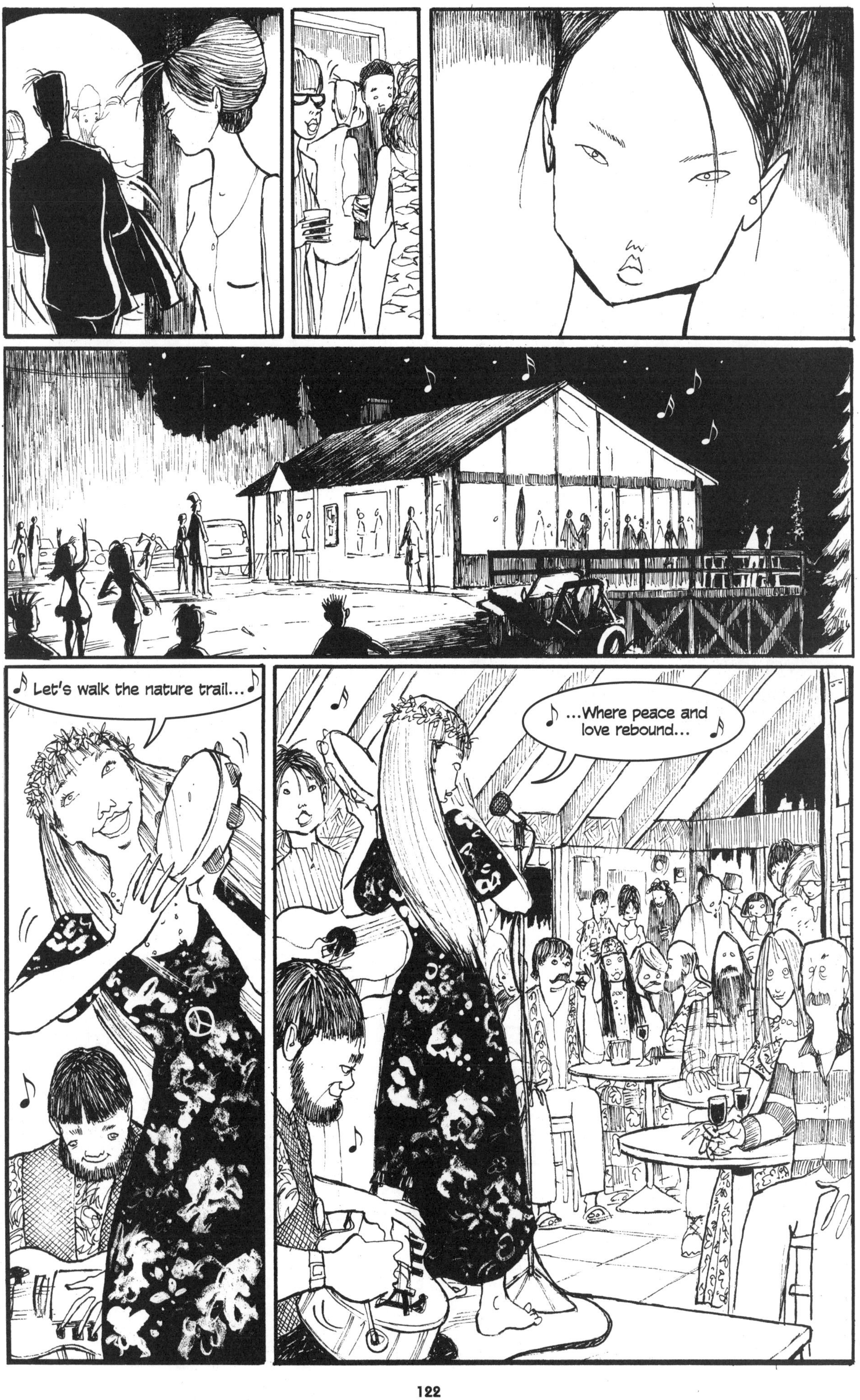
♪ Let's walk the nature trail... ♪
♪ ...Where peace and love rebound... ♪

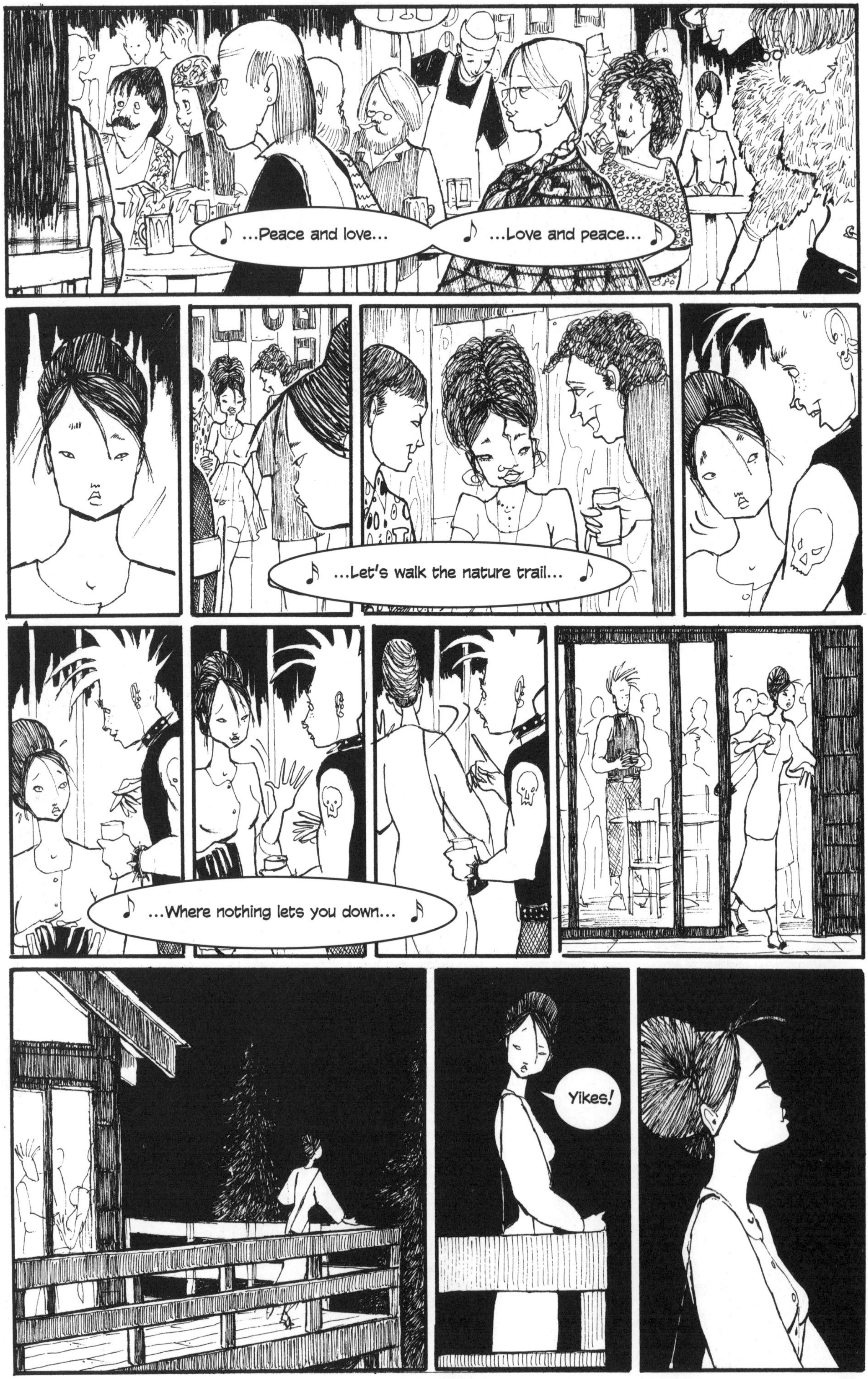
♪ ...Peace and love...
♪ ...Love and peace... ♪
♪ ...Let's walk the nature trail... ♪
♪ ...Where nothing lets you down... ♪
Yikes!

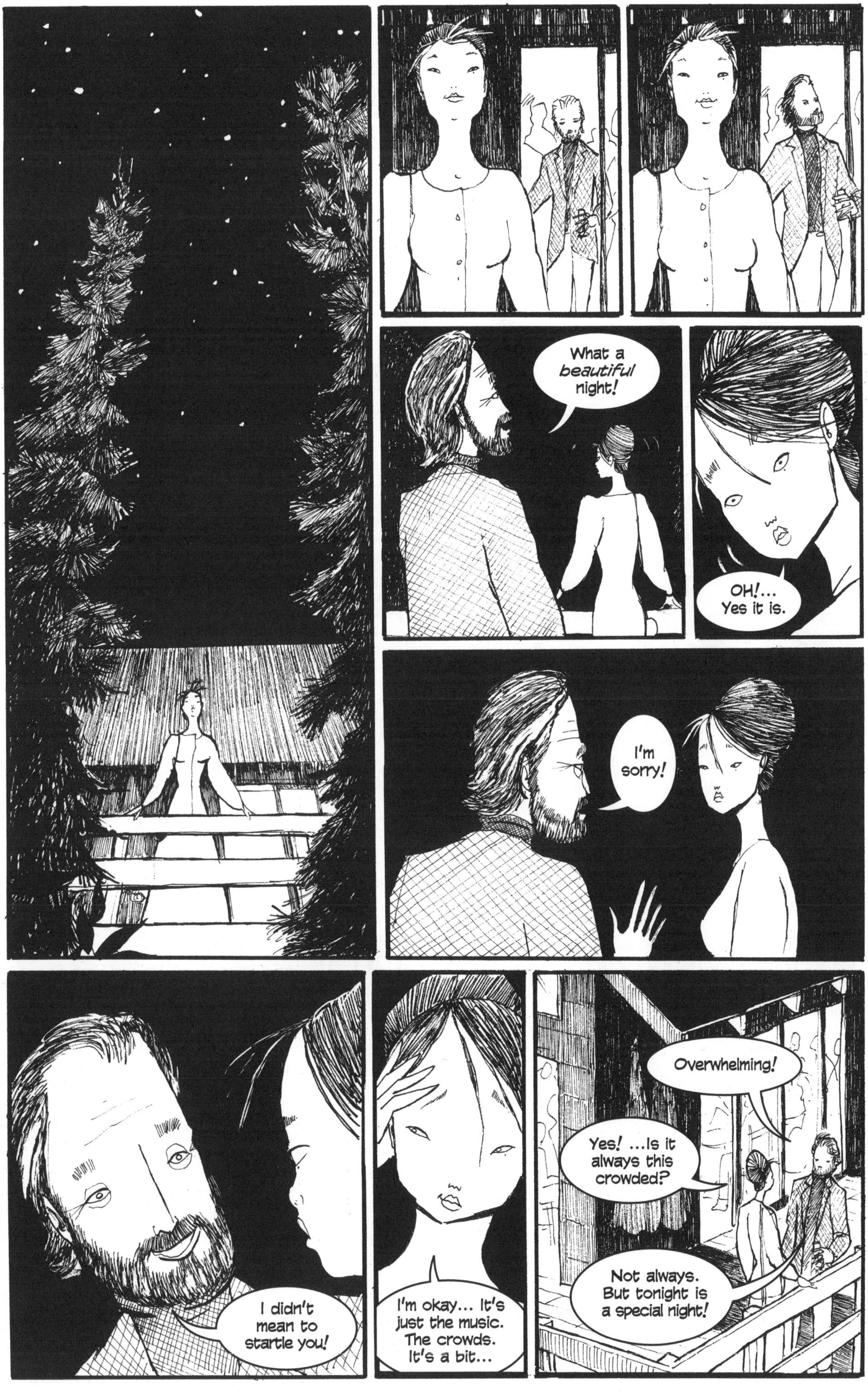

What a *beautiful* night!
OH!... Yes it is.
I'm sorry!
I didn't mean to startle you!
I'm okay... It's just the music. The crowds. It's a bit...
Overwhelming!
Yes! ...Is it always this crowded?
Not always. But tonight is a special night!

See all those older people in there?

Yes. Are they teachers?

No... They're hippies. Hippies and draft dodgers.

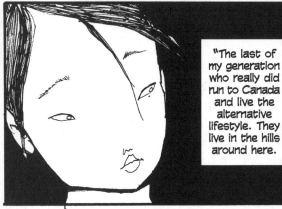

"The last of my generation who really did run to Canada and live the alternative lifestyle. They live in the hills around here.

"Simple lives. Raise their kids. Some farm.

"And when a folk band comes to town to play...

"...they all come wandering down, smoke some doobies, listen to the music and...

"...reminisce on their glory days. Before they go back up into the hills, and like ghosts..."

...they disappear, deep into the clouds, to places unknown.

That's beautiful.

It is, sort of like the swallows at Capistrano.

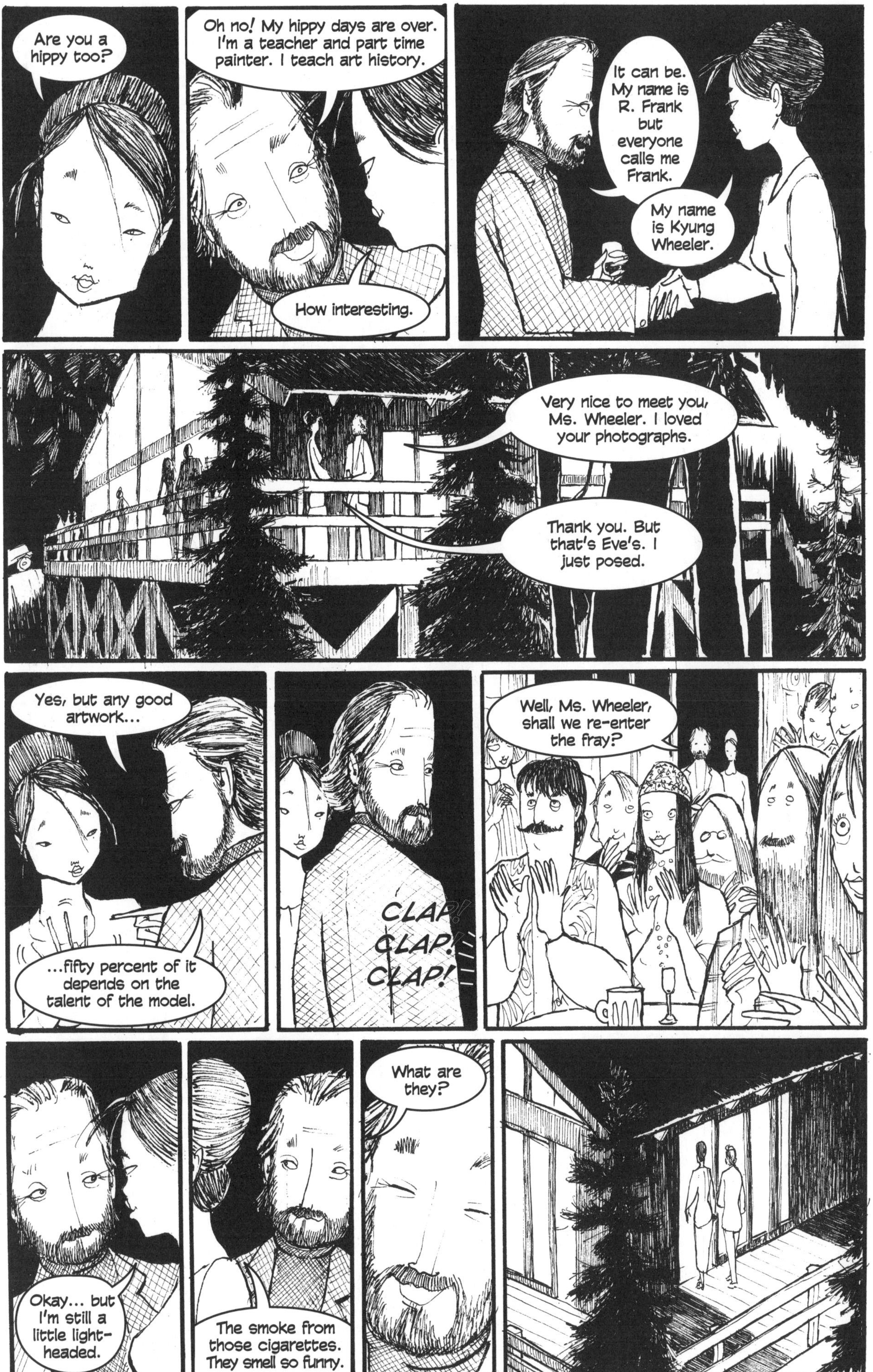
Are you a hippy too?
Oh no! My hippy days are over. I'm a teacher and part time painter. I teach art history.
How interesting.
It can be. My name is R. Frank but everyone calls me Frank.
My name is Kyung Wheeler.
Very nice to meet you, Ms. Wheeler. I loved your photographs.
Thank you. But that's Eve's. I just posed.
Yes, but any good artwork...
...fifty percent of it depends on the talent of the model.
CLAP! CLAP! CLAP!
Well, Ms. Wheeler, shall we re-enter the fray?
Okay... but I'm still a little light-headed.
The smoke from those cigarettes. They smell so funny.
What are they?

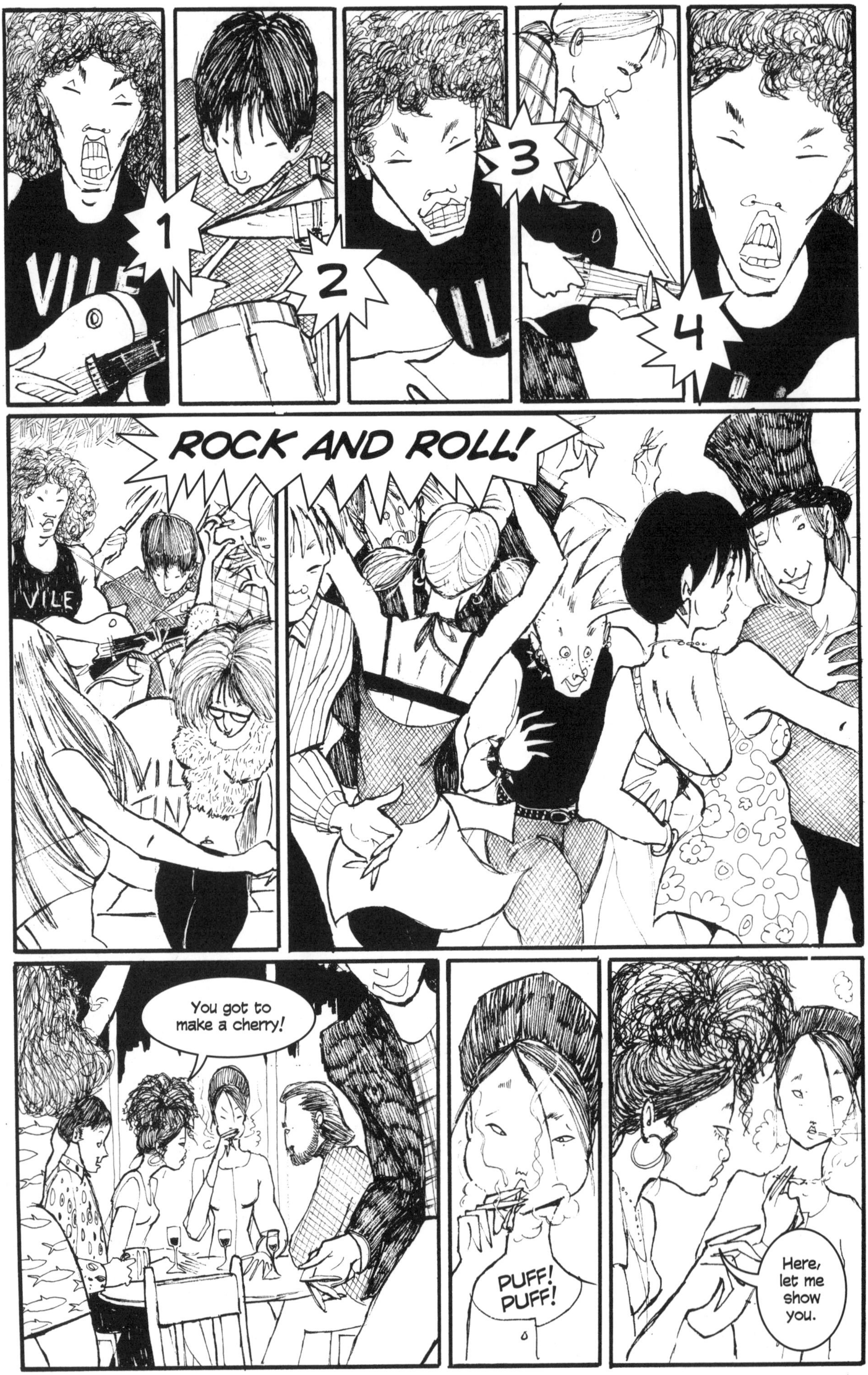

VILE
1
2
3
4
ROCK AND ROLL!
VILE
You got to make a cherry!
PUFF! PUFF!
Here, let me show you.

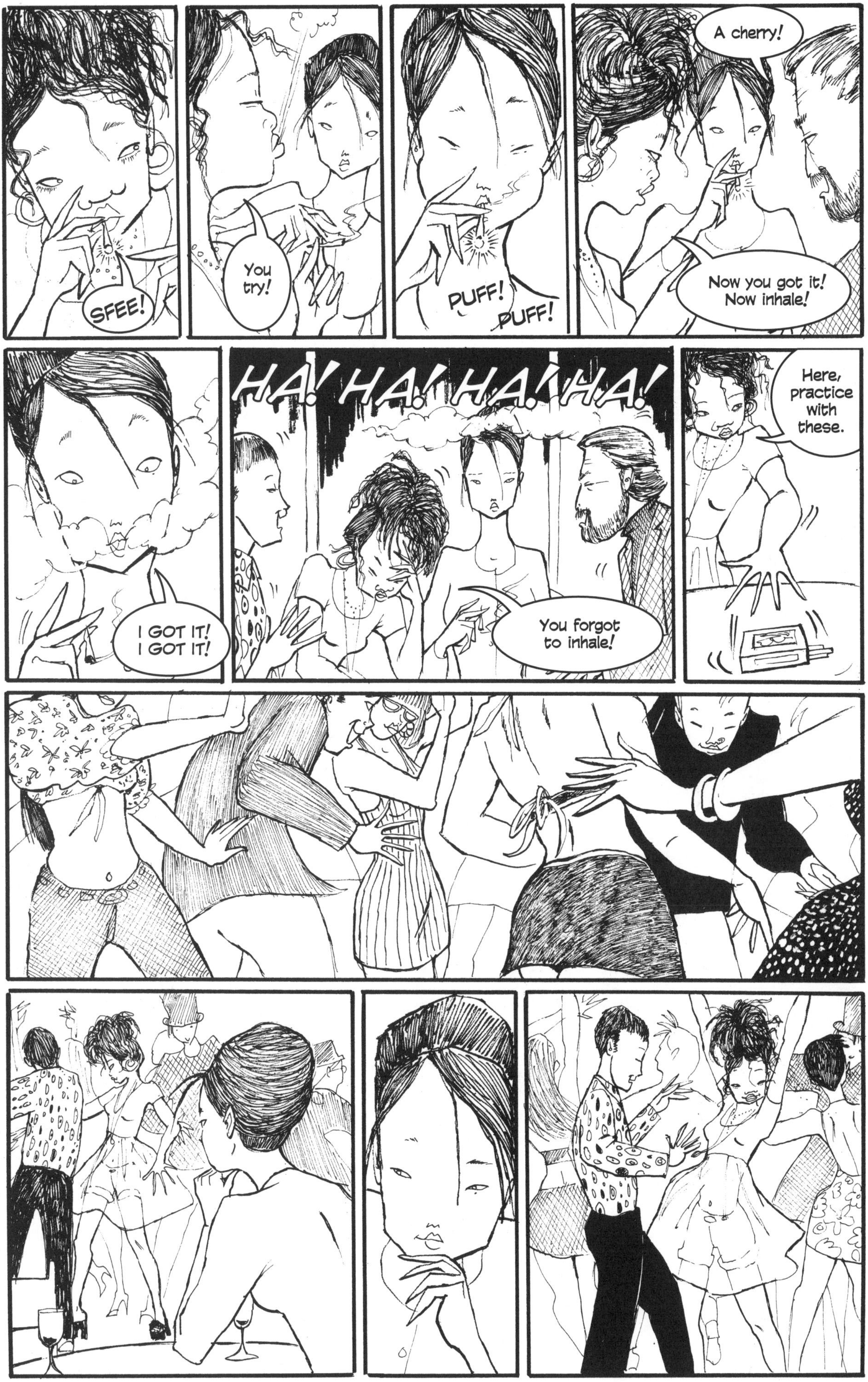
SFEE!
You try!
PUFF! PUFF!
A cherry!
Now you got it! Now inhale!
I GOT IT! I GOT IT!
HA! HA! HA! HA!
You forgot to inhale!
Here, practice with these.

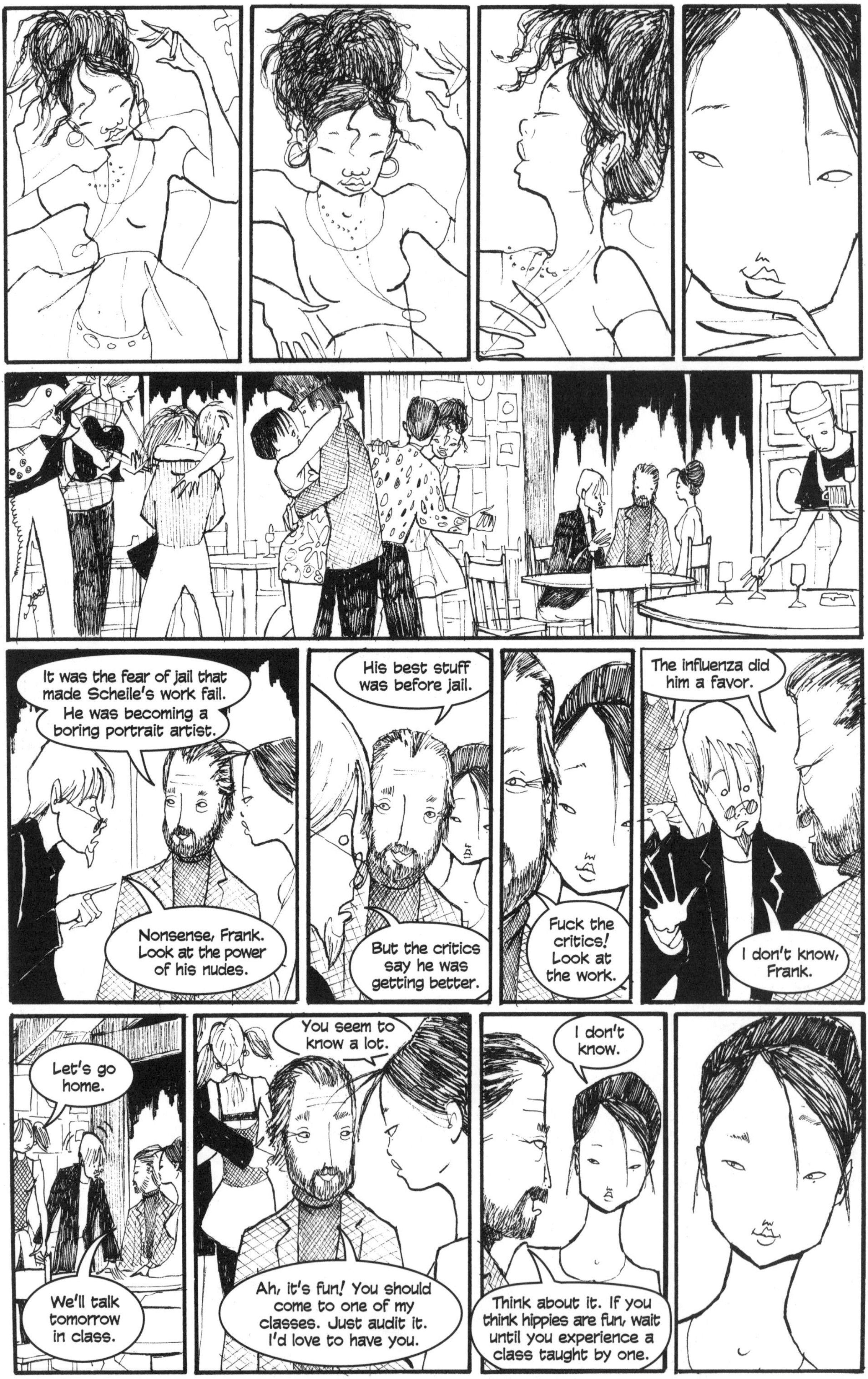
It was the fear of jail that made Scheile's work fail. He was becoming a boring portrait artist.
Nonsense, Frank. Look at the power of his nudes.
His best stuff was before jail.
But the critics say he was getting better.
Fuck the critics! Look at the work.
The influenza did him a favor.
I don't know, Frank.
Let's go home.
We'll talk tomorrow in class.
You seem to know a lot.
Ah, it's fun! You should come to one of my classes. Just audit it. I'd love to have you.
I don't know.
Think about it. If you think hippies are fun, wait until you experience a class taught by one.

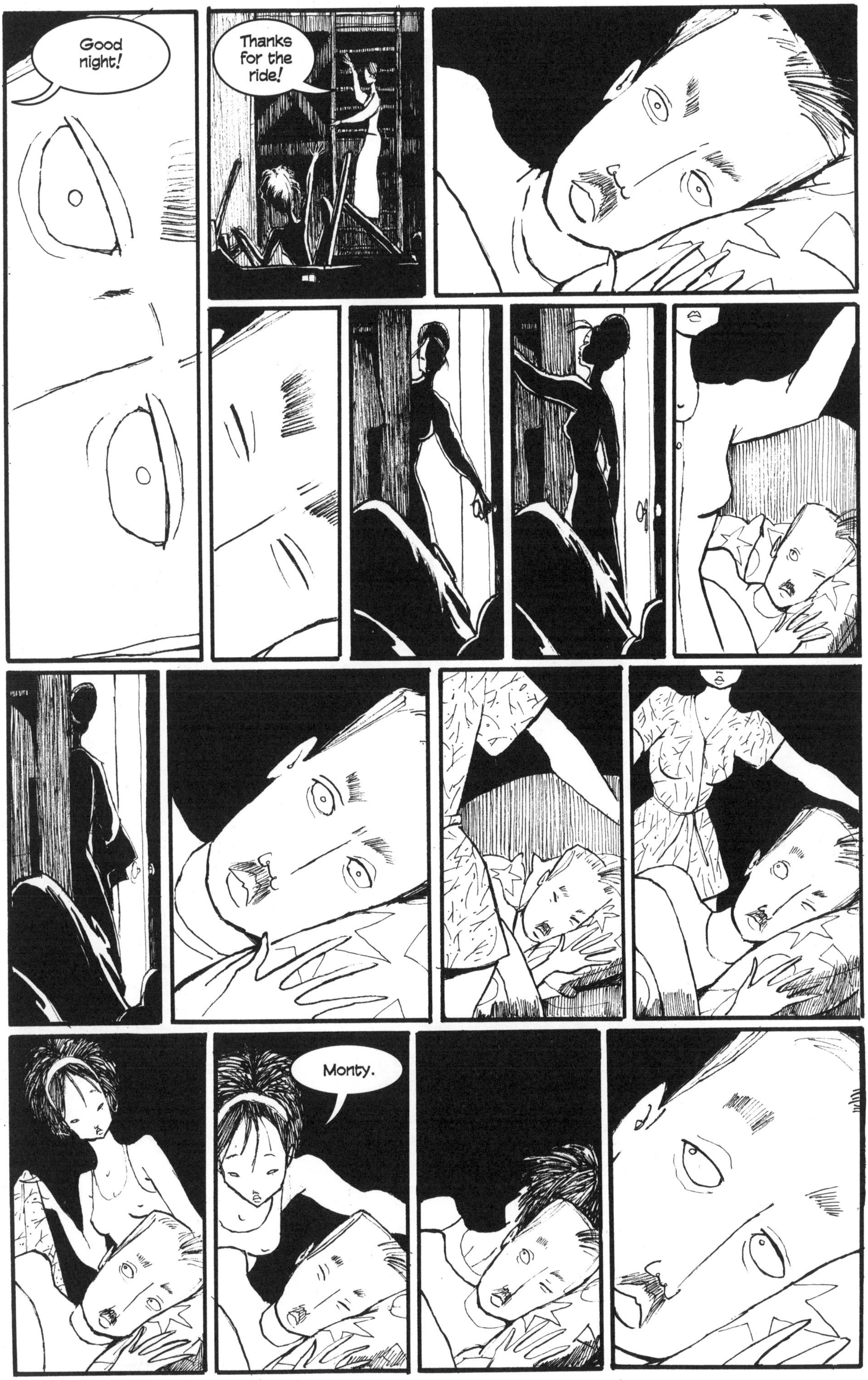
Good night!
Thanks for the ride!
Monty.

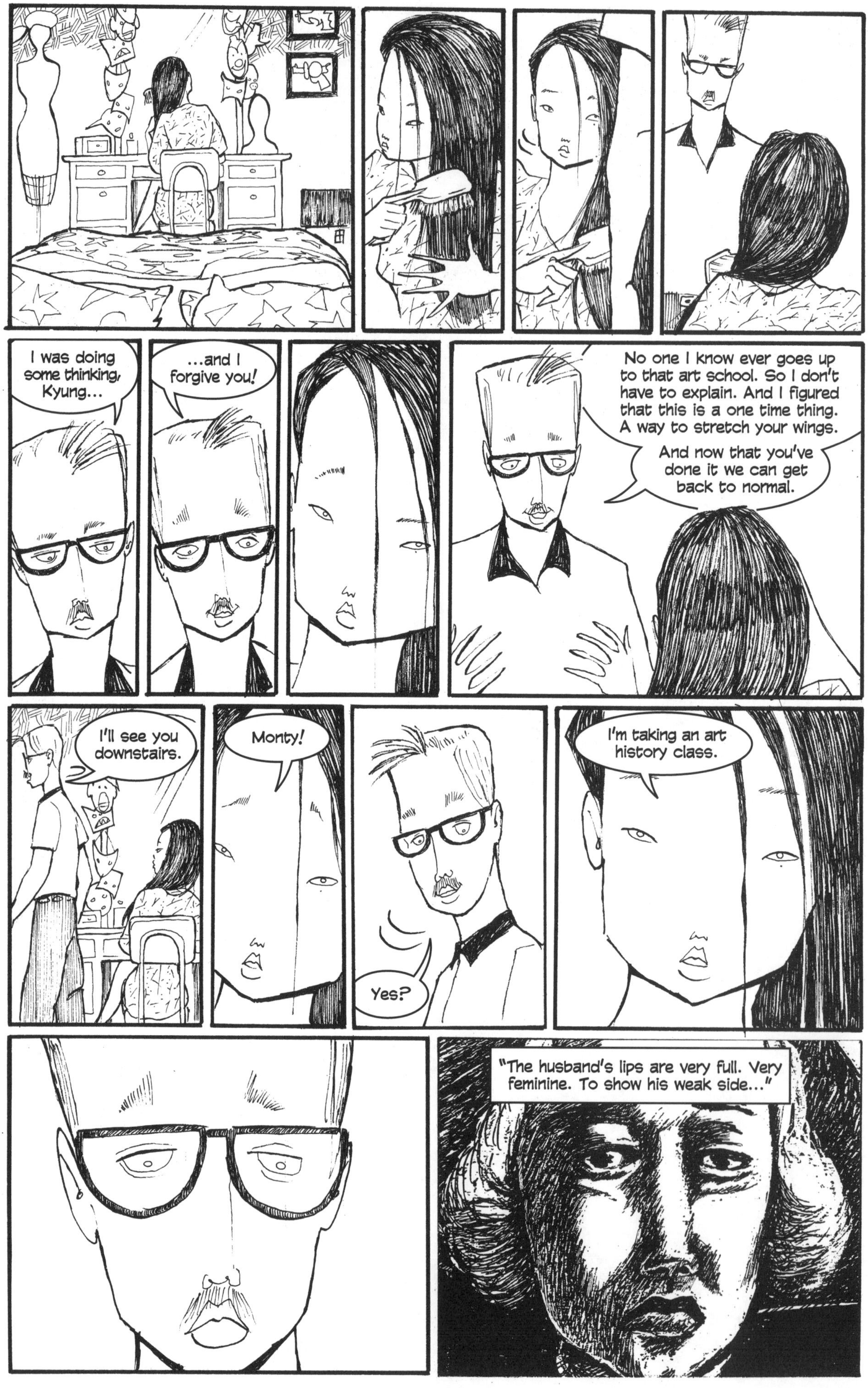
I was doing some thinking, Kyung...
...and I forgive you!
No one I know ever goes up to that art school. So I don't have to explain. And I figured that this is a one time thing. A way to stretch your wings.
And now that you've done it we can get back to normal.
I'll see you downstairs.
Monty!
Yes?
I'm taking an art history class.
"The husband's lips are very full. Very feminine. To show his weak side..."

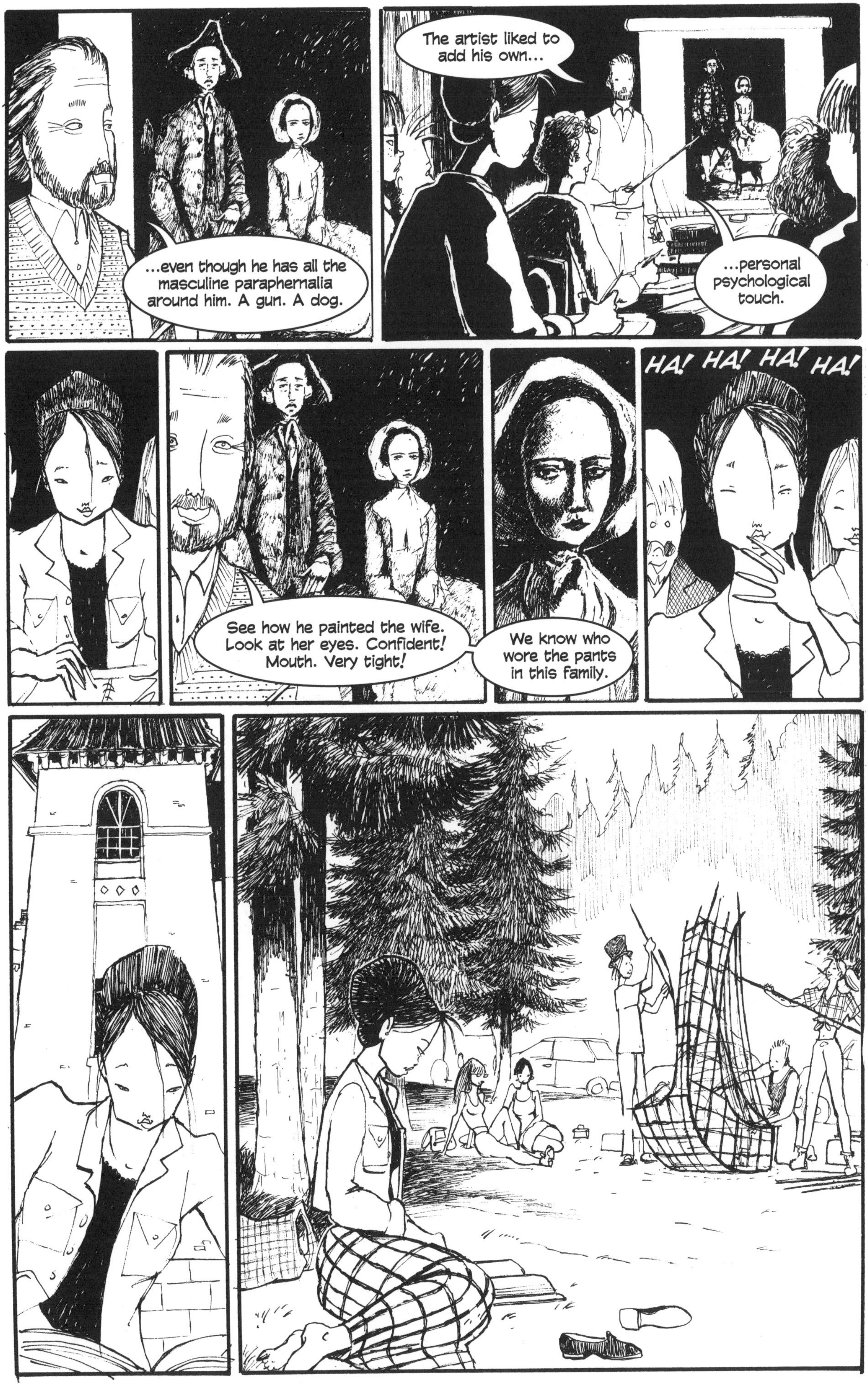
...even though he has all the masculine paraphernalia around him. A gun. A dog.
The artist liked to add his own...
...personal psychological touch.
See how he painted the wife. Look at her eyes. Confident! Mouth. Very tight!
We know who wore the pants in this family.
HA! HA! HA! HA!

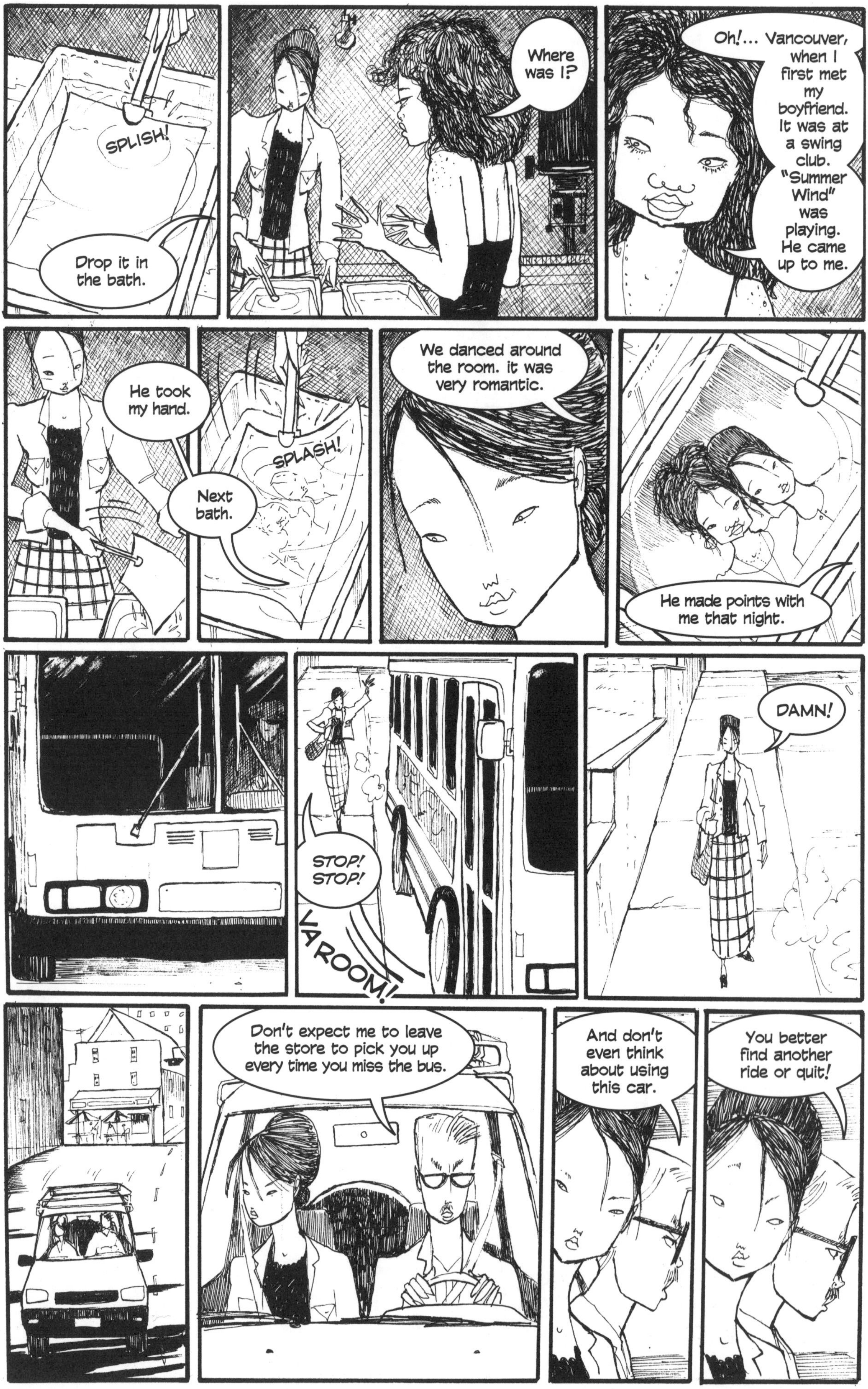
SPLISH!
Drop it in the bath.
Where was I?
Oh!... Vancouver, when I first met my boyfriend. It was at a swing club. "Summer Wind" was playing. He came up to me.
He took my hand.
SPLASH!
Next bath.
We danced around the room. it was very romantic.
He made points with me that night.
STOP! STOP!
VAROOM!
DAMN!
Don't expect me to leave the store to pick you up every time you miss the bus.
And don't even think about using this car.
You better find another ride or quit!

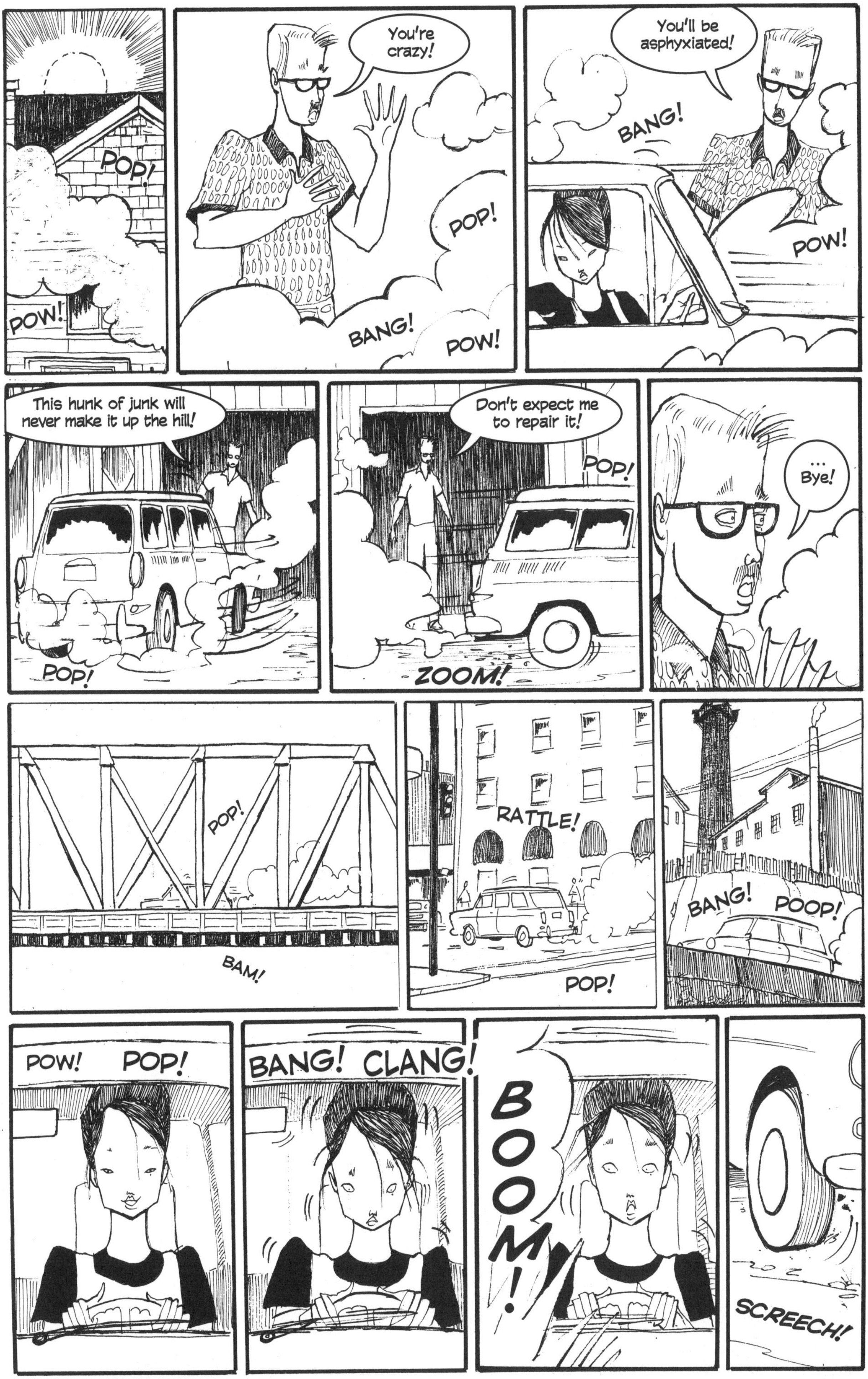
POP!
POW!
You're crazy!
POP!
BANG!
POW!
You'll be asphyxiated!
BANG!
POW!
This hunk of junk will never make it up the hill!
POP!
Don't expect me to repair it!
POP!
ZOOM!
... Bye!
POP!
BAM!
RATTLE!
POP!
BANG!
POOP!
POW! POP!
BANG! CLANG!
BOOM!
SCREECH!

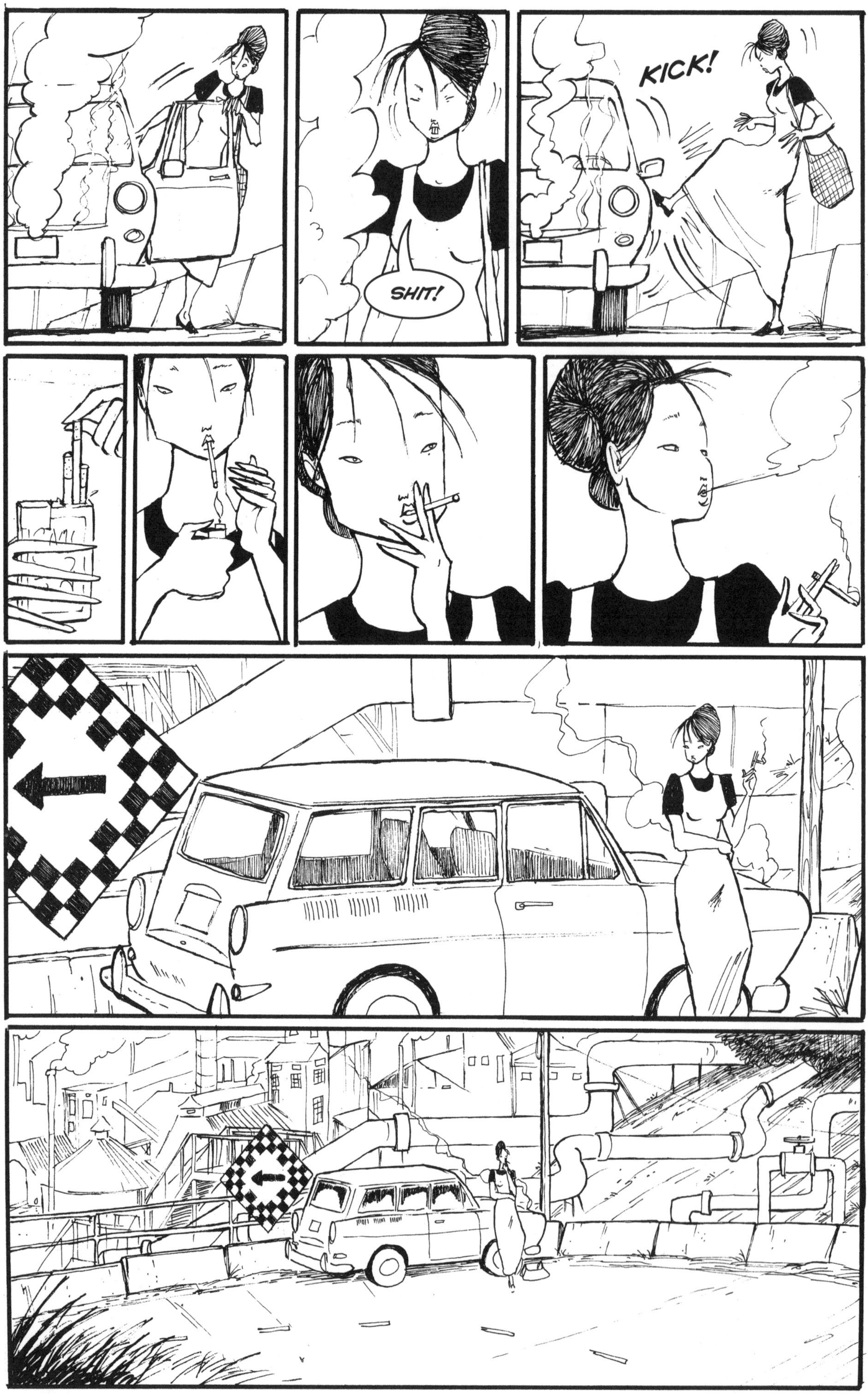
SHIT!
KICK!

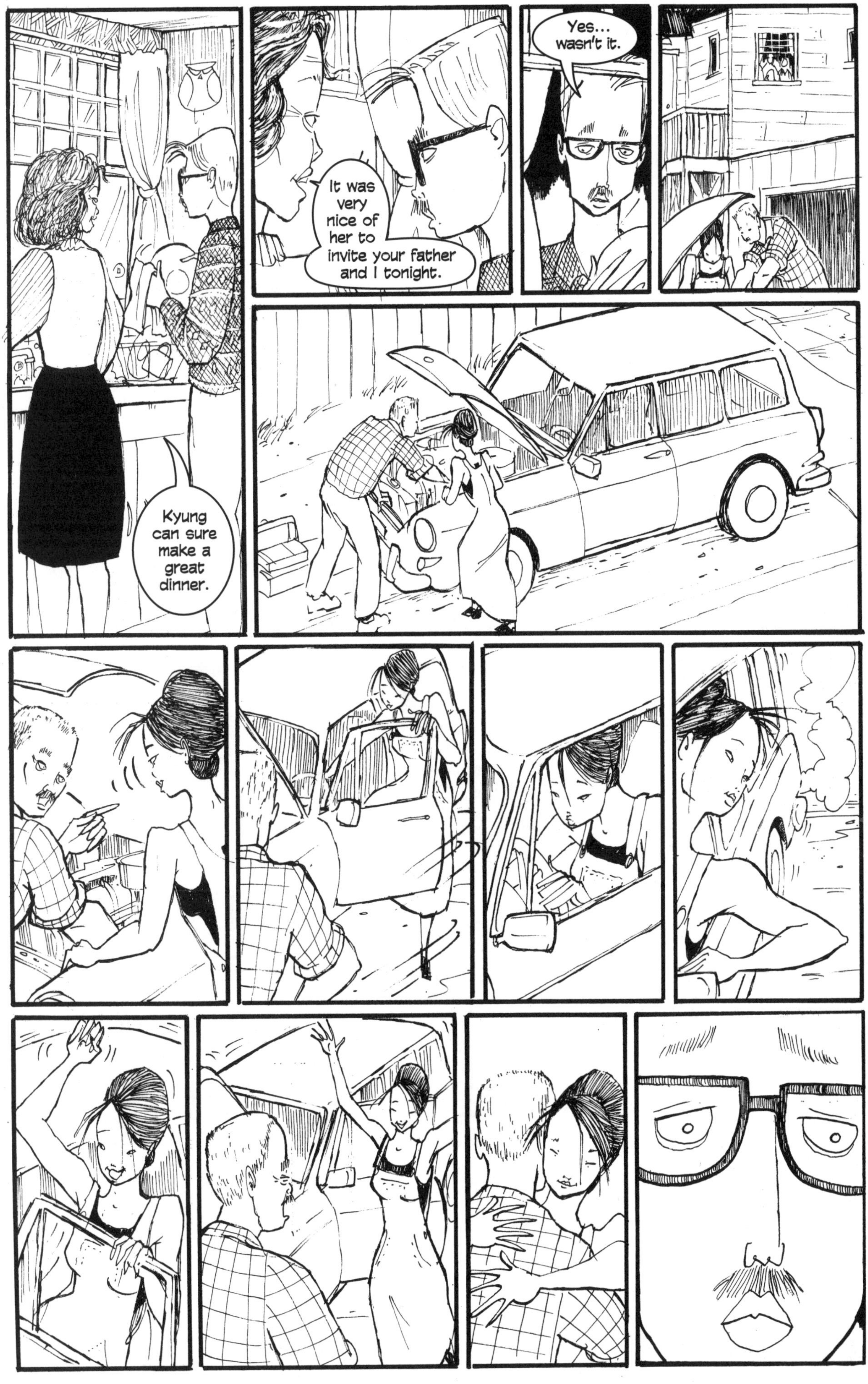
Kyung can sure make a great dinner.
It was very nice of her to invite your father and I tonight.
Yes... wasn't it.

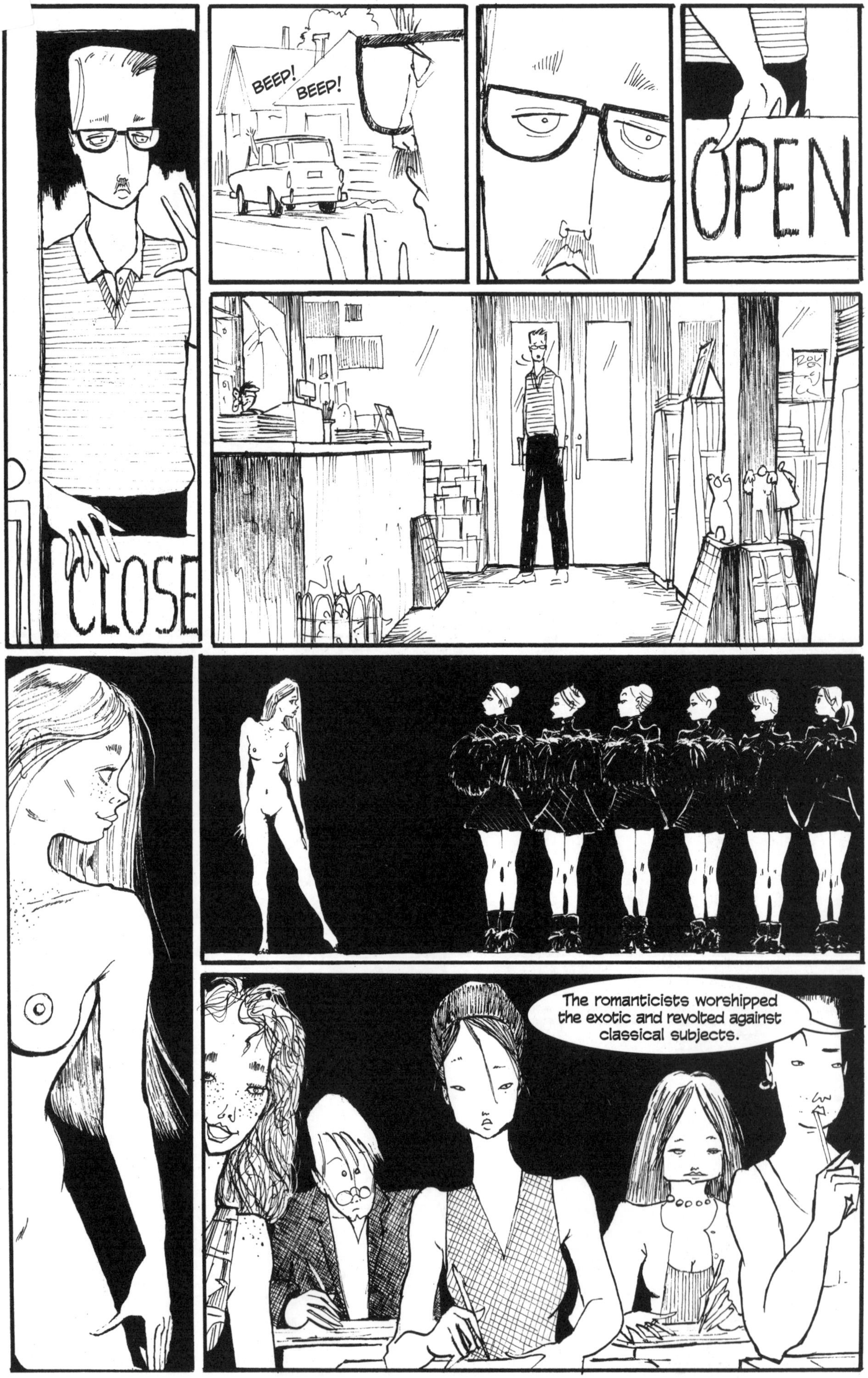
CLOSE
BEEP!
BEEP!
OPEN
The romanticists worshipped the exotic and revolted against classical subjects.

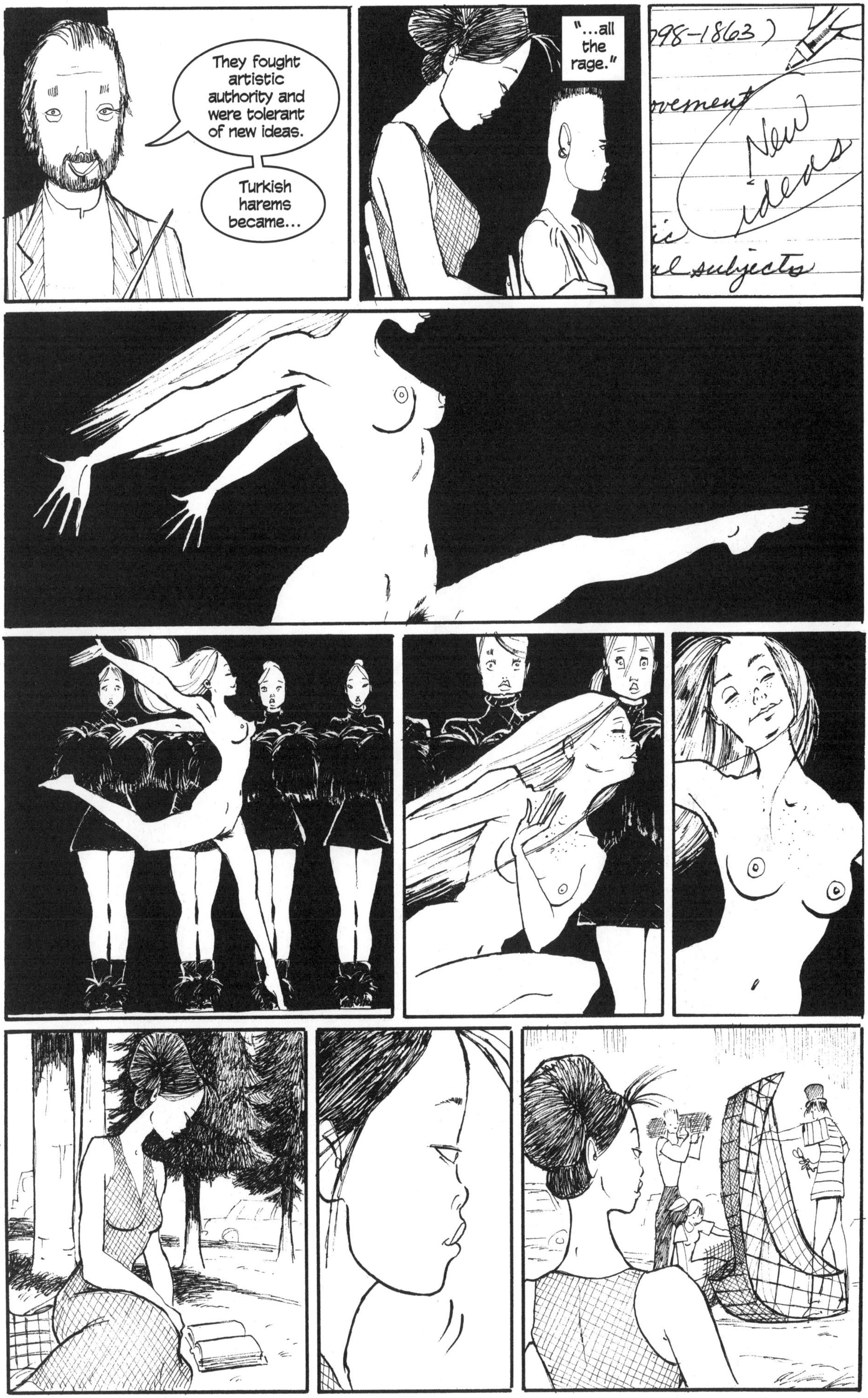
They fought artistic authority and were tolerant of new ideas.
Turkish harems became...
"...all the rage."
798-1863)
ovement
New ideas
l subjects

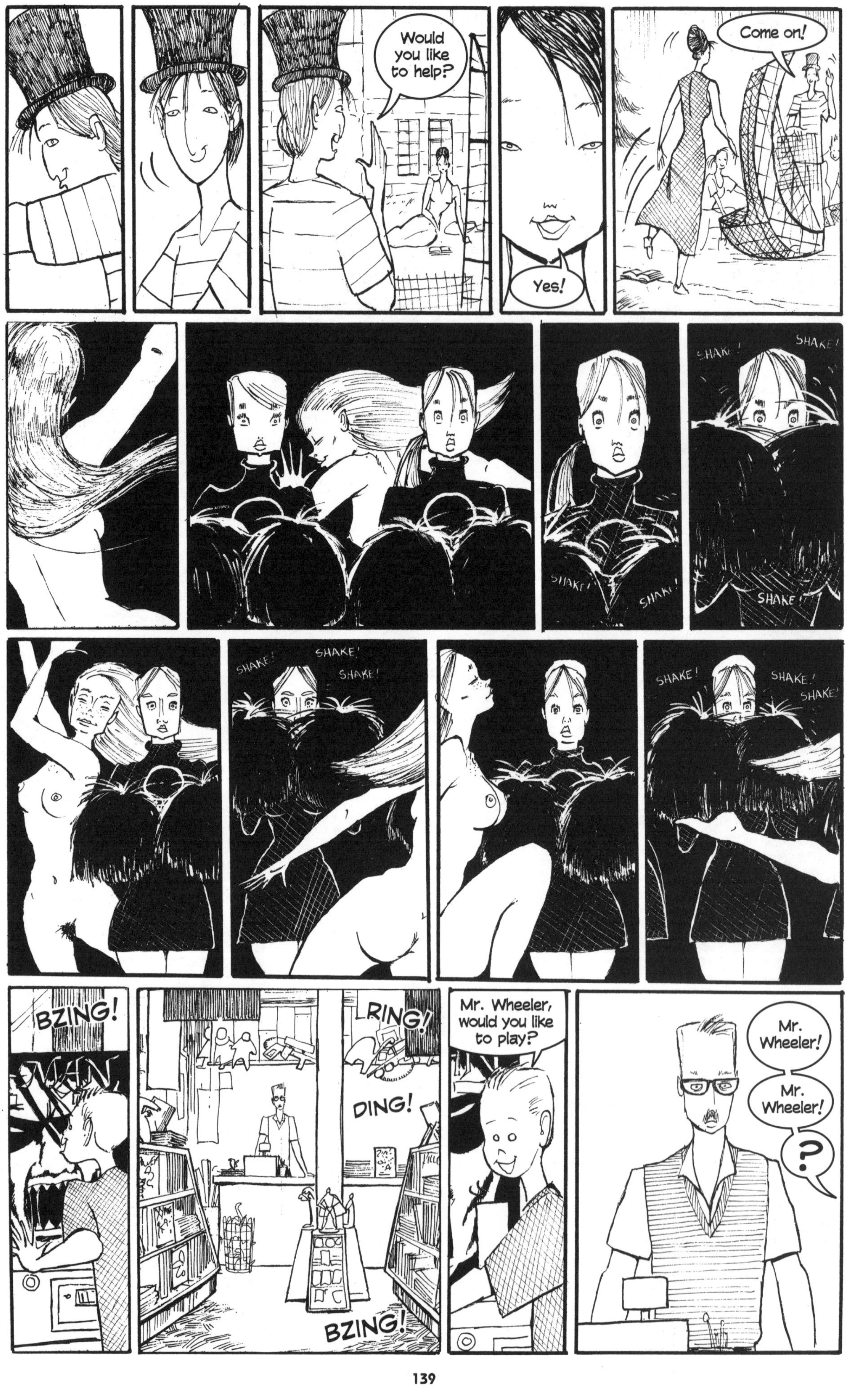
Would you like to help?
Yes!
Come on!
SHAKE!
SHAKE!
SHAKE!
SHAKE!
SHAKE!
SHAKE!
SHAKE!
SHAKE!
SHAKE!
SHAKE!
SHAKE!
BZING!
RING!
DING!
BZING!
Mr. Wheeler, would you like to play?
Mr. Wheeler!
Mr. Wheeler!
?

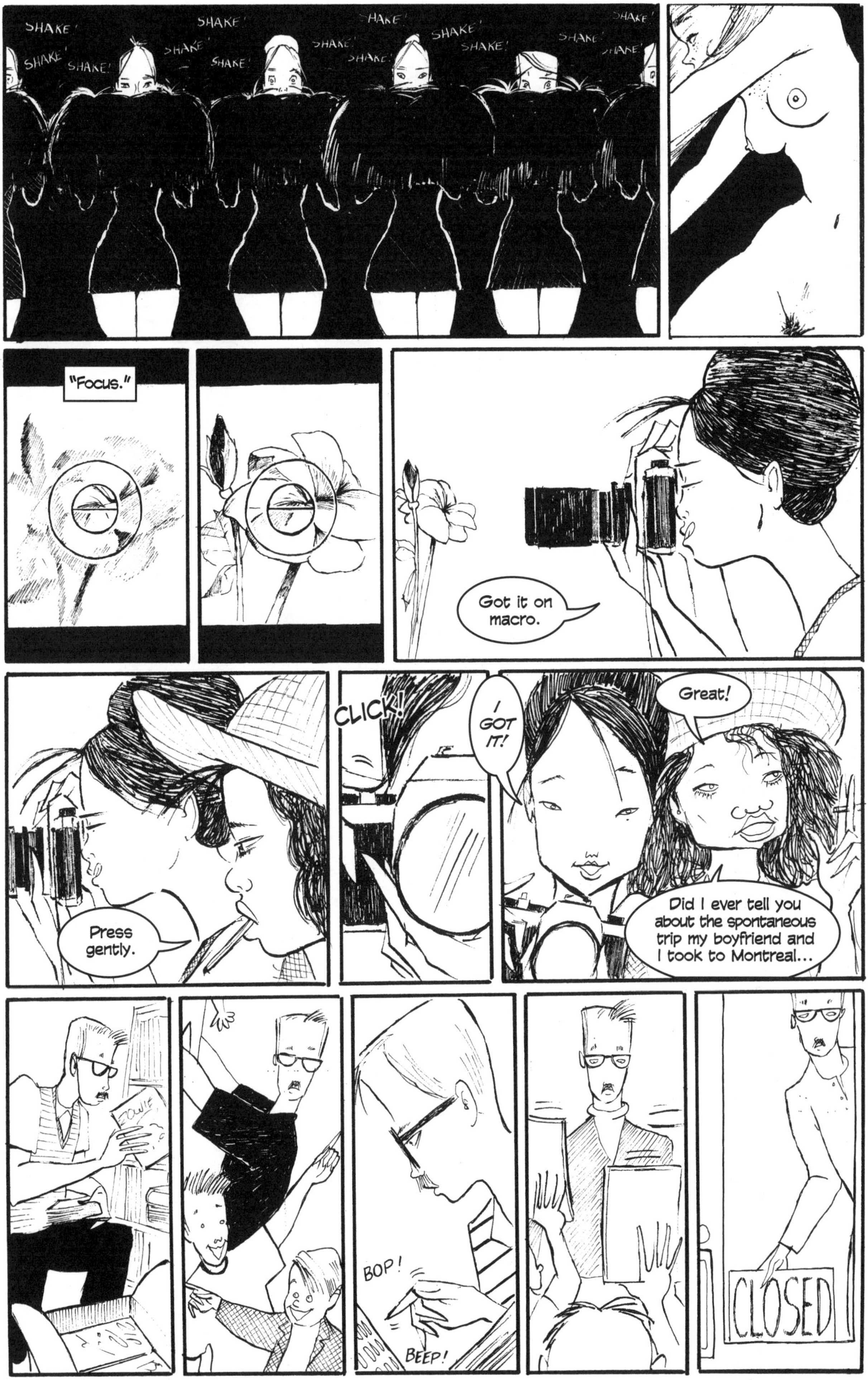
SHAKE!
SHAKE!
SHAKE!
SHAKE!
SHAKE!
SHAKE!
SHAKE!
SHAKE!
SHAKE!
SHAKE!
SHAKE!
SHAKE!
SHAKE!
"Focus."
Got it on macro.
Press gently.
CLICK!
I GOT IT!
Great!
Did I ever tell you about the spontaneous trip my boyfriend and I took to Montreal...
BOP!
BEEP!
CLOSED

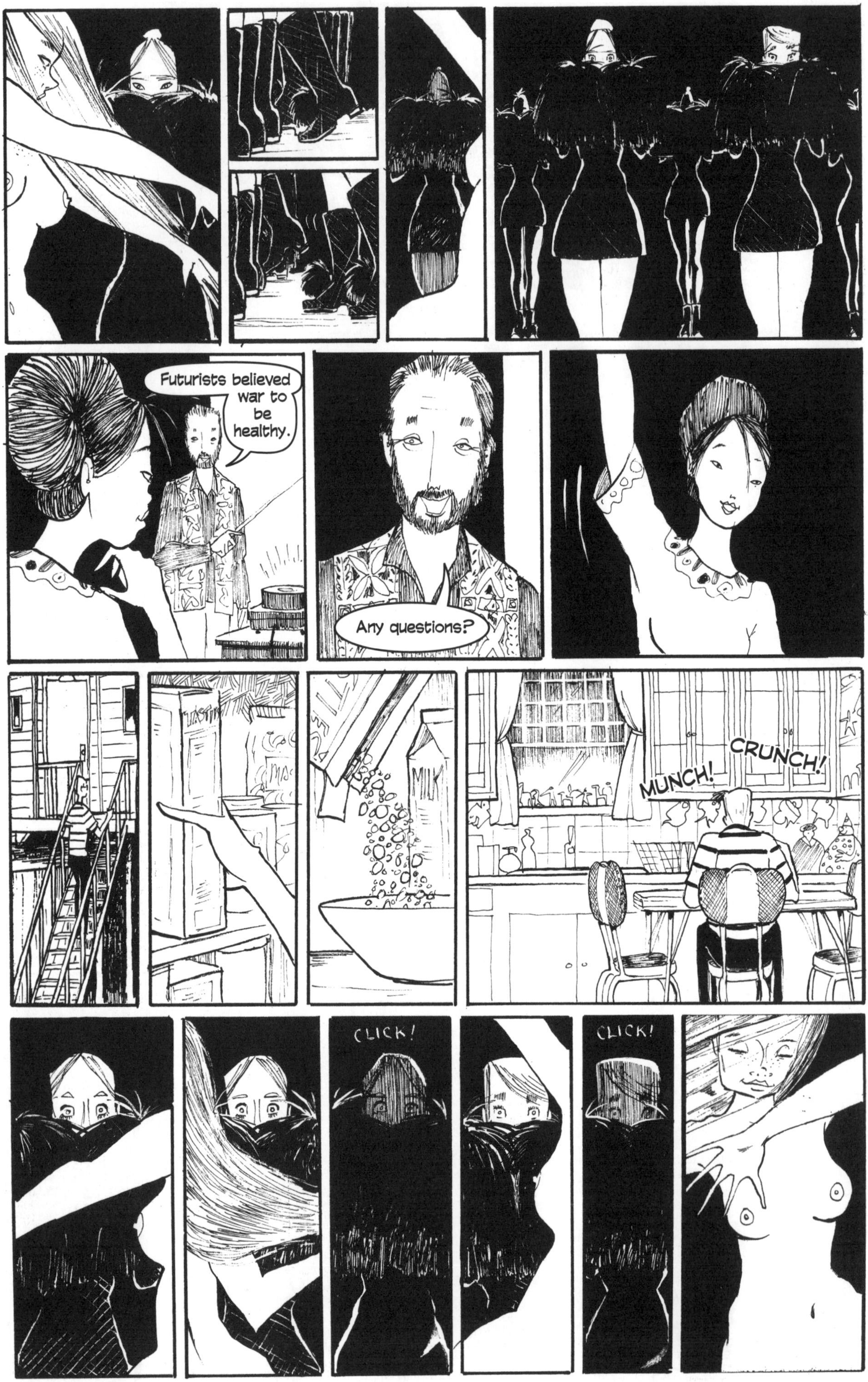
Futurists believed war to be healthy.
Any questions?
MUNCH!
CRUNCH!
CLICK!
CLICK!

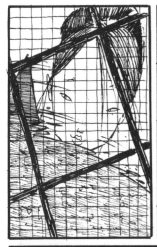

CLICK!

When I get back to Vancouver, my boyfriend...

...and I will be moving in together.

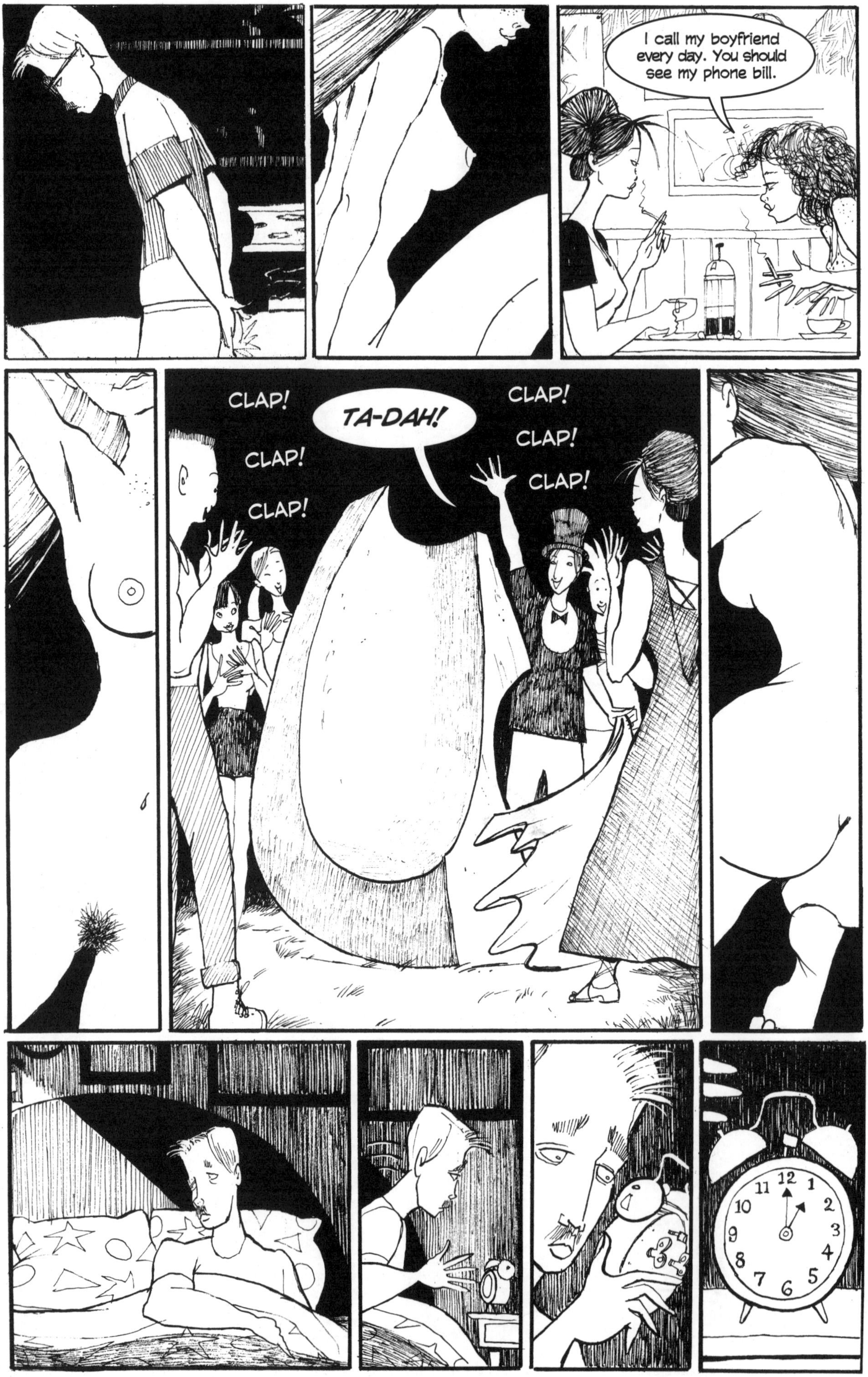
I call my boyfriend every day. You should see my phone bill.
CLAP!
CLAP!
CLAP!
TA-DAH!
CLAP!
CLAP!
CLAP!

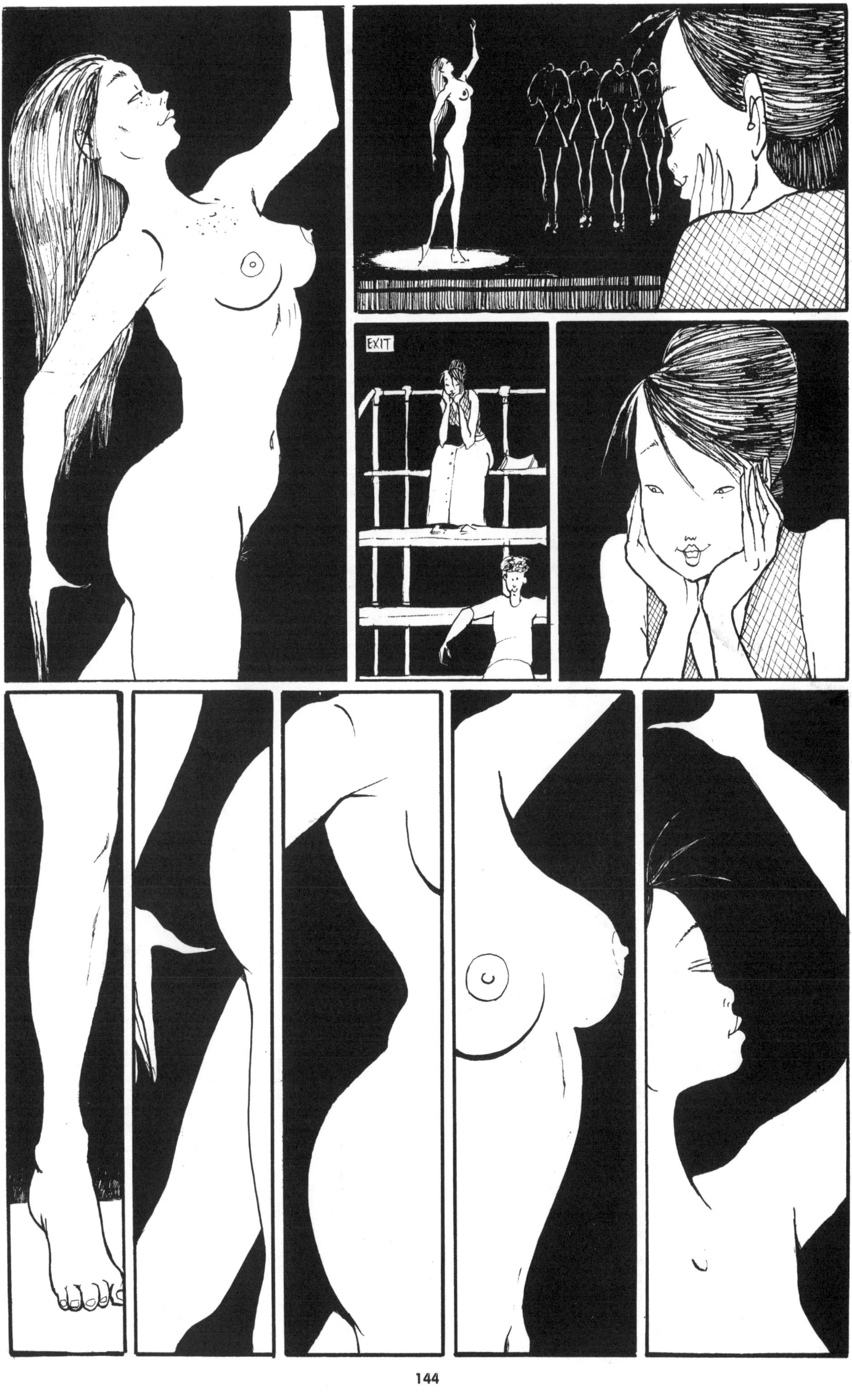
EXIT

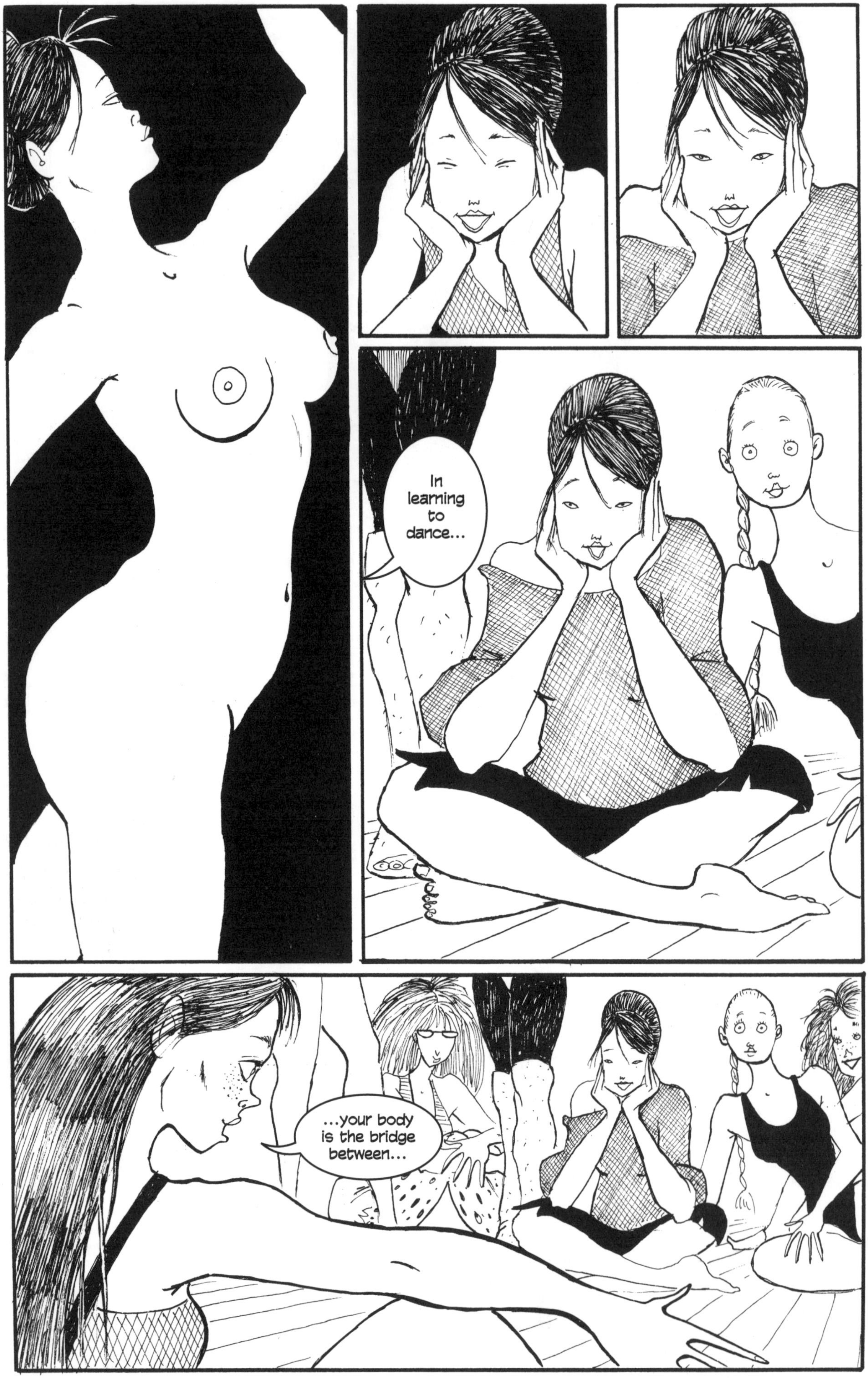

In learning to dance...
...your body is the bridge between...

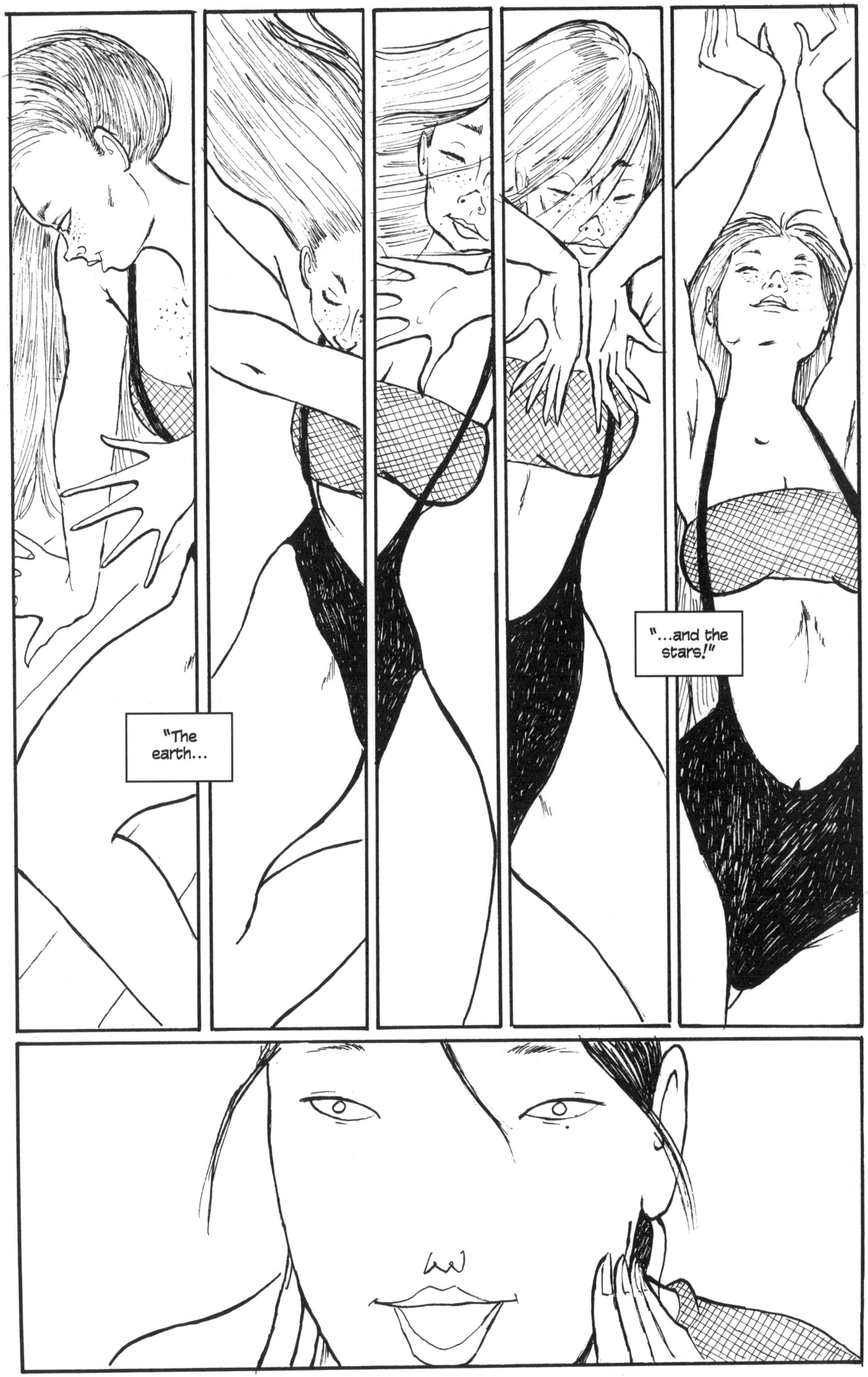
"The earth...
"...and the stars!"

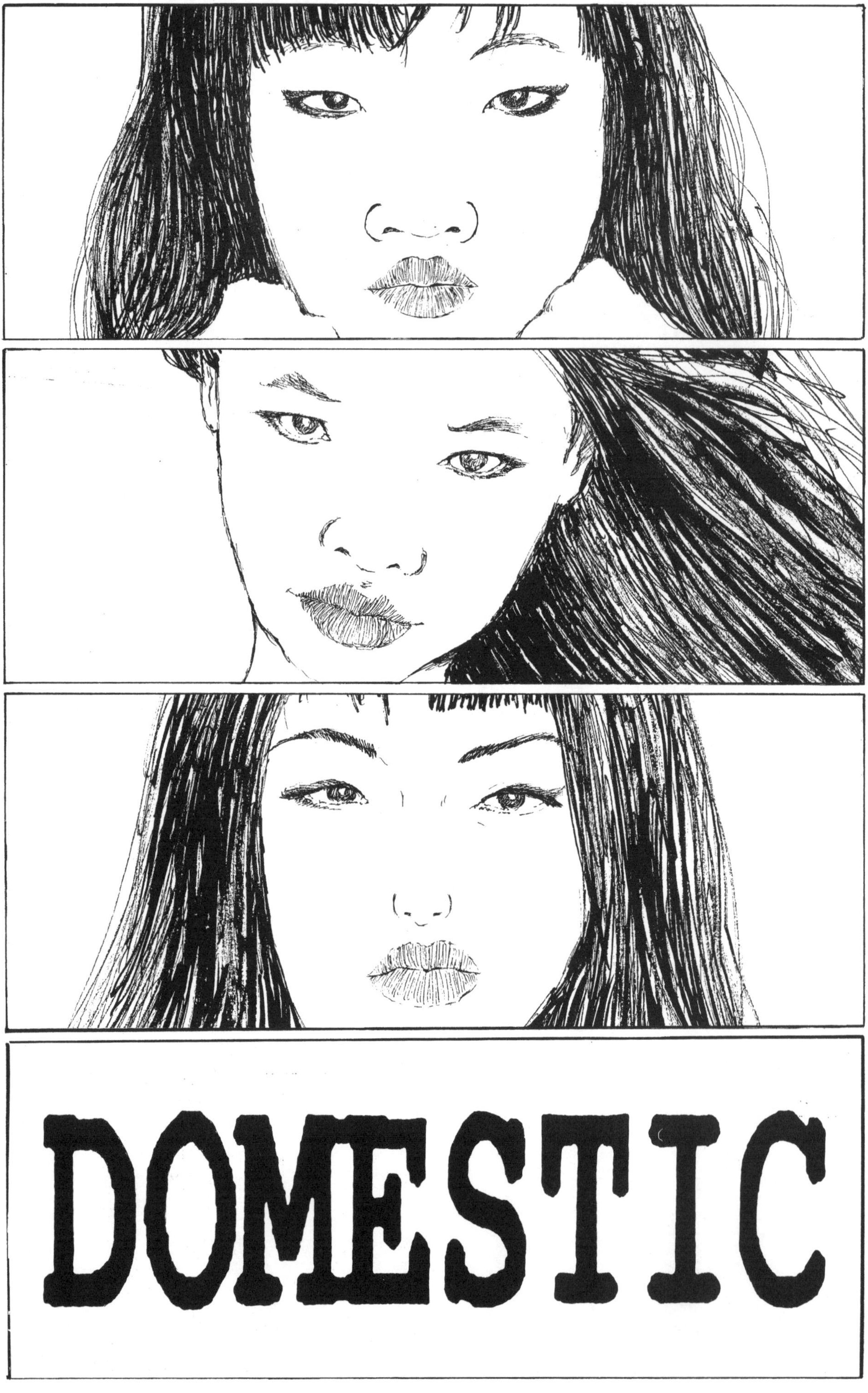
DOMESTIC

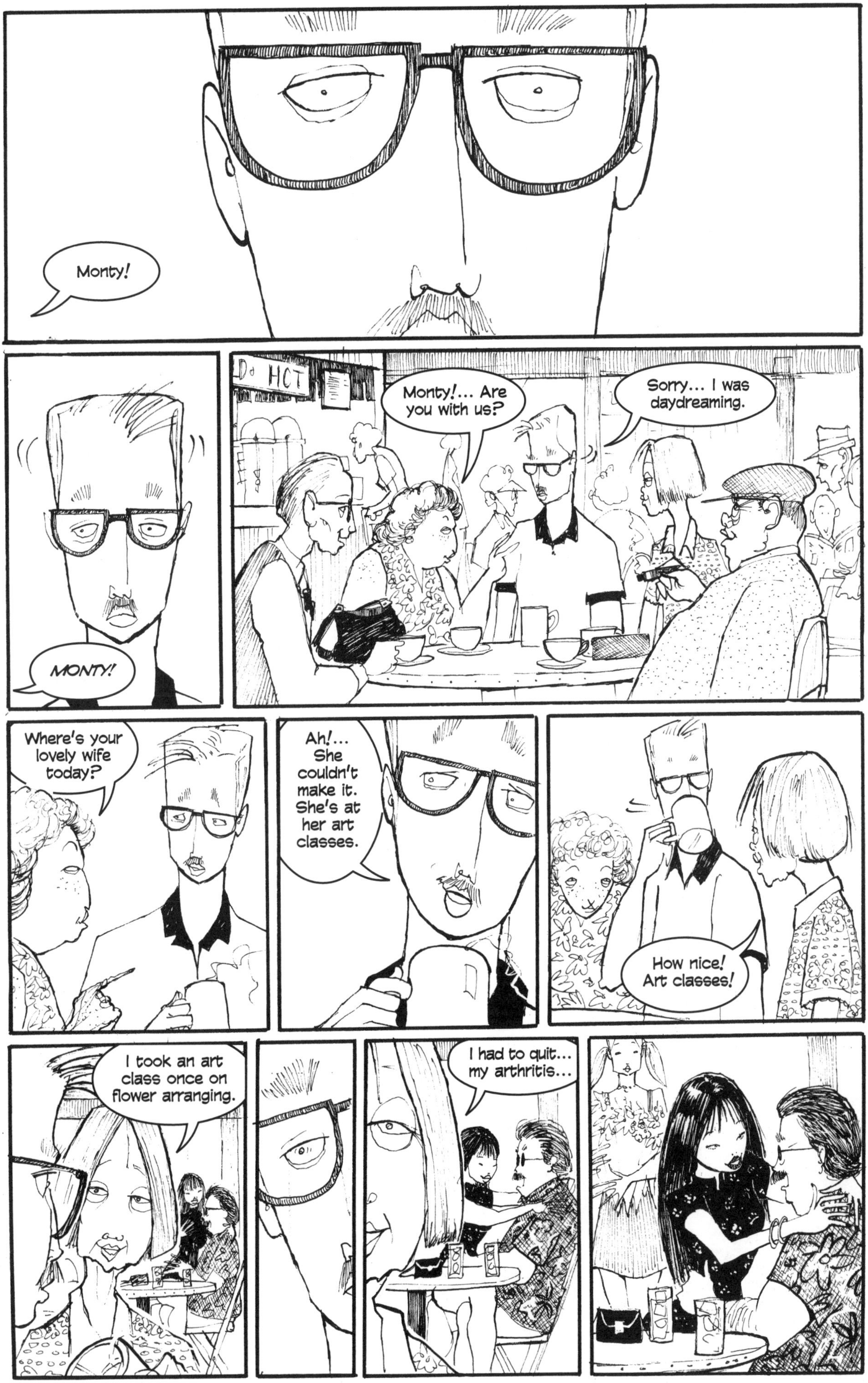
Monty!
MONTY!
Monty!... Are you with us?
Sorry... I was daydreaming.
Where's your lovely wife today?
Ah!... She couldn't make it. She's at her art classes.
How nice! Art classes!
I took an art class once on flower arranging.
I had to quit... my arthritis...

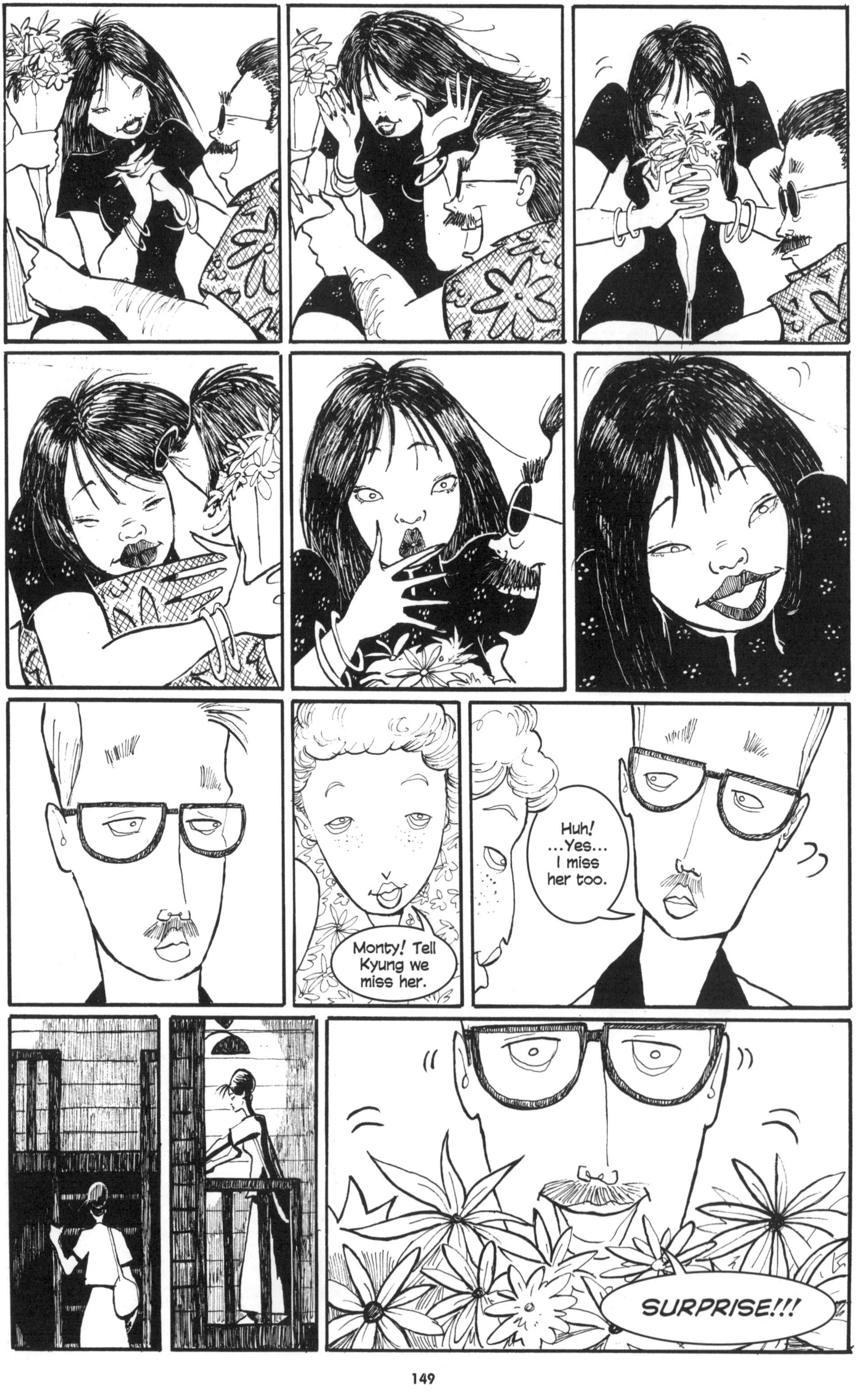
Monty! Tell Kyung we miss her.
Huh! ...Yes... I miss her too.
SURPRISE!!!

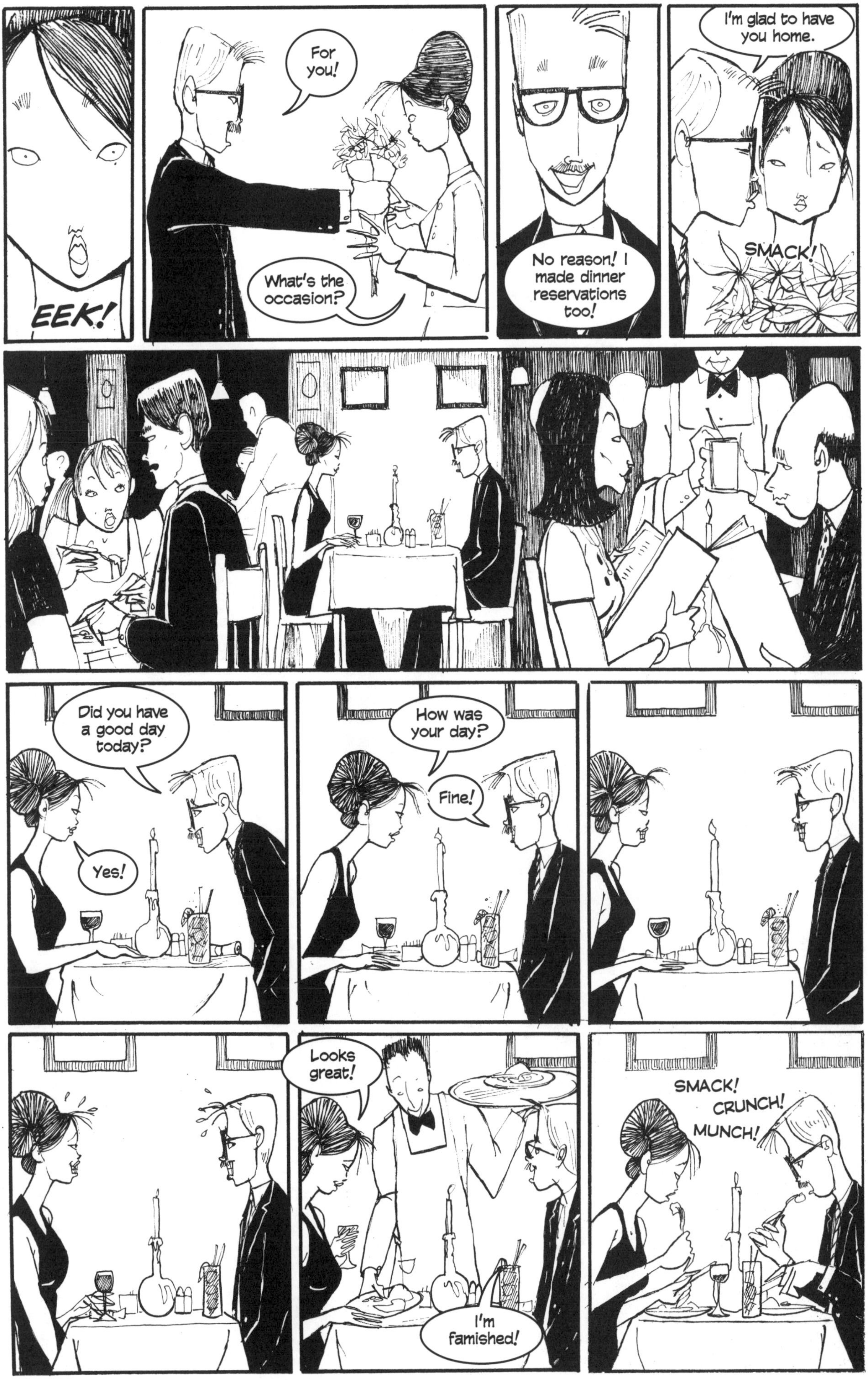
EEK!
For you!
What's the occasion?
No reason! I made dinner reservations too!
I'm glad to have you home.
SMACK!
Did you have a good day today?
Yes!
How was your day?
Fine!
Looks great!
I'm famished!
SMACK!
CRUNCH!
MUNCH!

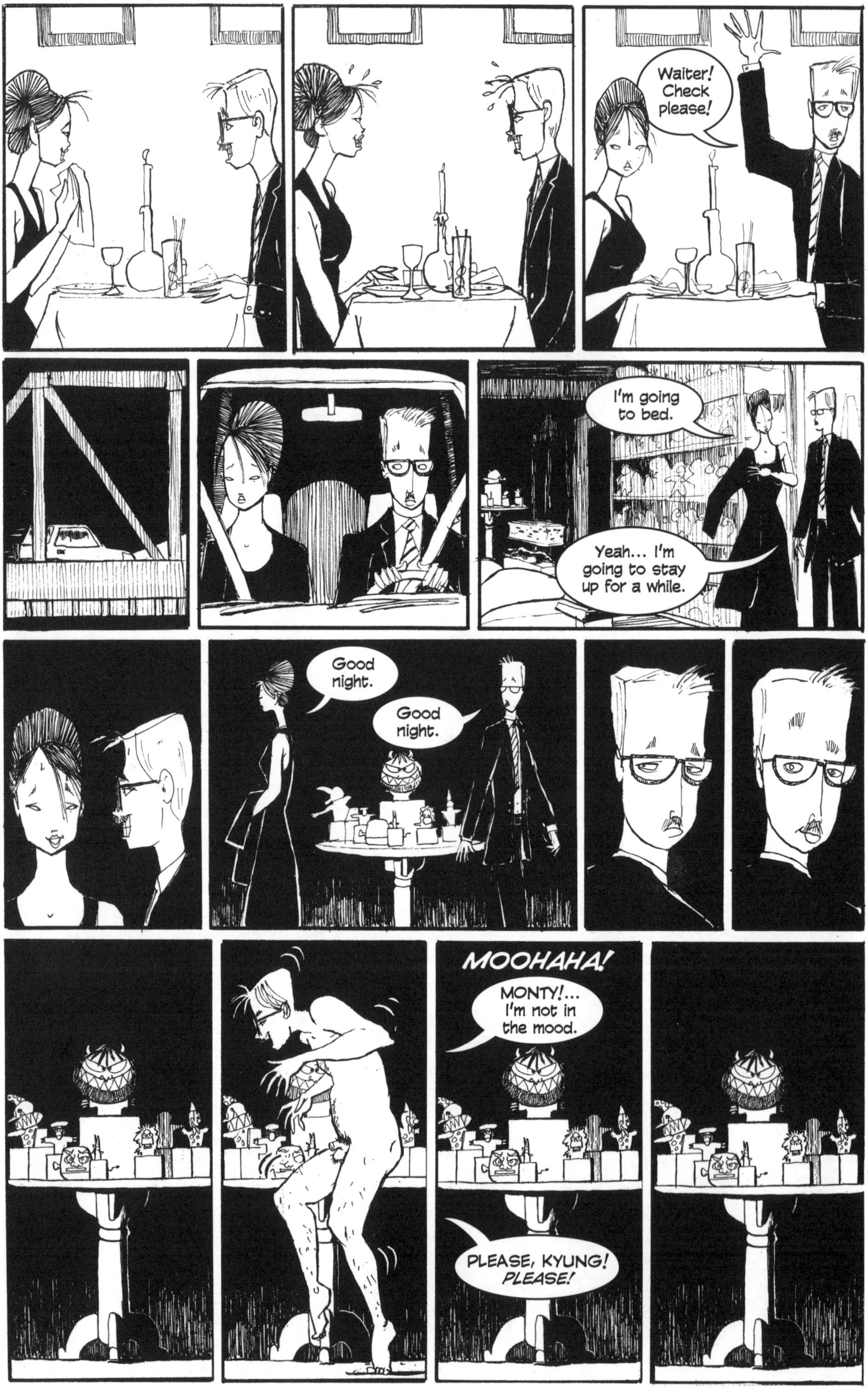
Waiter! Check please!
I'm going to bed.
Yeah... I'm going to stay up for a while.
Good night.
Good night.
MOOHAHA!
MONTY!... I'm not in the mood.
PLEASE, KYUNG! PLEASE!

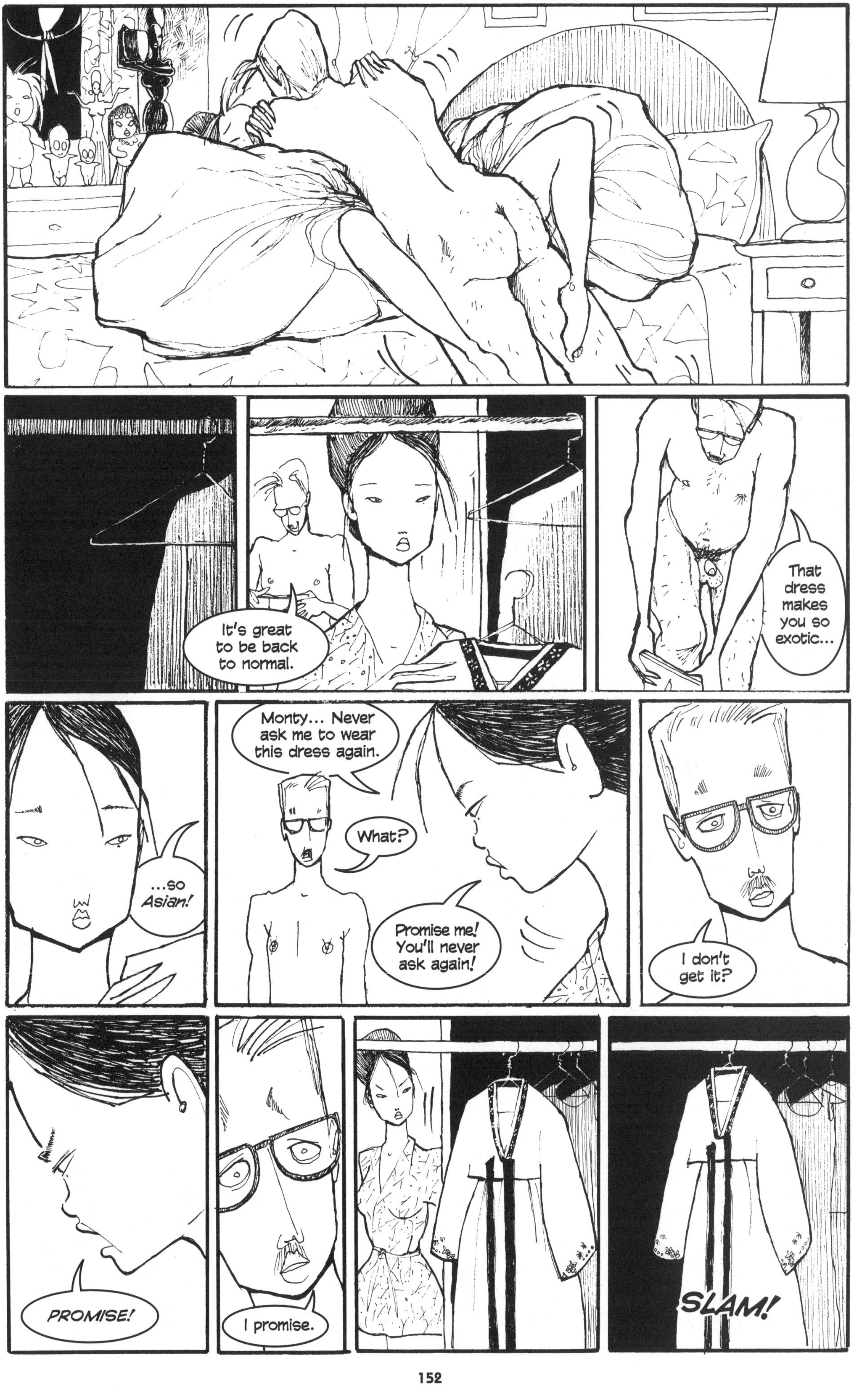
It's great to be back to normal.
That dress makes you so exotic...
...so Asian!
Monty... Never ask me to wear this dress again.
What?
Promise me! You'll never ask again!
I don't get it?
PROMISE!
I promise.
SLAM!

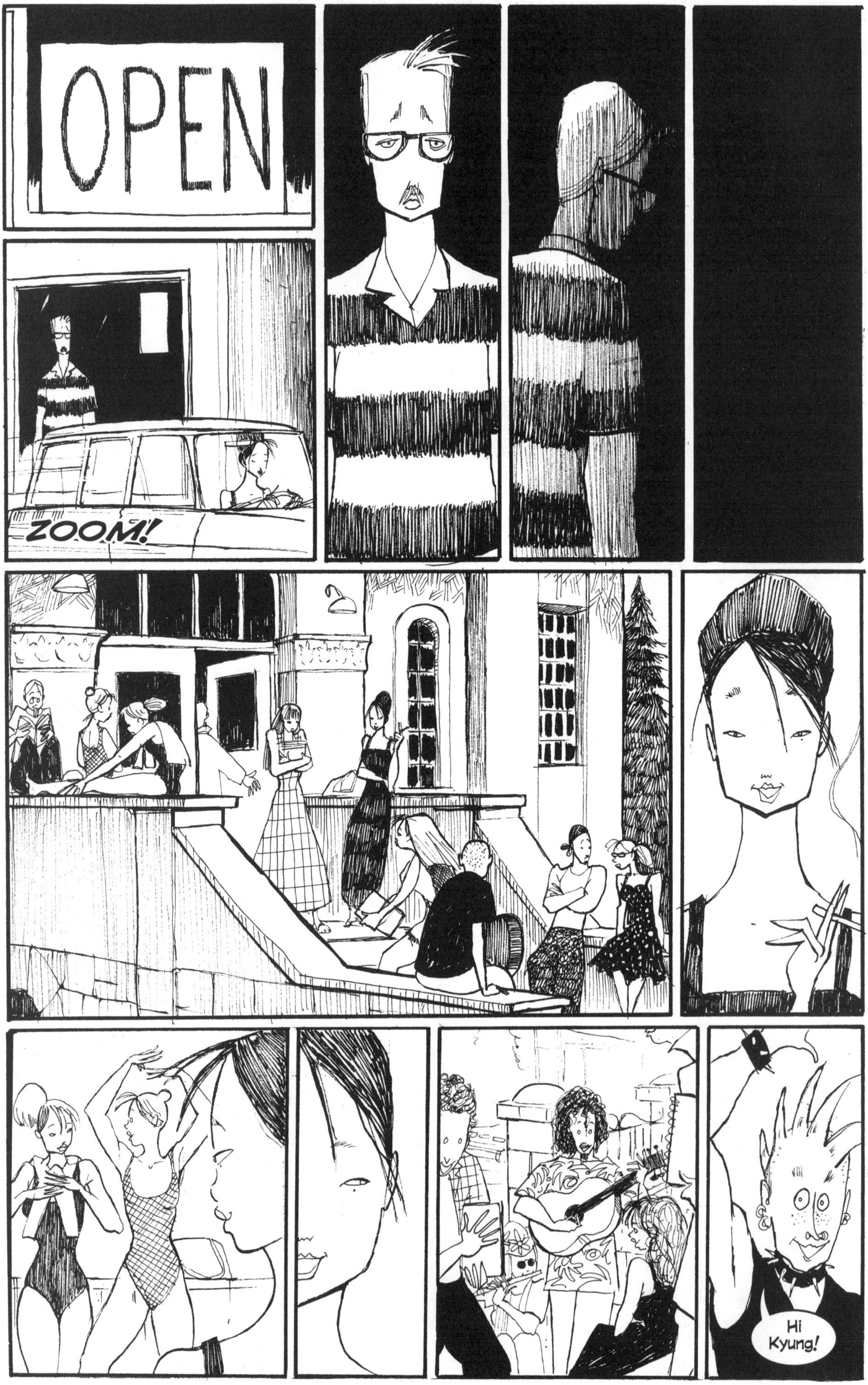
OPEN
ZOOM!
Hi Kyung!

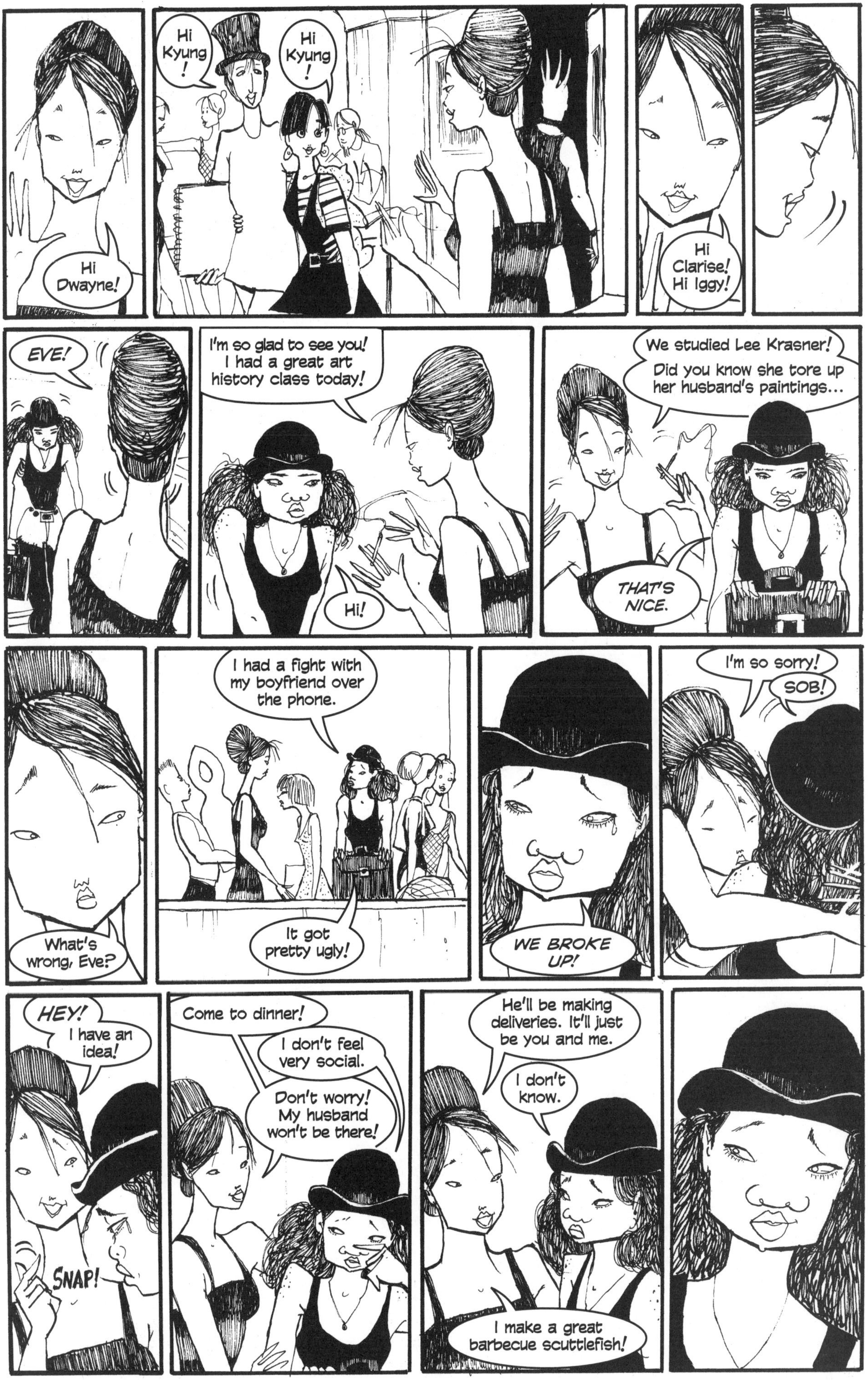
Hi Dwayne!
Hi Kyung!
Hi Kyung!
Hi Clarise! Hi Iggy!
EVE!
I'm so glad to see you! I had a great art history class today!
Hi!
We studied Lee Krasner!
Did you know she tore up her husband's paintings...
THAT'S NICE.
What's wrong, Eve?
I had a fight with my boyfriend over the phone.
It got pretty ugly!
WE BROKE UP!
I'm so sorry!
SOB!
HEY!
I have an idea!
SNAP!
Come to dinner!
I don't feel very social.
Don't worry! My husband won't be there!
He'll be making deliveries. It'll just be you and me.
I don't know.
I make a great barbecue scuttlefish!

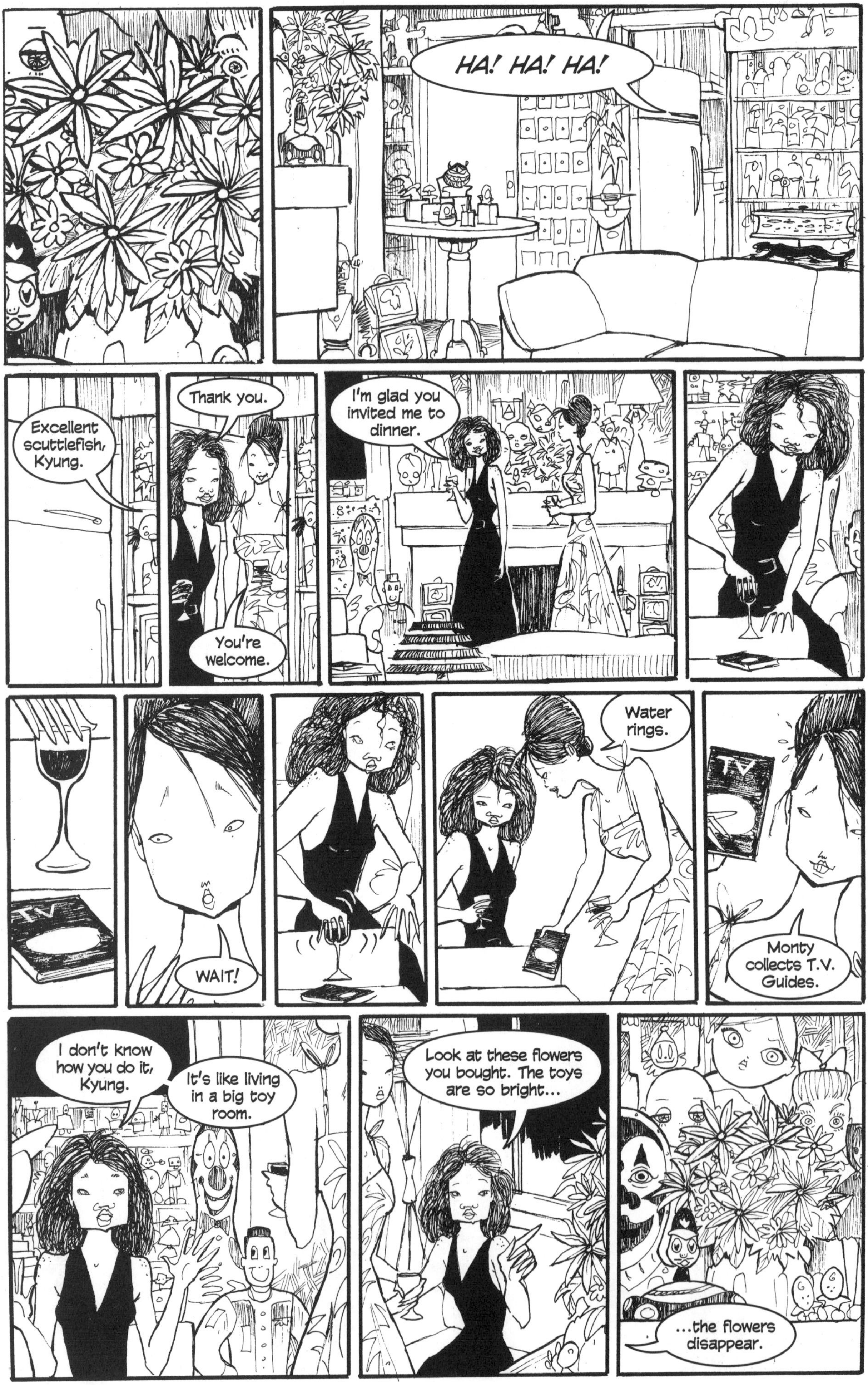
HA! HA! HA!
Excellent scuttlefish, Kyung.
Thank you.
You're welcome.
I'm glad you invited me to dinner.
WAIT!
Water rings.
Monty collects T.V. Guides.
I don't know how you do it, Kyung.
It's like living in a big toy room.
Look at these flowers you bought. The toys are so bright...
...the flowers disappear.

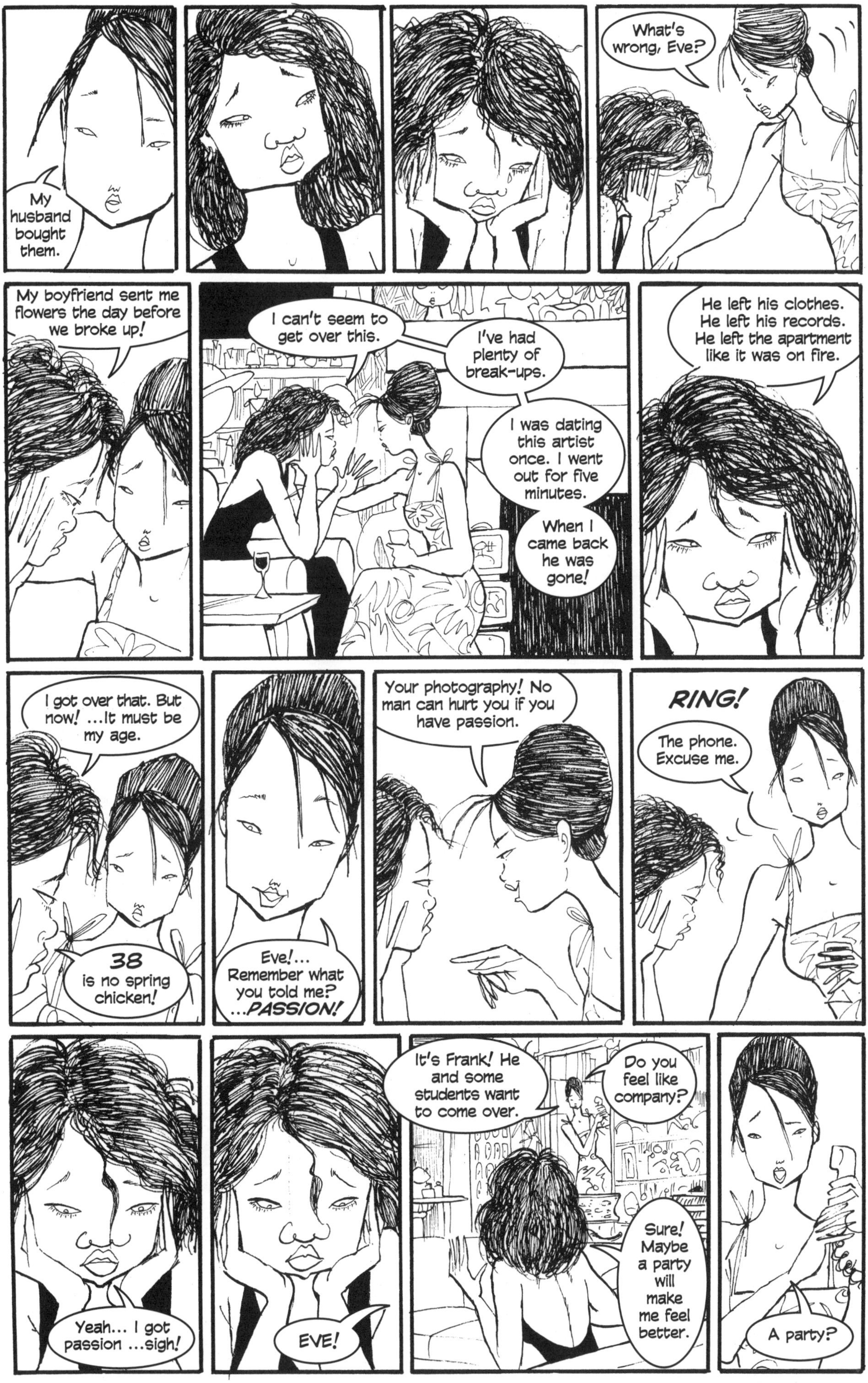

My husband bought them.
What's wrong, Eve?
My boyfriend sent me flowers the day before we broke up!
I can't seem to get over this.
I've had plenty of break-ups.
I was dating this artist once. I went out for five minutes.
When I came back he was gone!
He left his clothes. He left his records. He left the apartment like it was on fire.
I got over that. But now! ...It must be my age.
38 is no spring chicken!
Eve!... Remember what you told me? ...PASSION!
Your photography! No man can hurt you if you have passion.
RING!
The phone. Excuse me.
Yeah... I got passion ...sigh!
EVE!
It's Frank! He and some students want to come over.
Do you feel like company?
Sure! Maybe a party will make me feel better.
A party?

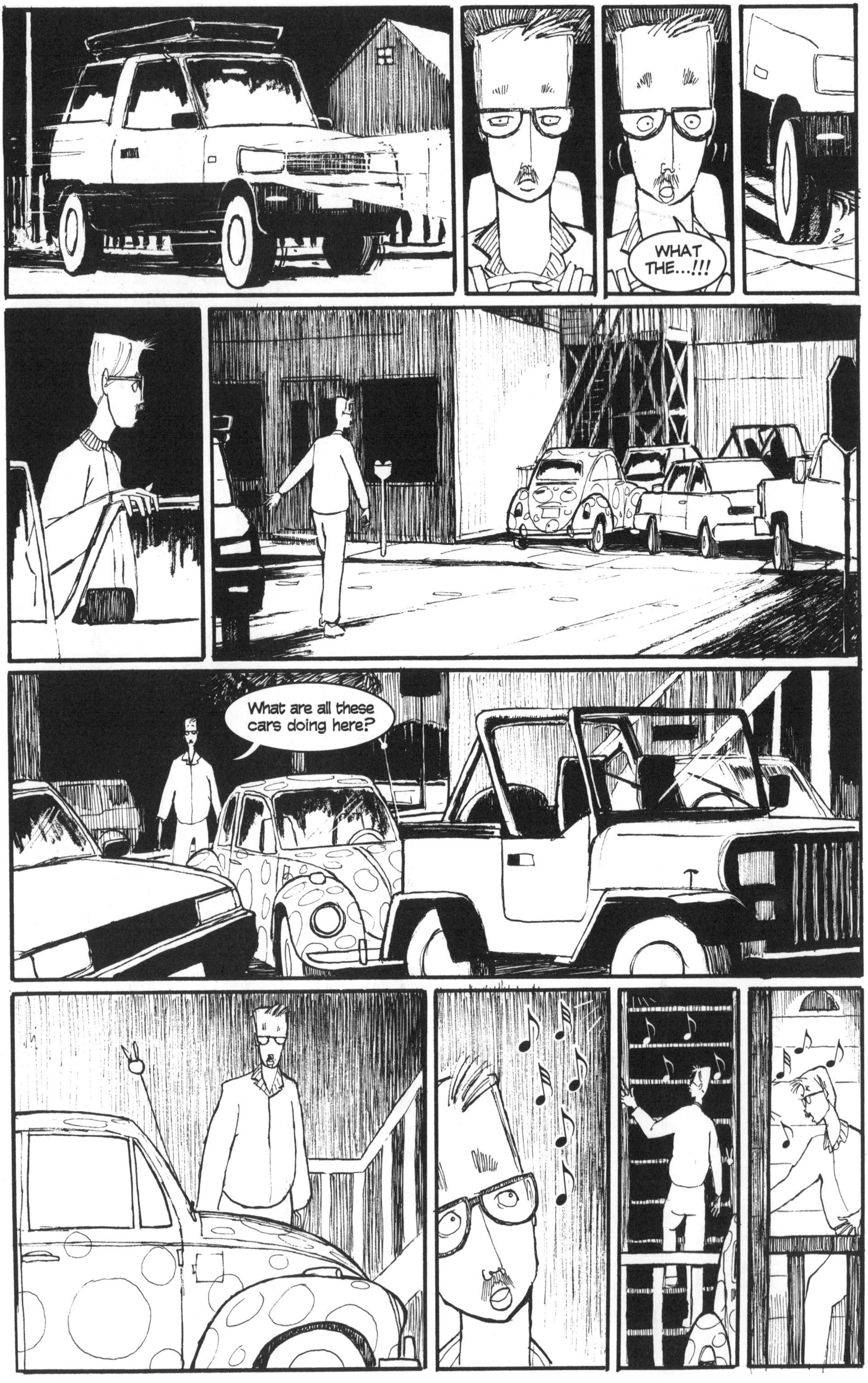

WHAT THE...!!!
What are all these cars doing here?

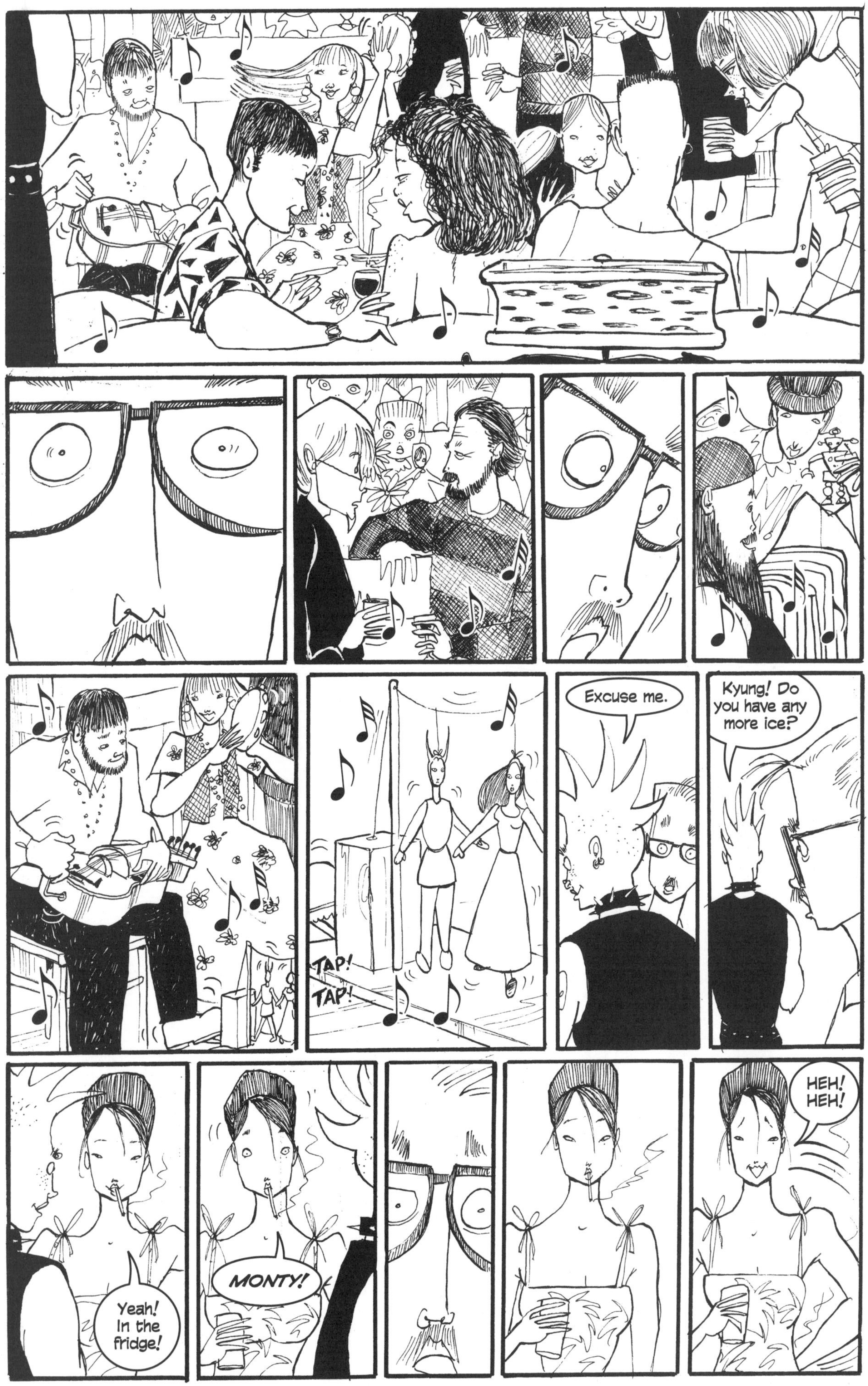

TAP!
TAP!
Excuse me.
Kyung! Do you have any more ice?
Yeah! In the fridge!
MONTY!
HEH! HEH!

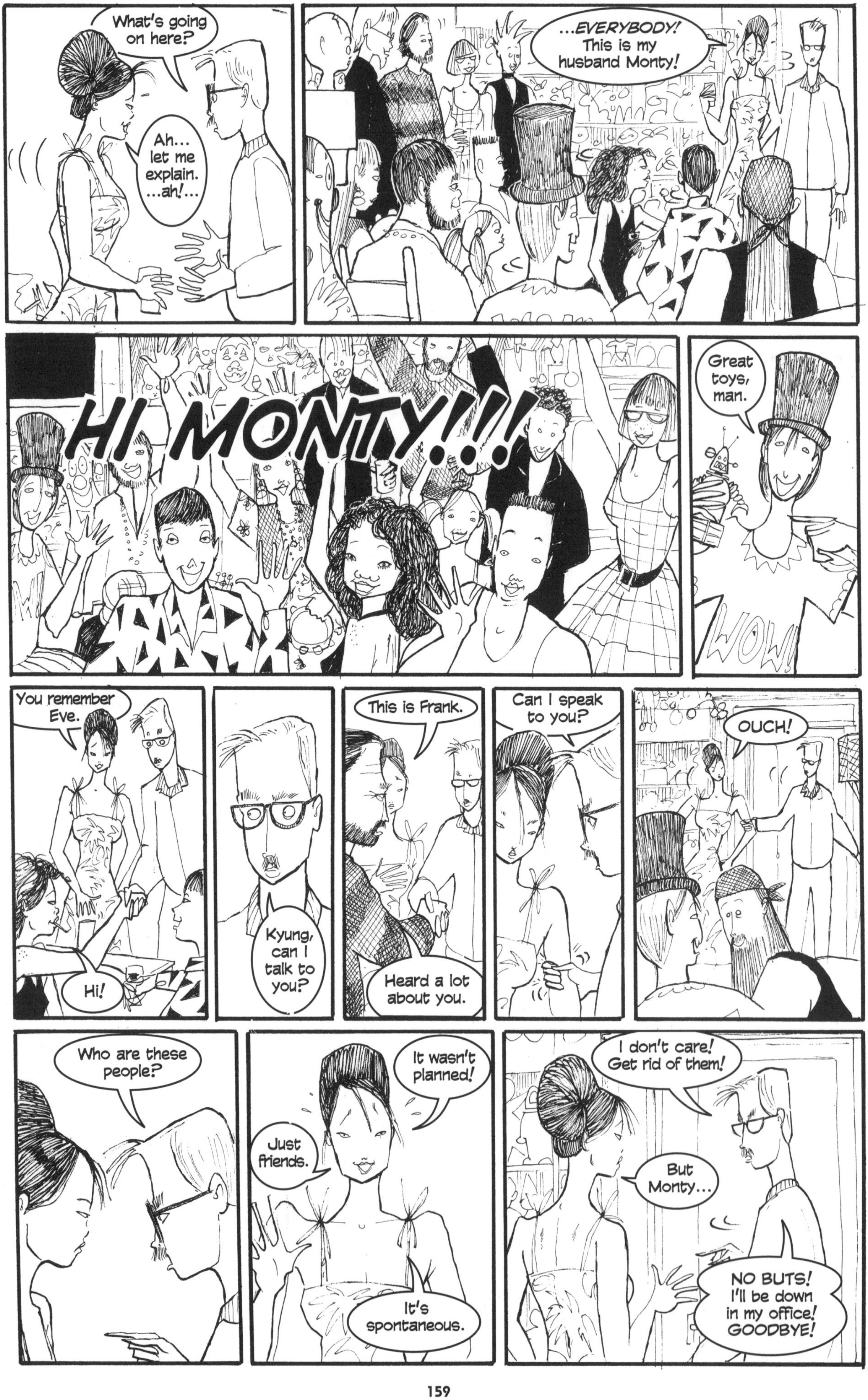
What's going on here?
Ah... let me explain. ...ah!...
...EVERYBODY! This is my husband Monty!
HI MONTY!!!!
Great toys, man.
WOW!
You remember Eve.
Hi!
Kyung, can I talk to you?
This is Frank.
Heard a lot about you.
Can I speak to you?
OUCH!
Who are these people?
It wasn't planned!
Just friends.
It's spontaneous.
I don't care! Get rid of them!
But Monty...
NO BUTS! I'll be down in my office! GOODBYE!

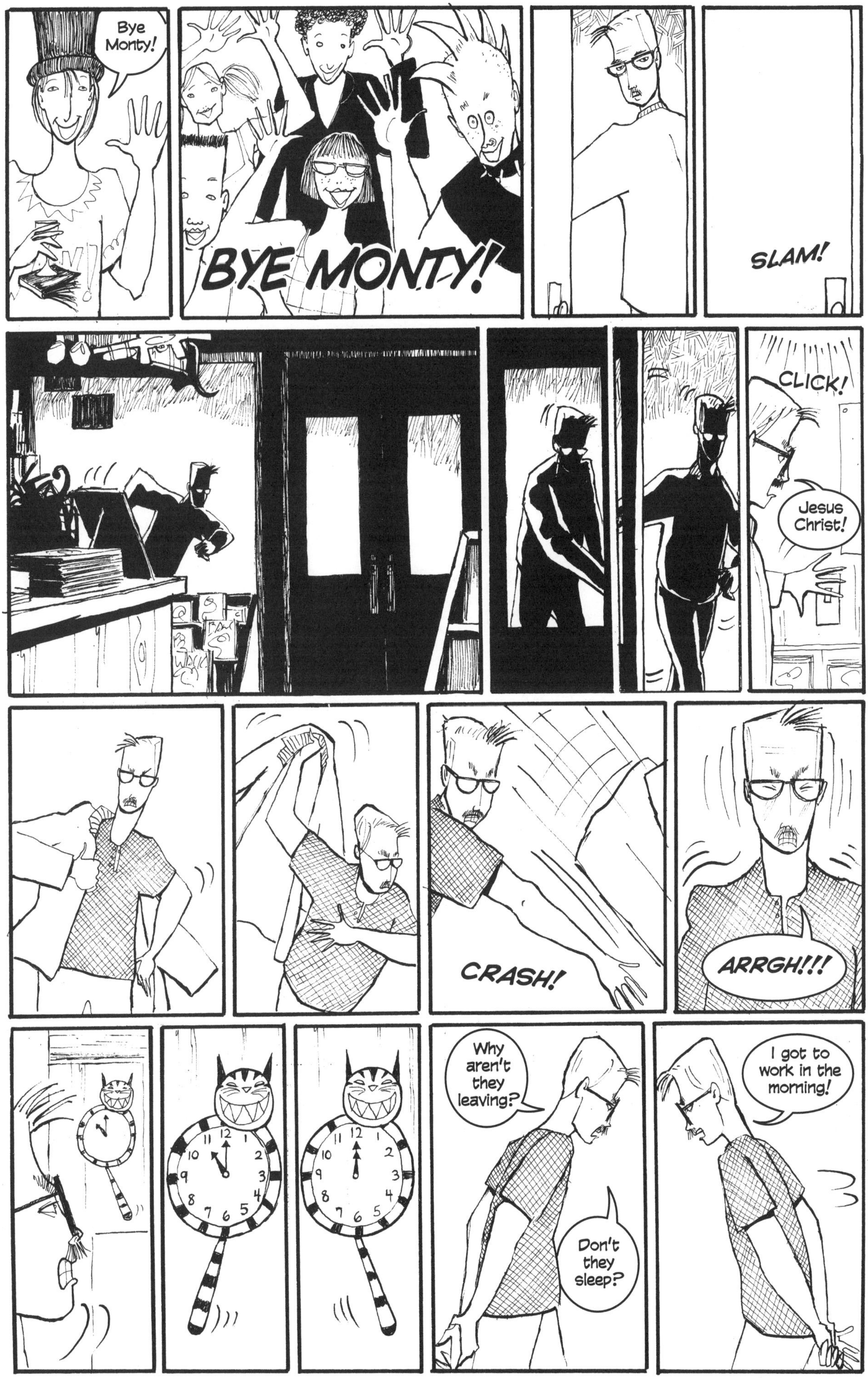
Bye Monty!
BYE MONTY!
SLAM!
CLICK!
Jesus Christ!
CRASH!
ARRGH!!!
Why aren't they leaving?
Don't they sleep?
I got to work in the morning!

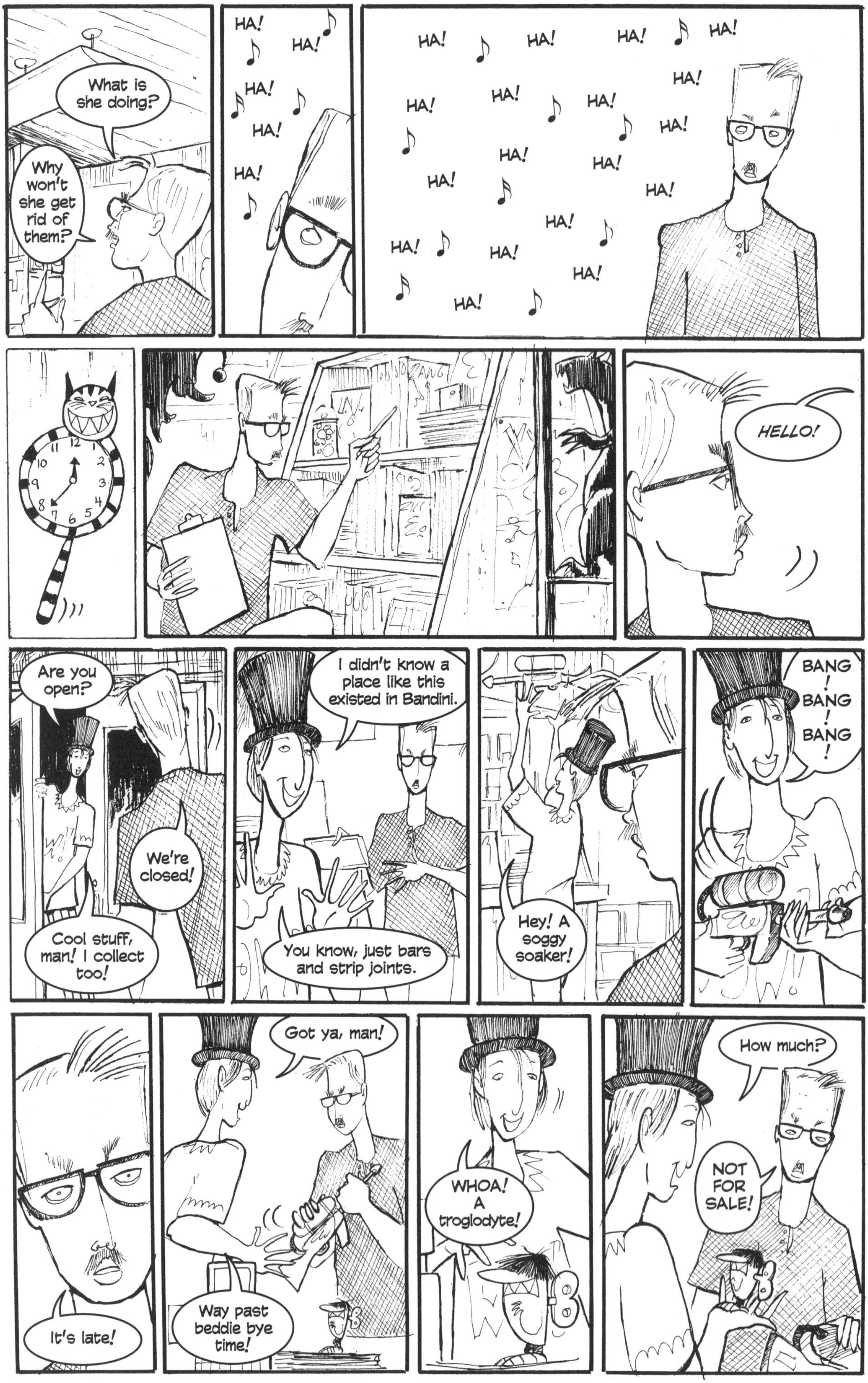

What is she doing?
Why won't she get rid of them?
HA! HA! HA! HA! HA! HA!
HA! HA! HA! HA! HA! HA! HA! HA! HA! HA! HA! HA! HA! HA! HA! HA! HA! HA!
HELLO!
Are you open?
We're closed!
Cool stuff, man! I collect too!
I didn't know a place like this existed in Bandini.
You know, just bars and strip joints.
Hey! A soggy soaker!
BANG! BANG! BANG!
It's late!
Got ya, man!
Way past beddie bye time!
WHOA! A troglodyte!
How much?
NOT FOR SALE!

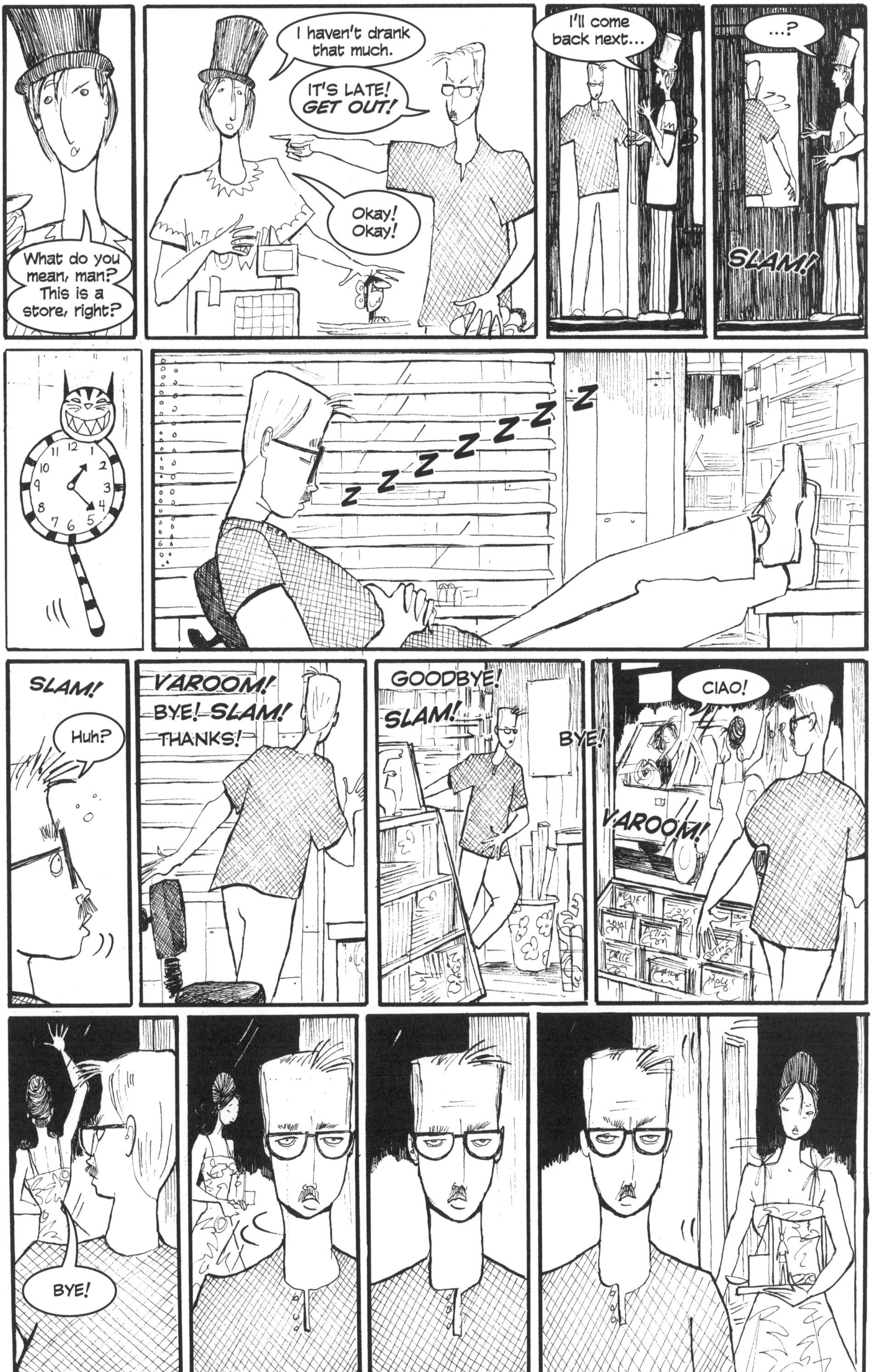
What do you mean, man? This is a store, right?
I haven't drank that much.
IT'S LATE! GET OUT!
Okay! Okay!
I'll come back next...
...?
SLAM!
Z Z Z Z Z Z Z Z
SLAM!
Huh?
VAROOM!
BYE! SLAM!
THANKS!
GOODBYE!
SLAM!
CIAO!
BYE!
VAROOM!
BYE!

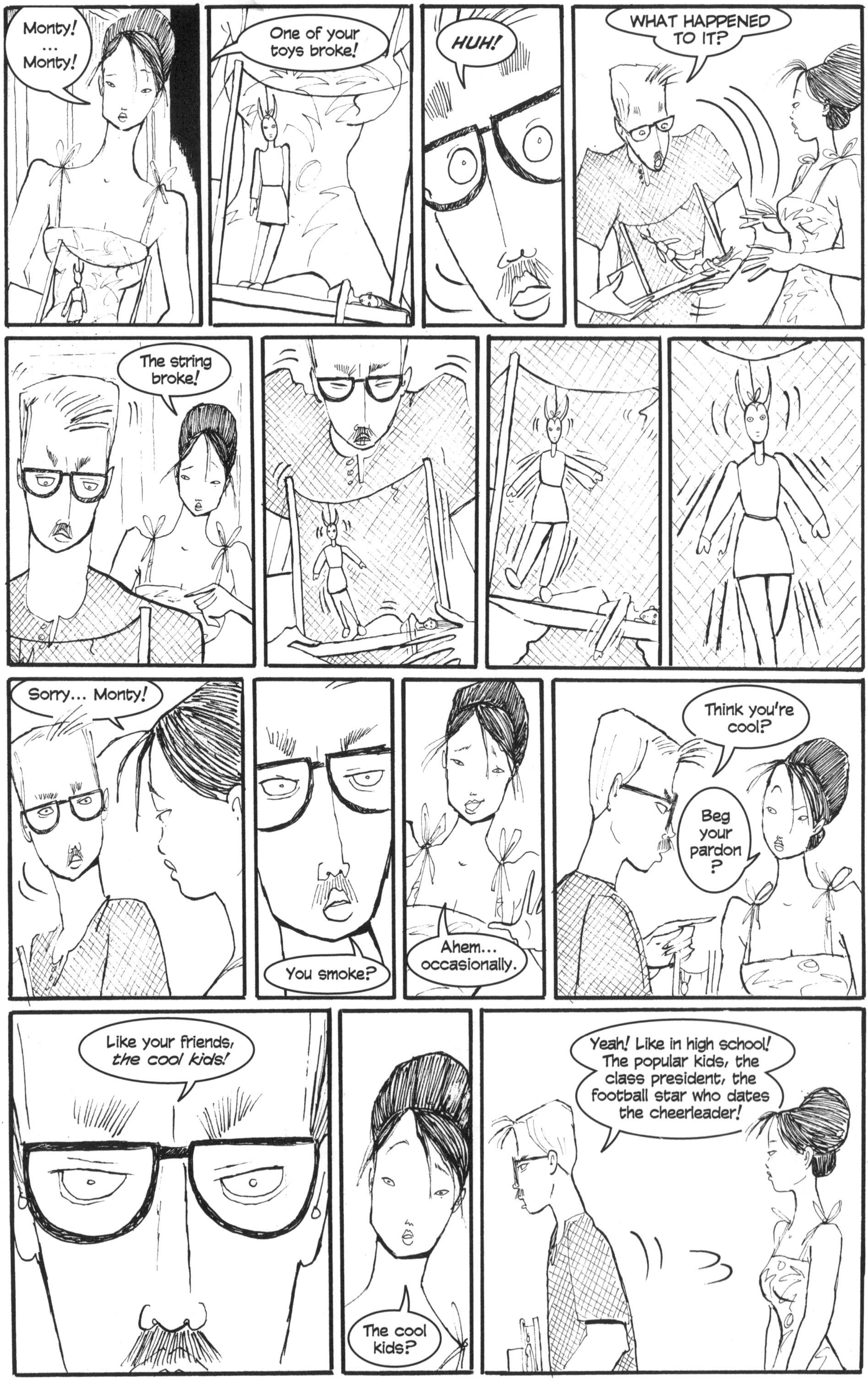
Monty! ... Monty!
One of your toys broke!
HUH!
WHAT HAPPENED TO IT?
The string broke!
Sorry... Monty!
You smoke?
Ahem... occasionally.
Think you're cool?
Beg your pardon ?
Like your friends, *the cool kids!*
The cool kids?
Yeah! Like in high school! The popular kids, the class president, the football star who dates the cheerleader!

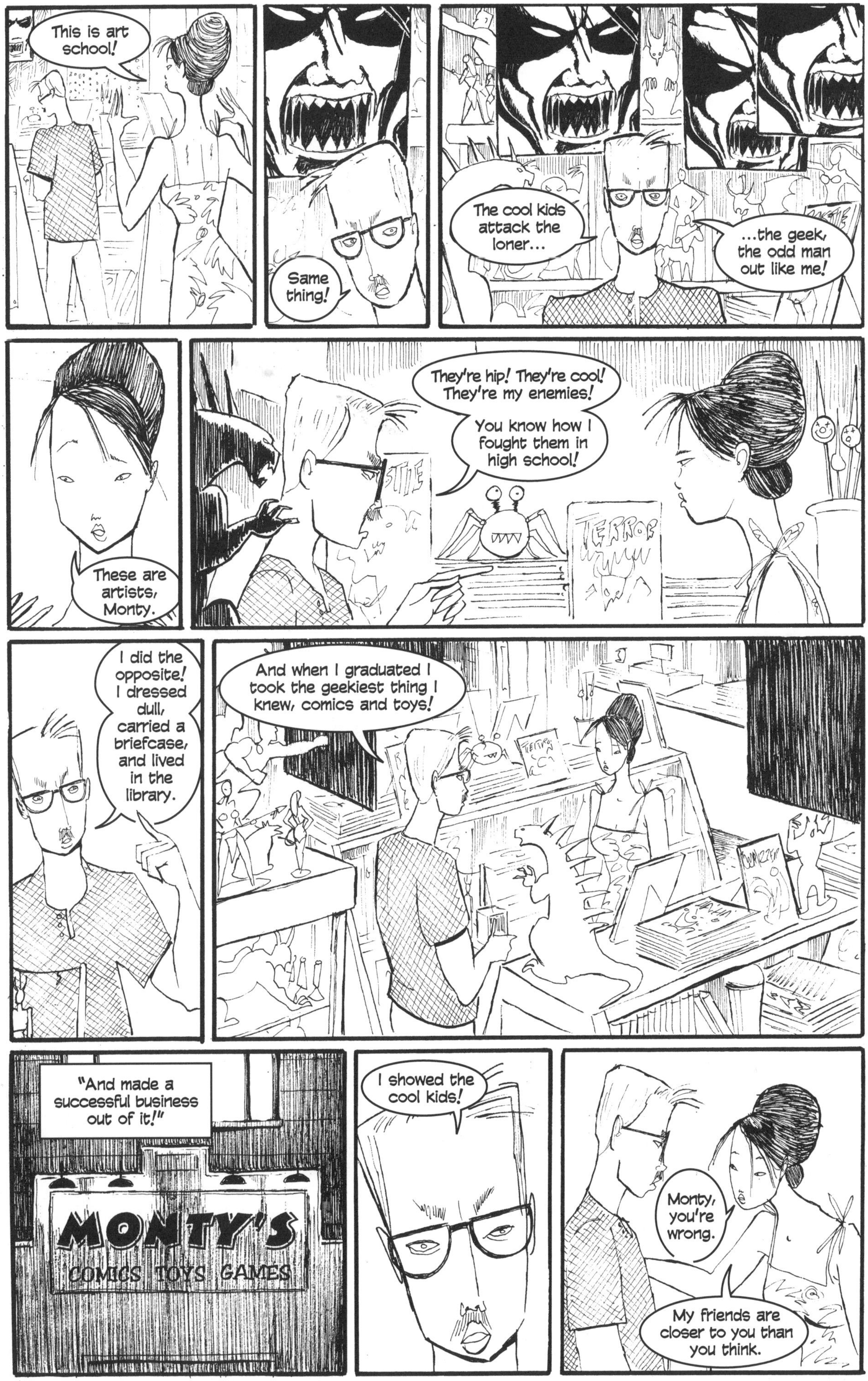
This is art school!
Same thing!
The cool kids attack the loner...
...the geek, the odd man out like me!
These are artists, Monty.
They're hip! They're cool! They're my enemies!
You know how I fought them in high school!
TERROR
I did the opposite! I dressed dull, carried a briefcase, and lived in the library.
And when I graduated I took the geekiest thing I knew, comics and toys!
"And made a successful business out of it!"
MONTY'S
COMICS TOYS GAMES
I showed the cool kids!
Monty, you're wrong.
My friends are closer to you than you think.

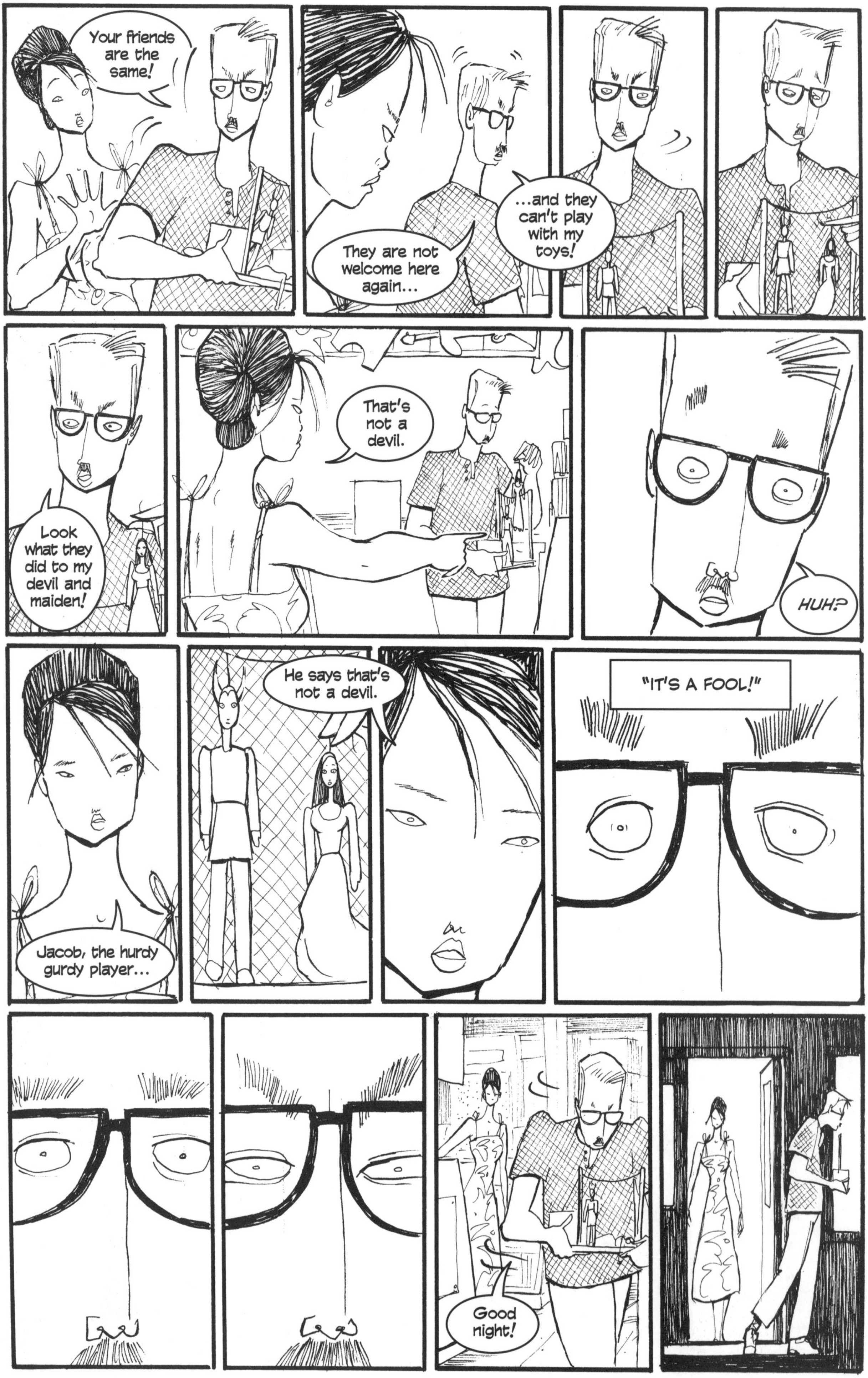
Your friends are the same!
They are not welcome here again...
...and they can't play with my toys!
Look what they did to my devil and maiden!
That's not a devil.
HUH?
Jacob, the hurdy gurdy player...
He says that's not a devil.
"IT'S A FOOL!"
Good night!

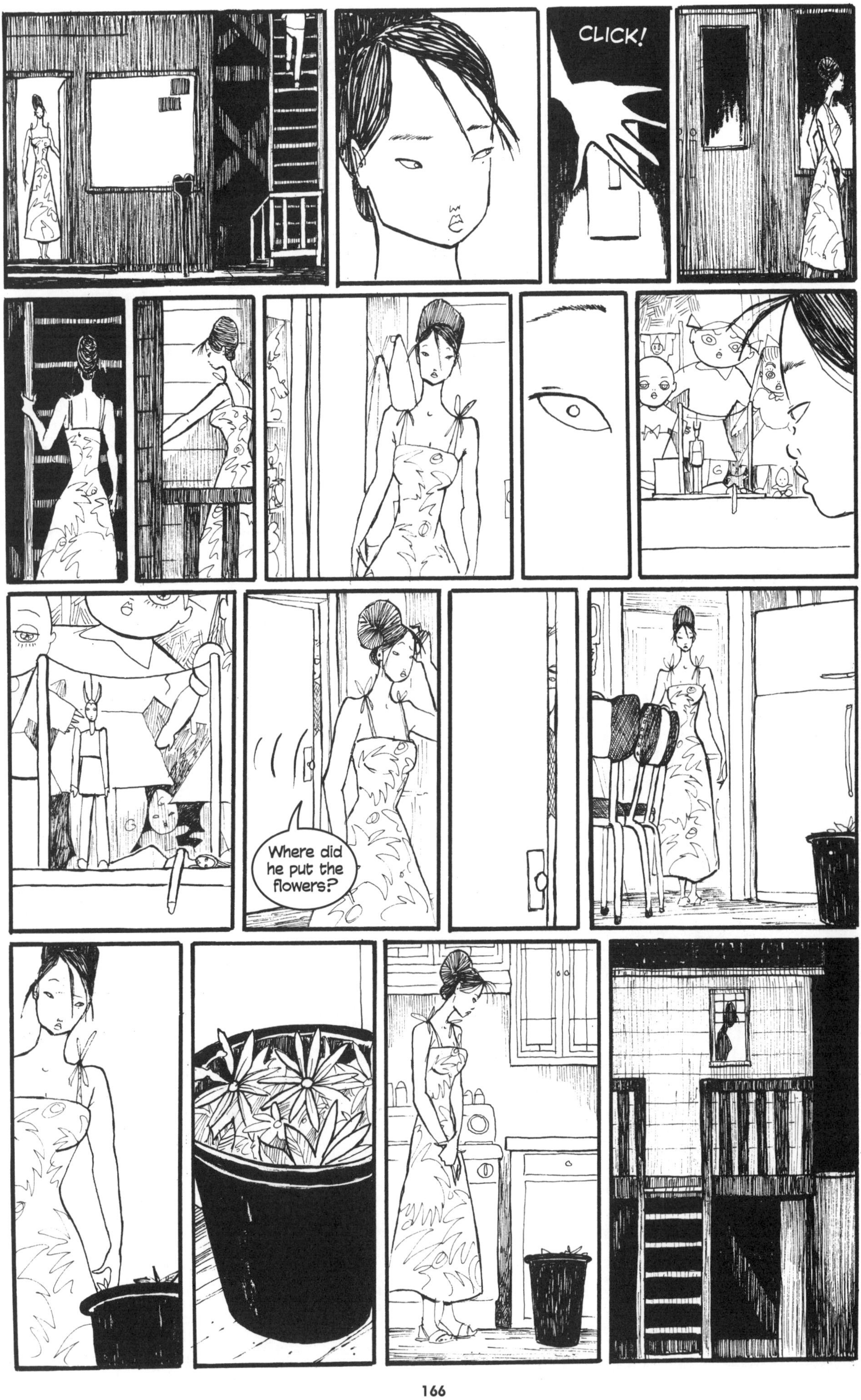
CLICK!
Where did he put the flowers?

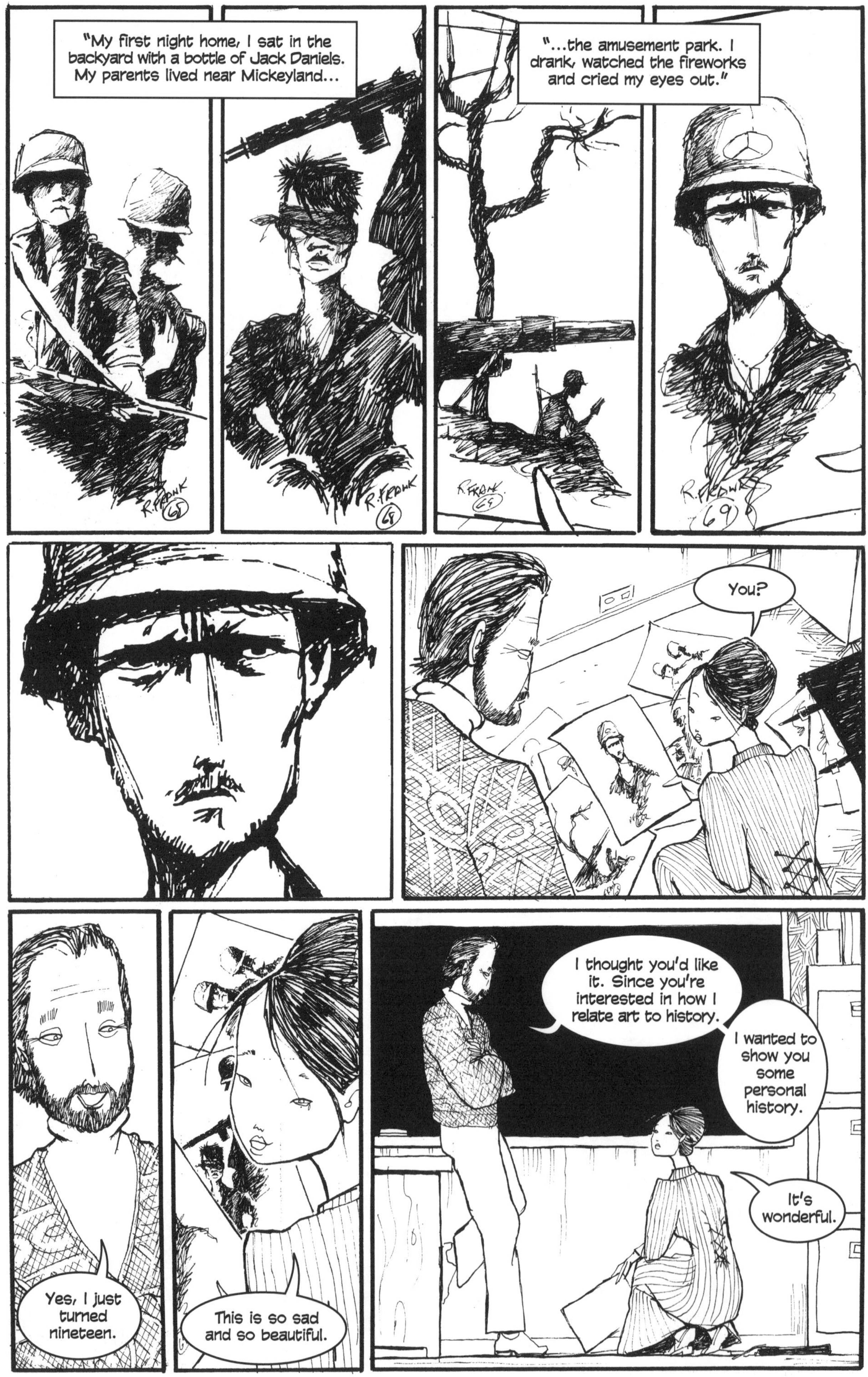
"My first night home, I sat in the backyard with a bottle of Jack Daniels. My parents lived near Mickeyland...
R. FRANK 68
R. FRANK 68
"...the amusement park. I drank, watched the fireworks and cried my eyes out."
R. FRANK 69
R. FRANK 69
You?
Yes, I just turned nineteen.
This is so sad and so beautiful.
I thought you'd like it. Since you're interested in how I relate art to history.
I wanted to show you some personal history.
It's wonderful.

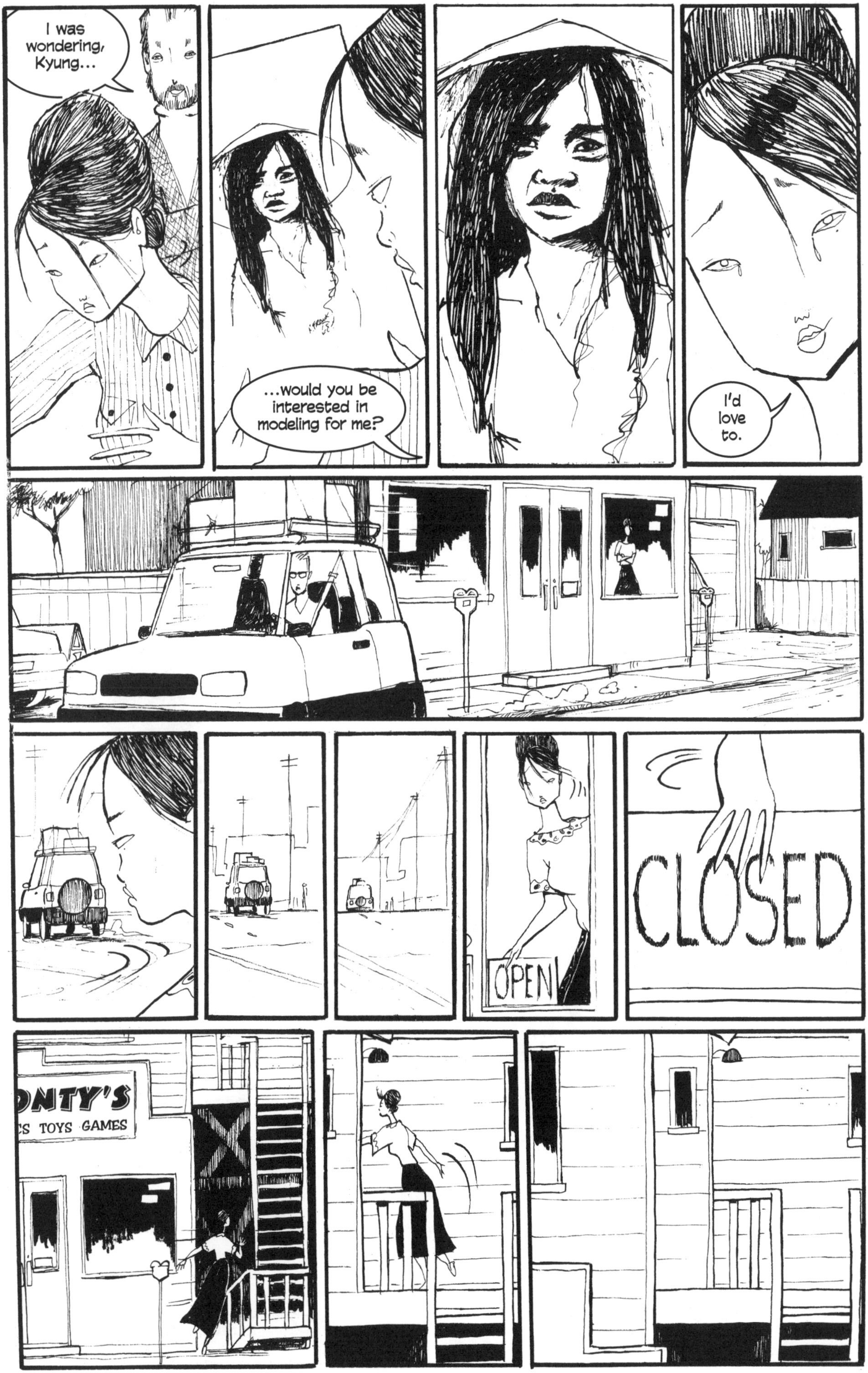
I was wondering, Kyung...
...would you be interested in modeling for me?
I'd love to.
OPEN
CLOSED
ONTY'S
CS TOYS GAMES

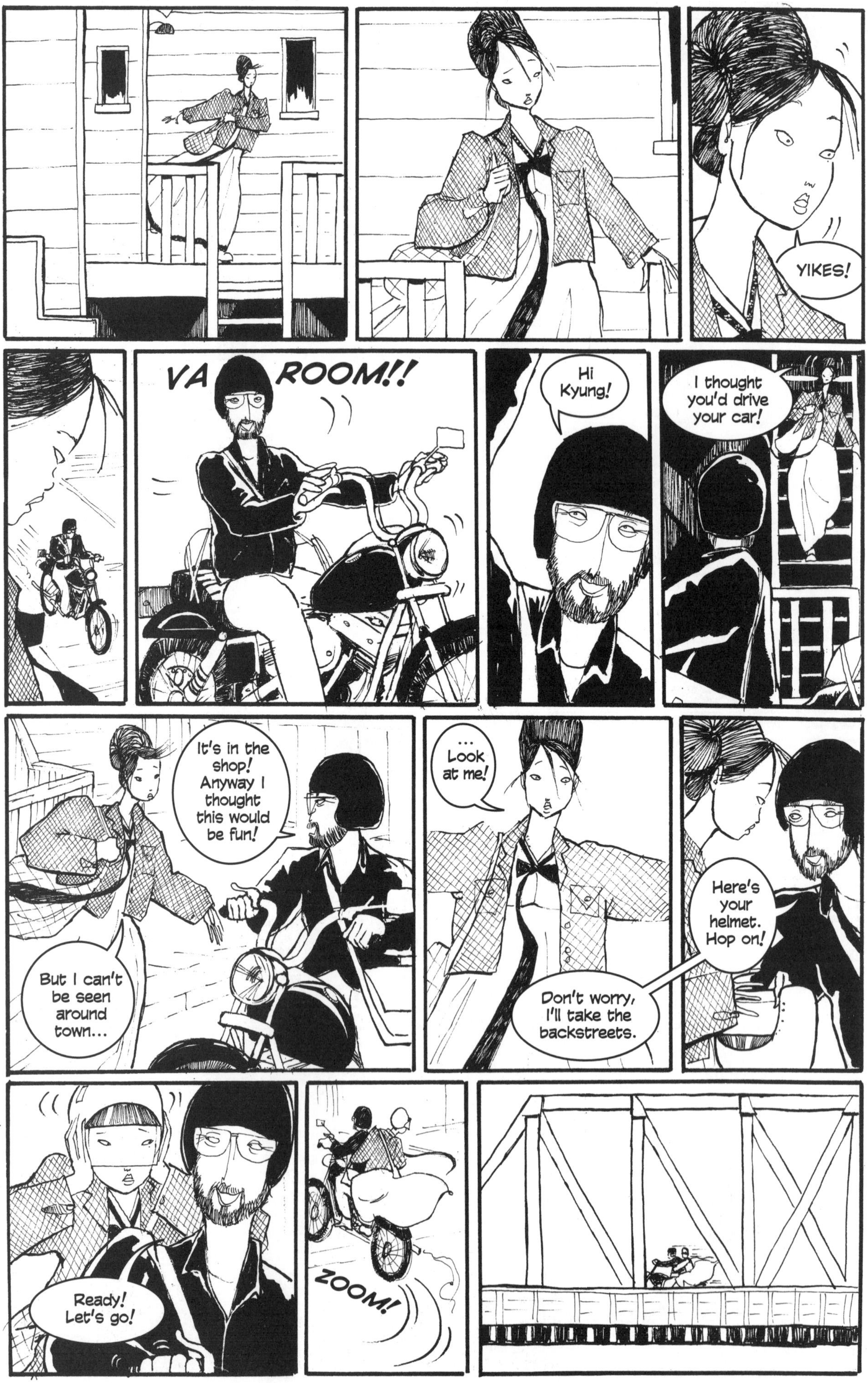
YIKES!
VA ROOM!!
Hi Kyung!
I thought you'd drive your car!
It's in the shop! Anyway I thought this would be fun!
But I can't be seen around town...
... Look at me!
Don't worry, I'll take the backstreets.
Here's your helmet. Hop on!
Ready! Let's go!
ZOOM!

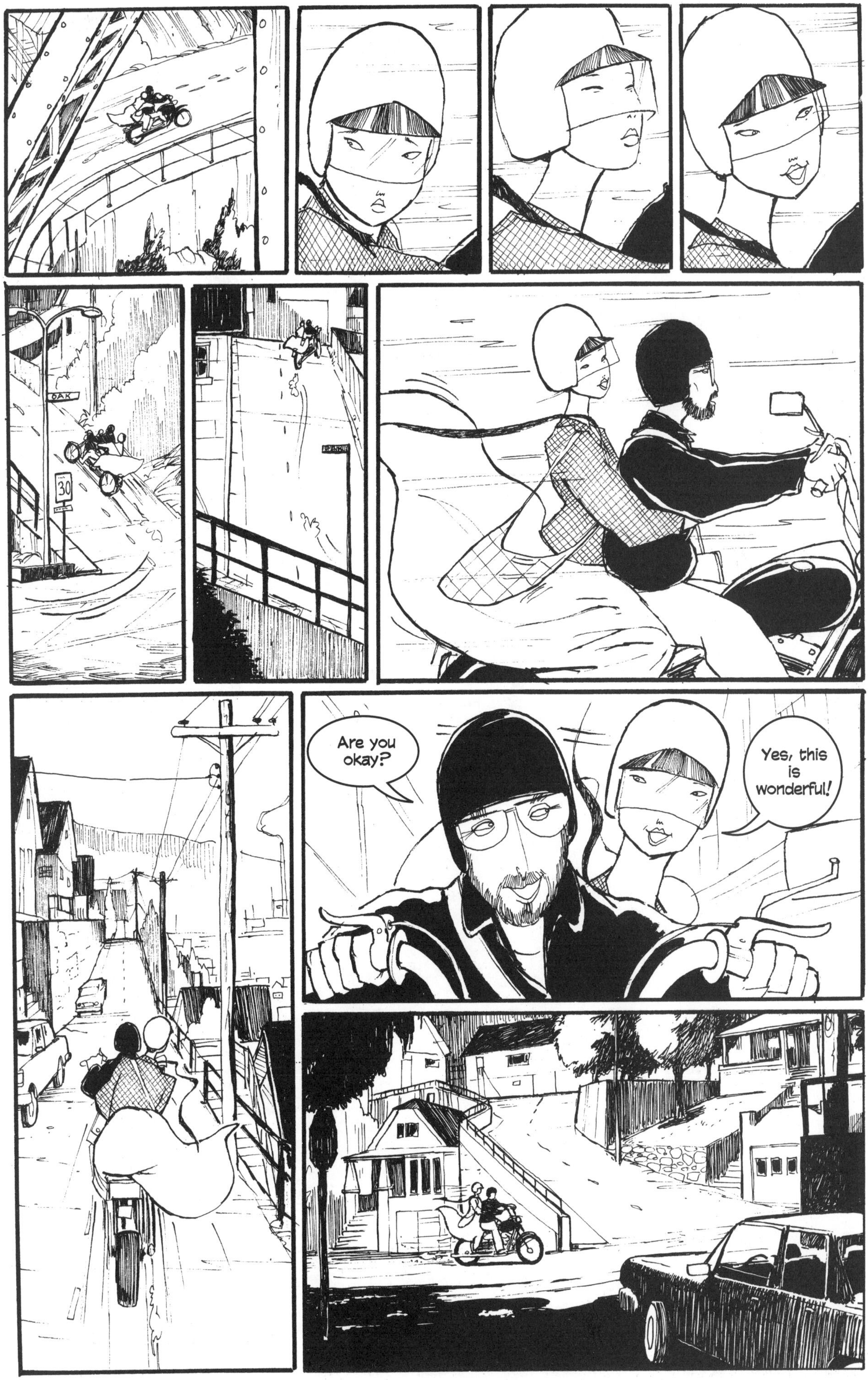
OAK
30
Are you okay?
Yes, this is wonderful!

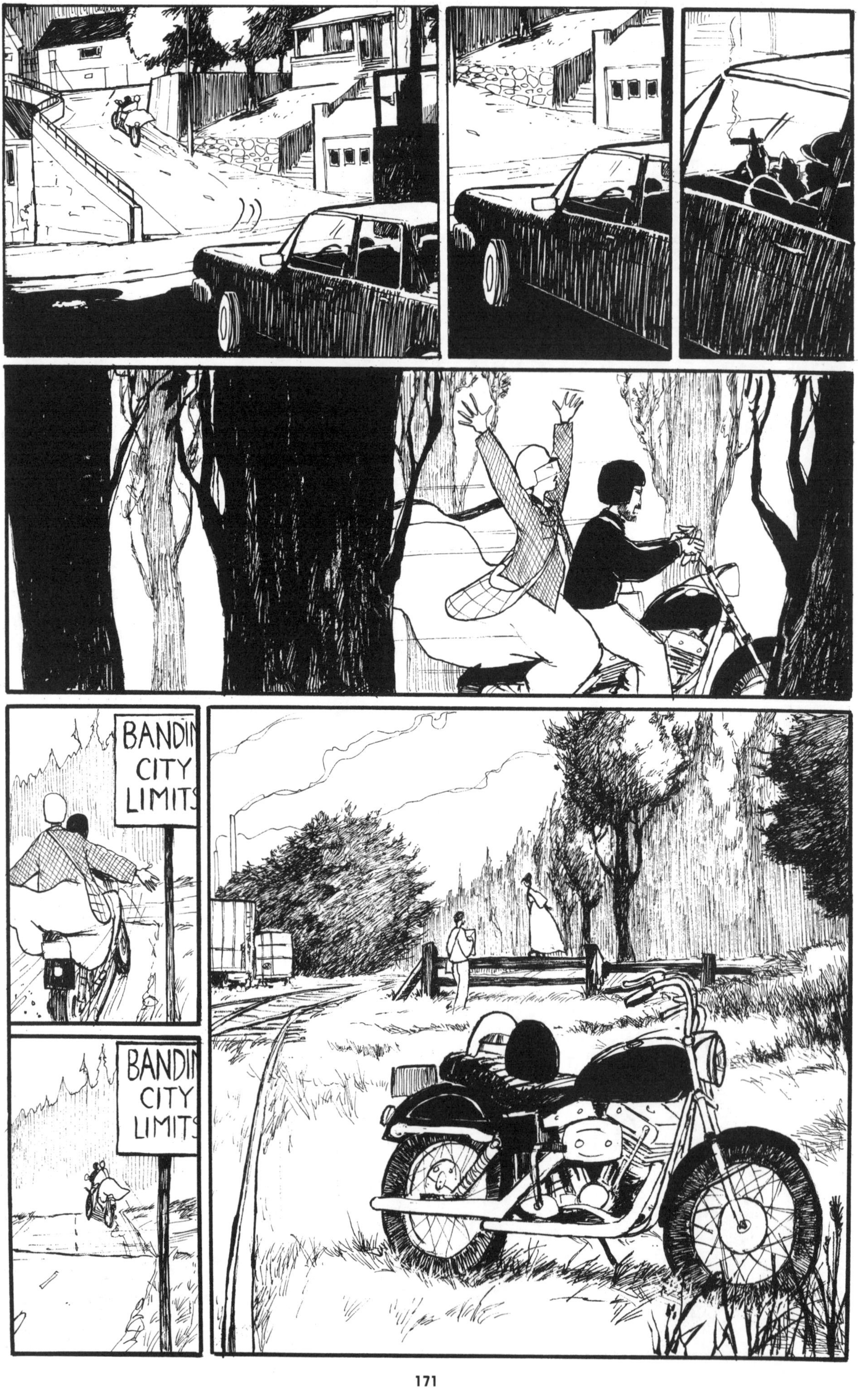
BANDIN
CITY
LIMITS
BANDIN
CITY
LIMITS

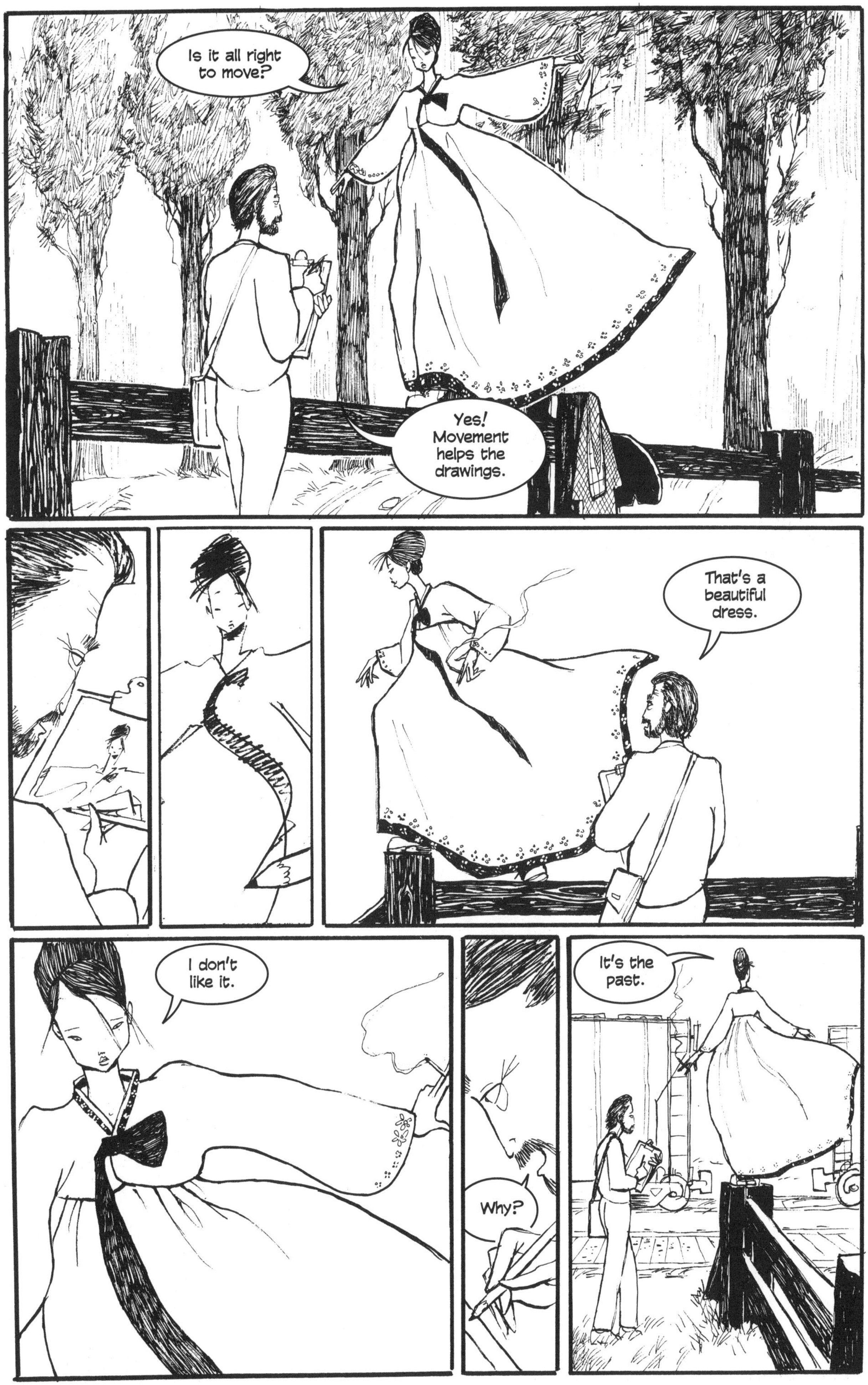
Is it all right to move?
Yes! Movement helps the drawings.
That's a beautiful dress.
I don't like it.
Why?
It's the past.

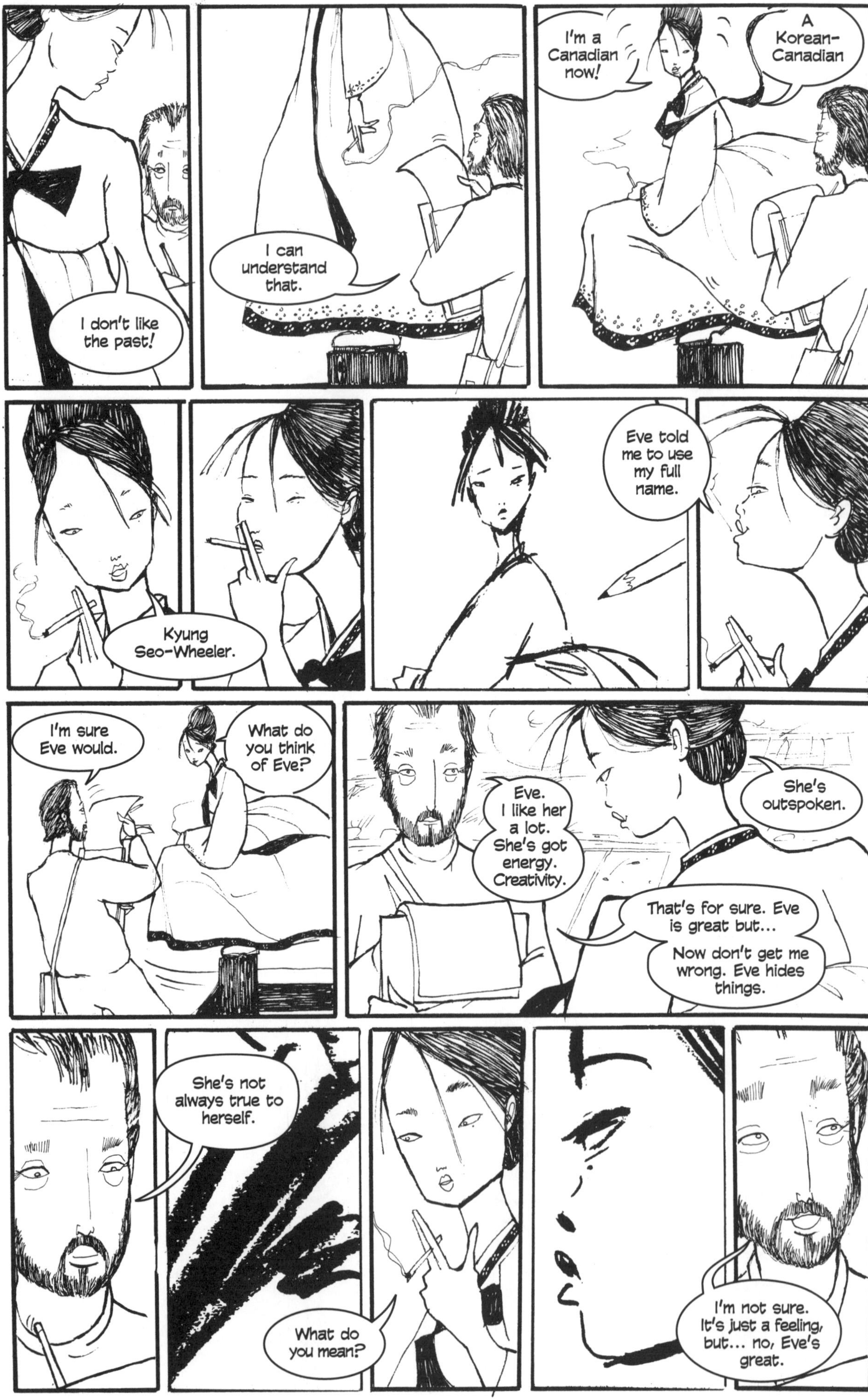
I don't like the past!
I can understand that.
I'm a Canadian now!
A Korean-Canadian
Kyung Seo-Wheeler.
Eve told me to use my full name.
I'm sure Eve would.
What do you think of Eve?
Eve. I like her a lot. She's got energy. Creativity.
She's outspoken.
That's for sure. Eve is great but...
Now don't get me wrong. Eve hides things.
She's not always true to herself.
What do you mean?
I'm not sure. It's just a feeling, but... no, Eve's great.

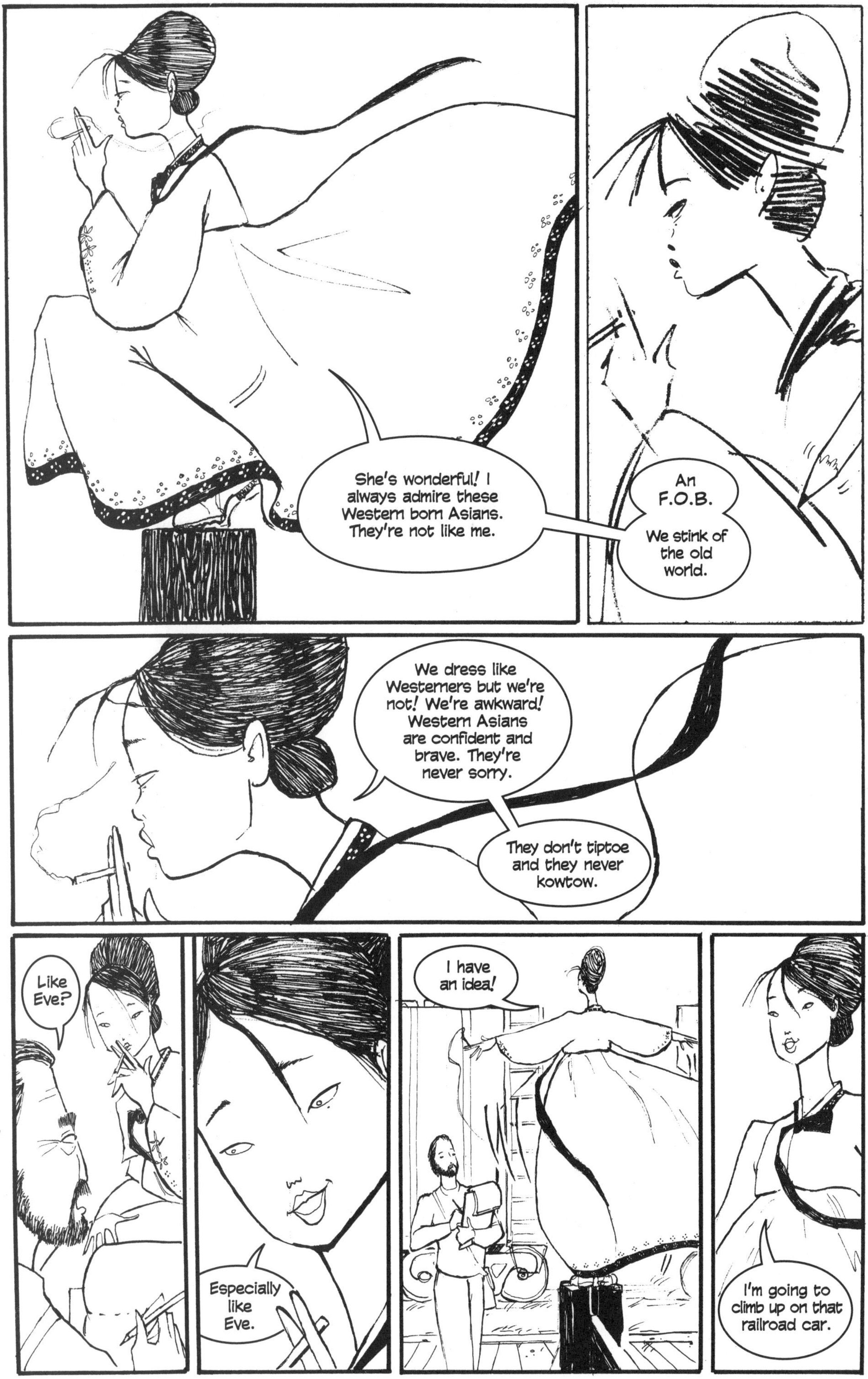
She's wonderful! I always admire these Western born Asians. They're not like me.
An F.O.B.
We stink of the old world.
We dress like Westerners but we're not! We're awkward! Western Asians are confident and brave. They're never sorry.
They don't tiptoe and they never kowtow.
Like Eve?
Especially like Eve.
I have an idea!
I'm going to climb up on that railroad car.

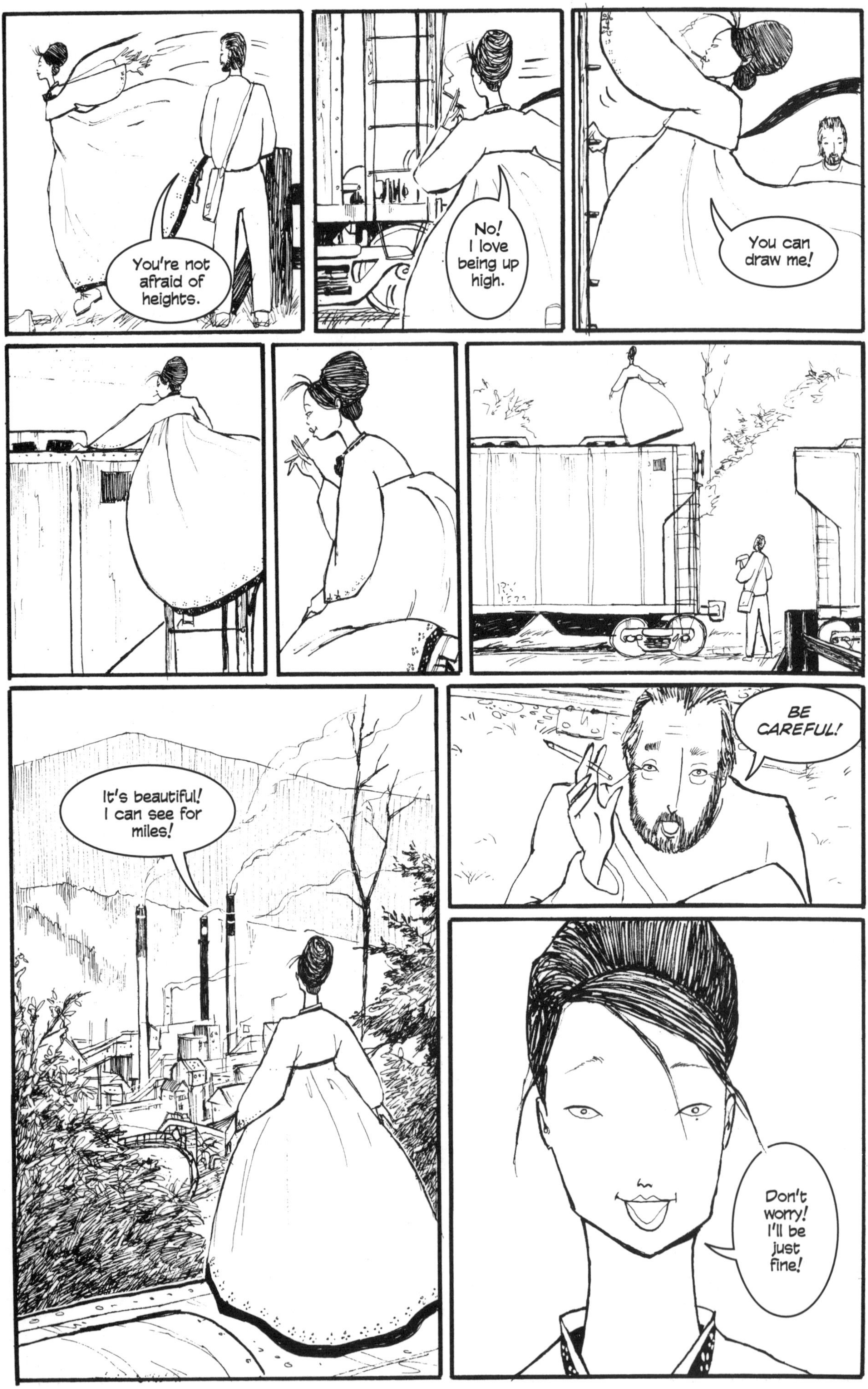
You're not afraid of heights.
No! I love being up high.
You can draw me!
It's beautiful! I can see for miles!
BE CAREFUL!
Don't worry! I'll be just fine!

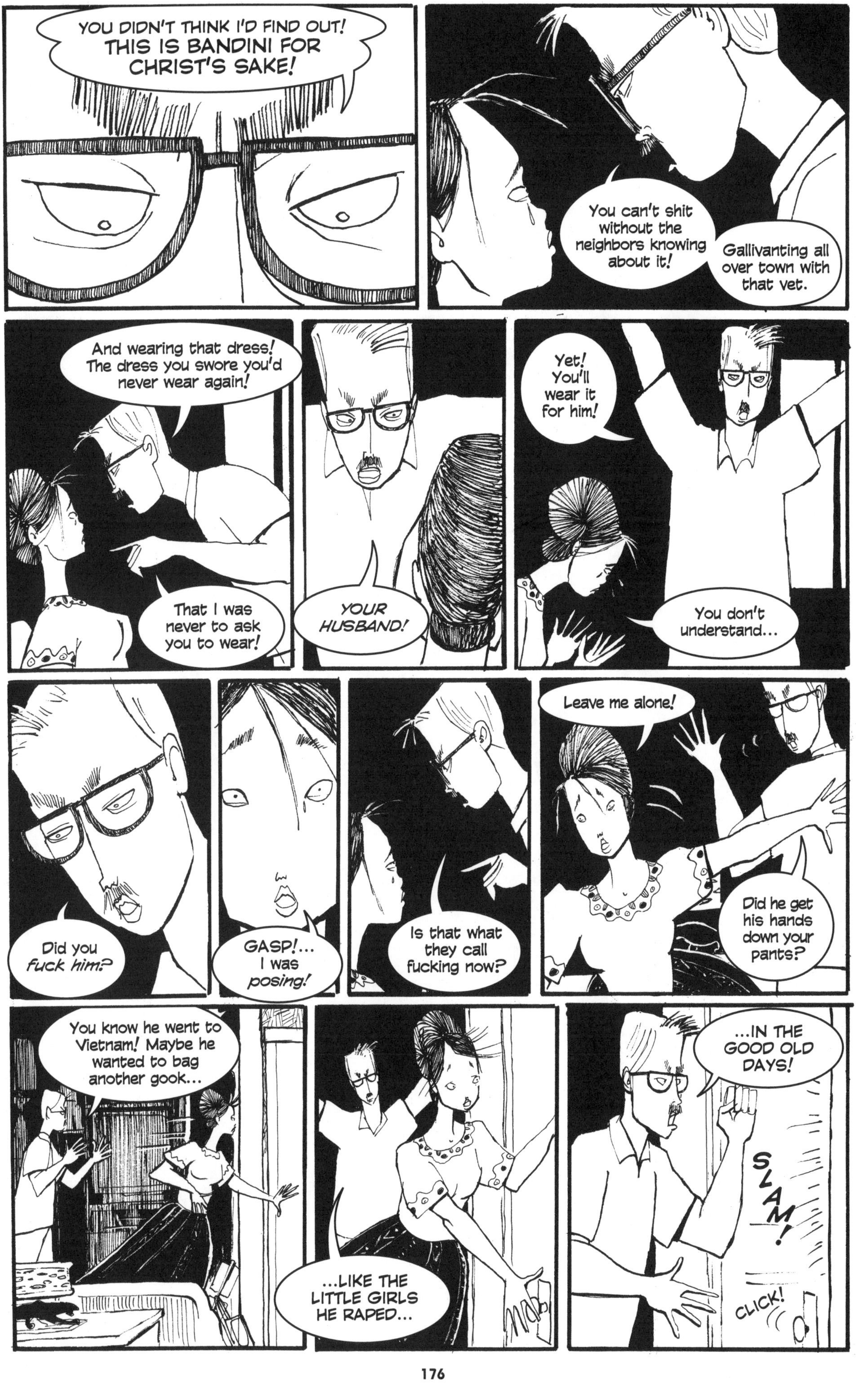

YOU DIDN'T THINK I'D FIND OUT! THIS IS BANDINI FOR CHRIST'S SAKE!
You can't shit without the neighbors knowing about it!
Gallivanting all over town with that vet.
And wearing that dress! The dress you swore you'd never wear again!
That I was never to ask you to wear!
YOUR HUSBAND!
Yet! You'll wear it for him!
You don't understand...
Did you fuck him?
GASP!... I was posing!
Is that what they call fucking now?
Leave me alone!
Did he get his hands down your pants?
You know he went to Vietnam! Maybe he wanted to bag another gook...
...LIKE THE LITTLE GIRLS HE RAPED...
...IN THE GOOD OLD DAYS!
SLAM!
CLICK!

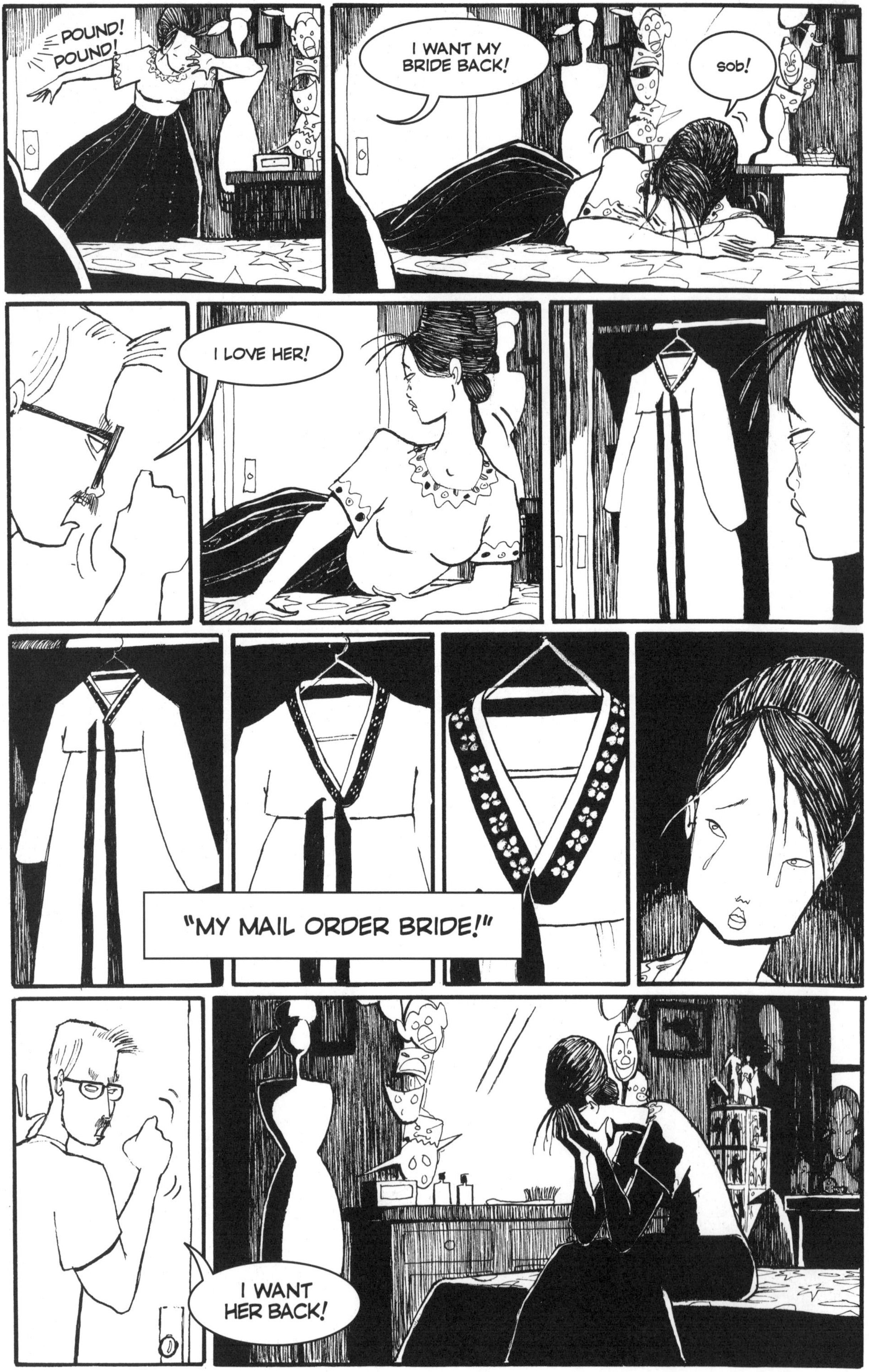
POUND! POUND!
I WANT MY BRIDE BACK!
sob!
I LOVE HER!
"MY MAIL ORDER BRIDE!"
I WANT HER BACK!

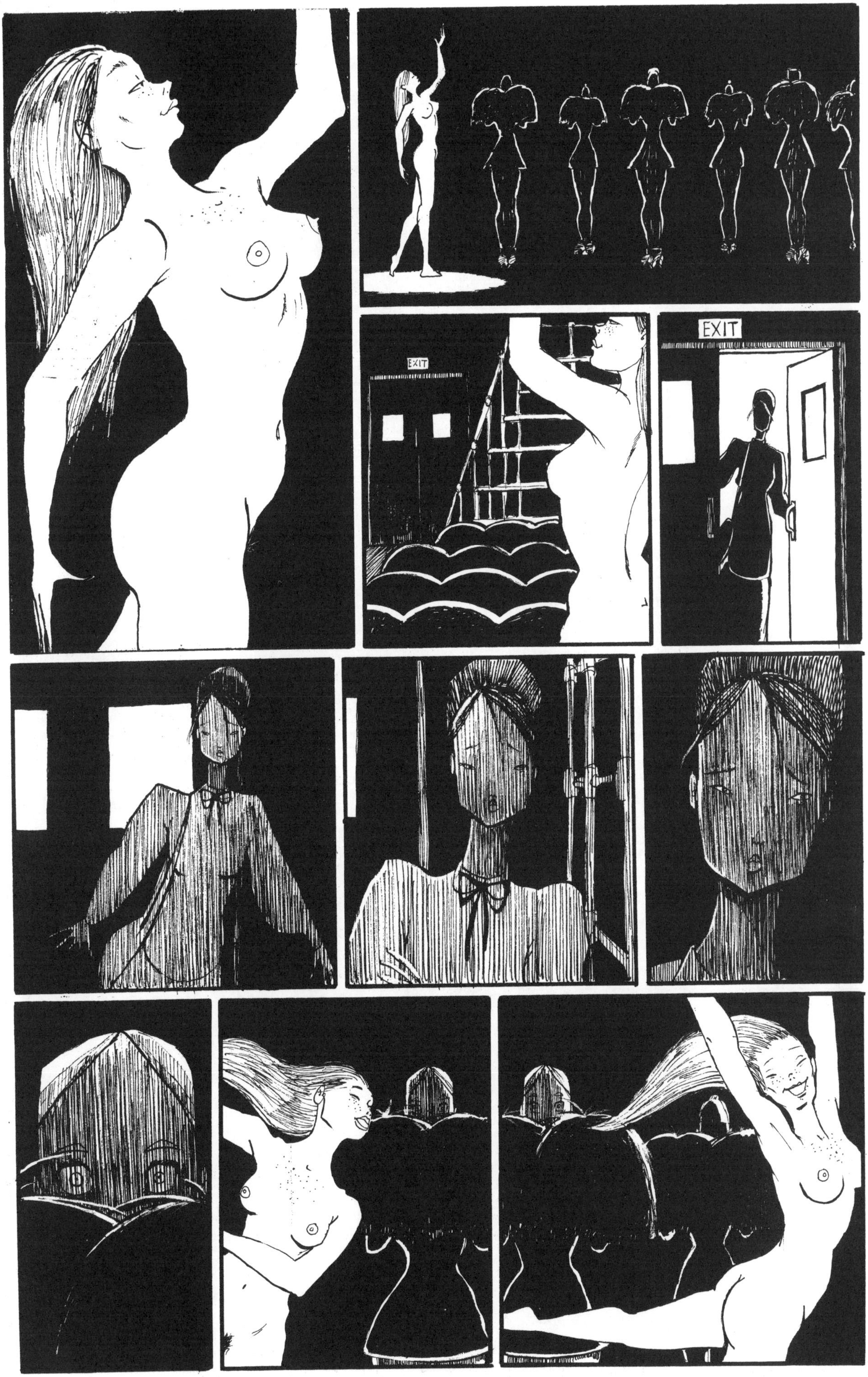
EXIT
EXIT

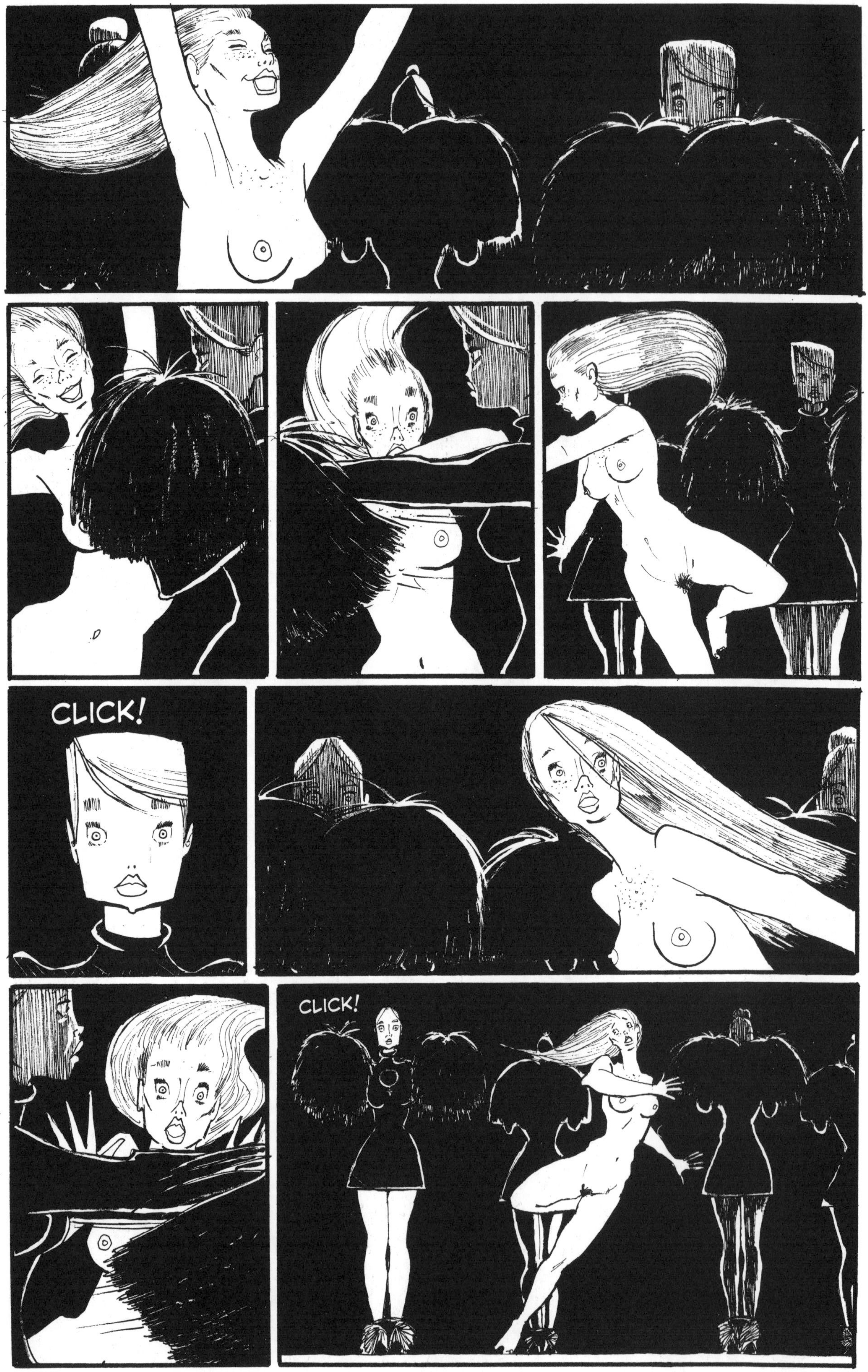
CLICK!
CLICK!

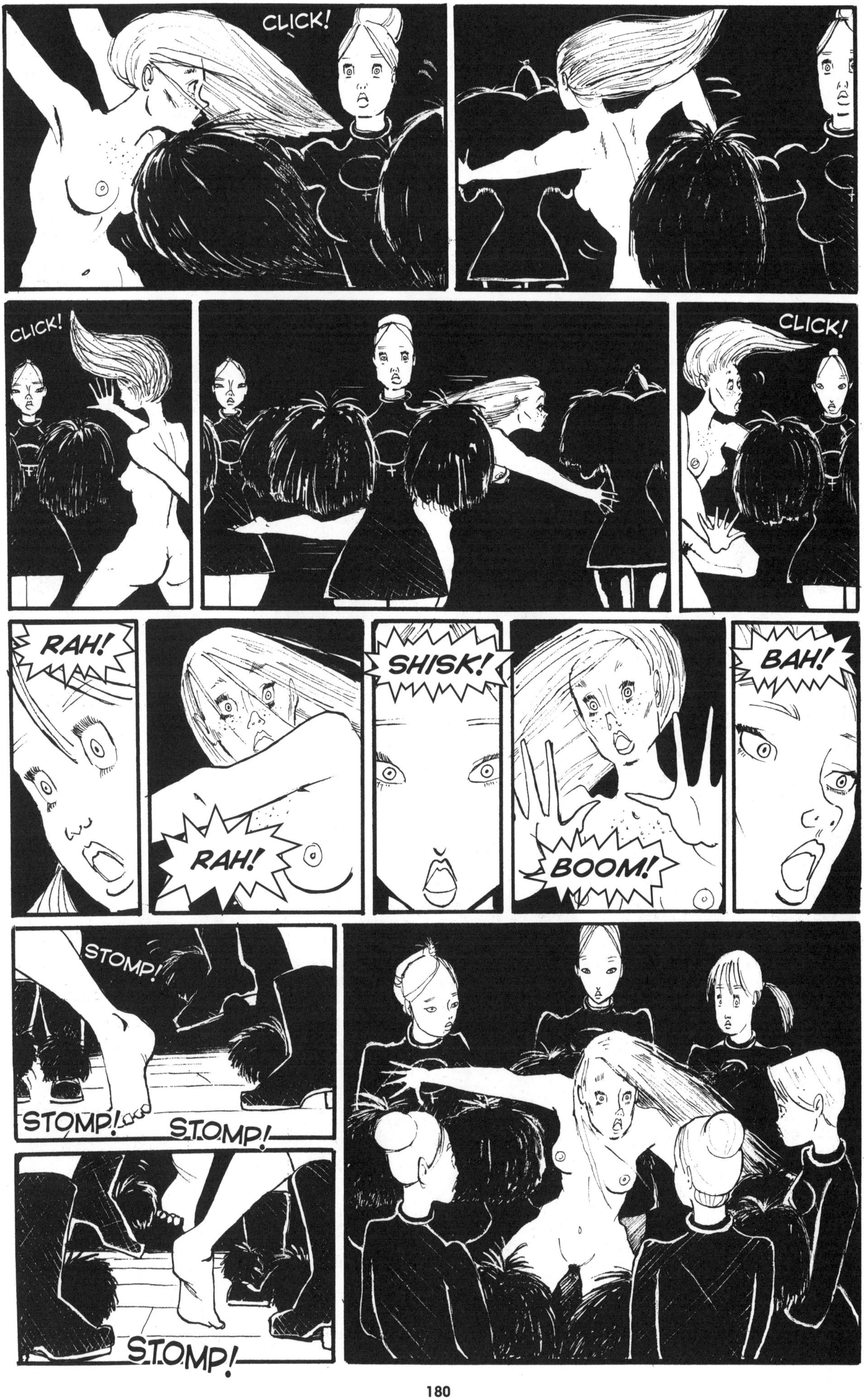
CLICK!
CLICK!
CLICK!
RAH!
RAH!
SHISK!
BOOM!
BAH!
STOMP!
STOMP!
STOMP!
STOMP!

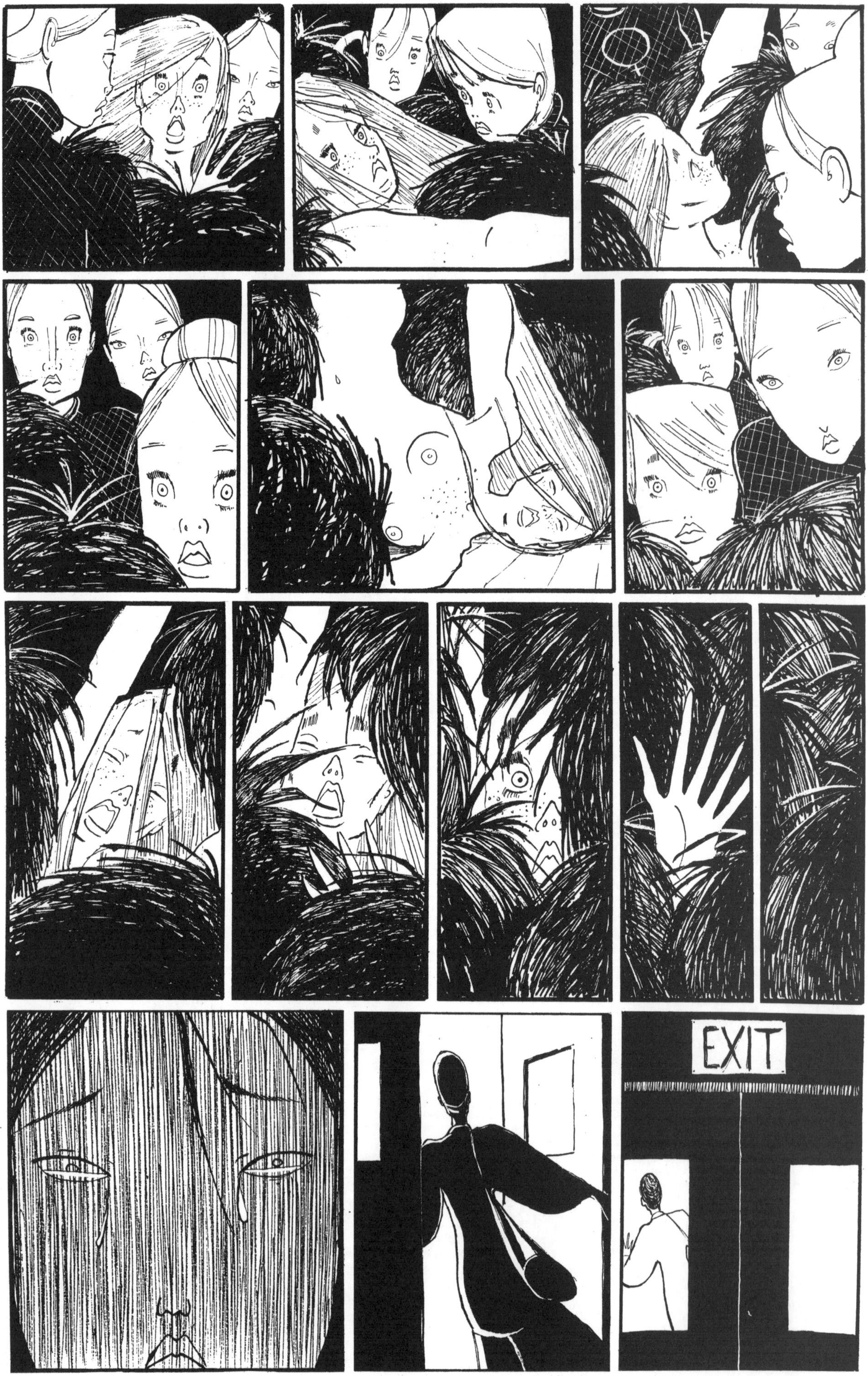
EXIT

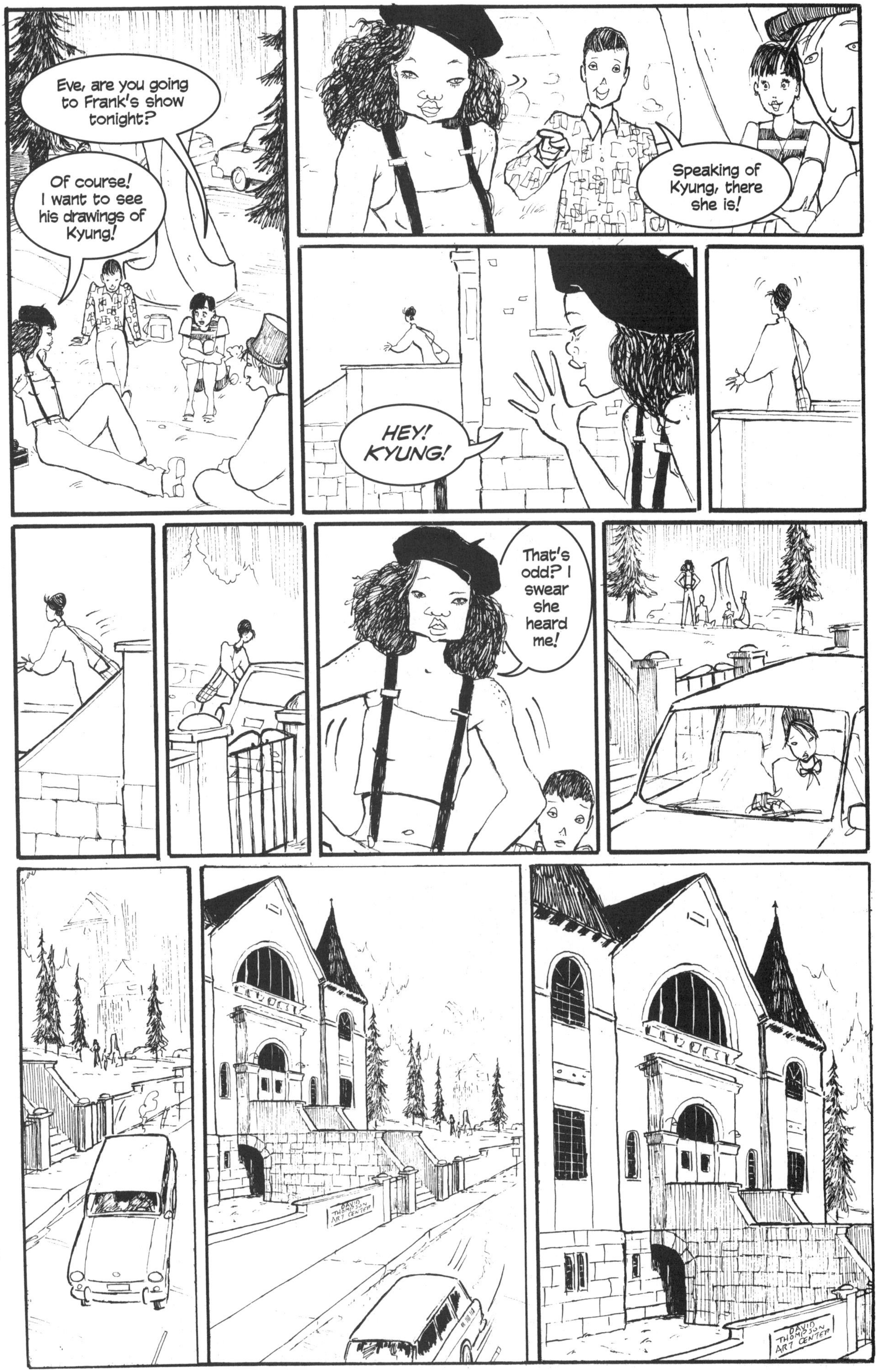
Eve, are you going to Frank's show tonight?
Of course! I want to see his drawings of Kyung!
Speaking of Kyung, there she is!
HEY! KYUNG!
That's odd? I swear she heard me!
DAVID THOMPSON ART CENTER
DAVID THOMPSON ART CENTER

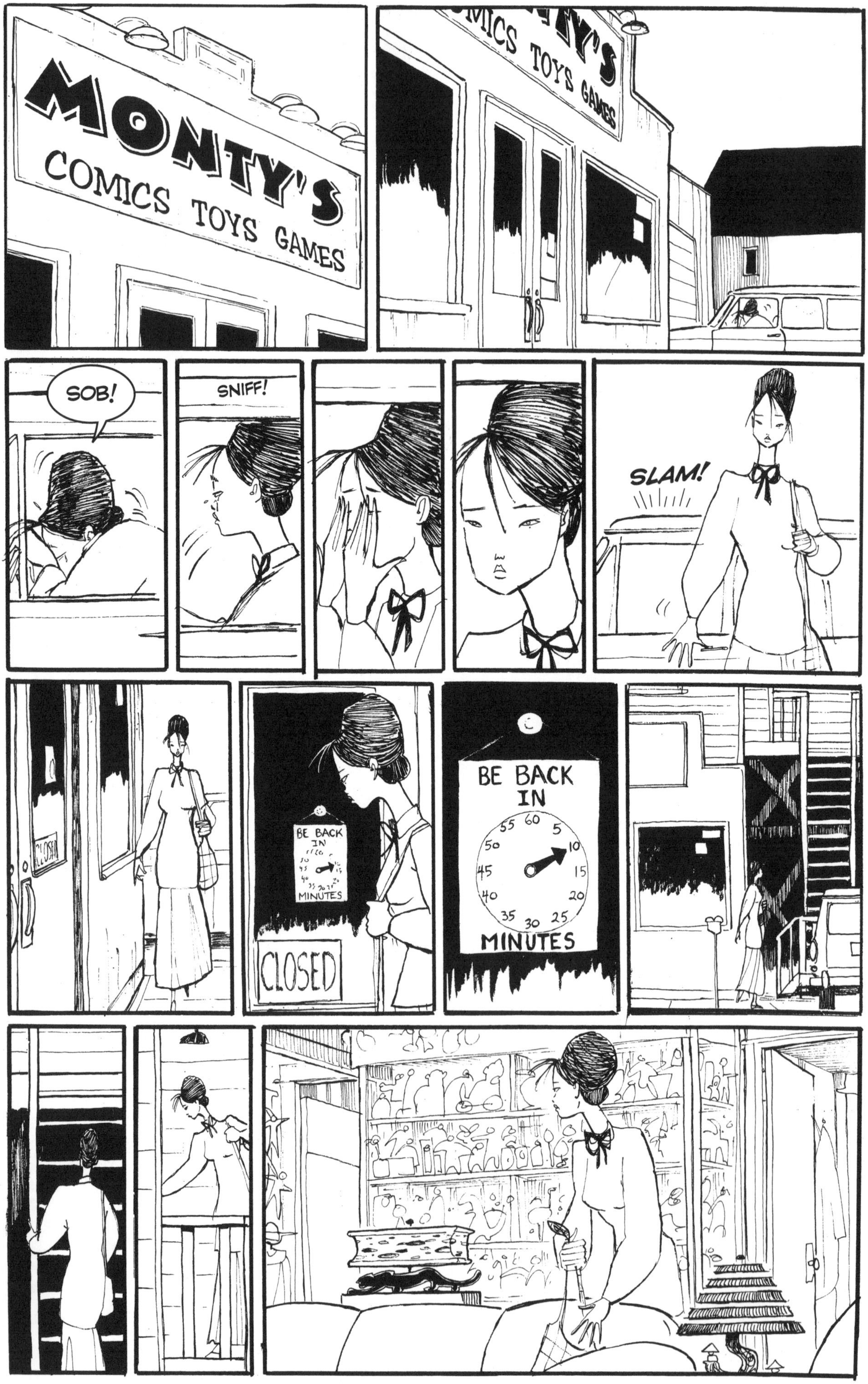
MONTY'S
COMICS TOYS GAMES
SOB!
SNIFF!
SLAM!
CLOSED
BE BACK IN
MINUTES
CLOSED

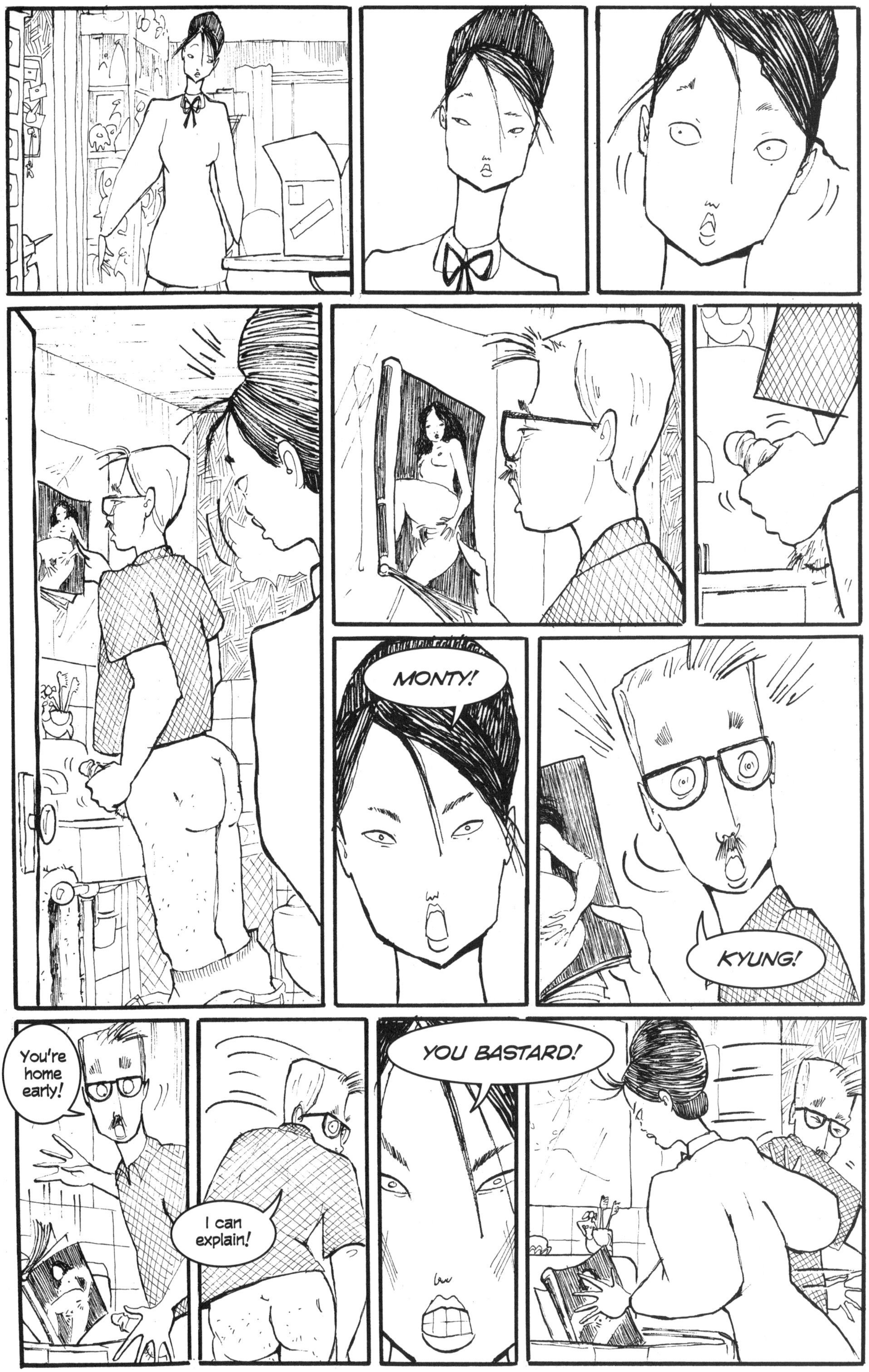
MONTY!
KYUNG!
You're home early!
I can explain!
YOU BASTARD!

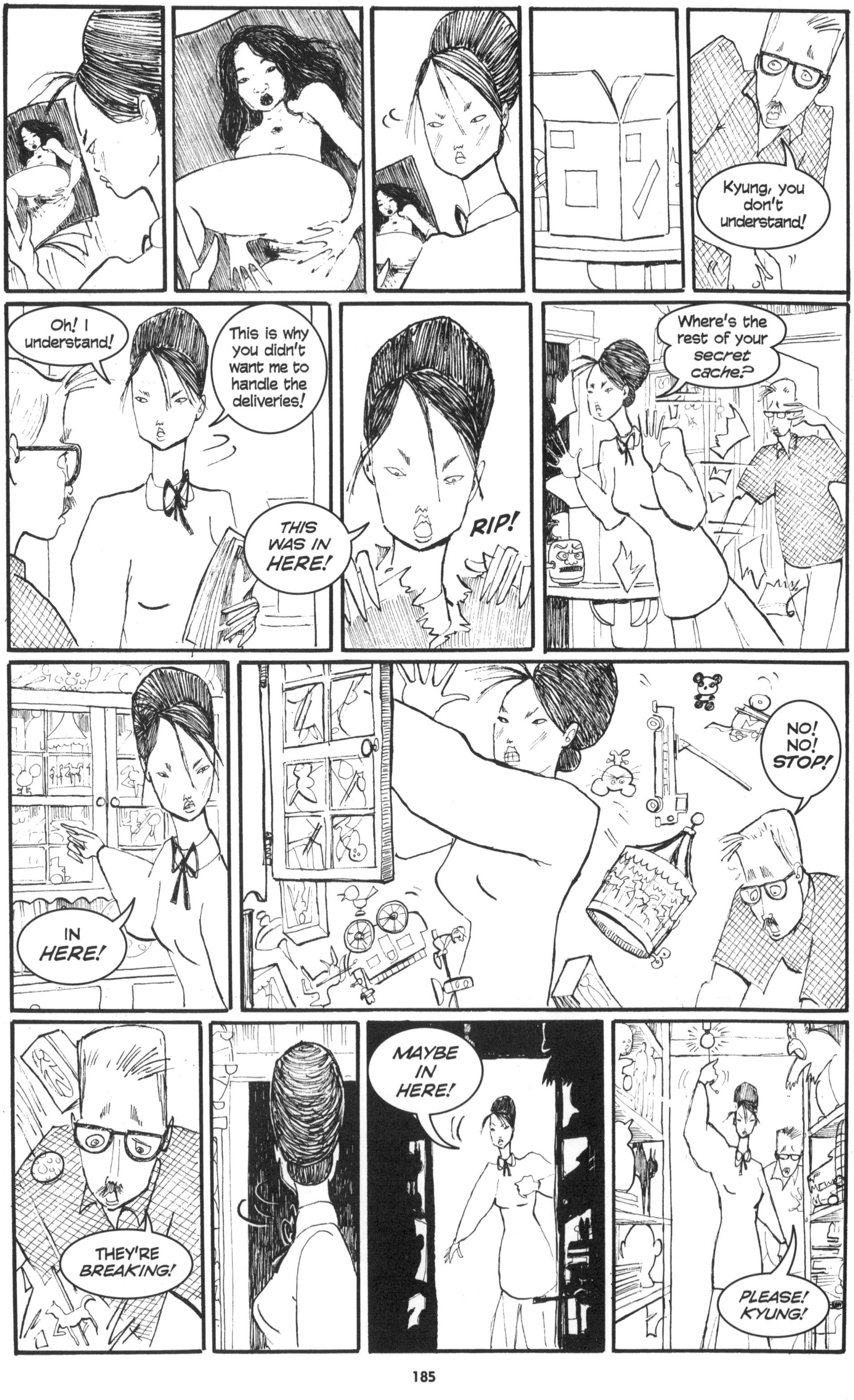
Kyung, you don't understand!
Oh! I understand!
This is why you didn't want me to handle the deliveries!
THIS WAS IN HERE!
RIP!
Where's the rest of your secret cache?
IN HERE!
NO! NO! STOP!
THEY'RE BREAKING!
MAYBE IN HERE!
PLEASE! KYUNG!

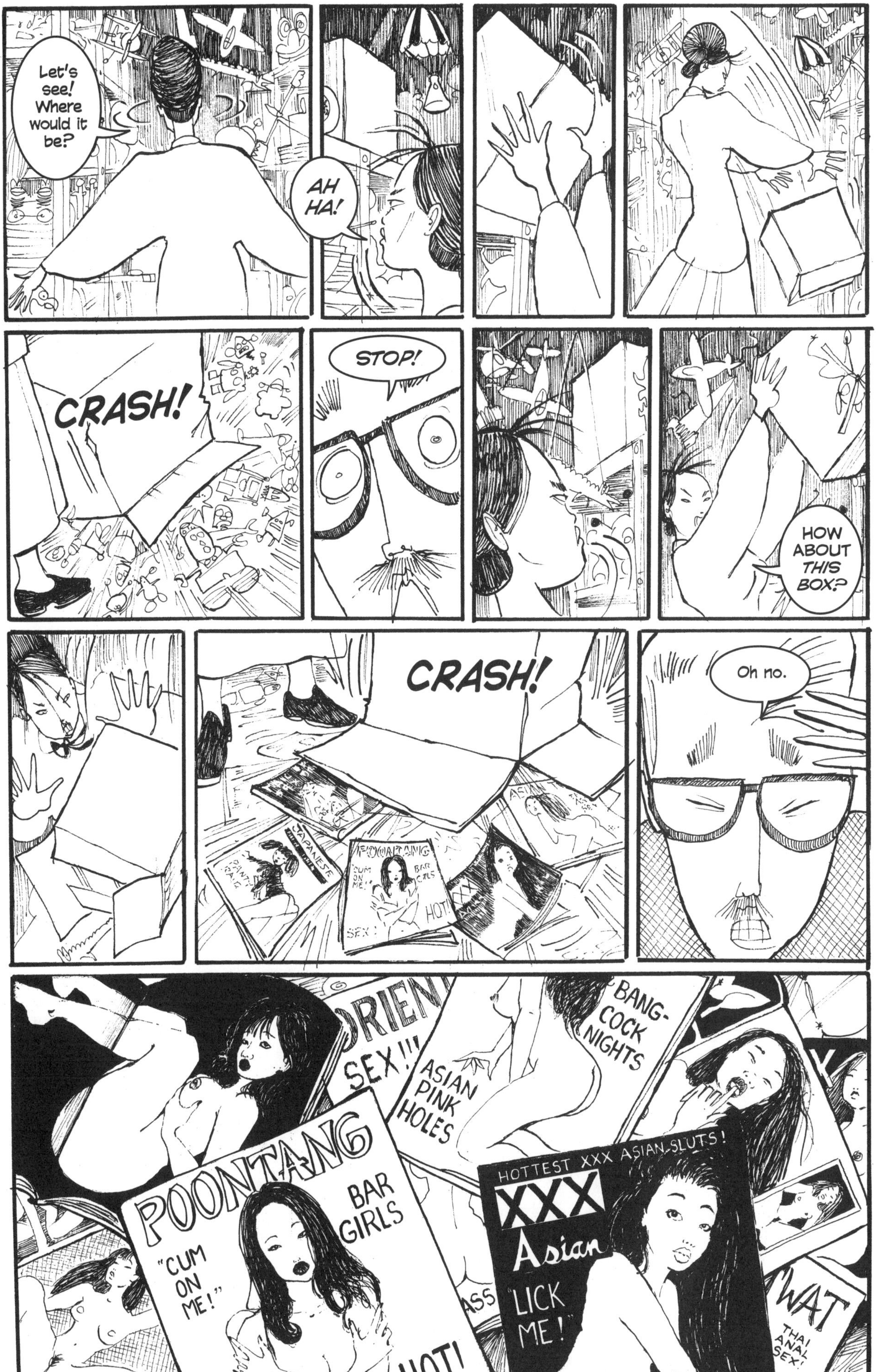

Let's see! Where would it be?
AH HA!
CRASH!
STOP!
HOW ABOUT THIS BOX?
CRASH!
Oh no.
ORIEN
SEX!!!
BANG-COCK NIGHTS
ASIAN PINK HOLES
POONTANG
BAR GIRLS
"CUM ON ME!"
HOT!
HOTTEST XXX ASIAN SLUTS!
XXX
Asian
'LICK ME!'
ASS
WAT
THAI ANAL SEX!

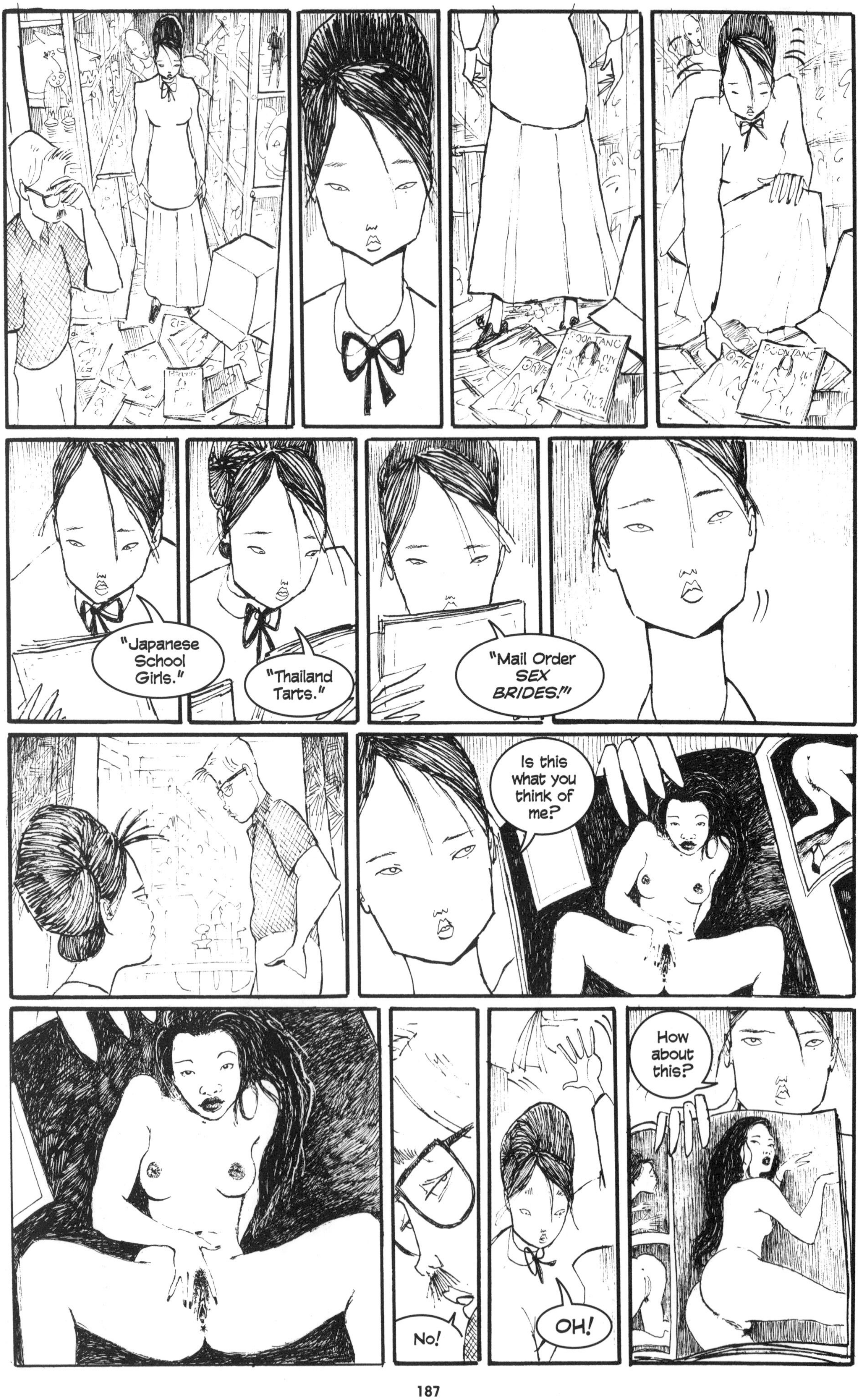
"Japanese School Girls."
"Thailand Tarts."
"Mail Order SEX BRIDES!"
Is this what you think of me?
No!
OH!
How about this?

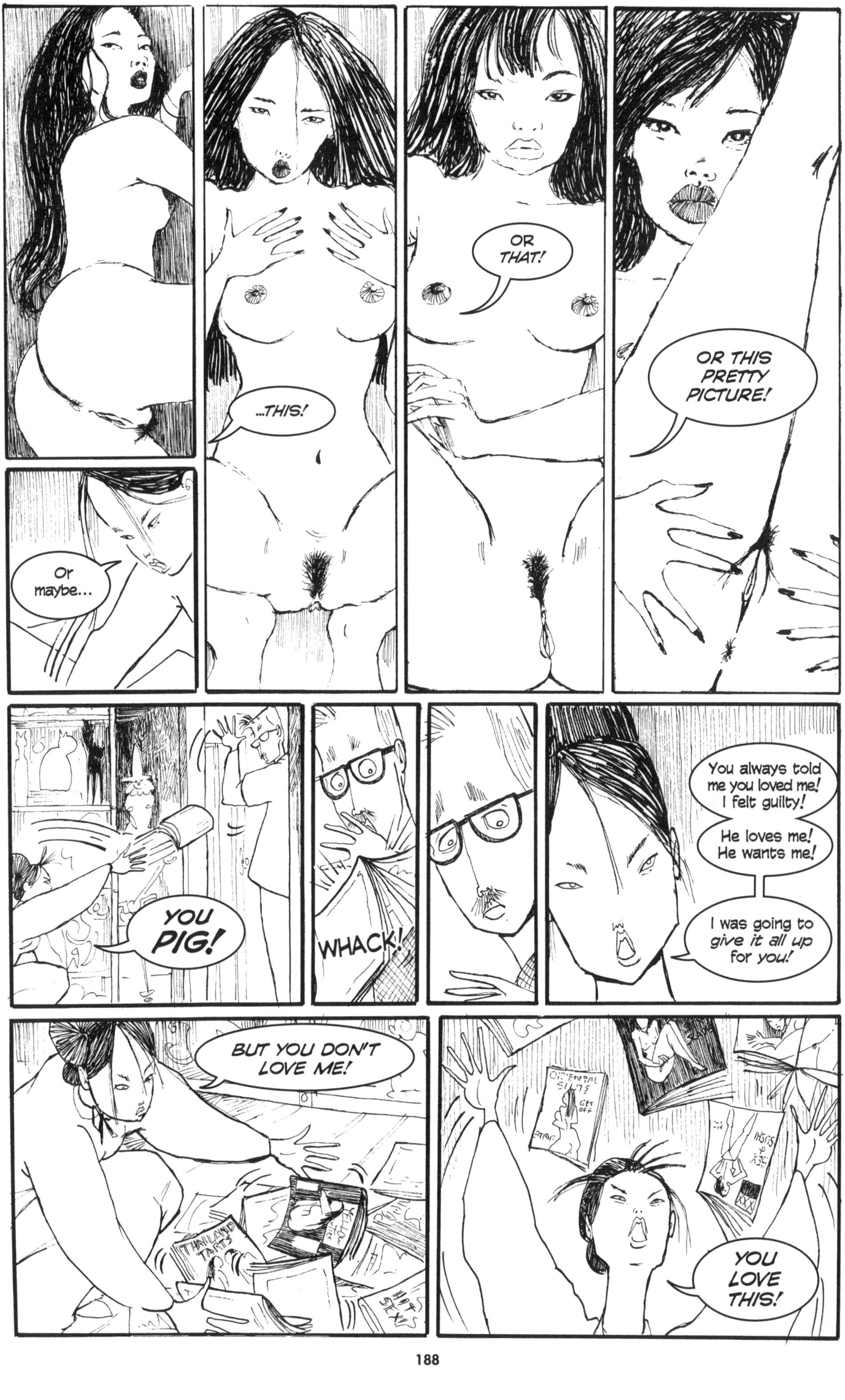
...THIS!
OR THAT!
OR THIS PRETTY PICTURE!
Or maybe...
YOU PIG!
WHACK!
You always told me you loved me! I felt guilty!
He loves me! He wants me!
I was going to *give it all up* for *you!*
BUT YOU DON'T LOVE ME!
THAILAND TARTS
YOU LOVE THIS!

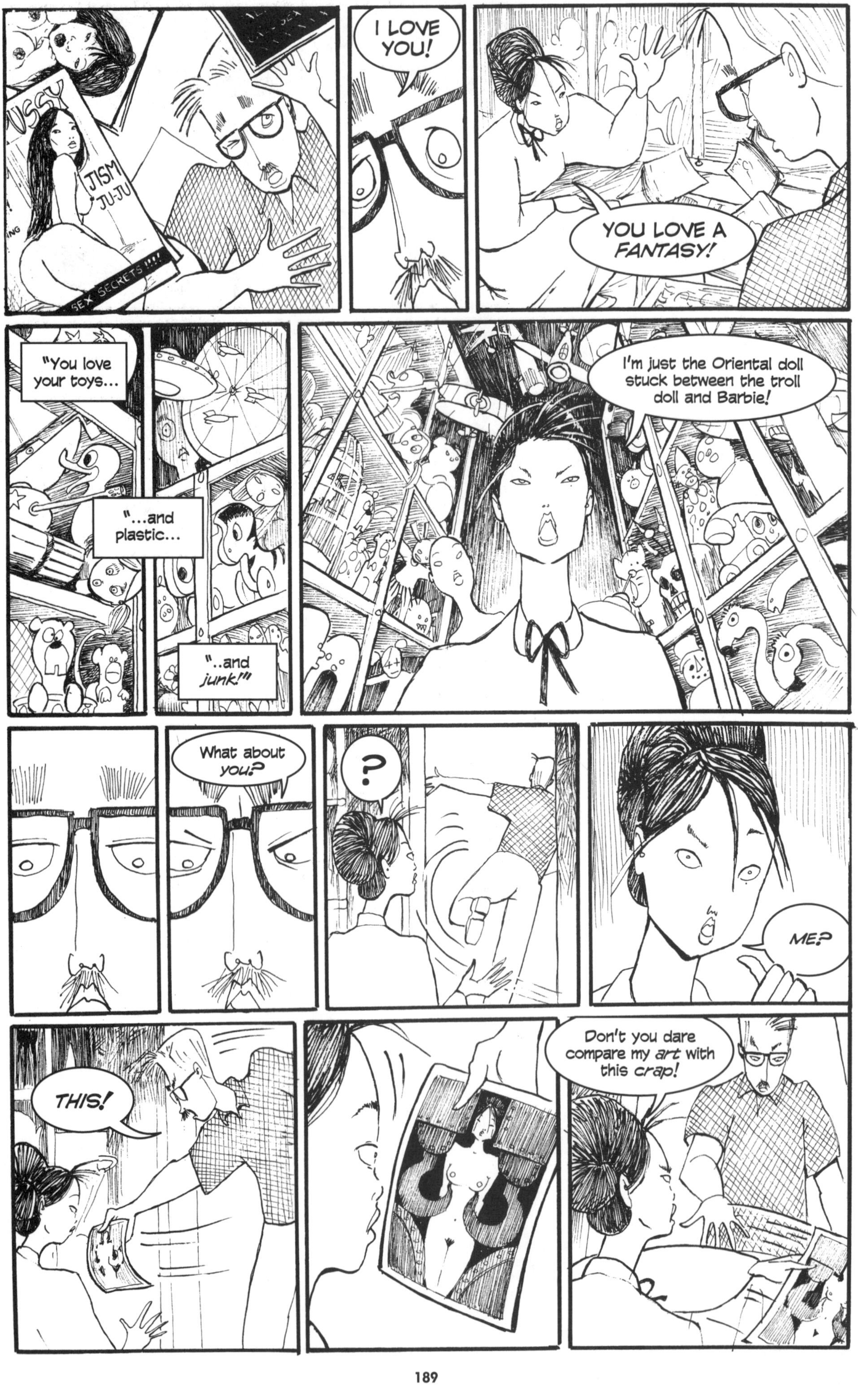
JISM
JU-JU
SEX SECRETS !!!
I LOVE YOU!
YOU LOVE A FANTASY!
"You love your toys...
"...and plastic...
"..and junk!"
I'm just the Oriental doll stuck between the troll doll and Barbie!
What about you?
?
ME?
THIS!
Don't you dare compare my art with this crap!

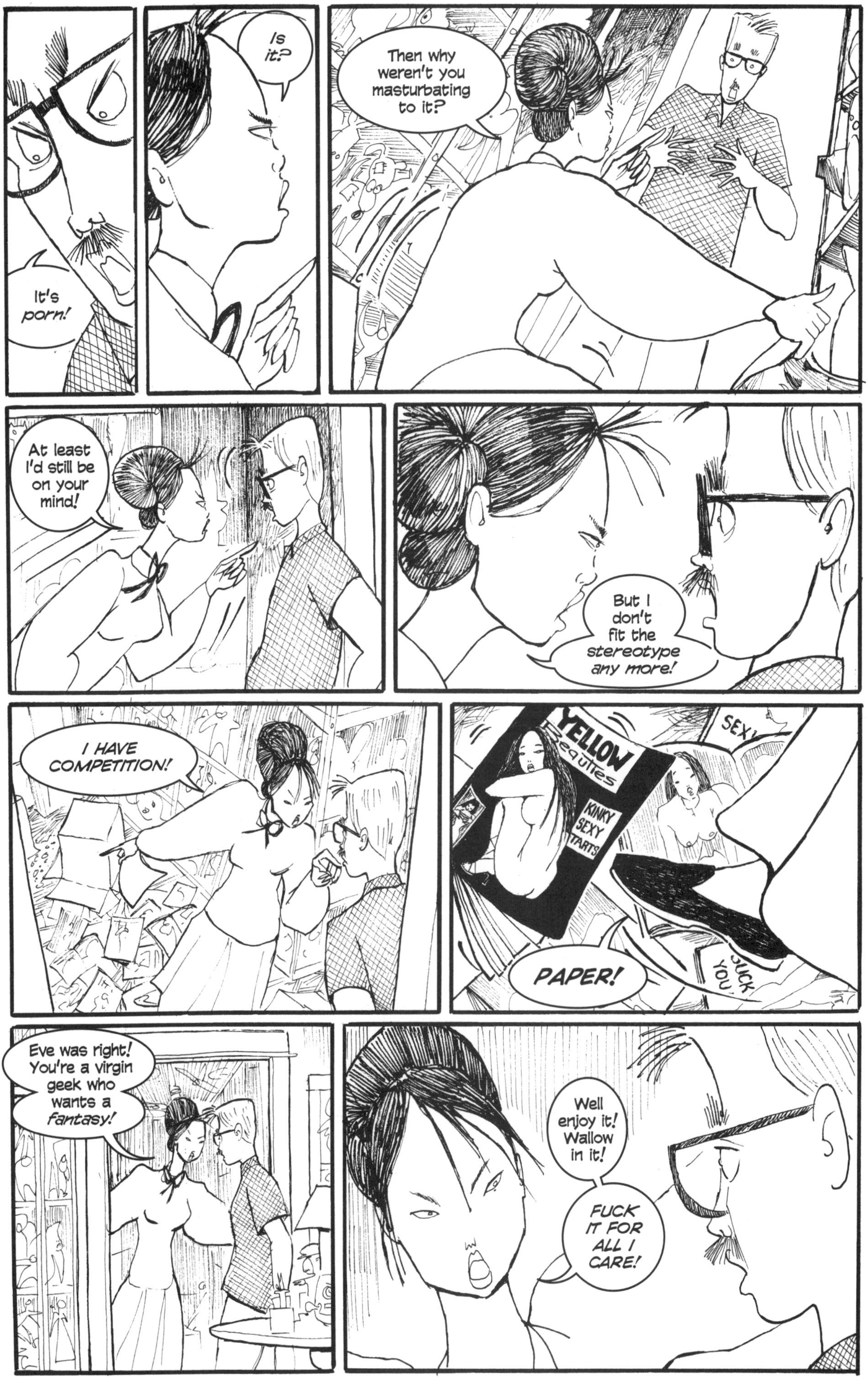
It's porn!
Is it?
Then why weren't you masturbating to it?
At least I'd still be on your mind!
But I don't fit the stereotype any more!
I HAVE COMPETITION!
YELLOW Bequttes
KINKY SEXY TARTS
SEX
PAPER!
SUCK YOU
Eve was right! You're a virgin geek who wants a fantasy!
Well enjoy it! Wallow in it!
FUCK IT FOR ALL I CARE!

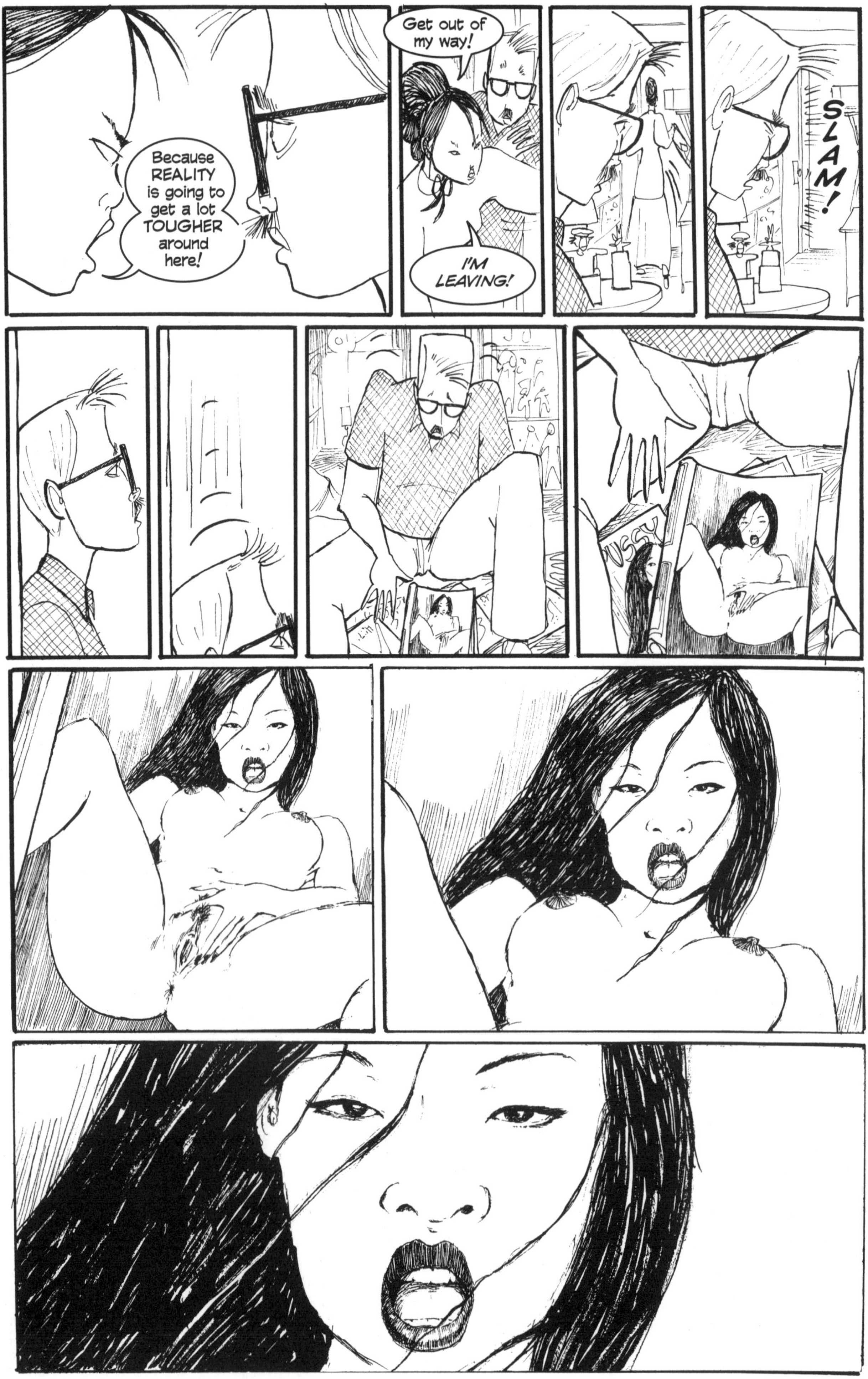
Because REALITY is going to get a lot TOUGHER around here!
Get out of my way!
I'M LEAVING!
SLAM!

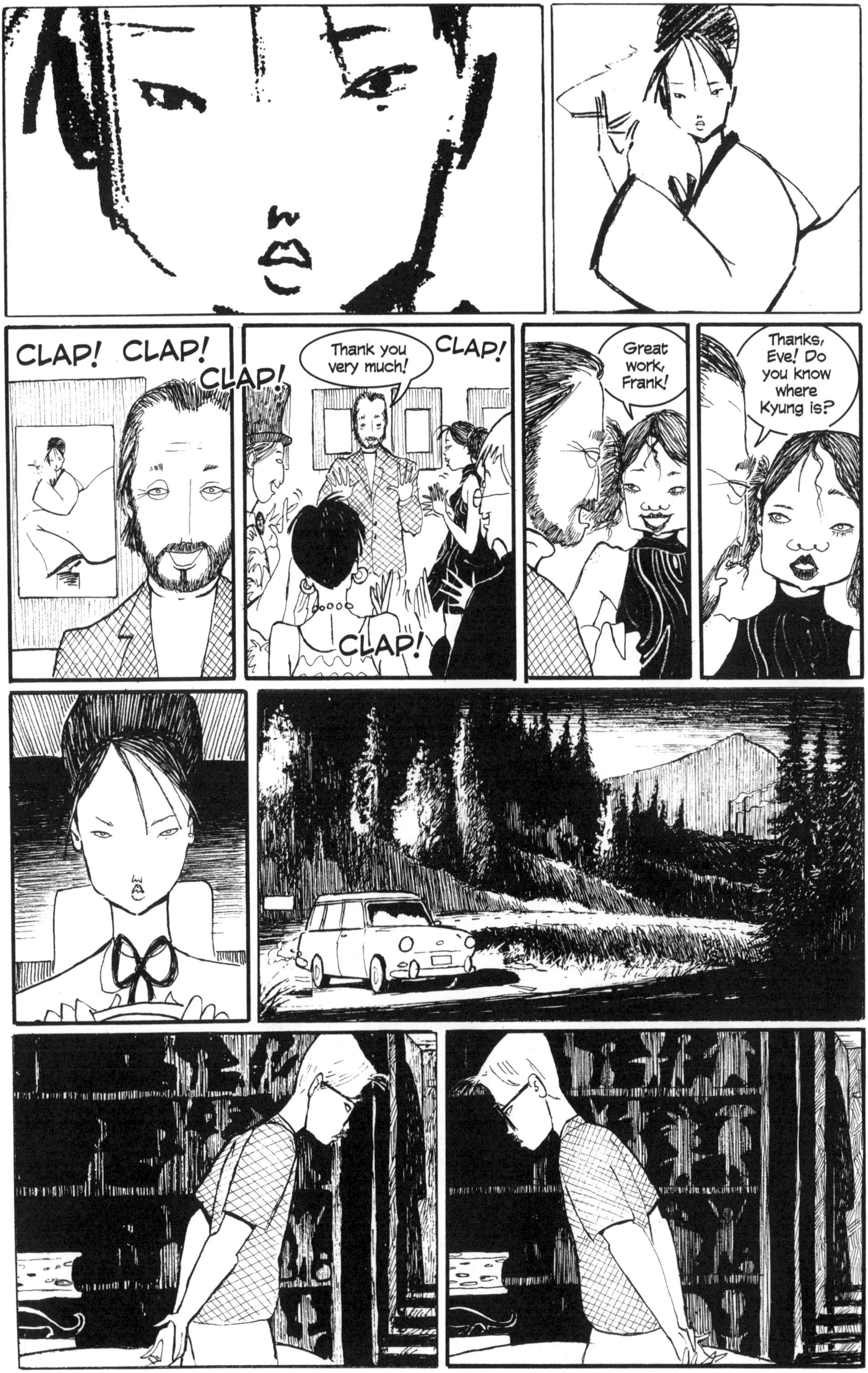
CLAP! CLAP!
CLAP!
Thank you very much!
CLAP!
CLAP!
Great work, Frank!
Thanks, Eve! Do you know where Kyung is?

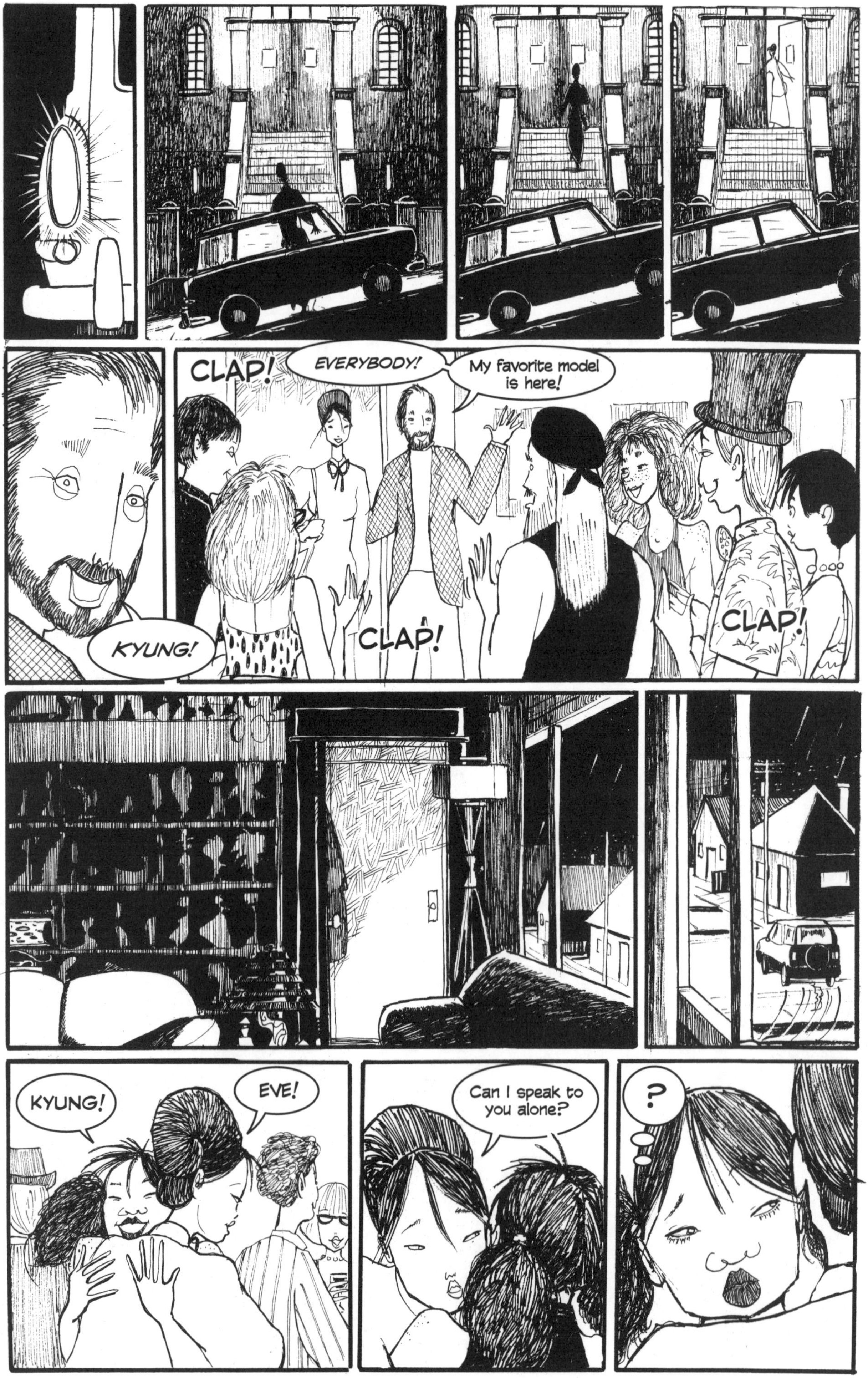
CLAP!
EVERYBODY!
My favorite model is here!
KYUNG!
CLAP!
CLAP!
KYUNG!
EVE!
Can I speak to you alone?
?

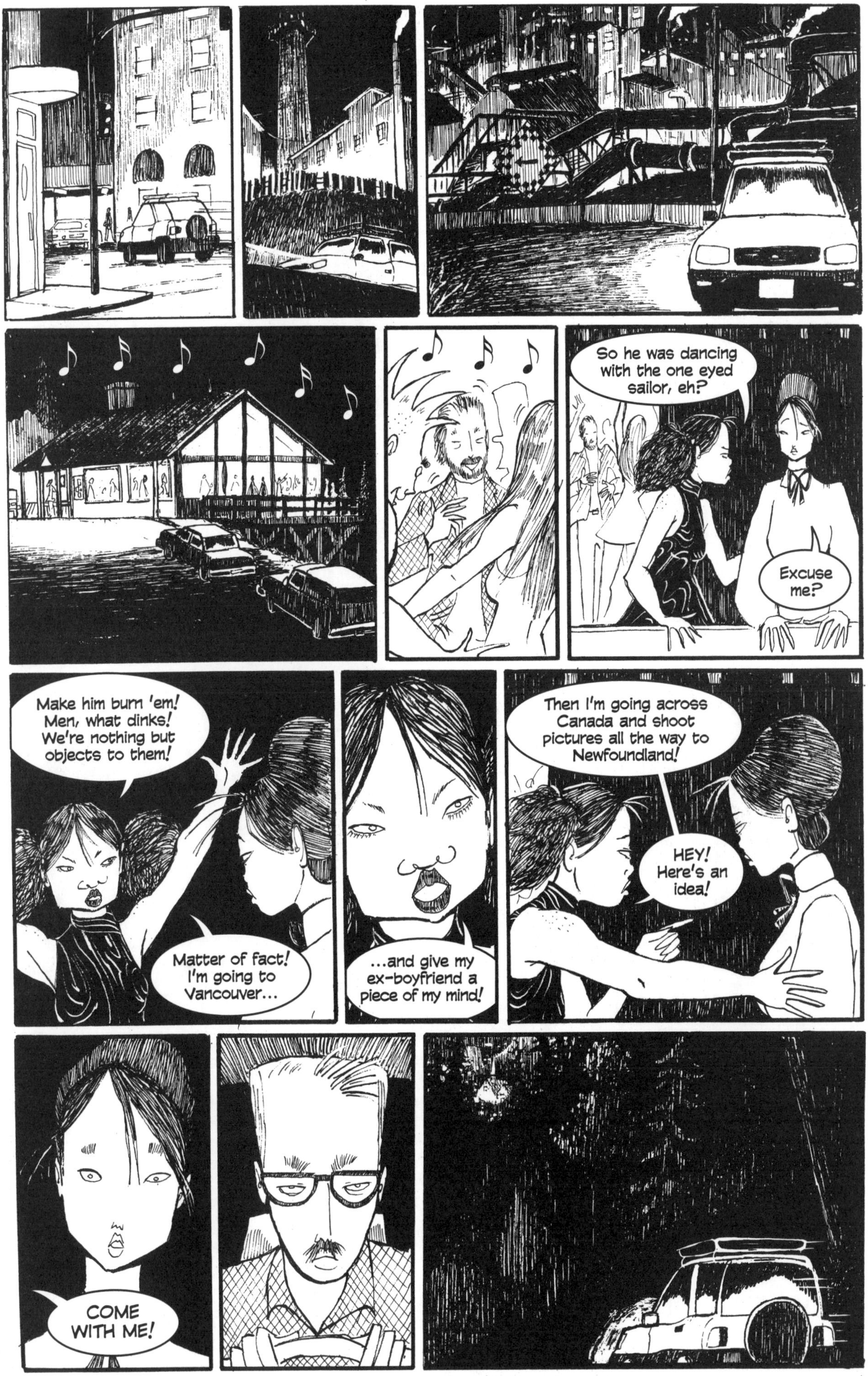

So he was dancing with the one eyed sailor, eh?
Excuse me?
Make him burn 'em! Men, what dinks! We're nothing but objects to them!
Matter of fact! I'm going to Vancouver...
...and give my ex-boyfriend a piece of my mind!
Then I'm going across Canada and shoot pictures all the way to Newfoundland!
HEY! Here's an idea!
COME WITH ME!

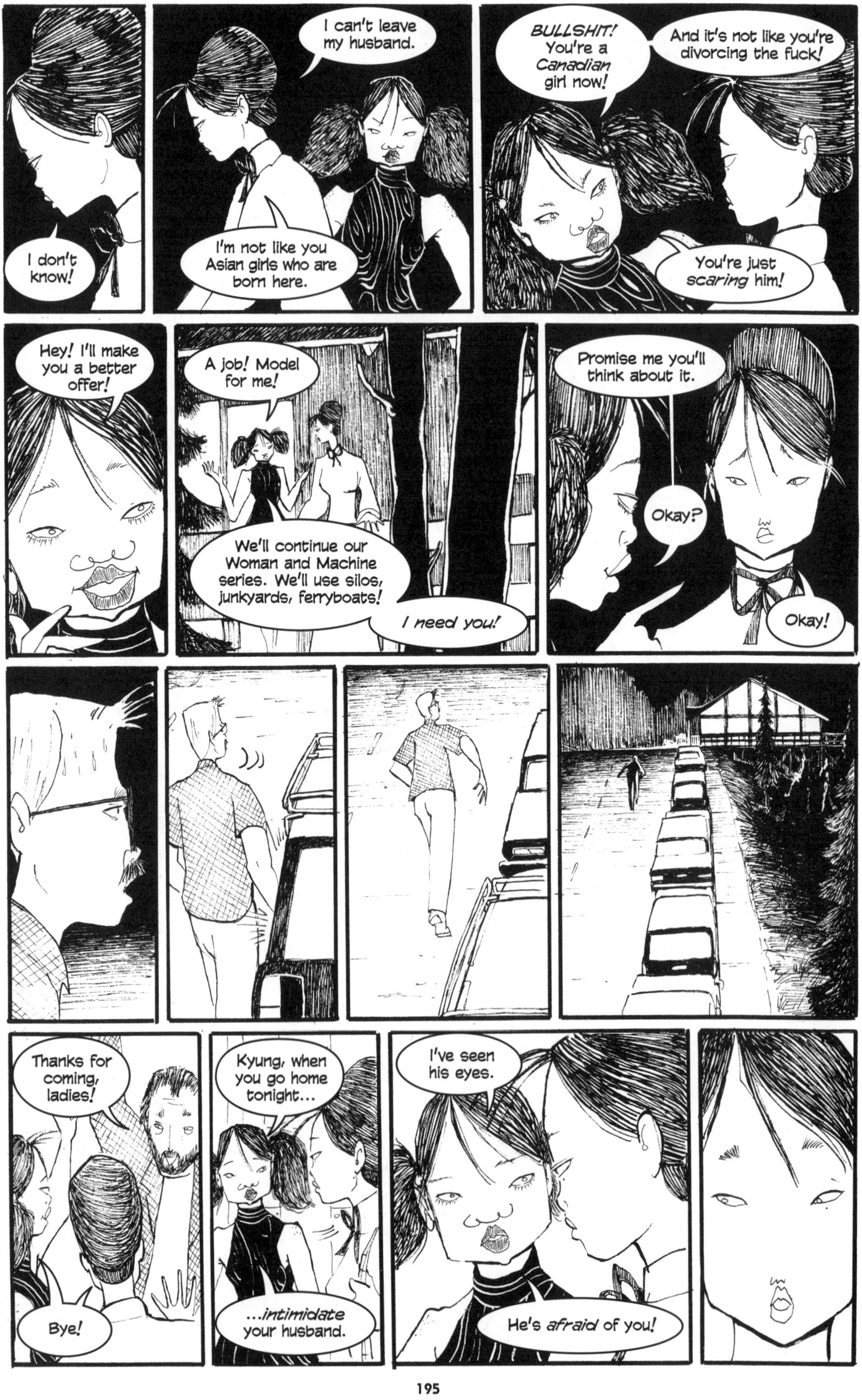
I don't know!
I can't leave my husband.
I'm not like you Asian girls who are born here.
BULLSHIT! You're a Canadian girl now!
And it's not like you're divorcing the fuck!
You're just scaring him!
Hey! I'll make you a better offer!
A job! Model for me!
We'll continue our Woman and Machine series. We'll use silos, junkyards, ferryboats!
I need you!
Promise me you'll think about it.
Okay?
Okay!
Thanks for coming, ladies!
Bye!
Kyung, when you go home tonight...
...intimidate your husband.
I've seen his eyes.
He's afraid of you!

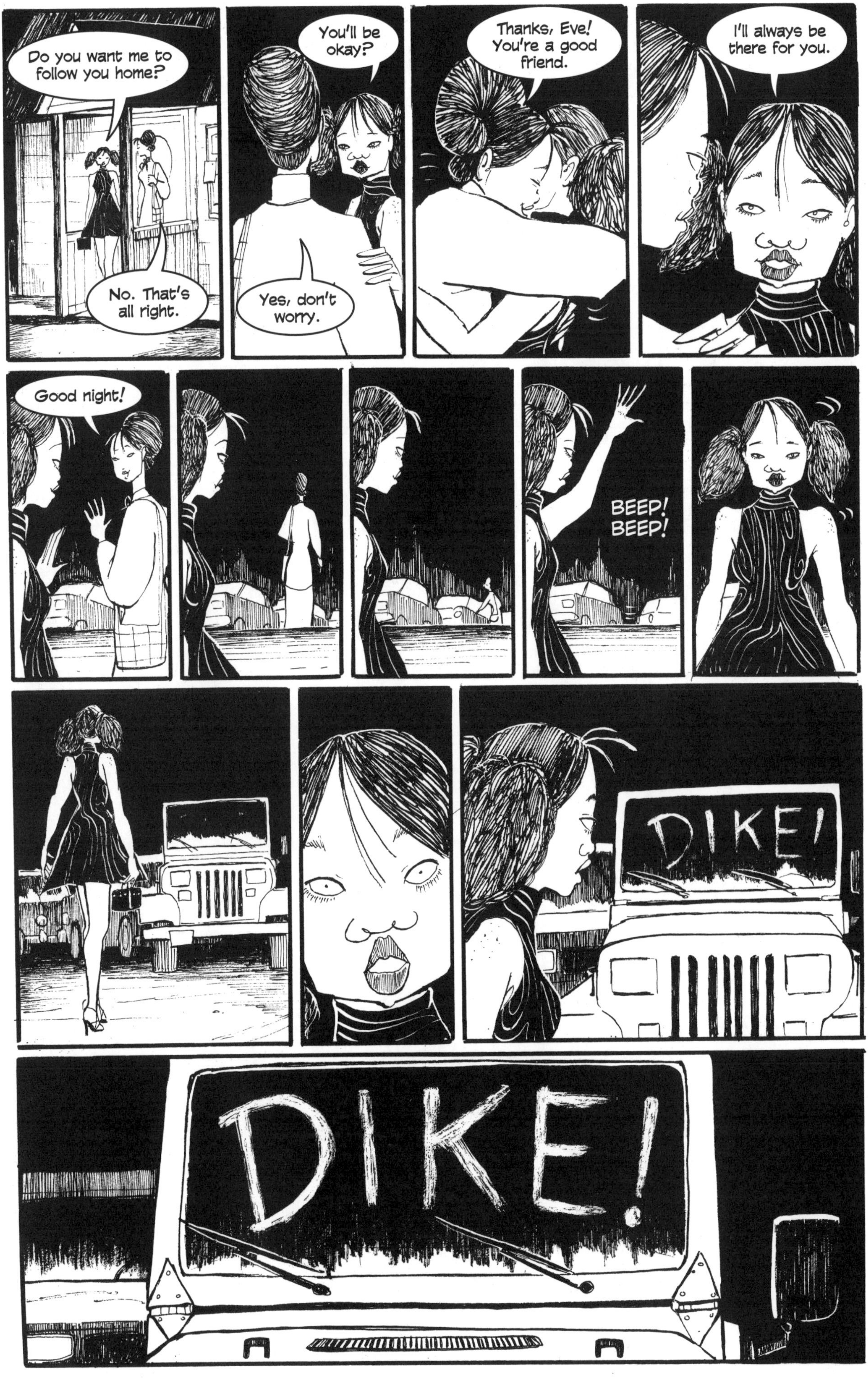
Do you want me to follow you home?
No. That's all right.
You'll be okay?
Yes, don't worry.
Thanks, Eve! You're a good friend.
I'll always be there for you.
Good night!
BEEP! BEEP!
DIKE!
DIKE!

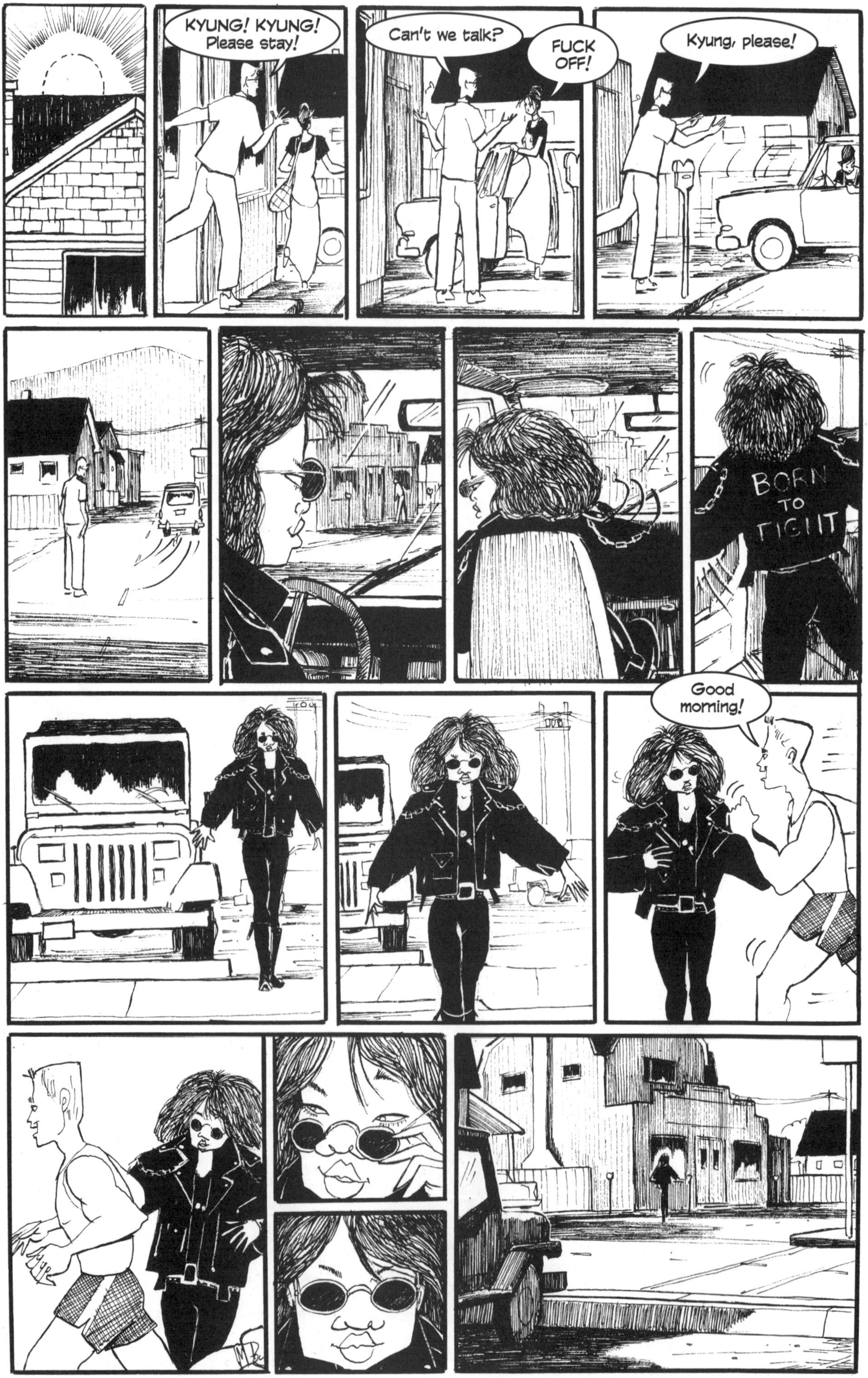
KYUNG! KYUNG! Please stay!
Can't we talk?
FUCK OFF!
Kyung, please!
BORN TO FIGHT
Good morning!

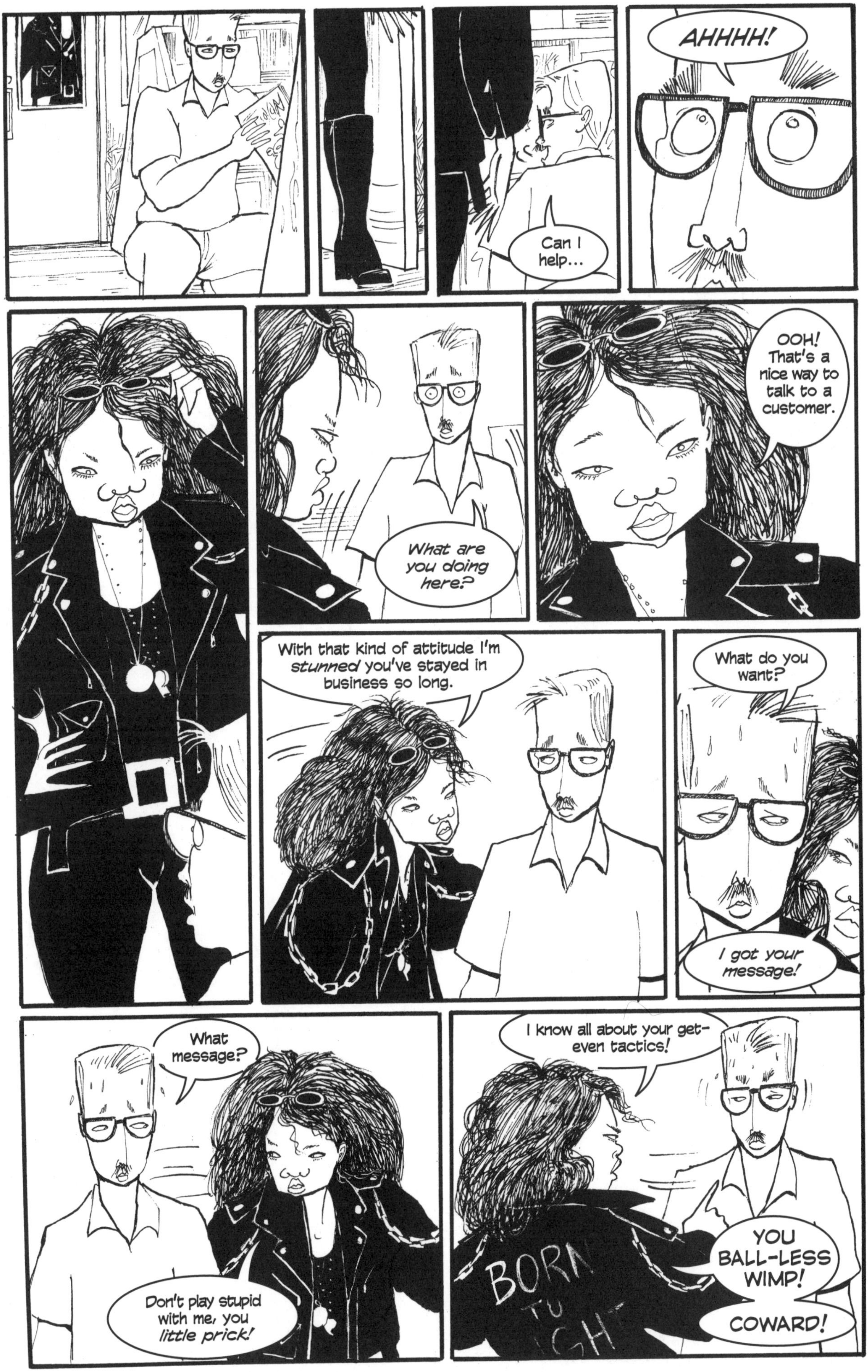
Can I help...
AHHHH!
What are you doing here?
OOH! That's a nice way to talk to a customer.
With that kind of attitude I'm *stunned* you've stayed in business so long.
What do you want?
I got your message!
What message?
Don't play stupid with me, you *little prick!*
I know all about your get-even tactics!
YOU BALL-LESS WIMP!
COWARD!
BORN TO

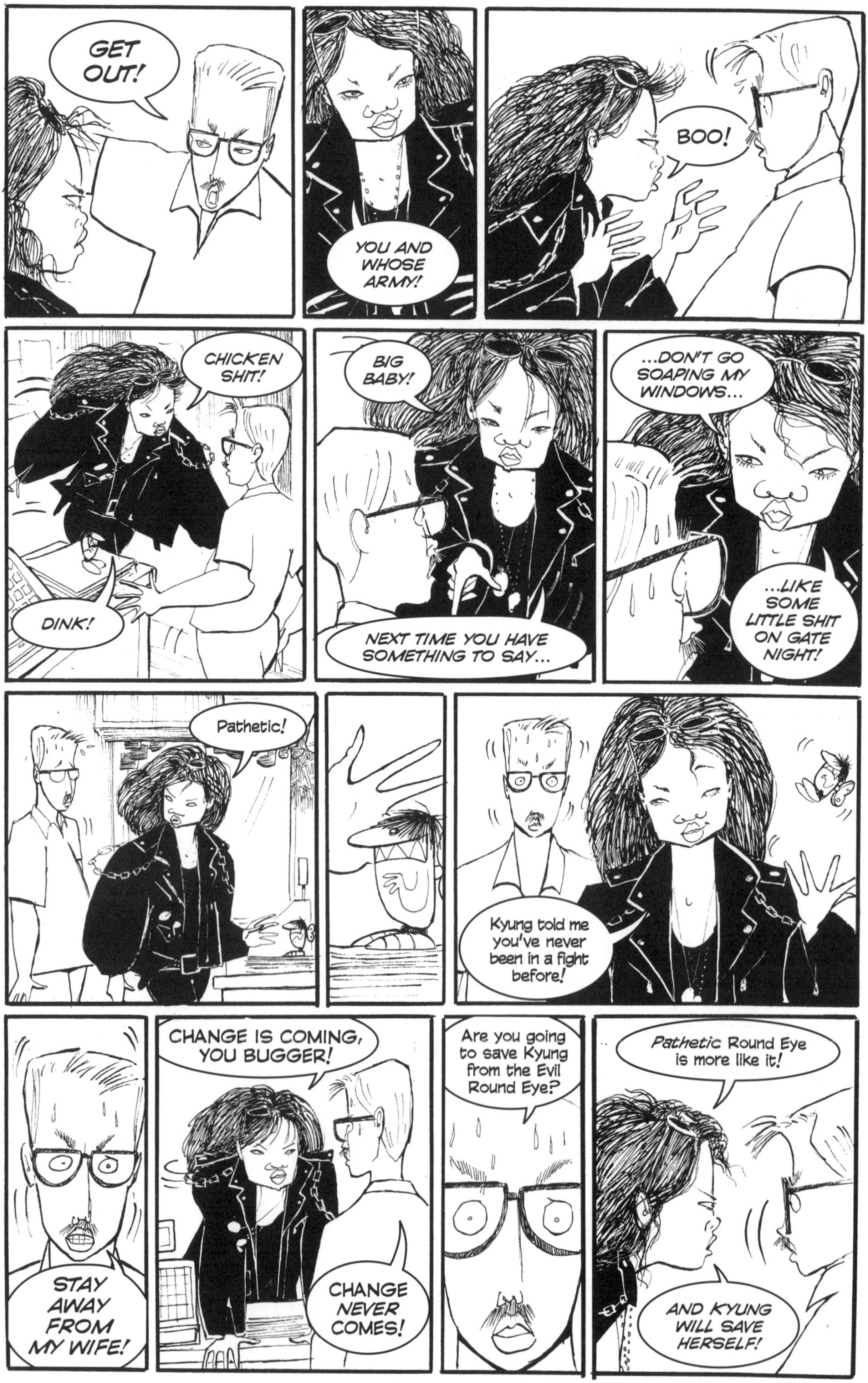
GET OUT!
YOU AND WHOSE ARMY!
BOO!
CHICKEN SHIT!
DINK!
BIG BABY!
NEXT TIME YOU HAVE SOMETHING TO SAY...
...DON'T GO SOAPING MY WINDOWS...
...LIKE SOME LITTLE SHIT ON GATE NIGHT!
Pathetic!
Kyung told me you've never been in a fight before!
STAY AWAY FROM MY WIFE!
CHANGE IS COMING, YOU BUGGER!
CHANGE NEVER COMES!
Are you going to save Kyung from the Evil Round Eye?
Pathetic Round Eye is more like it!
AND KYUNG WILL SAVE HERSELF!

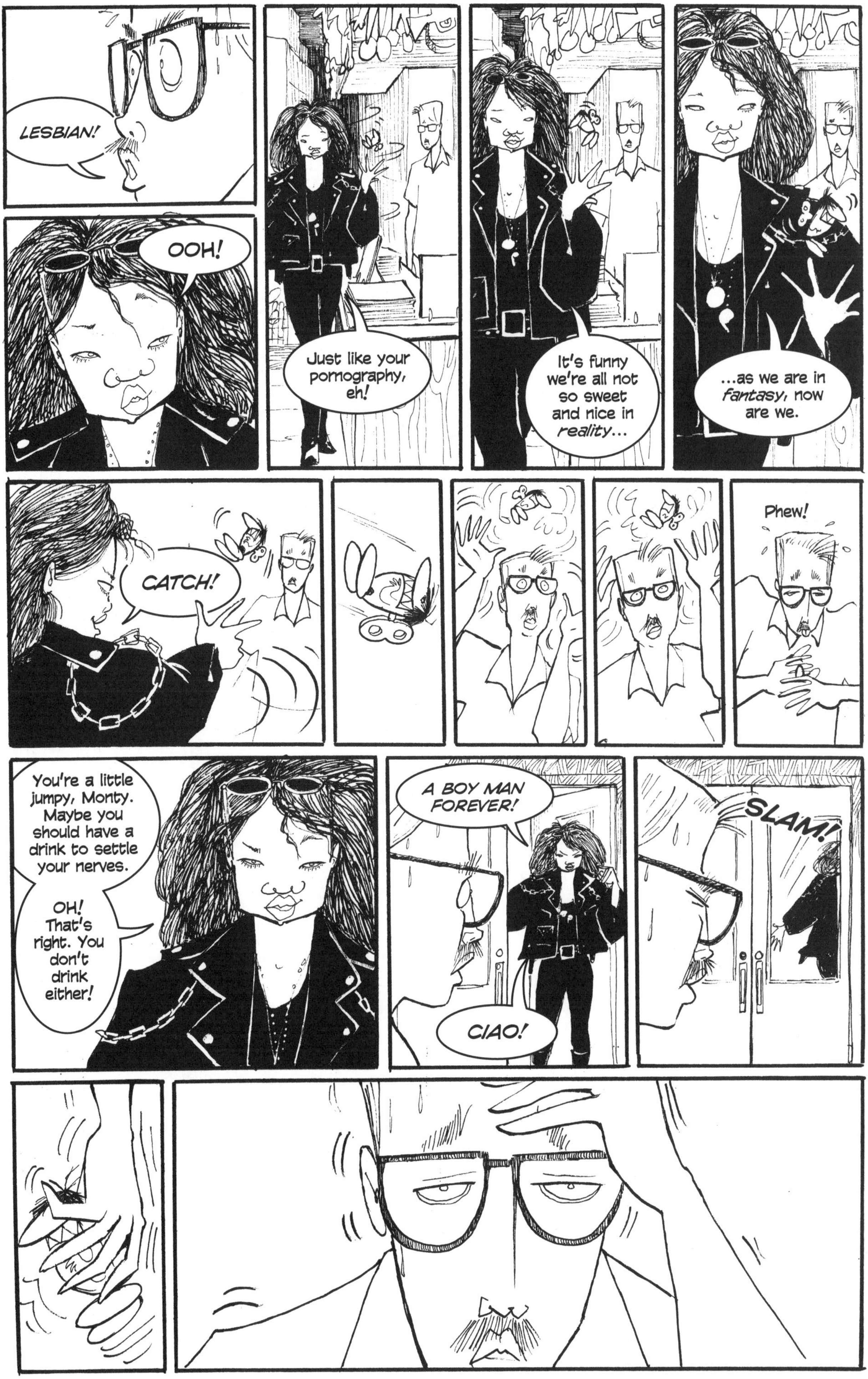
LESBIAN!
OOH!
Just like your pornography, eh!
It's funny we're all not so sweet and nice in *reality*...
...as we are in *fantasy*, now are we.
CATCH!
Phew!
You're a little jumpy, Monty. Maybe you should have a drink to settle your nerves.
OH! That's right. You don't drink either!
A BOY MAN FOREVER!
CIAO!
SLAM!

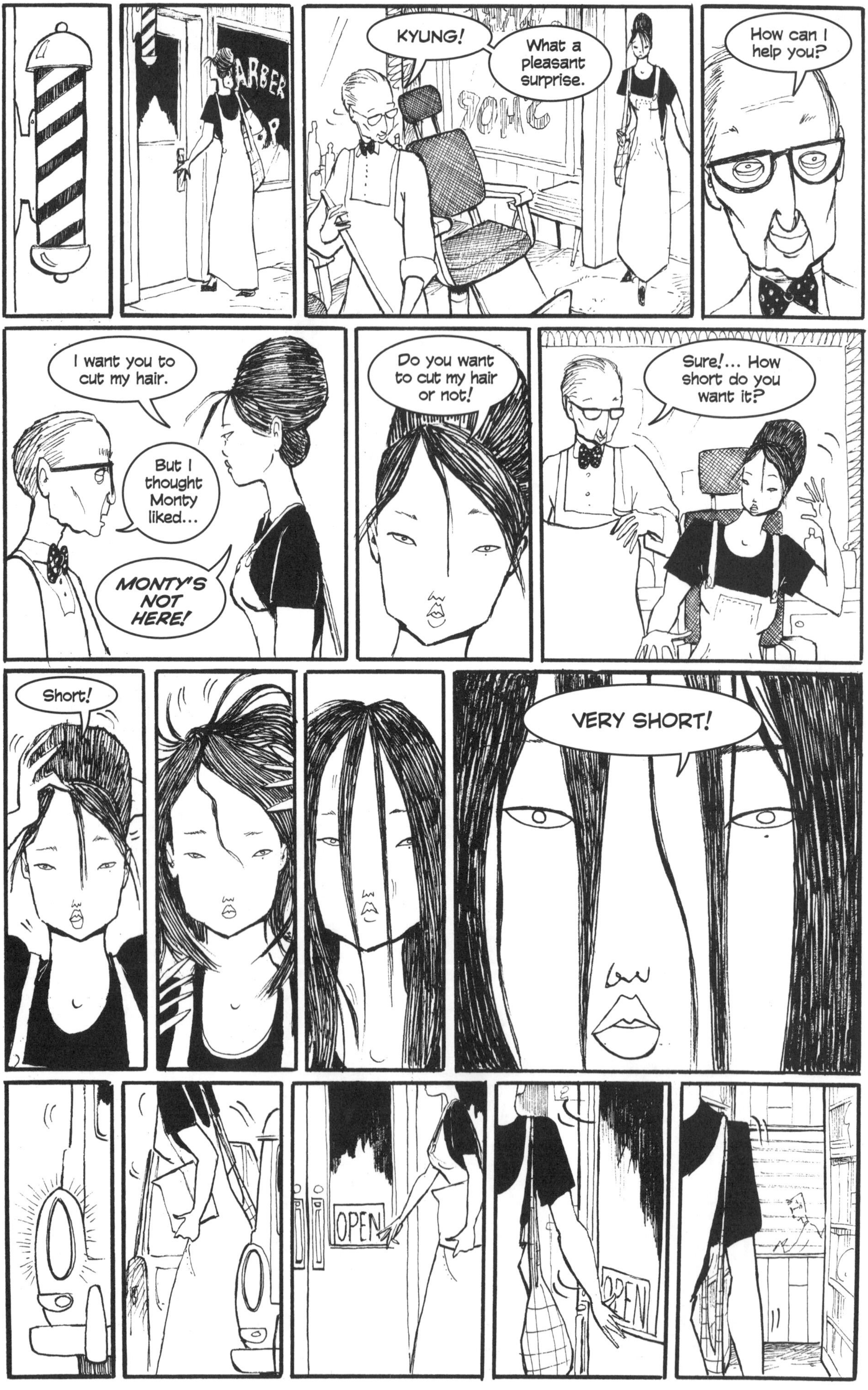
BARBER
KYUNG!
What a pleasant surprise.
SHOP
How can I help you?
I want you to cut my hair.
But I thought Monty liked...
MONTY'S NOT HERE!
Do you want to cut my hair or not!
Sure!... How short do you want it?
Short!
VERY SHORT!
OPEN
OPEN

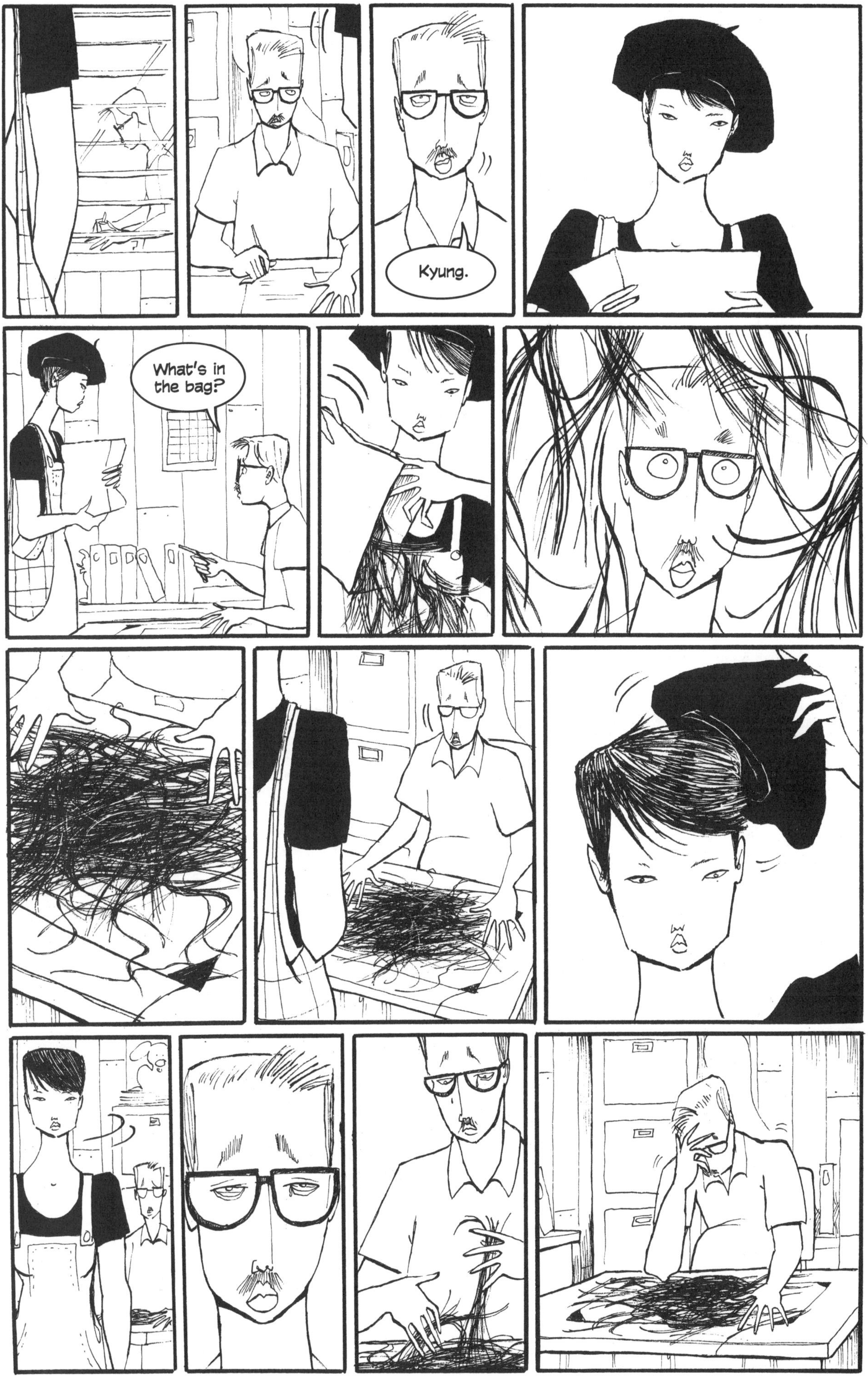
Kyung.
What's in the bag?

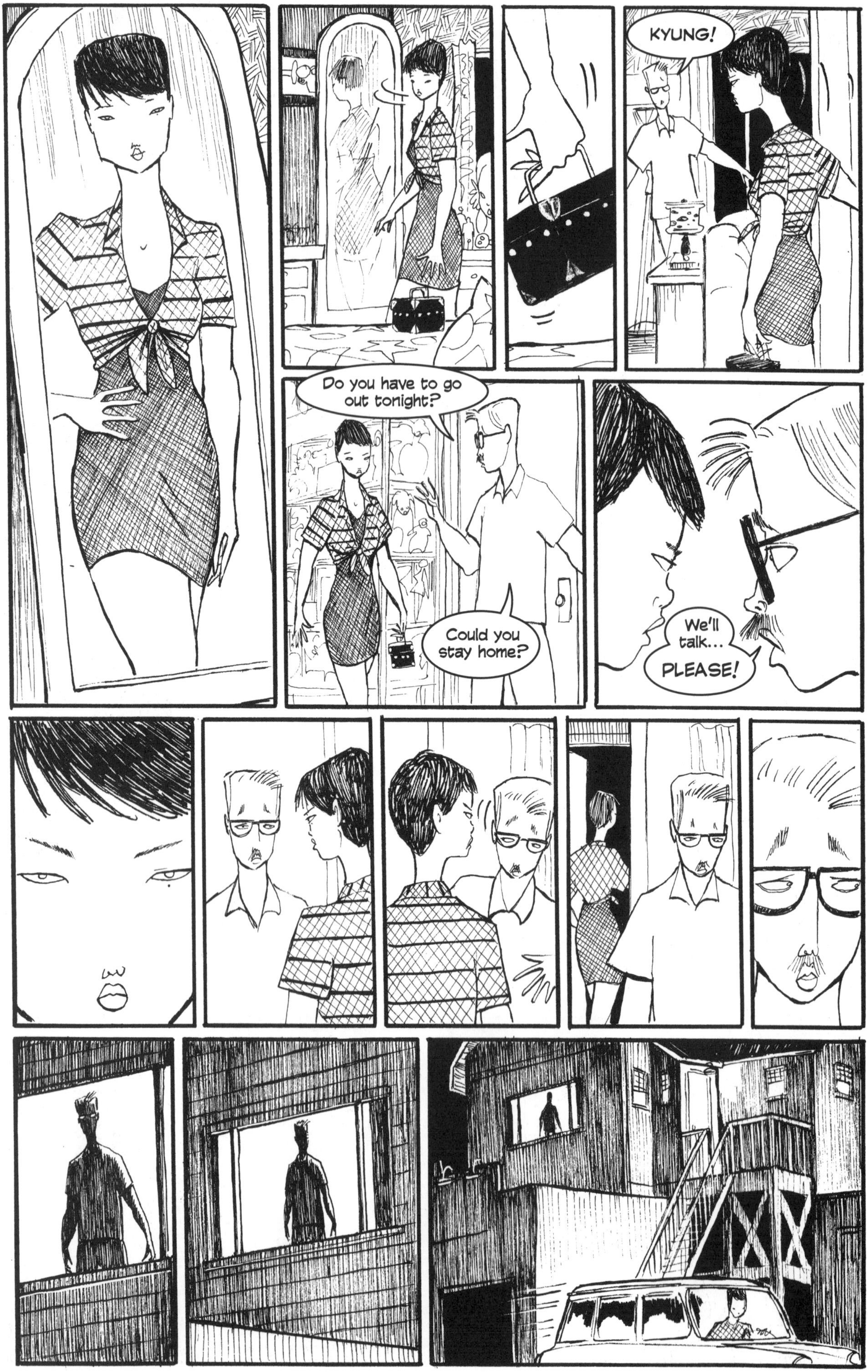
KYUNG!
Do you have to go out tonight?
Could you stay home?
We'll talk...
PLEASE!

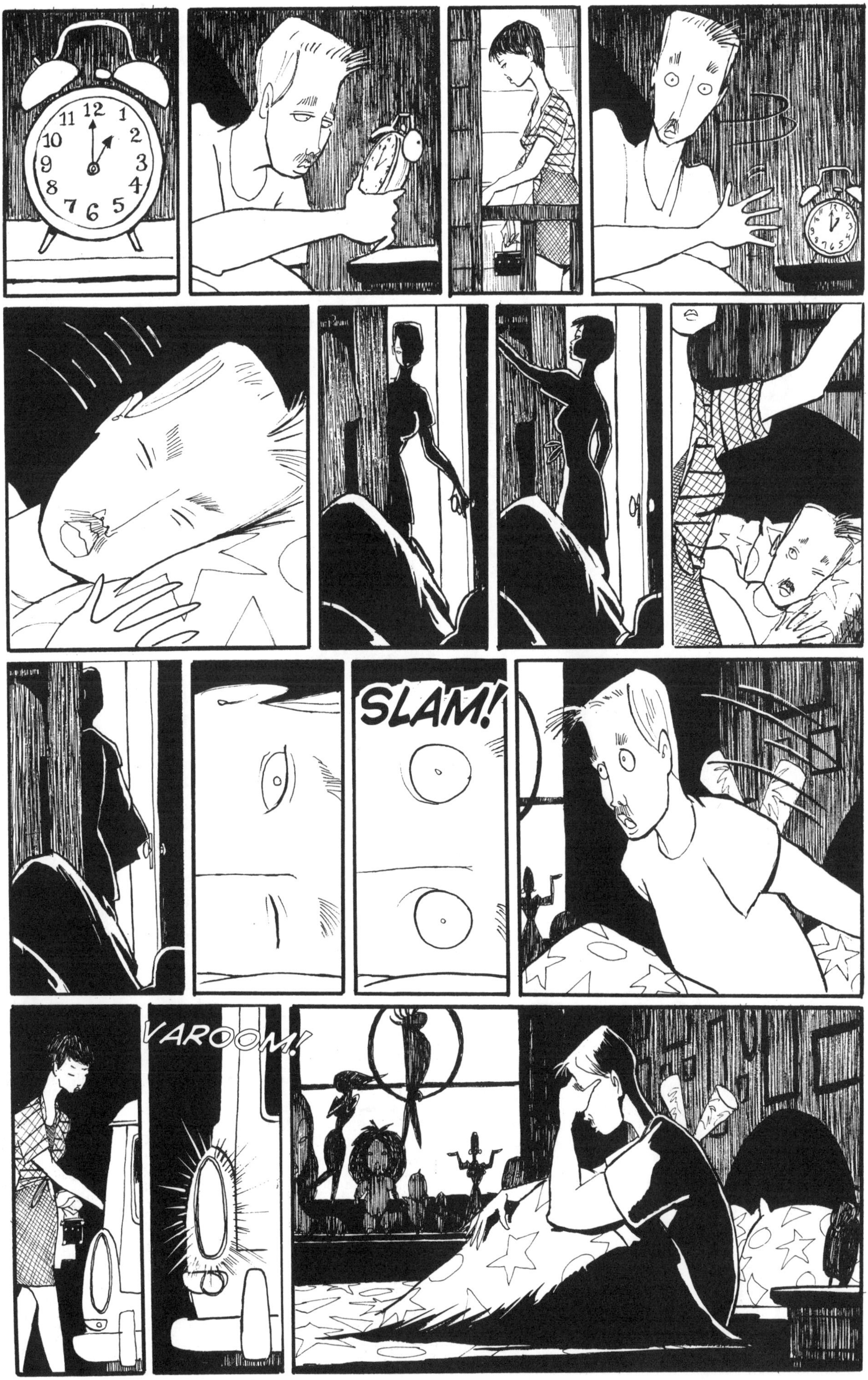
SLAM!
VAROOM!

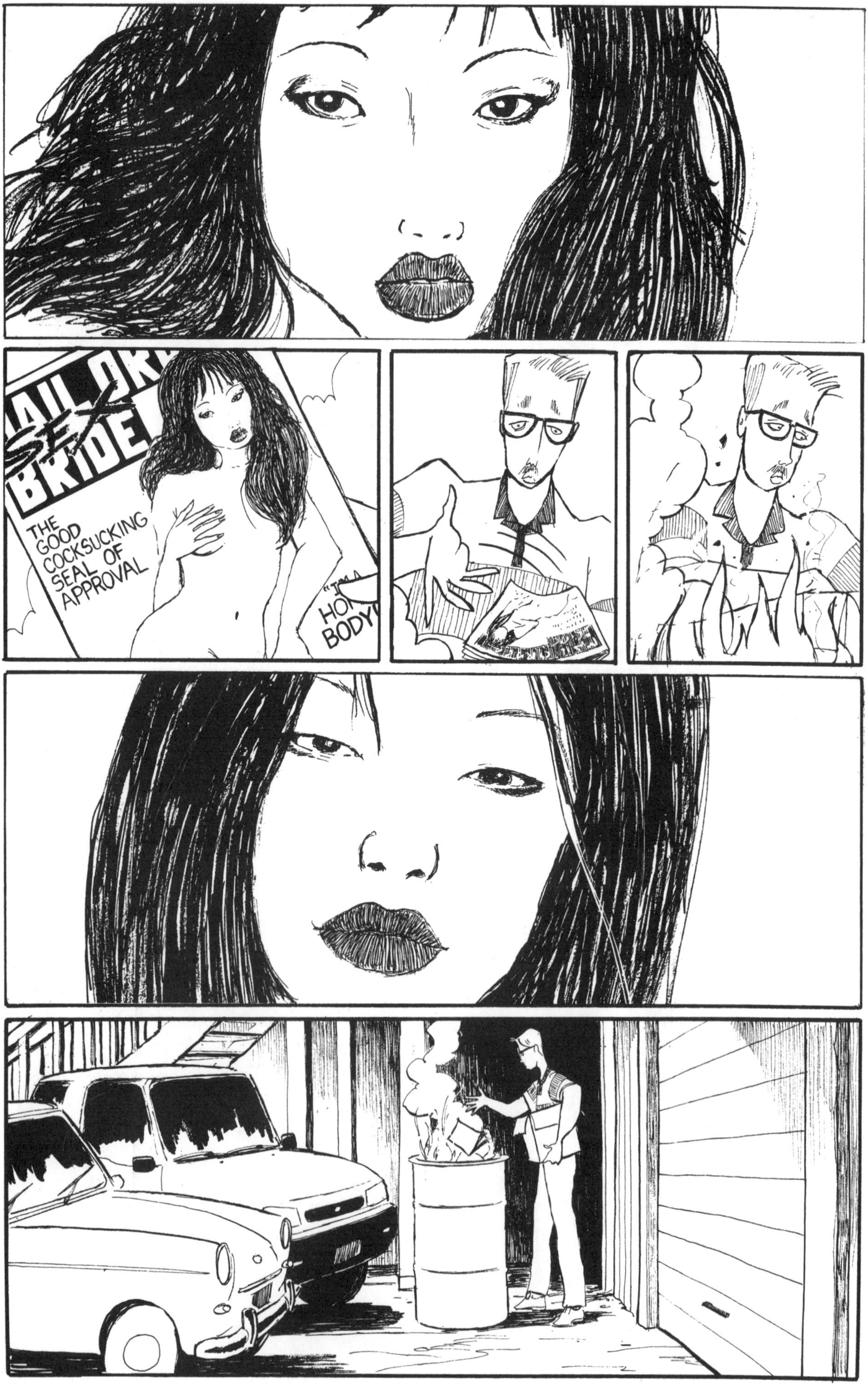
SEX
BRIDE
THE GOOD COCKSUCKING SEAL OF APPROVAL

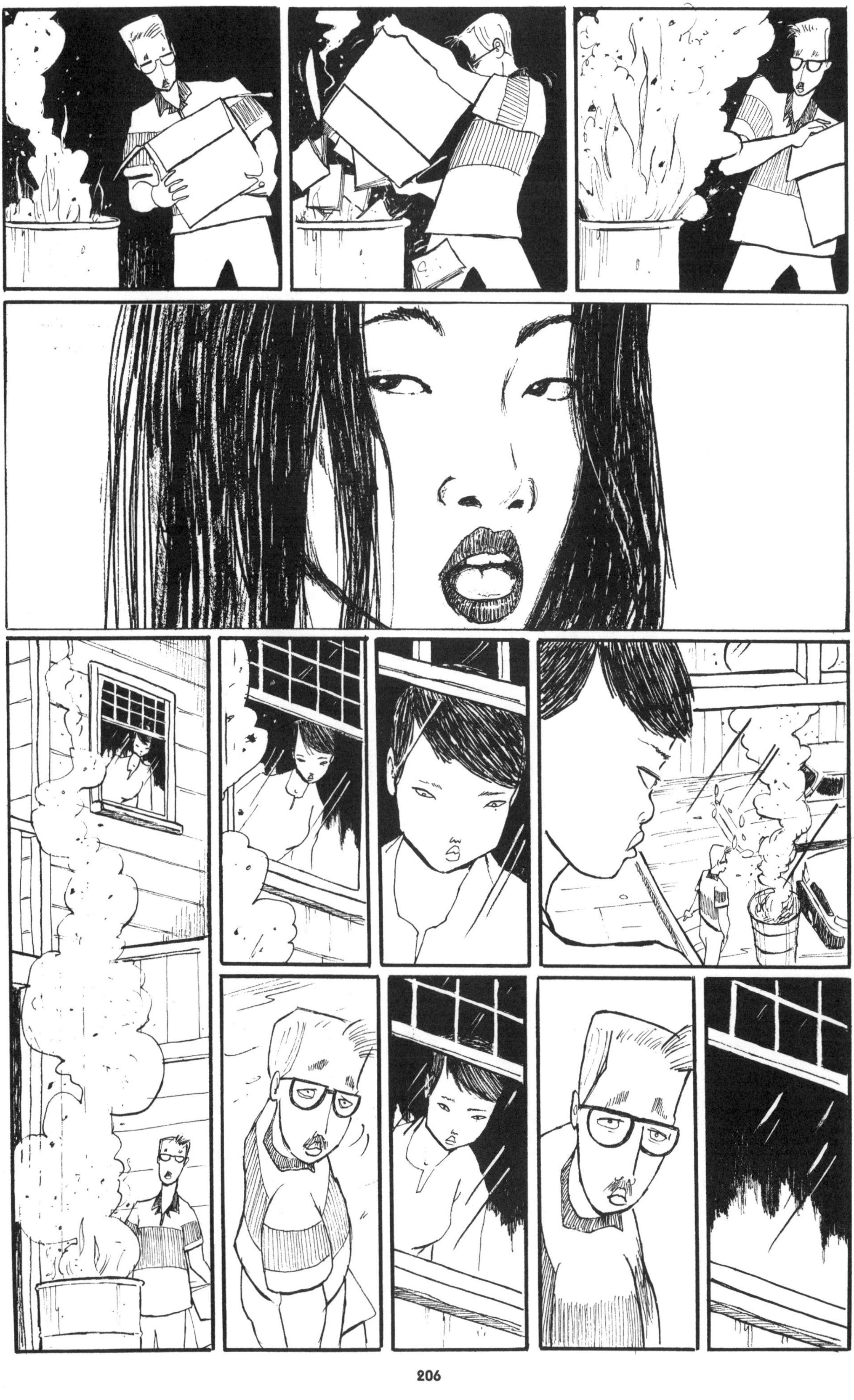

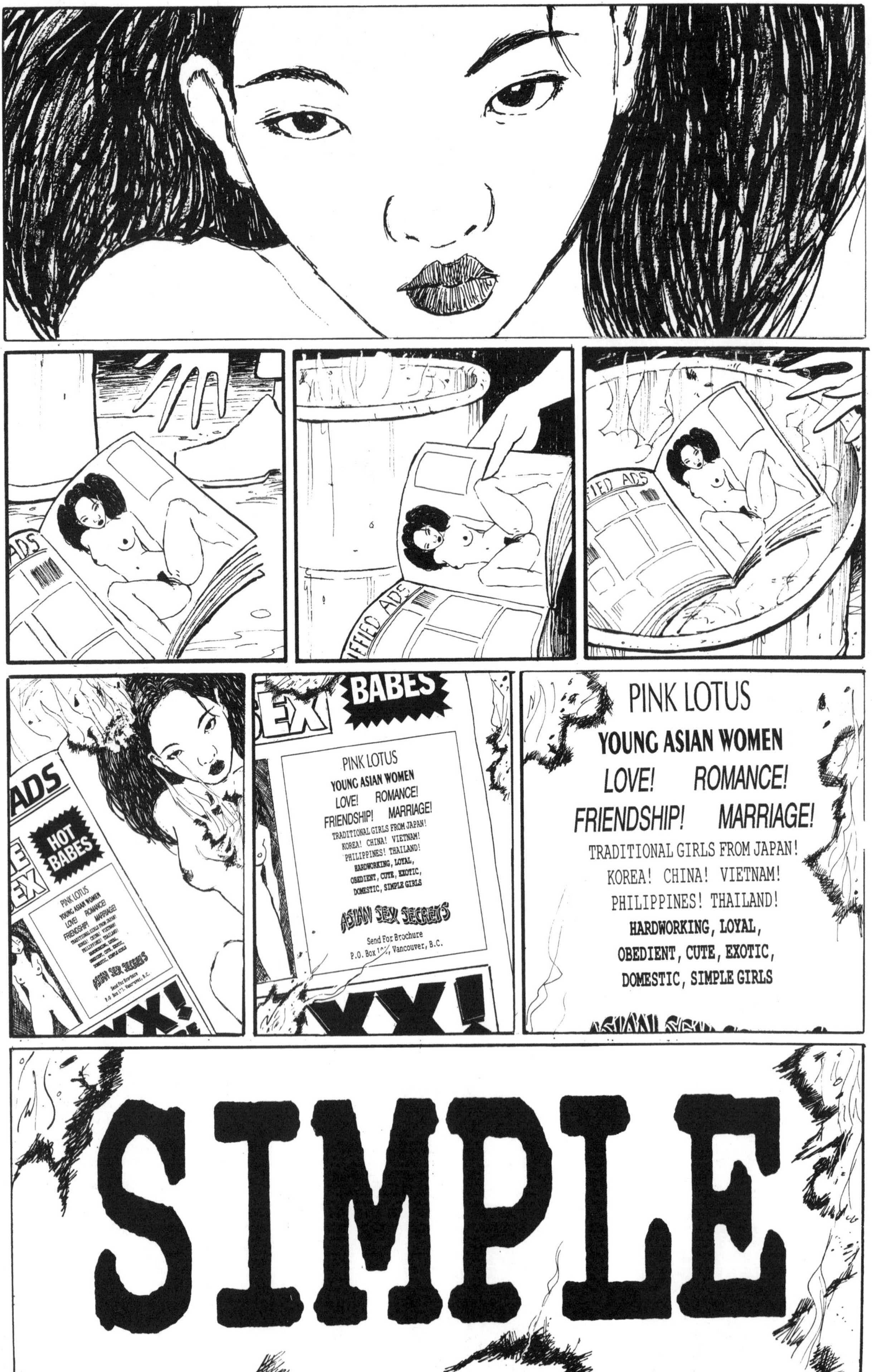
ADS
ADS
HOT BABES
SEX
BABES
PINK LOTUS
YOUNG ASIAN WOMEN
LOVE! ROMANCE!
FRIENDSHIP! MARRIAGE!
TRADITIONAL GIRLS FROM JAPAN!
KOREA! CHINA! VIETNAM!
PHILIPPINES! THAILAND!
HARDWORKING, LOYAL,
OBEDIENT, CUTE, EXOTIC,
DOMESTIC, SIMPLE GIRLS
ASIAN SEX SECRETS
Send For Brochure
PINK LOTUS
YOUNG ASIAN WOMEN
LOVE! ROMANCE!
FRIENDSHIP! MARRIAGE!
TRADITIONAL GIRLS FROM JAPAN!
KOREA! CHINA! VIETNAM!
PHILIPPINES! THAILAND!
HARDWORKING, LOYAL,
OBEDIENT, CUTE, EXOTIC,
DOMESTIC, SIMPLE GIRLS
SIMPLE

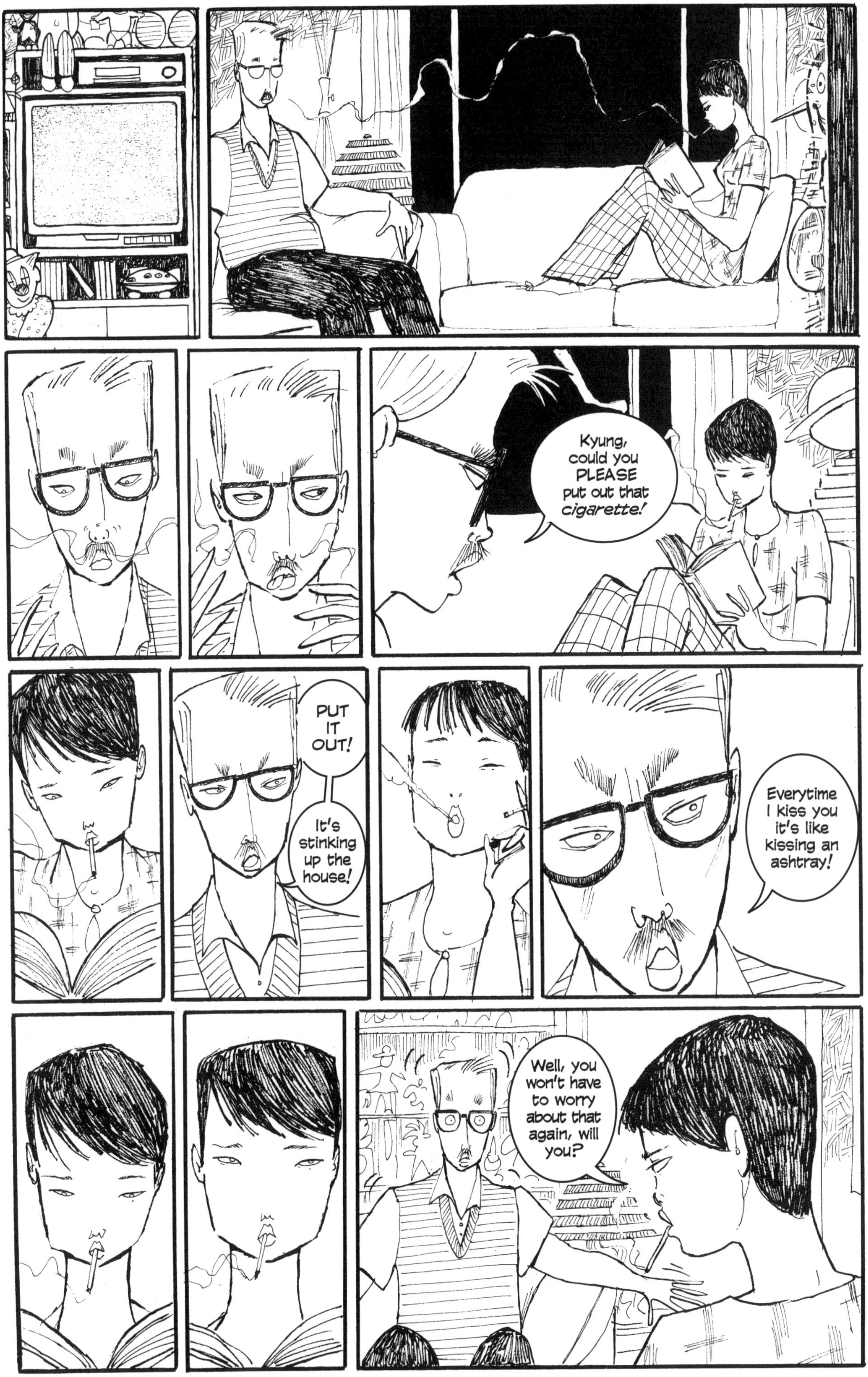
Kyung, could you PLEASE put out that *cigarette!*
PUT IT OUT!
It's stinking up the house!
Everytime I kiss you it's like kissing an ashtray!
Well, you won't have to worry about that again, will you?

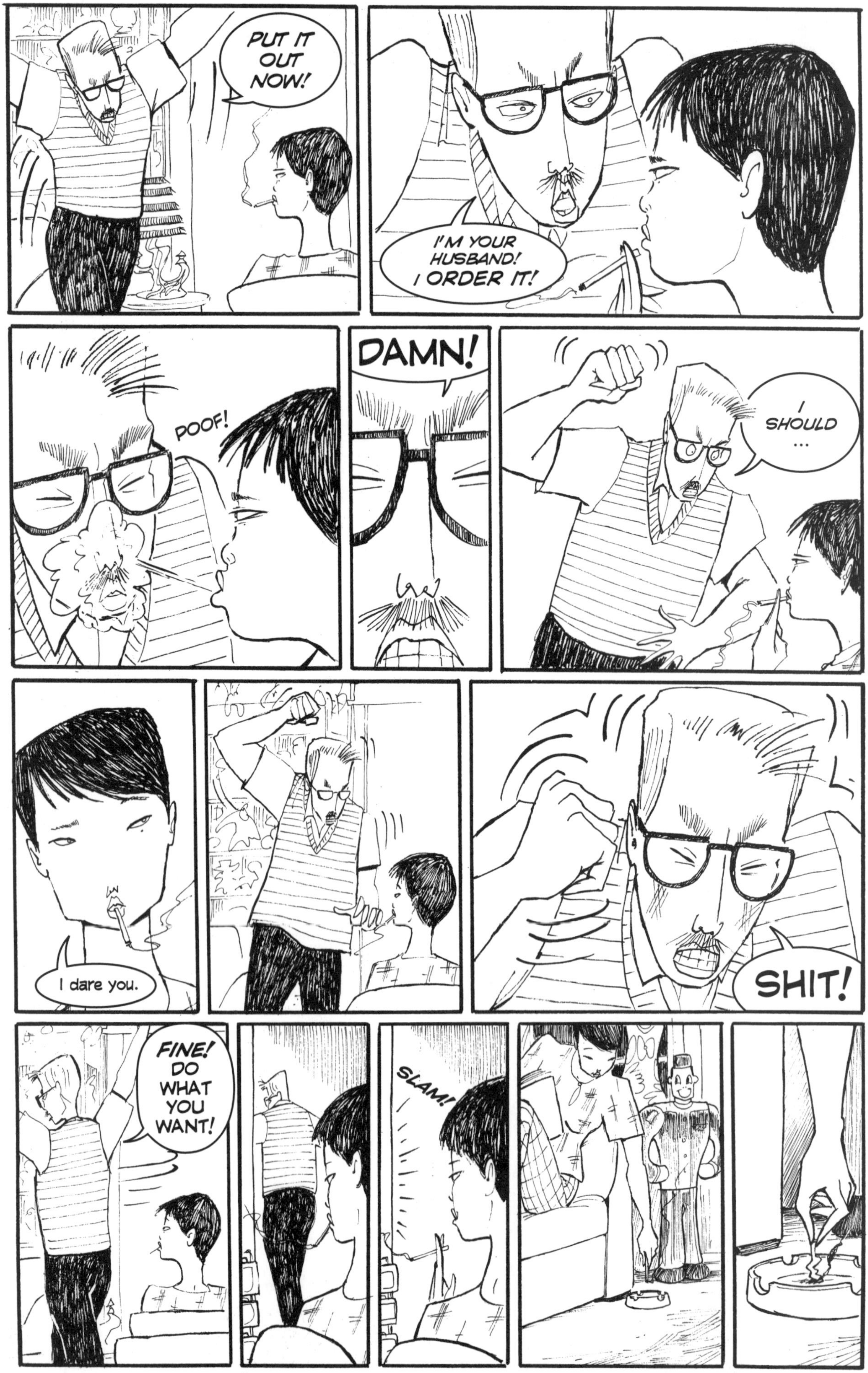
PUT IT OUT NOW!
I'M YOUR HUSBAND! I ORDER IT!
POOF!
DAMN!
I SHOULD ...
I dare you.
SHIT!
FINE! DO WHAT YOU WANT!
SLAM!

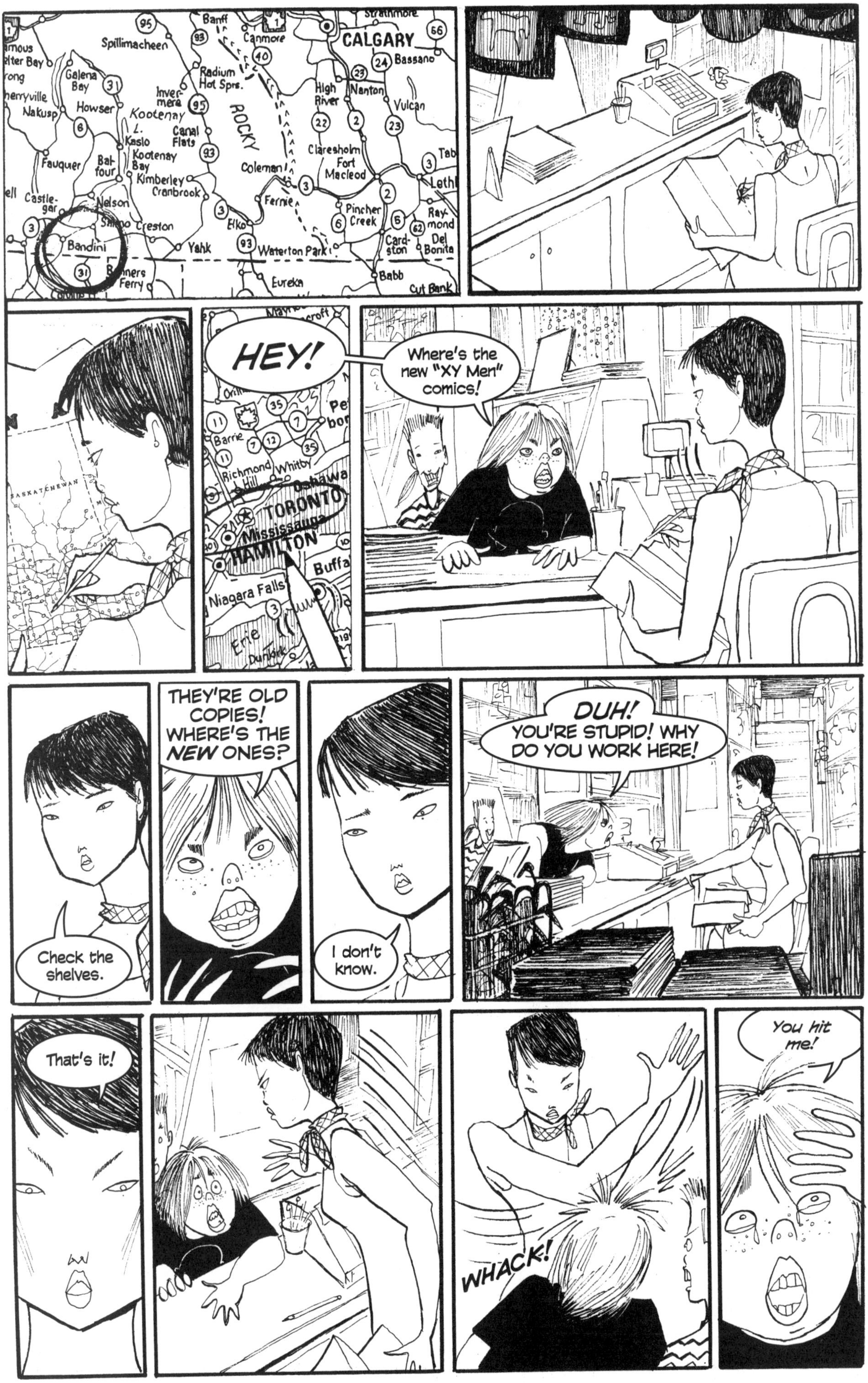

Banff
Canmore
Strathmore
CALGARY
Bassano
Spillimacheen
Radium Hot Sprs.
Galena Bay
Nakusp
Howser
Kootenay L.
Kaslo
Invermere
Canal Flats
ROCKY
High River
Nanton
Vulcan
Claresholm
Fort Macleod
Fauquier
Balfour
Kootenay Bay
Kimberley
Cranbrook
Coleman
Castlegar
Nelson
Creston
Fernie
Pincher Creek
Raymond
Bandini
Yahk
Elko
Waterton Park
Cardston
Del Bonita
Eureka
Babb
Cut Bank
SASKATCHEWAN
Barrie
Richmond Hill
Whitby
Oshawa
TORONTO
Mississauga
HAMILTON
Niagara Falls
Erie
Dunkirk
HEY!
Where's the new "XY Men" comics!
Check the shelves.
THEY'RE OLD COPIES! WHERE'S THE NEW ONES?
I don't know.
DUH! YOU'RE STUPID! WHY DO YOU WORK HERE!
That's it!
WHACK!
You hit me!

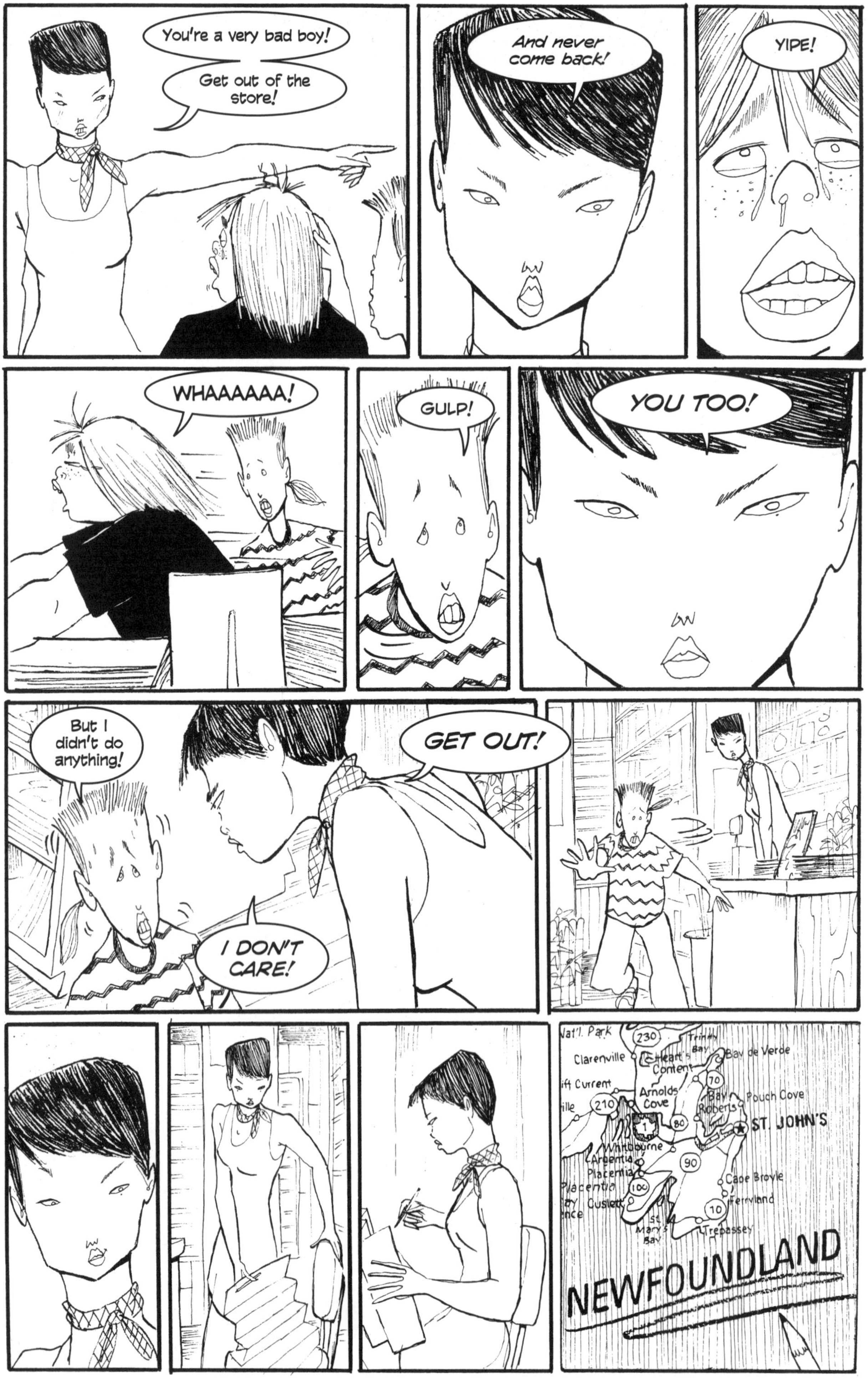

You're a very bad boy!
Get out of the store!
And never come back!
YIPE!
WHAAAAAA!
GULP!
YOU TOO!
But I didn't do anything!
GET OUT!
I DON'T CARE!
Nat'l. Park
230
Trinity Bay
Clarenville
Heart's Content
Bay de Verde
Swift Current
70
Arnolds Cove
Bay Roberts
Pouch Cove
210
80
ST. JOHN'S
1
Whitbourne
Argentia
90
Placentia
Placentia Bay
100
Cape Broyle
Cuslett
Ferryland
10
St. Mary's Bay
Trepassey
NEWFOUNDLAND

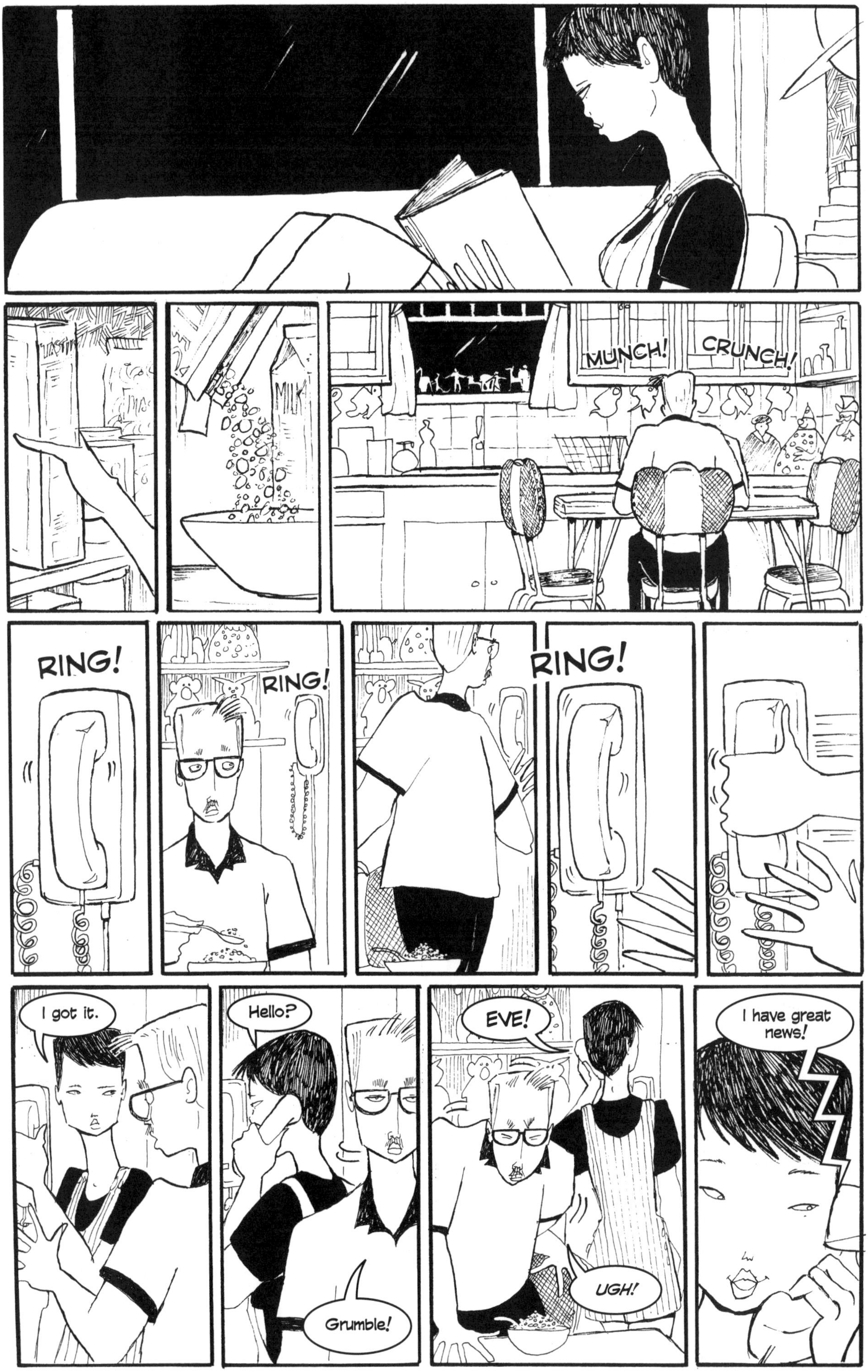
MILK
MUNCH!
CRUNCH!
RING!
RING!
RING!
I got it.
Hello?
Grumble!
EVE!
UGH!
I have great news!

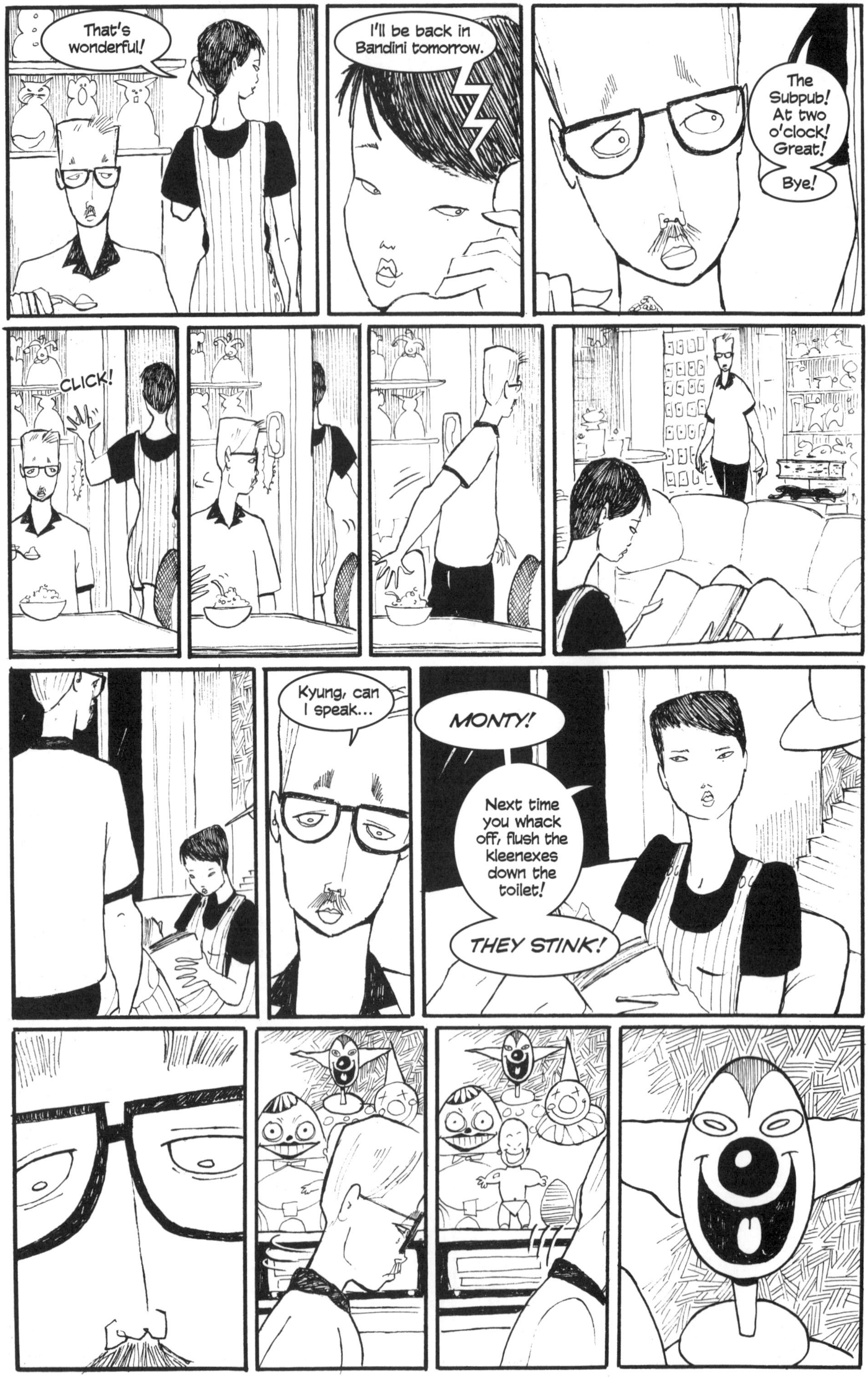
That's wonderful!
I'll be back in Bandini tomorrow.
The Subpub! At two o'clock! Great!
Bye!
CLICK!
Kyung, can I speak...
MONTY!
Next time you whack off, flush the kleenexes down the toilet!
THEY STINK!

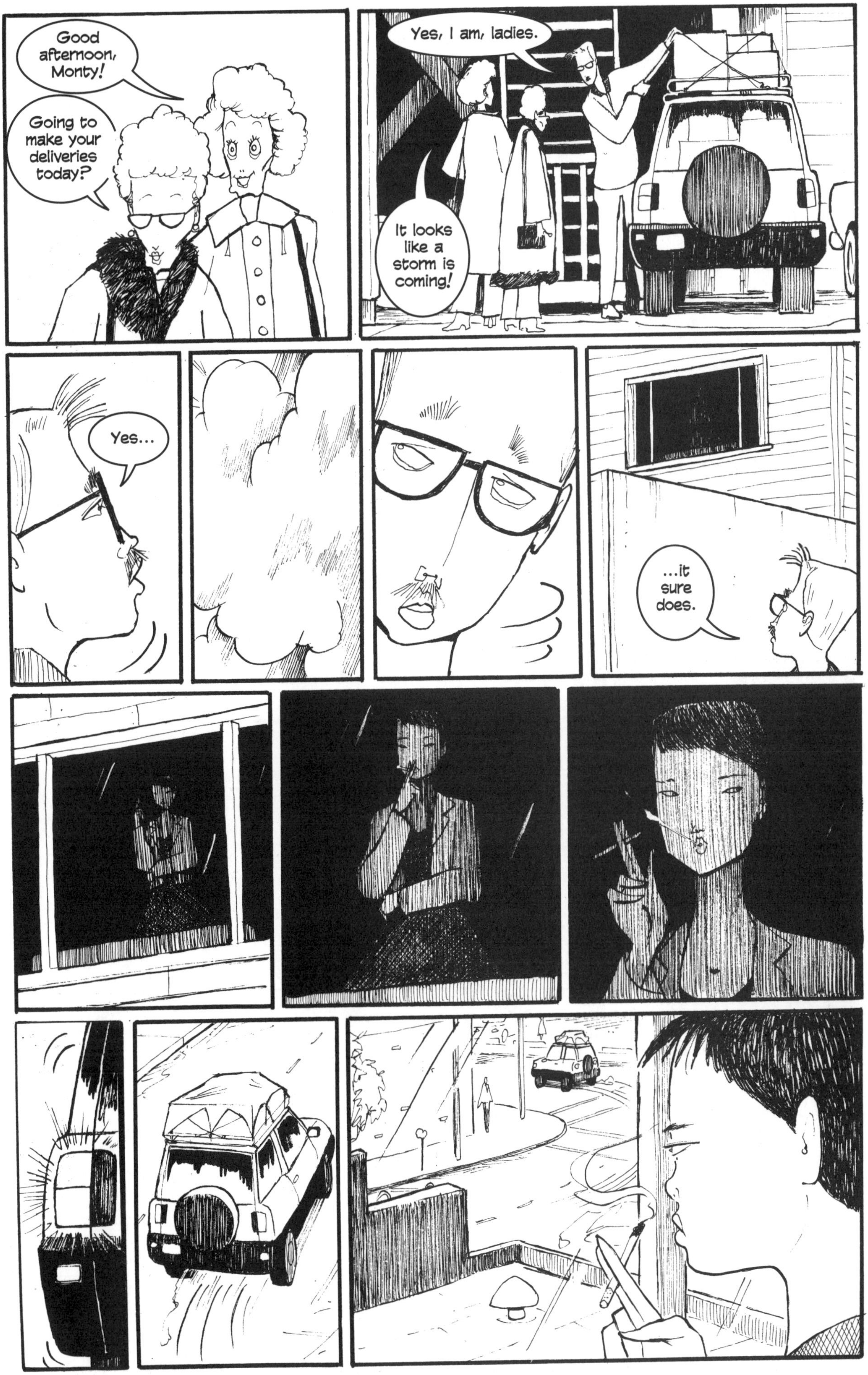
Good afternoon, Monty!
Going to make your deliveries today?
Yes, I am, ladies.
It looks like a storm is coming!
Yes...
...it sure does.

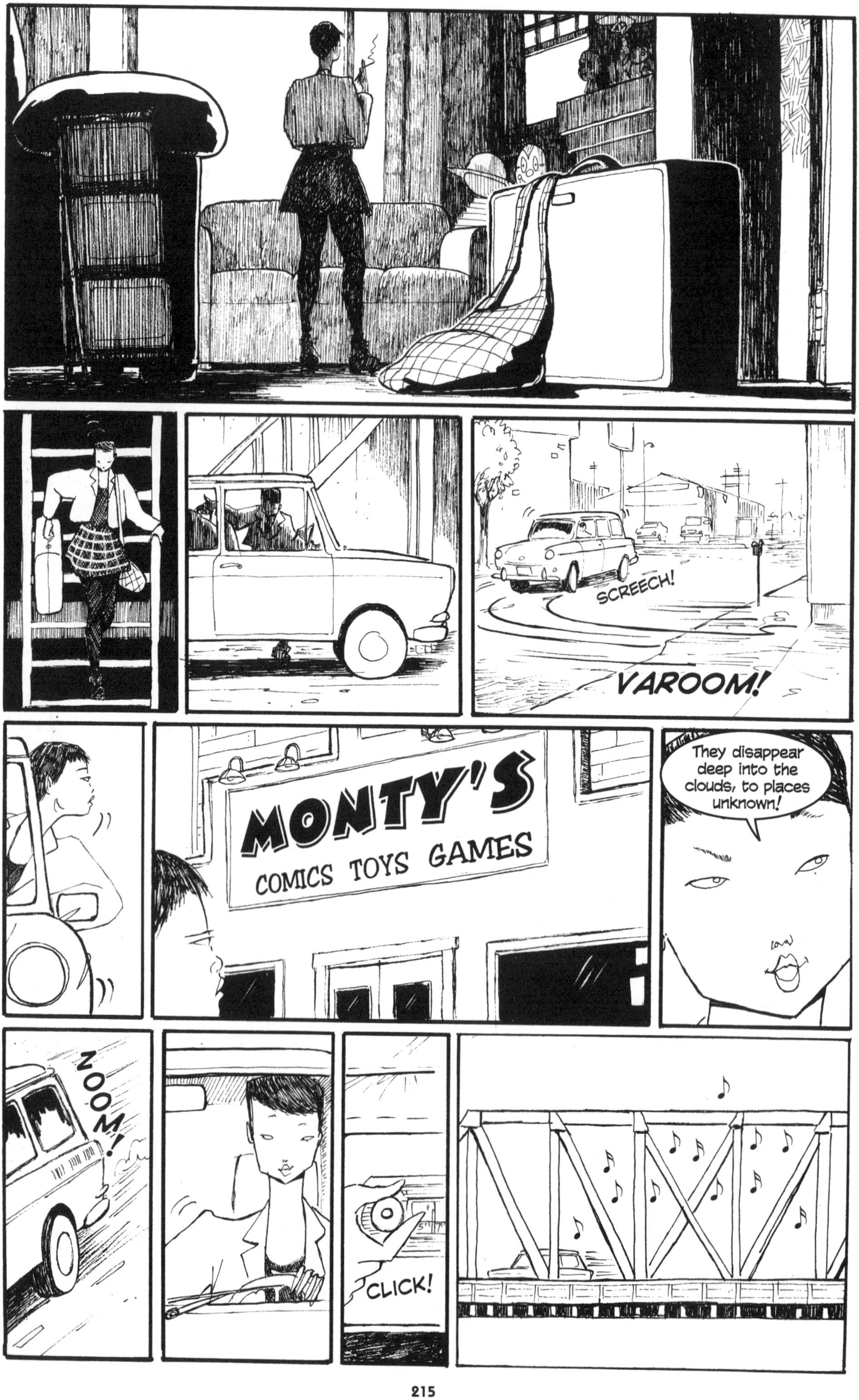
SCREECH!
VAROOM!
MONTY'S
COMICS TOYS GAMES
They disappear deep into the clouds, to places unknown!
ZOOM!
CLICK!

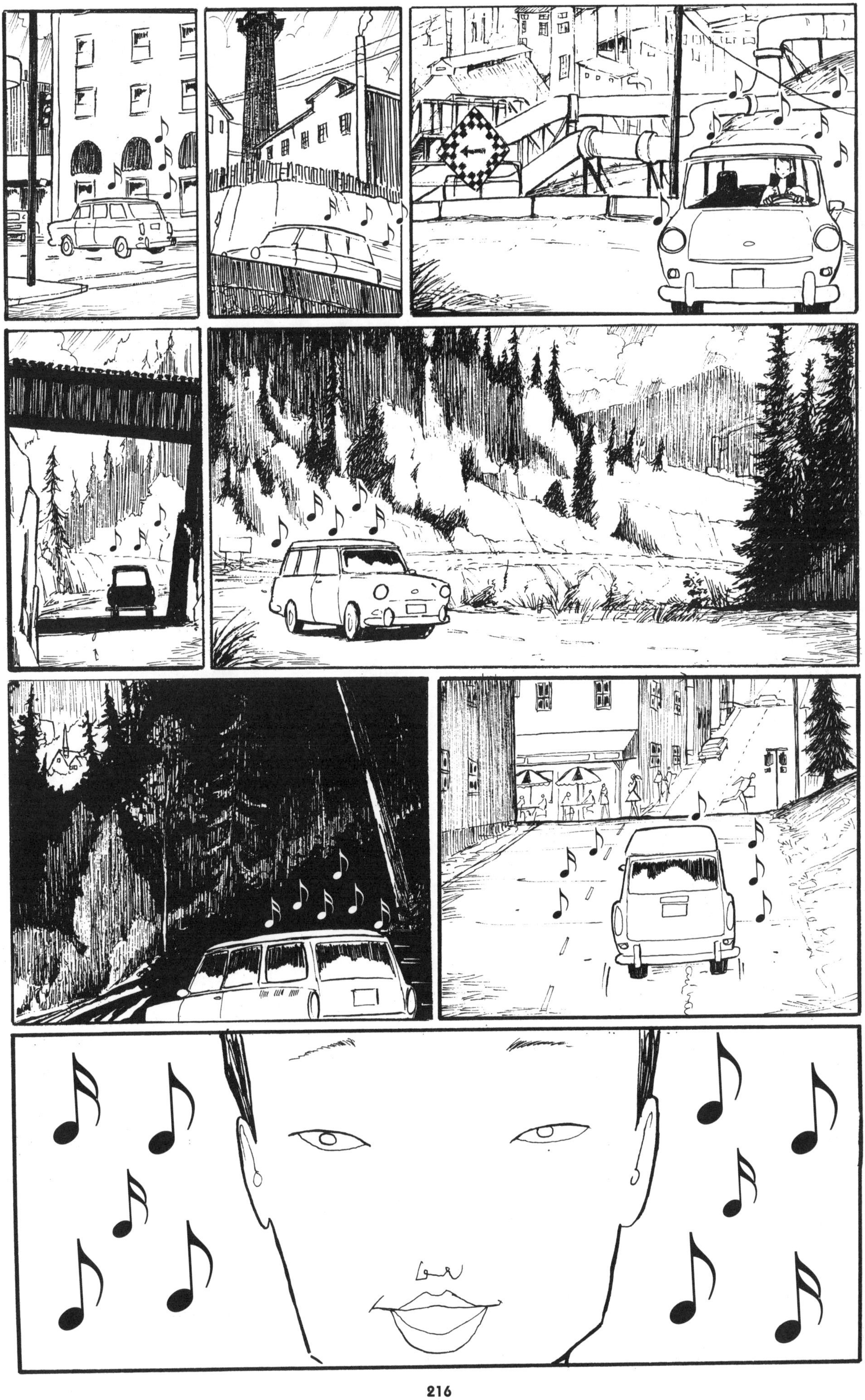

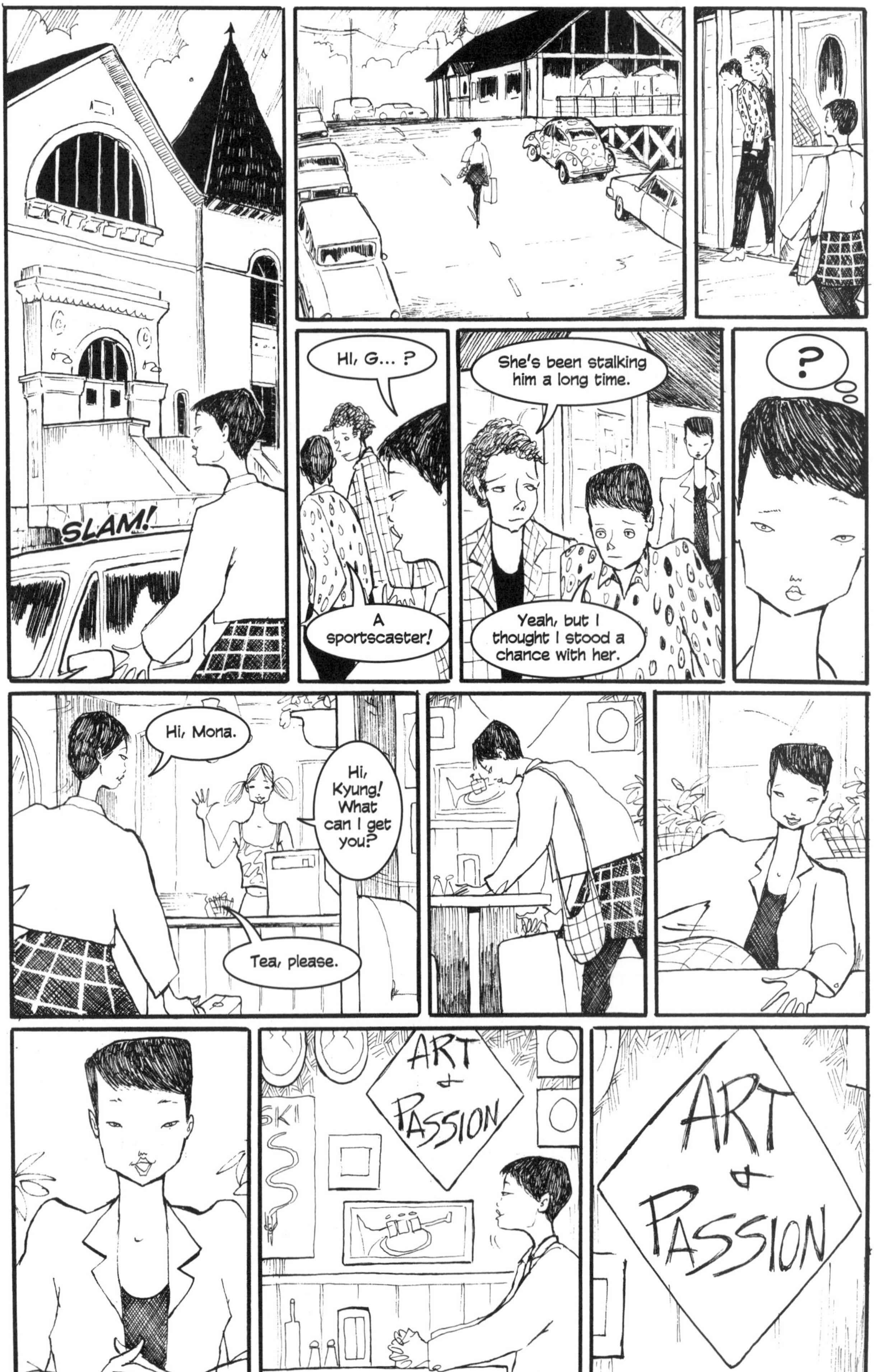
SLAM!
Hi, G... ?
A sportscaster!
She's been stalking him a long time.
Yeah, but I thought I stood a chance with her.
?
Hi, Mona.
Hi, Kyung! What can I get you?
Tea, please.
ART & PASSION
SKI
ART & PASSION

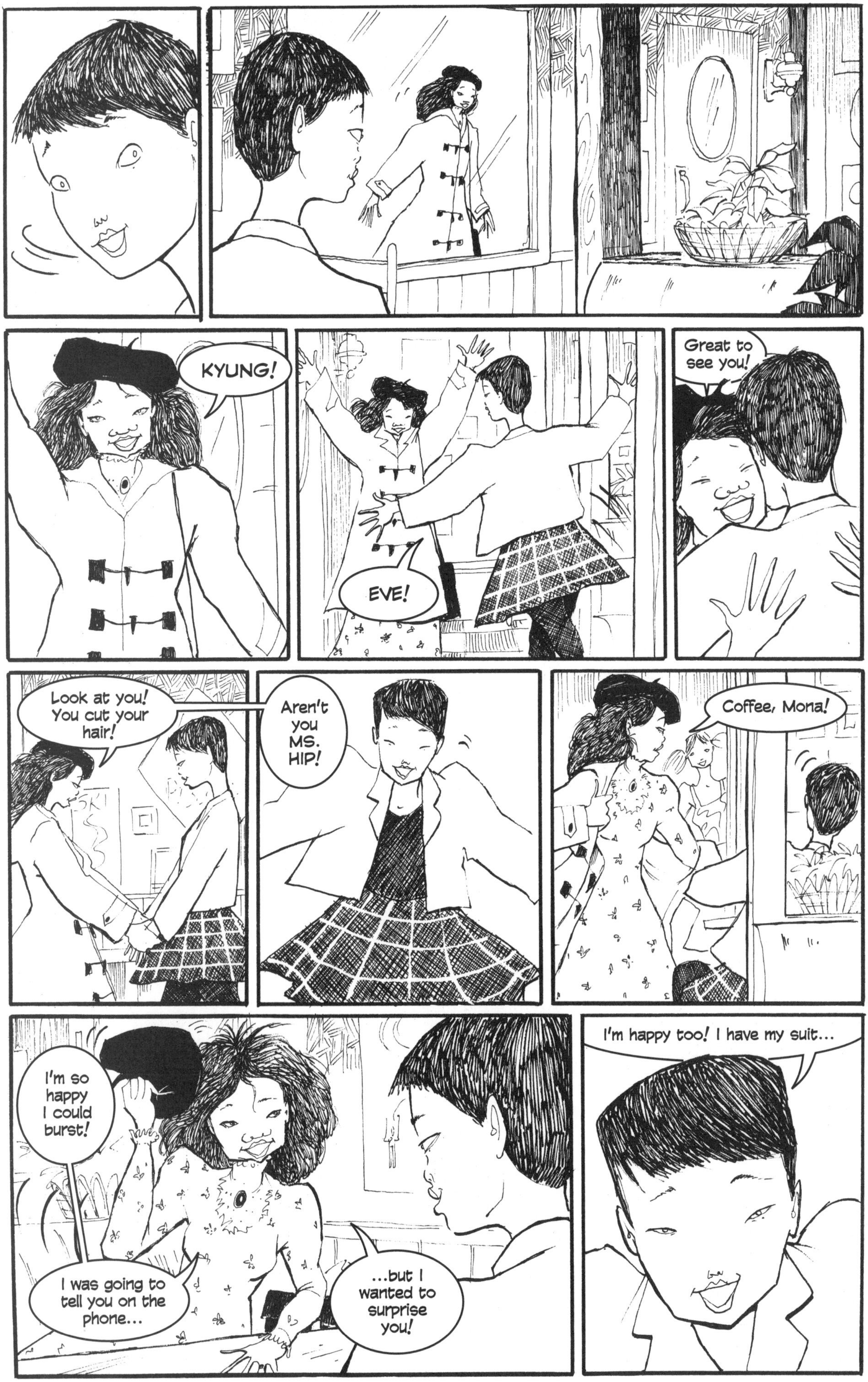
KYUNG!
EVE!
Great to see you!
Look at you! You cut your hair!
Aren't you MS. HIP!
Coffee, Mona!
I'm so happy I could burst!
I was going to tell you on the phone...
...but I wanted to surprise you!
I'm happy too! I have my suit...

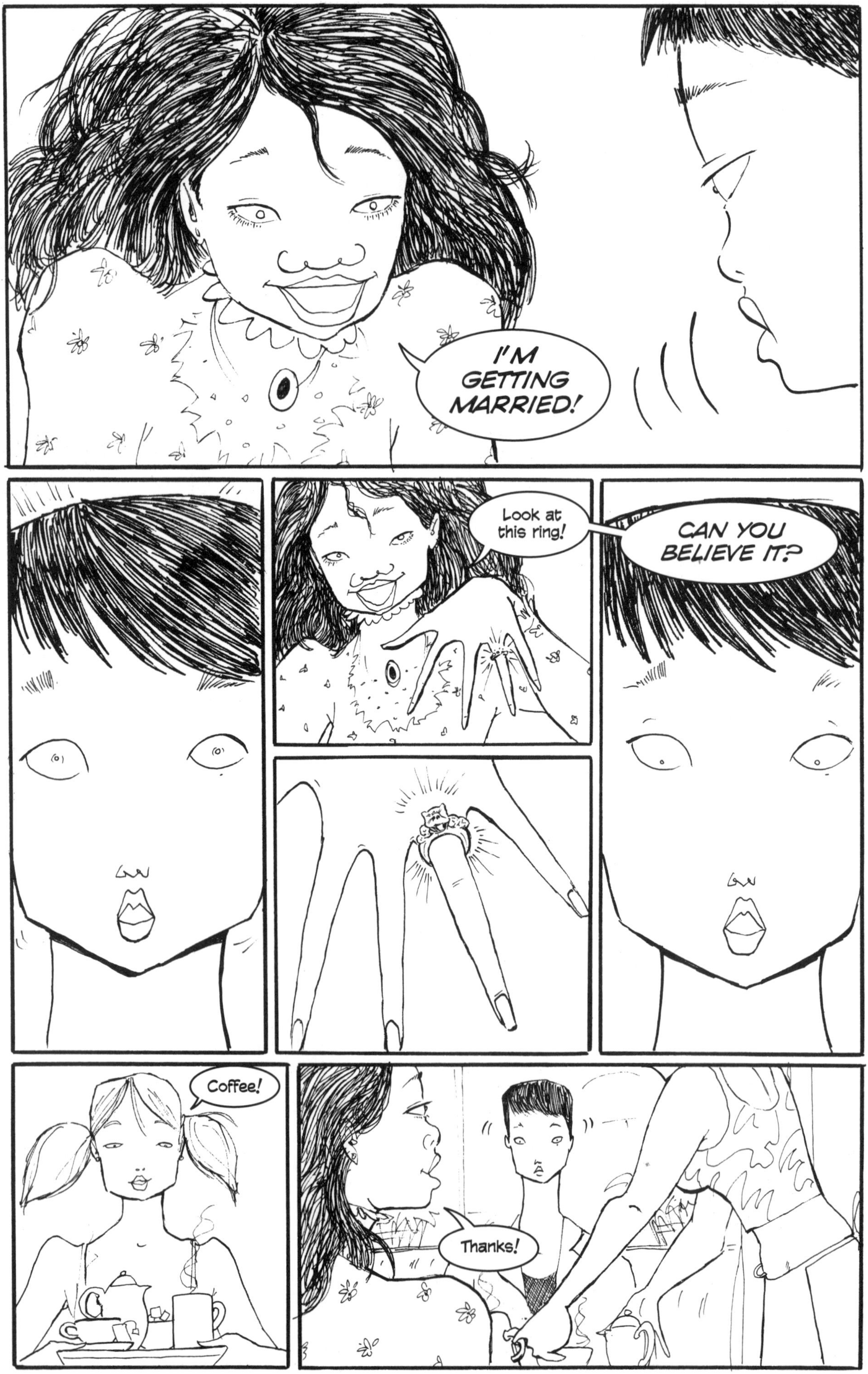
I'M GETTING MARRIED!
Look at this ring!
CAN YOU BELIEVE IT?
Coffee!
Thanks!

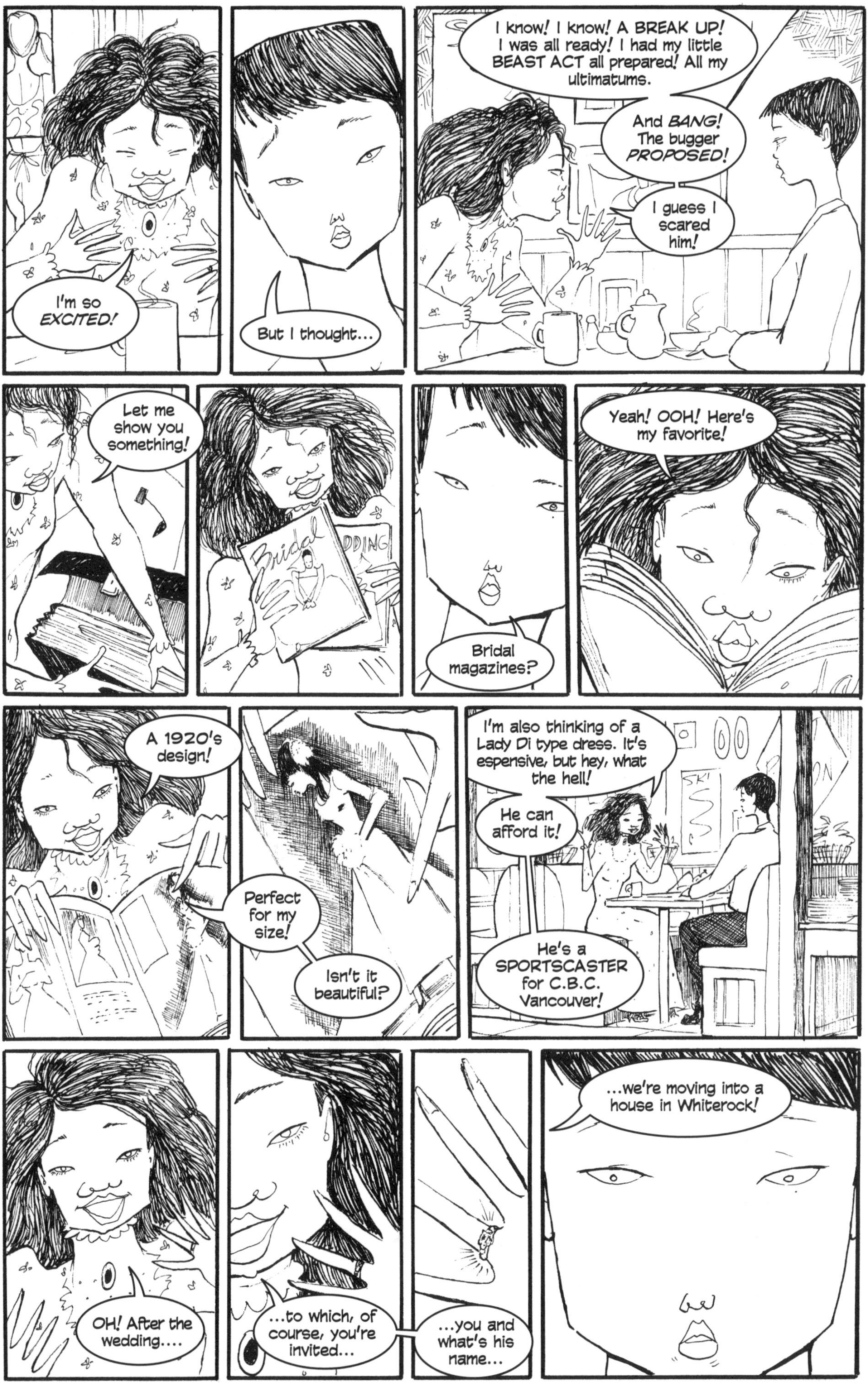
I'm so EXCITED!
But I thought...
I know! I know! A BREAK UP! I was all ready! I had my little BEAST ACT all prepared! All my ultimatums.
And BANG! The bugger PROPOSED!
I guess I scared him!
Let me show you something!
Bridal
Bridal magazines?
Yeah! OOH! Here's my favorite!
A 1920's design!
Perfect for my size!
Isn't it beautiful?
I'm also thinking of a Lady Di type dress. It's espensive, but hey, what the hell!
He can afford it!
He's a SPORTSCASTER for C.B.C. Vancouver!
OH! After the wedding....
...to which, of course, you're invited...
...you and what's his name...
...we're moving into a house in Whiterock!

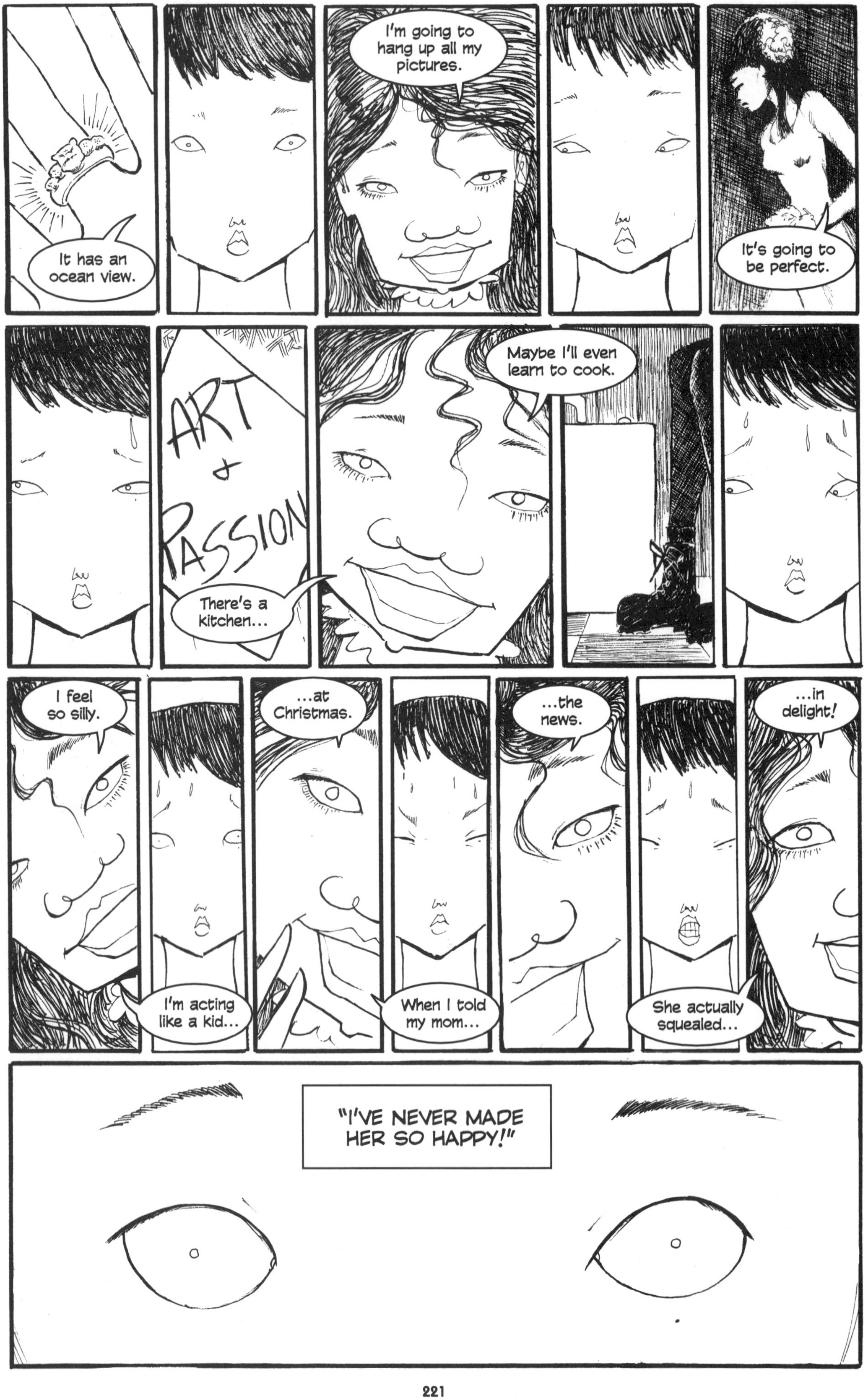
It has an ocean view.
I'm going to hang up all my pictures.
It's going to be perfect.
ART & PASSION
There's a kitchen...
Maybe I'll even learn to cook.
I feel so silly.
I'm acting like a kid...
...at Christmas.
When I told my mom...
...the news.
She actually squealed...
...in delight!
"I'VE NEVER MADE HER SO HAPPY!"

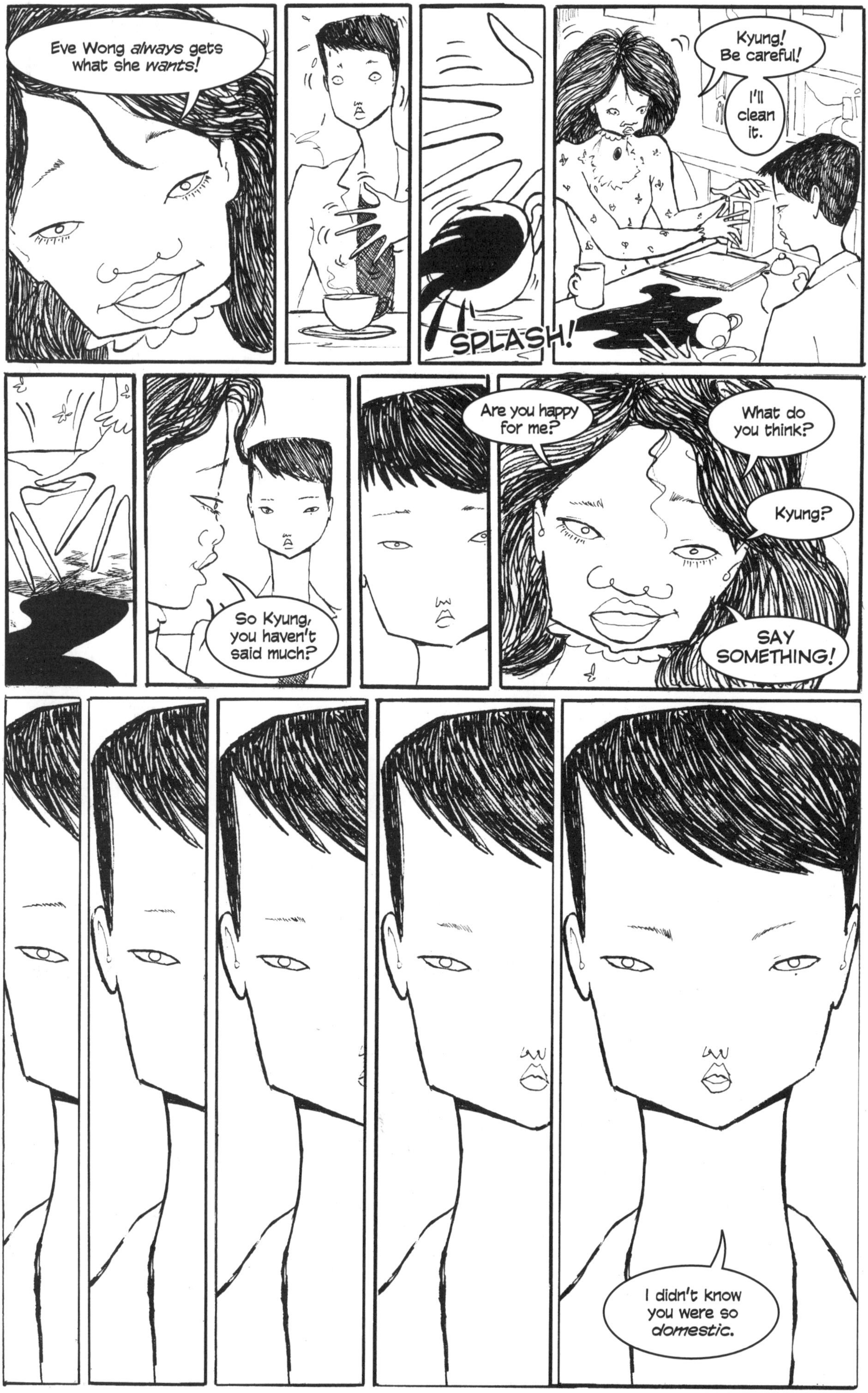

Eve Wong *always* gets what she *wants*!
SPLASH!
Kyung! Be careful!
I'll clean it.
So Kyung, you haven't said much?
Are you happy for me?
What do you think?
Kyung?
SAY SOMETHING!
I didn't know you were so *domestic*.

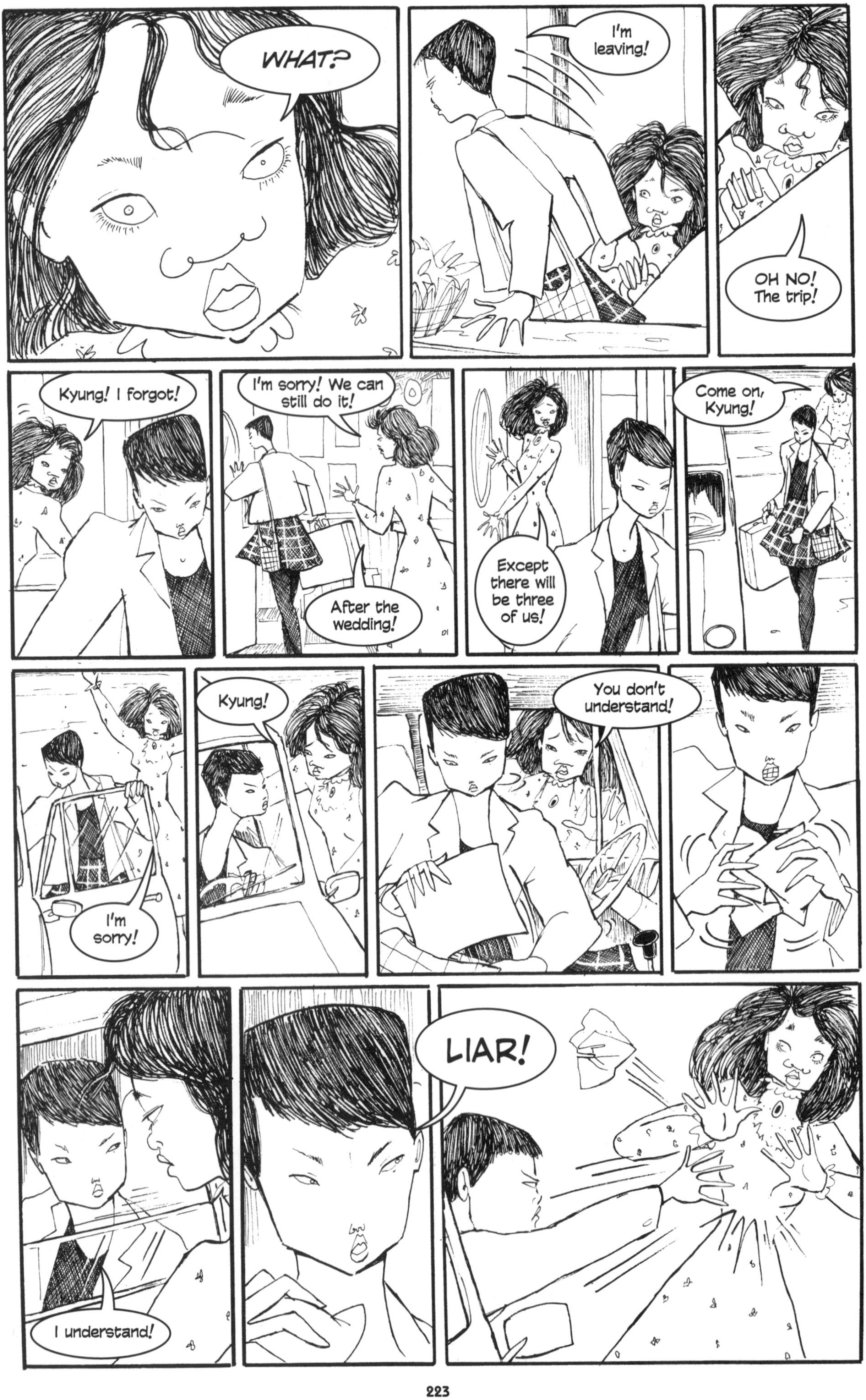
WHAT?
I'm leaving!
OH NO! The trip!
Kyung! I forgot!
I'm sorry! We can still do it!
After the wedding!
Except there will be three of us!
Come on, Kyung!
I'm sorry!
Kyung!
You don't understand!
I understand!
LIAR!

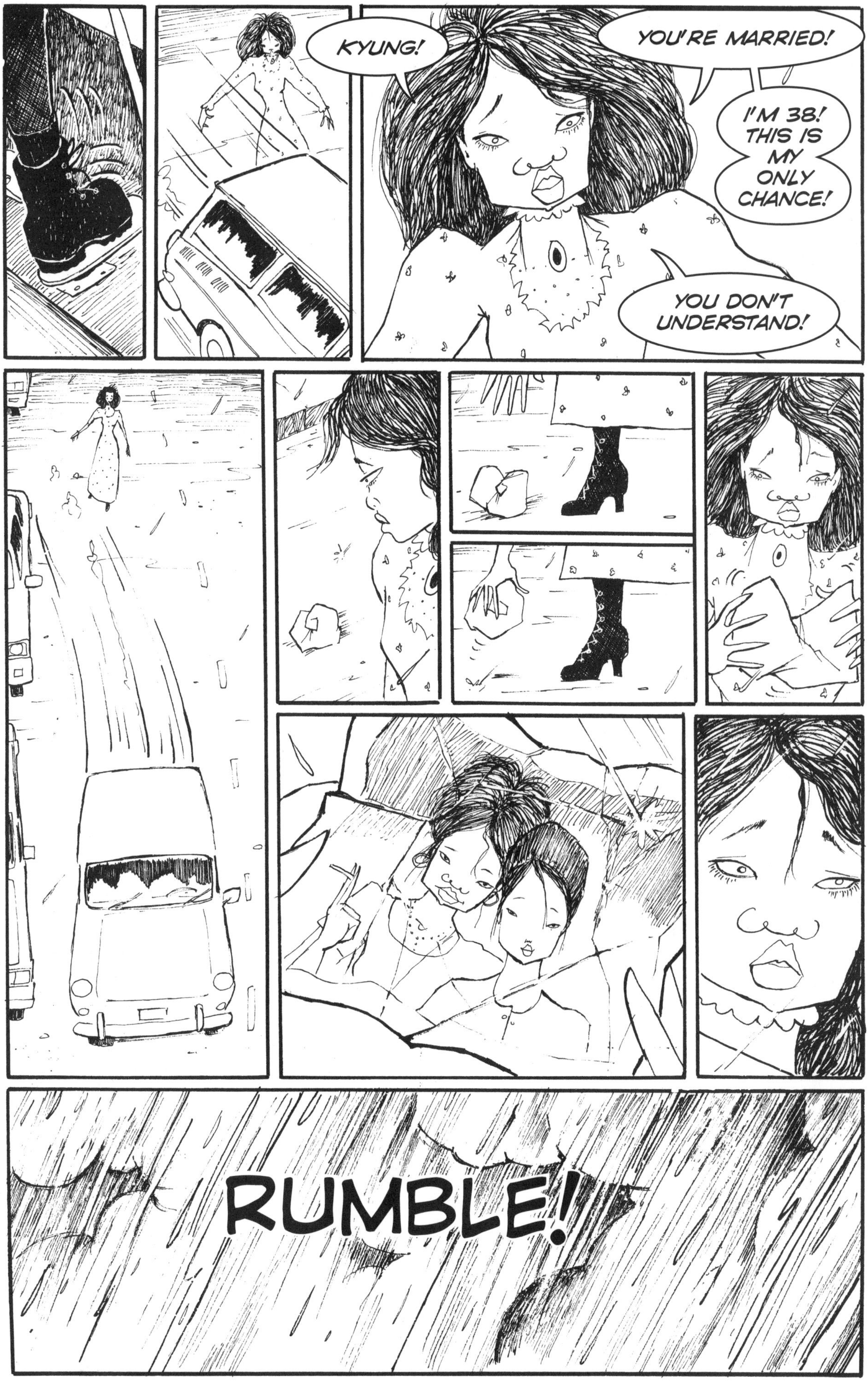
KYUNG!
YOU'RE MARRIED!
I'M 38! THIS IS MY ONLY CHANCE!
YOU DON'T UNDERSTAND!
RUMBLE!

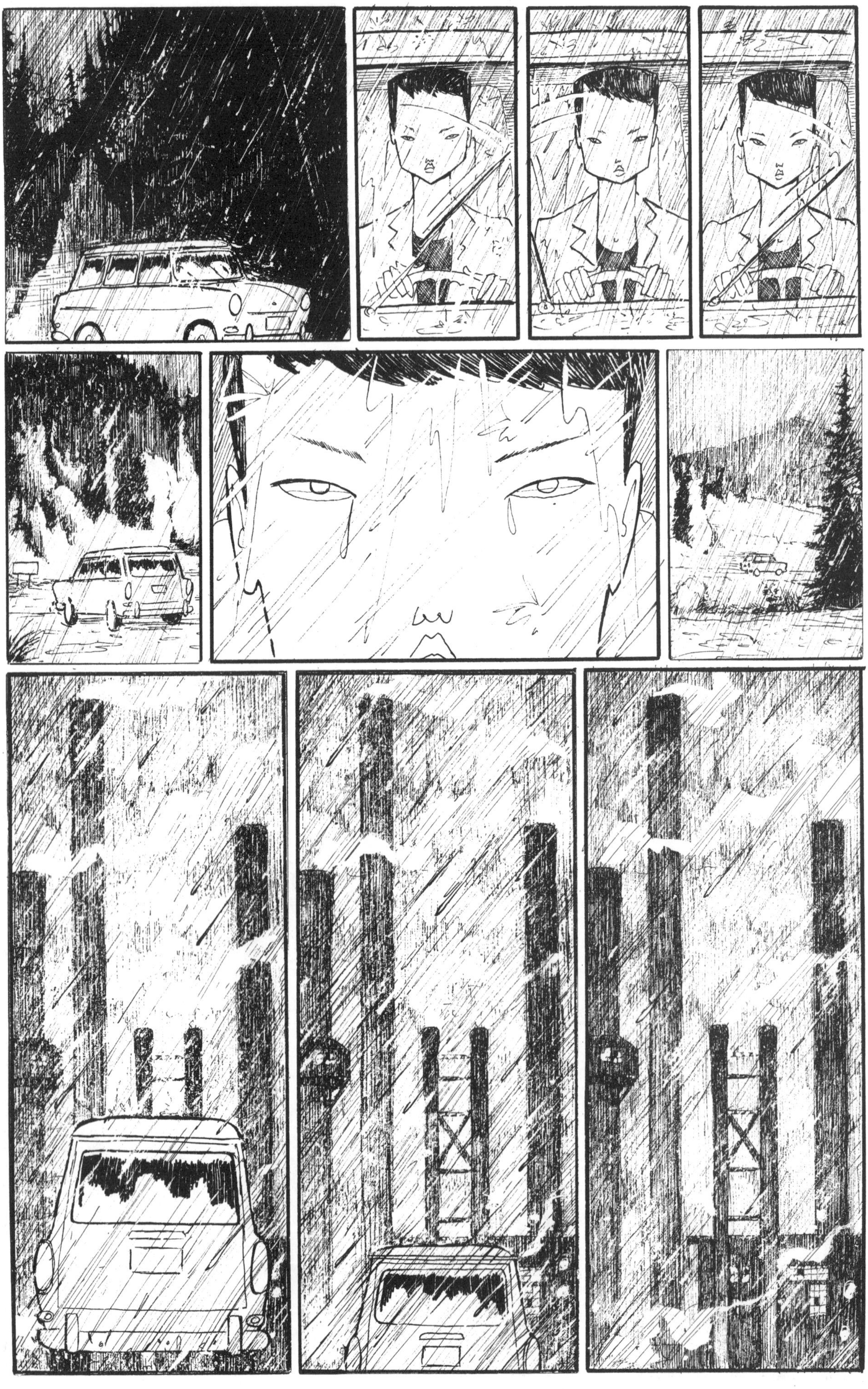

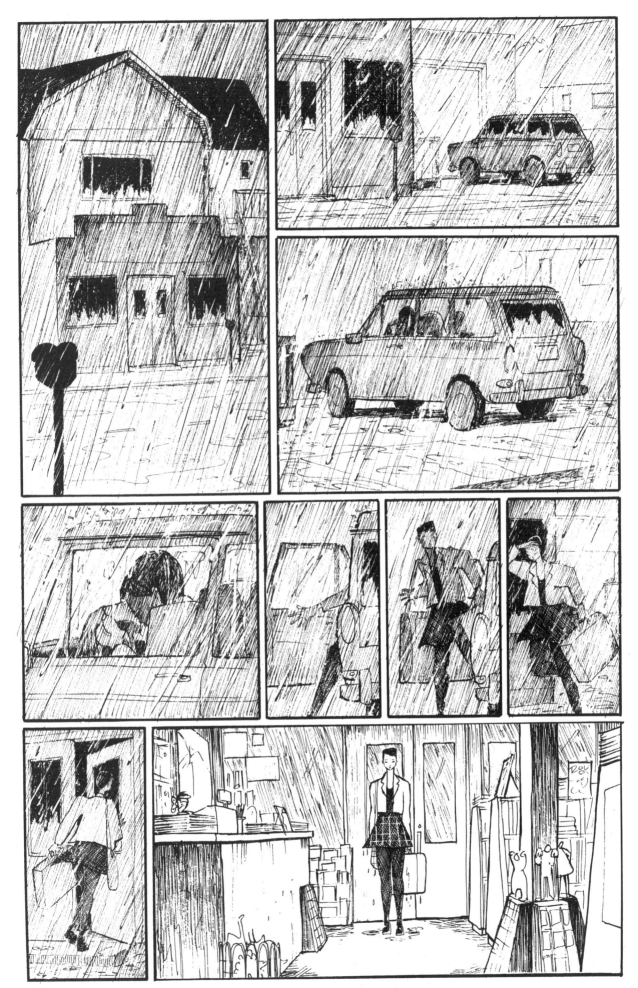

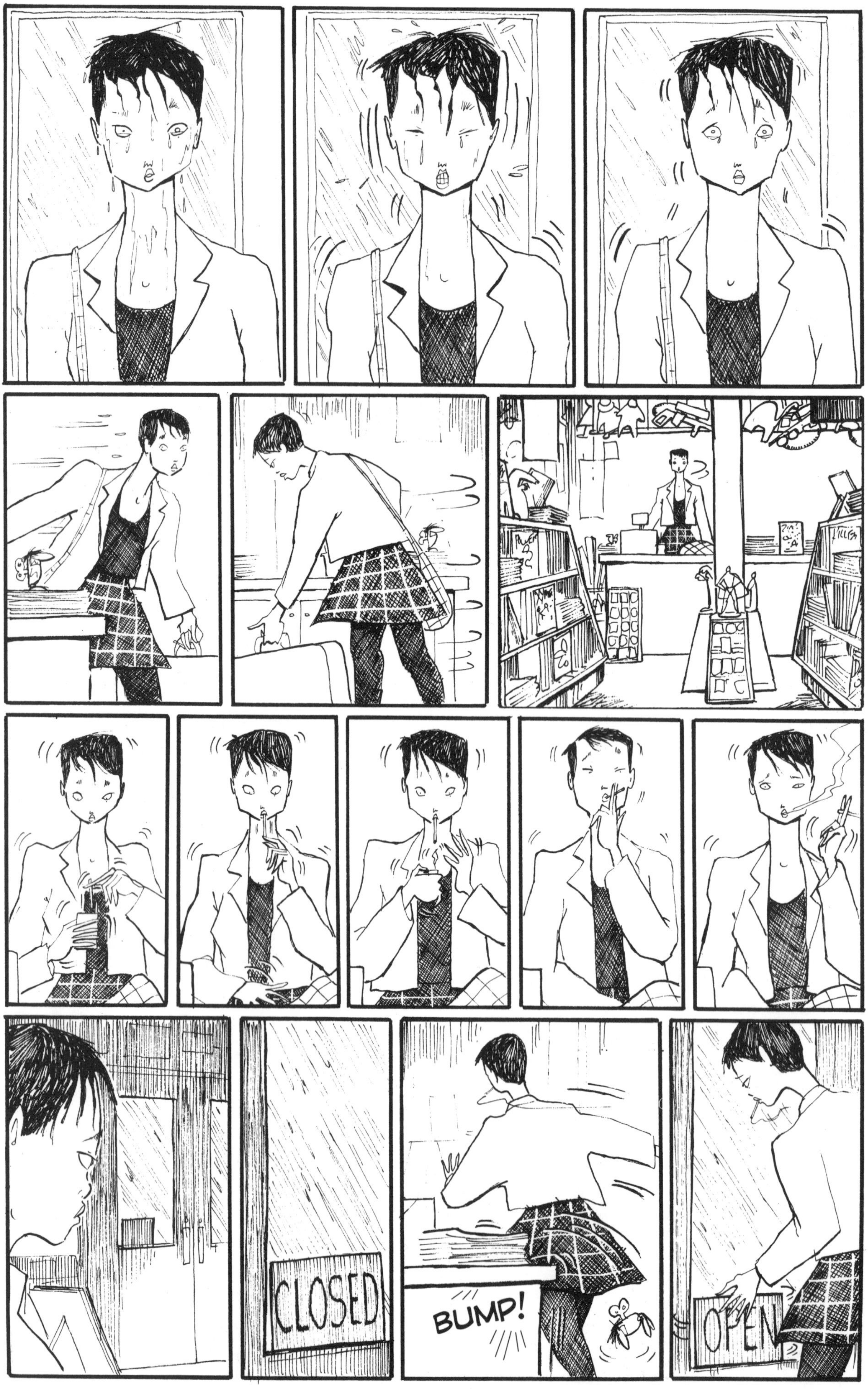
CLOSED
BUMP!
OPEN

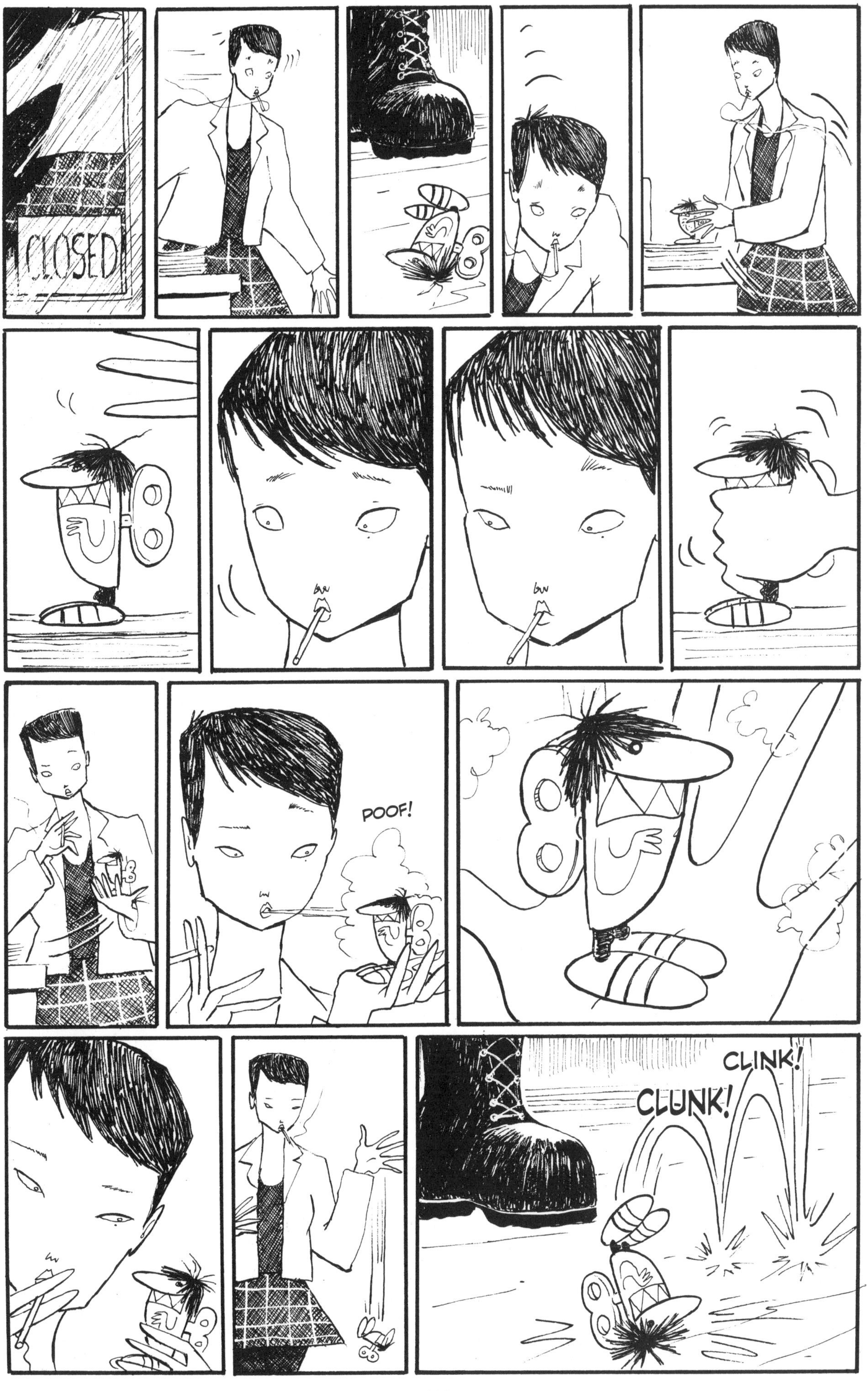
CLOSED
POOF!
CLUNK!
CLINK!

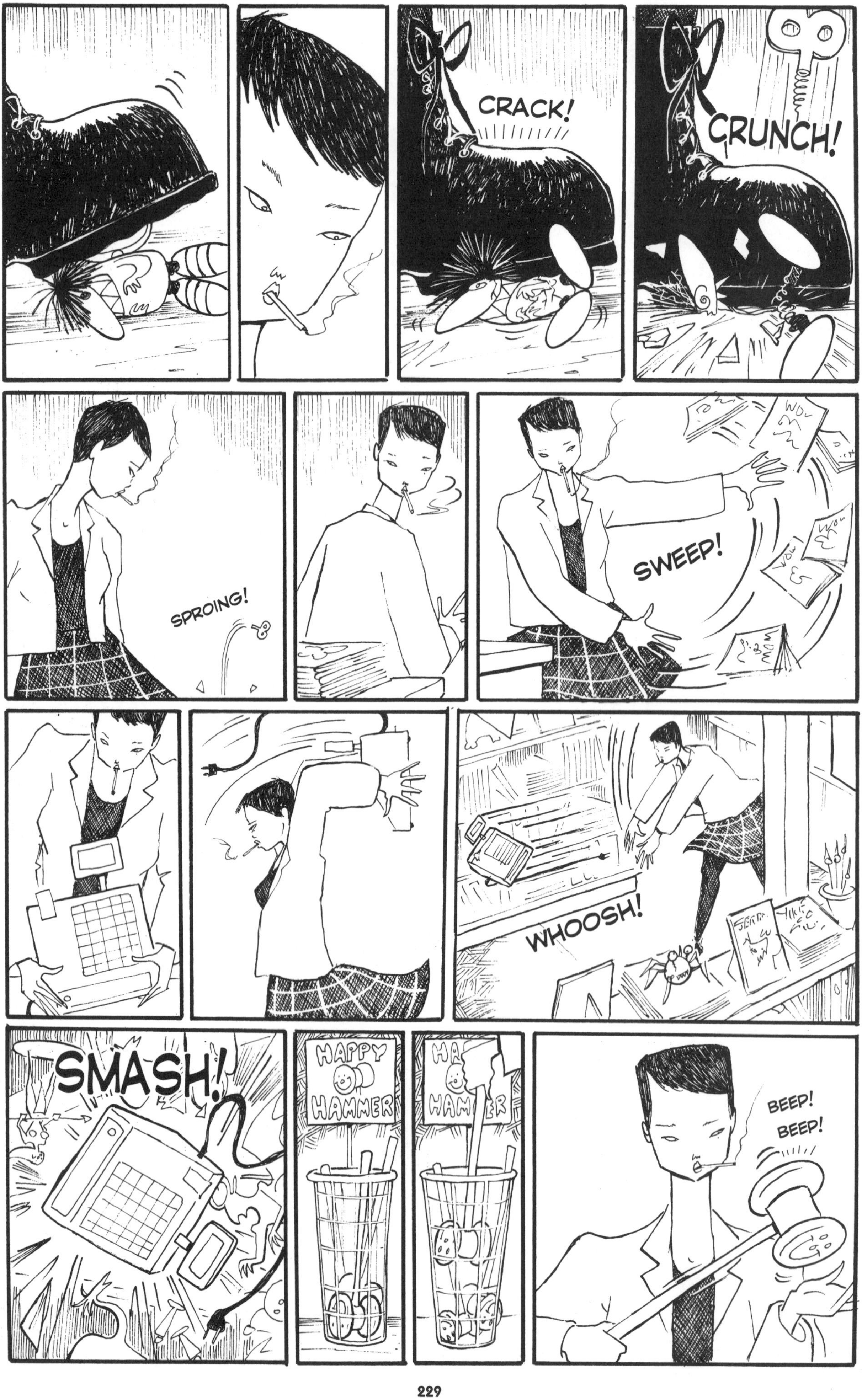
CRACK!
CRUNCH!
SPROING!
SWEEP!
WHOOSH!
SMASH!
HAPPY HAMMER
BEEP! BEEP!

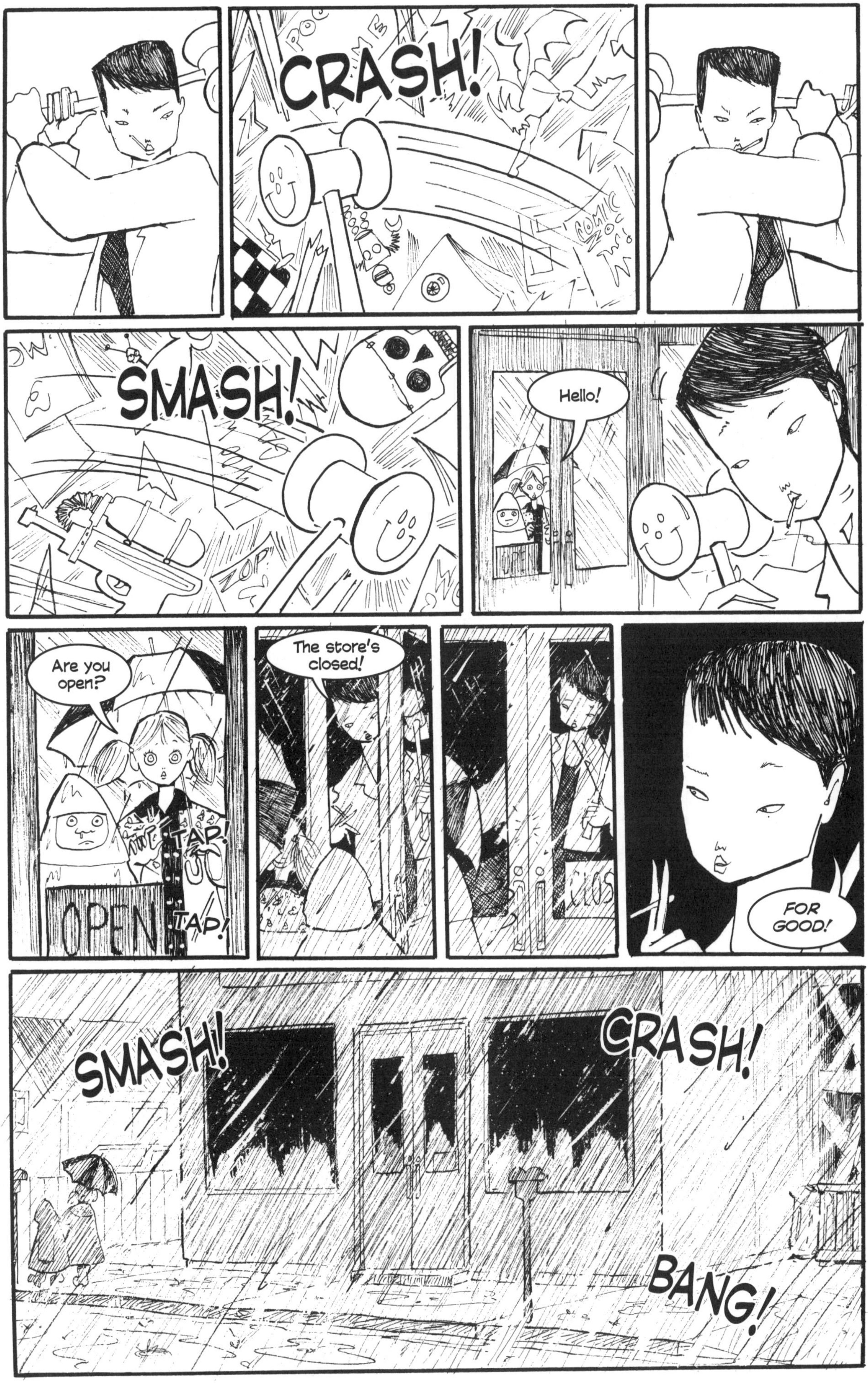
CRASH!
SMASH!
Hello!
Are you open?
TAP!
TAP!
OPEN
The store's closed!
FOR GOOD!
SMASH!
CRASH!
BANG!

SPLASH! SCREECH!

Well, she's home for once!

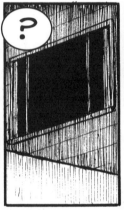

?

Why are there no lights on?

What's on the floor?

CRUNCH!

CRACK!

OUCH!

WHAT'S THIS?!!!

CLICK!

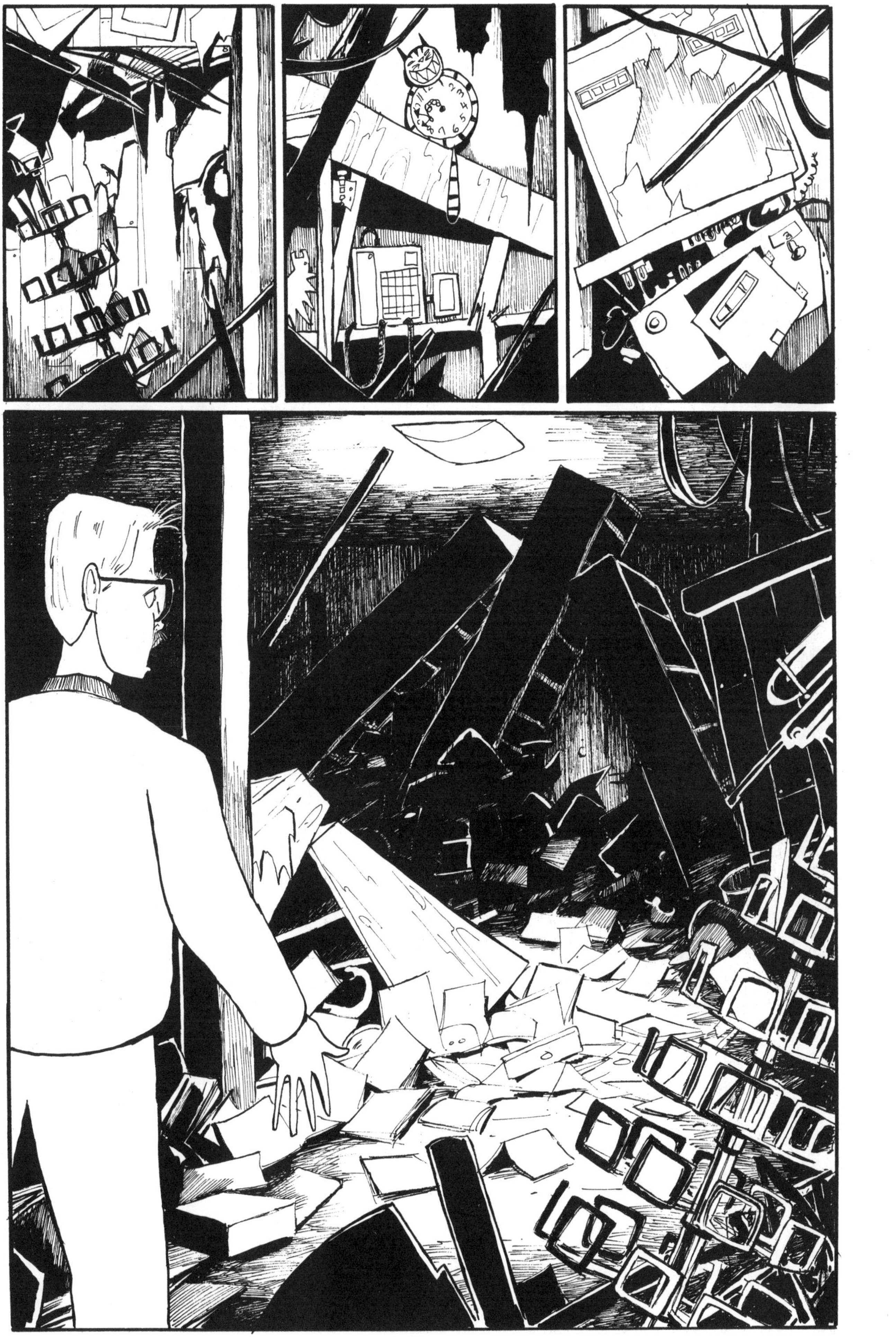

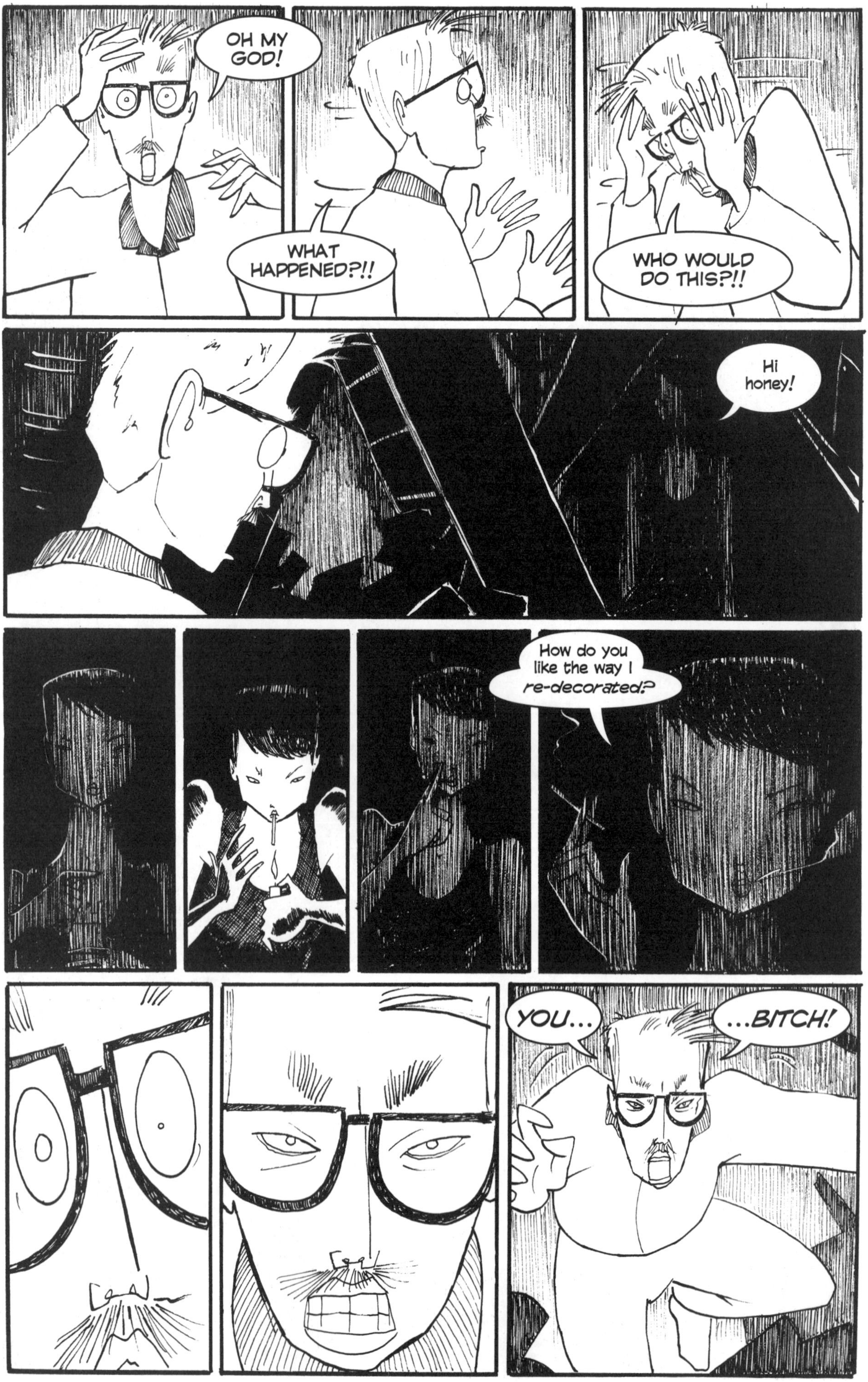
OH MY GOD!
WHAT HAPPENED?!!
WHO WOULD DO THIS?!!
Hi honey!
How do you like the way I *re-decorated?*
YOU...
...BITCH!

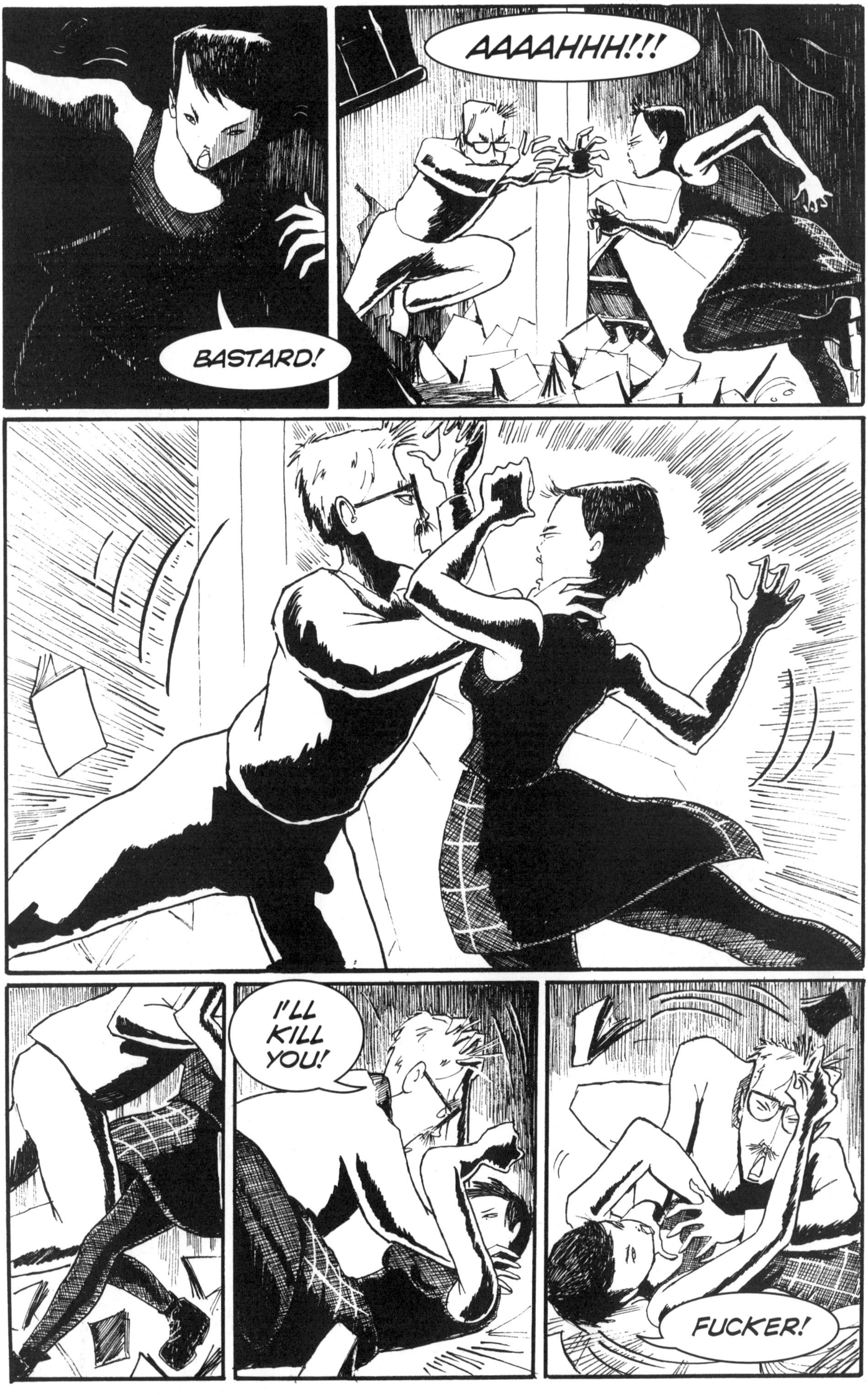
BASTARD!
AAAAHHH!!!
I'LL KILL YOU!
FUCKER!

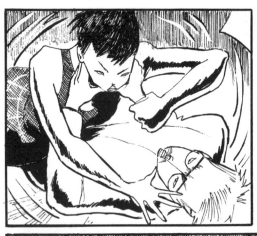

CRACK.

UGH!

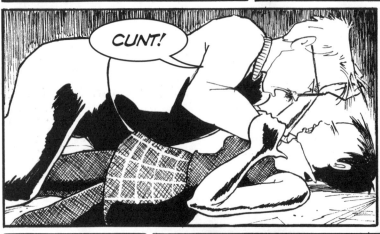

CUNT!

THUP!

UNGH!

WHACK!

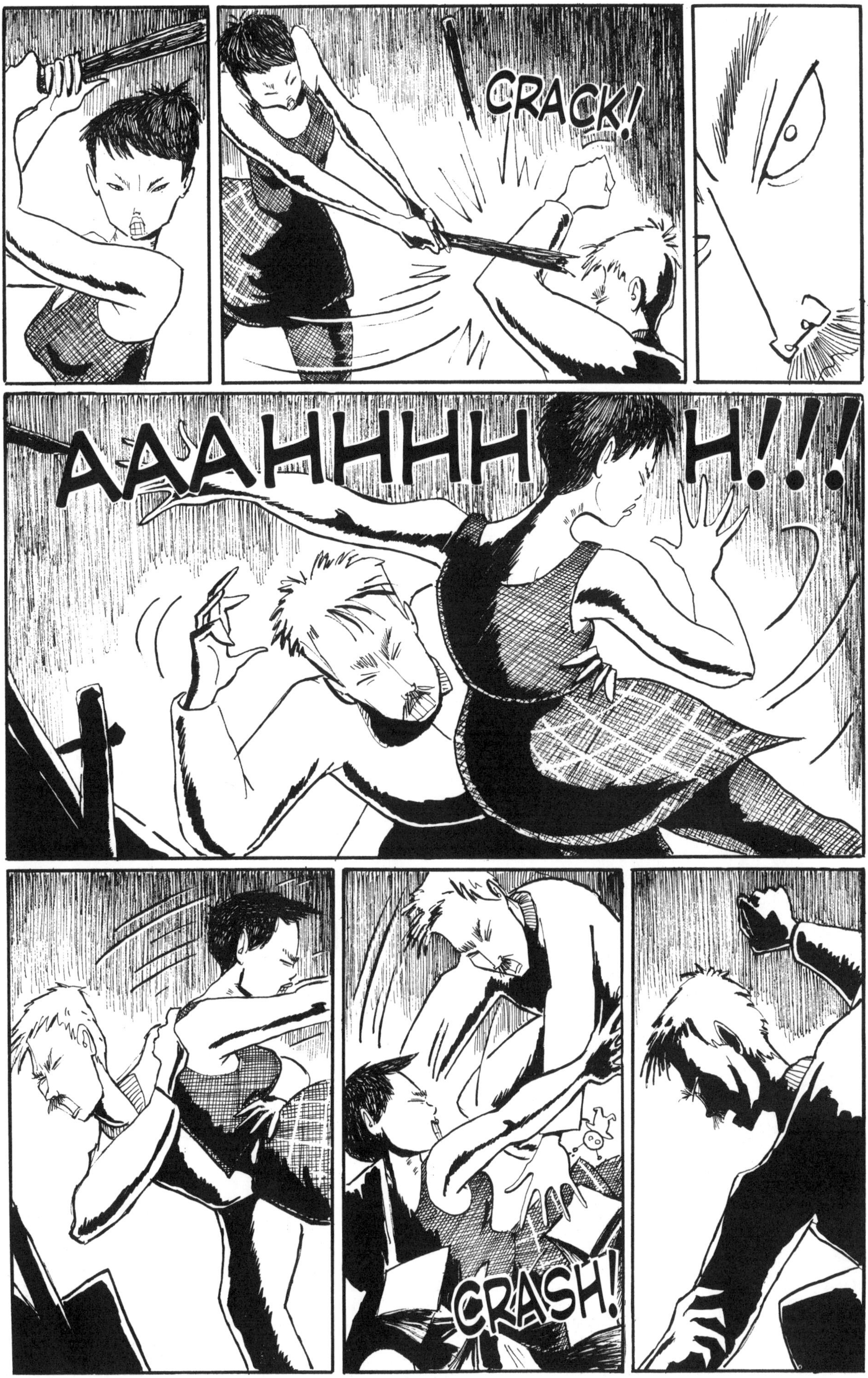
CRACK!
AAAHHHHH H!!!
CRASH!

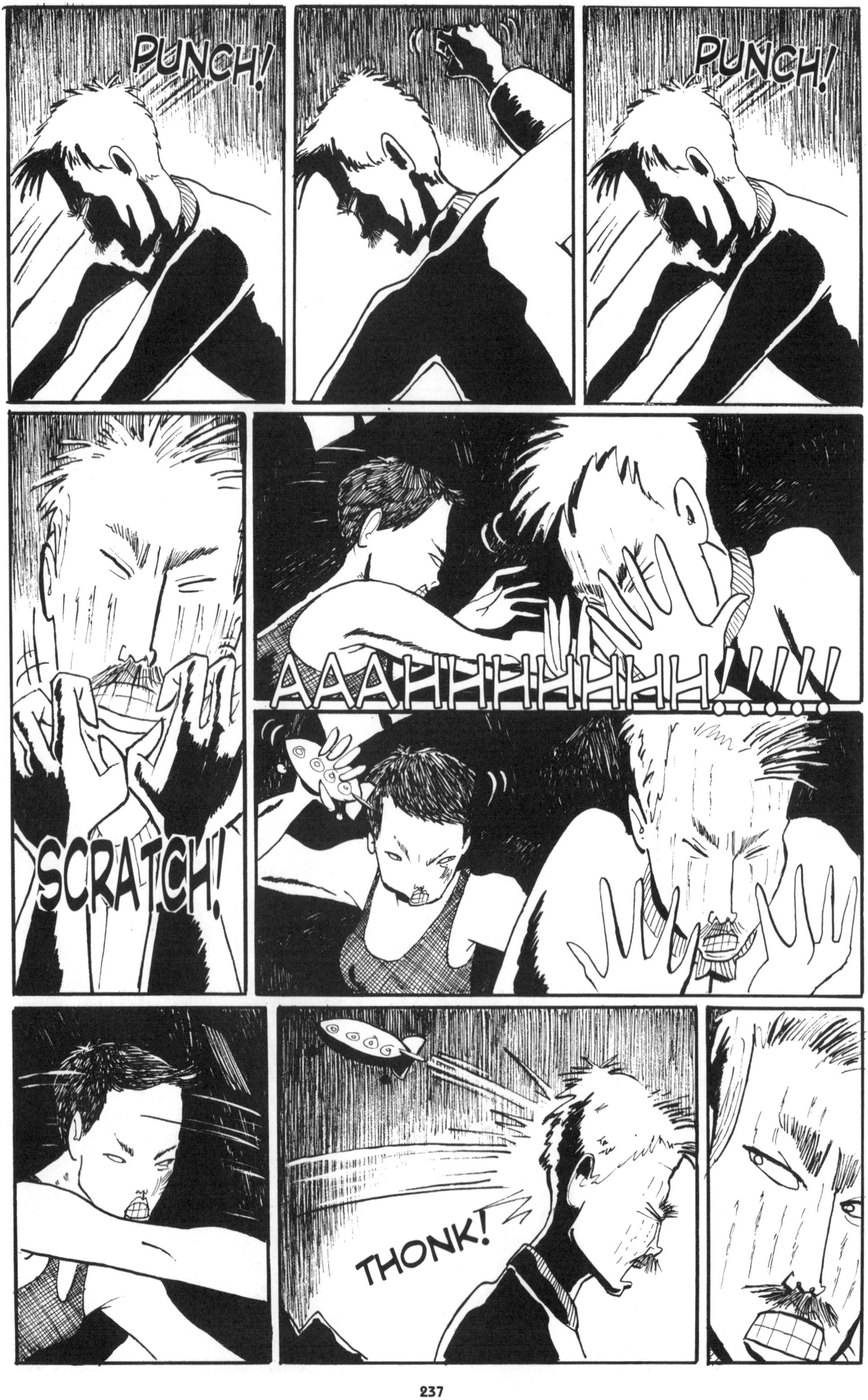
PUNCH!
PUNCH!
SCRATCH!
AAAHHHHHHHHH!!!!!
THONK!

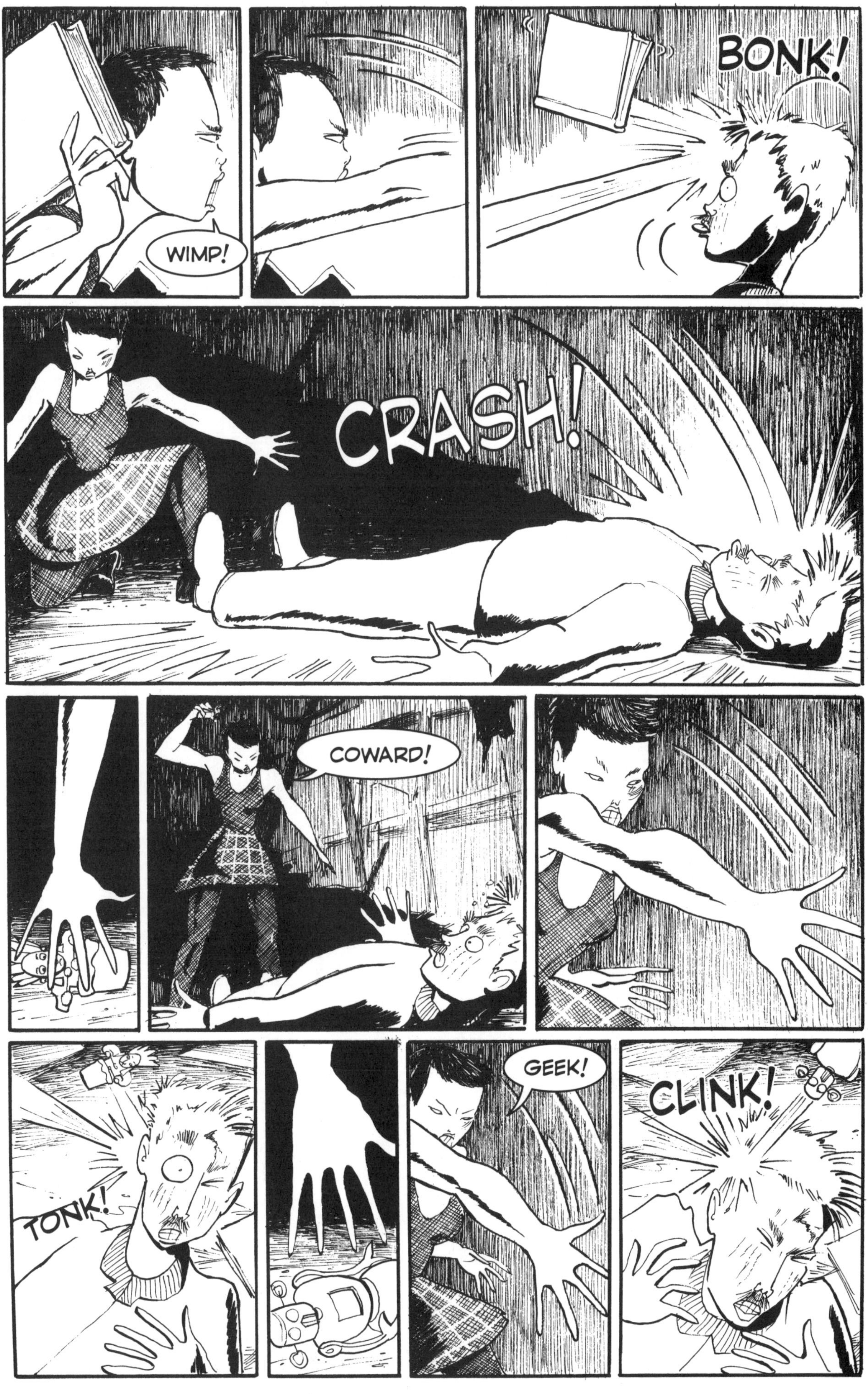
WIMP!
BONK!
CRASH!
COWARD!
TONK!
GEEK!
CLINK!

KICK!

AHH!

CRACK!

OHHHH!

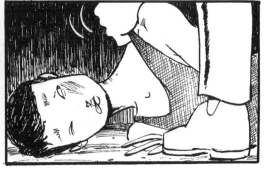

DIKE!

CRASH!

BITCH!

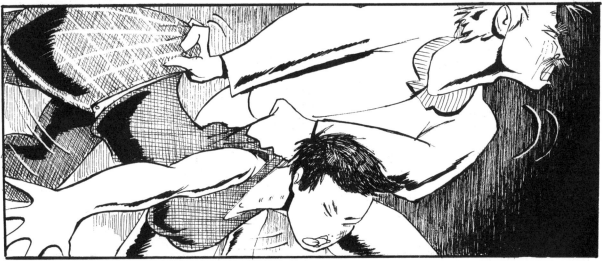

SMASH!

CUNT!

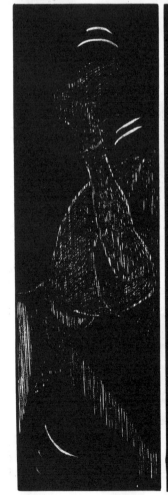

CRASH!

ROAR!

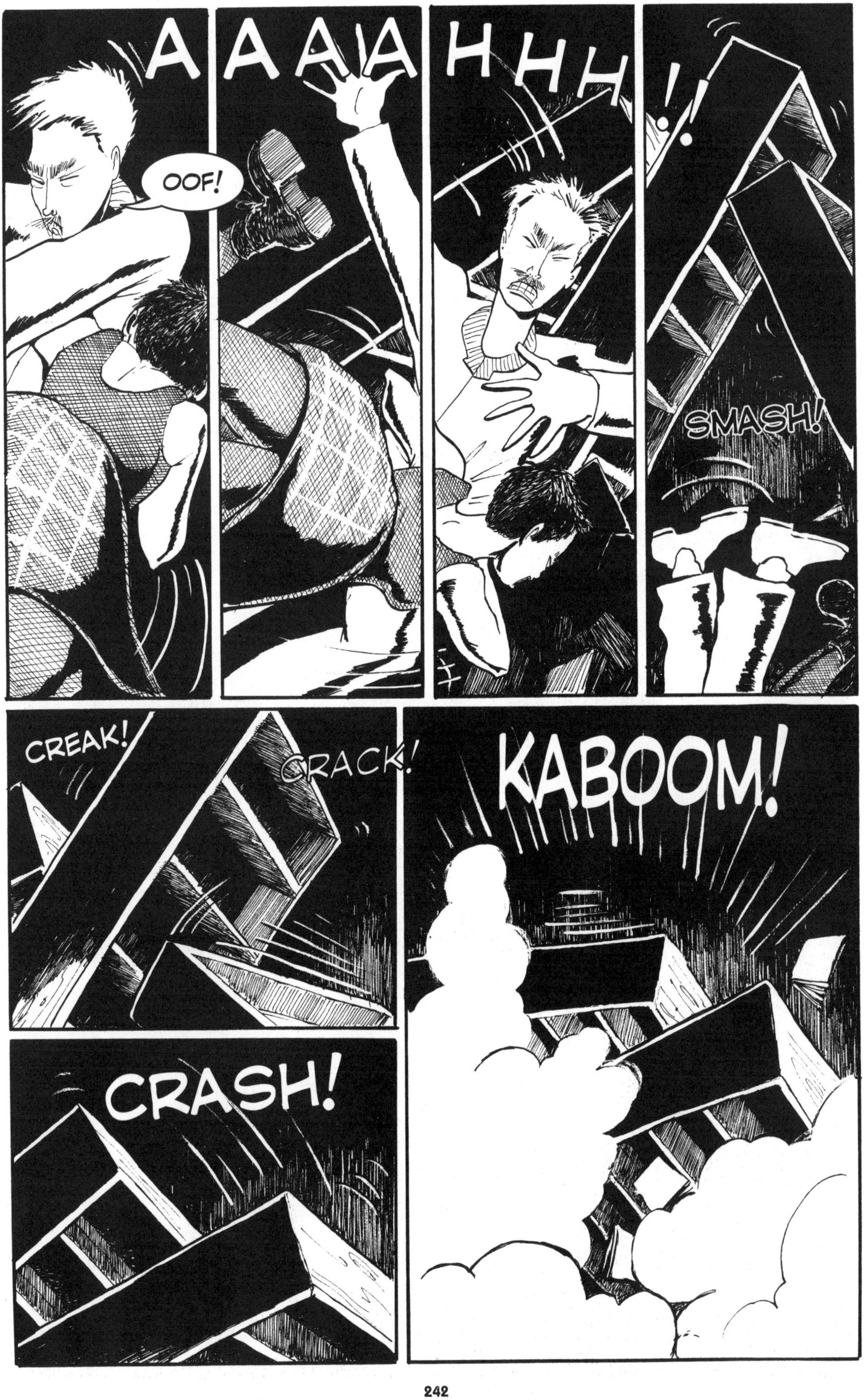
AAAAHHHH!!
OOF!
SMASH!
CREAK!
CRACK!
KABOOM!
CRASH!

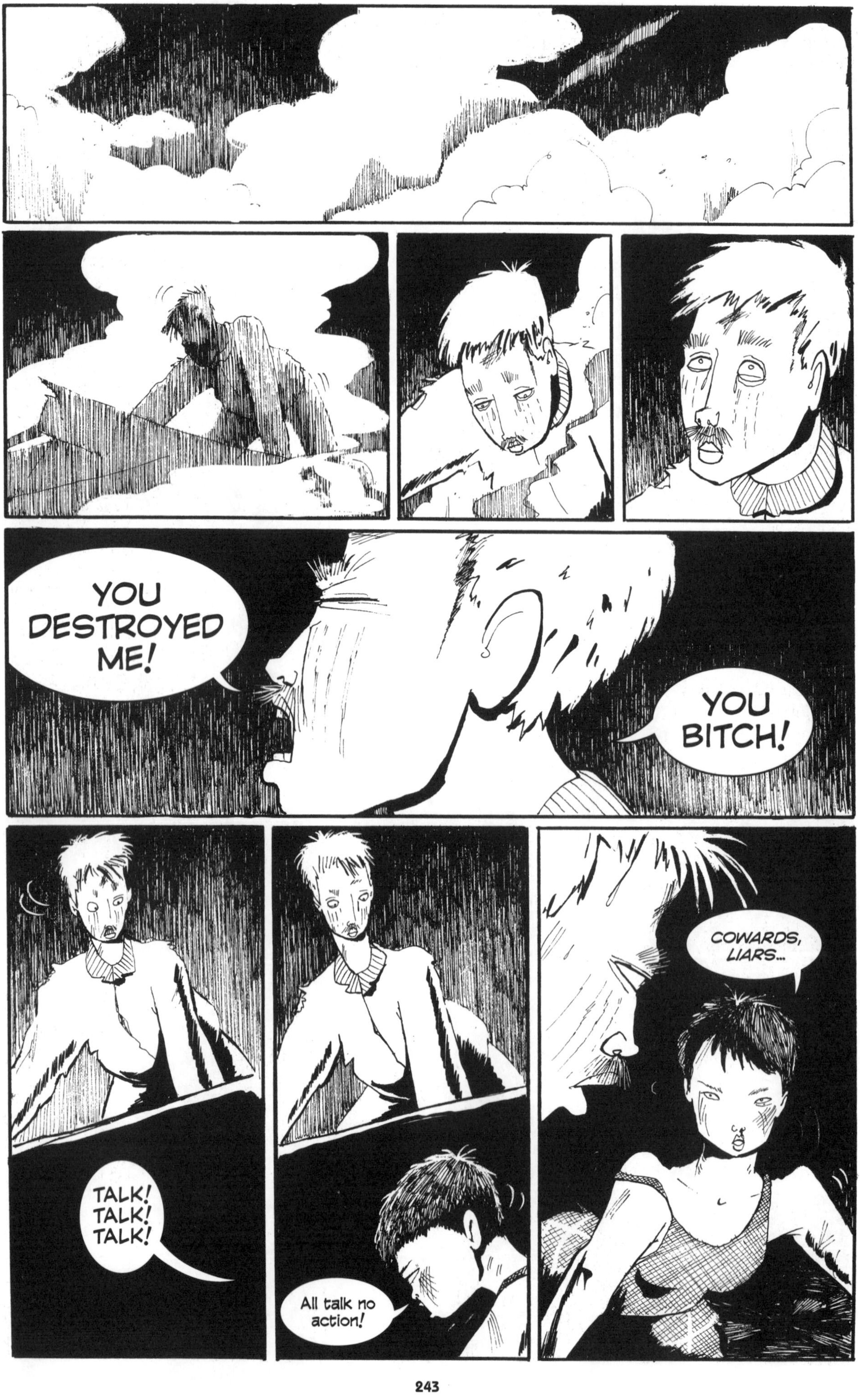
YOU DESTROYED ME!
YOU BITCH!
TALK! TALK! TALK!
All talk no action!
COWARDS, LIARS...

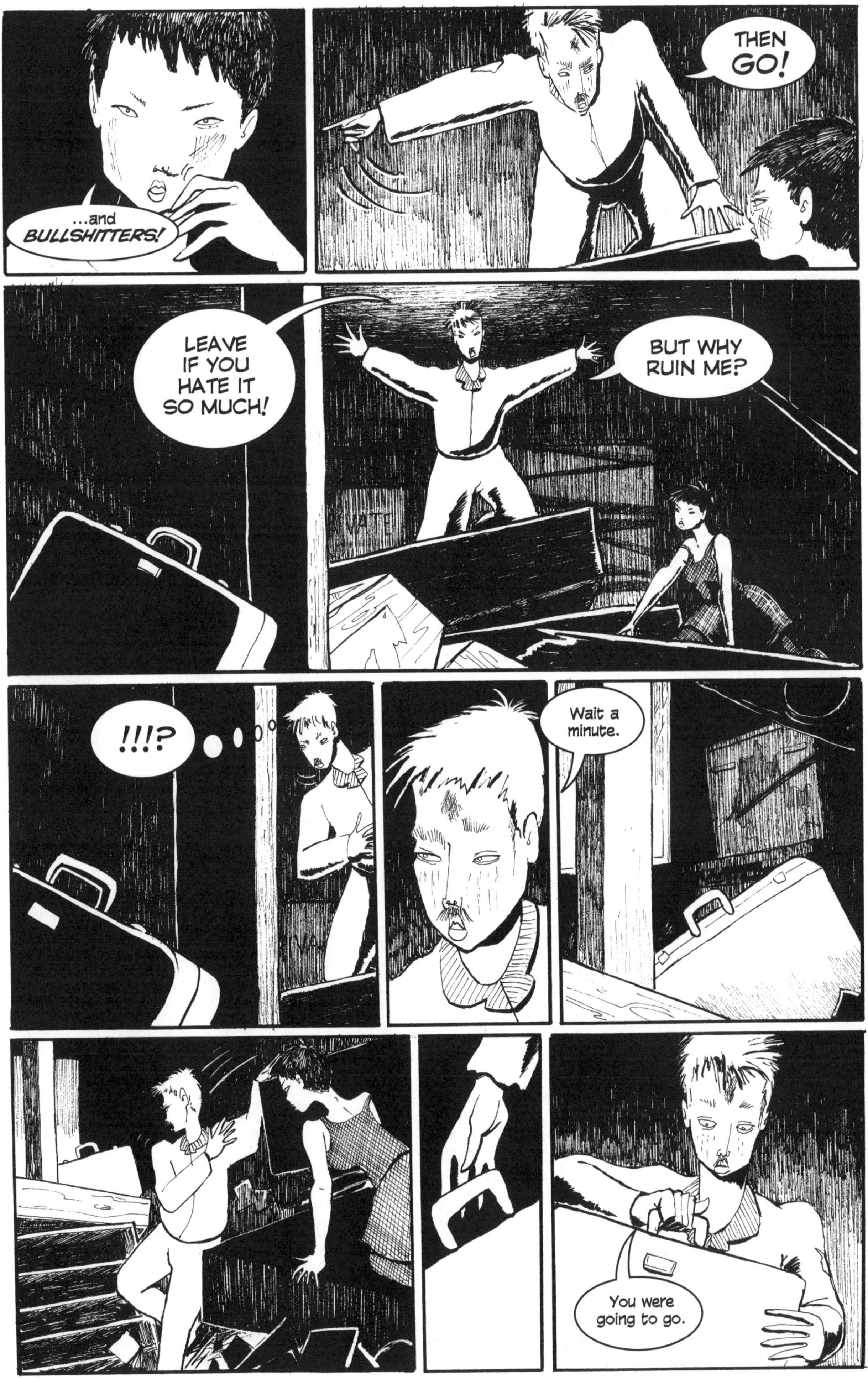
...and BULLSHITTERS!
THEN GO!
LEAVE IF YOU HATE IT SO MUCH!
BUT WHY RUIN ME?
!!!?
Wait a minute.
You were going to go.

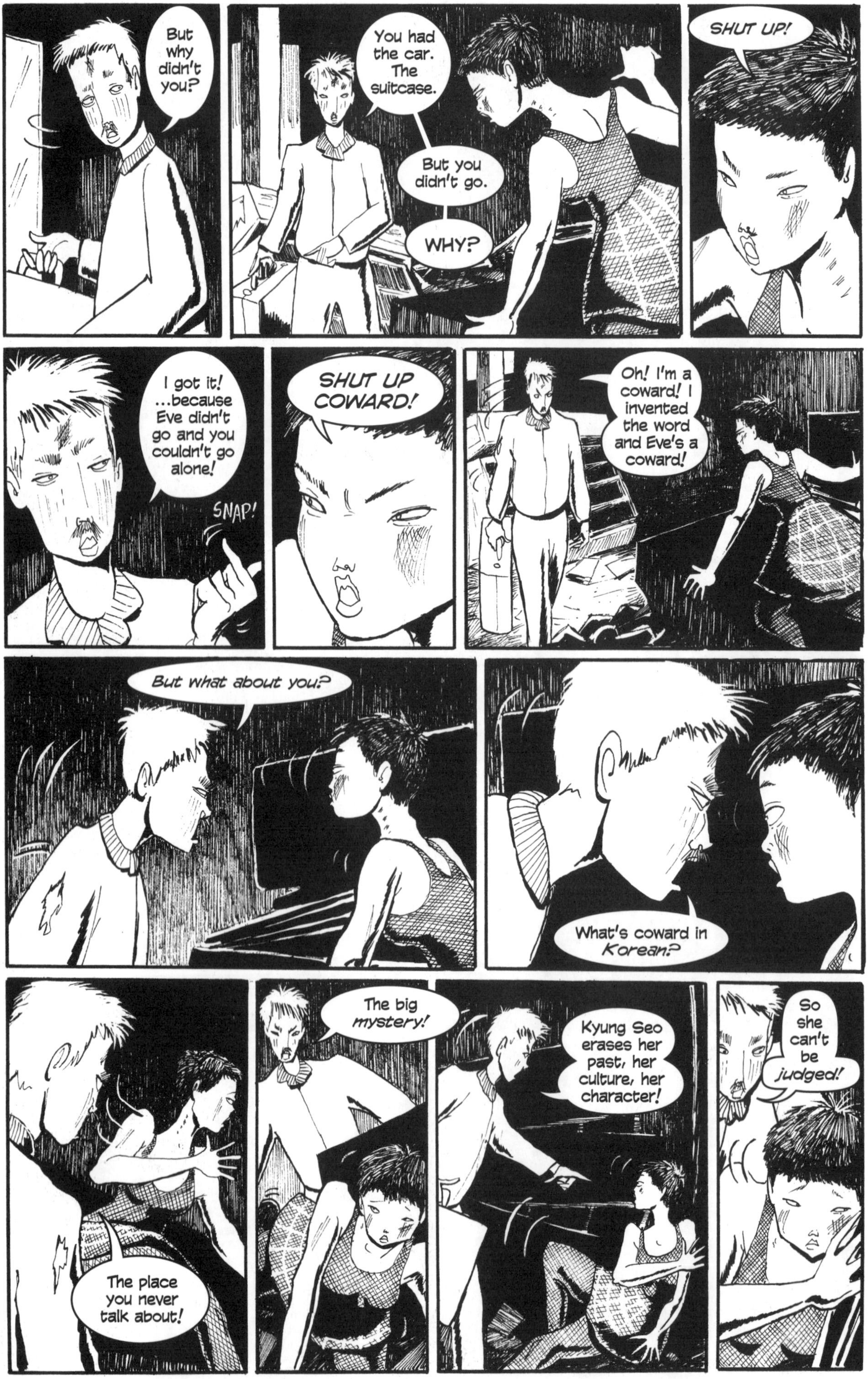
But why didn't you?
You had the car. The suitcase.
But you didn't go.
WHY?
SHUT UP!
I got it! ...because Eve didn't go and you couldn't go alone!
SNAP!
SHUT UP COWARD!
Oh! I'm a coward! I invented the word and Eve's a coward!
But what about you?
What's coward in Korean?
The place you never talk about!
The big mystery!
Kyung Seo erases her past, her culture, her character!
So she can't be judged!

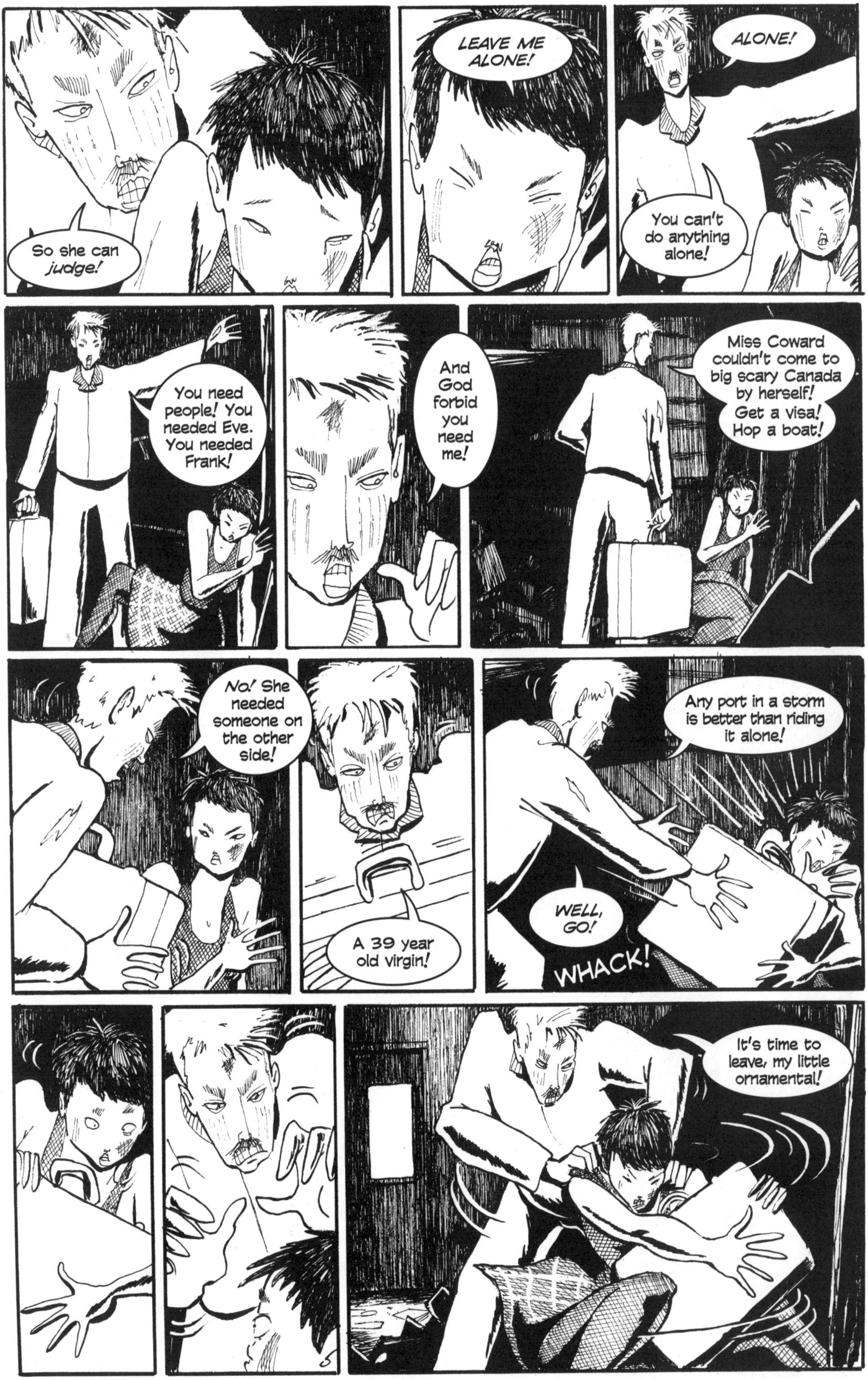
So she can judge!
LEAVE ME ALONE!
ALONE!
You can't do anything alone!
You need people! You needed Eve. You needed Frank!
And God forbid you need me!
Miss Coward couldn't come to big scary Canada by herself! Get a visa! Hop a boat!
No! She needed someone on the other side!
A 39 year old virgin!
Any port in a storm is better than riding it alone!
WELL, GO!
WHACK!
It's time to leave, my little ornamental!

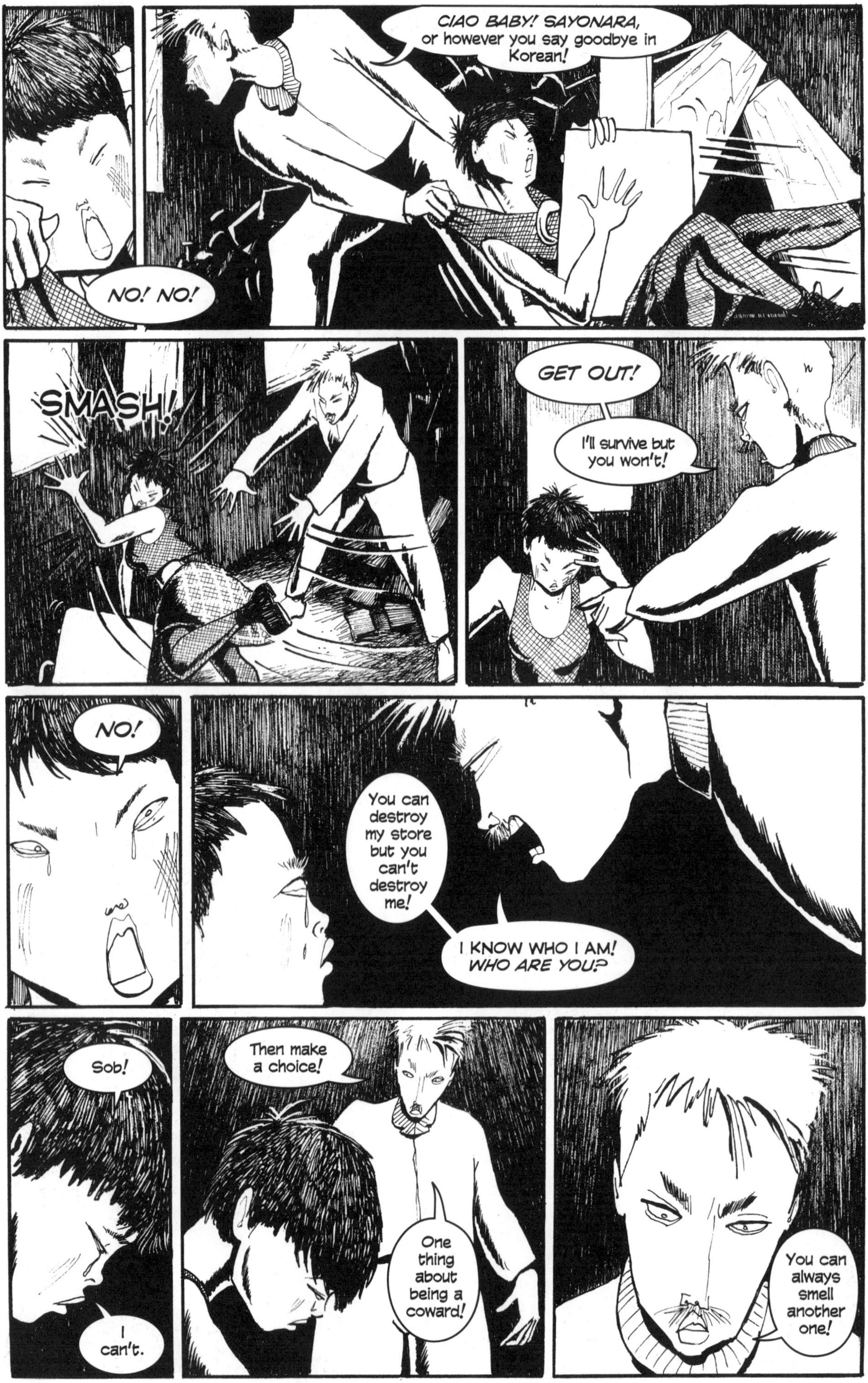
CIAO BABY! SAYONARA, or however you say goodbye in Korean!
NO! NO!
SMASH!
GET OUT!
I'll survive but you won't!
NO!
You can destroy my store but you can't destroy me!
I KNOW WHO I AM! WHO ARE YOU?
Sob!
I can't.
Then make a choice!
One thing about being a coward!
You can always smell another one!

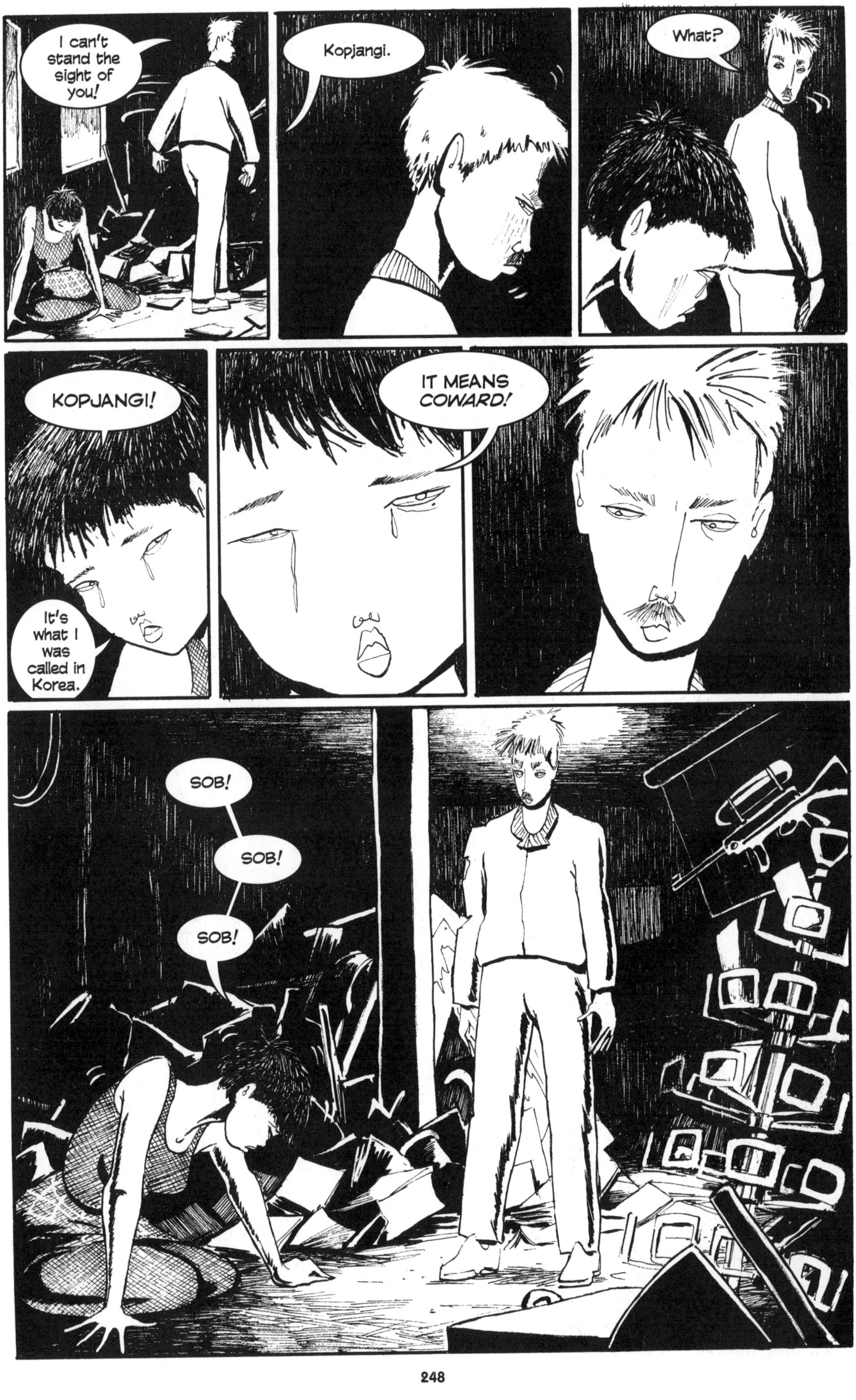
I can't stand the sight of you!
Kopjangi.
What?
KOPJANGI!
It's what I was called in Korea.
IT MEANS *COWARD!*
SOB!
SOB!
SOB!

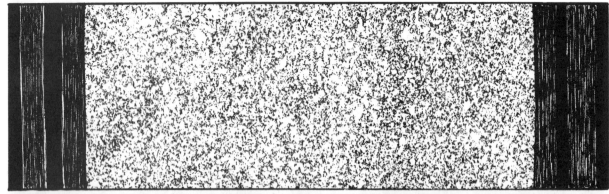

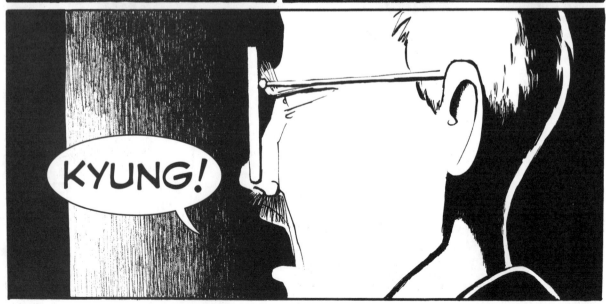

KYUNG!

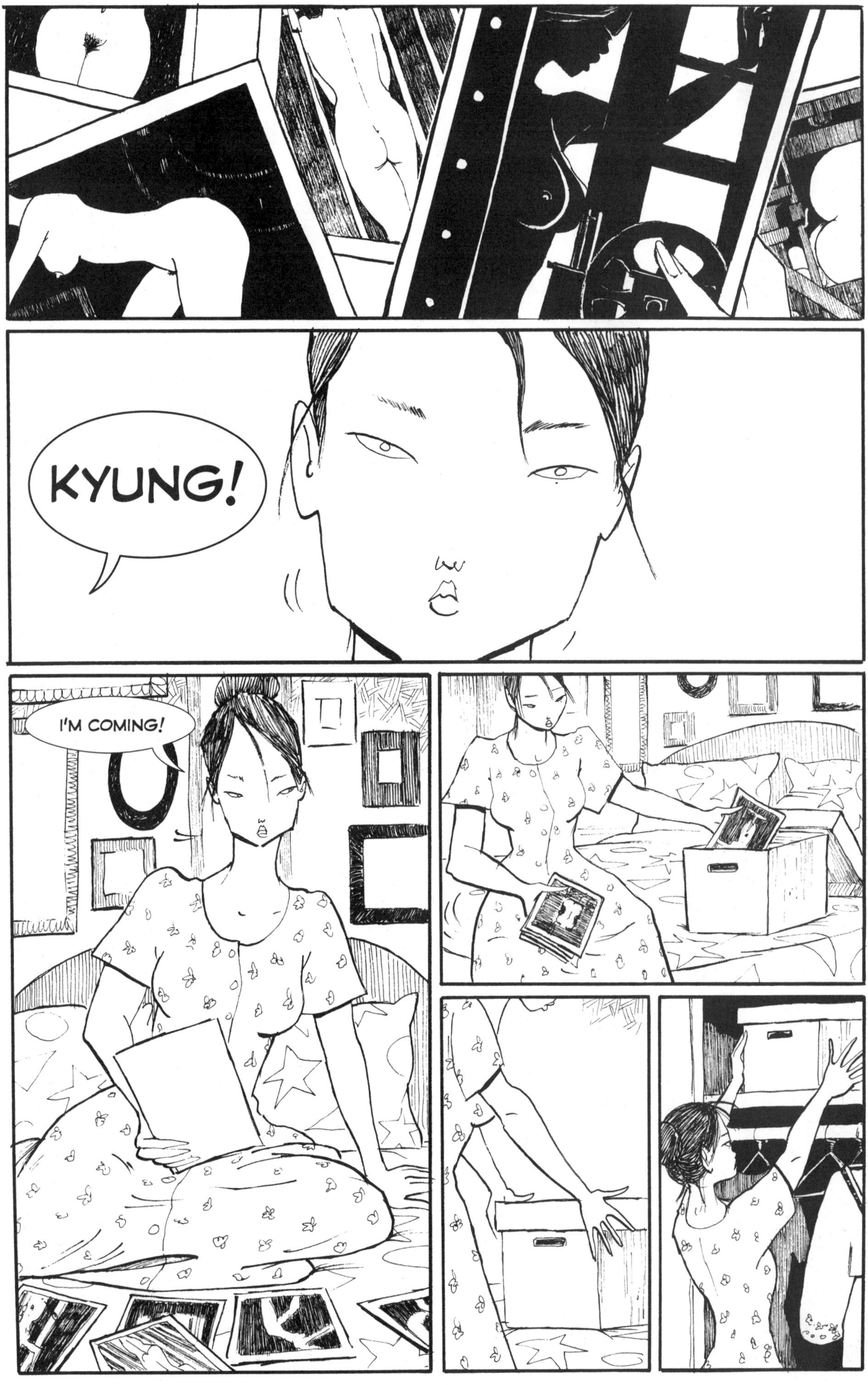
KYUNG!
I'M COMING!

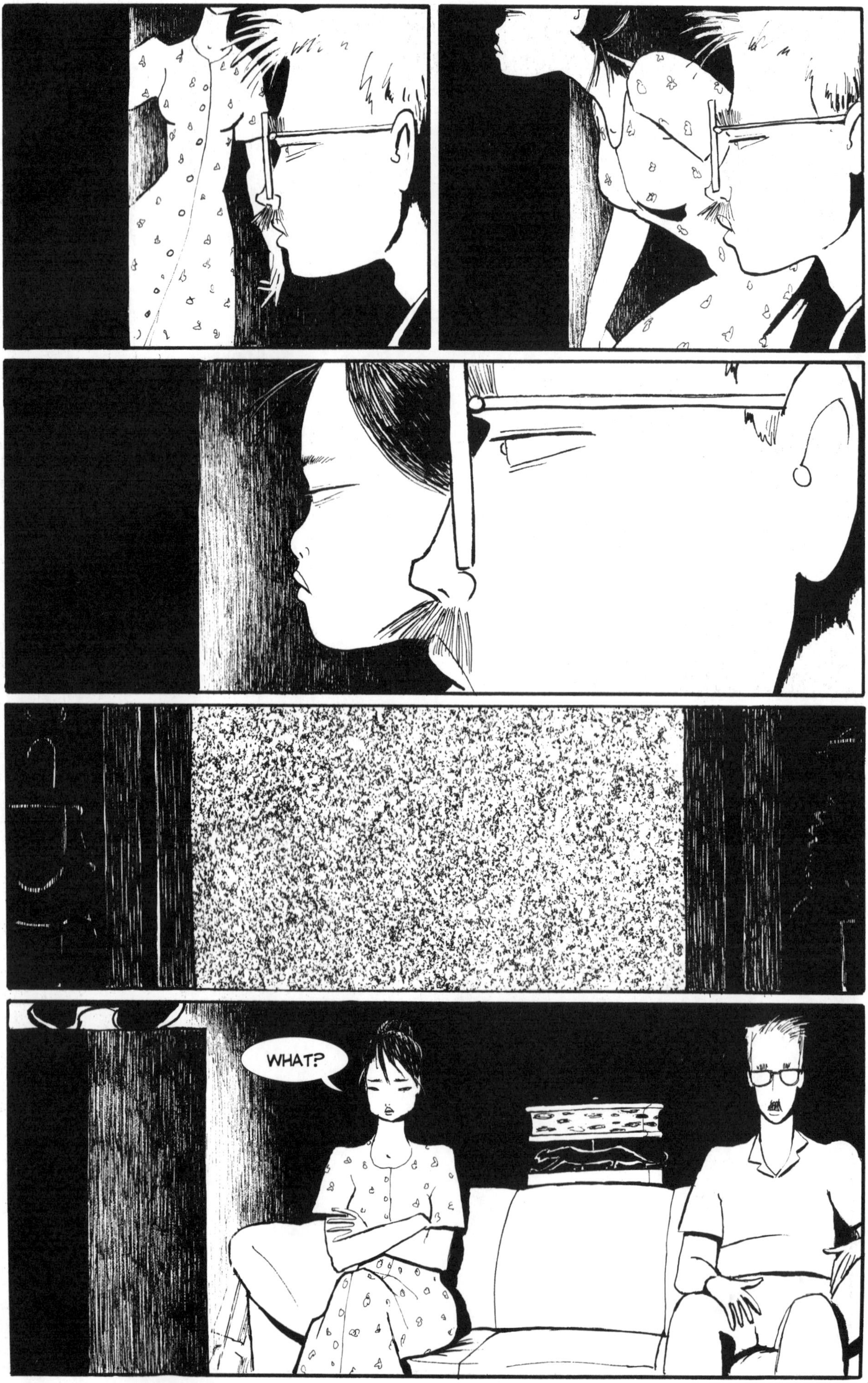
WHAT?

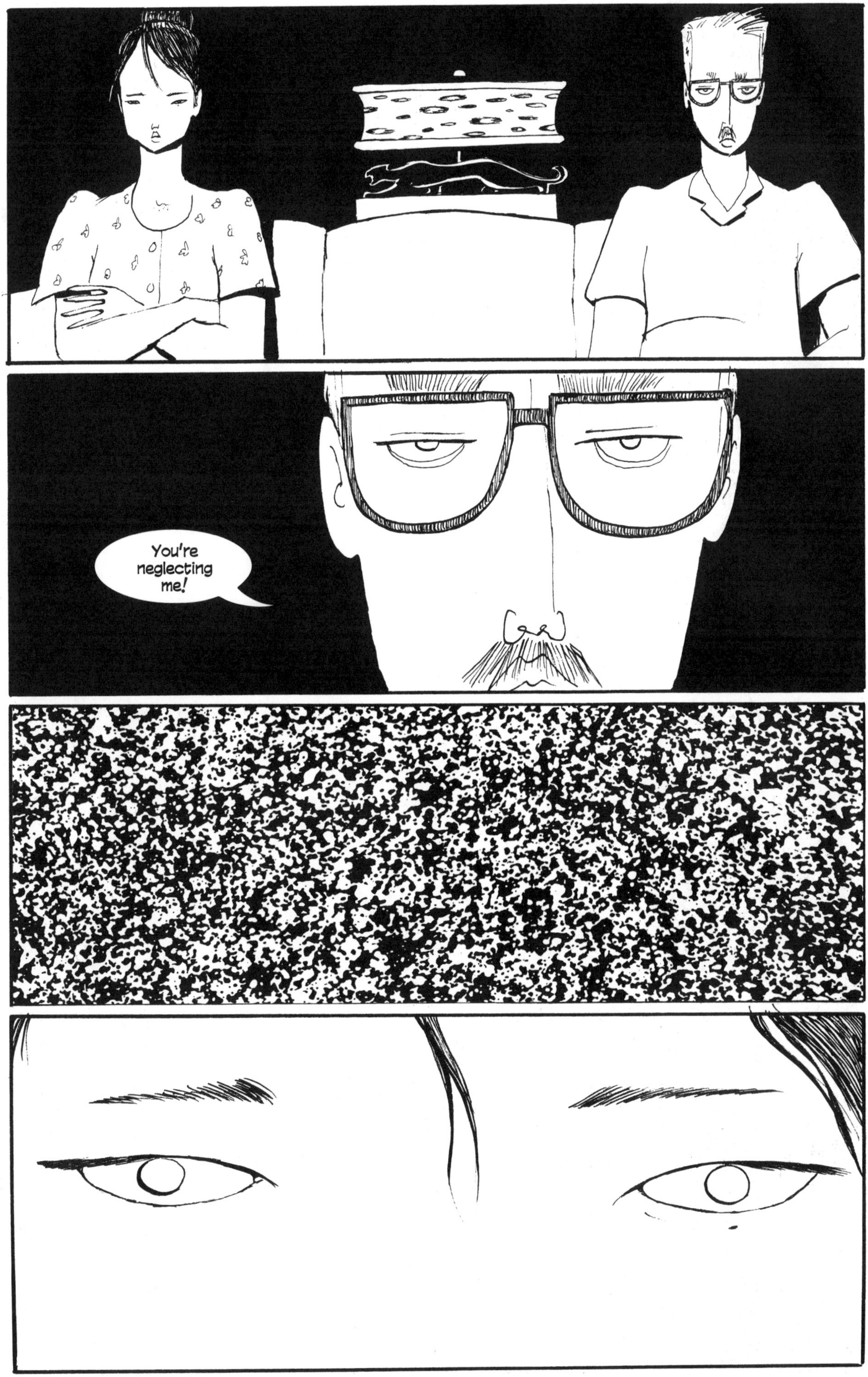
You're neglecting me!

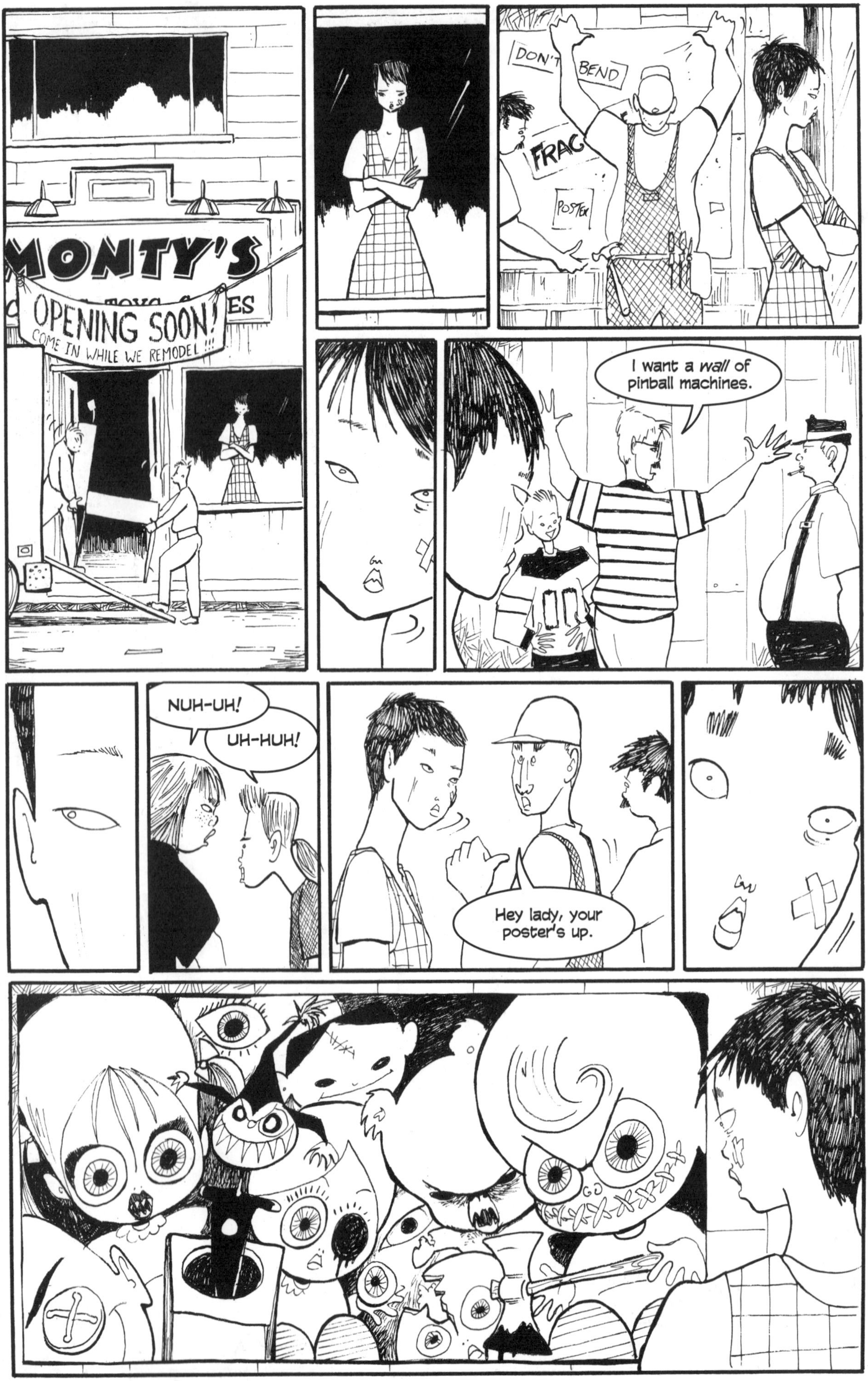
MONTY'S
ES
OPENING SOON!
COME IN WHILE WE REMODEL!!!
DON'T
BEND
FRAG
POSTER
I want a *wall* of pinball machines.
NUH-UH!
UH-HUH!
Hey lady, your poster's up.

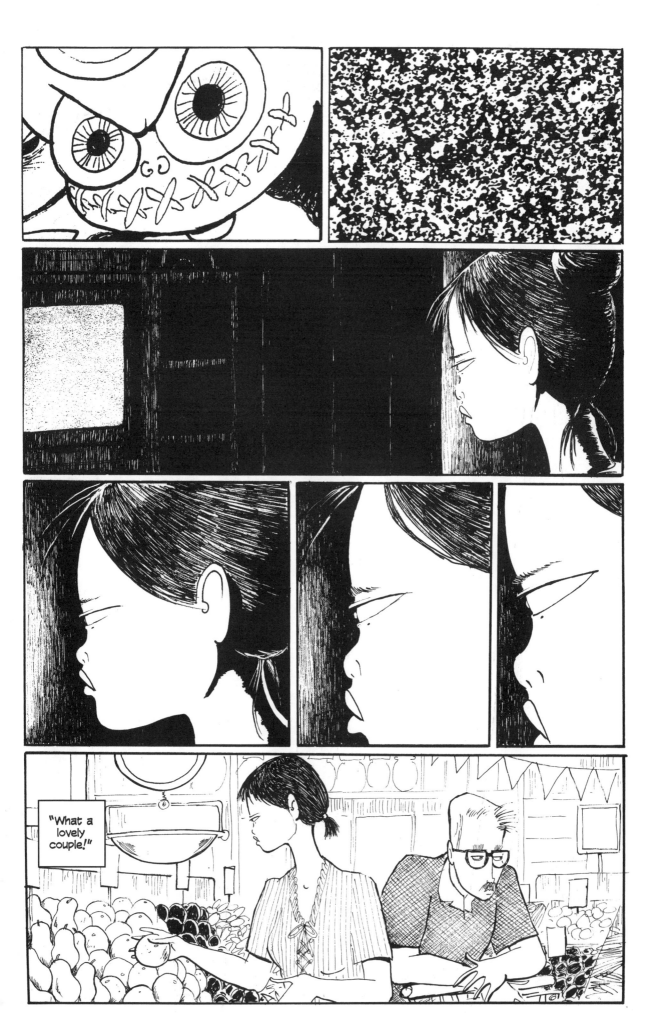

"What a
lovely
couple!"

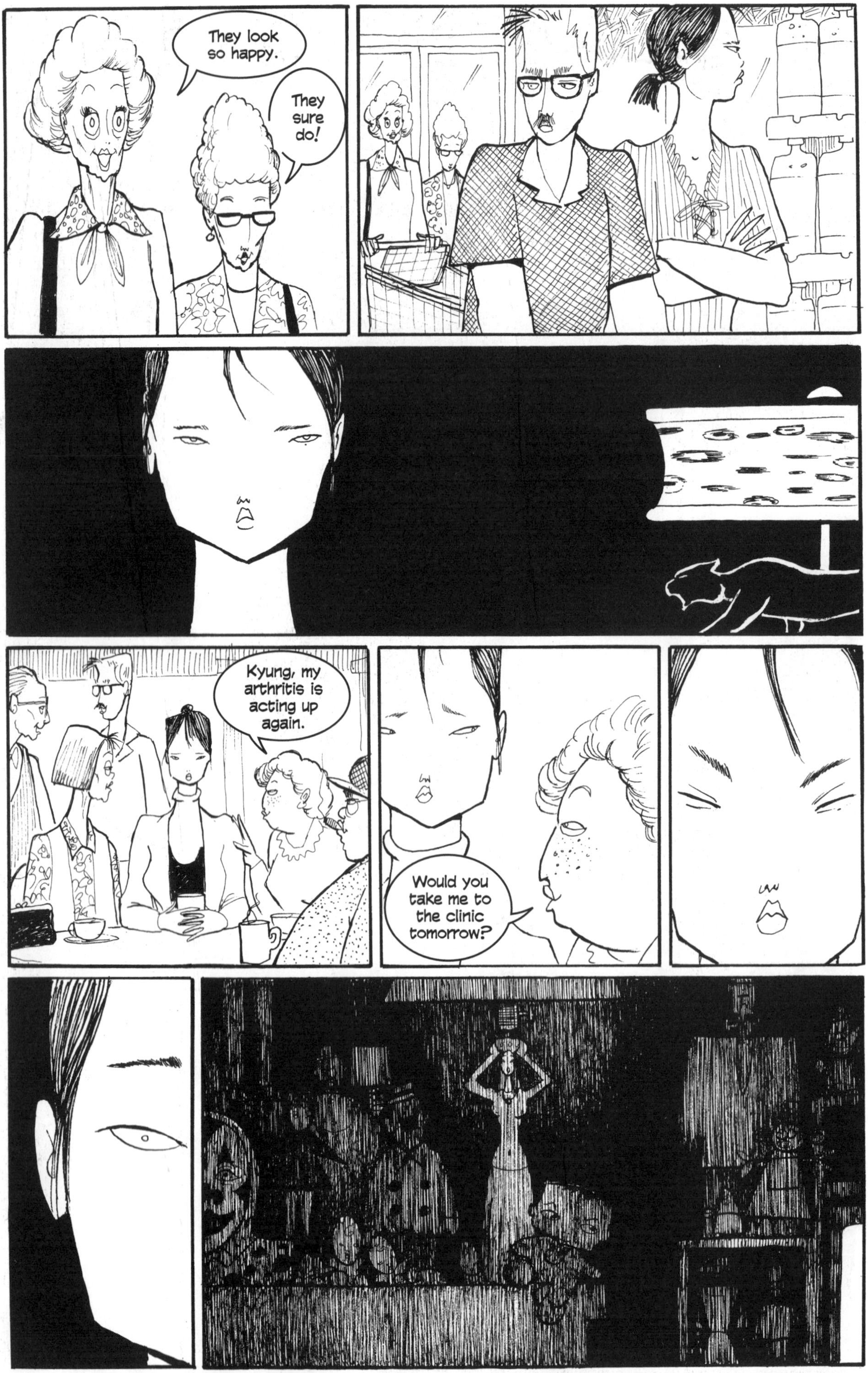
They look so happy.
They sure do!
Kyung, my arthritis is acting up again.
Would you take me to the clinic tomorrow?

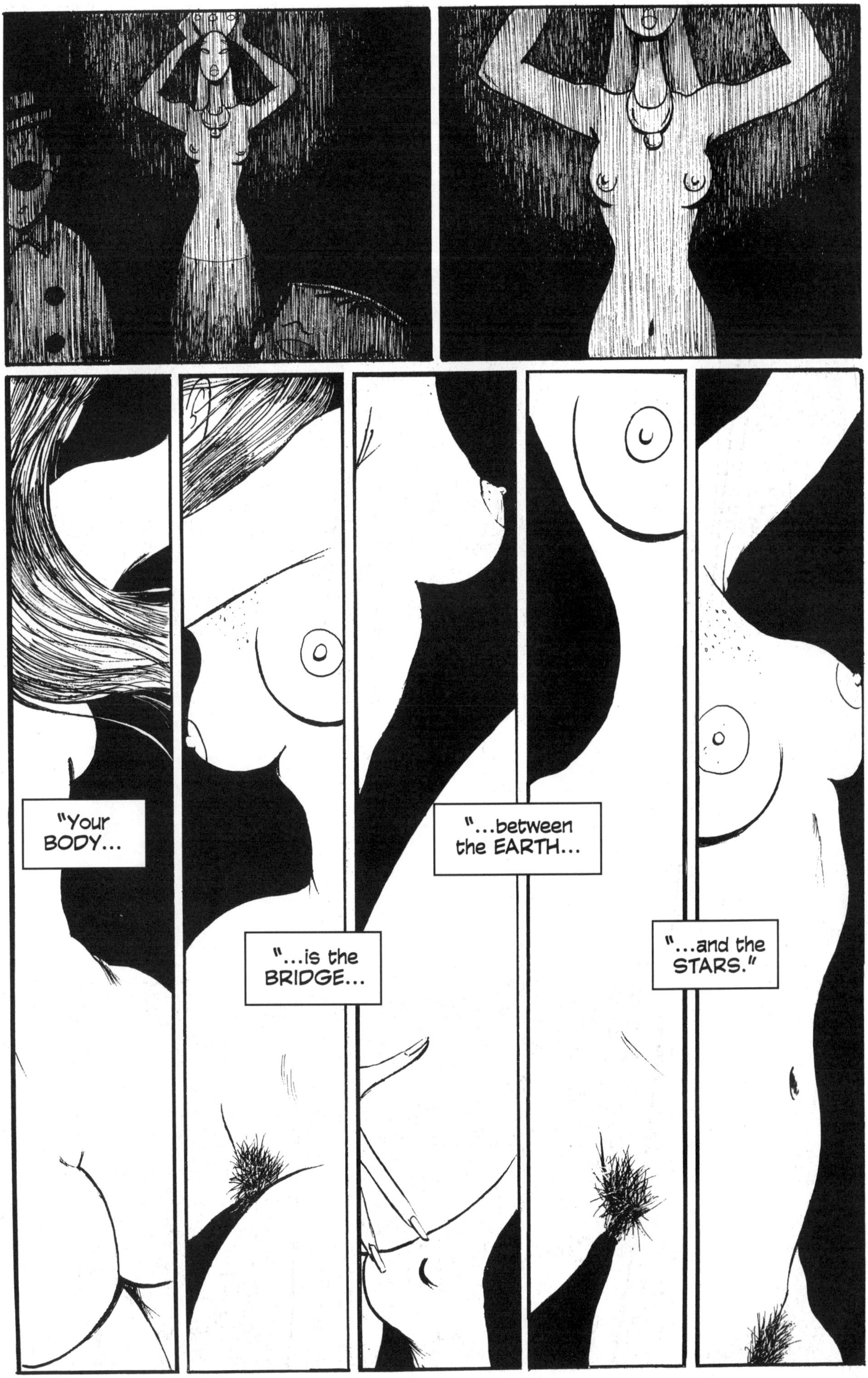
"Your BODY...
"...is the BRIDGE...
"...between the EARTH...
"...and the STARS."

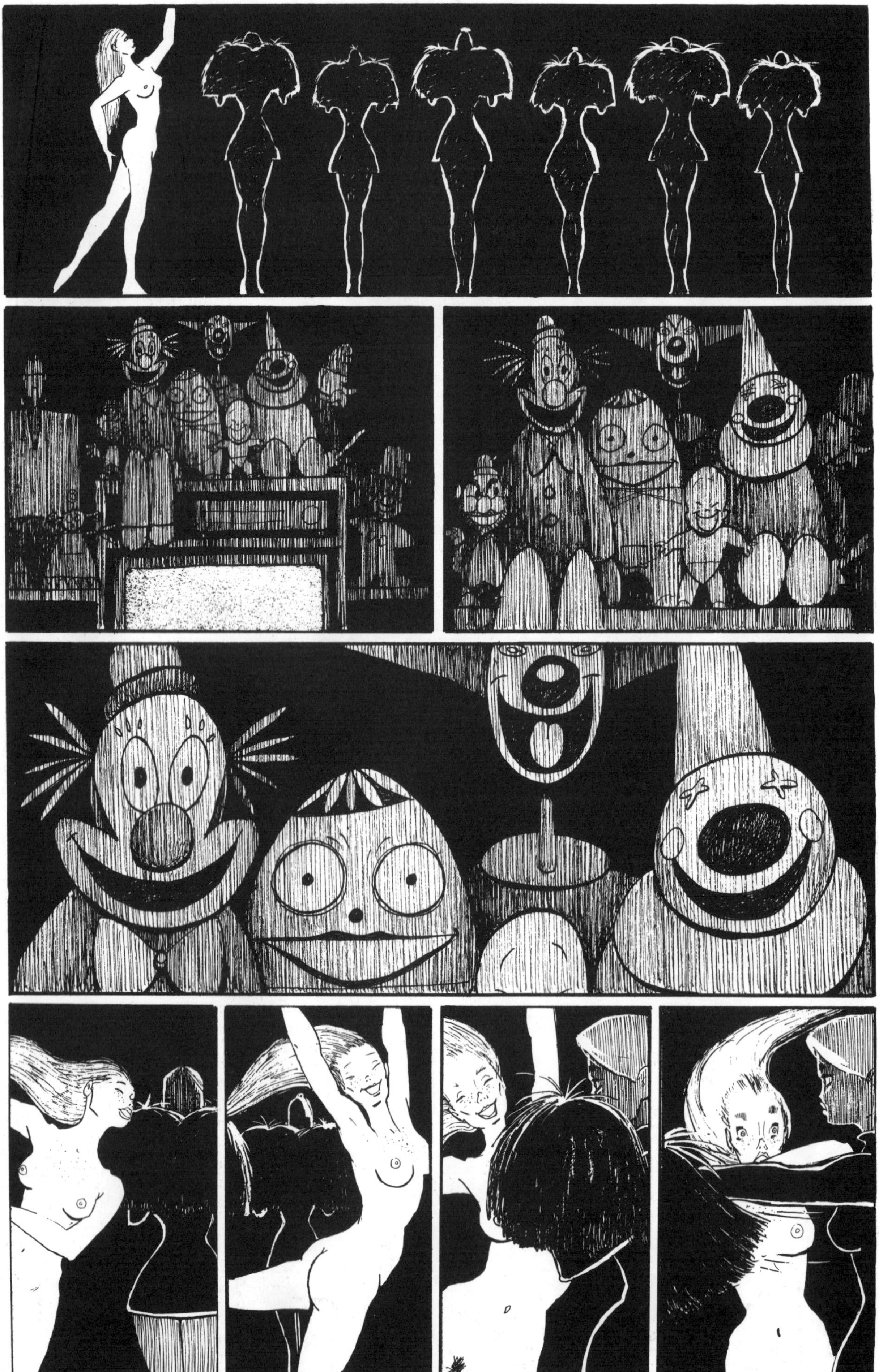

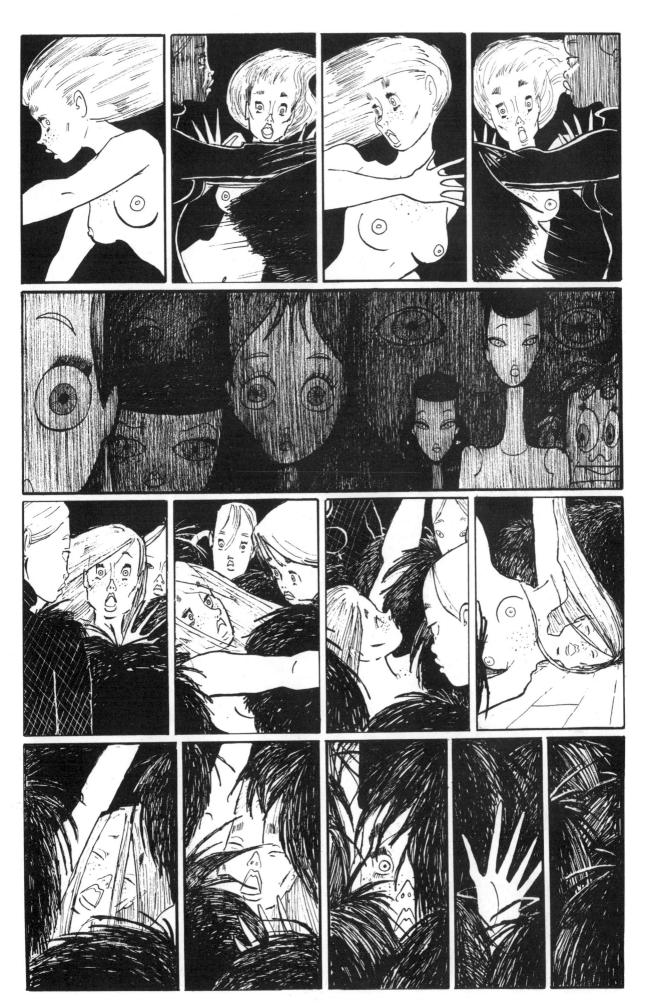

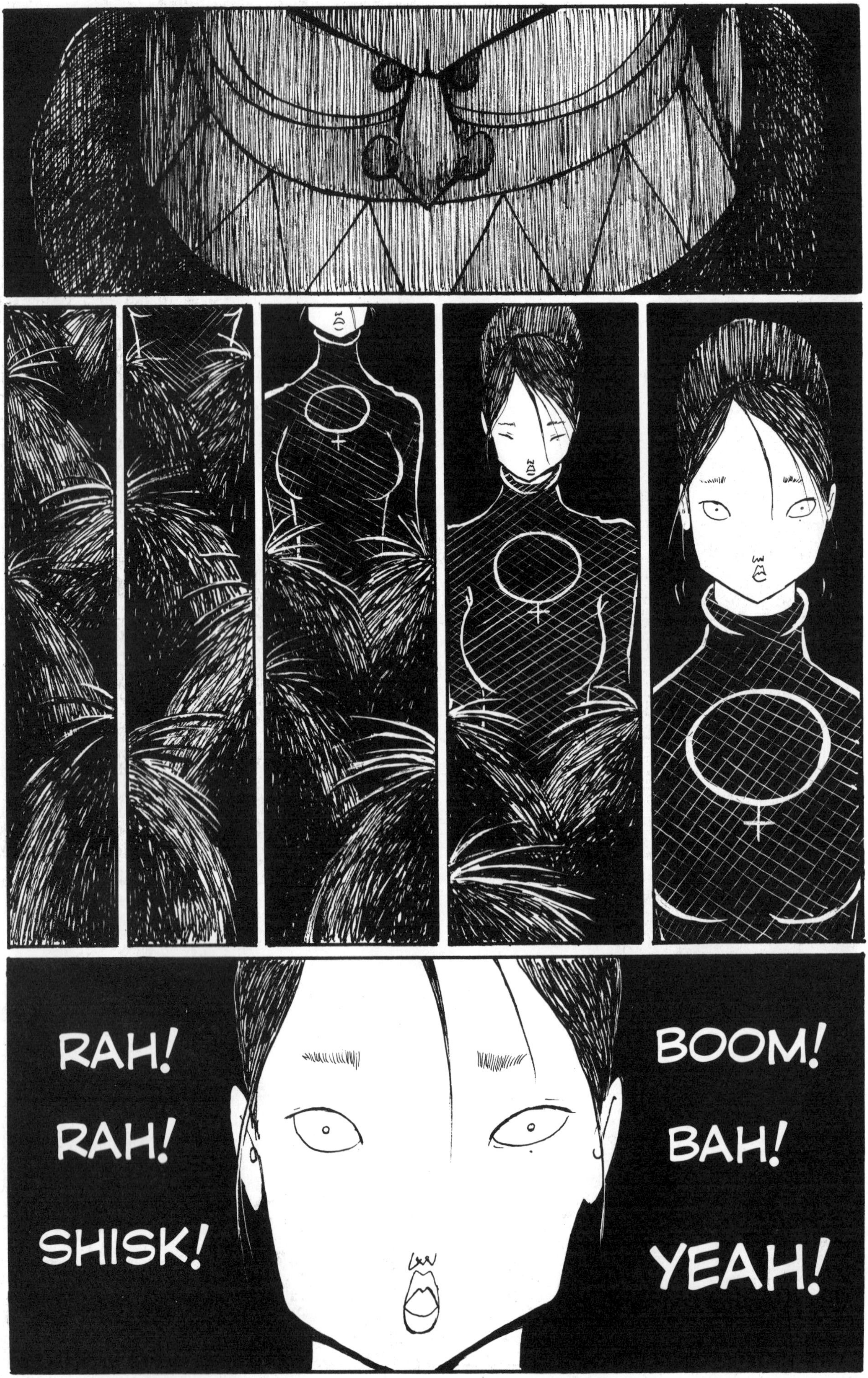
RAH!
RAH!
SHISK!
BOOM!
BAH!
YEAH!

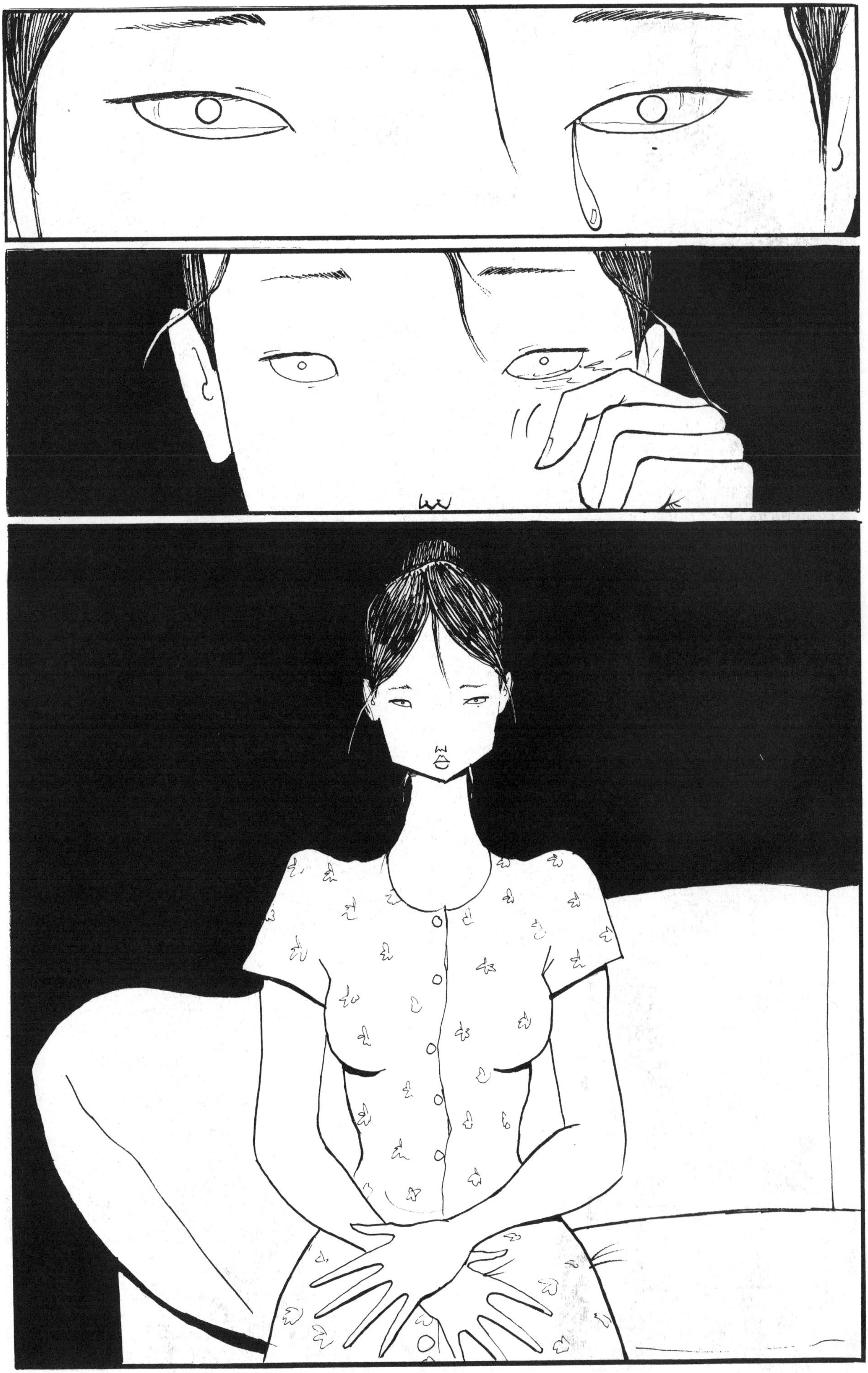

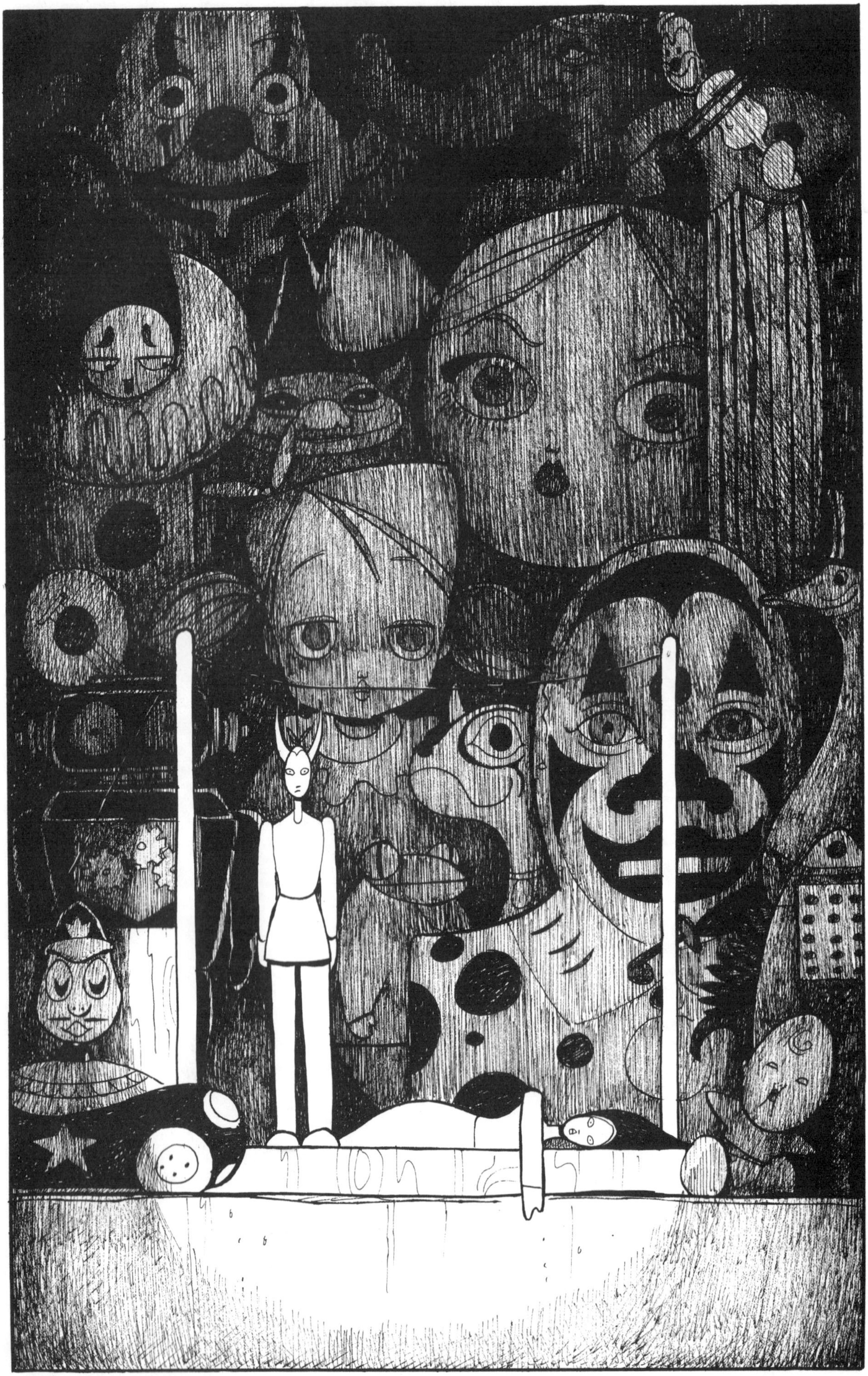